The Section Development Theory and Development Policy of the German Political Science Association is an association of political scientists in Germany working in this subject area. It organises regular section meetings and promotes exchange on research and teaching in development theory and policy.

The series
"Entwicklungstheorie und Entwicklungspolitik"

is edited by

Arnold-Bergstraesser-Institut (ABI), Freiburg

German Development Institute / Deutsches Institut für Entwicklungspolitik (DIE)

The Section Development Theory and Development Policy of the German Political Science Association (GPSA)

GIGA German Institute of Global and Area Studies, Hamburg

Institute for Development and Peace (INEF), Duisburg

Center for Development Research (ZEF), Bonn

Volume 22

Esther Kronsbein

Globalisation and Solidarity

Transformations in the Everyday Economy of Uganda

Nomos

This publication was supported by the graduate funding of the University of Kassel.

The Deutsche Nationalbibliothek lists this publication in the Deutsche Nationalbibliografie; detailed bibliographic data are available on the Internet at http://dnb.d-nb.de

a.t.: Dissertation an der Universität Kassel,
Fachbereich 05 Gesellschaftswissenschaften,
verfasst von Esther Kronsbein, Datum der Disputation: 24.03.2021

original title: „Globalisation and Solidarity:
Transformations in the everyday economy of Busoga/Uganda"

ISBN 978-3-8487-8651-0 (Print)
978-3-7489-3022-8 (ePDF)

British Library Cataloguing-in-Publication Data
A catalogue record for this book is available from the British Library.

ISBN 978-3-8487-8651-0 (Print)
978-3-7489-3022-8 (ePDF)

Library of Congress Cataloging-in-Publication Data
Kronsbein, Esther
Globalisation and Solidarity
Transformations in the Everyday Economy of Uganda
Esther Kronsbein
521 pp.
Includes bibliographic references.

ISBN 978-3-8487-8651-0 (Print)
978-3-7489-3022-8 (ePDF)

Onlineversion
Nomos eLibrary

1st Edition 2022

Acknowledgements

I would like to express my sincere thanks to all the people and institutions that have enabled me to conduct this research and write this work. It was only possible thanks to their support.

First of all, I would like in particular to thank Prof. Dr. Aram Ziai for his guidance and supervision. I also thank Prof. Dr. Julius Kiiza for his advice.

I am grateful to the *University of Kassel* for supporting my dissertation with a scholarship and to *Makerere University* for the affiliation.

I thank the following institutions in Uganda for their support: the *Department of Political Science and Public Administration* of *Makerere University*; *Makerere University Library*; the *Research Ethics Committee at the School of Social Sciences of Makerere University* (MAKSSREC); the *Uganda National Council of Science and Technology* (UNCST); the *Office of the Prime Minister*; the library of the *Parliament of Uganda*; the *Uganda Bureau of Statistics*; the *National Records Centre and Archives*; *Jinja District Archives*; *Jinja Municipality*; *Jinja District Administration*; *Kamuli District Administration*; *Buyende District Administration*; the *Obwa Kyabazinga Bwa Busoga*; the team of *Prime Solutions Ltd.* (Kampala).

I am particularly indebted to all my study respondents for sacrificing their time and sharing their knowledge, ideas, and experiences with me. I am also very grateful to the numerous gatekeepers who put us in touch.

The people I owe thanks to in Uganda are too numerous to name all of them. I would like to express my sincere thanks to everybody who supported me during my stay in Uganda. Nevertheless, there are some who have to be highlighted:

Many thanks to Nkonoka Hellen for accompanying me through the largest part of the research process and to Kaiso Moses for supporting us. Thank you to Nkonoka Victoria for teaching me Lusoga.

Very special thanks go to Waiswa David.

Many thanks to Mitchell J. Lincoln, Christopher Joseph, and Franziska Satzinger for sharing the workload of proofreading. Thanks Ewald Dietrich for your constant support.

I am particularly indebted to my family for their limitless support, encouragement, and understanding. I would like to say a special thank you to my mother.

Finally, many, many thanks to my husband Dominique for going through this demanding process with me, enduring all difficulties and providing encouragement at all times.

Contents

List of charts

List of acronyms

ACE	Area Cooperative Enterprise (regional umbrella for cooperatives)
ASF	African Social Forum
BG	Busoga Growers Co-operative Union
CAIIP	Community Agriculture Infrastructure Improvement Program
CEPAL	Comisión Económica para América Latina y el Caribe (Economic Commission for Latin America and the Caribbean)
EAC	East African Community
FAO	Food and Agriculture Organization of the United Nations
FLO	Fairtrade International (formerly: Fairtrade Labelling Organizations International)
GATT	General Agreement on Tariffs and Trade
GDP	Gross Domestic Product
GNP	Gross National Product
IBEACo	Imperial British East African Company
ICA	International Co-operative Alliance
IFPRI	International Food Policy Research Institute
ILO	International Labour Organization
INMECAFE	Instituto Mexicano del Café (Mexican Coffee Institute)
IMF	International Monetary Fund
MAKSS REC	Research Ethics Committee at the School of Social Sciences of Makerere University
NAADS	National Agricultural Advisory Services
NAEP	National Agricultural Extension Policy
NATO	North Atlantic Treaty Organisation
NCP	National Co-operative Policy
NGO	Non-Governmental Organisation
NIC	Newly developing country
NRA	National Resistance Army
NRM	National Resistance Movement
OBB	Obwa Kyabazinga Bwa Busoga (administration of the Kingdom of Busoga)
OWC	Operation Wealth Creation
PCI	Problem-Centred Interview
PMB	Produce Marketing Board
PRGF	Poverty Reduction and Growth Facility
PRSP	Poverty Reduction Strategy Paper
QCA	Qualitative Content Analysis
ROSCA	Rotating Savings and Credit Association

S&C	Savings and Credit Group
SACCO	Savings and Credit Cooperative
SAP	Structural Adjustment Programme
SSE	Social and Solidarity Economy
TV	Television
UCA	Uganda Co-operative Alliance
UIA	Uganda Investment Authority
UN	United Nations
UNCST	Uganda National Council of Science and Technology
UNDP	United Nations Development Program
UNLF	Uganda National Liberation Front
UPC	Uganda People's Congress
UPE	Universal Primary Education Programme
USE	Universal Secondary Education Programme
VSLA	Village Savings and Loan Association
WSF	World Social Forum
WTO	World Trade Organisation

1. Introduction

1.1 Problem statement and relevance

Globalisation has attracted much attention in both academic and non-academic public discussion in recent years. A growing portion of the numerous works on it is turning critically against the way in which globalisation takes place today, i.e., focused on economic interests exclusively and without paying attention to its social and environmental impacts.[1] James Ferguson's critique that the "enormous recent literature on globalization so far has had remarkably little to say about Africa" (Ferguson 2006, 25) is however equally applicable to literature critical of globalisation and to conventional[2] approaches. Particularly the everyday economy on which the majority of people in Africa lives, especially in rural areas, has not received much research interest. This includes subsistence activities, alternative economic activities, the informal economy, 'official' microeconomic activities, and the grey areas between those spheres. If research is done on such activities at all, then mostly with the objective of 'developing' the local economy, i.e., forming it in the image of the global North[3]. The aim of this research project is neither to evaluate nor to conceptualise 'development' activities. On the contrary, I take a critical stance on the conventional conceptualisation that equates 'development' with *capitalist development* (see chapter 2.2). Through this work, I hope to contribute to the recent discussion emphasising that, instead of trying constantly to teach it, "the global North [should try] to learn from the experiences of the global South" (Santos 2014, 19). The experiences of ordinary people in Busoga with globalisation and with alternative economic practices in their everyday life is thus central to this study. The mainstream way of

---

1 For example: Altvater/ Mahnkopf 2002; Amin 1998; Amin 2004; Brand 2005; Chossudovsky 2003; Ferguson 2006; Giegold/ Embshoff 2008; Greig et al. 2007; Hall et al. 2015; Pfeiffer-Schaupp 2005; Roberts/ Hite 2000; Ziai 2000.

2 For details on different approaches to globalisation, see chapter 3.

3 I prefer to use the terms 'global North'/ 'global South' to other options like 'First World'/ 'Third World' (see headword "Global North and global South/ First and Third World" in chapter 2.4 for explanations) and especially terms like 'developing' or 'underdeveloped' countries, which create the impression that those countries are inferior to so-called 'developed' countries (see chapter 2.2).

thinking in economics and conventional development theory is dominated by neoliberalism, the cornerstones of which are "the primacy of the competitive individual, the superiority of the private over the public" (Hall et al. 2015a, 14) "and a quasi-religious belief in the 'hidden hand', and the self-propelling virtues of 'the market'" (ibid., 17). The keyword 'solidarity' in the thesis title refers to the concept *Social and Solidarity Economy (SSE)*, which challenges all these assumptions and intends to replace them with principles of cooperation, reciprocity, and redistributive justice (see chapter 4 for details). In chapter 8.3, I examine economic activities encountered in Busoga that can be subsumed under this term, taking into consideration their potential to offer alternatives to existing concepts of capitalist development. Apart from SSE, the theoretical framework of this study encompasses postcolonial theory (see chapter 2.1), critical development studies (2.2) including the Post-Development approach (2.2.3), and Immanuel Wallerstein's approach to world-systems analysis (2.3). Postcolonial theory is the foundation of my research methodology and my general attitude towards the research topics. I interpret the research results from the standpoint of critical development studies and world-systems analysis (see chapters 8 and 9). I discuss globalisation from all three perspectives in chapters 3.2, 3.3, and 3.4.

Since the late 1980s, the government of Uganda has embarked on "one of the most ambitious programs of economic liberalization on the African continent" (Collier/ Reinikka 2001, 1; see also chapter 6.1). This suggests that Uganda's economy has since then been open to globalisation, which has likely impacted on people's everyday lives in general and on their alternative economic practices in particular. Beyond that, Uganda has a cooperative movement with a history of about 100 years (for details, see chapters 4.2.2, 6.2.3, 7.5, and 8.3.2) – almost as long as capitalism's history in the country (for details, see chapter 6). The Ugandan cooperative movement has been particularly pronounced in the Busoga region (see chapters 6.2.3, 7.5, and 8.3.2). Furthermore, from the beginning of the twentieth century up to the breakdown of the national economy during the terror regime of Idi Amin, this region has been essential to Uganda's integration into the capitalist world economy (cotton and coffee production, Jinja as one of the early industrial towns in the country, see chapters 6.2.2 and 8.2.1). For those reasons, the Busoga region in Uganda is a good setting for this study.

1.2 Research questions

The overall research question of this research project is to analyse how people in the Busoga region in Uganda react to the penetration of their local economy by global capitalism, with emphasis on alternative economic activities that are based on solidarity.

The research questions derived from that objective are: How have people in Busoga experienced changes in their socio-economic environment that can be traced back to globalisation, in the past 30 years? What kind of alternative economic activities based on solidarity do or did they practise? Did those activities persist in spite of, dissolve because of, or emerge as a reaction to globalisation? Do people consider such activities helpful in their situation, and why or why not?

The research hypothesis that underlies this thesis is: Everyday economy in Busoga shows signs of penetration by globalisation as well as alternative economic approaches, out of which some can be counted among the Social and Solidarity Economy (SSE).

1.3 Methodology and methods

This is a qualitative research project with a postcolonial orientation. There is no uniform definition of postcolonial (or decolonial) research. The idea itself is relatively new and joins other critical approaches like feminist research. The most important cornerstones of postcolonial research are elucidated in chapter 5.1. Briefly, these include first and foremost a self-reflexive researcher who openly communicates the results of her reflexions in the research report (see chapter 5.1.1). This is not specific to postcolonial research, yet it is one of its cornerstones. Self-reflexivity involves opposing the principles of neopositivist empiricism, among them the researcher's "carefully constructed public self as a mysterious, impartial outsider, an observer freed of personality and bias" (England 1994, 81). One way to express this opposition is to use "the reflexive 'I'" in academic writing (ibid., 82), as I have decided to do in this work. This expresses my readiness to "*accept responsibility* for the research" instead of pretending to either be able to "'give voice' to the researched" (ibid., 86, emphasis by E.K.) or to be a neutral, objective analyst of social 'reality' (ibid., 81-82). After all, every researcher is a human being with a theoretical, ideological, and personal background with characteristics in terms of ethnicity, gender, age, social class, etc. (Denzin/ Lincoln 1994, 3; England 1994, 85; Grosfoguel 2011, 5;

Kapoor 2004, 640-641). Although a researcher should certainly try to be as objective as possible, she should be aware of the limits to objectivity and be open about these to her readers. However, a critical research practice should not end at talking about oneself. Another important element of postcolonial research is to practise "a more receptive listening" (Alcoff 1991, 17; see also: Rufer 2012, 48; details in chapter 5.1.2). In the course of this research project, I conducted qualitative interviews because this means gathering information from the researched themselves. This should not conceal that it is I who analysed and interpreted the interviews. Pavarti Raghuram and Clare Madge state:

> "[...] we certainly do not presume that all difference can be dissolved to attain a complete (rational) understanding of the other, for there will always be degrees of incomprehensibility and continuing spaces 'in between'. But working through these inbetween spaces can bring moments of enlightenment; glimpses of the world through someone else's reality [...]." (Raghuram/ Madge 2006, 276)

The researcher must give up the illusion of herself being in the position of reaching a *full and objectively correct* understanding of 'the Other'. She must accept the insurmountable limits of her methods, her theoretical framework, her positionality and, above all, the limits that the researched decide to set for her. The limits imposed by power imbalances can also never be completely overcome. They are integral to the research situation and, when a person from the global North conducts research in the global South, they are severely exacerbated by *global* power imbalances (see chapter 5.1.3 for details). The researcher must reduce them as far as possible but nevertheless communicate the remaining limits of her endeavour (Denzin et al. 2017, 483-484; England 1994, 81-86; Husseini de Araújo/ Kersting 2012, 142). As I explain further in chapters 5 and 9.3, I have tried to comply with these requirements as far as possible and to be open with regard to the limitations.

The main research activity of this study involved conducting problem-centred interviews, a semi-structured form of qualitative interviews. These are divided into 30 'main interviews' with representatives of the general public living in the Busoga region of Uganda and ten 'expert interviews' with Ugandan academics, government representatives, and prominent figures from Busoga. The latter are regarded as 'experts' because their position provides them access to information that the respondents of the 'main interviews' do not have. Nevertheless, the 'main interviews' are the most important source of information in this study. This is mirrored by the term 'main' and their significantly higher number in comparison to the 'expert interviews'. The 'expert interviews' are intended to provide contextual information for the 'main interviews'. By the time this research started, the Busoga sub-region consisted of ten districts (UBOS 2018, 4). For reasons of feasibility, the area of research of this study had to be limited to a manageable size (see also chapter 5.2.1 for details of this discussion). I chose three districts, which represent a good overview of Busoga's different facets (see chapter 6.2 for details): Buyende, Jinja, and Kamuli Districts. The interviewees were identified through a combination of the gatekeeper approach and the snowball method. For analysing the interviews, I used Virginia Braun and Victoria Clarke's approach to *Thematic Analysis* (Braun/ Clarke 2006). As described in detail in chapter 5.2.4, it encompasses six phases of which the first two allowed me to work very closely with the original data, and the remaining four phases gradually increase the level of interpretation. This suited my wish to, on one hand, 'listen' to the researched actively and, on the other hand, be as transparent as possible in terms of the researcher's role in the research process. The interviews were recorded, transcribed with the help of the computer software *f4-transcript*, and analysed with the help of the computer software *MAXQDA*.

Another means of interpreting the interview material is contextual information collected in the scope of a document analysis, which I describe further in chapter 5.3. I have analysed a variety of written documents originating from the period between 1965 and 2018. I found some at *Jinja Archives* or the Africana section of *Makerere University Library*, was provided others by various Ugandan institutions, and found still others on the internet. These documents provide information about aspects of interest to my study that were fragmentary in the interviews and not easy to trace in the literature. I applied *content structuring Qualitative Content Analysis* (QCA) as described by Philipp Mayring (Mayring 2008) to the analysis of the documents. I chose this method in accordance with the nature of the data and the expectations I had towards the outcome of the analysis (contextual information). I analysed the documents with the help of the computer software MAXQDA.

1.4 *The setting*

In his book *The Anti-Politics Machine*, James Ferguson states that it is "not principally a book about the Basotho people, or even about Lesotho; it is principally a book about the operation of the international 'development' apparatus *in a particular setting*" (Ferguson 2014, 17, emphasis by E.K.). In an analogous manner, this study is not principally intended as a work on Uganda or the Basoga people. It is rather supposed to be a work on traces of global capitalism and solidarity in a local economy – *in a particular setting* in the global South, namely the Busoga region in Uganda. Nevertheless, the *setting* is more than a mere frame or location. It has great influence on the particular shape the objects under examination (globalisation and solidarity) take in the hands of the people concerned. The information about Uganda collected in chapter 6.1 and about Busoga collected in chapters 6.2 and 7 principally refer to events and circumstances that have (had) direct influence on the everyday lives of the people living in Busoga because this is what my research focuses on. Uganda has 15 sub-regions, of which Busoga is one (UBOS 2018, 4). By no means do I intend to generalise everything that may apply to this region (or parts of it) to the whole of 'Africa'[4], not even to the whole of 'Uganda'. Conversely, the experiences of people in Busoga *are part of* Uganda as well as of Africa. This means that, though what can be accepted as valid for Busoga is unlikely to be true for each and every other region of Uganda or especially of Africa – it is nevertheless a small but significant part of Ugandan as well as African lifeworlds.

1.5 Structure of the thesis

I outline the theoretical framework of this study in chapters 2, 3, and 4. Chapter 2 introduces the basic theoretical approaches on which the idea for this research project, the conceptualisation of its contents, its research design, and the interpretation of the collected data are based: Postcolonial theory (chapter 2.1), critical approaches to development theory (2.2) including the Post-Development approach (2.2.3), and world-systems analysis (2.3). Beyond that, central terms and concepts like 'Africa', 'the global South/North', etc., are being defined (2.4). In the following chapter, after having introduced the phenomenon of globalisation in general (3.1), I present it from the point of view of the three above-mentioned theoretical approaches (chapters 3.2, 3.3, and 3.4). I also consider the alter-globalisation discourse: In chapter 3.5, I take a brief look at international resistance movements. In chapter 4, I discuss alternative economic approaches in general and the Social and Solidarity Economy (SSE) in particular. I

4 For explanations on the use of the term 'Africa' in this thesis, see chapter 2.4.

present in chapter 4.3 three models of alternative economic practices (De-Growth, Fair Trade, and SSE) that oppose capitalist principles to differing extents. This highlights the most important characteristics of SSE in comparison to other alternative approaches and explains why I have included SSE as the main approach in the empirical part of the thesis. Chapter 5 starts with the presentation of the theoretical and ethical considerations, on which the methodology of this research project has been built (chapter 5.1). This includes a detailed discussion of the principles of postcolonial/ decolonial research methodology briefly outlined above. Beyond that, I explain in that sub-section how I have tried to implement those principles in the course of this research project. This is followed by the presentation of the research methods of this study: qualitative interviews (5.2) and document analysis (5.3). I describe in detail the data collection that involved 'main interviews' (5.2.1) and 'expert interviews' (5.2.2), transcription and translation (5.2.3), and data analysis (5.2.4). Apart from reporting what I have been doing, I elucidate how my postcolonial approach to research methodology has led to the decisions I took during the processes of data collection and analysis.

The method applied to chapters 2 to 6 is literature review. Chapter 6 presents a brief overview of Uganda's political history after independence (6.1) and provides a short excursion through academic literature about Busoga (6.2). The information provided in that chapter is intended to facilitate the understanding of the research results presented in chapters 7 and 8. In chapter 7, I outline the results of my document analysis. These results deliver helpful information about aspects that were central, yet fragmentary in the interviews, e.g., because respondents could not remember the details very well or lacked contextual information. Chapter 8 displays the results of the interview study. It is structured according to the results of the thematic analysis of the interviews. It begins with the presentation of the themes derived from the interview data (8.1). This is followed by two chapters that are named after the two main themes of the interview analysis (8.2 and 8.3). They are divided into sub-sections according to their respective sub-themes and each concludes on a sub-section outlining the key findings of the main theme (8.2.8 and 8.3.7). The theoretical framework of the study is applied to the research results throughout the entire chapter. Yet, some general theoretical implications of the overall results of the study are elaborated in chapter 8.4.1. Chapter 8 closes with the final conclusions on the two aspects under examination in this study: globalisation in Busoga's everyday economy (8.4.2) and the Social and Solidarity Economy in Busoga (8.4.3) as well as their implications for the situation of women and girls in Busoga (8.4.4.). Finally, chapter 9 provides conclusions on the central empirical findings, theoretical considerations arising from them, and the methods and methodology of this study.

2. Theoretical background of the study

This chapter provides an overview of the schools of thought that have influenced this study. My contention is that there is no single theory that can explain the complexities of globalisation and its manifold impacts on distinct societies. Consequently, my theoretical framework encompasses three schools of thought: postcolonial theory, critical development studies, and world-systems analysis. This chapter starts with an introduction to postcolonial theory (chapter 2.1). The latter determines my general attitude towards the research topics and my research methodology (see also chapter 5.1). This is followed by a discussion of the concept of 'development' (chapter 2.2.1) and different approaches to it, namely the conventional (see also chapter 2.2.1), the reformist (2.2.2), and the Post-Development approach (2.2.3). Chapter 2.2 concludes on the explanation of my approach to 'development' in this study (2.2.4). This is important because this study is supposed to make a contribution to critical development studies. It focuses on the effects of globalisation on the Busoga region in Uganda. As I elaborate in chapters 2.2 and 3.3, a discussion of globalisation in a country of the global South raises the issue of 'development' automatically, as the discourses of globalisation and 'development' overlap to a great extent, especially when it comes to the global South. The third school of thought that I present in this chapter is world-systems analysis, particularly Immanuel Wallerstein's approach. As I elucidate in chapters 2.3 and 3.4, world-systems analysis is a school of thought that adds a peculiar and interesting perspective to the globalisation debate, though it is again a limited one. In chapter 2.4, I explain my understanding and use of certain terms and concepts in this thesis, namely Africa, discourse, First World/ Third World/ global North/ South, hegemony, the subaltern, the West, and 'traditional'. Chapter 2.5 contains a brief conclusion on the issues discussed in this chapter.

An exhaustive account of any of the theories presented in this chapter would exceed the parameters of this study. A good introduction to the influential thoughts and writers of these theories would fill at least one book, each. As a result, my presentation of them is selective, providing only a glimpse. That element of selection tells more about me, the one who considers certain aspects important enough to occupy some of the limited space in my thesis, than about the theories presented. As a result, the purpose of this chapter is to show which aspects of the concerned theories have influenced this thesis the most. The image of those theories presented here shall neither be complete, nor distorted.

2.1 Postcolonial theory

Postcolonial theory is the major theoretical foundation of the ideas underlying this study. It determines my general attitude towards the research topics and my research methodology (see also chapter 5.1). This chapter starts with a general introduction to postcolonial theory (2.1.1), followed by a brief presentation of the 'classics', i.e., the most renowned thinkers, of postcolonial theory (2.1.2). It concludes on some reflections on Eurocentric epistemology and possible ways to decolonise it (2.1.3). This is important because in this study, I intend to challenge Eurocentric epistemology and value knowledge that has its origin in the global South. The latter applies to academic authors originating from global South countries as well as to the respondents of this study (for details on the latter aspect, see chapter 5).

2.1.1 What is postcolonial theory?

Postcolonial theory[5] is the most important theoretical basis of this study. It has influenced the theoretical approach as much as the methodological one (see chapter 5). As María do Mar Castro Varela and Nikita Dhawan aptly point out in their introductory book on postcolonial theory, it does not denominate a specific concept with regard to content, space, historical

---

5 Distinct authors refer to it either as 'postcolonial critique', 'postcolonial theory' or 'postcolonial studies'. Although some authors may have their reasons for their preference of one of them, e.g., because of their disciplinal or theoretical orientation, the three terms are being used to signify the same thing. Furthermore, there is the 'decolonial' movement, which has introduced the Latin American perspective to postcolonialism, which originally had a "strong focus on Asia and some few Arabian and African areas" (Castro Varela/Dhawan 2005, 319, translation by E.K.). Although some representatives of de-colonialism have criticised postcolonialism severely, it is rather a complement to it than an opposition, as their concerns in terms of content match, only their regional focus differs (ibid., 18-20, 318-319). As a result, it is common practice to quote decolonial writers alongside with postcolonial ones.

period, or political aims (Castro Varela/ Dhawan 2015, 286; for comparable statements, see also Kerner 2012, 10; McEwan 2009, 34). This can be regarded as its flaw or as its strength because that openness allows the concept to host even marginalised narratives and support different perspectives in challenge with each other (Castro Varela/ Dhawan 2015, 298). Cheryl McEwan defines postcolonialism as a "contestation of colonial and neo-imperial power and knowledge" (McEwan 2009, 35). Postcolonial critique aims at questioning Eurocentric discourses, epistemologies, and other power constellations, and at clearing the way for oppressed points of view (ibid., 25-26). Apart from variations in discipline or content, postcolonial writings stand out due to "their commitment to challenging cultural hegemony (be that from the West or from post-colonial elites), their commitment to anti-racism and anti-colonial politics, and their focus on matters of culture" (ibid., 35) – however, the latter does not apply to all of them to the same extent. What unites all these different approaches is "a common political and moral consensus towards the history and legacy of western colonialism", including the conviction that colonialism was not another finite episode of violence like many others in history (Young 2001, 5). Robert Young defines colonialism's main feature to be the way it has managed to survive its alleged termination and keep hold of its victims by transforming its appearance from a political-military to a political-economic one. Postcolonial theory aims to trace the consequences of colonialism in present politics, society, and academia, in the global North as well as in the global South (ibid., 5-6). Although, according to Castro Varela and Dhawan "[d]ecolonisation, after all, means primarily the disqualification of racist strategies of legitimisation" (Castro Varela/ Dhawan 2015, 300, translation by E.K.), they still warn the postcolonial theorist not to forget the equally important categories of class (ibid., 303) and gender (ibid., 300-303). Leela Gandhi states that: "Over the last decade, postcolonial studies has emerged both as a meeting point and battleground for a variety of disciplines and theories" (Gandhi 2019, 3). What can be said about approaches of postcolonial studies, critique, or theory in general is that they are *critical* approaches, which draw their readers' attention to social problems and unfair power relations (Kerner 2012, 12). Originating from literary and culture studies, postcolonial theory has made its way into numerous disciplines, which have all brought in their specific perspective (from historical to political science), such that postcolonial theory has become explicitly eclectic (ibid., 14-15). Ina Kerner emphasises postcolonial theory's ambition to challenge mainstream thinking, no matter in which discipline, e.g., by turning to perspectives that had been excluded or neglected before. She states that, in political theory, the first moves in the postcolonial direction started with the first consideration of decolonial texts, from the 1960s up to the 1980s, with some language-areas being ahead of others, e.g., English being ahead of German (ibid., 152-153). Postcolonial theory has a high sensitivity for historical as well as present-day global entanglement. It approaches respective questions from different points of view, be it socio-economic, political, epistemic, or cultural (ibid., 165), making it particularly suitable for my study.

Postcolonial theory's most important theoretical roots can be found in poststructuralism, psychoanalysis, and neo-Marxism (Kerner 2012, 34-40). Leela Gandhi expresses a common view when she calls poststructuralism and Marxism "mutually antagonistic theories", which have nevertheless been integrated in postcolonial theory (Gandhi 2019, 3). It seems that a postcolonial theorist has to choose, which camp to join. I am not willing to make that choice. In my view, to reject any of the two perspectives categorically would mean an attempt to keep up a three-dimensional vision with one eye closed. The poststructuralist approach is essential for analysing how 'the West' constructed, and still constructs, itself and 'the Other', using this construction in order to exercise power over 'the Other' and legitimise that power. As Leela Gandhi suggests, postcolonial theory has learnt from poststructuralism to question Western civilisation, culture, and epistemology (ibid., 25-26). This is one of postcolonial theory's essential features, for which Marxism cannot take the credit. Nevertheless, its use may be questioned as an academic end in itself, if there is no reference to the concrete economic living conditions of the suppressed as well as concrete political and economic measures that are taken on the global level. This is where the materialist approach comes in. The lives of people have both material as well as non-material aspects (e.g., in terms of culture, identity, epistemology), and (neo-)colonialism has manipulated all those aspects of life heavily. Consequently, to limit postcolonial critique to an approach that concentrates on one of these aspects exclusively, does not do its project justice. When it comes to the analysis of power, both the poststructuralist and the materialist approach have important aspects to contribute. The globalised world is much too complex to be analysed properly with the tool of 'one big theory'. In my view, what makes postcolonial theory particularly suitable for this task is its very openness to different approaches that agree on a handful of basic principles (see preceding paragraph), as well as its ambition to make 'the unthinkable' thinkable. Admittedly, in their original forms formulated by Karl Marx himself on the one hand and Jacques Derrida and Michel Foucault on the other, the theories would be difficult to combine. Indeed, it is highly questionable whether orthodox Marxism could be of any use to postcolonial theory at all. For example, Marx regarded the dissemination of European capitalism through colonialism as necessary, as prerequisite for social revolution (ibid., 73-74), and he believed that every country in the world would have to follow the same steps of industrial 'development' heading for the same goal (Chakrabarty 2000, 7). Those are just two of the most popular arguments against Marx, quoted by two renowned postcolonial critics. Such reproaches created the image of Marxism promoting a linear idea of development and history. On the other hand, Ngũgĩ wa Thiong'o states: "Marx made me reflect on many things including my conception of history and narrative practice" as he "challenged the linear development of history" and "released me from a one-dimensional view of reality" (Ngũgĩ wa Thiong'o 2014, 20). Robert Young argues as follows: "Marxism [...] has always been in some sense anti-western, since it was developed by Marx as a critique of western social and economic practices and the values which they embodied" (Young 2001, 6). In addition to that, he reminds us that postcolonial Marxism is not necessarily a 'pure' Marxism, but has been adapted and developed in different ways (ibid., 6-7).

In general, since their debut, both approaches have undergone diverse transformations and enhancements. Marxism has been transformed to neo-Marxism, which is being promoted by many theorists, who reject being called (orthodox) 'Marxists'. Apart from several neo-Marxist trajectories in the global North, there is what Robert Young calls "a flexible Marxism responsive to local conditions in the three continents" in the global South (Young 2001, 7). Poststructuralism is now associated with many more authors than Derrida and Foucault, among them Gayatri C. Spivak. Indeed, Spivak, herself a luminary in postcolonial theory, is an excellent example of postcolonial theory's ability to make 'the unthinkable' thinkable. While her works are based on Derrida and Foucault to a considerable extent, she also criticises those two theorists and their trajectory, e.g., for disregarding the international division of labour (Spivak 1988, 272; see also chapter 3.2 of this thesis). Spivak "has been referred to as a 'Marxist-feminist-deconstructionist', since she sees each of these approaches as necessary but insufficient by themselves, always in tension, yet productive together" (McEwan 2009, 67). According to Spivak's reasoning, Marxist theory of the international division of labour and the globalisation of capital can be valuable for analysing the relationship between the global North and the global South (Gandhi 2019, 74). Stuart Hall likewise criticises postcolonial theory sharply for having pushed aside the economic perspective on global capitalism. In Hall's view, this was postcolonialism's reaction to the breakdown of orthodox Marxism. Nevertheless, Hall insists that this break with orthodox Marxism should have led to "alternative reflections on questions of economic relationships and their consequences" *within* postcolonial analysis, instead of the two entering into competition with each other (Hall 2002, 243).

Crystal Bartolovich aptly points out that, although Marxism has a difficult standing within postcolonial studies, it has been and continues to be a crucial part of it. She attributes this difficult standing to Marxism's insistence on the criticism of capitalism, while according to her, that criticism has gone out of fashion among many postcolonial theorists. In response to the wide-spread accusation of Marxism being Eurocentric, Bartolovich admits that this is definitely true for some (neo-)Marxist approaches, while it is not for others (Bartolovich 2002, 9-11). Though not uncritical of Marxism at all, Dipesh Chakrabarty calls Marx "a relevant and fundamental critic of both capitalism and liberalism and thus central to any postcolonial, postmodern project of writing history" (Chakrabarty 2000, 30-31). Chakrabarty calls Marx' writings "one of the founding moments in the history of anti-imperial thought" (ibid., 47). Drawing on several other renowned authors, like Aijaz Ahmad and Arif Dirlik, E. San Juan Jr. accuses postcolonial theory of being incapable[6] of dealing with "globalized capitalism" (San Juan 2002, 221). According to San Juan, this incapability results from postcolonial theory's rejection of Marxism, which in turn, originates from a false image of Marxism having a linear, unidirectional, developmentalist idea of social change (ibid., 221-222). Those kinds of accusations against Marxism, alongside the accusation of Eurocentrism, can be found in the literature frequently. San Juan seeks to prove them wrong. He quotes Marx' explicit repudiation of any labelling of his theory as "suprahistorical" or as being applicable to every setting, regardless of its historical preconditions, referencing a letter that Marx wrote to a Russian journal in 1878 and underscoring it with evidence from other writings by Marx (ibid., 224-225). Immanuel Wallerstein ascribes this confusion in the perception of Marx' theory to Josef Stalin, premier of the Soviet Union from 1927 to 1953. According to Wallerstein, Stalin banned those parts of Marx' theories that did not fit his policy, among them the "Asiatic mode of production", which had been the proof of Marx' acknowledgement of exceptions to the rule of his suggested stages of development (Wallerstein 2007, 13). As a result, Wallerstein states, communist scholars had little

6 Dirlik would rather say *not willing* to deal with it (Dirlik 2004, 502-503).

scope left during the Stalinist era and only started thinking more freely after 1953 (ibid.).

(Neo-)Marxist theorists, on the other hand, return some criticism on postcolonial theory, e.g., accusing it of "complicity" with capitalism (San Juan 2002, 222, see also 230, 238-239) and its "ideology of the 'free market'" (ibid., 229). Arif Dirlik construes this complicity from a refusal to acknowledge that capitalism is the foundation of global relations, which leads to political, cultural, and social domination (Dirlik 2004, 503, 515-516). Furthermore, some of its critics judge postcolonial critique an academic end in itself, i.e., an occupation for academics without any relevance to its own target group, the subaltern in the post-colonies (Gandhi 2019, 56-57). Dirlik even calls postcolonialism "an expression [...] of new-found power" of "Third World intellectuals who have arrived in First World academe" (Dirlik 2004, 510, see also 513). Those accusations may apply to *some* postcolonial writings, but to most of them, they do not. Young expresses the contrary point of view when he writes: "Postcolonial critique is therefore a form of activist writing that looks back to the political commitment of the anti-colonial liberation movements and draws its inspiration from them, while recognizing that they often operated under conditions very different from those that exist in the present" (Young 2001, 10). This way of thinking can be traced back to Young's conviction that Marxism is not what postcolonialism tries to overcome, but its very basis (ibid., 6-10, 58). Nowadays, many postcolonial writers have accepted the challenge to analyse global capitalism and its consequences. For instance, Boaventura de Sousa Santos regards colonialism, as well as patriarchy, as tools of capitalist domination being unabatedly prevalent today and needing to be fought by a new kind of social science (Santos 2017, 34-35). In terms of the last-mentioned argument by Dirlik, the reproach against Third World intellectuals having discovered their new power, one might wonder why he considers this circumstance problematic. He reproachfully cites an interview, in which Indian academics exhort Spivak to mind the difference between herself, who, in her diaspora situation, could teach and write whatever she wanted without any consequences, and themselves, who were not free to the same extent (Dirlik 2004, 509). I would like to respond that the freedom of speech as well as the academic and sometimes political influence of Third World intellectuals, who live in the diaspora, should be regarded as a chance for being heard, not as an expression of arrogance. Nevertheless, there is one reproach to postcolonial critics with a poststructuralist, rather anti-Marxist attitude that some of them have to put up with: As long as they keep on concentrating on issues of language, culture, and identity instead of political problems, their writings give little trouble to conservative positions (ibid., 513). Boaventura de Sousa Santos states: "According to the epistemologies of the South, decolonizing thought and action won't be an efficacious cultural intervention if they are not an intervention in political economy as well" (Santos 2017, 117).

James Ferguson opens up a discussion that sounds very similar, with regard to the question of modernity in anthropological research. Although he does not refer to Marxism and poststructuralism, or to any particular theoretical approach at all, Ferguson's analysis contains striking parallels to the discussion that I have tried to trace briefly, above. Ferguson explicates why anthropologists have such a different view on modernity than most Africans. The latter tend to label their continent, country, or region as 'not modern', thinking of their daily living conditions, while anthropologists try to overcome outmoded ideas in Western science that used to deny coevalness to non-Western societies and label them as 'archaic' (Ferguson 2005, 174-175). Ferguson elaborates that the anthropologists' ambitions to prove that Africa *is* modern, in a cultural sense, are indeed honourable and necessary, as they have proved the existence of "coeval cultural difference" and "opened up for analysis a vast terrain of hybrids and bricolage" (ibid., 177). Nevertheless, he calls for more space for the problem of Africa's difficult political-economic position in a world of increasing global inequality and its corollaries (ibid., 180). When it comes to the living conditions of people, Ferguson states that modernity has become "a standard of living, a *status*, not a telos" (ibid., 176, emphasis in the original). The myth that everyone would be able to reach material modernity, i.e., 'development', one day, has given way to the insight that it is a status by birth that only a handful of people, who were not born in it, can ever reach – the fewest of whom are living in Africa (ibid., 176-179). If we compare it to the postcolonial debate sketched above, we may say that the Africans, whom Ferguson talked to, showed a preliminary materialist approach to 'modernity'. In contrast, the anthropologists tend to ignore that aspect (ibid., 174) and concentrate on issues of culture, identity, hybridity, and the like – bearing resemblance to the poststructuralist approach in postcolonial theory. It may depend on one's understanding of science whether one might prefer an approach that is closer to and more relevant for the concrete living conditions of the researched, or an approach that makes use of scientific distance in order to have a more abstract view. Eventually, if wanting to know *how Africa is* today, to concentrate on one of them exclusively may not suffice. In my view, this is another proof of the need to combine the two views, though with emphasis on the priorities of the researched (see also chapter 5.1).

The examination of "social injustices and inequalities" belongs to the focal points of postcolonial theory (Castro Varela/ Dhawan 2015, 299, translation by E.K.). Castro Varela and Dhawan trace the inequality between the global North and the global South back to the effects of colonialism, which they still see at work in exploitative global trade relations (ibid., 86). Nevertheless, the discursive practice of postcolonial theory should not be underestimated. As Aimé Césaire quotes from countless conversations he had about colonisation, and as Djibril Tamsir Niane quotes from a much more recent example, an official speech of Nicolas Sarkozy from 2007, colonialism's negative consequences are often traded off against its supposed 'achievements' for the colonised like roads, bridges, schools, and the like (Césaire 2000, 42-43; Niane 2010, 266-267). Whoever thinks that some kilometres of road network are worth countless human lives and unimaginable pains caused by torture, rape, forced labour, and deportation, cannot condemn colonialism, certainly. The intent of postcolonialism is to remind the world, especially the global North, which *actually profited* from colonialism and therefore tends to defend it or play it down, that this weighing up of human suffering against material items should *not* be acceptable at all. As part of that endeavour, postcolonialism highlights misconducts like those of Sarkozy in order to achieve the ostracism of racist, neo-colonialist, and inhuman discourse and behaviour. In addition to that, postcolonial research reminds the West of what it likes to forget. For instance, as Niane aptly points out, it were not the colonisers themselves, who sweated in the sun and died in accidents or due to exhaustion while building roads, railways, and bridges, but the colonised themselves (Niane 2010, 266-267). All that the colonisers invested was some knowledge and money – and they did it in anticipation of financial returns, not for charitable reasons.

After all, one might feel obliged to ask whether postcolonial analysis allows the use of European, and in some cases evidently Eurocentric, theories at all. Chakrabarty's answer is yes. He states that the worldwide influence of European thought has been too strong already for it to be excluded from postcolonial analysis. For him, "provincializing Europe becomes the task of exploring how this thought—which is now everybody's heritage and which affects us all—may be renewed from and for the margins" (Chakrabarty 2000, 16). Boaventura de Sousa Santos cautions that "the diversity of world experience is inexhaustible and therefore cannot be accounted for by any single general theory" (Santos 2014, 46). His recipe is to widen the theoretical horizon, not by excluding the contributions from the global North that do have their merits, but rather by complementing them with contributions from all directions (ibid., 42). For instance, Valentin Y. Mudimbe borrows Leo Frobenius' idea of 'African genesis' and develops it further into his concept of the 'invention of Africa' (Mudimbe 1988, 16). This does not mean that, in order to develop a valuable theory, he was in dire need of an idea from the global North as its foundation. Certainly, he could have done without it, but as it fitted his purpose, there was no reason why he should not have used it and made it his own. Shying away from using theories from the global North could be suggestive of unnecessary mystification.

The 'post' in postcolonial theory might be misleading, as it creates the impression of linearity from pre-colonial, through colonial, to post-colonial times and concerns (Castro Varela/ Dhawan 2015, 287). On the contrary, postcolonial theory does not regard colonialism and decolonisation as mere historical events that followed each other in-line, but as a continuous struggle of (neo-)colonial attempts of oppression and diverse forms of postcolonial resistance (ibid., 16). The formal obtainment of independence by the former colonies did not end the "epistemological and material conditions, on which European colonialism had rested" (Dhawan 2011, 12, translation by E.K.; see also Gandhi 2019, 17; Grosfoguel 2008, 95-96; 2011, 14; Ndlovu-Gatsheni 2013, 3-7, 50-51; Santos 2017, 19). Dirlik calls it "a world situation in which severe inequalities persist in older colonial forms or in their neocolonial reconfigurations" (Dirlik 2004, 514). For some postcolonial critics, "the unbroken term 'postcolonialism'" is an expression of this continuation of the colonial legacy, while others prefer the hyphenated spelling 'post-colonialism' in order to emphasise the process of decolonisation (Gandhi 2019, 3). Drawing on this reasoning, I chose to use the term without hyphen. For Stuart Hall, the 'post' in 'postcolonial' has the same quality like other 'post's, for example in 'post-structuralism': Chronologically, they come *after*, but they also go *beyond* the second part of their name, which causes a kind of tension that Hall deems productive (Hall 2002, 236-240). In his view, 'postcolonial' is a descriptive term, not an evaluative one that needs to be kept back for those who 'deserve' to be called 'postcolonial'. Hall states that even the colonisers have been affected by colonisation, though in a different way than the colonised (ibid., 225-226).

2.1.2 The classics of postcolonial theory

In any introduction to postcolonial theory, three names should never be missing: Edward Said, Gayatri C. Spivak, and Homi K. Bhabha. There is a certain consensus about their works *Orientalism*, *Can the Subaltern Speak?*, and *The location of culture* being the founding documents of postcolonial theory in the narrow sense. This might be true as far as the commitment to theory is concerned. Yet, they build on the – nevertheless theoretical – contributions of early anticolonial thinkers, who were rather recognised for their political commitment during their lifetime, most prominent among them Frantz Fanon and Aimé Césaire. Since then, many other brilliant and influential thinkers have made their contributions to postcolonial theory, though not all of them would call themselves postcolonial. And not all of them can be presented in the shortness of this sub-section. Based on their significance for my research approach, I chose to present in brief approaches of the following authors: Achille Mbembe, Valentin Y. Mudimbe, Boaventura de Sousa Santos, along with the 5 authors mentioned at the beginning of this paragraph. Beyond that, two authors from the decolonial school of thought, which is very closely related to postcolonial theory but has its particular Latin-American perspective (Castro Varela/ Dhawan 2015, 19-20), have their say in this chapter, namely Aníbal Quijano and Ramón Grosfoguel. Some ideas of another decolonial thinker, Walter Mignolo, as well as those of two other important representatives of postcolonial studies, namely Dipesh Chakrabarty and Shalini Randeria, are discussed in the next sub-section on decolonising epistemologies (chapter 2.1.3).

One of the most influential works of postcolonial theory is Edward Said's *Orientalism* (Castro Varela/ Dhawan 2015, 93-94; Gandhi 2019, 25, 64-66; McEwan 2009, 62). Said delivered the first discourse analysis of colonial, Eurocentric epistemologies and their production of the images of subjects and colonisers in a way that justified colonial rule (Castro Varela/ Dhawan 2015, 94-95). Thus, he demonstrated how knowledge was used as an instrument of power – though it was putative knowledge, which was based on representations and presented in the form of stereotypes (ibid., 97). In Said's own words, referring to the Foucauldian understanding of discourse, Orientalism was Europe's way "to manage—and even produce—the Orient politically, sociologically, militarily, ideologically, scientifically, and imaginatively during the post-Enlightenment period" (Said 1994, 3). As Leela Gandhi has elaborated, 'Orientalism' has three meanings in Said's work: First, it is a field of academic study. Second,

Said extends Orientalism to any kind of Western writing on the non-Western world. Third, he presents it "as an enormous system or inter-textual network of rules and procedures which regulate anything that may be thought, written or imagined about the orient", which is Said's main view of Orientalism (Gandhi 2019, 76). According to Said, the discourse of Orientalism creates a dichotomy between a self-image of the 'Occident' and its 'Other', the 'Orient' with its imagined opposing characteristics that justify its domination by the 'Occident' (ibid., 76-77). Said illustrates from historical and contemporary sources how the West created the image of itself being "rational, peaceful, liberal, logical, capable of holding real values, without natural suspicion", while construing the Orient as being "none of these things" (Said 1994, 49). The resemblance with the way the West staged itself in contrast with other colonies and their peoples, for instance in Africa, is more than obvious and will be elaborated further in subsequent chapters of the thesis at hand. Consequently, Orientalism tells more about its creators, the representatives of the 'Occident', than about its supposed object of study (McEwan 2009, 63). Those creators try to stabilise their self-image by construing the 'Other' as its perfect opposite. The constructed inferiority of the 'Other' is the main justification for its oppression, yet, this argumentation is only made possible through one particular discursive element: the pretence to *know* them and to *know* what is good for them (Said 1994, 34-35). Hence, 'knowledge' becomes an instrument of power. And in the hands of those in power, that 'knowledge' did not even need any rooting in reality, but could be made of fantasies and prejudices.

In the context of Africa, Valentin Y. Mudimbe's *The Invention of Africa* is regarded as the equivalent to *Orientalism* (Castro Varela/ Dhawan 2015, 95). Mudimbe describes vividly how Europe has been painting its own fantastic picture of Africa ever since, without caring for any similarity with what could actually be found on location, let alone how Africans see themselves and their environment (Mudimbe 1988). He illustrates his hypothesis with numerous examples, e.g., from arts from the sixteenth century onwards (ibid., 6-13), from epistemology (ibid., 13-15), from missionaries' discourse (ibid., 44-64), and from many other discourses. Mudimbe shows how anthropology, his equivalent to Said's Orientalism, turned into "a clearly visible power-knowledge political system" at the turn of the eighteenth century to the nineteenth (ibid., 16). He goes on arguing that anthropology has developed parallel to imperialism (ibid., 17) and "invents" its object of study, constituting it as the 'abnormal' ('primitive') counterpart to its image of the 'normal' ('civilised') self (ibid.,

27). Mudimbe asserts that anthropology has even managed to penetrate and instrumentalise supposed movements for African emancipation like the negritude movement (ibid., 86-87). Together with Said's *Orientalism* and Walter Mignolo's *The Idea of Latin America*, Mudimbe's *The Invention of Africa* completes the panorama of the production of a Eurocentric world view with the global North as the 'civilised' self and the global South as the supposedly 'inferior' Other (Castro Varela/ Dhawan 2015, 95).

Ten years after Said's *Orientalism*, an essay that was comparably essential for postcolonial theory was published: Gayatri C. Spivak's *Can the Subaltern Speak?* (Castro Varela/ Dhawan 2015, 152). Her own answer to the question was: "The subaltern cannot speak" (Spivak 1988, 308). However, this statement was often misconceived. Spivak means that, regardless of whether they try to *speak* or not, the subaltern *cannot be heard* because there is no space for them in the dominant discourse (Steyerl 2008, 12). Consequently, they need to be represented by intellectuals (Castro Varela/ Dhawan 2015, 192). Rosalind Morris highlights Spivak's "consequent emphasis on the question of audibility and legibility", focusing on the conditions that deny the subaltern, especially the subaltern woman, to be heard and to be taken seriously by the powerful (Morris 2010, 3). Drawing on Jacques Derrida's writings, Spivak presents deconstruction, namely the analysis of how the ethnocentric European subject constitutes itself by constructing the 'Other' as its counterpart, as an advancement in comparison to the quest for authenticity within the 'Other' (Spivak 1988, 292-294). Far beyond *Can the Subaltern Speak?*, Spivak has become one of the luminaries in postcolonial critique. Prior to Spivak's intervention, academic feminism had been dominated by theorists from the global North, who, for the most part, propagated a so-called 'international feminism' that was insensitive to their own complicity in unequal global power structures, as well as to the real concerns of women in the global South (Castro Varela/ Dhawan 2015, 163). Feminists from the global South, most famous being Spivak and Chandra Talpade Mohanty, have been criticising the image of the 'Third World woman'. Mohanty deplores Western feminists' representation of 'women', on the one hand, as a homogenous group that was fighting the same struggle against male oppression, and 'Third World women', on the other hand, as an inferior version of their supposedly emancipated 'First World sisters', being "ignorant, poor, uneducated, tradition-bound, domestic family-oriented, victimized, etc." (Mohanty 2004, 258). Spivak's approach is often described as "Marxist-feminist deconstruction" (Castro Varela/ Dhawan 2015, 151, translation by E.K.), although Spivak herself rejects any kind of allocation to a theoretical school of thought and prefers to challenge academic conventions with her demanding style of writing (ibid., 153). Spivak has coined several terms that have become central to the postcolonial debate. First and foremost, she adopted Antonio Gramsci's term 'the subaltern' for the postcolonial context (see corresponding paragraph on 'The subaltern' in chapter 2.4). Just like Said, Spivak looked critically at both sides of the coin: She traced how even *anti*colonial resistance could lead to a continuation of inequality by giving rise to a bourgeoise kind of nationalism (ibid., 183). Spivak stands for a strong emphasis on the duties of the state towards its citizens and the need to educate them to exercise their civic rights (Kerner 2012, 79). She puts that conviction into practice by teaching students in the global North as well as in the global South, through her professorship in the USA as well as through her education project for subaltern children in India (Castro Varela/ Dhawan 2015, 152).

Just like Said, another luminary of postcolonial theory has been strongly influenced by Frantz Fanon: Homi K. Bhabha. Nevertheless, Said and Bhabha drew different conclusions from Fanon's thoughts (McEwan 2009, 45). The most important impulse that Bhabha gave to postcolonial theory was his insistence on the agency of the colonised (Castro Varela/ Dhawan 2015, 227). Castro Varela and Dhawan have clearly summarised how Bhabha criticised Said for establishing an image of colonial power being totally in the hands of the colonisers, without considering the agency of the colonised. Bhabha deplores the lack of room for negotiation or resistance in Said's dichotomous image of powerful colonisers and powerless colonised. As practical evidence of this agency, Bhabha uses a radical postcolonial and deconstructive approach by adjusting Western theories to his line of reasoning in his writings (ibid., 221-223). Bhabha tries to overcome dichotomies by a "revision of traditional Marxist and liberal concepts" as well as by "a critical analysis of postcolonial studies" (ibid., 237, translation by E.K.). According to Bhabha, "colonial discourse produces the colonized as a social reality which is at once an 'other' and yet entirely knowable and visible" (Bhabha 2004, 101). As "one of the most elusive and effective strategies of colonial power and knowledge", Bhabha identifies what he calls *mimicry* (ibid., 122). In relation to the coloniser, the colonised is supposed to be "a reformed, recognizable Other", "*almost the same, but not quite*" (ibid., emphasis in the original). Cheryl McEwan summarises Bhabha's main argument as follows: "If the colonized continues to behave in his traditional ways, he brings no economic gain to the colonizer. But, if the colonized changes too much and is found to be exactly the same as the colonizer, the colonizer is left with no argument for his supremacy"

(McEwan 2009, 65). Yet, that supremacy is already damaged the moment the coloniser animates the subject to imitate his culture, which gives the colonised the chance to challenge the coloniser through mimicry (ibid., 66). Another famous term that Bhabha has coined and that has become an established term within postcolonial publications since then, is *hybridity*. The concept came into being through several essays, which Bhabha first published during the 1980s and early 1990s, and which were eventually collected in the book *The location of culture*. The key feature that distinguishes Bhabha's particular concept of cultural hybridity from its usual meaning is that it arises from a deeply asymmetrical power constellation, the colonial situation, on which it grows, while at the same time, destabilising it (Kerner 2012, 126). In opposition to Said, who had been concentrated on the colonisers as well as to Fanon, for whom the colonised were in the centre of attention, Bhabha analysed their interaction, "the 'in-between'" (Castro Varela/ Dhawan 2015, 223, translation by E.K). In Bhabha's view, cultures have to be regarded as heterogenous, while their boundaries are "areas of the negotiation of difference", not a matter of fact (Kerner 2012, 127, translation by E.K.). In the colonial situation, this means that the cultures of the coloniser and the colonised had an impact *on each other*, not just one on the other (McEwan 2009, 65). For Bhabha, cultures are neither natural nor static, but the hybrid, non-homogenous, dynamic, and ever-incomplete, constructed results of historical processes (Castro Varela/ Dhawan 2015, 247-248). Bhabha has been criticised for the de-politicising effects of his preference for language, culture, and psychology, as well as for his incomprehensible style of writing (see for example Dirlik 2004, 524-525). Yet, even his critics admit that Bhabha has enriched the postcolonial discourse with some central terms like *hybridity*, and that he is an inspiration to other postcolonial thinkers (Dirlik 2004, 524-525).

Achille Mbembe puts forth the hypothesis that, although Europe had always been 'othering' every new people, culture, or language it encountered in the world, the reaction to Africa has been the strongest (Mbembe 2001, 2). This goes hand in hand with Frantz Fanon's description of his experience in colonial military service: Though discriminated because they were black, he and his fellow Antilleans were glad not to be Africans because they believed that the Europeans disdained Africans the most (Fanon 2008, 9-10). Mbembe decries the image of Africa's characteristics being "elementariness and primitiveness", "lesser value, little importance, and poor quality" (Mbembe 2001, 1), her inhabitants being regarded as animals rather than human beings (ibid., 1-2). When it comes to describe the relationship between the colonisers and the colonised, Mbembe creates a strong image, turning the idea of cannibalism – an act of 'barbarism' that the colonised were often accused of – the other way around: Mbembe compares the status of the colonised in the eyes of their colonisers to that of animals, who could be killed, cooked, and eaten by the coloniser at any time (ibid., 26-27). According to Mbembe, Africa serves as the object of projection "of the West's obsession with [...] nothingness", meaning that not to be like the West, especially to such a great extent as Africa, corresponds to "*being nothing*" (ibid., 4, emphasis in the original). Aimé Césaire calls it the "boomerang effect of colonization" that the coloniser declares the colonised an animal in order to justify treating him or her in inhuman ways, yet, by doing so, the coloniser turns himself[7] into an animal that features no traces of civilisation or compassion (Césaire 2000, 41). In his famous essay *Discourse on Colonialism*, Césaire takes up the European argumentation that colonisation was a promotion of civilisation and inverts it, claiming that colonisation was doing nothing but *de*-civilising the coloniser, which could be proved by his overt brutality towards the colonised (ibid., 34-35, 41). In Césaire's view, National Socialism was the logical consequence of colonialism because only a society that closes its eyes on the outrages of colonialist violence mercilessly, like European society did, could bring out something like National Socialism's crimes (ibid., 36, 39).

A student of Césaire, who went far beyond his teacher's ideas in theory and practice, was Frantz Fanon. He is one of the earliest and most influential writers that, in retrospect, can be counted as postcolonial theorists (Kerner 2012, 43; Young 2001, 276). Kenyan scholar Ngũgĩ wa Thiong'o introduces his approach as follows: "Fanonism was a combination of psychoanalysis and Marxian-cum-Hegelian dialects applied to the colonial situation from inside the colony by a student of philosophy, a practicing psychiatrist, and an active revolutionary" (Ngũgĩ wa Thiong'o 2014, 23-24). Fanon is noted particularly for his two main books: *Black Skin, White Masks*, first published in 1952, and *The Wretched of the Earth*, first published in 1961. Edward Said lauded Fanon's *The Wretched of the Earth* for seeking new ways of leaving colonialism, as well as its legacy like ortho-

7 When it comes to the colonised, I make sure to consider both genders, as women, men, and children were equally affected by colonisation. When it comes to the colonisers, I leave it at the male form because during the time of colonisation, men were unquestionably the dominant actors. This shall not disclaim the complicity of white women in colonisation, yet, their role was ambivalent. Masculinity and patriarchy were constitutive elements of colonisation. This shall be expressed with the male form here.

dox nationalism, behind (Kerner 2012, 74). Robert Young states that, "A product of the western-educated colonial elite, Fanon used the resources of Western thought against itself" (Young 2001, 276). In *The Wretched of the Earth*, Fanon transformed Hegel's dialectic of master and bondsman in a way that, instead of the loser in the fight between two initially free parties having to recognise the other as master, the master (coloniser) has to recognise his bondsman's (colonised) claim to independence (Ngũgĩ wa Thiong'o 2014, 24). As Cheryl McEwan aptly points out, Fanon's greatest theoretical merit is having explicated psychologically the relationship between the coloniser and the colonised, with its respective effects on the psyche of the colonised. Blackness was defined by the coloniser as an indelible indication of inferiority, which the colonised was forced to accept, e.g., through speaking the coloniser's language instead of his or her own. Fanon pointed out that, in spite of all 'education', 'civilisation', and cultural adjustment, the colonised was never allowed by the coloniser to be "quite the same" (McEwan 2009, 47). For the oppression of a people, according to Fanon, "the destruction of cultural values, of ways of life", the degradation of "[l]anguage, dress, techniques" go hand in hand with "[e]xpropriation, spoliation, raids, objective murder" (Fanon 1967, 33). He describes how, on the side of the oppressed, cultures and individuals living in them get paralysed through this process. Meanwhile, the oppressor dehumanises them by flaunting his supposed superiority and reducing the oppressed culture to curiosities, i.e., exoticizing it (ibid., 34-35). Fanon calls the effect of that process "alienation", meaning that the oppressed feel obliged to accept their role as inferior, to reject their own culture and turn to the oppressor's culture as a substitute (ibid., 38-39). Several decades later, Sabelo Ndlovu-Gatsheni observes the same phenomenon in Africa: identities have been destroyed and leaders have been educated in higher institutions of learning established by the global North to desire the latter's culture rather than that of their country of origin (Ndlovu-Gatsheni 2013, 50). Nevertheless, Fanon detects a rediscovery of the abandoned culture by the oppressed that can even culminate in euphoria for the remains of their cultural roots that can still be found, even though they might not be alive, anymore (Fanon 1967, 41-43).

Another important concept with regard to colonialism and its impacts on the lives of the affected people and their descendants until today is Aníbal Quijano's *coloniality of power*. Quijano describes the concept of the *coloniality of power* as follows: With the emergence of America, two major changes in the social world order occurred, namely the relations between conquering and conquered populations in terms of labour and in terms of 'race'. While all forms of labour were renewed in order to be centred around capital, 'race' became the new concept for defining conquered people as inferior to their allegedly 'racially superior' conquerors. The invaders invented racial categories and applied them to the division of labour that they established. As a result, in the Americas, paid labour and control of means of production were allocated to people with the highest racial status, namely Europeans and a few chosen others (the 'Indian' nobility and the children of Europeans with 'Indians'), while people of lower racial status (non-noble 'Indians') were first enslaved, later turned into serfs, and those who were classified as 'Blacks' had to live in slavery, as their racial status was the lowest in that system. According to Quijano, the system spread from the Americas to the whole world, as the Europeans continued to colonise it (Quijano 2000, 216-217).

Ramón Grosfoguel states that, initiated in the sixteenth century, the *coloniality of power* had engulfed the whole globe in the 19th century, subjugating all spheres of social life to the concept of 'race'. People were given the label of being 'racially inferior' or 'superior', the latter being privileged, as Grosfoguel emphasises, *in all spheres of life* (Grosfoguel 2011, 11). This is how, according to Quijano, Western 'Europe' constituted itself as an entity and as the centre of global capitalist power, while imposing new identities on other regions that were henceforth known as 'America', 'Africa', 'Asia', and 'Oceania' (Quijano 2000, 217-218). Ndlovu-Gatsheni points out that by establishing the colonial matrix of power, 'Europe' destroyed all other notions of modernity as well as all other identities, for example in Africa, and made its particular case the universal model for the world (Ndlovu-Gatsheni 2013, 39). Quijano concludes on the coloniality of power that "the most significant historical implication is the emergence of a Euro-centered capitalist colonial/ modern world power that is still with us" (Quijano 2000, 218). This means that after formal 'decolonisation', colonialism was over, but *coloniality*, i.e., the exploitation of people in the global South by the global North, continued, resulting in the everyday lives of the respective people not being changed significantly (Grosfoguel 2008, 95-96; 2011, 14). The concept of *coloniality of power* is closely related to world-systems analysis, yet stands out against most of those approaches because of having identified the aspect of *racism* being "constitutive and entangled with the international division of labor and capitalist accumulation at a world scale" (Grosfoguel 2008, 102).[8] Grosfoguel extends this

8 Immanuel Wallerstein, one of the founders and main representatives of world-systems analysis, has taken the appropriate measures as a result of such criticisms. He

even further by observing a global power hierarchy in *each* sphere of social life (Grosfoguel 2011, 14). He cautions that this aspect of racism in all global power hierarchies, not only in political or economic structures, has to be regarded as "an integral, entangled and constitutive part of the broad entangled 'package' called the European modern/colonial capitalist/patriarchal world-system" (ibid., 11). On the epistemological level, Quijano criticises the "Eurocentric knowledge perspective" for telling an untrue story about the becoming of America and of the capitalist world system, which distorts the self-image of the colonised people (Quijano 2000, 222). For instance, Quijano holds against the evolutionist idea of the historical succession of different modes of production that, since colonisation, the latter have been existing in Latin America side by side and have been instrumentalized for capitalist production. He adds that it is the immanent racism of the international division of labour that decides who works under which conditions (ibid., 218, 230; see also Grosfoguel 2008, 102; 2011, 23). Grosfoguel summarises on *coloniality of power* as follows: "The colonial axis between Europeans/Euro-Americans and non-Europeans is inscribed not only in relations of exploitation (between capital and labor) and relations of domination (between metropolitan and peripheral states) but also in the production of subjectivities and knowledges" (Grosfoguel 2008, 96).

Boaventura de Sousa Santos regards colonialism as the source of the West's attitude towards the people in the global South as less human and, as a result, "nonexistent, invisible, radically inferior, or radically dangerous—in sum, as discardable or threatening" (Santos 2017, 25). He created the idea of an "abyssal line between metropolis and colony", the two parts of humanity created by the combination of capitalism and colonialism that did not change due to the formal end of colonialism (ibid., 20). For Santos, the idea that all peoples of the world have the same chances to evolve, be free, and enjoy universal human rights is tragically absurd because those privileges are from the outset reserved for those above the abyssal line. They can indeed suffer from exclusion, but they have access to the means of fighting for their rights, like the rule of law, the liberal state, etc., hence, their exclusion is "nonabyssal" (ibid., 20-21). Despite all

incorporated the relation between 'race' and the international division of labour in his later works, e.g., in a collection of essays called *Race, Nation, Class: Ambiguous Identities* that he published together with Etienne Balibar in 1991 (in chapter 2.4 of this thesis, one of Wallerstein's essays from this publication is cited from the 2002 reprint).

exclusion, there is a basic sense of "equivalence and reciprocity among 'us'", the members of the "metropolitan world" (ibid., 20). According to Santos, the people on the other side of the line cannot expect the same attitude because they are not taken for real humans. This makes their exclusion abyssal (meaning without any means of changing the system they live in for the better) and "nonexistent as it is unimaginable that they might ever be included" (ibid., 21). Santos declares regretfully that, just like the whole situation, the instruments of *managing* (rather than *ending*) exclusions below the abyssal line, that is in the global South, have not changed after formal independence: violence and appropriation (ibid., 21-22). Even the ending or reduction of some nonabyssal exclusions of people in the metropolitan world has been realised by the worsening of abyssal exclusions on the other side of the line, e.g., the European welfare state vs. increasing exploitation of workers without (enforceable) rights in the global South (ibid., 23-24).

At first glance, this picture painted by Santos may appear all too dark, but with a critical look at the global situation, one has to admit that it is appallingly realistic (see chapters 3.2, 3.3, and 3.4). The indifference of the largest part of the population and decision makers in the global North towards the life situation of the majority of people in the global South explains to a certain extent the reluctance towards any knowledge that has been produced in the global South, as described by Santos in his earlier and most famous book, *Epistemologies of the South: Justice against epistemicide* (Santos 2014). This small and selective range of approaches by some of the most renowned writers, who have contributed to postcolonial theory, shows how delicate the task of the latter is. First and foremost, postcolonial critique has to reveal oppressive power structures, under which people in or from the global South smart. In many cases, though not necessarily in every case, this might require a look into the times of colonialism, as many of these oppressive power structures originate from there. The traces of those power structures can be found in every sphere of life, from economics and politics up to education, arts, and general epistemology. For that reason, contributions to postcolonial theory can come from representatives of various disciplines, like literary studies, psychology, philosophy, sociology, political science, historiography, anthropology, and others. This interdisciplinary approach is one of the strengths of postcolonial theory because its field of study is too complex to analyse it while being restricted to a single discipline or to a single theoretical or methodological approach.

2.1.3 Decolonising Eurocentric epistemologies

Influential writers of postcolonial theory, from Edward Said to Ngũgĩ wa Thiong'o, have pointed out how 'knowledge' about the colonised has been used as a means of dominating them, to the extent that there was not even a need for sophisticated knowledge, but racist prejudice and exotic phantasies sufficed (Ngũgĩ wa Thiong'o 2014, 32-33; Said 1994, 3, 34-35). Although most former colonies have become politically independent, decolonising epistemology is a global project that is far from being completed. This sub-section is going to give a brief overview of one of the central fields of intervention of postcolonial theory: the decolonisation of Eurocentric epistemologies, especially in (Western) social sciences. This thesis is conceived of as a contribution to this discussion. In the final paragraphs of this sub-section, a current debate on the relationship between postcolonial theory and globalisation studies is taken up.

As Sebastian Conrad and Shalini Randeria aptly point out, during colonialism, a great number of disciplines were engaged in collecting the sought-after information about the colonised territories and peoples. Nevertheless, they put a strong emphasis on historiography because national liberation movements tended to be connected to endeavours to re-claim the history of the concerned people from the colonisers (Conrad/ Randeria 2002, 34-35). In his famous book *Provincializing Europe*, Dipesh Chakrabarty elaborates how Eurocentric historicism has put non-European peoples into "an imaginary waiting room of history", telling them they were "*not yet* civilized enough to rule themselves" (Chakrabarty 2000, 8, emphasis in the original). Anticolonial movements tried to turn that "not yet" into a "now" (ibid.). James Ferguson applies this idea to the "narrative of development" (Ferguson 2005, 167). In this supposed linearity of human history lies the promise of development: poor countries and their peoples just have to wait until it is going to be their turn to join the 'developed' ones on the peak of 'development', i.e., cultural modernisation and material wealth (ibid., 167-168). Santos finds this "*monoculture of linear time*" in numerous Western concepts: "progress, revolution, modernization, development, and globalization" (Santos 2014, 173, emphasis in the original). In total, Santos presents "*five monocultures* that have characterized modern Eurocentric knowledge: valid knowledge, linear time, social classification, the superiority of the universal and the global, and productivity" (Santos 2017, 25-26, emphasis by E.K.). Anything that does not fit into the frame made from these 'monocultures' is being "labeled as ignorant, primitive, inferior, local, or unproductive" by mainstream Western social sciences (ibid., 26). Chakrabarty gives a convincing example of the significance of colonial legacy for epistemology: The works of famous European historians are, in many cases, produced in ignorance of the histories of non-Western peoples and countries, while non-Western historians are obliged to refer to 'great works' in European history in order to be taken seriously. Chakrabarty extends his argument on the inferiority of non-Western science in international relationships of power to other sciences like literary studies (Chakrabarty 2000, 28). Ndlovu-Gatsheni points out that (social) science being taught in Africa are still Western (social) science that are presented as universal. Hence, he calls for a re-appropriation of epistemology and education by African intellectuals (Ndlovu-Gatsheni 2013, 57-58).

Ferguson reassures us that anthropologists are on the right track, leaving "the intellectual and explanatory failings of developmentalist evolutionary narratives" behind and regarding Africa "as a place of bricolage and creative intervention, where bits and pieces of what used to be called Western modernity are picked up, combined with local (and not-so-local) resources, and put back together" (Ferguson 2005, 172). Barry Hindess shows a less optimistic attitude towards Western social sciences. He takes Johannes Fabian's famous argument from the book *Time and the Other*, which says that anthropology denies non-Western societies a coeval status with Western 'civilisation', to which's 'primitive' preliminary stages they are reduced, and extends it to the social sciences, in general (Hindess 2016, 490-491). Fabian showed impressively how Western anthropologists tend to construct their 'object' that he provocatively calls "the savage" as living in the past, meaning at a stage of 'civilisation' that Western culture has left behind long time ago in order to reach where it imagines itself to be by now: at the peak of human development (Fabian 2014, 25-27). Concerning that chronology, Fabian writes: "The temporal distancing it involves is needed to show that natural laws or law-like regularities operate in the development of human society and culture" (ibid., 29). Drawing on classics like Max Weber and Raymond Williams as well as on empirical evidence, Hindess shows that the labelling of people, or their actions, as 'traditional' often serves as means of presenting them as irrational and backward (Hindess 2016, 493-495).

There is a lot of such criticism of Western social sciences having ignored, discriminated, alienated, and humiliated people as well as knowledge from the global South. Certainly, this criticism is necessary for making academia as well as the public recognise what has been elided for long time. Nevertheless, it raises the question whether postcolonial theory is able to go beyond criticism and contribute some constructive suggestions for a better practice. For historiography, one such suggestion was made by Shalini Randeria. She has come up with the concept of "Geteilte Geschichten", which can be translated from German either as 'shared' histories or 'divided' histories, an ambivalence with which Randeria plays intentionally (Conrad/ Randeria 2002, 17). She wants to sensitise her readers for that very ambivalence in global history. In the 'shared' version, diverse societies went through various experiences together, creating the modern world through their interactions. In the 'divided' version, the movement of people, ideas, and goods produced dissociation and dichotomisation. Either way, the most important aspect of that ambivalent relationship between cultures, societies, or nations, for Randeria, is the relationship itself, which is why she eventually speaks of "entangled histories" (ibid., 7, English in the original). Nevertheless, Randeria cautions against romanticising those relationships, as a great deal of them, though not all, have been formed by inequality, oppression, or coercion (ibid., 18). What counts for Randeria, as well as for some other writers to include Gurminder Bhambra, is to demonstrate how the histories of different cultures developed *depending on each other*, not just to establish parallel histories or processes of 'development' or modernisation (Kerner 2012, 81-84). According to Randeria, the knowledge on entanglement got lost because of the imperial separation of Europe and its colonies in the social sciences: Europe became the area of responsibility of political science, economics, and sociology. The "study of 'pre-modern' cultures" was entrusted to anthropology and ethnology, the study of the "old advanced civilisations" was entitled to sinology, Japanese studies, and Indology – hence, there was "no methodical space" for the entanglements between those geographical regions (Conrad/ Randeria 2002, 21, translation by E.K.). Grosfoguel likewise deplores this separation, drawing on arguments that have been forwarded by Immanuel Wallerstein. In Grosfoguel's view, this strict separation of disciplines is the reason why postcolonial theory, which is dominated by the humanities, has difficulties to capture economic aspects, while world-system analysis, which is dominated by social sciences, fails to deal with culture (Grosfoguel 2008, 99-100; 2011, 17-18). Randeria shows a more optimistic attitude towards postcolonial theory, stating that it has contributed significantly to the elaboration of shared/ divided histories, thanks to its multidisciplinary approach (Conrad/ Randeria 2002, 22).

In his famous work *Orientalism*, Said had already cautioned against treating any kind of knowledge as non-political (Said 1994, 9-11). McEwan equally points out that knowledge is not anything objective, but constructed, and that the West has been imposing its knowledge as the only acceptable one on the rest of the world. The aim of postcolonial theory in that regard is to question that epistemological violence as well as the erroneously supposed universality of Western knowledge (McEwan 2009, 35). Santos deplores that, due to centuries of teaching the rest of the world, the global North has forgotten how to learn from others (Santos 2014, 19). In order to revolutionise the Eurocentric, violent epistemology of today's world, it is necessary to recognise the other "as an equal producer of knowledge" (ibid., 156). In Grosfoguel's words: "The monologism and monotopic global design of the West relates to other cultures and peoples from a position of superiority and is deaf toward the cosmologies and epistemologies of the non-Western world" (Grosfoguel 2011, 25). Santos praises postcolonial as well as intercultural approaches for having opened up new possibilities to discover the plurality of knowledges. Nevertheless, what remains to be done is to overcome the prevailing domination of Western knowledge as scientific, correct, and valuable, while other forms of knowledge are being underestimated and branded as 'just local' or 'traditional' (Santos 2014, 199-201). In addition, Santos calls for an end of the excluding, oppressing attitude in Western social sciences. He suggests to have a "sociology of absences", which "delegitimize[s] specific mechanisms of oppression", and a "sociology of emergences" that frees the potential of social experiences, which have been disregarded so far (Santos 2017, 28). Walter Mignolo likewise looks for new, decolonised ways of producing and recognising knowledge. He suggests to leave behind any claims to "world or universal history" and look for "narratives geared toward the search for a different logic", which can be found in perspectives from the global South (Mignolo 2012, 22). This is his suggestion on how to improve on the attitude deriving from the colonial situation, in which writers from the global North were in the position to decide whether they accredited any history to people in the global South at all and, if yes, what kind of history (ibid., 3). This is particularly applicable to Africa, which has often been depicted as having no history before colonisation (cf. e.g. Ndlovu-Gatsheni 2018, 286; Ngũgĩ wa Thiong'o 2014, 34; Niane 2010, 259-260).

Ikons of postcolonial theory like Said, Spivak, and Bhabha are rightly criticised for preferring to reference 'great Western thinkers' rather than other authors from the global South (McEwan 2009, 71). And Young's enthusiasm on postcolonial critique's close relation to political anti-colonial struggles and its tendency to political activism (Young 2001, 11, 58) is not shared by everybody, as has been shown above. On the other hand, there are examples of practical activism for decolonising academia, e.g., the attempt at abolishing the English Department at the University of Nairobi that Ngũgĩ wa Thiong'o was involved in, in the year 1968 (Ngũgĩ wa Thiong'o 2014, 9, 42-43). He and his colleagues created a scandal by demanding to replace the exclusive teaching of white English literature to Kenyan students by a diverse curriculum, including writers from the global South as well as African-American writers (ibid., 9, 26, 56-57). This is a very interesting incident, as it happened within the scope of literary studies, which is the disciplinary origin of postcolonial critique, a descent that is often held responsible for postcolonial critique's supposed tendency to be 'apolitical'. Ngũgĩ wa Thiong'o reports that for him and his fellow students at Makerere University, Uganda, "It was fiction that first gave us a theory of the colonial situation", giving numerous examples of well-known African and Caribbean writers of fiction, among them Chinua Achebe, George Lamming, and many others (ibid., 15). This example shows vividly how political literary theory can be. It is this political, decolonising effect that postcolonial theory is supposed to have on any discipline that it touches upon.

Recently, there has been a discussion on the hypothesis that postcolonial theory was replaced by globalisation studies (Castro Varela/ Dhawan 2015, 79). In an attempt to refute that assumption, Castro Varela and Dhawan suggest that the attitude towards the nation state is one of the major differences between the two approaches. They claim that "[t]he focus of globalisation studies goes beyond the nation, while postcolonial theory anew examines the complex relationship between national and transnational power" (ibid., 84, translation by E.K.). This point of view does not consider the complexity of the field of globalisation studies. There is no single discipline, sub-division within a discipline, or coherent school of thought that can be called *globalisation studies*. Scholars from various disciplines like economics, political science, and sociology, with differing theoretical affiliations like (Neo-)Marxist, post-structuralist, or what Andrew Jones calls "classical social and economic theories" engage in studies on globalisation (Jones 2010, 4). As a result, their assessments of the role of the state within globalisation varies (ibid., 12-13). However, many of those scholars suggest that the state still plays an important role (ibid.; see also the approach of Hirsch that I discuss briefly in chapter 3.1). According to Dhawan and Randeria, postcolonial theory and globalisation studies have overlapping interests, yet their positioning towards each other is unclear. The points of view vary strongly, from globalisation studies being the uncritical variant of postcolonial theory, to the latter having been replaced by globalisation studies (Dhawan/ Randeria 2016, 559).

What they have in common are their interdisciplinary approaches as well as their endeavour "of differentiating between the economic, political, legal, and cultural dimensions of transnational processes and their differing impacts in various periods and regions of the world" (ibid., 559). Eckert and Randeria comment on the relationship between postcolonial theory and globalisation as follows: "We all live in a postcolonial world, not only those people in and from formally colonised areas" (Eckert/ Randeria 2009, 11, translation by E.K.). What is extraordinary about that comment is that it refers to the effects that occurrences in the global South have on the global North (ibid.), not the other way around. This goes hand in hand with Leela Gandhi's labelling of colonialism as "the historical harbinger" of globalisation (Gandhi 2019, 125). With regard to epistemology, Grosfoguel suggests that globalisation studies "produce knowledge from the Western man 'point zero' god-eye view", which means that they need decolonisation (Grosfoguel 2011, 7-8). He explicates this 'god-eye view' as a result of René Descartes' act of replacing God with man, which at his time inevitably meant the European man, as source of universal knowledge in the philosophy of science (ibid., 6-8).

The deduction I make from the above-described arguments for this study is that globalisation studies, like the social sciences in general, have to be subjected to postcolonial critique. As globalisation studies encompass numerous heterogeneous approaches (see above and chapter 3), some may need more decolonisation than others. However, even critical approaches to globalisation cannot be regarded as an alternative to postcolonial theory. Especially those approaches that try to offer a "grand theory" of globalisation by reducing "multiple, complex changes in the contemporary world to one, inappropriate conceptual framework" (Jones 2010, 239) have to be questioned from a postcolonial point of view. For instance, this applies to world-systems analysis, which I present in chapter 2.3. It suffers from that problem of trying to be a 'grand theory' while its perspective is limited. Nevertheless, it adds a very valuable perspective to globalisation studies (see also chapter 3.4), the full potential of which can be tapped when combining it with other theoretical perspectives. In this study, I combine it with postcolonial theory and critical development studies. I suggest that any research project that is undertaken the global South, especially when the researcher(s) come(s) from the global North, has to be subjected to thorough reflection from the postcolonial point of view, in terms of theory as well as in terms of methodology. This is what I have tried to do in this study.

2.2 (Post-)Development theory

This thesis is supposed to make a contribution to critical development studies. Consequently, it is of high importance to clarify my approach to development. As I show in this chapter and chapter 3.3, development is immanent of many aspects of my topic. This study is focused on globalisation in Busoga, a region that is located in the global South. As a result, 'development' enters the discussion naturally. The discourses of development and globalisation – especially globalisation in the global South – are very closely interrelated and overlap to a great extent (see also chapter 3.3). This chapter 2.2 provides a discussion of the concept of 'development' (chapter 2.2.1) and different approaches to it. The conventional approach is briefly explained in chapter 2.2.1. However, it is not the approach adopted in this study. Chapter 2.2.2 introduces the reformist developmentalist approach, the representatives of which look for *alternative development*. This is followed by the presentation of the Post-Development approach, which stands out against all other approaches because its aim is to find *alternatives to development* (chapter 2.2.3). Eventually, I present my own approach to development in this study (chapter 2.2.4), drawing on what has been discussed before.

2.2.1 The concept of development and some points of criticism

The term 'development' is not easy to grasp and has numerous meanings. In this study, I concentrate on the meanings it has in relation to social change. Other possible meanings like biological development (e.g., of a plant or a child), personal development of individuals, etc., are not considered. In relation to social change, as I elaborate further below, the concept of 'development' that is prevalent today is an idea of linear, capitalist socioeconomic evolution following the example set by the global North. According to its champions, every country or society has to go through this process. This idea results in concrete actions, which are called 'development aid' or 'development cooperation'. The official aim of these measures is to assist countries of the global South to 'develop' quickly and to catch up with the global North. In the following, I refer to this with expressions like 'capitalist development' or 'conventional approaches to development'. Critical development studies encompass approaches that criticise this conventional approach to development. As I elaborate in the sub-sections of this chapter 2.2, different schools of thought and individual authors have varying explanations for their rejection of conventional/ capitalist/ Western 'development' (hidden agenda, Eurocentrism, bad economics) and different solutions (delinking, protectionism, looking for alternatives to the very idea of Western development). However, in public as well as in mainstream academic discourse, the model of capitalist development following the example set by the global North is hegemonic.

Development claims to be an explanatory model for all problems of non-Western countries and peoples ('they just lack development') and, at the same time, the solution (Ferguson 2014, xiii). There are different opinions on when development became a concept or a discourse, from Enlightenment philosophy, through different schools of thought in the 19th century, up to the inaugural address of then US-President Harry S. Truman in 1949 (Ziai 2017, 71). Aram Ziai suggests "to distinguish between concepts of evolutionary social change (usually brought about by capitalist modes of production) and concepts designed to ameliorate negative effects of this change" (ibid.). The latter, namely policies for the economic up-lifting of poor populations of the world, "was in fact gradually constituted in the first half of the 20th century" (ibid., 72). Early mentions of the term 'development' in the sense that is relevant here can be found in the *British Colonial Development Act* from 1929 (Escobar 2012, 73), the British *Colonial Development and Welfare Act* from 1940 and the French *Fonds de développement économique et social* from 1946 (Cooper 2009, 59). Arturo Escobar points out that in colonial Britain, development of the colonies – meaning the utilisation of their resources, not necessarily the improvement of the living conditions of their populations – was already regarded as a task to be actively carried out by the government (Escobar 2012, 73). Nevertheless, Escobar is among the numerous authors, who regard Truman's inaugural address as the beginning of the modern development discourse (ibid., 3; see also Esteva 2019, 1; Ziai 2017, 112). This new programme of development resulted from the colonialists' experience of losing control over the colonies through strikes across Africa, nationalist movements in North Africa and Asia, as well as World War II (Cooper 2009, 58-59; see also Rowden 1999, 152-154; Ziai 2017, 103). Moreover, the predicament of the global South was observed as a threat, in terms of potential social conflicts on an international scale (Escobar 2012, 22) as well as with regard to the need of resource providers and new markets for the global North and with regard to the race of ideologies during the Cold War (Ziai 2017, 31-32). Of course, access to resources was a central motive in the latter, as well (ibid.,103). After World War II, the countries of the global South (by that time, called 'the Third World') were involved in the so-called

Cold War between the representatives of capitalism, namely the USA, Western Europe, and Japan ('the First World'), and the representatives of socialism, namely the Soviet Union and some other communist states ('the Second World'), both trying to secure their political and economic influence in the rest of the world (McMichael 2012, 43-46; see also 60-61). Other events of the 20th century that prepared the global system for the dissemination of the development discourse were "the global economic crisis emerging in the 1920s, Roosevelt's New Deal policies of the 1930s, the World Wars" and the advent of "the idea that all human beings are equal" (Ziai 2017, 103). With regard to economics, Arturo Escobar asserts that first attempts at thinking about an economic theory of poverty and development were made towards the end of the 1940s (Escobar 2012, 56-57, 73). This timeframe correlates with the political events listed above. This shows that the history of development is highly political. It is neither the history of a philanthropic idea, nor of a particular economic model, but that of concrete political interests and attempts at realising them in the arena of international relations.

As Aram Ziai points out, the prevailing approach in development theory defines development as a goal, which has already been reached by Western Europe and Northern America, and which has to be pursued by all other human communities worldwide. The characteristics of the 'developed' pioneer nations are presented as exclusively positive and even normative, while their lapses are obscured (Ziai 2016, 29). This attitude derives from modernisation theory, first and foremost from its luminary Walt Whitman Rostow and his five stages of economic growth (Schmidt/ Schröder 2016, 21; see also Rowden 1999, 149-150). According to Rostow, development always moves in a linear manner, from 'traditional' societies surviving on subsistence farming to industrial mass production (which was the state of the art in the global North at the time of his publication, in 1960), based on economic growth and technology (Schmidt/ Schröder 2016, 21-22). Modernisation presents itself as an 'achievement' that was handed from the metropolises of northwest-Europe to the rest of the world, pretending that there are no other worthwhile ways of living (Conrad/ Randeria 2002, 13). Javier Gonzalo Alcalde points out that development originates from the ideas of modernisation and economic 'progress'. He argues that, originally, the aim of 'development' was the exploitation of the colonies' resources, only[9], but gradually, 'development' got connected to social

9 Immanuel Wallerstein made the same observation on French colonialism: At the turn of the 19th century to the 20th, instead of "développement", the term "mettre

'progress' in the global South, i.e., assimilation to Western life-styles, from the 1920s onwards (Alcalde 1987, 218-220). Consequently, he calls it a part of the project of "the Westernization of the world" (ibid., 219).

The replacement of modernisation theory by neoliberalism as the dominant approach in development studies did not put an end to ethnocentrism and self-adulation on the part of the global North, nor to the focus on economic growth and technology. On the contrary, the existing paradigm was radicalised. Schmidt and Schröder describe this process as follows. Neoliberalism took over in the early 1980s, making free capitalist competition its primary development goal. This goal is supposed to be reached through politico-economic restraint and austerity on the part of the government. The latter has to give way to the market to steer socio-economic life. Economic freedom is equated with political freedom and individual liberty. This reduces the state's role to that of a facilitator of the greatest possible extent of individual liberty and deprives it of the regulatory functions it still had under the modernisation paradigm (Schmidt/ Schröder 2016, 25-26). This resulted in the new development agenda commencing "an active fight against the development state, import substitution industrialisation as well as progressive social reforms" in the global South (ibid., 25, translation by E.K.). David Ricardo plays an outstanding role in the neoliberal concept of international trade, especially his 'comparative advantage', the idea that every country should specialise on a few goods in order to become the most successful provider of those commodities in the market (ibid., 26). Rick Rowden compares that idea to "putting all of one's eggs in one basket" (Rowden 1999, 156). This metaphor illustrates the shortcomings of the concept, experienced in practice by several countries of the global South, in the most simple and eloquent way: If the basket drops (e.g., because the world price for the respective commodity drops), all the eggs break at once and the owner is left with nothing at all – apart from the debts (s)he incurred in order to buy chicken feed. Another central measure of neoliberal development policy is privatisation, which does not stop at sectors like education and health care (Schmidt/ Schröder 2016, 27). After almost forty years of experience with neoliberalism, even its proponents have troubles to defend it against criticism. Some of them start to pine for the modernist past and Keynesian models that still allowed state intervention in the market. For example, the authors of an article in the International Monetary Fund's journal *Finance*

en valeur" was commonly used, which can be translated as 'develop', but also as "to exploit, draw profit from" (Wallerstein 2017, 87).

and Development, after praising neoliberalism the way that is suitable for the host medium, admit that two of the main activities in the neoliberal agenda, namely unrestricted movement of capital and austerity, "have not delivered as expected" (Ostry et al. 2016, 38). Furthermore, they admit that these measures are "associated with increasing income inequality" (ibid., 40). They continue stating that "[t]he evidence of the economic damage from inequality suggests that policymakers should be more open to redistribution than they are", as well as for "increased spending on education and training" and "using taxes and government spending to redistribute income" (ibid., 41). Indeed, neoliberal policies, like the sharp restrictions on government spending for social services, have led to increasing poverty and social inequality in the countries that implemented them (Schmidt/Schröder 2016, 28).

Western economists declared economic growth one of the most important objectives of development planning (McMichael 2012, 48). Whenever a country realises considerable economic growth or rising per capita income, it is celebrated as a development success. Several scholars argue that increasing incomes across the globe over the past decades prove that capitalist development leads to better living conditions for all people in the world and has to be pushed further (e.g., Norberg 2005, 6-7). However, Philip McMichael cautions that "[a]verage indices such as per capita income obscure inequalities among social groups and classes" (McMichael 2012, 49). Though he refers to the establishment of such indices in the 1940s, when the development apparatus was still dominated by modernisation theory (ibid., 48-49), there has been no revision of those indices during times of neoliberalism (cf. e.g. Latouche 2019; see also discussion of that issue in chapter 2.2.3 of this thesis). Furthermore, McMichael states that "[c]ultural practices of wealth sharing and cooperative labor—dissipating individual wealth, but sustaining the community—were perceived as a *traditional* obstacle to making the transition" (McMichael 2012, 49, emphasis in the original). The destruction of social structures and local knowledge is also still deplored by development critics today (Bendix/Ziai 2015, 164). They have even been supplemented by the reproaches of the destruction of the natural environment and the displacement of supposed 'beneficiaries' in the name of 'development' projects like dams (ibid.). Hence, I want to emphasise here that the average indicators used for measuring success do not account for the living conditions of those disadvantaged by social inequality. As a result, 'development planning' became a purely technical endeavour. It lacks sensitivity for the fact that its objects of intervention are *people*, and people are living in social, cultural, and natural environments, not in a theoretical world of mere figures, where the targeting of a certain indicator inevitably has a certain effect. In addition, Daniel Bendix and Aram Ziai aptly point out: “Increased income can nevertheless mean growing impoverishment, if formerly free resources (water, education, health) are provided against payment” (Bendix/ Ziai 2015, 163, translation by E.K.). As I discuss in chapter 8 (especially 8.2.5), this study provides evidence for that hypothesis. Other achievements of development like reduced infant mortality are unquestionably important, but there is no convincing evidence that *Western-style, capitalist* development was a prerequisite for their realisation and that they could not have been achieved through alternative approaches.

As it is the global North that defines the criteria for being ‘developed’, it is logical that it has chosen categories, which make itself look ‘developed’ and others ‘underdeveloped’. Aram Ziai points out that this is the only rational explanation why “no measurement of *development* has ever tried to operationalise hospitality, crime, suicide, social networks or a noninstrumental relation to nature as indicators of a good society”, while indicators such as “life expectancy, years spent in school and above all, the GNP” are never in question (Ziai 2017, 33, emphasis in the original). N’Dione et al. deplore the same predicament. They suggest alternative indicators for measuring ‘wealth’ or ‘development’, e.g., the degrees to which a society is independent of outsiders, able to integrate the largest part of its population and to enable their integration in their social, spiritual, and natural environment (N’Dione et al. 1998, 369). Serge Latouche questions the right of one part of humanity to declare its particular norms universal. He points out that ‘development indicators’ like ‘standard of living’ or gross national product are not natural, but man-made, and in that case, North-made (Latouche 2019, 279-283; see also chapter 2.2.3). Consequently, the global North must make sure to be in control of the supervision of the performance in terms of the development indicators, which it has defined. The key institutions in charge are the International Monetary Fund (IMF) and the World Bank.

For Teivo Teivainen, “[t]he economic discourse of the IMF is a case in point of liberal orthodoxy” (Teivainen 2009, 110, translation by E.K.). He traces that approach back to liberal economic theorist Adam Smith’s ‘invisible hand’. According to Smith, people are utility maximisers, who just have to be ‘set free’ (the ‘liberal’ element), such that their individual utility maximisation culminates in general wellbeing (ibid., 110-111). According to Teivainen, the foundation of the IMF and the World Bank[10] by the representatives of 44 states in Bretton Woods, in the year 1944, established a form of "global economic surveillance" that was unknown before (ibid., 120, translation by E.K.). As McMichael describes, the two so-called Bretton Woods institutions have been founded in order to encourage international trade after Wold War II, especially to make countries of the global South export primary goods in order to be able to import technologies and manufactured goods from countries of the global North. For that purpose, they provided loans to countries of the global South, e.g., for infrastructural projects, for which expertise and materials from the global North were required. Even though the global South did profit from the institutions' support, especially in the sector of infrastructure, the main beneficiary was the global North, ensured by the latter's control over the decisions taken within the institutions (McMichael 2012, 58-60). McMichael illustrates this with the following figures: Although 27 nations attending the Bretton Woods conference were from the global South, the executive board of the World Bank is clearly dominated by the 5 biggest shareholders, who are from the global North (ibid., 59). The voting power of the 25 members of the *Board of Directors* of the World Bank, who represent the 189 member states (World Bank 2020), depends on their countries' respective capital shares (World Bank 2020a). Aram Ziai uses a formulation, which is typical for academic as well as journalist accounts, when writing: "The President of the World Bank is *traditionally* a US citizen (while the Managing Director of the IMF is European)" (Ziai 2017, 126, emphasis by E.K.). What is typical about his statement is the use of the word 'traditionally' (in some cases, it is replaced by 'customarily' or 'by custom', see for example Stiglitz 2002, 19). Tradition or custom, properties that the global North usually assigns to the global South, as a sign of its

10 To be precise, the foundations of the *International Bank for Reconstruction and Development (IBRD)* were laid in Bretton Woods in 1944, whereas it was joined by the *International Development Association (IDA)* in 1960. The latter gives out loans to the poorest countries at very low interest rates and completes the duo that is usually seen as 'the World Bank' – although the actual World Bank group comprehends some other institutions as well, namely the *International Finance Corporation (IFC)*, the *International Centre for the Settlement of Investment Disputes (ICSID)*, and the *Multilateral Investment Guarantee Agency (MIGA)* (Ziai 2017, 126). Nevertheless, as the IBRD has been the basis for the 'World Bank', it is common practice in the literature to take 1944 as the founding year of 'the World Bank' and call it a 'Bretton Woods institution'.

alleged backwardness, becomes something valuable when it supports the global North's claim to global power.

In order to ensure back-payment of debts, the IMF developed the principle of conditionality, which dictates economic policies to the borrower countries and has been copied by other international financial institutions and banks since then (McMichael 2012, 59). Teivainen calls the principle of conditionality, which started as an oral agreement between the IMF and the borrowing countries, but became binding towards the end of the 1950s, "one of the most effective mechanisms of global economic surveillance" (Teivainen 2009, 122). Borrowers had to sign a declaration of intent to follow the IMF's orthodox programme, e.g., by abolishing price subsidies, devaluating their currency, reducing import restrictions and customs duties, and limiting national debt (ibid., 123). Teivainen describes how these and other measures enforced by the IMF undermined democracy in the borrower countries: Within the respective governments, power was shifted from organs like the parliament, which can be held responsible internally, "towards corporations like the central bank or the Ministry of Finance, which were increasingly responsible to *external* forces", namely the creditors (ibid., 127, translation by E.K., emphasis in the original). Andreas Eckert and Shalini Randeria suggest leaving older categories behind by classifying the countries of the world as "credit grantors and credit receivers of the International Monetary Fund and the World Bank, two central institutions of the new post-colonial imperialism" (Eckert/ Randeria 2009, 10, translation by E.K.). They explicate that those two institutions are intervening in almost every political field in their borrower countries, be it health, education, law, environmental policy, or a completely new approach to economic and social policy, which has been enforced in the course of economic liberalisation (ibid., 27). At the same time, it is necessary to consider that endeavours from the side of the borrower governments were necessary to impose those measures, and that local elites were at least partly in favour of them because those measures helped them to repress lower social classes as well as social movements (Teivainen 2009, 127). This proceeding of the international financial institutions bears traces of colonial techniques of domination. It is evocative of Aimé Césaire's comment on the relationship of local elites with the colonisers, "the old tyrants get on very well with the new ones" (Césaire 2000, 43). In the course of his extensive analysis of newspapers as well as scientific magazines, Rick Rowden found the term "auto-colonization" for the frequently observed "signing away control of their political economies to the international financial institutions to whom their nations are indebted" by elected officials (Rowden 1999, 170). While in earlier decades, borrower countries could deal with the IMF's terms as 'recommendations', during the 1980s, the failure to fulfil them assiduously started to have serious consequences for them (Teivainen 2009, 131). This went far beyond conflicts between the two parties. Without a good reputation on the part of the IMF, it is difficult for a country, especially a country of the global South, to obtain a loan from other governments, private banks, or other financial institutions, or to participate in the capitalist world economy, at all (ibid., 124). Development aid is one of the instruments that are frequently used by the global North to discipline countries of the global South. For instance, when a country of the global South fails to follow the terms of an international trade agreement, cutting development aid can be one of the sanctions that it is being threatened with, alongside juridical measures or other economic sanctions (Wade 2009, 247). Chang likewise names development aid, alongside with trade policies and control over international institutions that the countries of the global South depend on, as a method of the global North to exert pressure on the global South (Chang 2002, 135-136). Conditionality is more than a justified measure of credit grantors, who want to ensure that their money is being paid back to them. It is a serious intervention into the policies and decisions of the governments of sovereign states, which make those governments accountable to the credit grantors rather than to the populations that they are supposed to serve. Nevertheless, those governments are in dire need of those credits because their colonial past and their weak standing in the system of international trade – both conditions, which have been procured by the parties steering the institutions that grant the credits – deprived them of their ability to survive without them. The following paragraphs are going to further verify these claims. However, Shalini Randeria points out that governments of global South countries do not always exploit the "space for manoeuvre" they still have (Randeria 2007, 3). She argues that "the stronger among subordinate states in the international system" act as "cunning states", deciding on the basis of the interests of national elites whether they exploit their "space for manoeuvre" or not – and in what way (ibid.). She describes several cases, in which the Indian government deliberately decided to rather act in the interest of national elites than in the interest of the majority of citizens and especially vulnerable groups (ibid., 9-12, 16-21). Nevertheless, she states: "There is hardly any policy domain in which the Bretton Woods institutions do not exercise influence on borrower governments: rule of law and democracy, judicial and legal reform, education and health, resettlement and environment, land reform and labour law" (ibid., 5).

The best-known conditionality that debtor countries had to accept were the structural adjustment programmes (SAPs) of the 1980s, with their neoliberal doctrine of "drastic reduction of public spending (especially on social programs, including food subsidies)", "currency devaluation", "export intensification", "privatization of state enterprises", and "reduction of wages to attract foreign investors and reduce export prices" (McMichael 2012, 118). McMichael deplores that the poorest social classes, those depending on subsidies and wages, suffered most from these policies (ibid.). He states that "[f]rom 1978-1992, more than 70 countries [of the former Third World] undertook 566 stabilization and SAPs to manage their debt", nevertheless, "[t]he debtor countries collective entered the 1990s with 61 percent more debt than they held in 1982" (ibid., 120). Under debt management measures, McMichael continues, almost 7,000 public enterprises were privatised in more than 80 countries, up to 1992. Although the elites of some countries of the global South might have been too enthusiastic when it came to public spending, the extreme privatisation and austerity pressure that was put on them from the 1980s onwards was not helpful to their countries either (ibid., 122). Their governments lost much of their power to global financial institutions while social inequalities among their citizens deepened (ibid., 147-148). In the course of the 1980s, classical development indicators like per capita income or infant mortality worsened considerably in some countries as a result of borrower governments being obliged to reduce public spending, e.g., on health or education facilities (ibid., 120). McMichael cites the examples of Zambia, Sudan, and Tanzania. Those countries were spending more on debt servicing than they could earn through their exports in 1983 (ibid., 118). In his view, although the 'development project' has been replaced by the 'globalisation project', the former did not vanish, but its meaning shifted from national development to international market orientation (ibid., 127). As early as 1980, the World Bank had turned from the goal of national development to that of "participation in the world market" (World Development Report 1980, cited in McMichael 2012, 112-113), which put an end to any possibility for countries of the global South to sympathise with any socio-economic model other than global capitalism.

Frederick Cooper asserts that the structural adjustment programmes (SAPs) of the International Monetary Fund (IMF) were rather a means of *denying* Africa's right to global resources than an attempt to make its economies more efficient (Cooper 2009, 67). Rick Rowden likewise suggests that the main objective of SAPs was *dismantling* the economic development of the global South, which was about to become a threat to the North's economic supremacy. Rowden draws on the argumentation of Walden Bello and Shea Cunningham from the *Institute of Food and Development Policy* (Rowden 1999, 159). Cooper points out the absurdity in the IMF's claims to strengthen the economies of African countries by making them cheapen their exports at a point in time when there was little demand for them (Cooper 2009, 67). This goes hand in hand with Achille Mbembe's argument. Mbembe explains how African economies, which were structurally disadvantaged for international competition since the first attempts to integrate them in it after independence, were ruined by SAPs: States that were forced to reduce their expenditures stopped making investments, without (international) private investors being seriously interested in taking over. In addition to that, the wages of government workers were lowered – another obstacle for private investment as well as a cause for a drop in purchasing power, as government workers had been the strongest consumers. Mbembe points to the disappointing, though not surprising results of SAPs with regard to their declared goals: In the concerned countries, neither the objective of overcoming the fiscal crisis could be attained, nor that of raising the gross domestic product. Some sectors of the economies have even reacted by going 'underground' (Mbembe 2001, 52-54). The restructuring of marketing boards, a measure that was supposed to make them more effective, "has extended bankruptcy to planters, industrialists, and bankers" (ibid., 57). Mbembe concludes on SAPs: "Without their being the sole cause, the deregulation policies introduced in the 1980s opened the way for a deepening of mass poverty" (ibid., 55).

The World Bank has been influencing the socio-economic policies of poor countries considerably, as well. In addition to punishing attempts at implementing socialist policies by countries of the global South with a refusal to give them loans, it also installed the *Economic Development Institute*, in the 1950s, in order to train officials from countries of the global South and send them back to their governments, aligned to the Bank's ideology (McMichael 2012, 60). Members of the elites of the borrower countries are trained to accept the Bank's policies and to implement and defend them in their countries. This strategy has been used by colonial administrations before. Majid Rahnema accuses especially the founding elites of the newly independent former colonies of having been indoctrinated with the ideology of their colonisers through formal education. He traces the rejection of indigenous identities as well as the obsession with wanting to 'develop' and to copy the standards of the global North in countries of the global South back to these founding elites (Rahnema 1998, 378). Another analogy of development and (neo-)colonialism is the disparagement of the people of the global South, their cultures, and their identities. As Rahnema aptly points out, development projects usually come with the message that their potential 'beneficiaries' are in need of them because "their traditional modes of living, thinking and doing" have made them poor (ibid., 384). The only solution to their self-inflicted predicament seems to be 'modernisation' of their minds and practices (ibid.). As has been shown in chapter 2.1 of this thesis, based on authors like Frantz Fanon and others, this practice of disparagement and forced assimilation was a typical strategy of domination that was implemented by colonialists. It served the subjugation of people of the global South, not their empowerment or promotion. Consequently, one might wonder how the *same* strategy is supposed to serve the *opposite* purpose in the context of development.

Against that background, it comes as no surprise that the discourse of development can be traced back to the discourse of colonialism (Ziai 2017, 30). Ziai verifies this assumption with colonial discourse's characterisation by "the division of the world into '*civilised*' peoples or nations and '*uncivilised*' tribes or masses", whereas "the latter are unable to *effectively govern their own affairs*, so that the former come to help them" (ibid., 27, emphases by E.K.). Although the harsh terminology might be out of fashion today, the assumptions that underlie development discourse are no different. The statement 'the world is divided into *developed* and *underdeveloped* peoples, whereas the latter are unable to *develop on their own*, so that the former come to help them' would be affirmed by most development practitioners as well as most conservative development theorists and countless politicians. The attributes of the 'civilised' (white, male) person collected by Ziai apply to the 'developed' person equally: "superior", "rational", "fit to govern" (ibid., 28). The 'uncivilised' person is the exact opposite of the 'civilised' (ibid.), a dichotomy that applies equally to the 'underdeveloped' and the 'developed' person or peoples. It has been explained above that this attitude derives from modernisation theory. Seeing that archaeology teaches us that Europe was not the first continent to be populated, one might wonder why European culture should be the most 'developed' or 'civilised' one. The global North used to explain this with religion, in the beginning, and with its opposite, the Enlightenment, later. A much more evident explanation would be that the model of linear human development/ civilisation with the global North at its peak is not only wrong, but an instrument of oppression. Ramón Grosfoguel asserts that the European industrial revolution as well as "the new identities, rights, laws, and institutions of modernity such as nation-states, citizenship and democracy" have all been achieved by the global North by means of exploiting the global South (Grosfoguel 2011, 13). In his view, the global North created the image of the global South as having an inherent problem of 'underdevelopment' in order to obscure this fact and to justify intensive intervention in the global South, in the name of development (Grosfoguel 2008, 103; 2011, 24). From this point of view, the narrative of the global North having achieved all this because of its advanced ('developed') intellectual and moral capacities, as well as its generous attempts to share this achievement made through its own hard work with the global South, starts to crumble. McMichael demonstrates how colonial powers destroyed agricultural knowledge and resources as well as crafts traditions in the global South on their quest for cheap raw materials and new markets for their manufactured goods (McMichael 2012, 31-36). The acknowledgement of this undisputed, historically traceable fact is enough to reduce to absurdity any claims on the part of the global North of having developed out of its own material resources and inventiveness – except if one wants to acknowledge its incomparable ability to exploit other peoples as its genuine 'inventiveness'. This calls into question the idea that the global South just has to copy the global North's development strategy in order to reach where it is. Whom are they supposed to exploit in order to get their cheap raw materials and new markets? And will the global North be ready to give up those foundations of its wealth, from which it is still profiting? Will it take the risk to give up the safe position it has been occupying for centuries, namely as the winner in the international division of labour? Those would be the fundamental pre-conditions for the catch-up-theory to make any sense. McMichael elaborates his argument as follows:

> "Unless we see the interdependence created through this division of *world* labour, it is easy to take our unequal world at face value and view it as a natural continuum, with an advanced European region showing the way for a backward, non-European region. But viewing world inequality as relational (interdependent) rather than as sequential (catch-up), calls the conventional modern understanding of 'development' into question. The conventional understanding is that individual societies experience or pursue development in sequence, on a 'development ladder'. If, however, industrial growth in Europe depended on agricultural monoculture in the non-European world, then

> development was more than simply a national process, even if represented as such." (McMichael 2012, 37-38, emphasis in the original)

McMichael's interdependence-argument does not only explain how the global North has managed to reach the position of power it occupies. It also explains the continuous suppression of the global South by the global North, through trade agreements that are unfavourable for the global South and through the domination of international organisations by the global North. Without that suppression, the global South could gain too much power. What if the global South was in the position to dictate the international terms of trade? The global North has become accustomed to such a high degree of consumption that a rise in prices of rare earth metals, animal feeds for meat production, salaries in textile or electronics factories and the like would be a disaster for it. At the same time, it needs markets for its own goods and services (not least the services of its 'development experts'). In such a vulnerable position, the best strategy is to hide one's own vulnerability and keep the counterpart in its place.

As Sally Matthews aptly points out, "Africa's place in the world has, since the end of colonialism, been closely linked with the idea of *development*" (Matthews 2018, 167, emphasis by E.K.). As a result, "Africa's place in international relations theory has, likewise, been one that has highlighted its supposed need for development with development aid being a key instrument through which the international community has related to Africa" (ibid.). In other words, whenever "Africa's place in the world" is being discussed, the discourse of 'development' comes in automatically (ibid.). Matthews argues that, although Africa's situation precludes a full rejection of developmentalist ideas, the image of "Africa as the epitome of underdevelopment" and the belief in standard solutions to Africa's problems should not be without alternatives (ibid., 168). She explains that the idea of development came to life through the need for a moral justification of late colonialism. Beyond the colonial era, the provision of development aid secured the global North the possibility to exert influence in Africa (ibid., 168-169). Zubairu Wai puts a large part of the blame for the persistence of "the Eurocentric evolutionist gaze" at Africa on "the discipline of international relations (IR), which remains a major site for the production of these problematic ideas about Africa", while being "incapable of coming to terms with African realities" (Wai 2018, 5). Wai describes international relations as a discipline that has been developed by the West as a study of how to dominate and exploit other countries most efficiently (ibid., 7-9). In that regard, Wai sees IR in the regrettable tradition of nineteenth-century anthropology (ibid., 18; see also Mudimbe

1988, 16-17, on anthropology). Djibril Tamsir Niane states with reference to Africa: "Nobody on the continent disclaims the responsibility of those in power: corruption, mismanagement, nepotism and many other ills are rife in our states" (Niane 2010, 267, translation by E.K.). As Branwen Gruffydd Jones aptly points out, the preferred explanation on the part of the global North, namely the imputation of "political immaturity" on the side of African peoples, must be firmly rejected (Gruffydd Jones 2018, 205, see also 213-214). Several African writers likewise are far from denying that African elites are part of the problem, yet the latter's misconduct, like corruption or the implementation of seemingly incomprehensible policies that harm their populations, has to be regarded in relation to their role in the neo-imperialist system that has been established by the global North (cf. e.g. Cooper 2009, 64-65; Ngũgĩ wa Thiong'o 1988, 79-80). Gruffydd Jones suggests that the aftermath of colonialism is not adequately taken into consideration in that context (Gruffydd Jones 2018, 187-188). Certainly, this point must be taken into consideration when discussing the role of elites in the global South. Though the problematic role of domestic elites must be discussed, the global North should not be given the chance to put all the blame for the global South's predicament on them. The destructive role – past and present – of the global North is *complemented*, not replaced or reconciled, by the malpractice of some governments and elites in the global South.

Criticism of development thinking, policies, and institutions is not only uttered by leftist scholars. Even developmentalists and proponents of capitalism do not always deny the deception in the development promises to countries of the global South made by the global North through development programmes as well as trade agreements. Robert Hunter Wade is a proponent of "the development of dynamic capitalistic economies in the non-core zones of the world economy" (Wade 2009, 240, translation by E.K.). Nevertheless, he challenges the neoliberal assumption that "the path to development is identical with the path of liberalisation and unreserved integration into the world economy" (ibid., 251, translation by E.K.). In addition to that, he deplores how powerful governments of the global North use "multilateral economic organisations, international contracts and bilateral agreements" in order to enforce economic policies, which are beneficial for themselves only, on the governments of the global South (ibid., 237, translation by E.K.). The way they keep them from regulating business companies from abroad is as harmful to their national economies as the non-fulfilment of the global North's promises to open their markets for them (ibid., 237-239, 249). Using the example of TRIPS (Agreement on

Trade-Related Aspects of Intellectual Property Rights), a WTO-agreement (World Trade Organization), Wade demonstrates how the global North has managed to secure its superior position by stipulating that its own duties towards the global South are non-actionable while its rights are actionable (ibid., 241-242). In this context, Wade argues that the USA of the 19th century as well as some Asian countries that made significant steps towards economic development in the 20th century were known for not respecting any intellectual property rights, but made their fortune through copying (ibid., 244). In general, Wade states that international trade agreements tend to be "vague on the points where vagueness benefits the industrial countries and precise in the points where preciseness has a negative impact on developing countries" (ibid., 251, translation by E.K.). Wade argues that almost all countries of the global North have reached their status of power and economic development without implementing intellectual property rights (ibid., 244), democracy, liberalism, or non-protective economic policies (ibid., 252). All these things are being sold to countries of the global South as prerequisites of economic development while, in reality, they are obstacles to it. Wade adds on that in fast-growing countries like India or China, economic growth started long time before trade liberation (ibid.). In that context, Wade cites Friedrich List's famous statement on 'kicking away the ladder' (ibid., 254; see also chapter 2.2.2 of this thesis).

In the following sub-section, I present reformist approaches. Like Wade, they criticise the prevalent development paradigm with its respective practices and institutions, yet they hold on to its (official) objectives. Their intention is to 'develop' countries of the global South as measured by the same standards, but with more success than has been achieved so far. We shall come back to the above-mentioned statement by List in that context.

2.2.2 Reformist approaches to development

Reformist approaches to development are being presented here for two reasons. First, it is a logical step on the way from conventional developmentalist thinking to Post-Development thinking, which is being presented in the following sub-section (2.2.3). As I elaborate below, both reformist developmentalists and Post-Development thinkers criticise the conventional development apparatus in the same way. The difference lies in the reformists criticising *the means only*, whereas Post-Development thinkers criticise both *the means and the aim*, i.e., the concept of Western 'development' itself. However, before the Post-Development school of thought emerged, reformist approaches to development have been tried out, and they are still tried out and discussed today. Consequently, I consider it important to present them here. The second reason why they are important for this study is that a certain question arose during my theoretical reflexions on the research topics and became a central theme with regard to 'development' as well as with regard to alternative economic practices: *How radical does an alternative have to be in order to be an alternative?* Is it legitimate to sacrifice radicality in favour of feasibility to a certain extent? If yes, to what extent? In terms of alternative 'development' or alternatives to 'development', I position myself within this discussion in chapter 2.2.4. The background information needed for that discussion is provided in this chapter (2.2.2) and the following chapter (2.2.3). The parallel discussion with regard to economic practices that try to provide alternatives to capitalism (or not) can be found in chapter 4. It also plays an important role in chapter 8.3.7, where it is applied to my research results. I provide a final conclusion on my evaluation of the question on alternatives in chapter 9.2.

A well-known and influential attempt at revolutionising development strategies for the global South was promoted by the *Economic Commission for Latin America* (CEPAL), a panel of Latin American economists, founded in the late 1940s: *import substitution industrialisation* (Escobar 2012, 80). Arturo Escobar describes the concept as being based on the intention to combat the degradation of the terms of trade for Latin American countries and their goods by fostering industrialisation in the respective countries. Its aim was to facilitate access to foreign exchange in order to promote the import of capital goods and achieve economic growth. Escobar aptly points out that, though the strategy was new, the aims remained the same, hence, *import substitution industrialisation* did not revolutionise development thinking. Although there were some innovative elements in it, such as a concern for structural factors of international economic relations as well as for the living conditions of the population, the concept continued relying on technical progress, capital accumulation, and economic growth as the only way forward. Because of that acceptance of central assumptions of the dominant economic discourse, concludes Escobar, the concept of *import substitution industrialisation* has been incorporated into the latter with ease (ibid., 80-81). Apart from that, there is some criticism concerning the performance of *import substitution industrialisation*. Among others, there are reproaches of "increased foreign-exchange vulnerability" as well as the worsening of certain sectoral imbalances – phenomena that the makers of the concept had intended to overcome (ibid., 81). Nevertheless, Escobar acknowledges CEPAL's influence on the development scene, which distinguishes it from most other alternative economist initiatives (ibid.). Many recent reformist approaches to development seem to be inspired by the CEPAL's work. Among them is Ha-Joon Chang's widely noted book *Kicking Away the Ladder*, which borrowed its title from the following quote by nineteenth-century liberal economic theorist and entrepreneur Friedrich List.

> "It is a very common clever device that when anyone has attained the summit of greatness, he *kicks away the ladder* by which he has climbed up, in order to deprive others of the means of climbing after him. [...] Any nation which by means of protective duties and restrictions on navigation has raised her manufacturing power and her navigation to such a degree of development that no other nation can sustain free competition with her, can do nothing wiser than *to throw away these ladders* of her greatness, to preach to other nations the benefits of free trade, and to declare in penitent tones that she has hitherto wandered in the paths of error, and has now for the first time succeeded in discovering the truth." (List 1885, cited in Chang 2002, 4-5, emphases by Chang)

Ha-Joon Chang postulates that this is exactly what rich countries are doing: obscuring the truth about their own way to success and forcing contrary measures on countries that are longing for development (Chang 2002, 2, 125, 127-129, 135). Chang points out that they "actively used 'bad' trade and industrial policies, such as infant industry protection and export subsidies", while allegedly indispensable prerequisites for development, such as patent right or central banks, were installed *only after* those countries had already reached a high level of economic development (ibid., 2). Cooper likewise points out that free trade "had never been an absolute standard, only the logical stance of the premier trading nation" (Cooper 1993, 120). Consequently, free trade is not the instrument to reach the top, but to employ when one has reached there – by other means.

Julius Kiiza comes to the same conclusion when comparing the case of Uganda, as an example of integration into the global market that was not well-prepared, with that of Taiwan, as a success story of what he calls "economic mercantilism" (Kiiza 2008, 179, 194). As "*economic mercantilism*" stands for "policies of economic nationalism" (ibid., 178, emphasis in the original), it is considered to be the converse of economic liberalism (ibid., 180). As such, it is contrary to the prescriptions of the IMF and the World

Bank. This inwardly oriented economic policy, which is also referred to as 'protectionism' or 'state interventionism', is often accused of having a tendency to "prop up inefficient firms, undermine innovation, and *distort* the free markets, nationally and internationally" (ibid., emphasis in the original). Kiiza admits that mercantilism's reputation is not good, neither in the neoliberal, nor in the Marxist camp, where it is regarded as exploitative. Nevertheless, he insists that both camps have too limited an idea of mercantilism, whereas the concept could be adjusted to the current needs of the respective national economy, e.g., from infant industry protection to a certain openness to globalisation. He hints to mercantilism being a strategy of shaping the state and, with it, the national economy (ibid., 180-181). With regard to the problems of weak or even 'failed' states in the global South that development agencies and politicians keep on decrying, it seems plausible to apply such a strategy to such countries. Nevertheless, there are several obstacles that prevent countries that want to 'catch up' from engaging in mercantilist or protectionist policies. Kiiza names the examples of rules dictated by the *World Trade Organization* (WTO), repudiating protective strategies, such as export subsidies or preferential treatment of local industry or capital. Furthermore, he refers to the above-mentioned TRIPS agreement, which prevents the countries that are currently trying to industrialize from copying their forerunners' technologies, like those precursors had done themselves (ibid., 181-182).

In his comparison of Uganda and Taiwan, Kiiza points out Taiwanese policies like land reforms, which could not have been implemented in Uganda due to structural adjustment programmes (SAPs), in combination with the influence of local elites that have been empowered through the colonial legacy (Kiiza 2008, 190). He continues stating that, "[i]n contrast to Uganda's donor-driven programs", in Taiwan, "the object of adjustment has never been global market integration", but the strengthening of the national economy (ibid., 191). Another point he makes is the highly efficient state bureaucracy of Taiwan (ibid., 190-192), in the style of successfully mercantilist, seventeenth-century France (ibid., 183). Uganda has not been allowed to build up such a bureaucracy under SAPs and subsequent operations of international financial institutions. In that context, Kiiza reports a reduction of public servants from 1993 to 2000 from 320,000 to 150,000 people (ibid., 190). What the neoliberal credit grantors were considering an appropriate strategy to save money that would have been spent on their wages, was indeed a disaster. Notwithstanding that 170,000 people and their extended families lost their income and purchasing power, public services had to be rendered by less than half the personnel while the population was exploding. Additionally, the remaining employees had seen how easily they could lose their source of income. This insecurity, in combination with a declining loyalty to the government as their unreliable employer, may have increased the temptation to accept bribes in some cases. Robert H. Wade wonders about "one of the most peculiar blind spots within development theory [being] its silence on *internal integration*", although "the development of a national economy is rather about internal than external integration" (Wade 2009, 258, translation by E.K., emphasis in the original). Wade goes on to explain that, in an internally integrated economy, wages are an important instrument of economic growth because they guarantee local consumption and demand for goods. In contrast, in an economy that is exclusively focused on export, wages are nothing but costs – an attitude, which establishes structures of exploitation and becomes an obstacle to social peace and democratic development. The role played by international trade agreements in the process of internal integration is destructive (ibid., 258-260). According to Kiiza, the key to success is "the capacity of domestic political institutions—particularly the state—to mediate the external pressures of globalism and pursue the long-term developmental goals of the national economy" (Kiiza 2008, 179, see also 195). Nevertheless, he admits that integration into the world economy can have favourable effects in terms of information, technology, or finance. Yet, he emphasises "that effective late industrialisation is unlikely unless a developing country participates in the world economy *on its own terms*, not the terms dictated by the external political economy pressures" (ibid., 195, emphasis by E.K.). Indeed, he holds the view that countries of the global South still have *some* agency. For instance, Kiiza calls upon them to strengthen their self-esteem in international negotiations, make sure they send their most qualified people there to claim their rights, and empower the state as important player in the national economy. Furthermore, he recommends that they put more emphasis on measures such as regional integration, education of professionals, concentration on science and technology, or "innovative industrial policies (such as tax holidays for priority industries)" (ibid.).

Nevertheless, what rich countries try to push through as the only way to go for other countries that want to 'catch up' with them is the approach of liberalisation, including free trade, deregulation, private property rights, and the like (Chang 2002, 1). As a result, Chang is not surprised by the unsatisfactory economic performance of countries that have been trying to catch up with rich countries, following the neo-liberal policies recommended by the latter, in the 1980s and 90s (ibid., 128) – the time of structural adjustment programmes. Economic growth rather slowed down, in comparison with the time of protectionist economic policies, while income inequality increased (ibid., 128-129). This matches with a reproach often addressed to governments of the global North as well as to international organisations, which are dominated by them. Rowden accuses the governments of then US President (1981-1989) Ronald Reagan and then British Prime Minister (1979-1990) Margaret Thatcher of having initiated the promotion of neoliberal economic policies for the global South in order to stop the emerging of newly industrialised countries (NICs), like the so-called 'Asian tigers' (because the first ones were Taiwan, Singapore, South Korea, and Hong Kong), which posed a threat to the economic dominance of the world-system by the USA and Great Britain (Rowden 1999, 154-156). Neoliberal economists, particularly the representatives of the *Chicago School for Economics* like Milton Friedman, had paved the way for the radically neoliberal policies of the Thatcher-/ Reagan-era (ibid., 151). Nevertheless, as Rowden points out, the reliance on the free-market forces that those governments pretended to practice, in combination with a strict restrain of the state, was dissimulation. In practice, Reagan's administration took numerous measures that were in stark contrast to neoliberalism, for instance it granted generous financial supports to the industrial sector and increased non-tariff barriers significantly (ibid., 152). The newly industrialised countries did the same: They subsidised their industries excessively, despite IMF and World Bank demanding privatisation and austerity. They protected their infant industries with trade barriers and protective tariffs, policies that IMF and World Bank ban in the name of free trade. They diversified their industries instead of relying on supposed 'comparative advantages' as prescribed by IMF and World Bank (ibid., 156). Rowden cites reports that "20 of the 24 OECD countries nearly doubled their levels of protective trade barriers and tariffs" in the 1980s, whereas the respective levels in the global South were almost halved, due to IMF and World Bank conditionalities (ibid., 158). Ziai likewise questions the World Bank's claim that the 'Asian tigers' succeeded due to the *Washington Consensus* and rather suggests that they succeeded due to protectionist strategies, just like most countries of the global North had done before (Ziai 2017, 109-111). In their above-mentioned article in the IMF's journal *Finance and Development* (see chapter 2.2.1 of this thesis), Ostry et al. admit that some neoliberal prescriptions do not work, giving examples in which even high-ranked IMF officials gave their blessing to unorthodox measures like state intervention, in particular cases (Ostry et al. 2016, 41). Nevertheless, their examples refer to Europe and the USA exclusively.

According to Rowden, the relationship between the global North and the global South is not based on the official slogan of neoliberal development, which he frames sarcastically, “the wealthy advanced countries are bending over backwards to help their former colonial subjects to develop into clean, proper, capitalist consumers” (Rowden 1999, 152). Instead, he states, it draws on the unofficial slogan: “No more NICs!” (ibid., 156) Rowden identifies the neoliberal free trade agreements of the 1980s and 90s as strategies of the global North to make sure that no more countries of the global South would reach the status of a NIC by weakening the state and place power into the hands of international investors and national elites (ibid., 157). Teivainen states: “[…] powerful governments indeed *followed Keynes back home*, but continued to tend to *promote Adam Smith abroad* – first and foremost in the Third World” (Teivainen 2009, 121, translation by E.K., emphasis in the original).

Chang is not interested in an alternative to development, but to “help today’s developing countries to develop faster” (Chang 2002, 141). With this attitude, which is also that of Kiiza, Wade, and other reformers, he expresses the wish of many people in global South countries. For them, development means higher standards of living, which they understandably desire. At first sight, the idea of a *Post*-Development approach must seem rash and foreign to them. The countries of the global South have no other choice than to think about the predicament of their populations. In one way or another, this means to think about some kind of ‘development’. In any case, the global North stands for development, in all its manifestations, including the respective organisations that are in charge of ‘developing’ the global South. Ziai cautions against too much enthusiasm for the ability (and genuine willingness) of the development apparatus to be reformed. Using the concepts of ‘participation’ and ‘ownership’ as concrete examples in development policy, he demonstrates that, despite all promises to do so, development ‘experts’ and institutions fail to give up their supposed superiority and put development in the hands of the people concerned (Ziai 2017, 78-79). This is why the Post-Development school of thought goes one step further than that, challenging the concept of development as such and trying to overcome it instead of reforming it (ibid., 80).

2.2.3 The Post-Development approach

During the 1990s, a new school of thought entered the arena of development studies, bearing the irritating name 'Post-Development' (Kerner 2012, 111; Ziai 2007, 3). Post-Development theory is among the approaches that emerged from postcolonial theory (Escobar 2012, xii). Ina Kerner calls it "postcolonial criticism of development policy" (Kerner 2012, 110, translation by E.K). As Cheryl McEwan points out in her book *Postcolonialism and Development*, the works of postcolonial critics like Said, Spivak, Bhabha, Chakrabarty, and many more are of high importance for people working in development politics and cooperation, as they face the same dilemmas the latter address, for instance (McEwan 2009, 72-73): Can we, should we, and by what means would we include the global South in general and the subaltern in particular into the dominant discourse?[11] What do the power constellations between the global North and the global South look like and is there a chance to interact in a way to overcome them?[12] Can the call of postcolonial scholar Dipesh Chakrabarty to provincialize Europe be applied to development studies? Ramón Grosfoguel demonstrates that the perpetual definition of the global South by the global North as inferior has by no means changed due to formal decolonisation. He does so by drawing a continuous line from "the sixteenth century characterization of 'people without writing' to the eighteenth and nineteenth-century characterization of 'people without history,' to *the twentieth-century characterization of 'people without development'* and more recently, to the early twenty-first-century of 'people without democracy'" (Grosfoguel 2011, 7, emphasis by E.K.).

Drawing on Arturo Escobar's work, Kerner defines the following three cornerstones of Post-Development: criticising the concept of development, critically analysing specific areas of intervention within development policy, and thinking about potential alternatives to development (Kerner 2012, 112-113). According to Ziai, the three founding works of the Post-Development school of thought are Wolfgang Sachs' *Development Dictionary*[13], Arturo Escobar's *Encountering Development*[14], and the *Post-Development*

11 For details on that issue, see the discussion of Spivak's *Can the Subaltern Speak?* in chapter 2.1.2 of this thesis and especially the discussion on 'speaking for others' in chapter 5.1.2 of this thesis.

12 The first part of the question is discussed in chapters 3 and 5, the second part especially in chapter 5.

13 First published in 1992, cited here in its third edition of the year 2019.

14 First published in 1995, cited here in the 2012 edition.

Reader[15] edited by Majid Rahnema and Victoria Bawtree. Though with emphases on differing aspects in particular, the three publications agree on the central point that development has been a disappointment to people in the global South and has rather harmed then helped them, whether in terms of livelihood, progress, or culture and identity (Ziai 2007, 4-5). As Ziai points out, following Escobar, Post-Development authors look for alternatives to development as a concept, not alternative ways to implement the concept, often expecting to find them in the lifeworlds of ordinary people in the global South (ibid.). Hence, they do not look for better ways to implement existing development programmes or for better ways to integrate poor countries into the world economy and have them copy the development path of the global North. Instead, they look for better ways to think about social change as a process that can look different in various societies and can have different yet satisfying outcomes for each society.

In *The Development Dictionary*, which has seen its third edition just recently, some of the most prominent representatives of critical development studies present their points of view on topics, which are central to development discourse, policies, and activities. They give a critical account on what is usually taken for granted and not questioned or contextualised in development studies, politics, and practice. For instance, Serge Latouche reminds us that the concept of 'standard of living', which is being treated as a natural phenomenon in development theory and practice, is an invention of the industrial age in the global North and by no means universal or natural (Latouche 2019, 279). He points out how the interest in "studying different modes of living" has been turned into an exclusive interest in different "*levels* of living", as the modes of living became more and more uniform and the modes of analysis became exclusively economic (ibid., 280, emphasis in the original).

The central entry in *The Development Dictionary* is Gustavo Esteva's on *Development*. Esteva is best known for his hypothesis that 'underdevelopment' as a condition has been constructed through the inaugural address to his second term by then US President (1945-1953) Harry S. Truman, on 20 January 1949. The most frequently cited quote of Esteva refers to that very date and occasion: "On that day, 2 billion people became underdeveloped." (Esteva 2019, 2) Although he admits that Truman has not invented the expression 'underdeveloped areas', for which he announced assistance, Esteva insists that it only gained its sweeping effects through this speech – with disastrous impacts on the identities and the self-esteem of whole

15 First published in 1997, cited here in its second impression of the year 1998.

peoples that were termed like this (ibid.). As a result, Esteva is a radical opponent of development. To those who try to reform development, manoeuvring "as if they were walking in a minefield", Esteva counters: "The minefield has already exploded." (ibid., 3) He suggests that "the simple fact of associating with development one's own intention tends to annul the intention, to contradict it, to enslave it", which "impedes thinking of one's own objectives", "clamours for management from the top down", and "converts participation into a manipulative trick to involve people in struggles for getting what the powerful want to impose on them" (ibid.). Esteva depicts biology as the source of the idea of development: The biologist knows the specific form that a plant or an animal is supposed to accomplish, the final stage of its 'development'. If it does not reach there, but takes an unexpected form, it becomes a 'monster', a failure (ibid., 3-4). From that point of view, development is indeed something that resists any attempt to adjust it, reform it, or re-shape it according to the supposed beneficiaries' needs. Esteva continues tracing the use of the word 'development' from Justus Möser to Johann Gottfried Herder in the eighteenth century, to common use, to Karl Marx in the nineteenth century (ibid., 4). Another important aspect of criticism on development is raised in Esteva's timeline of development thinking: the reduction of development, i.e., the movement of a society from a lower to a higher level in terms of standards of living and social evolution, to economic growth. Esteva traces this school of thought back to William Arthur Lewis, in the 1940s and 50s, whose definition of development as economic growth was taken up by leftist (Paul Baran) and conservative (Walter Rostow) thinkers alike in the 1950s and 60s (ibid., 8). Esteva follows development discourse and policies on the part of the United Nations through the following decades, coming to the conclusion that none of the attempts to improve on this one-dimensional view of development has ever managed to prevail over it (ibid., 9-14). Latouche comes to the same conclusion when tracing the attempts of World Bank and United Nations to revise the indicators for measuring 'standard of living', i.e., the success or failure of development, in a country. Despite serious attempts to find more diversified indicators, the development institutions ended up measuring the quality of life in a country first and foremost with the tool of the gross national product (GNP), a purely economic average indicator without reference to other spheres of life or to the dispersion of wealth among the citizens (Latouche 2019, 282-283). Latouche deplores the "one-dimensional reductionism" of this purely economic perspective on society that has become widely accepted worldwide (ibid., 285).

The second 'founding document' of Post-Development theory is Arturo Escobar's *Encountering Development*. One of the central hypotheses of the book is that poverty in the form that the global South is suffering from today, as well as the concept of development, are both corollaries of colonisation and "the consolidation of capitalism" that accompanied it (Escobar 2012, 22). In Escobar's words, "massive poverty in the modern sense appeared only when the spread of the market economy broke down community ties and deprived millions of people from access to land, water, and other resources" (ibid.). This argument goes hand in hand with the point of view presented by N'Dione et al. in their contribution to the *Post-Development Reader*. They point out that, by seducing people of the global South to neglect their social relationships in favour of the – oftentimes futile – quest for material riches, development thinking does the opposite of what it promises to do: It deprives them of their capacities to survive without help from outside (N'Dione et al. 1998, 368). N'Dione et al. deplore that the "development ideology implies – and therein lies its fraudulence – that development can bring something else, *something more than life*", creating the feeling of being 'poor' and 'deficient' in people, who indeed have been able to survive on their own until then (ibid., 369, emphasis by E.K.). This assumption may irritate people, who believe in a 'natural evolution' of human societies, which moves forward from primitiveness to civilization, from ignorance to wisdom, and from poverty to abundance. Yet, this is exactly the kind of thinking that representatives of Post-Development intend to overcome. This attitude tends to earn them the reputation of romanticising poverty. Escobar's reasoning shows very well the misunderstanding from which this reproach arises. According to him, before colonisation and 'integration into the world economy', people in the global South were not leading 'poor lives', but they were living according to their own standards. Being 'integrated' in the world economy forcefully and, at the same time, incompletely, with their indigenous systems being destroyed, but not replaced with something new that could work for them, is what made them 'poor'. Hence, Escobar is not trying to paint a picture of a romantic past, or of people being happy while they are poor. On the contrary, he tries to make visible the unpleasant truth that poverty is man-made and, as such, not an unfortunate condition that some people suffer from, while others can help them out with their superior technical knowledge. He identifies it as a *structural* problem with complex causes and without easy solutions. Escobar wants to cure the people of the global North from the belief that they innocently stumbled upon 'poor people' living in the global South, whom they now help to escape their 'natural' poverty and become like themselves, i.e., 'developed'. He wants both parties to see that the global North was, and still is, the *cause* of poverty in the global South and, as a result, it cannot be the solution for it. He calls the evolution of the discourse on the global South as 'poor' and the solutions for this essential problem being development and economic growth a "particular historical event"[16] (Escobar 2012, 24), depriving it of any sense of being a natural process or a corollary of pre-colonial lifestyles in the global South. N'Dione et al. do not depict life before development ideology as perfect either, but as liveable and as a potential ground for the people's own ideas of social change to grow on. Yet, according to their argument, Western development thinking has destroyed that ground. It has replaced a liveable life with a miserable one, self-sufficiency with permanent lack, and a future that was wide open with a destination that has been imposed on the people from outside and leaves no room for negotiation.

Economic theory plays the leading part in development studies and policies. Instead of accepting its self-image as "a neutral representation of the world and a truth about it" (Escobar 2012, 58), Escobar reveals that "the Western economy can be anthropologized and shown to be made up of a peculiar set of discourses and practices" (ibid., 59). He comments on "the notions of economy, market, and production" in the Western sense: "Their histories can be traced, their genealogies demarcated, and their mechanisms of truth and power revealed." (ibid.) From that anthropological point of view, Western economy should not be regarded as a production system, but "as an institution composed of systems of production, power, and signification", which are "inextricably linked to the development of capitalism and modernity" (ibid.). Escobar calls for the economy to be seen primarily as "a cultural production, a way of producing human subjects and social orders of a certain kind", not just "a material entity" that it pretends to be (ibid.). Concerning power, Escobar reminds us how much disciplining has been necessary in the global North to make peasants, farmers, and serfs leave the land they had been cultivating behind, work in factories, and evolve into the incarnations of *Homo oeconomicus*, the 'rationally' and economically thinking utility maximiser. Against this historical background, the alleged natural predetermination of that process becomes a suspect matter. With regard to signification, Escobar emphasises modernity's trait of "the separation of social life into

16 According to Escobar, this historical event took place right after World War II (Escobar 2012, 44).

functional spheres (the economy, the polity, society, culture, and the like), each with laws on its own" (ibid., 60). He calls for "the anthropology of modernity" to replace political economy as the central frame of reference and analyse economy as culture and the functional spheres of society as a social entity (ibid., 61). Yet, first and foremost, economics must be recognised as *a discourse* "that constructs a particular picture of the economy", not a truth (ibid.). The basic assumption of "the analysis of economics as culture" is that any model "is a construction of the world and not an indisputable, objective truth about it" (ibid., 62). This leads to the conclusion that the domination of one model entails the suppression or appropriation of others (ibid.). Escobar states that representatives of the Post-Development approach "are interested not in development alternatives but in alternatives to development, that is, the rejection of the entire paradigm altogether" (ibid., 215), meaning "the end of development *as a regime of representation*" (ibid., 216, emphasis by E.K.). The latter formulation clarifies that Escobar's intention is by no means to condemn people in the global South to eternal stagnation by rejecting development in the sense of social change. Rather, the idea is to rebel against the implicitness with which the global North, from its position of power, has created *a specific* idea of development and declared it *the only* thinkable one. Escobar even dreams of the day when the discourse is turned upside-down and the thinking that has made possible the "incredibly irresponsible policies and programs" of development becomes unthinkable (ibid., 217). This would mean that the currently hegemonic development discourse would have been replaced by another, a process that seems unimaginable as long as the old hegemony is still strong. Yet, this has nothing to do with the impossibility of alternatives, but with the power of the representatives of the hegemonic discourse to suppress any move towards their articulation. As soon as the power of that hegemonic class is no longer accepted by the majority, alternative discourses come up, first as alternatives, later as potential new hegemonies (see chapter 2.4, headword 'Hegemony').

It is no coincidence that Escobar writes about 'alternatives' in plural. As he insists, he does not believe in any single alternative that could work anywhere and under all circumstances (Escobar 2012, 222). He cautions academics that their quest for this one-size-fits-all solution is exactly what has caused the current crisis, and that they should be more sensitive to their role in the process. The strategy he recommends has two elements, a practical and a theoretical one. First and foremost, Escobar recommends to research existing local (hybrid) practices, in which he sees a high potential to bring up numerous and practicable alternative ideas (ibid., 222-223).

Rahnema likewise recommends that "a deeper and unbiased knowledge of how different cultures have solved their problems and of what they learned to cherish or dislike through the ages would be instructive for all those in search of alternatives to our own dilemmas" (Rahnema 1998, 381). Secondly, on the theoretical level, Escobar calls for a "deconstruction of development", for an end of development's epistemological hegemony, which requires active theoretical questioning from the side of academics as well as the application of the knowledge generated from the above-mentioned research on living alternatives (Escobar 2012, 223). This would allow "popular actors" to reclaim control over their lives from so-called 'experts' from academia as well as from development institutions (ibid.). Finally, Escobar adds that in these new alternatives, cultural differences have to play a central role because they are among "the key political facts of our times" (ibid., 225). What he aptly points out with that comment is that, after all, what the alternatives are inevitably going to have in common with the current notion of development is the desire for social change (of what kind whatsoever), yet the social cannot be thought without cultural characteristics. Its refusal to accept this fact and, as a result, its inability to consider cultural differences, is one of the reasons why the current approach to development has no chance to succeed on a global scale.

The Post-Development Reader is a kaleidoscope of many different approaches. This is exactly what the Post-Development school of thought intends to be. The point that they all agree on is that it is high time to revisit the concept of development, which has been regarded as invariable for decades, and dare to think about alternatives to it. The points they criticise in the concept of development are comparable with the ones that have been discussed in chapter 2.2.1. For instance, Teodor Shanin traces the legacy of the "idea of progress" from the seventeenth century (the period of Enlightenment) until today (Shanin 1998, 65) and the way its name "changed with fashion: 'progress', 'modernization', 'development', 'growth', and so on" (ibid., 66). Shanin unmasks the "immense arrogance" in the global North's attitude to consider itself "an example to all, a natural leader of all" (ibid., 68) because it believes it has found the universal solution to the mystery of social change (ibid., 67-68, see also 70). Nikita Dhawan gives the example of a government of a formerly colonised country. If it wants to be taken seriously by the global North, it has no choice but trying to imitate Euro-American norms, as the global North has established its norms as *the* universal standard (Dhawan 2011, 15-16). For Dhawan, it is not surprising that the copies which are produced by those endeavours are of poor quality, as the social and historical context of each country is different (ibid., 16). According to Shanin, this self-awarded status of universalism made the idea of progress (or development) a field of knowledge that ignores all questions and evidence that do not confirm its underlying ideology and that promotes its own 'experts' despite any failure or damage they produce (Shanin 1998, 69). In combination with the modern state, this ideology has been used continually to justify the privileges of the global North, which pretends to be on the crest of human development thanks to its own ingenuity (ibid.). Yet, some of the contributors of *The Post-Development Reader* want to go beyond criticism and suggest alternative approaches.

As has been shown above, N'Dione et al. hold the opinion that poverty is man-made and promoted by development ideology, as the latter deprives people in the global South of their capacities to survive on their own (N'Dione et al. 1998, 368-369). Beyond their scorching criticism of development, they offer very practical alternative approaches, as they themselves are practitioners. They state that they regard the "capital of relationships as the main wealth of the poor", which is why they try to "support all initiatives that make the most of people's social networks", e.g., involving popular leaders in the planning of activities (ibid., 370). Another important point for them is not to impose any world view on the beneficiaries, but to let them deploy their own and set priorities accordingly (ibid.). This may sound like the so-called 'participative' approach that has been in vogue in development projects for a while. Yet, it goes far beyond that half-hearted and oftentimes tokenistic poll among potential beneficiaries without any significant effect on the project design, as the latter has already been finalised prior to the poll. What N'Dione et al. opt for is the *liberation* of the beneficiaries through the naming of mechanisms that suppress and devalue them and through encouraging them to rediscover their capacities to make sense of their reality and their wishes (ibid., 370-371). Concerning global interconnectedness, N'Dione et al. admit that, under today's circumstances, it cannot be neglected. Nevertheless, for them, the purpose of global as well as local collaboration should be the facilitation of *local priorities* (ibid., 374).

Ivan Illich was among the early critics of development. In his view, development is first and foremost a strategy of the global North to create markets for its goods in the global South (Illich 1998, 94-95). This hypothesis is being supported by other scholars like Majid Rahnema and Rick Rowden. According to Rahnema, through development, the global North does not only benefit from new markets in the global South but also from easier "access to raw materials" (Rahnema 1998, 385). Rowden's hypothesis encompasses both arguments, supplemented by the factor of labour being cheaper in the global South (Rowden 1999, 176). As a result, societies in the global South are formed following the example set by the global North, with a middle class enjoying consumption of countless goods and an extending mass of people who are left behind, their living conditions getting worse and worse (Illich 1998, 96-97). Illich calls for "counterresearch on fundamental alternatives to current prepackaged solutions", with the task to "doubt what is obvious to every eye" (ibid., 100). Just like Illich, Wolfgang Sachs analyses the result of "the development race" as a "global middle class" consisting of people from the global North and increasingly "small elites in the South", which faces "large sections of socially excluded population" (Sachs 1998, 291). According to Sachs, the decisive dividing line is no longer any national boundary, neither the East-West division, but the *global* socio-economic dividing line that separates the rich from the poor (ibid.). Nevertheless, Sachs cautions against the illusion that, one fine day, every person in the world is going to be above the line. He asserts that "[e]conomic expansion has already come up against its bio-physical limits" (ibid., 292), as the Earth's capacities to serve as the sole provider of inputs and dumps for production activities are finite (ibid., 291-292). In this tense situation, globalisation with its new expansive facilities of communication and transport has a boomerang effect on its beneficiaries, the rich in the global North. After having avoided to face "the reality of a divided world" for centuries, since exploitation of resources and people was done to a large extent (though not exclusively) in distant places, the global North is increasingly confronted with this reality (ibid., 292). As a result, "[t]he crisis of justice and the crisis of nature stand, with the received notion of development, in an inverse relationship to each other" (ibid., 293). Any serious attempt to align the level of development in the global South with that of the global North seems to be unreasonable with regard to finite natural resources – just as any attempt to protect natural resources from exploitation for further development seems to be inacceptable for the masses of people in the world, who have been deprived of participation so far. According to Sachs, there is only one way out of this dilemma: to re-think development in the global North as well as in the global South (ibid.). He prescribes the global North to take up the position of the "home perspective", "making room for others by an orderly retreat", reducing its (ecological and other) global effects "to the radius of real responsibility" (ibid., 297). Sachs elucidates that this approach needs two measures for its implementation, namely efficiency and, even more, sufficiency with regard to the use of resources (ibid., 297-298). Nevertheless, he admits that the self-limitation and loss of power, which necessarily come along with sufficiency, will not be accepted by the people of the global North without reservation – even though nothing essential would be taken from them, only their "overdevelopment" (ibid., 299). For the global South, that would mean to at least think about the question whether growth and 'development' with the current connotations is really the kind of social change they want, or whether they could think of better alternatives. This audacious suggestion by Sachs is a typical example of the de-growth movement (see chapter 4.1.1).

In his afterword to the *Post-Development Reader*, Majid Rahnema comes to a similar conclusion as Sachs and, to a certain extent, Illich. Using the examples of paper consumption and car ownership in the USA, Rahnema points out that a catch-up of the global South is neither possible nor desirable, due to limited natural resources (Rahnema 1998, 379). In his view, "development, as it imposed itself on its 'target populations', was basically the wrong answer to their true needs and aspirations" (ibid.). He continues with the assumption that development ideology first and foremost serves the expansion of the interests of *powerful elites* and the transfer of socio-economic problems from the global North to the global South (ibid.). Here, Rahnema treats as a matter of course what would be unthinkable for most proponents of mainstream development ideology, namely: that development in the form we know today is not without alternative, but *just one option* among many, and not even the best. Rahnema calls for development to be "change that could help people to enhance their inborn and cultural capacities: [...] that could leave them free to *change the rules and the contents of change*, according to their own culturally defined ethics and aspirations" (ibid., 384, emphasis in the original). The strategies he suggests in order to reach that goal are to rather think alternatives (ibid., 391) than to fall for the belief of developmentalists in their omnipotence (even though, in some cases, they may mean well; ibid., 392-393); to keep initiatives at a manageable size and use the community members' individual strengths for their successful implementation (ibid., 393-394). On the side of the privileged, Rahnema calls for true solidarity, which means to him that all spaces to transform the system from within, be it within organisations or through public channels like the media or the internet, should be used (ibid., 395) rather than just 'sending a cheque' that could even end up in the hands of the wrong people (ibid., 393). In Grosfoguel's view, positive economic development in the global South can only be achieved if the permanent flow of wealth from South to North is reversed, e.g., with the help of international organisations or through taxes on global capital flows. Yet, he admits that this requires a complete revision of the whole world-system because it has been built by the global North, on the basis of its exploitation of the global South, and there is no willingness for change on the part of the global North (Grosfoguel 2011, 31). This observation unmasks so-called 'development aid' at the best as well-meant, but ill-informed acts of unfruitful philanthropy. At the worst, it can be regarded as a cynic strategy to enable the global North to continue exploiting the global South and, at the same time, look like its benefactor. Grosfoguel even accuses the International Monetary Fund (IMF) and the World Bank, two of the biggest representatives of the development industry, of having aggravated the situation for many countries of the global South since the beginning of the 1980s, the time of structural adjustment programmes. He concludes that any change that could be helpful to the global South first requires "to imagine anti-systemic global decolonial utopian alternatives beyond colonialist and nationalist, Eurocentric fundamentalist and Third World fundamentalist binary ways of thinking" (ibid.).

Ziai states that believing to have development knowledge corresponds to believing to know what is wrong with other people's lifestyles and how it can be corrected. This "authoritarian element in development discourse" makes it a discourse that is capable of exercising violence, e.g., by forcing people to accept development measures against their will, or by displacing populations in favour of development projects, especially infrastructure projects (Ziai 2017, 34). From the position of power that the 'West' is occupying, this arrogant attitude may look justifiable and even philanthropic because global power constellations make 'our' position the 'right' one. What if global power constellations would change and make the Chinese or a Muslim orientation the 'right' one? Would Western proponents of development thinking still hold the opinion that the hegemonic model has to be applied to all people in the world? In order to avoid the very emergence of such questions, the West does what it can in order to keep up its hegemony. Any form of resistance against European interventions in the global South is still, and has always been, treated as unjust and unthankful misconduct of the supposed 'beneficiaries', and has often been answered with rigorous oppression (Dhawan 2011, 15). This applies to the alleged 'civilising mission' of colonialism as well as to the cases of displacement of people in favour of 'development' projects mentioned with reference to Ziai above.

Sabelo Ndlovu-Gatsheni may not call himself a 'Post-Developmentalist', yet he questions the mainstream developmental reasonings for Africa's present situation like the lack of access to markets or to 'expert' knowledge. Instead, he states that "exploitative mercantilism, slave trade, imperialism, colonialism, apartheid and neocolonialism wrecked havoc on indigenous histories, institutions, values and systems, creating the fundamental problems of the neocolonial Africa we live in today" (Ndlovu-Gatsheni 2013, 6). In his view, to declare the lack of Western modernisation in Africa a lack of development is a move to justify political and economic intervention on the part of the global North (ibid., 41). Indeed, Ndlovu-Gatsheni is not critical of development as social change, but of *Western* developmentalism. He adds an interesting argument to the pro- and con-debate on development by stating: "Europe and America have appropriated *human ideas* of progress, civilization and developmentalism as exclusive virtues of Western modernity that had to be exported to other parts of the world" (ibid., 40, emphasis by E.K.). This statement reminds us how endangered even Post-Developmentalists are to fall into the trap of the very Eurocentrism they criticise. It is indispensable to always emphasise that it is the *specific notion* of development, which the global North claims its property, that is being rejected. As soon as Post-Developmentalists appear to claim that *any kind* of 'development' must be rejected because it is an invention of the global North, they enter complicity with the creators of the myth that the global North is the only human society capable of thinking about change, while all other societies are static and condemned to immutability (if not taught otherwise by the global North). Ndlovu-Gatsheni reminds us that "progress, civilization and developmentalism" are "*human* ideas" (ibid., emphasis by E.K.). Although their specific forms that have been imposed on the world since colonialism and that consequently dominate everybody's minds when they hear those terms are unquestionably productions of the global North, the idea of social change that underlies them cannot be claimed by a particular part of humanity as their own. In his view, this exclusive claim on progressive ideas by the global North, together with the denial of Africa's ability to produce them, is the link between "the politics of knowledge production" and the "politics of identity" that conjointly constitute "the colonial drive" against African knowledges and identities (ibid., 61-62).

Ziai states that two of the most important hypotheses of Post-Development are not even denied by its critics, namely that the conventional concept of development is Eurocentric, and also technocratic and authoritarian (Ziai 2007, 8-9). Nevertheless, there are several other points of criticism, internally as well as from the side of opponents of the school of thought. Ziai himself states that "PD discourse can serve both radical democratic as well as conservative political ends, and this constitutes its ambivalence" (Ziai 2017, 80-81). The Post-Development approach is in peril of being instrumentalised for paternalistic, nationalistic, or other conservative political programmes. Other points of criticism are discussed in the subsequent paragraphs. For instance, Sally Matthews cautions to bear in mind that the biggest number of alternative discourses, no matter whether they are informed by Post-Development theory or by Afrocentrism, build on the same categories as the discourse that they criticise, making their status as alternatives questionable (Matthews 2018, 174-175). She suggests "not to capitulate to development but to recognize, firstly, the power of development; secondly and relatedly, the ways in which supposed alternatives only partly overcome and oppose development; and, thirdly and finally, that opposition is possible even where escape is not" (ibid., 179). The most important term here is 'opposition'. It is not simply 'reform of development', but opposition to it, that Matthews advocates. Nevertheless, she cautions against the illusion that there is a space untouched by the development concept, where that opposition could take place (ibid., 182). For Post-Development thinkers, this means to always remember where they came from and never stop questioning the categories on which they build their discourse. Furthermore, it means never underestimating the adversary, the development paradigm, which is still far from being overcome.

James Ferguson, although his writings are very popular with Post-Development thinkers, is not in favour of Post-Development, due to his interpretation of the approach. Ferguson generalises for all prevalent Post-Development writers that they are believing that an era after development has started (Ferguson 2005, 172). He seems to take the 'post' in the concept's name literally, which is not the way it is meant, as has been shown above. Ferguson suggests: "A more precise way of posing the problem might be to say that while developmental narratives have hardly disappeared, they have undoubtedly lost much of their credibility for certain people in certain places" (ibid., 171). This sounds like the perfect Post-Development critique. That must be the reason why Ferguson's texts are so highly appreciated and frequently quoted in Post-Development writings. Arturo Escobar clarifies that, when he and other Post-Development thinkers are writing about a "post-development era", what they mean "is not a new historical period" that the world has reached or is about to reach (Escobar 2007, 20). It is rather a vision of a *possible condition*, in which social change would no longer be dictated by the development paradigm but take place through people freely constructing their own lifeworlds the way *they* want. Escobar emphasises the important role of "a re-valorization of vernacular cultures" and "taking seriously social movements and grassroots mobilizations" (ibid.). Countries of the global South would no longer be reduced to "imperfect deviations" from the norm of the 'developed' countries, being "in the process of approaching the norm – although they will never reach it" (Ziai 2007, 8). Their knowledges on all levels would be acknowledged and no longer despised as inferior to 'expertise' from the global North (Escobar 2007, 22-23, 26). Hence, the idea of a 'post-development era' should not be mistaken for a 'return to nature' or an end of all efforts to improve the living conditions of people. It is rather about an end of Eurocentrism, paternalism, exploitation, and neoliberal hegemony – and it is yet to be achieved. Those are all properties that Post-Development thinking allocates to the development project as it is implemented currently, as demonstrated in chapter 2.2.1. At least the first three of them might be evocative of properties of colonialism. Consequently, Post-Development takes up arms against the same forms of oppression that postcolonialism has been trying to fight.

A very strong counter-argument against Post-Development is that people in the global South *do want development*. Such claims are usually made without specifying what kind of 'development' they want, reason being that in the hegemonic discourse, this question does not arise. The concept of capitalist development based on the standards of the Western world is beyond question. When people in the global South wish for the amelioration of their living conditions, the solution must be capitalist development with all its implications like economic growth, integration into the global economy, etc. (see chapter 2.2.1). People in the global South know very well that 'development' is the code used by policy makers, 'development experts', and scholars (from both hemispheres) for the improvement of living conditions. As a result, they demand 'development', though they may have other priorities in mind than scholars, 'development experts', and policy makers. However, the reactions to the objection that people want 'development', even by some of the most eloquent Post-Development thinkers, look rather weak. For example, Rahnema claims that people are not really asking for it, but 'developers' from organisations and governments are just spreading that rumour (Rahnema 1998, 385). I have spoken to more than enough people in the global South, be it in the context of research (see chapter 8), work, or private conversations, to be sure that this is simply not true. People do call for development and they do not need any officials to tell them so. Rahnema continues arguing that, even if they were asked, the people would not know what would be good for them, such that they should rather leave the decision up to the wisest members of society (ibid., 388-389). Without question, this line of reasoning runs the risk of supporting paternalism and oppression. In any case, the question remains: What kind of 'development' do people mean when they call for it? Do they want structural adjustment programmes? Do they want schools? Do they want a general improvement of their life situation? And what does the latter look like in their own imagination? The answer to all those questions is the same: We will only get to know if we ask them. In the *Preface to the 2012 Edition* of his definitive book *Encountering Development*, Escobar states that "the desires and hopes for development and modernity that many people worldwide have adopted as a result of their encounter with development and modernity" are wrongly being ignored, although "these desires are real" (Escobar 2012, xvii). 'To improve living conditions' can have innumerable faces, from a return to nature up to building sky scrapers with tap water, highspeed internet connection, and pizza delivery service – or any imaginable thing between the two poles, *or at the side of the supposed line between them*. Every society should get the chance to negotiate, decide, and implement what its members consider real improvements in their daily lives. The problem with the hegemonic development discourse is that it does not allow for such chances but prescribes 'one-size-fits-all'-solutions.

James Ferguson calls "the developmental narrative" of human societies climbing the unidirectional, linear mountain trail of modernisation and increasing material wealth successively "a failure not only in the domain of academic theory but in practical economic terms as well" (Ferguson 2005, 172). His most popular idea can be found in his definitive book of the same name: *The Anti-Politics Machine*. The 'machine' in question is, of course, development or as Ferguson puts it, "the 'development' apparatus" (Ferguson 2014, 256). He compares it to the 'anti-gravity machine', which makes gravity disappear at the push of a button, in science fiction stories. In a comparably miraculous way, Ferguson sees the 'development apparatus' abrogate political implications in any (political) operation. He calls this the "instrument-effect", which, as he notes, "is two-fold: alongside the institutional effect of expanding bureaucratic state power is the conceptual or ideological effect of depoliticizing both poverty and the state" (ibid.). Ferguson suggests that this 'instrument-effect', especially the expansion of bureaucratic state power through development projects, leads to their repetition in spite of most of them being judged as failures (ibid.). Ferguson elucidates his machine-metaphor with his intention "to capture something of the way that conceptual and discursive systems link up with social institutions and processes without even approximately determining the form or defining the logic of the outcome" (ibid., 275). This might be another element of the explanation for development projects' tendency not to deliver the outcomes they have promised, but different outcomes: Within their scope, it is impossible for the planners to take into account and to control the actions of the other 'machine parts'. Ferguson does not consider the development apparatus to be in the position to push through the interests of some powerful actor(s), as some development critics believe, or of any specific individual or group, at all (ibid., 17-19). Another element of the explanation for the failure of 'development' to deliver as promised that he discusses is the 'packaged' nature of development projects and programmes. They tend to consist of one and the same package of ideas and procedures for every place of intervention, without considering any local peculiarities (ibid., 258-259). Illich's above-mentioned call for alternatives to development's "prepackaged solutions" (Illich 1998, 100) seems to echo here. As an alternative approach to development, Ferguson suggests empowerment. Expertise should be a service that bottom-up political movements and intrinsically motivated self-help initiatives of the concerned people can *call for in case they want it* instead of the experts trying to start activities for the 'beneficiaries' from scratch (Ferguson 2014, 281-282). Furthermore, Ferguson calls upon social scientists from the global North, who are committed for helping the global South, to go for political involvement in their own societies. Those people have particular knowledge and personal experience of regions of the world that other members of their societies have at best vague or stereotypical ideas of. According to Ferguson, this qualifies and, at the same time, *obliges* them to face "the task of combating imperialist policies and advancing the causes of Third World peoples", e.g., by "teaching, public speaking, and advocacy" (ibid., 286). This compliments Rahnema's above-mentioned call for 'true solidarity', which for him consists of transforming the system from within, using organisations as well as public channels like the internet or the media (Rahnema 1998, 395).

These conclusions offered by explicitly Post-Development authors as well as some, who fit well into the school of thought although they do not consider themselves members (e.g., Ferguson), show impressively the commonalities with – as well as the differences to – reformist developmentalist approaches. The criticism that both schools of thought pass on development is the same to a great extent, at least as far as unfair global power constellations and failure of development endeavours to improve on the situation of the global South are concerned. Yet, what divides them is the nature of the conclusions they draw from it. As I elaborated in chapter

2.2.2, reformist approaches look for better ways for the global South to catch up with Western development. The representatives of the Post-Development school of thought (and scholars with a related approach) suggest completely different solutions, as has been shown in this chapter. The dilemma of Post-Development approaches does not lie in their critique, but in the search for alternatives to development. If, on the one hand, they do not provide any alternative suggestion for the improvement of the situation of the global South, their legitimate, necessary critique is being disqualified because development seems to be without alternative. On the other hand, to provide an alternative is not easy, for many reasons. In general, any solution suggested by an academic is not much better than any other 'development' strategy because it was, again, imposed on the supposed 'beneficiaries' from outside. Some Post-Development theorists, e.g., Gustavo Esteva (Esteva 2019, 18), try to overcome that problem by analysing alternatives, which are already being practiced by certain groups. However, as is being shown in this chapter, the very assumption that any lifestyle can and should be universalised for all people is a major point of criticism by Post-Development theory.

2.2.4 Approach to development in this study

'Development' is a concept with a history, as has been shown above. The details are far from being undisputed. Different authors draw different lines of its formation, sometimes linear, sometimes erratic, sometimes plural and entangled lines. Some start in the age of Enlightenment, others start after World War II. I suggest that for tracing the history of a concept, it is necessary to go back as far as possible and consider all its harbingers as well as the changes it went through over time. Therefore, historical analyses like that of Gustavo Esteva (Esteva 2019; see also chapter 2.2.3 of this thesis) appear most coherent to me when tracing the concept, the idea, or the discourse of 'development' as social evolution. However, *activities* that are implemented in order to mitigate the negative effects of social change initiated by capitalist modes of production, are being implemented in the name of 'development' since the first half of the twentieth century (Ziai 2017, 72; see also chapter 2.2.1 of this thesis). Furthermore, my contention is that choosing one specific narrative by one specific author is not as important as drawing a general, essential conclusion: 'Development' is not just a word with a 'natural' meaning. It is a concept and a discourse that has been constructed actively and wilfully, with severe political and social consequences. The whole world is affected by development thinking, development practice, and the international power constellations that have been built on the two. The powerful are in the position to define 'development', its indicators and measures, hence, they define them in a way that allows them to look 'developed' while others look 'underdeveloped'. This seems to give them the right to treat those 'underdeveloped others' as inferior and to impose policies on them, allegedly for their own good. Against this background, the colonial legacy of development cannot be denied. Benevolent development theorists and practitioners ask themselves: "What else can we do for the people in the global South?" What they should ask themselves is: "How can it be that we (the Westerners/ the whites/ the global North/ the rich/ the powerful) are in the position to ask ourselves such questions? And what can be done in order to overcome the global power constellations that we have created in order to make others depend on our decisions instead of deciding for themselves?" Apart from that, I support Rahnema's assumption "that development, as it imposed itself on its 'target populations', was basically the wrong answer to their true needs and aspirations" (Rahnema 1998, 379). Following Sachs and Illich, I question the narrative of the global North living the perfect model, as this narrative ignores the social and ecological ramifications on the local, regional, and global scale, such as increasing social inequality within and across countries and the destruction of the global natural environment.

Another problematic aspect is epistemology. The West, as an ideological rather than a geographic entity (see chapter 2.4, keyword "The West"), celebrates itself as 'the free world', 'the cradle of democracy, rationality, and freedom of speech'. It is proud of its revolutionary thinkers and 'whistle-blowers' and contrasts its own alleged liberal nature with the thought control practiced under repressive regimes elsewhere. Nevertheless, when it comes to mainstream development theory and practice, the hegemonic model is without alternative. This attitude derives from the main discipline of origin of modern development studies, economics, in which neoliberal capitalism is likewise without alternative. Whoever questions those hegemonic concepts cannot expect to be taken seriously. Post-Development thinkers are an integral part of the movement that offers resistance to this form of suppression. Latouche aptly summarises it like this: "All conceptual distinctions break down, and easy assumptions and certainties fade away, as soon as one frees oneself from the taboos which govern the tribe of economists and statisticians" (Latouche 2019, 289). In his afterword to the *Post-Development Reader*, Rahnema makes the following statement, which can be applied to my personal situation as well as to my theoretical persuasion:

> "The tragedies and traumas that have resulted from the launching of development world-wide have helped many of the earlier believers to revise their positions. The studies contained in this Reader are testimony to the fact that a new generation of thinkers and 'doers' – particularly those whose personal field experience has led them to see things from the perspective of the peoples most concerned – have now come to question many of their previous ideological certainties." (Rahnema 1998, 379)

Even though I doubt that, as a privileged white person, I could ever be able to take the perspective of the alleged 'beneficiaries' of development endeavours, I do belong to the 'doers', who have been disillusioned by their experience in 'the field'. Yet, looking for an answer to the contradictions I encountered within hegemonic theory aggravated my confusion and frustration. To find that the alleged answers to the problems were really nothing but their *causes* left me with no other choice than to join the sceptics. I agree with Rahnema that, indeed, there are a few development projects that do more good than harm (Rahnema 1998, 381). Nevertheless, those few exceptions, which may arise either from favourable conditions or exceptional individuals or groups participating in them, cannot belie the faultiness of the development concept in its entirety.

Admittedly, among the critics of development, there is no unity. The strongest contradiction seems to be the one between the reformist developmentalists, like Chang, Kiiza (see 2.2.2), and Wade (see 2.2.1), and representatives of the Post-Development school of thought, like Escobar, Esteva, Rahnema, Sachs, and Ziai (see 2.2.3). The former criticise the power constellations in the international arena and call for a stronger standing for 'developing countries' and fairer chances for them to 'develop' in the general sense. The latter go one step further by rejecting the development paradigm as such and calling for a chance for people in all parts of the world to think and live alternatives, which *ideally* are more ecologically and socially acceptable. It is not easy to position myself in this debate. Representatives of the Post-Development approach would surely criticise reformists for not thinking *beyond* the concept of development as such. In return, the Post-Development thinkers would be criticised for representing an unrealistic concept that is not able to give concrete help to populations suffering from poverty with all its implications for health, human dignity, and prospects of participation, *right now*. In my view, both approaches are essential. I consider the fundamental critique of the development paradigm and apparatus as well as the search for alternatives done by Post-Development thinkers extremely important. To overcome the very concept of development as it is dominant nowadays should definitely be the medium-term goal of development studies (even if that would mean to search for a new name for them). Nevertheless, social change takes time, especially a change of such a dimension. Meanwhile, the system prevails and people suffer each and every day. These are good reasons for working on some room for manoeuvre for countries of the global South *within* the current system. After all, as has been demonstrated above, the two approaches are pursuing the same objectives, namely better living conditions and more dignity for the people of the global South, with the same critical attitude towards the current global power constellations. I admit that there is a certain danger of the two approaches trying to outdo each other. The reformists might claim that, in case they succeed, the people in the global South will be benefitting from development and there will be no need for Post-Development approaches. In return, the Post-Developmentalists might claim that trying to reform the development apparatus is so pointless an endeavour that no one should waste any time on it. However, the critics should try to be better than the objects of their criticism, namely the global economy and the development apparatus. Within these spheres, there is more than enough competition and rivalry. What is needed in the countermovement is cooperation. In chapter 2.2.3, the need for *alternatives to* conventional development thinking has been explained in detail. For instance, Wolfgang Sachs points to the facts that the growing global middle class faces "large sections of socially excluded population" (Sachs 1998, 291) and that "[e]conomic expansion has already come up against its bio-physical limits" (ibid., 292). He calls it the "crisis of justice and the crisis of nature" (ibid., 293). Additionally, the "authoritarian element in development discourse" makes it a discourse that is capable of exercising violence, e.g., by forcing people to accept development measures against their will, or by displacing populations in favour of development projects (Ziai 2017, 34). The crisis of justice arising from increasing social inequality; the crisis of nature due to the limited capacities of planet Earth to provide raw materials and tolerate waste products; the violent element of 'development;' and the disappointment with the nonfulfillment of its promises debunk the conventional, capitalist development model as an unsustainable concept that, in the long term, may even endanger social peace on the national and international level as well as the natural environment. Consequently, there is a very real need for alternatives, even if poverty reduction would be achieved otherwise. Additionally, Post-Development approaches do not pay attention to alternatives for the global South, only. Many of them are committed to achieve changes in the global North, the actual source of the problems and the centre of power. Although this aspect is indispensable, it may sometimes make them lose focus on the living conditions of the most disadvantaged people, who have no time to wait for scholarly discussions because they have no food to give to their children *this evening* (a time specification that is not going to become out-dated in the foreseeable future, I am afraid). This is where the reformists come in. It might be the divide between the practitioner I have been, who has lived, worked, and researched in the global South, and the Northern theorist I am about to become, that makes me think like that. However, in my view, it is indispensable that both approaches are being worked on by critical scholars and that they take notice of each other's work in order to be able to acknowledge the importance of the others' approach and the potentials of cooperation rather than competition.

2.3 World-systems analysis

This chapter presents world-systems analysis, particularly Immanuel Wallerstein's approach. This approach has provided concepts, which are vital for the theoretical framework of this thesis, namely the core-periphery-semiperiphery relation and the capitalist world-economy. The terms 'centre' and 'periphery', sometimes complemented by the term 'semiperiphery', are very popular within postcolonial studies and critical development studies. Many authors use them without specifying whether they have taken them from world-systems analysis or from dependency theory. As I demonstrate in chapter 2.3., the basic meaning of 'centre' (or 'core' or 'metropolis') and 'periphery' (or 'satellite') is the same in both trajectories and can be explained with a few sentences. In addition to that, what I intend to do in this chapter, is to present in brief Wallerstein's hypotheses on what the 'capitalist world-system' is, how core states, peripheral states, and semiperipheral states interact within it, and what this means for people in peripheral states like Uganda. In his later works, Wallerstein has commented on those aspects extensively. The comprehensive research he did on the history of Europe from the sixteenth century onwards, the foundation for his theoretical framework, can only be mentioned in passing here, as the focus of the thesis at hand is not on Europe, but on Uganda.

2.3.1 The history of world-systems analysis

As the founder and best-known representative of world-systems analysis, Immanuel Wallerstein reports that it came up in the early 1970s as a critique of preceding approaches, yet building on some of their assumptions – as all 'new' perspectives do (Wallerstein 2007, 1). He calls its basis, the core-periphery model, "an essential contribution of Third World scholars" (ibid., 11). The idea of 'centre' (or 'core' or 'metropolis') on the one hand and 'periphery' (or 'satellite') on the other was first mentioned by the *Economic Commission for Latin America* (CEPAL) (Escobar 2012, 80), namely by its first director Raúl Prebish (ibid., 90; Wallerstein 2007, 11-12). The CEPAL, a commission of Latin American economists, had its most far-reaching impacts in the 1950s (Escobar 2012, 80). Wallerstein ascribes the idea that economically powerful 'core' countries are in the position to dictate terms of trade that drain surplus value from the economically weaker countries, 'the periphery', to the representatives of the CEPAL. This model of "unequal exchange" comprised the belief that the countries of the periphery are in the position to protect themselves against exploitation by the core countries by means of national policies (Wallerstein 2007, 12). Up to this point, the core-periphery-paradigm was relatively callow and left much room for discussion and criticism (ibid.). André Gunder Frank and the 'dependency theorists' took it up, filled it with life and concluded that socialist revolution was the prerequisite for any change for the better (ibid., 12-13). The most important innovation that Frank added to Prebish's approach in the 1960s was the perception that the poverty of the periphery is an inherent characteristic of the capitalist world economy and, as such, a condition that capitalism *consolidates* and does not help to overcome (Cooper 1993, 93-94). While in the 1940s, Prebish had still believed that the situation of the periphery could be improved through national and international measures, Frank assumed that, in the interest of the centre, the periphery had to remain poor and powerless (ibid.). Writers like Walter Rodney, Immanuel Wallerstein and Samir Amin followed that line of argumentation, each of them giving it new facets, variants, and emphases (ibid., 94). André Gunder Frank's hypotheses that the history of the countries of the global South is not just a retarded copy of that of the global North and that they need an independent path of development (Frank 1966, 171) were revolutionary for his time. So was his assumption that the capitalist system had already managed to reach even areas that were regarded as remote and were not showing any positive signs of capitalist 'development' (ibid., 172). For Frank, the latter was no surprise because he identified the global capitalist system as the cause of the 'development' of the metropolises (rich countries and some big cities in poor countries, controlled by the rich ones) and the 'underdevelopment' of the 'satellites' (poor countries, especially rural areas) alike (ibid., 174). He assumed that the fate of a region depended on the question whether any metropolis had ever managed to make it its satellite. If so, as in the case of some Latin American regions that he had done research on, they were at first 'developed' and then dropped by the metropolis, as soon as the demand for the resources it had been needing from them was decreasing (ibid., 175). He uses Japan as an example for a country that had never become the satellite of any metropolis and, as such, had been able to escape 'underdevelopment' (ibid., 179).

Immanuel Wallerstein enhanced the core-periphery-model with the category of semiperipheral zones (Wallerstein 2011c, xiii), as I explain further in chapter 2.3.2. Wallerstein's definitive work is *The Modern World-System*, a historical reviewing of the evolvement of capitalism, or as Wallerstein calls it, the *capitalist world-system*. The work came out in four consecutive volumes, the first having been published in 1974. A complete edition of all four volumes was published in 2011, covering the development of that capitalist world-system over the period of the sixteenth century up to the early twentieth century and containing new prologues with clarifications and responses to critics by Wallerstein. Wallerstein's world-systems analysis combines the CEPAL's core-periphery analysis with Fernand Braudel's "world-economy" (Wallerstein 2007, 17). Braudel was the "second-generation leader" of the French *Annales* school of thought, which has influenced the discipline of historiography significantly in the second half of the twentieth century by raising awareness for the need to find a middle way between "'event-dominated' or episodic history" and "the search for timeless, eternal truths" (ibid., 15). Furthermore, the *Annales* school of thought urged historians and other social scientists to take notice of each other's work and integrate each other's findings into their analyses (ibid.). Braudel himself studied the Mediterranean of the sixteenth century and suggested that it was a "'world-economy' (*économie-monde*)" (ibid., emphasis in the original). Wallerstein defines a world-economy as "a large geographic zone within which there is a division of labor and hence significant internal exchange of basic or essential goods as well as flows of capital and labor" (ibid., 23). He emphasises that a world-economy consists of *several* political units, cultures, groups, languages, and so forth. The division of labour keeps the structure together. As a world-economy has nothing but this division of labour to keep it together, former world-economies have not been able to survive for long – only the modern world-system did, thanks to capitalism (ibid., 23-24). This is going to be explained further in the paragraph on 'hegemony' in chapter 2.3.2. Wallerstein defines a capitalist system as one that "gives priority to the *endless* accumulation of capital", which means that "only the modern world-system has been a capitalist system" (ibid., 24, emphasis in the original).

For world-systems analysts, it is a natural course of action "to analyze materials that had once been considered the exclusive concern of historians or economists or political scientists or sociologists, and to analyze them within a single analytical frame" (Wallerstein 2007, 19). Wallerstein questions the separation of the social sciences into political science, economics, and sociology. He traces it to the liberal conception, which says that modern social life is divided into three completely independent domains, namely the state, the market, and civil society, each needing its own respective science (Wallerstein 2011c, 243). Wallerstein calls them "the nomothetic disciplines" and portrays them as the attempt of nineteenth-century Western governments to apprehend the social reality of the time in order to keep it under control (ibid., 242-243). He substantiates his claim with the example of "economics" having been called "political economy" in the anglophone world and either the same or "social economy" in the francophone, up to the late nineteenth century (ibid., 243). It seems that the awareness of a connection between the domains of social life got lost during the nineteenth century. World-systems analysis is an attempt at putting back together what has been fragmented, in order to get a holistic picture of human society.

2.3.2 Characteristics of a world-system

In the *Prologue to the 2011 Edition* of *The Modern World-System I*, Wallerstein admits that the original idea for the book had been "a bad idea", an insight he gained during the process of writing (Wallerstein 2011, xviii). He had believed that knowing more about the way in which European nations had 'developed' since the sixteenth century would help to apprehend "the trajectories of the 'new nations' of the twentieth century", supposing "that all states followed parallel independent paths to something called 'development'" (ibid.). During the process of writing, he concluded that the *relations* between the countries could better account for everyone's place in the system than the position of a country on a linear racetrack to 'development'. Furthermore, he took up André Gunder Frank's idea of "the development of underdevelopment" (which has shortly been outlined above) as well as Frank's and Samir Amin's insights "that the 'traditional' was as recent as the 'modern', that the two emerged in tandem", not successively (ibid.).

According to Wallerstein, a capitalist world-economy is built around a "division of labor between core-like *production processes* and peripheral *production processes*" (Wallerstein 2007, 17, emphases by E.K.). Wallerstein emphasises that it is indeed possible to talk about "core and peripheral *states*", yet only because "such *processes* tended to group together in particular countries" (ibid., emphases by E.K.). Furthermore, he cautions to keep in mind that "core-periphery is a *relational* concept", i.e., the two terms make sense as a pair, only, not separately (ibid., emphasis in the original). Wallerstein emphasises "the hyphen in world-system and its two subcategories, world-economies and world-empires" (ibid., 16). He explains it as follows: "Putting the hyphen was intended to underline that we are talking not about systems, economies, empires *of the* (whole) world, but about systems, economies, empires *that are* a world (but quite possibly, and indeed usually, not encompassing the entire globe)." (ibid., 16-17, emphases in the original) Consequently, peripheral zones must be distinguished from areas, which are *external* to the specific world-system under examination, in Wallerstein's case the capitalist or modern world-system (Wallerstein 2011, 301-302). This does not mean that there are or were no trade relations between the respective world-system and those 'external' zones or the other world-systems that they belong to. However, their "trade relationship [is] based primarily on the exchange of preciosities" (luxury goods) while the internal peripheral zones produce commodities, which play a significant role for daily use within the world-system, though their production is poorly rewarded (everyday commodities or bulk goods) (ibid.). While core and periphery engage in "unequal exchange", meaning a "real transfer of surplus value from the peripheral zones to the core zones", the trade relations between the world-economy and external zones bring about a "win-win-situation" (Wallerstein 2011b, xv). The former are essential for both sides, whereas the latter can be cut off at any time without severe consequences for either party (ibid.). Wallerstein states that "the core countries continue to need, even at moments of downturn, certain of the products of the periphery—partly because due to ecological considerations they cannot be supplied elsewhere, partly because the cost of labor is more than ever lower than in the core" (Wallerstein 2011a, 129). In contrast, the trade in 'luxury goods' could be reduced or even cut off in case of economic downturn, without serious consequences for the economy as a whole – only for some individuals, who were specialised in trading those goods, which is bearable for the economy. This corresponds to Wallerstein's definition of a 'social system' as self-sufficient, which means that in the unlikely case of all its connections to the outside being cut, it would continue to operate in the same way as before (Wallerstein 2011, 347). Following this definition, only two social formations can be called systems: world-systems and "those relatively small, highly autonomous subsistence economies not part of some regular tribute-demanding system" (ibid., 348). Against this background, Wallerstein argues that, for example, the Azores and certain coastal regions of Brazil were part of the European world-economy (or the capitalist world-system) in the year 1600, whereas Japan and Persia were not (ibid., 301). He dates the incorporation of many zones, which had been external trade partners of the European world-economy until then, "most particularly and most importantly, the Indian subcontinent, the Ottoman empire, the Russian empire, and West Africa", to "the second half of the eighteenth and the first half of the nineteenth centuries" (Wallerstein 2011b, 129).

Following Fernand Braudel, who "said that capitalism was the 'anti-market'", world-systems analysis turns capitalism's self-image upside-down, unmasking it as a *monopolising* rather than a free market model (Wallerstein 2007, 18). This view goes hand in hand with Friedrich List's above-cited recommendation to 'kick away the ladder' and the reformist developmentalist approaches, which got inspired by it to do just the opposite of what neoliberal development programmes recommend to countries that want to 'catch up'. As has been shown in chapter 2.2.2 of this thesis, successful industrialisation, be it in the global North or in newly industrialised countries, has always relied on protectionist economic policies, which rather tend to foster monopolistic structures than free trade. Wallerstein explains as follows why a veritable free market would be the end of capitalism: In such an ideal free market, numerous buyers would face numerous sellers, both knowing all production costs and being devoid of restrictions of any kind. As a result, the buyers could "bargain down the sellers to an absolutely minuscule level of profit" (ibid., 25). As a result, the sellers would be deprived of their motivation to participate in the market (ibid., 25-26). For those reasons, producers prefer (quasi-)monopolies, or at least oligopolies, which allow them to realise high profits (ibid., 26). In order to create a favourable environment for (quasi-)monopolies and oligopolies to grow, regulatory action by the state is needed, for instance by means of patents or diverse protectionist policies (ibid., 26). That may remind us of Wade's and Kiiza's evaluations of the WTO-agreement TRIPS, discussed in chapters

2.2.1 and 2.2.2 of this thesis. Both demonstrate how the economically powerful countries of the global North are 'kicking away the ladder' by forcing the countries of the global South to practice one-sided 'free' trade and, at the same time, respect *the global North's* intellectual property rights. Thus, the global North ensures its monopoly on knowledge and, thereby, its high profits. It prevents potential producers from the global South from becoming their competitors in the global market – which, under these circumstances, is not a free, but a regulated market. Wallerstein explains that, whether a production process can be called core-like or peripheral, depends on its "degree of profitability", which equates to its "degree of monopolization" (Wallerstein 2007, 28). Competitive production processes are always peripheral, while monopolised ones are core-like, which puts core-like products in the stronger position and creates "a constant flow of surplus-value from the producers of peripheral products to the producers of core-like products" – the result being "unequal exchange" (ibid.). As (quasi-)monopolies need a strong state in order to protect their interests, they prefer settling in countries that can provide such protection to them (ibid.). This logic argument explains why, despite liberalisation policies that have been implemented in the past decades, many countries of the global South are still waiting for the spate of investors that has been promised to them. Though there are indeed investments in global South countries, those investors are very selective in terms of the countries and regions they turn to. Many African countries, especially those with little mineral resources, have seen few foreign investors so far.

World-systems analysts treat phenomena that leftist theorists tend to politicise and conservative theorists disclaim as 'leftists conspiracy theories' quite cold-bloodedly as natural processes that inevitably take place within a capitalist world-system and that will end no sooner and no later than the day the system comes to an end. For Wallerstein, it is a matter of fact that within the system, there must be strong states (core states) and weak states (peripheral states). Strong states "'intervene' in the internal affairs of weaker states", force them to open their frontiers for their products while the strong states keep their frontiers closed, they "relate to weak states by pressuring them to install and keep in power persons whom the strong states find acceptable" and "get them to confirm to the policy needs of the strong states" (Wallerstein 2007, 55). Core states are states with a high concentration of core-like production processes, whereas peripheral states are states with a high concentration of peripheral production processes (ibid., 28). Furthermore, there are "semiperipheral states", which are *not characterised* by "semiperipheral production processes", but by "a near even mix of core-like and peripheral products" (ibid., 28-29). This is possible because, over time, (quasi-)monopolies run out and become peripheral production processes, as happened to textiles, for example. Semiperipheries compete among themselves to receive the technologies for producing formerly core-like products (ibid., 29-30). For them, producing those products means "economic development", i.e., moving in the direction of core states instead of dropping back to the position of a peripheral state (ibid., 29). In order to win this day-to-day fight, semiperipheries try to reduce competition with outsiders and foster the evolvement of their domestic firms by implementing protectionist economic policies (ibid.). Semiperipheries receive "pressure from core states and [put] pressure on peripheral states" (ibid.), pouring their products on the latter's markets (ibid., 30). In order to prevent dropping to the level of a peripheral state and striving to become a core state one day, semiperipheral states "use state power in the internal and interstate arena quite consciously" (ibid., 56-57). This portrayal of semiperipheral states and their behaviour corresponds to the discussion of newly industrialising countries (NICs) in chapter 2.2 of this thesis. As outlined above, those countries, for example the so-called 'Asian tiger'-states, have reached a certain level of economic development by using protectionist economic policies in order to shield their infant industries from competition from outside. Those industries put out products that have been produced in the global North before, like clothes, steel, electronic devices, and similar goods.

World-systems analysis is frequently labelled as a neo-Marxist approach. Like most (neo-)Marxist approaches, world-systems analysis deals with the class struggle. While for many orthodox Marxists, it takes place on the national level, world-systems analysts regard it as one of many forms of social struggle and prefer observing all these forms on the level of the entire world-system (Wallerstein 2007, 20). This attitude results from the definition of a world-system as an entity that is held together by a common division of labour. As a result, the classes cut across national boundaries. Another issue is the attitude towards non-wage labour. From an orthodox Marxist point of view, it is dying out, whereas world-systems analysts assume that it persists among the numerous forms of labour under capitalism (ibid.).[17] This can be observed in the relation between households and employers. Within this relation, there is a form of exploitation that works

17 This insight has been provided by some other neo-Marxist approaches as well. For instance, the Bielefeld school ("Verflechtungsansatz") insists on the central role of subsistence production as "indispensable precondition for capitalist pro-

within a national economy as well as within a world-economy, if they are capitalist. Wallerstein describes how wage-earners are integrated in households that consist of several members who contribute to the household income by means of different sources, namely wages, subsistence activities, petty commodity production, rent, and transfer payments (ibid., 32-34). If the household depends on wages, the employer must at least pay the "*absolute* minimum wage", which is "an amount that represents at least a proportionate share of the reproduction costs of the household" (ibid., 35, emphasis in the original). In contrast to that, if the other members of the household provide income from other sources, the employer can pay the wage-earner(s) less. Hence, the household is "transferring surplus-value to the employer of the wage-earner over and above whatever surplus-value the wage-earner himself is transferring" (ibid.). This is a typical situation that I have observed in Uganda and that can be observed in most countries of the global South: Most households survive on the mix described by Wallerstein, with the highest proportion being subsistence activities, followed by petty commodity production, transfer payments, and – usually at the end of the line – wages and sometimes rent. Consequently, the households transfer immense surplus value to the employers. Some of those employers are local, others are from semiperipheral countries, and others are from core states, i.e., the global North.

Wallerstein explains that "the modern world-economy" is "not the first world-economy ever but the first world-economy to survive for such a long period and thrive, and it did this precisely by becoming fully capitalist" (Wallerstein 2007, 17). He defines a system as capitalist when it is devoted to "the *endless* accumulation of capital" (ibid., 24). All world-economies that existed before the capitalist one had turned into (world-)empires, which ultimately led to their decline (Wallerstein 2011, 16). According to Wallerstein's definition, an empire is a *political* entity that serves the collection of tribute for protection that exceeds the costs of that protection. In contrast, the modern world-system is not a political, but an *economic* entity, which comprises *several political entities* and connects them with each other by means of economic ties – which *may entail* "cultural links [...] political arrangements and even confederal structures" (ibid., 15). Wallerstein has his own definition of 'hegemony'. He emphasises that, for him, hegemony is a position that can be occupied by a country within a world-economy (Wallerstein 2011a, xxii). For defining that position, he

duction", especially in countries of the global South (Otto-Walter 1979, 9, translation by E.K.).

focusses only on the strong states within the interstate system. If one of the strong states stands out as by far being the strongest among them, it is the hegemonic state in the world-system (for the moment), but if they are all comparably strong, there is a "balance of power" (ibid.). So far, the hegemonic powers of the modern world-system have been the United Provinces (precursor of the Netherlands) in the mid-seventeenth century, the United Kingdom in the first half of the nineteenth century, and the USA in the mid-twentieth century (ibid., xxiii). Wallerstein defines hegemony "as a situation wherein the products of a given core state are produced so efficiently that they are by and large competitive even in other core states, and therefore the given core state will be the primary beneficiary of a maximally free world market" (ibid., 38). However, a hegemonic state will forfeit its position over time. It cannot keep up its economic advantages for long because they deprive its fellow strong states of the ability to provide it with markets and to be its strong allies against 'enemies' (ibid., xxiii-xxiv). The struggle for hegemony among the strong states within the capitalist world-system has kept it alive for long by preventing it from being turned into a world-empire by one of those states (ibid., xxvii). This looks as if at least one generally accepted assumption about capitalism and 'the market' was correct, namely that it flourishes thanks to competition. It has to be added, however, that Wallerstein is not thinking about general or 'free' competition, but about competition only among the strongest competitors. The weak, the 'developing', and even the moderately strong do not play any role in it.

One of the central hypotheses in the first volume of *The Modern World-System* is that the capitalist world-system came into existence in Europe in the sixteenth century. For Wallerstein, it is perfectly logical to locate its origins in the sixteenth century, an age of statism when ideas about free markets and 'laissez-faire' were still a long way off (Wallerstein 2011, 67), and its consolidation in "the age of *mercantilism*", i.e., economic nationalism, "from 1600 to 1750" (Wallerstein 2011a, 37, emphasis in the original). Many scholars associate capitalism with (neo-)liberalism and, consequently, would wonder about that historical mapping. As has been outlined above, Wallerstein considers a strong state the elementary prerequisite for capitalist development, not an obstacle to it, as neoliberals claim. Wallerstein states that "eventually by the end of the nineteenth century and the beginning of the twentieth, the entire globe, even those regions that had never been part even of the external arena of the capitalist world-economy, were pulled inside" (Wallerstein 2011b, 129). The world-economy incorporated all those zones due to *internal* pressures of expansion, not because they *wanted* to be included (ibid.). This does not apply to colonies, only, but they were most particularly impacted by this incorporation. Sabelo Ndlovu-Gatsheni gives the following account of Africa's position within the capitalist world-system:

> "[...] while initially Africa was dragged kicking and screaming into the nexus of Euro-North American-centric world system, its global orders and capitalist economy, once it was inside the bowels of the beast of coloniality, the African mental universe was fundamentally and deliberately changed to the extent that later the Africans imagined freedom and liberation in modernist and colonial terms of seeking deeper admission into the existing Euro-North American-centric modern world system." (Ndlovu-Gatsheni 2018, 284)

Apparently, Ndlovu-Gatsheni agrees with Wallerstein that Africa's 'integration' into the capitalist world-system did not take place voluntarily. The situation he describes, being "dragged kicking and screaming" and ending up "inside the bowels of the beast of coloniality" (Ndlovu-Gatsheni 2018, 284) describes that 'integration' as having been caught and eaten by a wild animal. Now, the process of 'digestion' transforms the prey. Africans have started to seek "deeper admission into the existing Euro-North American-centric modern world system" (ibid.). They have accepted that there is no alternative and have started dreaming of their countries becoming semiperipheries and, one fine day, core states – meaning that they seek 'development'. When dealing with Africa (though he generalises this argument to the entire modern world-system), Wallerstein describes how the people's hopes for 'development' have shifted from the government as the potential provider to the market (Wallerstein 2017, 59). However, his conclusion is the following: "Neither the 'state' nor the 'market' will promote egalitarian 'development' in a capitalist world-economy, whose guiding principle of the ceaseless accumulation of capital requires and generates ever-greater polarization of real income" (ibid.). Frederick Cooper calls the relationship of Africa and capitalism "an unequal fight – with equal emphasis on both elements of the term" (Cooper 2009, 70, translation by E.K.). According to Cooper, resistance to capitalism results in paying a heavy price, which Africa had to pay on two levels: On the economic level, Africa paid with its descent into insignificance and vulnerability, while on another level, it paid through the negative image the rest of the world has developed of the continent and its people (ibid.). Few African countries might be counted as semiperipheries[18]. The vast majority of African countries, including Uganda, are peripheral states. As such, they are under pressure from core states (from the global North) and semiperipheries (from the global South) alike, for whom they are a profitable source of surplus value. As long as this surplus value is being drained from them, there is no chance for them to improve on their economic situation within the current system. According to Wallerstein's hypotheses, the only short-term perspective they have within the capitalist world-system is to become semiperipheries by means of protectionist economic policies and acquiring formerly core-like production technologies. The better option is only viable in the medium to long term. I discuss it in the following sub-section.

2.3.3 The end of the capitalist world-system and the conceptualisation of its successor system(s)

Immanuel Wallerstein had a vision for the world and particularly for Africa. He analysed that the capitalist world-system is going through a crisis, which is eventually going to end with its natural death – as all systems have a limited life-span. In the 1990s, he forecasted this process to take another 25 to 50 years (Wallerstein 2007, 76-77; 2017, 64, 102), hence, according to his time frame, we are right in the middle of it. The profitability of production is decreasing because the entrepreneurs run short of places in the world where they can run to in search of cheap labour, low taxes, and places where they can dump their waste without anyone caring about it (Wallerstein 2017, 96-100). They are trying to change over to financial speculation, but this is not a sustainable alternative for realising endless accumulation of capital (ibid., 96). Beyond that, Wallerstein adds an economic argument to the discussion of 'limited natural resources' (see chapters 2.2 and 4.1.1 of this thesis), led by Post-Development thinkers, the de-growth approach, the 'Fridays for Future' worldwide pupils' movement, and other environmental activists. Wallerstein emphasises that the structure of the capitalist world-system exists in order to ensure the endless *accumulation of capital*, not equal distribution. As a result, it does not allow all members to produce and/ or receive the same amount of surplus value. Any upward movement of peripheral to semiperipheral or

18 According to Wallerstein, semiperipheries are defined by having "a near even mix of core-like and peripheral products" (Wallerstein 2007, 28-29).

even from semiperipheral to core status (which happens very seldomly) poses a threat to the system as a whole – especially when not mirrored by a corresponding number of downward movements (Wallerstein 2017, 92-94). As a result, "the sense that we are in a cul-de-sac has begun to creep in on more and more people—scholars, politicians, and above all ordinary workers" (ibid., 94).

For the system(s) to come after the death of the current one, we, meaning all the people in the world, must decide in what kind of system we want to live (Wallerstein 2007, 76-77, 89-90; 2017, 64-65, 102, 104). According to Wallerstein, *every* person in the world will contribute somehow to the change ahead with his or her behaviour during the phase-out of the old system as well as during the transition period (Wallerstein 2007, 90). Even those who are trying to keep out of the process "are merely making a hidden choice" (ibid.) by allowing others to get through *their* vision. This change could be for the better or for worse, depending on the choices and actions of people worldwide (Wallerstein 2007, 88-89; 2017, 64-65). According to Wallerstein, Africa has the potential to play a significant role in that transition. He ascribes this potential to the continent's marginal position in the current capitalist world-system, as the winners of a system are not the most creative thinkers when it comes to alternatives (Wallerstein 2017, 64-65). His conclusion on that point reads as follows:

> "If Africans stay mired in the claim for inclusion within the world-system in its present definition, they will tilt at windmills. If Africans show the way of combining short-run local meliorations with middle-run transformation of values and structures, they will not only help Africa; they will help the rest of us as well." (Wallerstein 2017, 65)

It is no coincidence that, in a subsequent chapter of the same book, Wallerstein shares the following passage from the conclusion of Frantz Fanon's *The Wretched of the Earth*:

> "Humanity expects other things from us than this grotesque and generally obscene emulation. If we want to transform Africa into a new Europe, America into a new Europe, then let us entrust the destinies of our countries to the Europeans. They will do a better job than the best of us. But if we want humanity to take one step forward, if we want to take it to another level than the one where Europe has placed it, then we must innovate, we must be pioneers." (Fanon, 2004, 239; a slightly different translation of this very passage is cited in Wallerstein 2017, 199-200)

Sabelo Ndlovu-Gatsheni likewise calls upon Africa, first, to reassemble what has been torn apart by colonialism and its aftermath, and, second, to go for polycentrism and pluriversality rather than repeat the attempt to force Africa into the Western-dominated world-system (Ndlovu-Gatsheni 2018, 293). Nevertheless, Wallerstein did not want to be deemed a revolutionary. For him, the death of a system over time and the emergence of one or more new systems is a natural process that can only be delayed to a limited extent and cannot be accelerated (Wallerstein 2017, 95). Hence, when a "push from below" appears to succeed, the system was already dysfunctional, and its defence mechanisms did not work anymore (ibid.). According to Wallerstein, the capitalist world-system is dying, but what is needed is not a rash revolution, but careful negotiations about the way to go after the patron's demise – a task for social movements of all kinds (ibid., 106-107). Of course, he does not release the people of the core states (the global North) from their responsibility to contribute to a better model for the future, yet he ranks the contributions from peripheral states (the global South) more promising.

2.3.4 Criticism of world-systems analysis

Like any other model or theory, world-systems analysis faced much criticism over time. Some critics reject it totally, others want to correct certain aspects, which they regard as erroneous. Some points of criticism arise from misunderstandings, others from differing perspectives or priorities, and again others from real fallacies within the concept. There are two strong points of criticism that Wallerstein had to give in to: The reproach of world-systems analysis being another 'grand narrative' and that of a limited perspective, which gives priority to economic issues and leaves cultural[19] aspects aside (Wallerstein 2007, 21). Another point that Cooper criticises is that dependency theory and related approaches (which includes world-systems analysis) are too apologetic in terms of the questionable role played by local elites, as they put all the blame for the predicament of the periphery on the centre (Cooper 1993, 97). Moreover, Cooper deplores that the world-systems perspective is too static, pretending that the

19 In his later writings, Wallerstein tried to come to terms with the issue of culture, e.g., in his contributions to the essay collection: Featherstone, Mike (ed.) (1990): *Global Culture*. London: Sage. Nevertheless, world-systems analysis remains a concept in which economic issues are central and others follow their lead.

same processes would take place in the same sequence everywhere they occurred (ibid., 95). This corresponds to the caveat of world-systems analysis representing another 'grand narrative'. The latter was not Wallerstein's intention, nevertheless, it is the outcome of his endeavours. Against the background of peripheralisation in Africa, Cooper deplores that "Wallerstein can treat the difference between family labour on a coffee farm and wage labor in a gold mine [...] as little more than variation on a theme" (ibid.). I would agree that the variation is of little significance to world-systems analysis, as both are sources of household income as described in chapter 2.3.2 of this thesis. Both, the wage-labour below minimum wage in a mine and the petty commodity production on a family-run coffee farm, contribute to the transfer of surplus-value from the household to the employer (Wallerstein 2007, 32-35). It is not surprising that both are forms of production, in which the producers turn out a product that they could never afford themselves (at least not in the form of the processed and packed coffee in the supermarket shelf) because the major profit goes to entrepreneurs and traders (partly from the global North and/ or semiperipheries), not to the producers (in the global South). Of course, Cooper's argument that there are significant differences between the two forms of production is accurate. However, the aim of world-systems analysis is this very specific perspective on the exploitation of the peripheries (and semiperipheries) by the centre (and semiperipheries). Some basic assumptions of the model may be simplistic, static, or limited in perspective. These characteristics are natural to *any model*, especially an economic model. Certainly, it is unfortunate that world-systems analysis has not been able to overcome that limitation. On that account, I agree with Cooper that the world-systems perspective is not sufficient to analyse the situation of the global South holistically. Still, it is not discredited by that fact because I must add that no single theory or model is suitable for that task. Various perspectives and approaches are needed to analyse the situation of the global South properly.

Wallerstein to a certain extent recognised the criticism on the boundaries of the capitalist world-system he had drawn and the categories he had used, namely "trade in bulk goods" versus "trade in preciosities" (Wallerstein 2011, xxiv-xxvi). Nevertheless, he insisted that it is a central characteristic of a world-system to be a world in itself rather than a world*wide* system. As a result, though he admits some of his critics had good arguments for some regions to be included at a certain point in history when he had explicitly excluded them, to include all would spoil the logic of his basic idea (ibid., xxv-xxvi). To critics, who accused him of neglecting the political sphere in favour of the economic one, Wallerstein objects that they are not separate spheres, but political institutions are part of the capitalist world-system and follow its rules, just like other institutions do (ibid., xxii). To critics, who want to correct the analysis of the capitalist world-system to earlier periods than the sixteenth century, Wallerstein counters that in his view, there is no analysis of that time that could convince him to consider it part of the evolvement of capitalism (Wallerstein 2011, xxvi-xxvii). One of the strongest criticisms and counter concepts came from André Gunder Frank, whom Wallerstein regarded as an early fellow world-systems analyst, whose early works he had highly appreciated (ibid., xxvii-xxix). However, in his book *Re-Orient: Global Economy in the Asian Age*, Frank presented a five thousand years old China-centred world system, in which European domination was just a short interlude in the nineteenth and twentieth century. He accused Wallerstein and other authors of having overlooked this due to Eurocentrism. Wallerstein's answer to this caveat is that his *capitalist* world-system is different from Frank's world*wide* economic, though *not capitalist* system (in his later writings) (ibid., xxix). To Wallerstein, this meant a "radical revision of world-systems analysis", not just a correction of some fallacies within it (ibid., xxx). As such, he regards Frank's approach as a new, alternative concept of *world system analysis* (which should be spelled without hyphen and plural because it looks at one system that encompasses the whole globe). World-systems analyst Giovanni Arrighi, though he appreciates Frank's "legitimate preoccupation with the premodern ancestry of the modern world system", does not share Frank's "rejection of capitalism as a useful notion for the analysis of world historical change" (Arrighi 2002, 25). When searching for a comprehensive economic history of the world, one might surely find the better answer in Frank's approach. However, when looking for a history of capitalism, or for an explanation for the mechanisms of oppression and exploitation that the global South is suffering from today, Wallerstein's approach is a good choice.

There are also positive judgements on world-systems analysis, out of which I just want to quote the ones I found in the literature cited in earlier chapters of this thesis. Sebastian Conrad and Shalini Randeria rate Wallerstein's world-systems analysis as one of the better contributions to the fight against Eurocentrism. Although Wallerstein keeps the idea of the central feature of the system, capitalism, spreading from Europe to the rest of the world, he presents it "not as a European invention, but as a formation, which depended on outlying forces" (Conrad/ Randeria 2002, 15, translation by E.K.). In the course of his extensive analysis of newspapers and scientific magazines, Rick Rowden came to the conclusion that, to a great extent, the assumptions of dependency theory and world-systems analysis are being confirmed, though unwillingly, through the facts reported (Rowden 1999, 174-176). All the 'bad news' from the global South and all the accounts of policies implemented by the global North seem to match the basic assumptions of these approaches.

From the point of view of the Post-Development approach, Ziai criticises dependency theory for not really overcoming the idea of 'development', but rather looking for alternative ways (e.g., self-reliance and delinking) for peripheral countries to make their way to the status of a metropolis, i.e., 'developing' (Ziai 2017, 32). As has been shown above, Wallerstein's approach can also be interpreted that way. Nevertheless, Wallerstein is less enthusiastic about that option of 'development' than dependency theory or some other approaches of world-systems analysis. For him, the rise of a peripheral country to the status of a semiperiphery and one day even a core country is not impossible (indeed, it has happened), yet not likely either. In any case, it is at best a short-term solution for the rest of the lifespan of the current system. As has been outlined in chapter 2.3.3, his assumption is that the system is coming to an end anyway, and that the best we can do is to work on the outlines for (a) new, hopefully better system(s). This attitude matches that of many Post-Development thinkers, who assume that the current system (by which they usually mean a mixture of unequal global power constellations, neo-colonialist policies, and the 'development' apparatus) is resistant to change and the task ahead is to think about alternatives to it. Both Wallerstein and Post-Development thinkers, appreciate contributions from the global South to that discussion on alternatives most. Another commonality between the two approaches is that world-systems analysis attacks the belief in the inevitability of progress that originates from the Enlightenment, considering progress "a possibility rather than a certainty" (Wallerstein 2007, 18). In case a transition, e.g., from feudalism to capitalism, did actually take place somewhere, the omission of inevitability gave way to the possibility of *examining the causes* of this transition – which would have been pointless in orthodox Marxist and (neo-)liberal theory alike (ibid., 18-19).

Ramón Grosfoguel, a prominent representative of decolonial theory and the world-systems perspective alike (Kerner 2012, 154), calls for a decolonisation of world-systems analysis, together with political economy paradigms in general, postcolonial and cultural studies (Grosfoguel 2011, 4-5). In his view, Quijano's concept of 'coloniality of power' (see chapter 2.1.2) has a great potential to revolutionise such approaches (Grosfoguel

2008, 95). With regard to epistemology, Grosfoguel puts forth the hypothesis that many, though not all, approaches of world-systems analysis "still continue to produce knowledge from the Western man 'point zero' god-eye view" (Grosfoguel 2011, 7-8). He continues: "If we analyze the European colonial expansion from a Eurocentric point of view, what we get is a picture in which the origins of the so-called capitalist worldsystem are primarily produced by the inter-imperial competition among European Empires." (ibid., 8) According to Grosfoguel, world-systems analysis needs to evolve in a way that allows the subaltern to be heard through it (Grosfoguel 2008, 103). He suggests shifting the theory's perspective from that of the white man to one from the global South, e.g., an indigenous woman in the Americas (Grosfoguel 2011, 8-9). In that context, he cautions against an exclusively economic point of view, commemorating that capitalism was not the only thing that reached the colonies with the arrival of the colonisers, but aspects concerning racism, violence, gender and sexuality, religion, epistemology, language, arts, and other aspects of life (ibid., 8-10). Grosfoguel sees in each of these spheres of social life (he mentions 15 but admits that there might be even more) a global power hierarchy (ibid., 13; see also 9-11). Certainly, he is right insofar as decolonisation and a diversification of the perspective in favour of the global South is concerned. Yet, Wallerstein would most likely answer that capitalism *is the very essence* of his approach and that his approach cannot work if capitalism is replaced by other priorities. I agree with both. World-systems analysis as it is, should not be torn apart, but *completed* with other perspectives, preferably from the global South. This would help to get a holistic picture of the processes under discussion.

To choose Wallerstein's particular approach to world-systems analysis made sense for me in many respects. Since he had developed his approach in the 1970s, he has been constantly reflecting on it, reviewing the criticism that has been passed on it, and trying to apply his model to current developments. In addition to that, his line of reasoning appears logic to me, against the background of my own experience. It is quite possible that this has to do with a parallel between Wallerstein and me, namely that our scientific interest in the global economy and the capitalist system has been formed by our experience gained as representatives of the global North in Africa. Indeed, it would be preferable if he had managed to overcome the traces left by the generalisation of 'grand narratives' and simplifying economic models in his world-systems perspective. Those traces can even be found in many of his reactions to critics. Several of those reactions can be reduced to a refusal to re-think any of the basic assumptions of his model. Nevertheless, this does not make him any worse than many bright thinkers, who insist on the basic assumptions of their models because it makes no sense to adjust them to each and every criticism that comes up. This does not make his model any poorer than others. As I have stated repeatedly, I do not consider *any single* model or theory capable of capturing the complexity of what we perceive as social 'reality', neither in the global South, nor elsewhere. It comes as no surprise that each and every model or theory has to face legitimate criticism. However, in my view, world-systems analysis in general, and Wallerstein's version in particular, is among the approaches that have delivered one of the most important perspectives to the discussion – even though it needs to be complimented by other perspectives. For those reasons, the world-systems perspective is one part of my theoretical framework, but only one amongst others. The postcolonial perspective is the essential part, followed by critical development studies and the world-systems perspective, both requiring the former to make sense for my particular approach. As chapter 8 and 9 will show, the combination of the three approaches has proven valuable for interpreting the data I collected in the course of this study and answering my research questions.

2.4 Central terms and concepts

The main purpose of chapter 2 has been so far to introduce the theoretical framework of the thesis at hand. This includes clarifications on specific terms and concepts that I am using frequently. Several of them have already been explained above, especially 'decolonial or postcolonial', 'development', 'Post-Development', 'capitalism', 'neoliberalism', 'the modern/ capitalist world-system', 'core/ centre/ metropolis versus periphery/ satellite and semiperiphery'. In chapters 3 and 4, I explain other central concepts, namely 'globalisation' and 'Social and Solidarity Economy', the concept from which the word 'solidarity' in the title of this thesis originates. Some central terms and concepts remain to be explained in this sub-section, drawing on the theoretical framework that has been outlined above. Some may need more explanations than others. Those terms and concepts are, in alphabetical order: 'Africa', 'discourse', 'global North and global South/ First and Third World', 'hegemony/ hegemonic', 'the subaltern', 'the West', and 'traditional'.

Africa

Africa is "a place-in-the-world", not in the geographical sense, but meaning "a category that (like all categories) is historically and socially constructed [...] that is imposed with force, that has a mandatory quality" (Ferguson 2006, 5). James Ferguson postulates that "'Africa' continues to be described through a series of lacks and absences, failings and problems, plagues and catastrophes" (ibid., 2). Still, it is the above-mentioned "consequential power and mandatory force of regional categorization" that prevents even Ferguson – much to his regret – from ending the use of the term *Africa* (ibid., 7). Yet, he refuses to use it in an attempt "to define a historical or cultural region of 'Africa'" (ibid., 4). Dipesh Chakrabarty has demonstrated this strategy when defining the terms 'Europe' and 'India' in *Provincializing Europe*. He informs us that he is using them "as hyperreal terms in that they refer to certain figures of imagination whose geographical referents remain somewhat indeterminate" (Chakrabarty 2000, 27). He anticipates criticism on his use of the terms, especially the term 'Europe', as homogenous entity, which, in reality, it was not (ibid., 27-28). Chakrabarty's refutation of this charge is that, just like Orientalism has survived within the "discourse of history", a certain image of 'Europe' "as the scene of the birth of the modern" survived as well (ibid., 28). His pointed conclusion on it is: "Analysis does not make it go away." (ibid.) In this thesis, the term *Africa* is used in the sense of Ferguson's 'Africa' or Chakrabarty's 'Europe' and 'India'.

Frederick Cooper traces the sad carrier of the image of 'Africa' in the Euro-American sphere: From the continent of the slaves in the eighteenth and nineteenth century, it 'advanced' to a hopeless case in terms of uncontrollable population growth, hunger, violence, corruption, and failed states in the twentieth and twenty-first century (Cooper 2009, 37-39; for similar accounts of Africa's image in the international sphere, see Gruffydd Jones 2018, 187; Matthews 2018, 167). Western media declared 'Africa' a danger to the global public, with its rocketing numbers of desperate inhabitants laying siege to the gates to the West because nobody seems to be able to govern them properly (Cooper 2009, 38-39). Zubairu Wai has also analysed how Africa is being represented in the West as "the hopeless continent" and "a danger not only to itself but also to the West", as its allegedly hostile living conditions are considered a potential hotbed of future terrorism (Wai 2018, 2). However, an upcoming "'Africa Rising' narrative" exists parallel to it (ibid., 3), in accordance with the dichotomous image of Africa that the global North has been producing ever since:

the 'barbaric savage' versus the 'noble savage', the source of death versus the source of wealth, fear versus (simulated) sympathy. In summary, Wai delivers another proof for the fact that what has been resistant to any kind of 'development' since formal colonialism, is not Africa itself, but the West's image of it. The latter still consists of phantasies of 'the complete Other' with its most extreme positive and negative peculiarities (ibid., 4-5). Of course, African thinkers have not been passive, but tried to recover an emancipated image of Africa, yet they were faced with indifference on the part of the West (Mbembe 2001, 11-13). A good example of an attempt to break free from the West's epistemological grip is the 'Fundi wa Africa' school of thought that works on recapturing Africa's diverse history (Ndlovu-Gatsheni 2013, 5-6). Another concrete example of epistemological emancipation is the essay collection *The ungrateful continent? African answers to European Paternalism* (Cichon et al. 2010, translation by E.K.). Many members of the African intellectual community expressed their indignation about the overt racism in a speech that Nicolas Sarkozy, then President of France, held during a visit to the *Cheik Anta Diop University* of Dakar, Senegal, as recently as 2007 (ibid.). Another example is the essay collection *Recentering Africa in International Relations* that calls for the long-overdue end of "the notion that the region's only importance to world politics is its peripherality and that it should be saved through Western modernist interventions", meaning 'development' interventions (Wai 2018, 14).

Cooper explicates that slave trade was only made possible through the way, in which the ones who enslaved others talked about them. If they had recognised them as fully-fledged human beings, they could not have dared to treat them in this way. Hence, they had to create a discourse about them being less than human (Cooper 2009, 40). Just like Edward Said states for Orientalism that nothing beyond the discourse dictated by it can be said about 'the Orient' (Said 1994, 3), the discourse on Africa seems to be limited to those images, too. This can be applied to later developments as well. One might wonder how the majority of people in the West are able to live their lives at the expense of people in countries of the global South without even caring about it. Certainly, they could not if they felt as much sympathy for them as they feel for people of their own social sphere. Consequently, they need the media to do the work that Cooper describes, namely to paint a picture of the people in those countries as being hopelessly miserable due to their own inferiority, denying all historical or current exploitation and oppression that they have been suffering for the benefit of Western populations. Sally Matthews points out that writing about 'Africa' as a single entity is a product of European imperialism and originates from the search for information that helped to dominate the 'Other' (Matthews 2018, 173). Nevertheless, after having been established in this way, the idea of 'Africa' was taken up by African nationalists, who tried (and are still trying) to create an African identity as a counterpart to Africa's suppressors (Ndlovu-Gatsheni 2013, 99-102). Sabelo Ndlovu-Gatsheni states:

> "Even those like Cheikh Anta Diop who worked hard to define what Africa was and sought to capture its meaning in African terms could not contain the slippery nature of the idea of Africa together with its mirage character that made it to always melt away into the domains of representation, cartography, profiling and race (Diop 1974). The making of Africa and its people involved the work of explorers, cartographers, missionaries, travellers, colonial anthropologists, colonialists, African kings and chiefs, ordinary Africans as makers of history, historians, imperialists, pan-Africanists and African nationalists and other too numerous to mention." (Ndlovu-Gatsheni 2013, 100)

One important group that he mentions later-on is the African diaspora, which has been created by the slave trade, and which added its own facet to the discourse on 'Africa' (Ndlovu-Gatsheni 2013, 108). Ndlovu-Gatsheni's account illustrates that, though it has once been an invention of colonisers (ibid., 102, 104-111), the idea of 'Africa' was embraced, appropriated, transformed, and adjusted to their needs by Africans. As he explicates with the help of a quote from famous Nigerian intellectual Chinua Achebe, the people living on the continent needed an African identity to build up their self-esteem after colonialism. For that reason, they had to excel *as Africans* (ibid., 99; see also 104-105 and 111). With this kind of self-esteem, interviewees and other people I met in Uganda talked about themselves and their fellow country(wo)men as 'Africans', their culture as '(traditional) African culture', and the like. Critics might lament the inadequate generalisation of the diverse peoples of a whole continent. Though they might not be completely wrong, there is a necessity to make a sharp difference between Africans speaking or writing about a seemingly generalised 'Africa' and non-Africans doing so. When speaking about 'Africans' or 'African culture', there is always a certain danger of lapsing into the above-mentioned negative, or, on the contrary, a romanticising discourse about 'Africa'. However, when Africans use such expressions, it is an act of self-definition, which is different from outsiders (like Westerners) labelling them. The latter should be avoided. I am a white European, a circumstance that puts me in a difficult situation in this regard. Nevertheless, I write about 'Africans' in this very section. Whom do I mean by that? Ndlovu-Gatsheni rightly criticises all popular definitions of 'an African', the "racial, geographical/ territorial and consciousness/ commitment" definition alike (ibid., 115). He argues that each of them includes people, who might not be 'real Africans' while excluding others, who are (ibid.). Wherever possible, I avoid using terms like 'African(s)'. However, in a section like this, it turned out to be impossible. In my view, my positionality as a white European (in terms of origin, residence, look, and privilege) does not allow me to do 'the right thing'. The least bad I can do is to refrain from defining other people and call all those 'Africans', who define themselves as such. This might be another unsatisfactory solution that bears the same problems as the options rejected by Ndlovu-Gatsheni, but it has to suffice until a more convincing one is found. Africans share that common experience of oppression through colonialism and neo-colonialism as well as the struggle for emancipation described by Ndlovu-Gatsheni – though the level of oppression they have been experiencing may vary according to their geographical location, social class, ethnic group, gender, religious or political affiliation. Although their cultures, languages, and histories differ, all of their histories share this turning-point and its manifold consequences to a certain extent. Meanwhile, Westerners have been the beneficiaries of that oppression, and they still are. When they talk about 'Africa', they draw on a history as colonisers and exploiters, hence, the above-mentioned images of 'the inferior African' will always show through every generalising statement they make.

Ndlovu-Gatsheni suggests that the concept of 'Africa' has been producing crises and conflicts again and again (Ndlovu-Gatsheni 2013, 104). He cautions against "mutations of African nationalism from civic principles founded on the slogan of 'diverse people unite' into narrow, autochthonous, nativist and xenophobic forms that breed violence rather than deep horizontal pan-African comradeship envisioned by the pan-Africanists" (ibid., 101). Furthermore, he points out that "African identity or identities are products of complex histories of domination, resistance, complicity, creolization, and mimicry" (ibid., 123). Drawing on writings by British-Ghanaian intellectual Anthony Kwame Appiah, Frederick Cooper asserts that, after the shared experience of age-long oppression, Africans were longing "to find a place in the sun – not only as people, but as Africans, whose characteristic was now reckoned as a vivid contribution to the cultures of the world" (Cooper 2009, 41, translation by E.K.). Ndlovu-Gatsheni calls it "making African citizens out of colonial subjects" (Ndlovu-Gatsheni 2013, 112). Immanuel Wallerstein states that Pan-Africanism created 'the African' as counterpart to 'the European', i.e., the oppressor (Wallerstein 2002, 189). In terms of 'African literature', Ngũgĩ wa Thiong'o states that, despite Africa's diversity, "African literature always saw itself as beyond the national territorial state, assuming, at the minimum, the continent for its theatre of relevance and application" (Ngũgĩ wa Thiong'o 2014, 54).

In summary, 'Africa' and 'Africans' are words that people in my position must use very carefully or, wherever possible, avoid to use. Like Ferguson, I will not be able to avoid their use completely. Other descriptions like 'people residing on the African continent' are no suitable alternatives either. First, all of them would refer to one of the categorisations of people as 'Africans' or non-'Africans' that Ndlovu-Gatsheni rejects. There are people living on the continent, who are not 'Africans' (disqualified by nationality, origin, etc.), whereas some 'real Africans' live abroad. Second, even if we call them 'people residing on the African continent' or 'people of African origin' or the like, there is no escape from the word, the category, and the attached discourse of 'Africa(n)'. Therefore, I will be obliged to use those words sometimes. Hence, I try not to use them excessively and unthinkingly. I avoid inappropriate generalisations and the reproduction of stereotypes wherever possible. Nevertheless, when my interviewees talk about 'Africa', 'Africans', or 'African culture', I am not going to treat this as unreflecting generalisation, but as the expression of their self-perception. Who am I to tell them how (not) to define or label themselves?

Discourse

Drawing from Michel Foucault, Aram Ziai explains that by speaking, we "construct social reality" (Ziai 2017, 101). A specific way of speaking about something constructs knowledge about it and, at the same time, excludes other possibilities to 'know' it, see it, or refer to it (ibid.). Discourses produce knowledge that, in turn, produces 'truth' – the latter not referring to "the accurate representation of reality by language" but to those discourses that society accepts as truth (ibid., 102). This acceptance depends heavily on relations of power (ibid.). Which political or social actions are acceptable or inacceptable in a society depends on the knowledge produced by its accepted discourses (ibid.). As Foucault insists, this does not mean that "making a change in the order of discourse" is impossible (Foucault

2010, 209). His concern is rather to raise awareness for the way in which speaking does not describe but *construct* social practice – and how this process is formed by "conditions" and "rules" (ibid., 208-209). Consequently, any supposedly 'new' statement, which is supposed to be added to a certain discourse, correlates with those conditions and rules already (ibid., 209, see also 25). This very brief definition of the term 'discourse' in the Foucauldian sense served to explain what I refer to whenever I use that term. Beyond that, it mirrors my conceptualisation of 'truth', which I do not consider an innocent, objective matter of fact, but a *social construction* that is highly influenced by relations of power. What this paragraph is neither able nor supposed to provide is a comprehensive account of Michel Foucault's theories, not even with regard to those two terms. Their presentation had to be reduced to the most important cornerstones because in my theoretical framework, Foucault's original writings do not play a major role beyond that point. Of course, their traces can be found in several works I am citing frequently.

Global North and global South/ First and Third World

During the Bandung conference in 1955, representatives of 29 Asian and African nations came together, trying to find their own way to carry on after independence, apart from the allegedly obligatory choice between the two options that the capitalist and the communist bloc of the Cold War offered them (Dhawan/ Randeria 2016, 572-573). Nikita Dhawan and Shalini Randeria call this "a globalization of the postcolonial imagination" (ibid., 573). Robert Young differentiates further that the actual founding of the Movement of the Non-Aligned Countries, hence the official self-definition as 'the Third World', took place in 1961, yet he admits that the Bandung conference "set up the institutional basis" for it (Young 2001, 192). As Dhawan and Randeria point out, the Bandung conference, as well as its implications, is "hardly remembered today" (Dhawan/ Randeria 2016, 572). This circumstance might account for the fact that the positive, emancipatory connotation of the expression 'Third World' has fallen into oblivion. Today, it is widely rejected, especially by development practitioners because they believe it refers to the 'Third World' being poorer or inferior to the 'First' or the 'Second World'. The benevolent, but apolitical and ahistorical attitude of large numbers of development practitioners (and some theorists as well) leads to the paradoxical situation that their 'beneficiaries' are denied their right to define themselves – in order to paternalistically 'help them to emancipate themselves *in the right way*'. Representatives of the Non-Aligned-Movement, like Kwame Nkrumah, the first President of independent Ghana, considered their step to unite as a 'Third World', non-aligned to any of the others, to be a realistic option to defeat neo-colonialism (Nkrumah 1965, 253). Arif Dirlik explains that the model has been "jumbled up" by the disappearance of the 'Second World' with the downfall of socialism and the constant encounters of 'First' and 'Third World' on each other's terrain through migration and the extension of global capitalism (Dirlik 2004, 520).

Today, '(global) North' and '(global) South' are the accepted expressions in development studies (McEwan 2009, 13). Regarding the re-orientation from three worlds to 'North' and 'South', Dirlik cautions us to "remember that 'North' and 'South' designate not merely concrete geographic locations but also metaphorical referents: 'North' denoting the pathways of transnational capital; 'South' denoting the marginalized populations of the world, regardless of their location (which is where 'postcoloniality' comes in!)" (Dirlik 2004, 519). Wolfgang Sachs writes: "'North' and 'South' are therefore less and less geographical categories but rather socio-economic ones, referring to the line which divides the strong world market sectors from the competitively weak, economically superfluous sectors in society." (Sachs 1998, 291) Sachs refers to his hypothesis that development endeavours have created a dividing line between a rich global middle class, which participates in mass consumption and other 'blessings' of development, and a global mass of people permanently excluded from those things (ibid.). This dividing line between global middle class and global class of the excluded and impoverished masses has been spotted by Ivan Illich as well (Illich 1998, 96-97). With his argumentation, Sachs gives the juxtaposition of 'global North' and 'global South' a political dimension, which is less emancipatory but more up to date than that of 'First World' and 'Third World'. I have chosen to use the expressions 'global North' and 'global South', not because they are ideal but because they suit the current situation as described by Sachs better than the existing alternatives.

Hegemony/ hegemonic

'Hegemony' is a popular word in the social sciences and may have diverse connotations. In chapter 2.3.2, Immanuel Wallerstein's very particular use of the word has been outlined. Whenever I use the word without further explanation, I do not refer to Wallerstein's definition, but to Antonio Gramsci's. For Gramsci, 'the state' is "the peculiar form of political rule" invented by the bourgeoisie, the ruling class in "modern capitalism" (Opratko 2014, 37, translation by E.K.). One of its central characteristics is that it is based not only on force, but at least to the same extent, on 'hegemony' (ibid.). 'Hegemony' denotes the bourgeoisie's strategy to create a broad social consent, meaning the acceptance of the bourgeoisie's ideology and conduct by all (especially the oppressed) social classes (ibid., 35). In order to fulfil the two above-mentioned functions, 'the state' has developed two spheres, namely the "'private' organisms in civil society" in charge of hegemony and those of "'political' society" (the state in the narrow sense) in charge of exercising force (Morton 2007, 89; see also Opratko 2014, 37). However, the distinction between the two spheres does not mean that 'hegemony' is devoid of force. It is a mixture of consent and coercion, with the mixing ratio depending on the requirements of the particular situation (Morton 2007, 94-95; Opratko 2014, 40). Consent works by means of "universalisation and compromise" (Opratko 2014, 43, translation by E.K.). As Benjamin Opratko explains, the bourgeoisie practices a kind of *universalisation* that generalises its particular interests for all social classes, yet making *compromises* by taking into consideration needs, everyday experience and ideologies of the subaltern to a certain extent. The bourgeoisie's willingness to make compromises depends on the question whether the respective compromise supports or undermines its dominant position (ibid.). The stability of bourgeois hegemony is guaranteed as long as it is fixed in "everyday common sense"[20] (ibid., 45, translation by E.K.). The latter is defined by Opratko, drawing on Gramsci's writings, as "an image of the self and the world, which encompasses not only the consciousness, but everyday practices, routine actions and also unconscious dispositions" (ibid., 44, translation by E.K.). In order to influence 'everyday common sense', civil society uses cultural, moral, and ethical means (ibid., 36), e.g., "schools, street layout and names, architecture, the family, workplace, or church" (Morton 2007, 93). The formation of hegemony

20 There is a confusion in Gramsci's terminology that is very difficult to explain in English and in German alike. Opratko explains it as follows: There are two kinds of 'common sense'. One corresponds to the definition cited above and is immanent to every person. The other is the ideal to be reached, at least as part of the above-mentioned 'common sense', namely a critical, well-informed view of the world and the self (Opratko 2014, 44-47). I translated the former as "everyday common sense", hoping to capture its relatively unreflecting character of day-to-day practice, though it might not be excellent English. For the latter, the ideal version, I would suggest "good judgement" rather than "common sense" again.

"is a dynamic process constantly constructed as well as contested through different forms of class struggle or 'counter'hegemonic initiatives" (ibid., 78). This is what Gramsci called the "struggle for political 'hegemonies'" that every party aiming at social change of any kind has to engage in (Opratko 2014, 45, translation by E.K.). Counter-hegemonic movements cannot just overthrow the old hegemony without replacing it with a new one, which is equally fixed in 'everyday common sense' of all social classes (ibid., 44; Williams 1988, 145). The establishment and maintenance of hegemony, be it the old one or a new one, has economic as well as political and cultural aspects (Williams 1988, 145).

This extremely shortened account of Gramsci's complex theory of hegemony leaves out many aspects, which would be of high importance if this theory was central to my theoretical approach. Indeed, it is marginal. This paragraph serves to clarify what I mean by writing for example 'the hegemonic discourse'. The idea I have in mind when using such an expression is the one presented above, i.e., that this discourse has been established by 'the civil society' (in the Gramscian sense) by means of a mixture of consent and coercion, whereas consent was most likely realised through a mixture of universalisation and (to a lesser extent) compromise. By those means, the discourse has been fixed in the minds of the people, namely in their 'everyday common sense'. That idea of 'everyday common sense' and the power it has with regard to social change is indeed very important. All previous sub-sections of chapter 2 led to the conclusion that the representatives of the theoretical schools of thought presented seek to shape social change. Postcolonial thinkers strive for decolonisation of all spheres of life and science; Post-Development thinkers intend to overcome the development paradigm and clear the way for alternatives; Immanuel Wallerstein wants everybody to participate in the conceptualisation of a better socio-economic system that can be established after the forthcoming natural death of capitalism. Hence, they can be called "'counter'hegemonic initiatives" (Morton 2007, 78). However, my interest in this line of thought ends here. The research question of this study is not how to implement counter-hegemonic projects (though it would be a worthwhile topic for further research). Nevertheless, hegemonic and counter-hegemonic discourses play a significant role for the topics under discussion.

The subaltern

Gayatri C. Spivak is one of the most influential representatives of postcolonial theory (for details, see chapter 2.1.2). For Spivak, the word 'subaltern' is more suitable to cover the diverse situations of oppressed people than 'masterwords' like 'the workers' or 'the colonised' that create the false impression of those groups being homogeneous and easily representable (Castro Varela/ Dhawan 2015, 184-185). Antonio Gramsci has coined the term 'the subaltern' as a name for people, who are not part of a hegemonic class, including the rural population, which had not played a significant role in the Marxist approach until then (ibid., 186-187). This inclusion of the rural, mainly agricultural population is crucial for Gramsci's approach and for its adoption to the context of the global South by postcolonial studies. For Gramsci, the subaltern are more than just dominated by the hegemonic class; they are completely excluded from political representation, one of the main reasons being that they are dispersed and not speaking the same language, a circumstance that makes them unable to unite like the workers did in some places (Steyerl 2008, 8-9). The *South Asian Subaltern Studies Group* modified the term 'subaltern' from a postcolonial point of view (Castro Varela/ Dhawan 2015, 187). Nevertheless, its main representatives, like Spivak, used it analogous to Gramsci, in a relational way, 'subaltern' being the counterpart to 'hegemonic' (ibid.). Spivak writes about them as "the 'true' subaltern group, whose identity is its difference" (Spivak 1988, 285), in contrast to "[d]ominant indigenous groups" and, even more so, "[d]ominant foreign groups" (ibid., 284). A central part of Spivak's argument is that there is no way the subaltern can express themselves such that they can be heard by the powerful (Castro Varela/ Dhawan 2015, 197-199). This impossibility to gain a hearing and, as a result, to speak is an essential characteristic of subalternity (ibid., 200). Spivak's answer to the question, why the subaltern accept their own oppression, is that they perceive it as their "inescapable fate", such that they are unable to see the political rights that are, or should be, entitled to them (ibid., 204, translation by E.K.). As a result, they are not even able to see themselves as part of a national state (ibid., 212). After having been developed by Spivak and the *South Asian Subaltern Studies Group* in order to describe a particular category of people within India, the concept of the subaltern was applied not only to Latin America, but to places all over the world (Morris 2010, 10).

“The West”

Terms like ‘Europe’ or ‘the West’ “are discursive constructions, which iron out numerous internal differences and deviations” (Conrad/ Randeria 2002, 12, translation by E.K.), just like terms such as ‘Africa’ (see above for corresponding paragraph on ‘Africa’ in this sub-section). In this thesis, terms like ‘Europe’ or ‘the West’ are used consciously, being aware that they signify a discursive construction with its attributive imaginations. Cheryl McEwan states that “the terms western and ‘the West’ are used interchangeably with the North” (McEwan 2009, 14). Although they refer to the same group of countries, the difference I found between the two expressions is a qualitative one. As stated above, ‘the (global) North’ is an expression from development studies (and practice), intending to bear *maximum neutrality* – whether it achieves that neutrality or not being another matter. Additionally, it needs a counterpart in order to make sense, ‘the (global) South’. In contrast, ‘the West’ is an expression with undeniable political implications, and it is so strong that it has even got rid of its counterpart, ‘the East’, without suffering any damage. As Raymond Williams elucidates, the West-East division has a long history with significant changes over time (Williams 1988, 333-334). I use ‘Western’ in the sense of ‘Western’ as capitalistic and ‘Eastern’ as socialist/ communist – although the counterpart ‘Eastern’ got lost with the end of the USSR (ibid., 334). I do not agree with McEwan’s definition of ‘Western’ being used for “countries that have chosen democracy as a form of governance, favour capitalist modes of economic organization, espouse the values of free international trade and co-operate both economically and militarily” (McEwan 2009, 14). This definition is not suitable to explain why, in the largest portion of the literature, ‘non-Western’ is being used generally for the countries of the global South although many of them fulfil all the criteria given by McEwan for ‘Western’ countries. In my use of the term, ‘Western’ or ‘the West’ refers to the core countries of the capitalist world-system.

Traditional

‘Traditional’ is a very problematic term. It is excessively and absolutely uncritically used by most development practitioners as well as their colleagues in charge of marketing and fundraising, those who write the advertising texts and reports for websites or flyers. The same applies to a good number of journalists and academics. When it comes to the global South, 'traditional' is mainly used by people from the global North to describe practices that need to be changed through 'development' measures. Typical examples are 'traditional agriculture' meaning outdated methods that need to be 'modernised', i.e., 'improved', or 'traditional gender roles' meaning women are being suppressed and need to be liberated through a 'development' project. Arturo Escobar points out how significantly "W. Arthur Lewis' model of the dual economy" has contributed to this general assumption in 'development' thinking (Escobar 2012, 77-78). According to Escobar, Lewis contributed to development thinking the assumption that 'development' means to push ahead the replacement of the 'traditional' sphere, which is assumed to represent backwardness, of social and economic life in a society by the 'modern' one (ibid.). In another context, Escobar mentions that "many 'traditional cultures' survive [modernisation or 'development'] through their transformative engagement with modernity" (ibid., 219). He suggests "to speak of popular culture as a present-oriented process of invention through complex hybridizations that cut across class, ethnic, and national boundaries" (ibid.). He cautions against illusions of "authenticity" within so-called 'traditional' artefacts or practices and suggests "hybridity" as a concept that could be more helpful to understand societies in the global South than 'tradition' (ibid.). I try to avoid the use of the term 'traditional' in this thesis. Instead, I use a term that might sound a bit old-fashioned: autochthonous. Its meaning is very close to 'indigenous'[21], but as it is a technical term that has never entered colloquial language, it is not as charged with (partly problematic) implicit meanings as 'indigenous' is. Although the word might neither be catchy nor completely unproblematic, I regard it as the better choice in order to avoid the derogatory (Williams 1988, 319-320) as well as the potentially romanticising connotations of 'traditional'. Anyway, for 'traditional', I would like to make the same point as for 'Africa' when it comes to the question of the speaker. Many respondents of this study spoke about 'traditional' or 'cultural' (in Lusoga, it is the same) issues. I even used the word in the interview framework, after consultation with my translator, because alternatives like 'autochthonous' would have been incomprehensible to the interviewees. As a result, I use 'traditional' when quoting statements uttered by the interviewees. Their use of the word might also be uncritical, yet it has a completely different quality than its use by foreigners, especial-

21 For instance, the term is used in a study by Hans Dieter Seibel in that way (Seibel 1987, e.g., 1).

ly whites. The people concerned often use 'traditional' with the intention to claim something as their own. Many oppose 'traditional' and 'Western'/ 'white'/ 'exotic' (in Lusoga, the Swahili-word 'Muzungu' is used for all of this) to mean 'what is ours' and 'what is not ours'. Some have also adopted the hegemonic Western attitude of viewing 'traditional' as outmoded and inferior, others show much pride in it. In any case, be it for the lack of a better word or for their pride in something that they have produced themselves, I respect the use of the word 'traditional' by the interviewees.

Terence Ranger suggests that all tribal identities and the biggest part of so-called 'traditions' known in Africa today were invented of recent, either by the colonisers or by Africans, who copied the colonisers' habit to invent traditions, for their own interest (Ranger 1984). On the one hand, this argument is valuable because it tries to put an end to all romanticisation and unquestioned acceptance of whatever is presented to a researcher (of any provenance) as 'African tradition'. It obliges us to look deeper into the issue before jumping to conclusions. Sally Matthews likewise cautions against "the extent to which colonialism adapted and (re-)invented traditions" (Matthews 2018, 177). On the other hand, Ranger's argument is highly problematic. First of all, it suffers from its generalisation for the whole of Africa despite the heterogenous pre-colonial, colonial, and post-colonial histories of the continent's various countries and regions. Although colonialism is a common experience of oppression and as such, of course, an experience of cultural uprooting, the intensity and methods of (cultural) interventions by the colonisers differed strongly in distinct places. Consequently, differing outcomes may be expected. Apart from that, to accept Ranger's argument without reservation would mean to deprive Africans of any right to claim their own past and identity. It would mean to declare whites the only source of cultural creativity, history, and identity in Africa. This is not the attitude espoused in this thesis. This study is neither historical nor anthropological. The question of authenticity of local culture or 'tradition' is not central to it, as it is concerned with the living conditions of the people under globalisation, a phenomenon that has nothing to do with tradition. After all, Raymond Williams aptly points out that "it only takes two generations to make anything **traditional**: naturally enough, since that is the sense of tradition as active process" (Williams 1988, 319, emphasis in the original). Nevertheless, in terms of solidarity structures, I asked the respondents whether there are 'traditional' ones. What I wanted to capture here is not the truth, but their *personal assessment* of the origin of solidarity structures. Do they experience a genuine sense of solidarity in their social environment or not? If yes, they would rather answer that solidarity structures are 'traditional', i.e., genuinely theirs, or that there are some 'traditional' kinds of solidarity structures. Whenever they answered with "no", they either added that solidarity structures have been introduced by government programmes or non-governmental organisations (i.e., not theirs) or that they had never been there at all.

2.5 Conclusion

The aim of this chapter was to present the overarching theoretical framework that constitutes the background to this study. It has become clear that this research project neither relies on a single discipline, nor on a single theory. It is based on a broad foundation of multidisciplinary theories that complement each other, with postcolonial theory as the overarching theme, the traces of which can be found in the other approaches. As Sabelo Ndlovu-Gatsheni points out, "the understanding of the African and Third world predicaments" cannot be achieved with the help of a single theory (Ndlovu-Gatsheni 2013, 42). In his view, the centre-periphery approach is one of the theories that can be helpful to understand the situation of the formerly colonised countries, though it needs to be completed with other perspectives (ibid.). Ndlovu-Gatsheni calls for a dialogue between post-structuralism, postmodernism, postcolonialism and political economy, in order to make them "complement each other and reinforce each other's intervention if the African condition is to be clearly understood" (ibid., 47). This attitude corresponds to the experience I had during my professional life. What I have seen in the global South as well as in the global North with regard to 'development' practice, global power constellations, and their effects on people's lives, has made me unable to believe that any one-sided approach, no matter how brilliant it is, will ever be sufficient to capture the complexity of those phenomena. Together, the theoretical approaches presented above may still not suffice to get a 'realistic' picture. This would require an objective 'reality', which does not exist, and a perspective that nobody has, namely a truly internal perspective from all points of view. My perspective is inevitably formed and limited by my positionality. A researcher should be aware of those limitations to 'objectivity' and understanding. I explain this further in chapter 5. Nevertheless, the theoretical framework and the methodology of a study should enable the researcher to apprehend the researched phenomena *as well as possible* under these circumstances. In my view, the combination of the theoretical approaches I have presented in this chapter allows me to do this.

Ramón Grosfoguel, who is a prominent representative of the decolonial movement and the world-systems perspective alike, comments on the two: "Postcolonialism shares with the world-system approach a critique of developmentalism, of Eurocentric forms of knowledge, of gender inequalities, of racial hierarchies, and of the cultural/ideological processes that foster the subordination of the periphery in the capitalist world-system" (Grosfoguel 2008, 99). Critical development studies, especially the Post-Development approach, could be added to the list because they share exactly the same critique. We find comparable ideas underlying Randeria's entangled histories in chapter 2.1, McMichael's "interdependence created through [the] division of *world* labour" (McMichael 2012, 37) in chapter 2.2, and Wallerstein's analysis of the capitalist world-system in chapter 2.3. Another parallel between several authors of those trajectories, for instance between Randeria and Wallerstein, can be found in their analyses of modernity's separation of the social sciences into separate spheres – a separation that has obstructed the view of social scientists. People's social reality is not chopped up like this, but it is an entity, in which the political, the economic, the social, and the cultural overlap at all times. As a result, concentrating on a certain sphere for a certain research purpose can make sense, but only if the influence of the other spheres is taken into consideration, at least to a certain extent.

The strongest influence on the theoretical and the methodological framework of this thesis comes from postcolonial theory. It influences strongly the way I perceive the roles played by countries of the global North and the global South in the process of globalisation. I have been sensitised by it for racism, social inequality, and mechanisms of power and oppression on a global scale. This refers to historical events (colonialism, the Cold War period) as well as to the current situation (globalisation). Furthermore, it has made me question the epistemological dominance of the global North and choose a research topic that puts knowledge and experience from the global South in the centre of attention. All of these aspects are central to the Post-Development approach as well. The latter builds on them its extensive critique of the 'development' paradigm – including the institutions in charge of its implementation – and the search for alternatives, preferably from the global South. At first glance, one might think that development is not part of my topic. On the contrary, when dealing with the global South, it is impossible to ignore notions of 'development' thinking. 'Integration of all countries into the world economy' is the theme of globalisation and, at the same time, the current slogan of the development paradigm. Due to neoliberalism, the latter has turned its back on national development policies to a large extent. Many indicators that I asked interviewees about in order to learn about their perception of globalisation in their socio-economic environment can equally be perceived as indicators of 'development'. For that reason, and because the concept of 'development' is more familiar to them than the comparably new concept of 'globalisation', many interviewees talked more about 'development' than about 'globalisation' when it came to those indicators. The solidarity structures, which I examine in the course of this study, regardless of whether they are autochthonous or modern[22], are practised by the respective people because they aspire to 'development'. Indeed, the whole topic of this thesis revolves around 'development' and different approaches to it, namely *globalisation and solidarity*. Consequently, I had to define my position in terms of 'development'. The Post-Development approach's focus on alternatives to 'development' from the global South complements the call for decolonisation of epistemology by postcolonial thinkers and encouraged me to give priority to knowledge and experience from the global South in my research project. Eventually, there is world-systems analysis. Its understanding of the core-semiperiphery-periphery perspective may be a little reductionist, but like any model, it is helpful to imagine some basic structures and processes shaping the world-economy and the lives of its inhabitants. The inescapability of the capitalist world-system it describes may be disenchanting. However, in my view, it can make a significant contribution to the explanation for the failure of most countries of the global South to become *equal parts* of the system in the past sixty years – in spite of all 'development' endeavours. While some few countries of the global South have managed to become semiperipheries[23], the majority has remained in the status of peripheries. The world-systems perspective supports the Post-Development approach by giving an explanation, based on thorough analysis of economic history, for the fact that the capitalist world-system is *not able* to support socio-eco-

22 I use the expression 'modern' due to the lack of a better term for a phenomenon that is both relatively new and the result of influence from outside.

23 The capitalist world-economy is divided into the production of core-like, i.e., highly profitable products and peripheral, i.e., less profitable products by the "axial division of labour" (Wallerstein 2007, 28). In semiperipheries, a more or less balanced mix of peripheral and core-like products is being produced, while peripheries are clearly dominated by the production of peripheral products and core states by core-like products (ibid.).

nomic 'development' in the global South. As a result, it supports the call for a new socio-economic system, or rather several new socio-economic systems, if global inequality, poverty, and a racist world order are supposed to be overcome. Nevertheless, another school of thought should not be forgotten, namely the reformist developmentalist perspective presented in chapter 2.2.2. It corresponds to the *short-term* strategies recommended by Wallerstein and other representatives of world-systems analysis (see chapter 3.4 of this thesis) to peripheral states, namely the revival of nationalist economic policies. As long as the 'big change' in the system is still a long way off, they can play a significant role in mitigating the suffering of people in the global South.

Whether we consider it from the politicising point of view of postcolonial and Post-Development thinkers, or from the cold-blooded systemic standpoint of world-systems analysis; whether we analyse it historically, economically, or sociologically, the conclusion is the same: The ideological basis of development and globalisation alike, a mixture of modernisation theory and – to a growing extent – neoliberalism, is not able to fulfil the promise of promoting (nearly) equal distribution of wealth. As has been shown in this chapter, despite all promises of prosperity to the global South, the neoliberal policies it has implemented in the past decades have primarily benefitted the global North. All countries that have achieved significant economic development in the past decades – regardless of their geographic and social location either in the global North or in the global South – have achieved it through protectionist policies and the suppression of their competitors in the global market, not through free trade and laissez-faire. This is how far I have come by means of theory, literature, and research results presented by other scholars. In my own study, my aim is not to prove these assumptions right or wrong. Of course, they have been present in my mind when I conceptualised the interview framework and analysed the interviews. To assert that they were not would be self-deception. Nevertheless, my objective is not to collect evidence for any theory from the researched, but to add a new point of view to the discussion.

3. Globalisation

'Globalisation' is an overused term that says both everything and nothing at the same time. In the global North, the term is widely used in science and media alike, such that the concept of globalisation is "well established in the popular imagination" (Jones 2010, 1). Yet, the ideas it implies can differ significantly. One of the main purposes of this chapter is to clarify my understanding and use of the term 'globalisation'. Specifically, this means describing globalisation from the point of view of the three schools of thought presented in chapter 2: Postcolonial theory (chapter 3.2), critical development studies (chapter 3.3), and world-systems analysis (chapter 3.4). Those three sub-sections are preceded by a general introduction, which presents key features of globalisation that help to distinguish economic globalisation (my focus) from other forms of globalisation, e.g., cultural globalisation. Chapter 3.5 considers resistance to globalisation. This is a corollary of the phenomena described in the preceding chapters that I examine only briefly as it is not central to the topic of this thesis. For the chapter as a whole, the relationship between the global South and the globalised world economy is particularly important. During the interviews conducted for this study, I asked respondents how they have experienced globalisation in their region in the preceding 30 years. This meant that I had to explain to them my understanding of globalisation and find connections it may have with their everyday lives. Further information about the interview framework can be found in chapter 5 and in the appendices.

3.1 General introduction to globalisation

> "The most important aspects of globalization are the breaking down of national economic barriers; the international spread of trade, financial and production activities, and the growing power of transnational corporations and international financial institutions in these processes." (Khor 2001, 7)

The term globalisation denotes an economic process of business and finance leaving behind national boundaries to interweave in a global economy (Ziai 2000, 34). This process is enabled by the liberalisation of world trade, movements of capital, and by new communication technologies –

leading to high competitive pressure for enterprises as well as states (ibid.). However, trade liberalisation can be regarded either as a common practice and the path to economic strength or as a one-sided instrument being forced upon the weaker members of the world economy by its stronger members, who maintain their superiority by means of protectionist policies. Numerous scholars like Chang, List, and Kiiza, whose standpoints have been discussed in chapter 2.2.2, or Ugandan scholar Yash Tandon (Tandon 2016, 21, 51), advocate the latter assumption, pointing out that the economic success of wealthy countries was evidently built on protectionist policies rather than free trade. International corporations play a significant role in globalisation as they "move not only capital and goods across borders, but also technology" (Stiglitz 2002, 10; see also Greig et al. 2007, 164-165; Wolf 2018, 48-50). Many of those corporations practise "global sourcing", receiving their inputs from various places around the world (Glenn 2007, 70; see also Greig et al. 2007, 165). This does not only apply to inputs that cannot be sourced locally, e.g., certain raw materials, but likewise to inputs that can be sourced cheaper elsewhere, for instance labour. As new facilities have made it fast, cheap and easy to move money (financial liberalisation), materials and (semi-)finished products (transport facilities), and information (communication facilities) around the globe, such corporations can source, produce and sell wherever it is most profitable for them, almost without restrictions (Greig et al. 2007, 165). Some authors call for an understanding of globalisation as an ethical-religious, philosophical, political, economic (e.g., Pfeifer-Schaupp 2005, 12-13) and cultural mosaic (ibid., 19-20). Here, those other dimensions are regarded as *consequences* of the economic dimension, which entails changes in culture, morals, politics, and other spheres of life due to its specific capitalist division of labour, mode of production, and social ideology (for details, see below or consult chapter 2). Globalisation is being driven by capitalism and has to be distinguished from "simple trading activity which has occurred throughout the millennia" (Glenn 2007, 10). John Glenn describes capitalism's main features as follows: Private ownership of means of production by a few; the lack of alternatives to selling their labour for many; the extraction of surplus value from workers by the owners of the means of production; and the production of goods for exchange, not for immediate consumption. Yet he states that the most important properties of capitalism are the ones that make it drive globalisation, namely its *permanent* need for accumulation of capital and the *competition* in the market economy. This competitive pressure leads to the need for permanent expansion and innovation, plus the permanent quest for cheaper inputs, especially labour (Glenn 2007, 9-11; see also Burchardt 2004, 84). As a result, firms move around the globe in search of cheaper inputs, in order to be as competitive as possible and to accumulate as much capital as possible (Glenn 2007, 11). At the same time, they need markets for their products. As the home market is always in danger of becoming saturated, "new social wants and needs" must be created, either at home, or in new markets (ibid.). Currently, globalisation is taking place in a *neoliberal* manner (Burchardt 2004, 80-83; see also Altvater/ Mahnkopf 2002, 263; Glenn 2007, 9; Pfeifer-Schaupp 2005, 23-26), with many negative ecological and social effects (cf. e.g. Greig et al. 2007, 174-175; Pfeifer-Schaupp 2005, 27-38). Among those effects are dramatically increasing social inequality and 'failed states', which are neither able to deal with violent conflicts, nor with the need for education, health care and food provision due to neoliberal pressures from outside (Hall et al. 2015a, 9-13).

As Andrew Jones aptly points out, "in terms of the academic study of globalization, the literature is now so vast, diverse and (periodically) impenetrable that to read every thought written on the topic would require a lifetime in a library" (Jones 2010, 1). Academics have categorised approaches to globalisation according to a variety of criteria. In his overview of key thinkers, Jones uses a "thematic approach" (ibid., 2), with categorisations like "systemic thinking" for Immanuel Wallerstein, "positive thinking" for Thomas Friedman and Martin Wolf, "reformist thinking" for Joseph Stiglitz, "cultural thinking" for Arjun Appadurai, etc. (ibid., 15-18). John Glenn focuses on globalisation's effects on North-South relations. He roughly follows the categorisation of approaches to globalisation by Anthony McGrew, distinguishing between "the globalists", for whom globalisation is an unprecedented phenomenon; "the sceptics", who do not believe that there is a significant change that can be called 'globalisation'; and "the transformationalists", who "view contemporary economics as 'a process of on-going transformation'" (Glenn 2007, 34). The transformationalists combine the two extreme points of view: To the observation of the sceptics that the world has been interconnected before, they add the globalists' claim that exchange has never been as vibrant as today – and come out with a balanced position. The arguments of the respective schools of thought for or against the openness of the world economy are based first and foremost on levels of foreign direct investment and cross-border flows of goods and finance (ibid., 66-67). In this thesis, I take a position that Glenn would call 'transformationalist'. As I base my approach partly on world-systems analysis, I do not see the beginnings of globalisation as occurring in the twentieth century but rather in the sixteenth century, when the formation of the capitalist world-system started. Interconnectedness existed even before that, yet not with the attributes of capitalism, which have been described in the preceding paragraph (and in chapter 2.3). Nevertheless, the process has significantly sped up from century to century, first by colonial expansion and later by attempts at 'peaceful' capitalist expansion after formal decolonisation. Technical innovations of the twentieth and twenty-first century such as means of faster communication, transport of goods and people, and transfer of capital have contributed to the acceleration of globalisation. This process was fostered by the increasing saturation of home markets of the core countries and neoliberal ideology.

The role of the state is also transforming under globalisation. According to Joachim Hirsch, a major process within that transformation, a process he calls "denationalisation", alters the relationship between society and the state (Hirsch 2001, 117, translation by E.K.). As capital leaves behind national boundaries, the same applies to the class struggle, such that social inequality grows within societies and across the globe. According to Hirsch, this inequality leads to the paradox that though globalisation makes societies "'more multinational' and 'more multicultural'", it also promotes nationalism and racism (ibid., translation by E.K.). As a result, the state with its monopoly on the use of force is needed to safeguard peace. Hirsch observes another process he calls "*privatisation of politics*" (ibid., translation by E.K., emphasis in the original). The obligation for national governments to make concessions to powerful actors in society existed before globalisation but is intensified by the formation of international markets and transnational capital (ibid., 118). Furthermore, international organisations become increasingly powerful. On the one hand, manifestations of this phenomenon can be found in the big transnational institutions like the IMF, the World Bank, the NATO, etc., in which the powerful countries of the world dominate the rest, and in regional economic cooperation between neighbouring countries (ibid., 119-120). In these organisations and institutions, states play a significant role as representatives of differing national interests (ibid., 119-120, 125). On the other hand, those manifestations can be found in so-called non-governmental organisations (NGOs). Hirsch suggests that NGOs are an "extended state" rather than private organisations, as they take over tasks that national governments fulfilled prior to the above-described developments (ibid., 120-121, translation by E.K.). As a result, the separation between society and the state as well as the ways in which they interact have been changed profoundly by globalisation (ibid., 121). Hirsch emphasises, however, that the state is still needed for regulating the class struggle, safeguarding social peace, and sustaining the global accumulation process (ibid., 122-124).

There are positive and negative evaluations of globalisation as well as attempts at "value free" approaches (Jones 2010, 14) like Joseph Stiglitz's endeavours to present a balanced image of globalisation in his oeuvre (ibid., 17). As the following sub-sections take up a rather sceptical stance, I summarise some optimistic assumptions in this paragraph. The most optimistic analysts of globalisation, among them Martin Wolf, characterise globalisation as "an exciting opportunity for improving human welfare across the globe" (ibid., 130). Wolf's thinking can be traced back to classical economists like Adam Smith and David Ricardo as well as neoliberal thinkers like Jagdish Bhagwati and Anne Krueger (ibid., 139). For instance, Wolf praises Adam Smith's "invisible hand" for being at work in today's globalised world economy, supplying consumers with virtually everything they desire and producers all over world with customers (Wolf 2018, 45). From the point of view of the privileged global upper and middle classes, this is certainly true. It just ignores the point of view of all the people in world, who are either excluded or exploited by the system (see subsequent chapters). In general, the major problem with the majority of approaches that are optimistic about neoliberal globalisation is their limited perspective. After all, they have some arguments in favour of global capitalist development that are hard to refute and encompass the following aspects: As a result of global capitalist development, the world population on average has a higher life expectancy and standard of living (Stiglitz 2002, 4; Wolf 2018, 164). Globalisation provides people in the global South with access to knowledge and the internet enables activists to connect worldwide and exert pressure on political actors on their behalf (Stiglitz 2002, 4). When countries of the global South open up their markets to products from the global North this may destroy local business, but at least impoverished populations receive access to the respective products (ibid., 5). The activities of foreign business companies "can also lead to the introduction of new technologies, access to new markets, and the creation of new industries" (ibid.). Capitalist societies of the global North have developed a high level of freedom and democracy (Wolf 2018, 54-55). Nevertheless, the latter must not lead to the conclusion that less capitalism automatically means less freedom and democracy. However, many pro-globalisation thinkers refuse to *think beyond* the economic systems that have been tried out by humanity so far. They present global capitalism as *the only alternative* to either "feudal societies" in which "kings and lords had the power of life and death" or "state-socialist and national-socialist regimes of the twentieth century" (Wolf 2018, 53). They contrast "democratic, consensual, free-market-oriented governance" under capitalism with "authoritarian rule with centrally planned economies" that have resulted in "making people equally poor" – as if there was no escape from this dichotomy (Friedman 2005, 49). Furthermore, the proponents' portrayal of globalisation implies that it is inappropriate (or even unthankful) to criticise a phenomenon that has positive aspects (e.g., Wolf 2018). They tend to rather downplay the dimensions of globalisation's downsides than to offer solutions to them (Jones 2010, 145). However, the positive effects of global capitalism do not outweigh its downsides. As the following sections of this chapter will show, more awareness[24] for capitalism's negative effects and a more flexible thinking in terms of alternatives are necessary.

Stiglitz clearly expresses his unwillingness to support any of the extreme positions (for or against neoliberal globalisation) and admits that many proponents of globalisation are too enthusiastic about it and do not see that some promises of globalisation, especially to the global South, have *not* been fulfilled. He contrasts the rapidly increasing number of people living in poverty with the annual increase of total world income in order to demonstrate the "growing divide between the haves and the have-nots" (Stiglitz 2002, 5). This hints to the issue discussed in chapter 2.2.3 that macroeconomic indicators for the standard of living like the gross national product (GNP) are average indicators without reference to the dispersion of wealth within the population (Latouche 2019, 282-283). A growing part of the numerous works from differing theoretical camps is turning critically against a neoliberal globalisation that is led by powerful corporations, focused on economic interests exclusively, leaving aside social and environmental issues (e.g., Altvater/ Mahnkopf 2002; Amin 1998; Amin 2004; Brand 2005; Chossudovsky 2003; Ferguson 2006; Giegold/ Embshoff 2008; Greig et al. 2007; Hall et al. 2015; Pfeiffer-Schaupp 2005; Roberts/ Hite 2000; Ziai 2000). The point of criticism is not a kind of international mindset but rather the economic system and its effects on humanity and the natural environment. Sometimes the critique refers to capitalism in general. In all instances, it addresses neoliberal ideology. Castro Varela and Dhawan call it "violent neoliberal globalisation", yet they caution against confusing it with "forms of emancipatory internationalisation" (Castro Varela/ Dhawan 2015, 79, translation by E.K.). Joseph Mensah summarises:

24 As those sections will show, there is already much awareness among critical scholars and activists but it is not yet sufficiently recognised in public debate.

"At the heart of these controversies [about globalisation] lies the ideology of neoliberalism, which seeks to further expand global capital accumulation through free trade, financial deregulation, privatization, and other tenets of the so-called Washington Consensus, spearheaded by the World Bank, International Monetary Fund (IMF), World Trade Organization (WTO), and kindred organizations [...]." (Mensah 2008, 1)

3.2 *Globalisation and postcolonial theory*

Postcolonial analysis of globalisation regards the latter as the continuation of the global North's exploitation of the global South. This has its historical roots in colonialism (Castro Varela/ Dhawan 2015, 78; Dhawan/ Randeria 2016, 562). The way in which the International Monetary Fund (IMF) and the World Bank have been introducing what they call "the market" in their borrower countries has "a colonial history of involuntary integration into the capitalist world system" (Eckert/ Randeria 2009, 25, translation by E.K.). Sabelo Ndlovu-Gatsheni puts it as follows: "Globalization, is today, still driven by coloniality on a world scale." (Ndlovu-Gatsheni 2018, 292) In his view, the global North still dominates and exploits Africans as it did during colonial times through inequitable power relations in the political, social, and cultural sectors (Ndlovu-Gatsheni 2013, 8). Ndlovu-Gatsheni contrasts the part of the world that calls itself 'the free world' (the voluntarily capitalistic world) with what he calls the 'un-free world', namely those countries (many in Africa) that have been dragged by colonialism into the capitalist world-system against their will and still are being dragged inside by globalisation (ibid., 48). Andreas Eckert and Shalini Randeria state that many people in the global South, whether they are academics or not, regard globalisation "as the re-colonization of their future", seeing in it a variety of imperialism (Eckert/ Randeria 2009, 13, translation by E.K.). This perspective is equally reflected in the consideration of neoliberal globalisation as "global coloniality" (Escobar 2012, xxxii) and "a new form of financial imperialism" (Hall et al. 2015a, 11).

Gayatri C. Spivak insists that the international division of labour necessarily must be taken into consideration when discussing "global capitalism" (Spivak 1988, 272). According to Spivak, the international division of labour works as follows: Some countries, mainly from the global North, make investments in other countries, mainly in the global South, "both through the comprador indigenous capitalists and through their ill-protected and shifting labor force" (ibid., 287). Spivak suggests that nineteenth century imperialism and the present-day development project had in common the following effects on the countries of the global South: The destruction of local industries, changes in land distribution, and the extraction of raw materials. At the same time, Spivak argues, the present-day development project, which in her opinion serves the international division of labour, does not even serve the people of the global South the way nineteenth century imperialism did (albeit not altruistically) by establishing education systems, infrastructure for transport, and law. For Spivak, this attitude is necessary in order to keep up the international division of labour, which guarantees cheap labour in the global South through totalitarian states, low living costs for the workers, and poor (enforcement of) labour laws (ibid., 287-288). In Spivak's view, outsourcing production stages, which require a lot of labour, from the global North to the global South is a strategy to avoid resistance. Its underlying objective is, on the one hand, to spend little money on the labour force and to take advantage of tariff exemptions. However, on the other hand, its objective is to separate the producers from their products and their multinational bosses by taking the products back to the investing country instead of supplying the local market (ibid.). This strategy robs the global South host countries of any possible advantage emerging from that business. Governments in the global South know that the preconditions for investors to come are tax holidays, tariff exemptions, free trade agreements, low wages, poor labour law enforcement, and, in some cases, other incentives such as the allocation of cheap land (see also below for description of the situation in India by Dhawan/ Randeria 2016, 567). Though a large faction of the beneficiaries of so-called *land grabbing* are domestic enterprises or even the respective governments themselves (Engels/ Dietz 2011, 403), the latter make huge portions of land available to global investors (McMichael 2012, 271). Governments of global South countries concerned hope to acquire foreign currency, new technologies, and employment opportunities for their citizens by attracting those investors (Engels/ Dietz 2011, 408). These objectives are suggested to them by 'donor' countries and the Bretton Woods institutions through loan conditionalities like structural adjustment programmes (see chapters 2.2 and 3.3 for details).

Concrete practices like those described in the previous paragraph are being enabled by both political pressure and a hegemonic ideology. With striking parallels to Antonio Gramsci's concept of hegemony (see chapter 2.4, keyword 'hegemony'), Hall et al. state:

> "Every social settlement, in order to establish itself, is crucially founded on embedding as common sense a whole bundle of beliefs – ideas beyond question, assumptions so deep that the very fact that they *are* assumptions is only rarely brought to light." (Hall et al. 2015a, 14, emphasis in the original)

The "common sense" of neoliberalism is based on "the primacy of the competitive individual, the superiority of the private over the public" (ibid.), "a quasi-religious belief in the 'hidden hand', and the self-propelling virtues of 'the market'" (ibid., 17). The hegemony of those assumptions draws "whole populations materially and imaginatively into a financialised and marketised view of the world" (ibid., 14). For example, many citizens worldwide have started to believe that privatisation of state-run enterprises is desirable because it is done for the sake of providing them with better services. Another expectation is that privatisation provides jobs (for locals!). For instance, Ngila Mwase shows some confusion in the face of Ugandan President Yoweri Museveni admitting in 2000 that the economic reform package, which encompassed comprehensive privatisation, did not deliver a significant number of jobs despite its promise to do so (Mwase 2007, 62). As Hall et al. aptly point out, privatisation first and foremost serves the commodification of areas that have previously been out of reach of the private sector for profit making (Hall et al. 2015a, 14). For the global South, this means losing another profit-making opportunity to the global North – where internationally operating companies are more competitive than local ones, if there are local ones at all – and to lose any control over the prices of basic services provided to their citizens. Furthermore, Hall et al. state that the bourgeois neoliberal ideals of "the 'free market' and the free-standing individual have had to be actively *produced* and *imposed*" (ibid., 15, emphases by E.K.). This goes hand in hand with Arturo Escobar's above-described[25] argument that "the tales of the market, production, and labor which are at the root of what might be called the Western economy" are rather "a peculiar set of discourses and practices" than the "neutral representation of the world and a truth about it" that it pretends to be (Escobar 2012, 58-59). Under the 'common sense' of neoliberal globalisation, commercialisation and profit-maximisation touch upon every sphere of life (Hall et al. 2015a, 19; San Juan 2002, 229).

María do Mar Castro Varela and Nikita Dhawan describe how globalisation has spurred the above-described neoliberal common sense in

---

25 See chapter 2.2.3.

politics globally. Accordingly, the concerns of business companies and international elites are prioritised over those of the population (Castro Varela/ Dhawan 2015, 80, 204). For the rural populations of countries in the global South, globalisation has brought about new forms of economic and social marginalisation. Democracy (in whatever condition it might be in the particular country) is being disabled by market conformity. This phenomenon can be observed all over the world, yet it most acutely affects the subaltern in the global South. They are already the weakest members of the global society when it comes to political representation (ibid., 204). This makes them highly vulnerable to any intervention at their detriment, as their prospects to enforce their rights are very limited. Hall et al. observe "a massive shift of power and resources from public to private, from state to market" (Hall et al. 2015a, 10). In global South countries, the shift from the *national* public/ state sphere to the private/ market sphere is dominated by *foreign* investors, sabotaging the agency and legitimacy of the respective governments at national and international levels. Furthermore, the above-mentioned business companies and international elites of course include *domestic* companies and elites. As a result, globalisation fosters class struggles, exploitation and marginalisation of lower classes and rural populations within global South countries.

A case study of a shift from the state to the market in the global South is being depicted by Nikita Dhawan and Shalini Randeria. They describe the opening of the until then centrally planned economy of India through neoliberal policies as follows: State enterprises were privatised and domestic and foreign investments in the formally public sector were allowed. Agricultural subsidies were dialled down, several import restrictions and controls were abolished, and the middle class gained access to scores of consumer goods. As a result, there has been a phenomenal rise in the use of mobile telephones, in TV channels, shopping malls, and in the music, fashion and film industries (Dhawan/ Randeria 2016, 563). From a developmentalist and, more so, a neoliberal point of view, this seems to verify the effectiveness of structural adjustment programmes and the positive impacts of (global) capitalism. For an examination by a neoliberal globalisation analyst or a report by the IMF or the World Bank, this might already be the conclusion. Dhawan and Randeria, however, follow a postcolonial approach and thus continue with an analysis of the downsides of economic liberalisation, highlighting the uneven development and social inequality that have been exacerbated across regions as well as between rural and urban areas. Economic liberalisation has also worsened unemployment rates in numerous sectors and intensified the problem of indebtedness among impoverished rural populations. Regional governments try to encourage investors to come to their region by granting them tax breaks and low land prices. Large parts of society, especially the most vulnerable and marginalised members, suffer from the loss of agricultural lands and commons in favour of *Special Economic Zones*, in which the workers are not protected by labour law. In addition, they suffer from environmental pollution, displacement, and denied access to natural resources such as forests. Exacerbating this already precarious living situation, the World Trade Organization (WTO) has made biogenetic material patentableIn combination with multinational corporations introducing genetically modified seeds to the Indian market, intellectual property rights on food crops disadvantage the rural population (ibid., 564). The case of India is not exceptional but mirrors the typical effects observed in countries that were 'liberalised' through structural adjustment programmes and comparable policy instruments (for more examples, see chapter 3.3). The positive outcomes (economic growth, rising levels of consumption, and numbers of health facilities) on which official reports focus, benefit only a small part of the population, however. The majority of the population is worse off than before. Higher per capita incomes contrast with higher income inequality and exploding cost of living. Consequently, those programmes succeed with capital accumulation but fail in poverty reduction.

The cultural dimension of globalisation interacts with these economic and political dimensions. As Boaventura de Sousa Santos aptly points out, it is nowadays difficult to distinguish between 'the local' and 'the globalised' (Santos 2014, 178-179). What appears 'local' at first sight may be a "localized globalism" – which should not belie the fact that *there are* local phenomena (ibid., 179). Before labelling anything – if one finds that process of labelling possible and useful, at all – it has to be examined thoroughly. Arjun Appadurai insist that "at least as rapidly as forces from various metropolises are brought into new societies they tend to become indigenized in one or another way: this is true for music and housing styles as much as it is true of science and terrorism, spectacles and constitutions" (Appadurai 1990, 295). Eckert and Randeria are sceptical when it comes to the aspect that many critics call "cultural imperialism", meaning the suppression of autochthonous cultures by global 'Westernisation' (Eckert/ Randeria 2009, 22, translation by E.K.). They accuse the concept of 'cultural imperialism' of simplifying cultural mechanisms. In their view, these mechanisms are not simple cultural changes flowing unidirectionally from centre to periphery and causing predictable effects in their 'recipients'. They call for 'recipients' in the global South to be seen as active participants in the process, who decide actively what to adapt from outside, and who are also able to release a pulse in the other direction (ibid., 22-23). In another piece, together with Sebastian Conrad, Shalini Randeria asserts that Europe has been influenced by Asian and African cultures since the very beginning of colonial endeavours (Conrad/ Randeria 2002, 10-11). Traces of Homi K. Bhabha's concepts of *hybridity* and *agency* (see chapter 2.1.2) are evident in all these assessments. In terms of economic activities, people in the global South are also more than passive recipients of Western knowledge. Quite the contrary, they have always been surviving on their own strategies and they still do – although, in most places, they had to adapt to changing circumstances. This makes their economic activities particularly interesting.

In terms of the role of people within the process of globalisation, Arif Dirlik suggests that global capital transforms the global population into producers, consumers (some are both, others not), and the 'useless' rest that has nothing to contribute to the project of global capitalism's expansion (Dirlik 2004, 519). However, this exemplary division is not as sharp in reality as it seems to be on paper. Large parts of the world's population may look as though they belong to the 'useless' group because they are unemployed or impoverished peasants. They may also *feel* 'useless' because they do not profit from the gains of capitalist 'development', and they are despised by society. Nevertheless, they can still play a role as consumers. The unemployed in the global North receive aid from their governments. Peasant households in the global South survive on a mix of wages/ salaries (including odd jobs), subsistence activities, petty commodity production, rent, and transfer payments (Wallerstein 2007, 32-34). Though those groups have comparably small amounts of money at their disposal, they use what little funds they have for consumption. And as they are many in number, the total volume of their consumption is considerable. Many providers of consumer goods or services have discovered a target group for their products in low-income groups in the global South. For instance, as I have observed in Uganda during my research period and in other African countries during my professional practice, even people with very low incomes have mobile phones. In the market, there is a mobile phone for every budget, and service providers have adapted their prices per unit to the pockets of their customers. During the interviews conducted for this study, an expert interviewee explained that phenomenon to me (see Expert 8 in chapter 8.2.4). This is only one example of how masses of allegedly 'useless' members of the global capitalist community are drawn into the pool of consumers. The sense of citizenship moves away from rights and political representation, approximating "the private realm of commodity consumption and the mass media" (García Canclini 2001, 15). People let go of their biological, social and cultural survival strategies in favour of the 'modern lifestyle' of a consumer-citizen (Hawley 2008, 26). This observation has particular significance for my study, as I expand in chapter 8.

3.3 Globalisation and development

The discourse of 'development' is closely interrelated with that of 'globalisation'. In many texts, the two terms could be interchanged without serious consequences for the authors' arguments, at least when texts about globalisation turn to the role of the global South. For instance, the debate about globalisation's (dis)advantages for countries of the global South can equally be found in development discourse (see chapter 2.2): While proponents of globalisation advertise it as bringing wealth for all, opponents claim that it benefits the haves at the expense of the have-nots, and some authors claim that globalisation creates *global classes* of 'winners' and 'losers' (Burchardt 2004, 79). As has been outlined in chapter 2.2.3, Ivan Illich and Wolfgang Sachs have observed the formation of this global class divide, as well, and attributed it to 'development'. Aram Ziai states that globalisation gained popularity as concept in the mid-1990s and that "the rise of neoliberalism and the discourse of globalisation are intertwined with the decline of development discourse" (Ziai 2017, 106). Philip McMichael expresses a similar thought by writing that "the development project was replaced by the globalization project" (McMichael 2012, 80). Yet, he adds that this is "not because development is dead but because its coordinates have changed" from national to global and from public to private (ibid., 112). 'Development' does no longer take place on a *national* level, but on the level of the *global* economy (ibid., 112-113, 126). In his view, the globalisation project came up with the *Washington Consensus* (for details, see below) (ibid., 127). Ziai explicates how historical events such as the Russian Revolution (1917-1918), anti-colonial struggles in the colonies, the great depression of 1929, and the world wars led the global North to the conclusion that it needed investments in the global South for its financial stabilisation (Ziai 2017, 72-73, 103). Thus, the people of the global South needed convincing that those interventions were good for them as well, a process that was achieved through the idea of 'development' (ibid.,

73). Now that many people in the global South have been disappointed by 'development', the new label for the same project is 'globalisation'. Both concepts – that of globalisation and of development[26] – are capitalist and imbued with neoliberalism, as I have demonstrated in chapters 2.2, 3.1, and 3.2. Globalisation promotes the idea of Western-style economic and social 'development'. In return, many activities labelled 'development' spread neoliberal thinking (Satgar 2014, 11) and are meant to open markets in the global South for companies and products from the global North (Illich 1998, 94) – phenomena of globalisation. The 1980s were the decade in which "neoliberalism, or global free-market capitalism" became the doctrine of the global economic system (Hall et al. 2015a, 9) and "the decade of the rise of neoliberal discourse in the field of North-South relations" (Ziai 2017, 115). By then, this neoliberal discourse started influencing the policies of powerful 'development' institutions like the World Bank (ibid., 117). Among the central concepts of neoliberalism are "trade liberalism, privatisation of state enterprises, the deregulation of markets and the increasing commodification of social relationships and nature" (ibid., 106). All spheres of life are drawn into the economic sphere and subjected to economic principles with far-reaching effects on the respective societies on a macro- and micro-level.

The connections between capitalist 'development' and globalisation go beyond discourse. They can also be found at the institutional level. Joseph Stiglitz calls the International Monetary Fund (IMF), the World Bank, and the World Trade Organization (WTO) "the three main institutions that govern globalization" (Stiglitz 2002, 10). Martin Khor likewise names these three institutions as the ones steering the globalisation process. He claims that their power and authority not only allow them to dictate policies to the governments of sovereign states, but they have even outdone the *United Nations*' influence on internationally agreed policies (Khor 2001, 12). As a result, globalisation follows the market-oriented, neoliberal approach of the three financial institutions, not that of the *United Nations*, which, according to Khor, is founded on principles of partnership and human rights and needs – and encourages public intervention in favour of those objectives (ibid., 15). The tasks of the WTO, the World Bank, and the IMF, namely regulating international trade and financial stability, are based on a global economic system with vibrant exchange (Stiglitz 2002, 196, 199). As discussed in chapter 2.2 of this thesis, the WTO, and all the

26 I refer to 'development' in the conventional sense as represented by development agencies (e.g., World Bank, NGOs of various sizes and origins) here.

more the IMF and the *World Bank*, are the most powerful institutions in the 'development' industry, as well. Apart from the significant role the IMF and the World Bank play in forming international economic policies through their loan conditionalities (Khor 2001, 12-13; Stiglitz 2002, 43-44), countries that want to enter international capital markets need a positive assessment from them (Stiglitz 2002, 17-18). The WTO mainly intervenes in the sphere of development by subjecting countries of the global South and their development policies to international trade agreements and legal frameworks[27] like intellectual property rights.

Stiglitz identifies the policies of Ronald Reagan and Margaret Thatcher in the 1980s as the impetus for the *World Bank* and the IMF to depart from the Keynesian policies they had been promoting until then and instead beginning to propagate neoliberal ideology (Stiglitz 2002, 11-13). A passionate proponent of the original ideas behind those institutions, Stiglitz deplores their shift to "the free market mantra of the 1980s, part of a new 'Washington Consensus'—a consensus between the IMF, the World Bank, and the U.S. Treasury about the 'right' policies for developing countries" (ibid., 16). For him, the problem lies in the tension between the Keynesian idea of market failure that needs to be corrected through political action, on which the IMF was originally built, and its current staff consisting of "economists who have both a high level of confidence in the markets and little confidence in public institutions" (ibid., 196). The three cornerstones of advice under the *Washington Consensus* in the 1980s and 1990s were market liberalisation, meaning "the lowering of tariffs and elimination of other protectionist measures", fiscal austerity, and privatisation (ibid., 53). Stiglitz is not generally critical about those measures and their objective, economic growth (ibid.). This is not surprising for a former chief economist and senior vice president of the World Bank. Nevertheless, Stiglitz expresses concern about such measures, especially when they are applied at the wrong moment in the evolution of a national economy, or when they are simply "ends in themselves" (ibid.). For example, he holds the success of East Asian countries (like Japan, South Korea, and China), which did not follow the *Washington Consensus*' advice, against the failure of Latin American countries (like Argentina) that did (ibid., 79). Julius Kiiza comes to the same conclusion when comparing Uganda, which was subjected to premature orthodox liberalisation, to Taiwan, where

27 See the discussions of TRIPS by Wade and Kiiza in chapter 2.2 or of patents for biogenetic material by Dhawan/ Randeria in chapter 3.2. For more details on the WTO, see below in this chapter.

the national economy was given time to grow strong before opening it to international competition (Kiiza 2008; see also chapter 2.2.2). Glenn likewise states that the 'Asian tiger'-states were the only ones that had ever managed to 'catch up', and that they had only been able to do so thanks to a policy mix that included protectionist policies, not prioritising free trade or *laissez faire* (Glenn 2007, 221-222).

Stiglitz explains that the turn to neoliberal ideology in the 1980s marks the moment when the two institutions started to act conjointly: The World Bank began to provide "*structural adjustment loans*; but it did this only when the IMF gave its approval", leading to the above-discussed 'conditionalities' (Stiglitz 2002, 14, emphasis in the original). Thus, "the IMF became a permanent part of life in most of the developing world" (ibid.). Yet, according to Stiglitz, the IMF has not only been unsuccessful in terms of its original mission to guarantee stability to the world economy, it has even done the opposite, especially by pushing through policies like "premature capital market liberalization" (ibid.). IMF policies have even exacerbated the situation for countries in crisis, in particular for those already affected by poverty (ibid., 15). Many policies that arose from the *Washington Consensus* were pushed through in the global South although they were not helpful for countries in such "early stages of development" (ibid., 16). As examples, Stiglitz uses overhasty forced trade liberalisation, in contrast to the protectionist policies that countries like Japan or the USA had used in order to allow their domestic industries to grow strong before they were exposed to competition from outside. Local farmers are affected by overhasty liberalisation, as they are unable to compete with highly subsidised products from the global North (ibid., 16-17). To enforce all this before the concerned countries had been able to evolve strong industries, a diversified labour market, social safety nets, and stable capital markets, according to Stiglitz, is simply "bad economics" (ibid., 17). Yet, it is hard to believe that some of the most powerful economic institutions in the world are staffed with incompetent economists. On the one hand, Stiglitz rightly deplores the focus in economics on teaching common macroeconomic models, which build on unrealistic assumptions, e.g., the nonexistence of unemployment or the perfect equivalence of demand and supply (ibid., 35). On the other hand, this explanation is not satisfactory in view of the continuing existence and power of those international financial institutions. Ha-Joon Chang's above-cited book *Kicking Away the Ladder* hints to a possible explanation: Successful trading nations promote trade liberalisation internationally because it helps them to consolidate their success while the weaker nations are disadvantaged by it (Chang 2002; see also chapter 2.2.2).

Stiglitz adds another aspect to the discussion by stating that those "institutions are dominated not just by the wealthiest industrial countries but by commercial and financial interests in those countries, and the policies of the institutions naturally reflect this" (Stiglitz 2002, 18-19). He blames this domination of the institutions by particular interests in wealthy countries on the personnel composition of the institutions. Trade ministers speaking at the WTO must report to the producers in their home countries, some of them wanting to be protected from the influx of competing products from abroad, others wanting to export their products to other markets under favourable conditions. Central bank governors and finance ministers speaking at the IMF expect to find highly paid jobs in financial firms back home after having finished their period of service. As a result, even the interests of 'ordinary citizens' in their own countries do not matter to some of those representatives of wealthy countries, not to mention those of people in other, more disadvantaged countries (ibid., 19-20). The citizens of the global North are fortunate that they either profit automatically from the strengthening of their national economies or, at a minimum, their comparably high incomes and the comparably stable social safety nets provided by their governments enable them to compensate for negative effects of certain policies on their everyday lives. The majority of citizens of global South countries, especially lower classes and rural populations, have none of these advantages. On the contrary, compounding the consequences of discriminatory international economic policies are the requirements to pay back their governments' loans to the IMF and the World Bank. Furthermore, their representatives in the respective institutions are as prone as those from the global North to being interested in their carrier rather than the needs of their citizens. Though Stiglitz's attitude towards globalisation is fundamentally positive, he demonstrates understanding for protestors against the way globalisation is currently shaped by the Bretton Woods institutions, especially the IMF (ibid., 20, 214-215). He states:

> "Disillusion with the international system of globalization under the aegis of the IMF grows as the poor in Indonesia, Morocco, and Papua New Guinea have fuel and food subsidies cut, as those in Thailand see AIDS increase as a result of IMF-forced cutbacks in health expenditures, and as families in many developing countries, having to pay for their children's education under so-called cost recovery programs,

> make the painful choice not to send their daughters to school." (Stiglitz 2002, 20)

Among the instruments used by the IMF to push through such policies in the concerned countries, structural adjustment programmes (SAPs) are best-known (see chapter 2.2 for details). James Ferguson recounts a trip to Zambia in 1989, when the country was encountering the effects of SAPs: "Prices of essential goods were skyrocketing, employment was declining, and real incomes were rapidly shrinking. [...] with high food prices, many went hungry; with free medical care abolished, many sick people could not receive treatment" (Ferguson 2006, 70). Structural adjustment programmes caused "a far-reaching political crisis" in numerous African countries (ibid., 38). As more and more activities were "outsourced" to the private sector to fulfil the requirement of cutting public expenditure drastically, qualified personnel was drained from government institutions (ibid.). Those states became "hollowed out" and were left with workers who often received "less than subsistence salaries, with the inevitable consequences of corruption and an explosion of 'parallel businesses.'" (ibid., 39) Neoliberal policies have indeed achieved their desired 'reorientation from the state to the market'. However, this has not occurred on the part of the economy but rather that of government workers who cannot make a living through their full-time employment and must therefore either neglect it in favour of other activities or accept bribes (ibid.).

Commenting on privatisation of the health sector, Samir Amin warns that "the results of capital's offensive in this area are always catastrophic for the popular classes" (Amin 1998, 33) as public administration can provide at least some democratic control in a way that private administration cannot (ibid., 32). Ikubolajeh Logan reminds us "that privatization is an economic and not a social welfare development strategy" and as such relies on a "benevolent market", which does not exist, to allocate resources like health care (Logan 1995, 56). Market-oriented (neoliberal) economic strategies allocate the distribution of goods to the private sector, in which "demand is often defined by purchasing power and not by the actual needs of different segments of society", as should be the case for the distribution of public goods (ibid., 63). The market favours high-income earners, whereas low-income earners are not only denied access to services, but they also lose ground in their struggle for those services (because government and donors can argue that 'services are there') (ibid.). Privatisation is not a suitable tool to grant access to health care services to low-income earners (ibid., 68-71). As Rick Rowden aptly points out, neoliberalism first and foremost benefits the national elites of a country and international investors (Rowden 1999, 156-157). Privatisation of the health sector is a typical case, in which national elites profit from more – and often better – health facilities, investors profit from a new source of income, and the health care situation of low-income earners worsens. Private health facilities must finance their services and their profits through the payments made by patients, whereas the government finances the largest part of the costs via taxes and does not seek profits. The services in the privatised health facilities are too expensive to be accessible to low-income earners. Government-run health facilities are either closed or neglected because the government relies on the private facilities (and, in most cases, is forced by the Bretton Woods institutions to cut health care costs). As a result, and as I have observed in Uganda, a large part of the population either has no access to health care at all or is permanently indebted to health care facilities (see chapter 8).

The third highly controversial authority in the global market, apart from the IMF and the World Bank, is the World Trade Organization (WTO). The plan for an organisation in charge of international trade relations had already been drawn up at Bretton Woods, yet from the 1940s through to 1995, only the *General Agreement on Tariffs and Trade* (GATT) was in place (Stiglitz 2002, 15-16; Tandon 2016, 15-16). Stiglitz's account of the WTO sounds idyllic: "It does not set rules itself; rather, it provides a forum in which trade negotiations go on and it ensures that its agreements are lived up to" (Stiglitz 2002, 16). 'Providing a forum for negotiations' seems to be a fair and democratic endeavour. Yash Tandon paints a completely different picture when he writes: "The WTO was created 1 January 1995. It was designed to benefit the United States, the European Union and Japan at the expense of the rest of the world" (Tandon 2016, 15). As an active member in the 'negotiations' at the WTO 'forum' on behalf of African countries (Uganda, Kenia, Tanzania) from the very beginning, Tandon offers a scathing testimony: "The WTO is a veritable war machine" (ibid., 1). This attitude arises from his experience as a representative of the global South, which, according to Tandon, must accept either the policies dictated by the powerful representatives of the global North or economic sanctions (ibid., 1-3). He reports that "decisions are made by a few select members […] in so-called 'green rooms'", and that for example the "Singapore Issues" were negotiated in 1996 without a single African country represented in the 'green room' (ibid., 2). Tandon argues that the WTO is at least partly to blame for food insecurity in the global South, as its interventions in the agricultural sector are always in favour of trade and market access, especially for the global North, and never in favour of food security or 'development' for the global South (ibid., 35-38).

Stiglitz draws the conclusion on globalisation that it could be designed more justly and in a manner that benefits all by giving a voice to every country affected by the decisions of the above-mentioned institutions (Stiglitz 2002, 21-22). He believes that the three big institutions, the IMF, WTO, and World Bank are needed in order to master globalisation and advocates for their reform (ibid., 222). Naturally, he ranks as higher the potential for improvement of his home institution, the World Bank (ibid., 241) than that of the rival, the IMF, which he first and foremost wants to see being limited to its original tasks (ibid., 231-233). As Glenn points out, however, even the World Bank's own academic panel accuses the Bank of using untested data in order to present as the most successful its policies, especially the achievement of economic growth by means of liberalisation (Glenn 2007, 220). Khor likewise calls for a democratisation of the three financial institutions, with more rights for the countries of the global South, in order to design globalisation more justly. Yet, for him, this would also mean to allow the United Nations to play a more significant role in the globalisation process (Khor 2001, 119-123). In spite of his general optimism, Stiglitz rates as low the readiness of the global North to implement reforms that benefit the global South (Stiglitz 2002, 251). This may be an outcome of his experience in trying to reform the World Bank. According to Hans-Jürgen Burchardt, the efforts made by the World Bank in favour of a post-Washington Consensus, which encompasses poverty reduction, the promotion of social capital, social integration, and state intervention as a tool of achieving those objectives, were indeed remarkable (Burchardt 2004, 222-224). Yet, they were cancelled by conservative parts of the World Bank administration together with several powerful actors such as the U.S. Treasury, neoliberal opinion leaders in economics, and several governments of the global North (ibid., 225). As a result, chief economist Joseph Stiglitz and Ravi Kanbur, the World Bank's economist in charge of Africa, both resigned from their positions in the year 2000. The reforms in World Bank policies remained embryonic (ibid., 225-226). Against the background of the issues discussed in this chapter so far, this does not come as a surprise. The issue of the above-mentioned 'conditionalities' seems to confirm that impression.

As Glenn points out, conditionalities have outlived structural adjustment programmes (SAPs), which were replaced by *Poverty Reduction and Growth Facility programmes* (PRGF) in 1999. National *Poverty Reduction Strategy Papers* (PRSPs) must be signed as a requirement for debt relief or new loans to borrower countries. Those 'national' papers must present the country's strategy to reach economic *growth* and require World Bank and IMF approval – hence, no surprises concerning their content can be expected (Glenn 2007, 211-212). Glenn warns that there is no reason to talk about "a 'post-Washington consensus'" simply because SAPs have been reduced to PRGFs (ibid., 225). Apart from the fact that the IMF must still agree with the PRSPs, numerous countries of the global South have already gone through liberalisation due to SAPs or to their membership in "the liberal trade regime governed by the WTO" (ibid.). Hence, what Glenn sees underway is not a process of reform but a *slight relaxation* of the rules because a big part of the job is done (ibid.). Stiglitz recommends to countries of the global South to take their policies into their own hands (Stiglitz 2002, 251). Several authors call for more freedom for countries of the global South to choose their own approaches to development, to their integration into the world economy, and to the balance between the state and the market they find appropriate (e.g., Burchardt 2004, 249; Khor 2001, 123-126). Stiglitz states that, as a result, all countries of the global South could go through the same 'development' process as the 'Asian tigers' and, eventually, the Untied States (Stiglitz 2002, 21-22). The desirability of such an evolution has been discussed in chapter 2.2, and the likelihood of it to happen in chapters 2.2 and 2.3. Even Stiglitz's own point is rather inconsistent. On the one hand, he advocates for economic growth and the need for the three international financial institutions to master globalisation. On the other hand, he calls on countries of the global South to follow their own path because the global North is not going to support them. Hence, though Stiglitz is a representative of a rather conservative idea of 'development' (conceptualising it as economic growth and as an imitation of the global North), he acknowledges the power imbalance that is immanent to globalisation: The global North and the international organisations it controls (among them the IMF and the World Bank) dominate clearly over the global South.

Martin Khor describes another facet of the above-mentioned power imbalance that is immanent to globalisation. While low-income countries have little influence on the global economy, the global economy has a strong influence on them, e.g., with regard to prices or demand for their export goods (Khor 2001, 7). Khor suggests that the disadvantaged starting point of countries of the global South within globalisation has contributed significantly to their current fragile position. Following the social and economic devastation of colonialism, these countries entered the world economy and encountered low prices for their export goods coupled with the permanent need to incur and repay debts in order to be able to participate in world trade (ibid., 20). In many of these countries, dictatorships or economic mismanagement (which are certainly interrelated with the external factors mentioned above) exacerbated the already volatile situation (ibid., 21). Khor points out that colonial structures of trade between the global North and the global South have persisted as many countries of the global South must still rely on primary commodities for export, especially to the global North, while industrial products must be imported. Yet, primary commodities are less profitable than manufactured goods, thus, many countries of the global South suffer from low or instable prices and demand for their main export goods. In the worst case, both local supply of food and export revenues suffer from large portions of land being used for the production of unprofitable cash crops (ibid., 27-29).

When it comes to Africa, its disadvantageous position in globalisation is principally explained with the same arguments as its 'lack of development' (see chapter 2.2). The range of explanations goes from African elites being guilty of corruption, mismanagement, or allegedly harmful protectionist policies, to reproaches of neocolonialist and neoliberal policies used by the global North to keep Africa in its place (Mensah 2008, 2-3). Joseph Mensah argues that all those aspects must be considered to a certain extent (ibid., 4). Certainly, he states with authority that the role played by African elites should not be forgotten. However, Samir Amin points out that "criticisms of independent Africa, which address its corrupt political middle class, its lack of economic direction, and the tenacity of its rural community structures, forget that these features of contemporary Africa were forged between 1880 and 1960" (Amin 2004, 15). He refers to the violent integration of Africa into the capitalist world-system by means of colonial domination, exploitation, and oppression of phenomena such as the formation of a local middle class (ibid., 14, see chapter 3.4 for details). This does not release African elites of the need to rethink their attitude. Yet it explains why, so far, they had neither the time nor the incentives to try out their position and the best strategies to fulfil their responsibilities towards their populations. Another common narrative explaining the failure of poor countries or regions to profit from globalisation is the claim that they are not (yet) well-integrated into the world economy (e.g., Wolf 2018, 172). I address this line of reasoning more thoroughly in the next sub-section. Frederick Cooper summarises:

> "Capital has not invariably won the battles it fought during the first and second occupations of Africa—to make production predictable and orderly throughout the continent—but it has altered the spatial

> structure of production so that winning everywhere is less important. Capital's greater intensity and mobility allow it greater selectivity in concentrating on islands of production or on basic raw materials, while the extent of Africa's integration into commodity markets and labor flows that has already taken place makes further penetration desirable but not the goal that it was in the 1890s or 1940s. So Ghana and Uganda can be forgotten if the state cannot function or cultivators resist growing cash crops, and most of Zaire can be left to Mobutu's predators as long as the copper mines keep running." (Cooper 1993, 146)

This cynical statement originally written in 1981 (see Cooper 1993, 143) shows the essence of globalisation in general and its attitude towards Africa in particular (only that the word 'globalisation' was not yet fashionable at that time). Ferguson makes a similar point when referring to the classification of "'usable/useful Africa' and 'unusable/useless Africa,'" by French colonialism (Ferguson 2006, 39). He demonstrates that the image of Africa being ignored by global capital is incorrect. Rather, capital concentrates on "[u]sable Africa" and ignores "unusable Africa", based on its own logic, namely which parts are easily and effectively exploitable, e.g., because they are rich in valuable resources and politically unstable (ibid., 39-41, 196-197, 207-208). Khor deplores increasing inequality, which arises from globalisation benefitting a few countries or groups of people within countries while for the majority, the situation is worsening (Khor 2001, 16-18). To such complaints, Cooper asserts, "[a] Ricardian would reply that the periphery may indeed get less than the center from exchange, but more than it would have got from no trade at all" (Cooper 1993, 94). In other words, the periphery should be grateful that at least someone is so generous to exploit it, in its own interest. Later in his text, Cooper lists the numerous reproaches international corporations operating in Africa most frequently face, among them the charge that they make "the local economy less interconnected rather than more" (ibid., 139). Cooper continues: "The corporations' defenders can acknowledge many such criticisms and still insist that weak local linkages are better than none at all" (ibid.). Again, the global South is supposed to appreciate the crumbs (no matter how tiny) it gets from the cake that the global North is taking from it. And again, the global North does not remind itself that, without the global South, there would be no cake, and instead urges the global South to appreciate that there would be no crumbs without the noble investors from abroad. The option that, without exploitation and suppression, Africans would have been able to make their own cake, albeit perhaps a different one, instead of depending on the North's crumbs, seems unthinkable. This is not surprising given the many factors making such a notion unthinkable: The racist image of 'the incompetent African' in the global North; the factual existence – historically and contemporarily – of exploitation and suppression that limits the political, economic, and social agency of people and governments in the global South; the quasi-religious belief in the universality and infallibility of neoliberal economic thinking and 'development'; the structure of the capitalist world-system, in which most African countries have a fixed position as peripheries and very few have a chance to become semiperipheries, but probably not more.

The emphasis on 'subsistence farming' in the global South and especially in large parts of rural Africa creates the impression that agriculture in such regions is something very 'local', even 'private'. Yash Tandon reminds us that the opposite is the case. Agriculture in the global South, whether subsistence or not, even when practiced at the edge of starvation, is strongly globalised. Tandon provides the following list of reasons for increasing food insecurity in the global South: First, there is *global warming*, a result of environmental pollution that has been produced all over the world, but especially in the global North, over the past centuries and has started to confuse the weather patterns that farmers have been relying on for generations. Second, *chemical fertilisers and means of transport*, which are both supposed to raise productivity and market access for farmers, become more and more expensive due to fuel prices (Tandon leaves their effect on global warming unmentioned). Third, small producers are affected by *land grabbing* practiced by larger players in commercial agricultural production. Fourth, land is being *repurposed from food production to the production of commercial commodities* (Tandon mentions biofuels, yet the same applies to other cash crops such as coffee or sugar cane). Fifth, the IMF's structural adjustment programmes have forced states to abolish food production subsidies and food reserves on local levels. As a result, even the smallest farmer *depends on market forces, intermediaries, and international corporations* that hold the patents for seeds and fertilisers. Sixth, food prices are affected by *financial speculation*. Seventh, the USA and the European Union keep up their subsidies and, by doing that, their monopoly on the global market for agricultural commodities (Tandon 2016, 37). Several of these aspects were subject to lively narrations by interviewees of this study (see chapter 8.2).

In summary, though the question whether globalisation benefits or harms Africa is debatable, few scholars still doubt the continent's intensive involvement in the world economy and the fact that its populations have been affected by it in one way or another (Cooper 1993, 84). Ferguson concludes that what we find in Africa nowadays is "not a lamentably immature form of globalization, but a unique 'advanced' and sophisticated mutation of it" (Ferguson 2006, 41). This thesis was informed by my interest in the features of this 'mutation', especially with regard to its impacts on the everyday lives of ordinary people. Although the phenomena described in this sub-section – neoliberalism, world trade, global financial institutions, SAPs, PRGFs, and PRSPs – appear as though they were reserved for academic and political discourse, their consequences are evident in everyday life. In this study, interviewees eagerly highlighted effects of liberalisation and privatisation such as food prices, school fees, hospital bills, the profitability and trade channels of (cash) crops, and the availability of new products (see chapter 8 for details).

3.4 Globalisation from the world-systems perspective

> "The ideological celebration of so-called globalization is in reality the swan song of our historical system. We have entered into the crisis of this system." (Wallerstein 1998, 32)

As John Glenn has put it, "globalization is portrayed in the literature as involving an increasing number of countries becoming ever more integrated into the global economic system" (Glenn 2007, 70). Consequently, the world-systems perspective seems predestined for dealing with globalisation, as it analyses exactly this process. Yet, it must be kept in mind that world-systems analysis has a very specific perspective, as discussed in chapter 2.3. This is simultaneously its merit and its flaw. On the one hand, it is a limited perspective that cannot stand on its own but needs other perspectives to complement it. On the other hand, it introduces a point of view to the debate that differs from most others. This enables the analyst to step out of the mainstream 'globalisation hysteria' and approach the phenomenon from a different direction.

The majority of approaches to globalisation, regardless of their theoretical or political background or their discipline of origin, consider it a kind of 'end of history', a condition that is inevitably going to shape the future in its own image. In that regard, globalisation continues the strategy of its precursors and cornerstones, namely capitalism and 'development'. After the Cold War, those ideas had become so hegemonic that the largest part of the world population started believing (and still does) they were without alternative. As outlined in chapter 2.3.3, Immanuel Wallerstein hypothesised that the capitalist world-system must follow the path of every other world-system, meaning it has to die (Wallerstein 2007, 76-77; 2017, 64, 95, 102). In his view, the transition we are currently in is much more significant, with a much more uncertain outcome than anything that the powerful try to make us believe with their 'globalisation' narrative (Wallerstein 2003, 45-46). What should be expected from that transition is not a homogenous world formed in the image of the successful capitalists, but *the end* of the capitalist world-system and the beginning of a new era, the parameters of which have not yet been defined. That is why, for Wallerstein, it is less important to decide how to react to processes of global capitalism, but rather how to react when they wear off (ibid.). Greig et al. point out how Wallerstein builds on the work of Karl Marx, arguing that socio-political factors such as worldwide increasing costs of labour and a rising tax burden due to social services provision, as well as a steady increase of commodity prices due to excessive exploitation, are finally going to make production uneconomical (Greig et al. 2007, 166). Wallerstein calls social services provision "the pay-off utilized to tame the 'dangerous classes', that is, to keep the class struggle within limited bounds" (Wallerstein 2003, 63). Consequently, that pay-off must be raised in case of rising unemployment and social insecurity.

Nevertheless, the most serious problem is the rising mistrust in the state, which weakens the latter (Wallerstein 1998, 45-48). According to Wallerstein, liberalism had been the dominant ideology that had made people believe in the chance that the future would bring a reduction of the capitalist world-system's economic and social polarisation, since the middle of the nineteenth century. The growing disenchantment concerning this hope is what has started to weaken the states worldwide since the end of the 1970s (Wallerstein 1998, 47-48). The problems of increasing costs of labour, the rising tax burden, and the rising costs of exploitation and destruction of the natural environment have so far been successfully dealt with by means of neoliberalism (ibid., 46). In contrast to its self-image, Wallerstein defines neoliberalism as an approach of capitalists to master the above-mentioned challenges with the help of states (ibid.). The latter are needed to implement neoliberal policies, which serve "to weaken the bargaining position of workers", reduce the capitalists' tax burden "without a reduction of state services (direct and indirect) to capitalist producers, and severe limits on the internalization of costs", e.g., for disposal of industrial waste and other forms of pollution (ibid.). The crux of the matter is that capitalists need a strong state for the "implementation of their interests", "for reasons of political legitimacy" (Hirsch 2001,

124, translation by E.K.), or as Wallerstein puts it, for securing the quasi-monopolies on which they build their capital accumulation (Wallerstein 2003, 65-66). The insight that capitalists need the state can even be found on the part of some neoliberal thinkers, for example Martin Wolf. He points out that all major institutions of the capitalist market economy "depend on institutional arrangements underpinned by the state as creator and enforcer of the law" (Wolf 2018, 48). Joachim Hirsch is optimistic that the state's monopoly on the use of force will persist and grant the state an important role despite its transformation through internationalisation (Hirsch 2001, 121-124). Wallerstein, in contrast, suggests that even this basic function of the state is in peril due to the disappointment of entire populations with the failure of their governments to ameliorate their living conditions (Wallerstein 2003, 65). His position, however, should not be confused with that of "hyperglobalist" thinkers, who declared in the 1990s that globalisation would dissolve all borders (literally, i.e., of nation states, and figuratively) (Jones 2010, 12). Wallerstein does not claim that the state disappears, but that its position is weakened by the decline of confidence its citizens have in it. He observes fierce "antistatism" on the part of "the world workforce" (Wallerstein 1998, 48) or "the masses of the world" (Wallerstein 2003, 65). The declining credibility of the state, which is supposed to facilitate and legitimise capital accumulation, becomes the most serious problem for the capitalist world-system (ibid., 65-66). Considering the perspective of 'globalisation' as the expansion of the capitalist world-system, this assertion leads to the conclusion that globalisation is not immortal, either. Rather, it is another anecdote in the *longue durée* of socio-economic history and will one day give way to something else. Like Philip McMichael (McMichael 2012, 80), Wallerstein states that globalisation has replaced 'development' as the 'great concept' that is expected to advance the socio-economic progress of the world, especially that of countries of the global South. Nevertheless, Wallerstein goes one step further than McMichael by claiming that even the concept of 'globalisation' has already started to follow the downfall of 'development' in the eyes of its disenchanted 'beneficiaries' (Wallerstein 2017, 90).

For the first decades of the twenty-first century, i.e., the last decades of the current world-system, Wallerstein defines three fights, the outcomes of which are going to shape the transitional period to the next world-system(s). The first fight is the competition among the European Union, the USA, and Japan for domination in the capitalist world-system. The second fight is the struggle between the global North and the global South. The third fight is the dispute about the parameters for the world-system(s) to come after the current one between "the spirit of Davos" (*World Economic Forum*: the privileged, who want the new system to be as exploitative as the old one, or even worse) and "the spirit of Porto Alegre" (*World Social Forum*: those who want more egalitarian and democratic principles for the new world-system(s)) (Wallerstein 2003, 273, see also 288-290). The time of transition that has already begun becomes increasingly chaotic until the system finally fails to restore equilibrium and collapses (Wallerstein 1998, 63). Though he admits that this might sound frightening, Wallerstein assures us that, on the contrary, it is a great chance because, as long as the system is still strong enough to restore its equilibrium, there is no way to achieve essential change. According to Wallerstein, we live in exciting times. We might become not only witnesses, but designers of significant historical changes – yet, we have to pay for that opportunity with uncertainty about the outcome of the change and with personal insecurity during the chaotic time of transition (ibid., 62-64). Wallerstein calls for everybody to participate in the negotiations about the system(s) to come after the current one, which are already ongoing in civil society (Wallerstein 2007, 76-77, 89-90; 2017, 64-65, 102, 104, 106-107). Yet, he cautions that the task is not to make up "utopias", i.e., "dreams of heaven that could never exist on earth" (Wallerstein 1998, 1). He names the visions that are needed "utopistics" and defines the process to produce them as "serious assessment of historical alternatives, the exercise of our judgement as to the substantive reality of alternative possible historical systems", "the sober, rational, and realistic evaluation of human social systems" (ibid.).

The institutions in charge of the above-described complex task are academia (Wallerstein 1998, 2) and social movements (Wallerstein 2017, 106-107). States or other political institutions cannot play a significant role in it because it is a symptom of the demise of the system that people turn away from those institutions and seek refuge in "extrastate self-defence structures" (Wallerstein 1998, 50). In Wallerstein's view, it is the task of social movements to implement the following four-point-strategy: First and foremost, there must be an open debate about alternatives for the future. This may sound easy yet it is difficult to implement in practice. Second, social movements must encourage their supporters to exercise their right to vote, not in the hope of being able to change the unchangeable current system for the better, but to moderate (at least partly) its negative repercussions on the present situation (Wallerstein 2003, 270-271). Third, there is a need for "interim, middle-range goals" (ibid., 271). Wallerstein suggests the objective of decommodification, which for him means more than opposing the current tendency to make everything into commodities, even hospitals, water, or the human body. Beyond that, he suggests reversing the commodification of industries, especially those that seem to have failed or to be failing. What he suggests is not nationalisation, but the installation of "structures, operating in the market, whose objective is performance and survival rather than profit" (ibid.). Fourth, there need to be concrete long-term goals for a more egalitarian and democratic world – though Wallerstein acknowledges that there will always be limits to equality and democracy (ibid.). Points 1 (open debate about alternatives for the future) and 4 (long-term goals) comply with the major objective of the Post-Development approach to find alternatives to conventional notions of development (see chapter 2.2.3). The above-mentioned "extrastate self-defence structures" (Wallerstein 1998, 50) can be forums for discussions about and testing of such alternatives. This is where the two approaches, Post-Development and Wallerstein's version of world-systems analysis, have similar research interests. Those self-defence structures can have various manifestations, e.g., social movements with explicit political goals, but also *alternative economic practices*, in which this study is particularly interested.

Samir Amin comments that the 'catch up'-promise that proponents of globalisation make to countries of the global South is, in reality, "nothing of the sort" (Amin 2004, 7). He bases his argument on the classic core-periphery model as described in chapter 2.3. In most cases in which peripheries seem to 'develop' economically, what really happens is that all members of the system, including the centres, 'develop' in the same proportion (ibid., 6). As a result, the distance between the members of the system – and the marginalised position of the peripheries – remains unchanged. Amin warns that the common lamentations about countries of the global South not being sufficiently integrated into the world economy, i.e., about them being 'marginalised', make no sense. He emphasises that they *are* fully integrated, only that their role as peripheries is different from that of centres – nevertheless, both are fixed. As a result, there is no point in the policies of the Bretton Woods institutions claiming to 'integrate them into the world economy' in order to give them access to the 'blessings' of the global market (ibid., 14). Africa was even among the first regions to gradually be integrated into the global system, from the inception of the latter in 1500 up to the demise of formal colonialism in the 1960s. The results of that integration were extensive exploitation of African natural and human resources by the colonisers, a century of delay of "any commencement of an agricultural revolution", and the violent prevention of the formation of a local middle class throughout the whole colonial period (ibid.). Although unequal regional development has been a natural phenomenon throughout human history, Amin acknowledges "that polarization has become the immanent byproduct of the integration of the entire planet into the capitalist system" only in modern times (Amin 1998, 1). The global North secures its position of power in the current world-system through a number of monopolies, namely the monopoly on innovative technologies (especially for production), the control of international financial institutions and financial markets, its monopoly on information (through media and science), and its monopoly on certain military technologies (Amin 1998, 4-5; Wallerstein 2003, 281). In addition, there is the global North's "[m]onopolistic access to the planet's natural resources" (Amin 1998, 5), which is of course secured by means of the other monopolies. Samir Amin concludes on globalisation as the expansion of the capitalist world-system: "The logic of this globalization consists of organizing apartheid on a global scale." (Amin 2004, 7) Unlike Wallerstein, Amin believed in the possibility to change the current world-system and called for it to be changed into worldwide socialism (Amin 1998, 42).

A famous concept for countries of the global South that arose from such considerations is 'delinking'. Samir Amin has presented his own version of it, distancing himself from the general perception of the concept of delinking, which equates it with autarky (Amin 1990, 62). He defines his concept of delinking as the "pursuit of a system of rational criteria for economic options founded on a law of value on a national basis with popular relevance, independent of such criteria of economic rationality as flow from the dominance of the capitalist law of value operating on a world scale" (ibid., 62). Amin emphasises that relations with the outside world, especially import of technologies and export in order to afford them, is indispensable, though in the delinked model it should be of secondary importance in relation to national priorities (ibid., 66-67). The delinked society in Amin's model would be a predominantly agricultural society that renounces "the dominant forms of private ownership of land and factories" and realises "the most egalitarian possible income distribution (notably between rural earnings and workers' pay)" (ibid., 63). The pricing system as well as the wage system would be inferred from the net output being shared between urban and rural sectors according to the contingent of labour contributed by them (ibid.). Amin admits that this is a model "of national and popular development that may lead to socialism", but he repudiates any tendency to "[n]ostalgic culturalist nationalism", which he rather considers "a symptom of the crisis [of development] and not an answer to it" (ibid., 67).

Sabelo Ndlovu-Gatsheni, though showing great appreciation of Samir Amin's thoughts, critiques them in two ways. In general, Ndlovu-Gatsheni accuses Amin of being unable to free himself from the Eurocentrism he criticises (Ndlovu-Gatsheni 2013, 11). More specifically focused on Amin's concept of 'delinking', Ndlovu-Gatsheni queries the possibility of responding to a challenge that has global causes with measures on a local or national level (ibid., 10). Ramón Grosfoguel likewise criticises dependency theory and world-systems analysis in general for having created the expectation that socialist reforms at the national level could serve to detach the respective country from the global system (Grosfoguel 2008, 101; 2011, 21). However, such a reproach could rather be addressed to Amin and authors with approaches similar to his than to Wallerstein, who would most likely have agreed with Grosfoguel. Samir Amin, for his part, counters such arguments with the reasoning that, though we must strive for a "better world order", it remains an illusion as long as the countries involved do not review their national policies (Amin 1990, 68). Wallerstein's position is similar, though with the inverse emphasis: While he admits the necessity of "short-run local meliorations" for countries of the global South, especially in Africa, his focus of interest is on "middle-run transformation of values and structures" on the national, international, and global level (Wallerstein 2017, 65). Furthermore, the concept of delinking does not fit into Wallerstein's argumentation, as for him, there is no escape from the capitalist world-system. One may sympathise either with Amin's concrete suggestions for a delinked and socialist world order, or rather with Wallerstein's insistence on the need for open-ended public negotiations over the parameters for the world-system(s) to come. In either case, world-systems analysis allows us to leave any kind of – neoliberal as well as critical – mainstream thinking about globalisation behind and approach it from a different point of view. Beyond that, it shows Africa's 'integration in the world economy' from a different perspective than the alleged 'marginalisation' that is decried by most neoliberal and many critical observers alike.

3.5 Resistance to globalisation in the global South and in the global North

With reference to both the global South and the global North, Verity Burgmann states: "Incessant marketization—a hallmark of capitalist globalization—has spawned new forms of community-based resistance" (Burgmann 2008, 245). As Nikita Dhawan and Shalini Randeria aptly point out, alter-globalisation activists, be it from the global South, the global North, or an alliance of both, "do not simply oppose globalization" but try to promote "alternative visions of globality that could provide a just alternative to the current processes of corporate-driven cultural and economic globalization, tame its forces, and mitigate its injustices" (Dhawan/ Randeria 2016, 575). This is the reason why most of them prefer the expression '*alter*-globalisation movement' or sometimes expressions like "the 'social movement', the 'citizens' movement' or the 'global justice movement'" to that of '*anti*-globalisation movement' (George 2004, ix). Susan George clarifies this point: "The movement is not 'anti' but internationalist and deeply engaged with the world as a whole and the fate of everyone who shares the planet" (ibid.). Since the mid-1990s, a worldwide increase in protest movements of that kind can be observed (Brand 2005, 7; Dhawan/ Randeria 2016, 575). Privatisation and austerity measures that have been forced upon the populations of countries of the global South by the Bretton Woods institutions, through structural adjustment programmes and similar measures, have been raising protest in several countries since the 1980s (Burgmann 2008, 245). Burgmann quotes the examples of workers of the Indian state power company, who went on strike in 2000, hoping to prevent its privatisation, and that of the frequent "riots against austerity measures in Argentina" (ibid.). Stuart Hall et al. mention "the water and gas wars in Bolivia, and the struggle of 'the poors' in Thailand" as well as some "progressive governments and grassroots social movements in Latin America" as examples for the alter-globalisation movement in the global South (Hall et al. 2015a, 12). Joseph Stiglitz states: "Virtually every major meeting of the International Monetary Fund, the World Bank, and the World Trade Organization is now the scene of conflict and turmoil" (Stiglitz 2002, 3). He points out that protest in the global South is as old as "austerity programs", yet had been unnoticed until protesters *from the global North* had appeared on the scene (ibid.). Meanwhile, diverse forms of protest movements have formed, on the local, national, and international level; in the global South, in the global North, and as South-North-cooperations.

A prominent example is the *World Social Forum* (WSF), an annual meeting of alter-globalist activists from different spheres of civil society around the world that took place for the first time in Porto Alegre, Brazil, in 2001, and that has the famous slogan "Another world is possible" (Hawley 2008, 23). Wallerstein calls the alter-globalisation movement "the spirit of Porto Alegre" and predicts it will be particularly important in the worldwide political struggles of the decades ahead (Wallerstein 2017, 95). Under the umbrella of opposition against neoliberalism with its negative social consequences, the WSF unites new and old movements from the global North as well as from the global South (Wallerstein 2003, 268-269). Beyond the regular meetings, there are publications of the *World Social Forum*, which mainly deal with the topics of "the production of wealth and social reproduction", "access to wealth and sustainability", "civil society and public space", and "political power and ethics in the new society" (Hawley 2008, 24). As Hawley points out, there is no common policy at the WSF. Reformist approaches stand side by side with revolutionist ones, de-growth with pro-growth champions, nationalists with proponents of local governance and those who believe in reformed global institutions. The main common goal of the WSF is to make global society truly democratic and, as such, accountable to all its members, also and especially the weakest, whose needs and liberties are not being respected in the current system (ibid., 25). Edward Osei Kwadwo Prempeh emphasises that "one of the major strengths of the deglobalization movement is its embrace of, and respect for, difference" (Prempeh 2008, 60). He insists that this movement of movements is more than just another initiative by the global North; rather the global South, and particularly African movements and organisations, contribute to it significantly (ibid., 60-61). Prempeh reminds us that Africa has a long tradition of anticapitalist resistance dating back to the anticolonial struggles, which were struggles against political and military oppression as much as against capitalist exploitation of African populations. As a result, he regards the African alter- or de-globalisation movement as a continuation of the tradition of African anticolonial liberation struggles, not as a mere copy of social movements of the global North. The turn from a general anticapitalistic orientation to the specific opposition to globalisation took place in the 1980s, starting with "the so-called IMF riots against the neoliberal emphasis on austerity, privatization, deregulation, and trade liberalization", which raised "mass consciousness against neoliberal globalization in Africa" (ibid., 61). What started as scattered struggles began to coordinate in 2000 (ibid.).

The *African Social Forum* (ASF), which took place in Bamako (2002), Johannesburg (2002), Addis Ababa (2003), and Lusaka (2004), "[u]nder the theme 'Another Africa Is Possible'" played a very important role in this process (Prempeh 2008, 62). Unfortunately, the last meeting was taken over by professional NGOs, meaning 'development' professionals paid by so-called non-governmental organisations that, to a large extent, receive their funds from the global North (ibid., 68). As I was not able to find traces of further meetings of the ASF in the literature or on the internet, I assume that this takeover by the 'development' apparatus has (temporarily?) put an end to its dynamic grassroots activities. This is quite possible, as many of those NGOs are representatives of the international development apparatus rather than of grassroots movements. A 'Google'-search displays some scattered regional fora, e.g., in Southern or Western Africa. Though this aspect of African resistance deserves further investigation and illustrates the important point that such forms of resistance are anything but unknown in Africa, it is not central to the topic of this thesis.

The above overview outlines some examples of resistance to globalisation in the sense of political struggle, specifically the international alter-globalisation scene. While the literature in this domain is vast, within this thesis I focus on the way people react to globalisation *within the sphere of their everyday life*, not in the public or political sphere. For example, Hassan Zaoual sees "defence mechanisms" at work within African societies being penetrated by capitalism and, in order to protect their social fabric, "marginaliz[ing] projects as they do capitalism as a whole" (Zaoual 1998, 35). In this thesis, I am interested in considering the following questions: Does such everyday resistance exist in the researched region? If yes, what does it look like? In either case, how do people adapt to the new capitalist structures? Do adaptation and resistance exist side by side? If yes, what does that look like?

3.6 Conclusion

This study focusses on globalisation as economic process. In chapter 3.1, I explained that my understanding of globalisation refers to growing economic interconnectedness on an international level, being enabled by the liberalisation of world trade and international capital flows as well as by the spread of communication technologies. The political, social, and cultural dimensions of globalisation are also of high significance for this study, yet they are regarded as *consequences* of the above-sketched *economic* processes. First and foremost, globalisation as it is taking place today is a phenomenon of capitalism, which needs expansion to fulfil its core objective of endless accumulation of capital. This makes firms move around the globe in search of cheap raw materials and labour as well as for new markets. The approach to globalisation in this study was categorised as 'transformationalist', i.e., based on the assumption that the interconnectedness of the world economy is not a new phenomenon, yet it has accelerated in the past 30 to 40 years. Major factors of acceleration were the increasing saturation of home markets of the core countries, neoliberal ideology, and technical innovations such as means of faster communication, transport of goods and people, and transfer of capital.

In sub-sections 3.2, 3.3, and 3.4, globalisation was described from the points of view of the three schools of thought presented in chapter 2. In chapter 3.2, I presented the approach of postcolonial theory to globalisation. In brief, postcolonial analysis of globalisation regards the latter as the continuation of the global North's exploitation of the global South that has begun under colonialism. Postcolonial thinkers analyse how neoliberal common sense has been spread by globalisation and how it has been used by the global North to exert political pressure on the global South. Through neoliberal policies, new forms of economic and social marginalisation for the lower classes and rural populations in the global South have been introduced. While the emphasis on the victimisation of actors in the global South is strong in some approaches, others emphasise the *agency* of people living in the global South. Alternative economic practices, as they are being examined in this study, can be regarded as such a form of agency. Chapter 3.3 described the relationship between globalisation and development from a critical perspective. The conventional discourse of 'development' is closely interrelated with that of 'globalisation', the major difference being that the former emphasises capitalist economic development *on a national level*, while the latter emphasises capitalist economic development *on a global level* (McMichael 2012). Parallels between the spheres of globalisation and 'development' can also be found on the institutional level. The International Monetary Fund (IMF), the World Bank, and the World Trade Organization (WTO) play leading roles in the global coordination of both processes. In chapter 3.3, I presented various examples of effects of their interventions on the lives of people in the global South from the literature. In chapter 8, I present my own research results with regard to such effects.

As Ngila Mwase aptly points out, it is not easy to identify the traces of globalisation on the micro level, e.g., in rural households in Africa (Mwase 2007, 66). It is possible, however. James Ferguson states that African countries "have arguably suffered the most from the lethal IMF dogmatism", which has been described above (Ferguson 2006, 25-26). As a result, people have witnessed exploding cost of living, due to rising food prices and the privatisation of education and health care. Small-scale farmers have lost state-subsidised farming inputs, extension programmes, and the option to sell their crops through cooperative societies. The popular claim that Africa's alleged 'lack of development' originates from its 'lack of integration into the world economy' has been discussed. In both chapters 3.3 (from the perspective of critical development studies) and 3.4 (from the perspective of world-systems analysis), I concluded that the assumption of Africa's 'lack of integration into the world economy' does not apply. Africa has been integrated into the capitalist world-system since colonialism (Amin 2004; Ferguson 2006; Wallerstein 2011). In chapter 3.4, I highlighted the contribution that world-systems analysis can make to the globalisation debate. Though its perspective is too limited to stand on its own, its peculiar approach enriches the debate considerably. Wallerstein's assertion that the capitalist world-system is just one world-system like others and will give way to one or more other world-system(s) one day (Wallerstein 2003/ 2007/ 2017), denied the irrevocability that globalisation is associated with in many other approaches. Wallerstein suggests that it is not only possible but even necessary to think and discuss about alternatives to the way in which the capitalist world-system works. He sees the highest potential for creative alternative ideas in the global South, especially in Africa (see chapter 2.3.3). He shares this interest in alternatives to capitalist development, especially alternatives from the global South, with the representatives of the Post-Development approach (though many of the latter would explain differently why those alternatives are needed; see chapter 2.2.3). Chapter 3.5 was a brief excursus into international resistance to globalisation, e.g., in the shape of the *World Social Forum* and the *African Social Forum*. However, within this thesis, I focus on the way people react to globalisation *within the sphere of their everyday life*, not in the political sphere.

This chapter has outlined a critical perspective on globalisation in general and particularly with regard to its impact on the global South. Nevertheless, as I clarified in the conclusion to chapter 2, my objective is not to substantiate a particular theory by collecting evidence for it from the respondents of this study, but to add a new point of view to the discussion. Of course, it cannot be *their* point of view. Tied to my positionality as a privileged white outsider to their communities, I can only present *my* point of view, not that of the researched (see chapter 5.1 for details of this discussion). However, I can decide how to prioritise the various influences that shape my point of view. Hence, I tried my best to prioritise the perspectives of the researched.

4. Searching for alternatives: The Social and Solidarity Economy (SSE)

The famous slogan by Margaret Thatcher "There is no alternative", followed by the respective policies that seemed to allow no reversal, gave the impression to the world population that neoliberalism is indeed without alternative (Altvater 2006, 9). The alter-globalisation movement, the representatives of which do not accept this taboo on alternatives, has many facets. In addition to spawning various forms of political resistance like demonstrations, petitions, and public awareness raising, it has produced several ideas regarding opposition to neoliberal capitalism in everyday practices. As Boaventura de Sousa Santos and César A. Rodríguez-Garavito aptly point out, "alternative economic initiatives and visions are extremely diverse" and can be found in the form of macro- and micro-economic approaches (Santos/ Rodríguez-Garavito 2007, xviii). Those approaches usually have theoretical/ academic as well as practical expressions. Many ideas promoted by the representatives of those various approaches are not new but rather combine existing knowledge with recent experiences, attempting to think beyond both. This study is inspired by one of those approaches, namely the concept of the *Social and Solidarity Economy* (SSE). The term 'solidarity' in the thesis title derives from this concept. Understanding SSE is a prerequisite for answering the part of my research questions that asks: "What kind of alternative economic activities based on solidarity do or did people in Busoga practise? Did those activities persist in spite of, dissolve because of, or emerge as a reaction to globalisation?" With regard to the first question, I need to explain what I consider "alternative economic activities based on solidarity", namely SSE activities. The second question requires analysis of the relationship between such activities and capitalism[28]. I cover both of these tasks in this chapter.

This chapter introduces the basic ideas underlying SSE (4.2.1), a concrete example of SSE in practice (4.2.2), the discussion of SEE's relation to capitalism (4.2.1 and 4.2.3), and its relation to similar concepts of alternative economic practice (4.3.1 to 4.3.3). I bookend this portrait of SSE through a brief introduction to alternative economic practices in Africa at

28 As has been explained in chapter 3, in this thesis globalisation is defined as the global expansion of capitalism.

the beginning (4.1) and a conclusion that links SSE to the theoretical and empirical approach of my study (4.4). In order to illustrate SSE in practice, chapter 4.2.2 discusses cooperatives in general and in Uganda, in particular. Neither in Uganda nor in general do cooperatives represent the only form of SSE activities, yet these have been researched most extensively and thus can best illustrate what an SSE activity can look like as well as what kind of ambiguities and difficulties must be confronted when dealing with them. In addition to that, they are the form of SSE activities that I could be sure of finding in the scope of my research in the Busoga region, as it is known that cooperatives exist all over Uganda (see chapter 4.2.2). Whether other forms of SSE exist there, and what they look like, has been part of my research questions. Further information on the cooperatives, as well as on other forms of SSE activities I encountered during my research in Busoga, can be found in chapter 8.3.

4.1 *Africa as a location of alternative economic practices*

Africa is repeatedly being presented as "a peculiar exception" to the supposed norm of "global markets and economic growth" (Cooper 2009, 42, translation by E.K.). As Frederick Cooper aptly points out, this norm has been established by the powerful, in this case Europe and Northern America, but has no claim to universal validity. He challenges the assumption that capitalism is the 'natural' peak of economic development and that any society that does not reach there (fast) has to apologise for that 'failure' (ibid., 42-43). Cooper's underlying argument is that the structure of African societies, supported by the continent's geography, have ever since resisted any claim, be it by local elites or by intruders, to exercising total power over their populations. In his view, Africa's current situation does not display a failure but rather "the result of a partial success of a big number of people struggling to block, to divert, or to use in their own interest foreign endeavours for gaining economic supremacy" (ibid., 47, translation by E.K.). Cooper's generalisation of 'Africa' might look problematic at first sight, yet he does not reproduce the image of a homogenous 'Africa' or of 'traditional African societies' (see chapter 2.4, keywords "Africa" and "Traditional"). He stresses that, what African societies have in common, to his mind, is not based on tradition, but on inventiveness and diversity (ibid., 58). His approach complements Hassan Zaoual's above-mentioned assertion that "defence mechanisms" are at work within African societies, which are getting penetrated by capitalism and, in order to protect their social fabric, "marginalize projects[29] as they do capitalism as a whole" (Zaoual 1998, 35). Against that background, it does not come as a surprise that "[t]he 'alternatives to development' put forward by the post-development authors are located in grassroots movements, urban and rural local communities and the informal sector" (Ziai 2007, 5). Sally Matthews weaves the practical experience of the Senegalese NGO Enda Graf Sahel and Post-Development theory together, coming up with the hypothesis that many communities of "the poor and the oppressed [...] are indeed actively and effectively responding to their situation" (Matthews 2007, 135). After having realised that their classical development approach of imposing projects on the target population had completely failed (ibid., 132-133), the staff of Enda Graf decided to switch to an approach of "accompanying popular dynamics", "seeking to build upon *the community's ways* of addressing their problems" (ibid., 133, emphasis by E.K.).

The most interesting element within Cooper's, Matthews', and Zaoual's argumentations is that they resist the usual portrayal of Africans as allegedly passive and powerless victims of external forces that intervene in their lives: colonisers, 'developers', the Bretton Woods institutions, foreign business enterprises. There is no doubt that Africans have been and still are subject to those interventions, yet the typical Eurocentric portrayals of Africans' helplessness much too readily deny the latter of their agency. In the majority of descriptions of these interventions, Africans (or people in the global South in general) have only two options: 1. They 'succeed', which means that they become part of the global middle class by adapting to the new circumstances dictated by the intruders. As has been discussed in chapters 2 and 3, it is safe to assume that the structure of the capitalist world-system does not allow a great number of people to do so. That seems to imply that the majority ends up with option two: 2. They 'fail', meaning that they eke out a miserable existence in absolute poverty and isolation. The approaches of Cooper, Matthews, and Zaoual, just as many Post-Development authors (see chapter 2.2.3) and many representatives of alternative economic approaches such as SSE (see subsequent chapters) open our eyes to another possibility: What if the people in the global South 'fail' in the eyes of their capitalist 'developers' because they do not improve significantly with regard to the latter's 'development indicators' and yet they find their own ways to get along? In that case, their alleged 'failure' would turn out to be a form of resistance, regardless of whether it

29 Referring to projects of capitalist development.

would be done for political reasons or out of necessity to survive within a system that is hostile towards them.

As has been stated above repeatedly, there is a need to beware of any dichotomisation of the 'modern', 'developed' (no matter whether those terms are used with a positive or with a negative connotation) capitalist global North on the one hand and a romanticised version of a 'traditional African' society that is based on reciprocity and solidarity, on the other hand. As I show in the remainder of this chapter, SSE is a modern phenomenon. Consequently, SSE activities cannot be misused for trying to prove the existence of a romanticised 'traditional African society' based on reciprocity. Nevertheless, autochthonous forms of cooperation and solidarity are of interest in this study as well. Frédéric Thomas proposes that autochthonous solidarity structures in rural African societies are a good foundation on which modern SSE activities can grow (Thomas 2015, 10-11). What is more, this is where Santos' clarion call for learning from "suppressed, silenced, or marginalized realities" in the global South can come in (Santos 2014, 157). People's experiences with autochthonous solidarity structures can have significant effects on the way they practise and judge modern solidary activities. For those reasons, I asked interviewees in this study about both autochthonous and modern forms of solidarity structures. During conversations with the interviewees and analysis of the interviews, those two forms have been strictly separated.[30]

4.2 The Social and Solidarity Economy (SSE)[31]

The theory of the *Social and Solidarity Economy* (SSE) is not yet widespread. Some of its practical manifestations, especially those of the *Social Economy* like cooperatives and other social enterprises, are being applied in the scope of 'development' practice. Others are not well known. However, the concept arouses more and more interest, especially on the part of the alter-globalisation movement on its quest for alternatives to neoliberal

---

30 Details on this point can be found in chapter 8.3, especially in sub-section 8.3.1.

31 Excerpts of this chapter have been presented in the scope of the talk "Eine "Financial Democratization von unten"?" ("Financial democratisation" bottom-up?) at the 27th Scientific Congress of the DVPW (Deutsche Vereinigung für Politikwissenschaft/ German Political Science Association) "Frontiers of Democracy" (25-28/09/18), within the panel "'Financial Democracy' und die Finanzialisierung von Entwicklung" ('Financial Democracy' and the financialisation of development) on 26 September 2018, in Frankfurt/Main, Germany.

economic practices, in its academic arm as well as in its activist arm. Peter Utting comments on the recent "surge of interest within scholarly and advocacy circles to explain what exactly SSE is, to analyse its alternative potential, measure its scale, document good practices, examine its regional manifestations and variations, and identify public policies and legal arrangements that can enable SSE" (Utting 2015, 3). This sub-section provides an introduction to the concept of SSE (4.2.1) and presents a concrete example of its practical implementation, namely cooperatives (4.2.2). I describe the latter in general as well as specifically in the context of Uganda. The sub-section closes with a brief discussion of a common reproach to certain SSE activities, namely that they are acting as a kind of 'repair workshop' for capitalism, de-politicising the fight against its negative effects by mitigating them (4.2.3).

4.2.1 Introduction to the Social and Solidarity Economy (SSE)

The term 'solidarity' in the title of this thesis refers to the concept of Social and Solidarity Economy (SSE). SSE can be defined as "forms of economic activity that prioritise social and often environmental objectives, and involve producers, workers, consumers and citizens acting collectively and in solidarity" (Utting 2015, 1). Another important characteristic is its accessibility for social classes that are not mobile, e.g., due to poverty, and need a source of income in their area (Fall 2013, 89-90). The best-known manifestations of SSE are "cooperatives, community associations and mutuals" (Satgar 2014, 4; see also: Thomas 2015, 8; Utting 2015, 1). Community associations can be broken down further, e.g., into "myriad types of self-help groups organising to produce goods and services", "community-based saving schemes" and various "other forms of volunteering and giving" (Utting 2015, 1). Another model (which is more popular in Latin America and Asia than in Africa) is the occupation of insolvent factories by their workers, who turn them into cooperatives (Singer 2007, 6-7; 2008, 215). A 2003 survey on SSE in Brazil showed that out of 15.000 solidary enterprises with 1.5 million members, 14% were such kinds of cooperatives, 55% were other registered societies, and 27% were informal groups (Singer 2008, 217). Norman Chipakupaku gives two examples from Uganda: one association of shoeshine people and one cooperative of fisher people, who pooled their money in order to buy boats. From other African countries, he quotes examples of transport cooperatives buying bicycles conjointly and village associations harvesting, drying and storing fruit conjointly (Chipakupaku 2008, 136-137). Apart from such manifestations of SSE on a micro level, there are macro-economic approaches to it as well. For instance, the German Akademie Solidarische Ökonomie (Academy for the Solidarity Economy) suggests a host of measures, among them monetary policies that reduce the power of money and force it back into a serving function (Bender 2012, 97), a different understanding of property with corresponding legislation (Winkelmann 2012, 122-126), a switch from inflexible full-time employment to flexible part-time employment in order to realise full employment (Winkelmann 2012a, 158), and many more (Bender et al. 2012). Such macro-economic aspects cannot be examined in the scope of this study because it is focused on grassroots activities on a micro-level. Nevertheless, to know that SSE does have both micro- and macro-economic dimensions increases its political relevance.

SSE activities have potential for providing alternatives to capitalist development.[32] The *World Social Forum*, an institution of the alter-globalisation movement briefly introduced in chapter 3.5, promotes SSE (Singer 2008, 215; Utting 2015, 2). According to Elmar Altvater, SSE activities are "practical attempts at designing work and life on the basis of solidarity" (Altvater 2006, 10, translation by E.K.). As such, they actively oppose the mainstream thinking of neoliberal capitalism (ibid., 9-10). Thinking about alternatives to capitalist development is one of the cornerstones[33] of the Post-Development approach (Escobar 2012, 215; see also chapter 2.2.3). In order to oppose the dominance of capitalist thinking within the development discourse, Arturo Escobar calls for the "denaturalization of the economy [...] for instance, in the imagination of diverse economies and *social and solidarity economies* beyond the capitalistic one" (Escobar 2012, xii, emphasis by E.K.). Escobar states that alternatives can be found in communities in the global South, though it has to be kept in mind that many of them are not purely local but hybrid practices (Escobar 2012, 223). Majid Rahnema makes a similar point when stating that a deeper understanding of various local problem-solving strategies that do not comply with conventional ideas of capitalist development would be instructive for people from all over the world, who are ready to think about alternatives

32 There is also a certain danger of SSE being incorporated by capitalist development. I discuss this issue below. Here, I would like to emphasise its *potential* in terms of *alternatives*.

33 In addition to that one, other cornerstones of the Post-Development approach encompass criticising the conventional concept of development and critically analysing specific areas of intervention within development policy (Kerner 2012, 112-113; see also chapter 2.2.3 of this thesis).

(Rahnema 1998, 381). In this study, concrete SSE activities that have been encountered in Uganda are being examined with regard to their alternative potential.

A common distinction is the one between the *Solidarity Economy* pursuing radical political goals, like overcoming capitalism, and the *Social Economy* being an attempt at mitigating social problems like poverty within the scope of capitalism (Satgar 2014, 4-5, 12-15; Utting 2015, 2; Williams 2014, 37-38, 50-51, 59). Yet, the dividing line is not clear. According to Michelle Williams, "cooperation, democratic decision making, collective ownership, bottom-up processes, caring and sharing" are the most important principles of groups practicing the *Solidarity Economy* (Williams 2014, 59) – however, all are likewise fulfilled by initiatives of the *Social Economy* (ibid., 46-47). For her, the distinctive characteristics are the *Solidarity Economy's* opposition to capitalism (ibid., 51) and its emphasis on creating networks between producers and consumers (ibid., 55-56, 59). Thomas proposes that the non-uniform use of the terms derives from differing expectations that the *Social and/ or Solidarity Economy* has to fulfil in differing national, regional, or social contexts (Thomas 2015, 14-16). One example of this is the difference between the anglophone sphere, in which the *Social Economy* has become rather tame and capitalism-friendly, and the francophone sphere, where it still stands for the fight for an alternative economy (Williams 2014, 44). However, in most cases, the distinction between the *Social* and the *Solidarity Economy* is first and foremost based on the fact that the idea of the *Social Economy* is older and that there have been many cases in which it has been taken over and harnessed by capitalism and by the development apparatus (Satgar 2014, 3-4, 14; Williams 2014, 37-38, 43-44). This occurred despite the *Social Economy's* fight to reverse the subordination of social needs to the economy, which it has been fighting since the beginning of industrialisation in Europe (Williams 2014, 43-44). Those who have been disappointed by that development, place their hopes in the new approach of the *Solidarity Economy* to be more successful in resisting capitalist (mis)appropriation (Satgar 2014, 4-5; Williams 2014, 37-38). According to Thomas' analysis, 'Solidarity' is being added to the 'Social Economy' in order to free the latter from its tainted pedigree as "firefighter or shock absorber" that has been used to mitigate the negative consequences of neoliberal 'development' strategies (Thomas 2015, 21, translation by E.K.).

According to Utting, both approaches reject the neoliberal agenda in the narrow sense, prioritising social and environmental issues, not profits. Still, he distinguishes *Social Economy* approaches as acceptant of the basic rules and institutions of the capitalist system, from more radical approaches inside the *Solidarity Economy* (Utting 2015, 2). Hence, the *Social Economy* definition allows an inclusion of approaches such as Fair Trade or for-profit social enterprises in the definition of the umbrella term SSE, whereas the *Solidarity Economy* rather supports approaches like alternative currencies (ibid., 1). The *Solidarity Economy* "emphasises issues of redistributive justice, so-called 'deep' sustainability, alternatives to capitalism and the debt-based monetary system, as well as participatory democracy and emancipatory politics" (ibid., 2). Nevertheless, both the *Social* and the *Solidarity Economy* alike can be regarded as counterhegemonic to neoliberal capitalism or globalisation, as they both oppose the two main characteristics of neoliberal capitalism that have made it expand in the shape of neoliberal globalisation, namely *endless accumulation of capital* and *competition* (see chapter 3). According to Utting, "SSE is becoming an arena where two of the most powerful world views that are contesting market liberalism – namely 'embedded liberalism' and 'alter-globalisation' – are finding common ground" and "speak to, rather than past, each other" (ibid., 35). With 'embedded liberalism', he refers to the *Social Economy* after his definition, whereas he regards the *Solidarity Economy* in the narrow sense as a product of 'alter-globalisation'. For him, the potential to "effectively challenge 'business as usual'" lies in that very unification of the two trajectories under the umbrella of SSE (ibid.).

Norman Chipakupaku describes the "People's Economy", which he defines as the African version of Social and Solidarity Economy, as a necessity for survival in Africa (Chipakupaku 2008, 138-139). According to him, some such practices have always been part of African societies, while others are current reactions to the unfulfilled promises of African governments and (foreign) investors (ibid., 136-137). Their common principles are: 1. joining economic efforts in order to earn a living[34]; 2. being run by and for the sake of the local population; 3. creating local economic cycles that provide employment to locals, keeping money and facilities at their disposition; 4. preserving nature for future generations (ibid., 138). It cannot be denied that the *People's Economy* is focused on the goal of making a living rather than on that of transforming the economic or political system. Nevertheless, the *People's Economy* attempts to achieve its goal by means that oppose capitalism's logic. It counters competition

34 *Earning a living* in contrast to the capitalist principle of *accumulating capital*, from which only a few people benefit, whereas the *People's Economy* is supposed to distribute (modest) income to *many* people.

with cooperation, profit maximisation with a modest expectation to make a living, accumulation of capital with distributive justice. Consequently, though it might not be a form of conscious political struggle, in times of an almost perfect hegemony of neoliberal capitalism in all spheres of life (see chapters 2 and 3), it is indeed a form of resistance. Alternative practices are lived, notwithstanding the fact that neoliberal hegemony does not allow alternatives (see, e.g., Altvater 2006, 9-10; see also chapters 3.2 and 3.3 of this thesis).

In Boaventura de Sousa Santos' international research project *Reinventing Social Emancipation: Towards New Manifestos*, one central topic to which the second volume of the project documentation is dedicated, is alternative economic practices (Santos 2007, vii-viii). Santos calls them "solidary economy" (ibid., viii). In the introduction to that volume, Santos and César A. Rodríguez-Garavito deliberately reject the limitation of economic practices, which deserve to be taken into consideration as forward-looking 'alternatives', to those that consciously and radically oppose capitalism (Santos/ Rodríguez-Garavito 2007, xxii). They want to prevent the loss of "emancipatory potential" that lies within the forms of economic and social organisation, as well as within the values of cooperation and solidarity, which alternative practices encompass – even the ones that can also function within the scope of capitalism (ibid., xxiii). In Santos' and Rodríguez-Garavito's view, the "ability to survive in a capitalist context" is even an important characteristic of alternative economic practices because it ensures their feasibility (ibid., xxi). They state that such practices must "carve out niches of solidary production and political mobilization within the context of global capitalism" (ibid., xx) in order "to open up spaces for further transformations of capitalist values and socioeconomic arrangements" (ibid., xxi). For Brazilian economist Paul Singer, the most important characteristic of an enterprise in the *Solidarity Economy* is that it "rejects any separation between work and ownership of the means of production, the recognized basis of capitalism", meaning that all of its workers are also its owners (Singer 2007, 3).

Those difficulties of definition, delineation, and categorisation become even more difficult when we turn from theory to practice. While insisting on the above-explained distinction between the *Social Economy* and the *Solidarity Economy* in theory, Michelle Williams admits that, in practice, elements of the two often overlap, as "both seek to build local economic and social practices" (Williams 2014, 45). As my research focus is on practice, I have decided to use the umbrella term Social and Solidarity Economy (SSE) for alternative economic practices of that kind. The use of this umbrella term has been suggested by Utting (Utting 2015, 1-2, 35; see above), Thomas (2015), and by the representatives of the Mont-Blanc Meetings (MBM) of the *International Forum of the Social and Solidarity Economy Entrepreneurs* (Jeantet 2013).

If SSE is supposed to become more than a collection of curious local phenomena, namely an actual alternative movement, a favourable political framework would be helpful. This should provide, in the ideal case, "progressive taxation, particular forms of subsidy, land reform, policies associated with the care economy, and the restructuring of government transfers and incentives" (Utting 2015, 32). Yet, a favourable political and legal framework for SSE is rather a long-term objective than something that can already be found somewhere. Indeed, several countries have made first steps in that direction (e.g., Brazil, Belgium, France, Bolivia, Ecuador, Thailand, Mali) (Thomas 2015, 9-10), yet their aim was rather to facilitate SSE as an additional (and marginal) branch of the national economy, not to change the latter's orientation. Those governments – even in countries that are famous for SSE, like Brazil or Bolivia – keep on implementing policies that completely oppose the principles of SSE, at the same time as they promote it (ibid., 19). Apart from that, Thomas cautions that state intervention may indeed harm the autonomy of SSE initiatives (ibid., 16). This point plays an important role in the next sub-section (4.2.2).

On the one hand, SSE activities can be regarded as an alternative approach to a more just form of 'development' (Utting 2015, 5, 9-10). This must be the underlying expectation of the increasing promotion of SSE activities, such as cooperatives, by governments and non-governmental organisations (NGOs) in Africa (Thomas 2015, 11). On the other hand, one could think of the "social and solidarity economy as a laboratory to question the dominant paradigm in development processes" (Fall 2013, 96). For example, a farmers' association with the goal of providing market access to small-scale farmers can be a product of a typical development agency, with the goal of capital accumulation, expansion, and growth. Or it can be a self-help initiative of peasants, who prefer to cooperate with each other rather than be exploited by middlemen. A third possibility, as described by Thomas, is that the 'self-help initiative' was founded because the farmers have heard about funds that either the government or NGOs grant to such groups (Thomas 2015, 13). The danger lying in the latter variant is that the group may dissolve as soon as the members have received their material support. In any case, there is a kind of capitalist orientation in this example because the goal is 'access to markets'. Nevertheless, the opposition to capitalism lies rather in the principles on which the activities of the groups base (cooperation, distributive justice, democratic principles). It would be unrealistic to expect radical anti-capitalistic activities from such groups of producers in the global South because their members are dependent on the system that surrounds them and not in the position to change it on their own. This would require a more far-reaching network, not just individual producer associations. However, such groups can make an essential contribution to the formation of the basis for such a movement. In addition to that, as Karl Birkhölzer insists, social enterprises "like all enterprises strive for economic success", yet this success is defined differently, i.e., in social terms (Birkhölzer 2006, 68, translation by E.K.). For instance, paying wages and salaries is not an annoying cost factor that has to be reduced, as in capitalist enterprises, but it is a core objective of social enterprises to provide a source of fair income to as many people as possible (ibid.). Social enterprises do not operate for the benefit of individual owners or stockholders, but in favour of the common good (ibid., 70). Certainly, 'the common good' can mean almost anything, e.g., equal income for all members of a group, investment in local infrastructure or social purposes, even re-investment in the group's activities with the goal of making more 'profit' for 'the common good'. 'The common good' can definitely not refer to private accumulation of capital, however. Consequently, the activities of the above-mentioned farmers' association can be rated as forms of resistance because of their alternative principles. The goal of such an association with regard to expansion or growth usually is to one day become a cooperative. The next sub-section introduces cooperatives in general and the Ugandan cooperative movement in particular.

4.2.2 Cooperatives: an example of SSE in practice

Whenever authors or activists list examples for alternative economic activities or SSE activities (regardless of their respective definition of those terms), the *cooperative* is among the examples they cite. Singer even states that "[t]he production cooperative is the basic unit of the solidary economy" followed by other forms of cooperatives, such as commercial, consumer, and credit cooperatives (Singer 2007, 4). The literature and the internet have confirmed what I had already known from my professional experience: cooperatives can be found all over Uganda. For all the other possible forms of SSE, it was difficult to anticipate prior to my research which types I would encounter in Busoga. To uncover the nature of alternative economic practices in this region was part of my research quest.

However, with regard to cooperatives, I could be sure to find some in Busoga. As they are so dominant in SSE literature and wide-spread in the region I chose for my research project, they shall serve here as an illustrative example of SSE in practice.

The *International Co-operative Alliance* (ICA) defines the values of cooperatives as follows: "Cooperatives are based on the values of **self-help**, **self-responsibility**, **democracy**, **equality**, **equity**, and **solidarity**. In the tradition of their founders, cooperative members believe in the ethical values of honesty, openness, social responsibility and caring for others" (ICA 2020, emphasis in the original). The internationally acknowledged "seven cooperative principles" it represents are the following: "1. Voluntary and Open Membership", "2. Democratic Member Control", "3. Member Economic Participation", "4. Autonomy and Independence", "5. Education, Training, and Information", "6. Cooperation among Cooperatives", "7. Concern for Community" (ICA 2020; see also: Santos/ Rodríguez-Garavito 2007, xxvii). Hence, members are supposed to join the cooperative without any pressure to do so, or not to do so; they should be part of rule-setting and decision-making; with their financial contribution, they become owners of and decision-makers in the cooperative; they can decide for their cooperative to enter into collaboration with governments or other organisations (as long as this does not damage the cooperative's autonomy); they have a right to being trained by the cooperative and an obligation to be disseminators of cooperation in their social environment; they should strive for "local, national, regional and international" collaboration with other cooperatives; and they should show concern for their home community (ICA 2020; see also: Santos/ Rodríguez-Garavito 2007, xxvii). The daily administrative business is done by an executive committee that is elected by all members (ICA 2020a; Singer 2007, 3).

When it comes to the history of cooperatives, different forerunners are being identified in eighteenth (ICA 2020a) or nineteenth century Europe (Santos/ Rodríguez-Garavito 2007, xxvi). However, the Rochdale consumers' cooperatives, which were founded in England in 1844 as an attempt at escaping poverty, are usually taken for the prototype of modern cooperatives and the basis of the international cooperative movement (ICA 2020a; Santos/ Rodríguez-Garavito 2007, xxvi). The "Rochdale Pioneers" were poor weavers, who made everyday commodities available to themselves and to other poor people by purchasing those commodities in bulk and making every buyer a shareholder of the business (ICA 2020a). Hence, cooperatives are rooted in the European labour movement. This circumstance laid the foundation for the ambiguity that has been inherent to cooperatives ever since, and still is: On the one hand, the first cooperatives have been a highly political effort of people to fight their exploitation by capitalist structures, using the means of the anti-capitalist values of solidarity, cooperation, and a more equal distribution. On the other hand, they first and foremost served the survival of the poor and exploited *within* the system.

Cooperatives made their way from Europe to other countries of the world, among them African countries. According to Bruno Baeriswyl, those "products of the socio-economic conditions of Europe in the 19th century" were introduced to the colonies by "colonial administrations, European settlers, and missionaries" (Baeriswyl 1988, 16). In the case of Uganda, it is not clear where the first co-operators picked the idea from. They may have been inspired by missionaries or it may have been their own idea to form groups. In either case, it can be assumed that it was the respective legislation introduced by the colonial administration that turned those groups into cooperatives in the narrow sense, i.e., complying with international cooperative standards. Patrick Develtere has retraced that, in many African countries, cooperatives have been introduced by the colonisers, who established a suitable legal and economic framework together with them – while in other countries, like Liberia or Ethiopia, the government took over this role. Cooperatives were conceptualised first and foremost in order to optimise crops exports, with very strong government influence – despite the original idea of cooperatives as member-oriented and autonomous agencies (Develtere 2008, 2-3). This led to the problem that cooperatives were associated with the state rather than with self-organisation (ibid., 11). This problem was even aggravated after the end of formal colonialism. After independence, in most former colonies in Africa, as in Asia and Latin America, cooperatives were, to a large extent, continuously controlled by the government (ibid., 13). In some cases, state control was even extended, as cooperatives became part of nationalist development strategies (ibid.). In the 1960s, numerous institutions like the *International Labour Organization* (ILO) or development organisations discovered cooperatives as a means of the promotion of economic and social development (ibid., 16-17). Develtere states that, in the 1960s, rural cooperatives in many African countries, including Uganda, "were sponsored by numerous institutions including the World Bank, the United States Agency for International Development, national governments, churches, political parties, and private individuals and organizations" (ibid., 17-18). Membership was at least strongly encouraged, if not even made compulsory by governments (ibid., 18). About a decade later, as Develtere observed, there was a reorientation of cooperative policy in many African countries from "an instrument of realizing national economic and social objectives" to "poverty alleviation and fulfilling the basic needs of the poor" (ibid., 19) and from compulsory to voluntary membership – though incentives for voluntary commitment were still acceptable (ibid., 20). This process rekindled interest that persists until the present day and leads to the revival of old cooperatives as well as the foundation of new ones (ibid., 1).

Although Develtere insists on the lack of any autochthonous origin of cooperatives in Africa, he admits that they worked best where other forms of solidarity structures existed before, such as "work-sharing groups and burial societies", which, in many countries, "have always involved large parts of the population" (Develtere 2008, 2). This evaluation complements Thomas' above-cited hypothesis that autochthonous solidarity structures in rural African societies are a good foundation on which modern SSE activities can grow (Thomas 2015, 10-11). Develtere emphasises that "[u]nlike modern forms of cooperation and mutualism, these endogenous systems do not have built-in mechanisms for expansion or growth" (Develtere 2008, 2). While there are certain uniform characteristics of cooperatives all over the world, as well as among cooperatives with a colonial legacy, Develtere adds that there is also a specific "cooperative culture" in every country (ibid., 3). Brazil is a good example for such a peculiar cooperative culture: SSE in general, and the cooperative movement in particular, is closely entangled with workers' unions and the movement of landless rural workers. This has to do with Brazil's economic and social history (Singer 2007). Although the cooperative movement historically originated from the workers' movement, as shown above, such a strong dependency of the cooperative sector on workers' unions is not necessarily the case in every country. Some cooperative cultures base rather on peasants than workers, as in the case of Uganda.

In Uganda, the colonial division of labour had been monopolising the processing and marketing of cash crops in the hands of the colonisers and immigrants from India, who had been brought to the country by the British. The role of Ugandans was reduced to planting and harvesting the cash crops, especially coffee and cotton, for little money, such that they felt disadvantaged (Develtere 2008, 6; Kyazze 2010, 2; Nannyonjo 2015, 267). The farmers started cooperating, as Justine Nannyonjo puts it, "to help each other survive the market forces" (Nannyonjo 2015, 271) and seek protection from exploitation by "alien commercial interests" (ibid., 267). Develtere likewise states that Ugandan cooperatives came up "as a protest against the disadvantageous terms of trade imposed on the peasants"

(Develtere 2008, 6). The first association of Ugandan farmers marketing their produce cooperatively started operating in 1913, followed by others, forming the basis for the creation of the *Buganda Growers Association* at the beginning of the 1920s (ibid.; Kyazze 2010, 2; Nannyonjo 2015, 267). The latter later became the *Uganda Growers Cooperative Society* (Develtere 2008, 6-7). In 1946, the *Cooperative Societies Ordinance* created the legal basis for cooperatives in Uganda (Nannyonjo 2015, 267). The government founded an agency in charge of cooperatives, which, over the subsequent decades, would change its name and degree to which it interfered in the cooperatives' daily activities according to the policies of the respective government in power (ibid., 268-269). After 1962, the post-independence government[35] discovered cooperatives as a tool for promoting rural development, leading to the *Cooperative Societies Act* of 1963 (ibid., 268). The Ugandan government granted cooperatives "a virtual monopoly in cotton ginning and coffee factories", yet "set up state Marketing Boards to manage the export business", which were supplied by the cooperatives (Develtere 2008, 14). In 1965, Ugandan cooperative unions had a market share of 61% in cotton, 40% in Robusta coffee, 90% in Arabica coffee, and were turning to other products like milk, hides and skins, cattle, fish, or savings and credit (Nannyonjo 2015, 269). The 1970 *Cooperative Societies Act* "gave the minister direct control over the affairs of registered cooperative societies, thus robbing the cooperative movement of its autonomy" and made cooperatives and unions a kind of "government parastatals" (ibid.). This model of fierce government intervention in cooperatives was quite popular in countries of the global South by that time (Baeriswyl 1988, 19-21). In 1971, Uganda had 36 unions, including four national ones, an apex organisation, and more than 2,500 primary cooperative societies, with over 750,000 people depending on them (Nannyonjo 2015, 269). The terror regime of Idi Amin followed. Interestingly, during that time of violence, disorder, and economic demise, the number of cooperative societies (3,054 in 1978) and unions (41 in 1978) increased, whereas their performance decreased (ibid.). It seems that, though cooperatives suffered from the political situation just as the rest of the country did, the population still believed in them as a sheet anchor. After Amin, the Obote II government (1980-85) rediscovered cooperatives as tools of rural development and went back to tight control while simultaneously offering them commodities and services (ibid., 269-270).

35 For a brief outline of the political history of Uganda, see chapter 6.1 of this thesis.

The next decisive change for cooperatives in Uganda arose with the IMF structural adjustment programme (SAP) under President Yoweri Museveni in the late 1980s: Liberalisation policies set them free from government control, yet they also robbed them of government support, including their monopolies, exposing them to free competition while they lost their sources of finance, training, and management support (Nannyonjo 2015, 270). Herment Mrema reports from his own survey that "membership development, training, regular inspections and management advisory services" are among the services that Ugandan cooperatives would like again to receive from the *Department of Cooperatives* (Mrema 2008, 156). The slow but sure decline of cooperatives in Uganda was accelerated by structural adjustment programmes considerably (Mrema 2008, 153; Nannyonjo 2015, 269-270). The only cooperatives that profited from liberalisation were *Savings and Credit Cooperatives* (SACCOs) (Kyazze 2010, 4). At the beginning of the 1990s, new legislation put the power over cooperatives into the hands of the members (Mrema 2008, 155; Nannyonjo 2015, 270). During the remainder of that decade, the Ugandan cooperative movement reinvented itself, trying to adapt to the new circumstances (Nannyonjo 2015, 271-273). The most serious difficulty it encountered in the course of that process was the vacuum of power that the withdrawal of government had left behind. In many cooperatives, members were not prepared to take over their new role and claim their rights within the democratic structures, whereas many board members were ready to take advantage of the situation, resulting in mismanagement and corruption (Mrema 2008, 155-156). Meanwhile, cooperatives became the target of intensive support from the Ugandan government anew (Nannyonjo 2015, 275-281). Today, the Ugandan cooperative sector is divided into primary societies and cooperative unions, with the most popular activities being agriculture as well as savings and credit, followed by others such as housing, transport, and hospitality (Mrema 2008, 156-158). The bigger ones among them provide services to other cooperatives, such as trainings, financial services, marketing or transport services (ibid., 157). However, a large part of the registered cooperatives in Uganda is inactive. In 2000, more than half of them were considered 'dormant' (ibid., 158). There are various potential reasons for this. Thomas cautions that, in practice, SSE activities are exposed to many dangers: "weaknesses in terms of capacities and resources, problems with management, the fragmentation of experience, the lack of a strategic vision, gaps in the marketing chain, shortcomings or contradictions in the political and legal framework" (Thomas 2015, 14, translation by E.K.). Mrema defines "lack of ownership" as one of the main problems of cooperatives in present-day Uganda (Mrema 2008, 171). He deplores the majority of members joining cooperatives due to financial incentives or even coercion on the part of the government, not voluntarily as it should be (ibid., 159). The questions whether their SSE activities worked well, and why, or why not, were central in the interviews that were conducted for this study. Several interviewees talked about "the old cooperatives" and some compared them with "the new cooperatives" (see chapter 8.3.2).

The history of Ugandan cooperatives may be tarnished to a certain extent by excessive state intervention; misappropriation by capitalist structures and a fortiori the development apparatus; mismanagement; and lack of ownership. Nevertheless, it is not a utopia, but a true story that displays the dangers and pitfalls on the way to an alternative economy – under difficult conditions. Although, on the one hand, cooperatives are being promoted by the Ugandan government, the idea behind that promotion is by no means an alternative economy. On the contrary, in 1987, the NRM government under President Museveni embraced the economic policies of the Bretton Woods institutions, which include a massive liberalisation of the economy (Mutibwa 2016, 432-436). Consequently, cooperatives are being promoted in anticipation of 'development' in the conventional sense. However, the 'gentle, yet persistent' kind of resistance described in chapter 4.1 might show through here and there. The early history of cooperatives as a means of self-protection of farmers against exploitation seems to suggest this. Chapter 8 discusses this point further, drawing on the experience of interviewees with cooperatives as well as other forms of SSE.

4.2.3 SSE: Capitalism's repair workshop?

According to Elmar Altvater, cooperatives are oftentimes founded out of misery, as "an organised, collective self-help initiative against hunger, unemployment, loss of worker's dignity and human dignity" (Altvater 2015, 276, translation by E.K.). Such descriptions have led to the conclusion that SSE and its instruments (like cooperatives) are stooges to capitalism, which appease its victims without pushing for serious change (cf. e.g. Delheim/Schlosser 2008). Indeed, SSE activities may start out as counterhegemonic projects but become capitalist as soon as they are successful (Altvater 2015, 278). Singer has observed this process in Brazil. For him, the first decision that usually leads a cooperative on that path is to employ workers or managers who are not part of the cooperative, i.e., not owners of the means of production (Singer 2007, 5). Sometimes, capitalist corporations are being 'rescued' by turning them into cooperatives when they are about to become insolvent (Altvater 2015, 278). Is SSE therefore capitalism's repair workshop? According to Thomas, SSE activities in the global South are first and foremost reactions to economic crises that deny access to social services or employment opportunities to certain parts of the population (Thomas 2015, 14). For instance, he explains how structural adjustment programmes have forced many governments of countries of the global South to reduce their social services in favour of austerity policies, such that the citizens' social needs were 'outsourced' to SSE actors (ibid., 11). In that case, SSE has been misappropriated by neoliberalism. The hardships imposed on the population through neoliberal policies were mitigated with the help of SSE. Hence, the situation was de-politicised and potential pressure on the governments to countermand those policies was averted. Against that background, Judith Delheim and Irmtraud Schlosser ague that SSE activities must always encompass an element of political mobilisation against exploitative structures (Delheim/ Schlosser 2008, 91). However, I suggest that the concrete situation must be taken into consideration in every particular case. While the situation seems to be clear in theory, it is by no means clear in practice. People have needs and what counts for them, first of all, is to satisfy those needs and those of their families. If they do not see a realistic chance to have them fulfilled by means of political pressure within an acceptable period of time, the logical short- to medium-term solution may be to deal with them by themselves. The prescription of Delheim and Schlosser to always include political mobilisation into such activities seems to be a good solution. However, the time factor plays a significant role with regard to this point as well. While in some countries, regions, or individual cases, the declaration of radical political goals may encourage people to join a group, in others it may discourage them. In the latter case, a group may first of all need a good period of time to form, to operate successfully, and to build trust among the members, before political elements can come in. Consequently, a current lack of political engagement and networking within a group does not mean that there is no counterhegemonic potential in it. After all, the members have joined the group because of problems in their everyday lives, of which they are painfully aware. The very act of coming together and implementing their economic and often social group activities is already a political act. Altvater postulates that SSE activities "show that, even in predominantly capitalist society, not all spaces are capitalised completely" and that collective forms of economic activities can still exist "embedded in society" (Altvater 2015, 276, translation by E.K.).

Singer has observed cooperatives, which, over the years, could act more solidary or more capitalist from time to time, depending on the surrounding conditions (Singer 2007, 5-6). Hence, SSE activities can have different qualities, with stronger or weaker tendencies to mitigate capitalism's negative effects. To a certain extent, this effect is inevitable. As I show in chapter 4.3, one of the main qualities of SSE is that it can both exist within the scope of the capitalist world-system and be part of an alternative vision. As a result, if SSE is supposed to exist within the scope of the capitalist world-system, it *has to mitigate* capitalism's negative effects to a certain extent. If it did not, that would mean that it would bring no improvement to people's lives. If that was the case, SSE would neither convince people of practising it today, nor to include it in their visions for the future. SSE can indeed act as a repair workshop for capitalism, from time to time. People need those 'repairs' in order to be able to carry on with their lives. Nevertheless, I am of the view that a slight mitigation of their suffering does not suffice to block their view for the problems surrounding them. The interviews conducted in the scope of this study have been revealing in that regard (see chapters 8 and 9.2).

4.3 Why SSE and not another alternative concept?

SSE is not the only alternative economic concept. Though presenting all the alternatives exceeds the parameters of this study, I have chosen to outline two examples, namely de-growth and Fair Trade. As I show below, both have strong parallels to SSE. For instance, the cooperative enjoys great popularity within all three approaches. Nevertheless, there are also significant differences between them. Carving out these differences elucidates why SSE has been chosen to play a significant role in the empirical part of this study. As I present de-growth and Fair Trade as a means to an end, I limit my overview to the aspects most central to my overall argument.

4.3.1 De-growth

Representatives of the de-growth movement reject the common belief in the desirability of economic growth. The term 'de-growth' (French: 'décroissance') is a "designation for a shrinking economy, which does not denote a recession, but a release from the permanent obligation to economic growth" (Muraca 2014, 26, translation by E.K.). The greatest concern of authors and activists of that approach is the destruction of the natural environment, yet they also consider social inequality and competition (ibid., 77). Wolfgang Sachs states that the "world economy increases every two years by about the size ($60 billion) it had reached by 1900 after centuries of growth" (Sachs 1998, 292). What may sound like fantastic news to advocates of capitalism, globalisation, and development is catastrophic in relation to the finiteness of the Earth. As Sachs aptly points out, the Earth must serve simultaneously as the sole provider of raw materials and the waste disposal site needed for the realisation of that growth – putting a natural limit to it (ibid., 291-292). Instead of being intimidated by the threats of "recession, unemployment, poverty" forecasted by pro-growth economists for the case of the absence of growth, they believe in the possibility of restructuring societies in a positive way, without economic growth (Muraca 2014, 77, translation by E.K.). The first report delivered by the *Club of Rome* in 1972 had raised some awareness for the problem of the exploitation and destruction of the natural environment by the expanding world economy (ibid., 25; Paech 2015, 71). However, mainstream economists found a capitalist solution to this problem: 'Qualitative' or 'sustainable' growth, meaning a continuous expansion, combined with investments in technologies, which are expected to make economic activities more environmentally acceptable (Paech 2015, 71). De-growth thinkers and activists suggest that such kinds of 'solutions', though they may sound tempting, cannot work because they do not tackle the real problem (ibid.). The central reason why they rather aggravate it is that the development and production of new technologies is done *additionally*, leading to even higher levels of consumption of resources and pollution of the natural environment (Muraca 2014, 27; Paech 2015, 72-73).

Niko Paech points out how the consumption patterns of the new global middle class contribute to a shortage of inputs (Paech 2015, 72). This may remind us of Ivan Illich's and Wolfgang Sachs' observations on dividing lines between social classes becoming international (see chapter 2.2.3 and 2.4, keyword 'Global North and global South/ First and Third World'), or world-systems analysis' standpoint that the class struggle must be observed on the level of the world-system as a whole, not on national level (see chapter 2.3.2). According to Serge Latouche, this problem would be solved automatically in a de-growth society. One of the necessary steps to build such a society would be a "[r]estructuring of social relations", which would have to include fair redistribution of wealth and access to natural resources "between the North and South and, within each society, between classes, generations and individuals" (Latouche 2015, 36). This reform of redistribution would reduce the purchasing power of the "world consumer class" and "the big predators" (ibid., 36-37). At the same time, it would end poverty, as the extreme wealth of a few would be shared among the poor, such that everyone would just have enough. Mainstream economists continue to claim "that sustained reductions in poverty cannot be attained without robust economic growth" (Stiglitz 2002, 78). Yet, when it comes to the 'trickle-down-effect', i.e., the expectation that economic growth means improvement of the commonweal because its positive effects will 'trickle down' even to the poor, many of them have been disabused of it by historical evidence, e.g., from several Latin American countries in which growth has led to rising inequality and poverty (ibid., 78-80; see also: Paech 2015, 73-74). Teodor Shanin deplores that the promises "of limitless linear growth blinded us to the complexity of the social world" (Shanin 1998, 70).

Measures recommended by the representatives of the de-growth approach are manifold. On the personal level, they comprise first and foremost the reduction of consumption and a gradual reorientation from full-time wage labour to part-time wage labour, in combination with increasing subsistence activities and social activities in favour of an independent, balanced life (Paech 2015, 76-78). Certainly, these recommendations make more sense for the global North than for the global South, where the rates of consumption and full-time wage labour are low anyway. Against this background, Wolfgang Sachs prescribes the "home perspective" to the global North in particular, demanding the latter to provide certain leeway to others to evolve, by means of "an orderly retreat" (Sachs 1998, 297; see also chapter 2.2.3). The primary measures he recommends implementing are efficiency and, even moreso, *sufficiency* with regard to the use of resources (ibid., 297-298). Paech has collected the following de-growth recommendations for changes on a larger scale: They comprehend measures such as short value chains (regional economies), cooperative banks, and regional currencies. Production is supposed to be reduced to a minimum and emphasis laid on the prolongation of the useful life of existing goods and infrastructure through repair and improvement. Monetary reforms, financial market reforms, and land reforms are supposed to accompany the de-growth process (Paech 2015, 77-78). All of this must take place under the umbrella of democratic principles (Muraca 2014, 87-89). The question of gender relations, especially when it comes to the evaluation of unpaid 'care work' mostly done by women (e.g., taking care of children, the sick, the elderly; household chores; etc.), is an important point of discussion within the de-growth movement (McMichael 2012, 296-297; Muraca 2014, 84). Serge Latouche's programme for a transition to a de-growth society is the following: Reconceptualising values and concepts such as poverty and wealth, scarcity and abundance; adjusting social relations as well as the productive apparatus to the new values; arranging redistribution of wealth and access to natural resources in a just way, globally, between generations and classes; bringing production back to a local level; reducing the exorbitant levels of consumption, wastefulness, and mass tourism on the part of the global North; job-sharing and part-time work in order to give access to *work and leisure* to everyone instead of having people sick of excessive labour and unable to participate in social life on the one hand and masses of unemployed on the other; reusing and recycling materials to the greatest possible extent (Latouche 2015, 35-41). Latouche refers to "the ecologists' old slogan of 'Think globally, act locally'" (ibid., 44). While people, particularly in the global North, should be aware of the global social and ecological consequences of their everyday practices, they should act locally – meaning in their private life as well as in their direct social and political environment – in order to make change. This means first and foremost to reduce the 'ecological footprints', i.e., the level of consumption of natural resources and that of pollution, of individuals, groups, firms, nations, and humanity as a whole. Nevertheless, Latouche admits that this is problematic for the global South. He states: "Reducing Africa's ecological footprint (and GDP) is neither necessary nor desirable" (ibid., 57). For the global South in general, and for Africa in particular, the *contraction* that is unquestionably needed in the over-developed global North is not an option. Latouche recommends to those countries to turn to Post-Development approaches (see chapter 2.2.3) instead of trying to follow the global North on its quest for economic growth, which is leading to ecological disaster (ibid., 57-63).

The relation of de-growth to capitalism is ambivalent. De-growth scholars and activists espouse differing opinions about it (Muraca 2015, 86-87). Serge Latouche uncompromisingly takes sides by stating: "De-growth is fundamentally anti-capitalist" (Latouche 2015, 91). He rationalises this conviction with the argument that growth and capitalism are inseparable (ibid., 90). Yet, he adds that not only capitalism but also "productivist socialism" build on economic growth, making both incompatible with a de-growth society (ibid., 89). Some representatives of less radical approaches to de-growth paint a picture of "a well-regulated form of capitalism" based on social and ecological values and allowing diverse forms of economic practice (McMichael 2012, 298). In either case, a form of capitalism compatible with de-growth would have to be altered beyond recognition (Muraca 2015, 87). Certainly, it would need to be a *strongly* regulated form, not a neoliberal one, because the state plays a very important role in the de-growth model. For instance, a typical demand uttered by representatives of the de-growth movement is the one for an unconditional basic income or for free basic services such as education, mobility, and housing (ibid., 80-81). The underlying expectation is of course that the state provides such benefits. City planning would need to be adjusted because in a de-growth society, town dwellers would have completely different needs than they currently have. They would all be moving by foot, on bicycles, and by bus (not with individual cars), and they would need space for practicing agriculture, for meeting neighbours, for exchanging and repairing things (ibid., 82).

Khor rightly points to the danger that the global North could "make the environmental issue a new instrument of domination over the South" (Khor 2001, 125). He reminds us that the biggest part of the environmental problems from which the world currently suffers is a product of the global North and that the global North has the financial and technological means to work on solutions (ibid.). Accordingly, the global North should not shift the responsibility on to the global South. This argumentation goes hand in hand with Latouche's point of the "huge 'ecological debt'" that the global North has incurred with the global South by exploiting natural resources in the global South and causing pollution to its own advantage (Latouche 2015, 37). Another reproach that the global South could address to the global North is hypocrisy. After having enjoyed the fruits of 'development', wealth, prosperity, and affluence for a considerable period of time, it is easy for the global North to tell the global South: 'You don't need this! It is not as good as you expect.' It looks like a return to the old 'not yet'-strategy (Chakrabarty 2000, 8; see also chapter 2.1.3), which has become a 'not anymore'-strategy: 'We told you that you need growth and development, but now we don't want it anymore, so, you don't need it either.' The global South might feel bilked of the experience of decades of wealth that the global North has been enjoying – at the cost of the global South. The de-growth approach thus clearly has important lessons to teach to the global North. The latter is destroying the basis for life of humanity as a whole. The de-growth movement, which comprises several critical economists, provides some concrete, realistic suggestions on how to work against this. The implementation of these suggestions is hindered by lack of political will, not by lack of feasibility. However, when it comes to the global South, the approach becomes problematic.

4.3.2 Fair Trade

Some scholars count Fair Trade[36] among the diverse forms of SSE (Reed 2015; Singer 2008, 216; Utting 2015, 1). Daryll Reed, for example, argues that producers can be motivated to join SSE organisations like cooperatives in order to profit from Fair Trade (Reed 2015, 104). In order to become part of *Fairtrade International* (FLO) for example, small-scale producers must "be organised democratically, a requirement that typically is fulfilled through incorporation as a cooperative" (ibid.). Some authors even claim that most of the positive effects of Fair Trade on producers arise from that membership in cooperatives rather than from the 'fair' terms of trade (Wuttke 2006, 151). Cooperatives provide a number of benefits to their members, out of which one is a higher bargaining power when it comes to the prices they receive for their produce. Regional and national producer associations have been founded under the aegis of Fair Trade – though not all of them comprise SSE organisations exclusively (Reed 2015, 106-107). They can nevertheless provide advocacy services to the latter (ibid., 107).

The best-known objectives of Fair Trade are the economic ones, namely paying a 'fair' price to small-scale producers in the global South (e.g., for coffee) and granting them reliable access to the world market through respectful trading relations (Wuttke 2006, 34). Additional objectives include fighting child labour; supporting indigenous people and women; sensitising consumers in the global North for unfair global trade relations; showing that respectful and transparent trade relations are feasible and encouraging conventional trade to change accordingly; promoting human rights, social justice, and environmentally friendly production methods (ibid., 35). Although all Fair Trade organisations essentially agree on those points, details differ among them, e.g., the question whether a 'fair' price shall be set by the producers in the global South or by the buyers in the global North (ibid., 37). To agree on those principles also does not always mean that they are actually fulfilled. For instance, Astrid Ohnmacht has found no significant effect of Fair Trade on the empowerment of women and indigenous people in her study (Ohnmacht 2007, 61-63).

The first alternative trade networks that endeavoured to pay producers in the global South a 'fair' price for their produce were established by

---

36 There are different spellings for the term. I have chosen the capitalised spelling in order to demonstrate that I am referring to a particular concept (or rather a trademark), not to 'a kind of trade that is fair'.

actors in the USA in the 1940s, followed by Europe in the 1950s, where Oxfam UK was the pioneer (Fridell 2015, 40-41; Wuttke 2006, 38). However, those were not yet certified or well-coordinated efforts. First steps towards coordination were done in the scope of the 'world shops', which started as a Christian initiative in the Netherlands in 1969 and spread from there all over Europe during the 1970s and 1980s (Fridell 2015, 40-41; Wuttke 2006, 38-40). Those 'world shops' are still alive and well yet have a limited target group of well-educated, ethically concerned, and well-off customers. The first organisation in charge of certification, *Max Havelaar*, was established in the year 1988 in the Netherlands, followed by other organisations of that kind in the global North (Fridell 2015, 53-54; Reed 2015, 108; Wuttke 2006, 44). In 1997, due to the need to coordinate among Fair Trade organisations and to match their standards, the *Fairtrade Labelling Organizations International* (FLO) was founded, which later changed its name into *Fairtrade International*, maintaining the acronym FLO (Reed 2015, 108-110; see also: Fridell 2015, 54; Wuttke 2006, 47).

The movement started in the global North. Producers from the global South became members much later (Reed 2015, 108). Using the example of Germany, Mirja Wuttke explains how the Fair Trade movement split into two in the 1970s: One part wanted to first and foremost raise awareness for unfair trade relations and use their own 'solidary'- or 'alternative trade'-networks for their political argumentation rather than for market access for a big number of producers. The other part seriously wanted to open the world market to producers who had been disadvantaged until then and sought ways to raise their market share while granting them fair prices. The political 'alternative trade' movement can be accused of abusing producers from the global South as 'teaching material', promising them a change in the future, which has not come within the last forty years (Wuttke 2006, 41-43). Their activities are meant well but do not seem to have any significant effect. What has finally become the Fair Trade movement at first sight has more to show for its approach. Today, Fair Trade certified products can be found in almost every supermarket in Germany. As Wuttke points out, almost all countries of the global North have turned out to be good markets for products with 'Fair Trade' labels (ibid., 49-50). The market for the producers from the global South has indeed widened considerably. Nevertheless, what looks like a success story at first glance deserves further consideration. On the international level, Gavin Fridell observes that the Fair Trade movement has its roots in dependency theory. As a result, its early representatives (up to the 1980s) were convinced that the poor had no chance in the capitalist world-system, meaning that an alternative trading system had to be established for their products in parallel (Fridell 2015, 39-40). Meanwhile, the movement has given up its original ambitions of "creating a distinctly alternative market" in close collaboration with the state (ibid., 50), in favour of a "market-friendly approach" (ibid., 51). Fridell traces this decision back to the priority of Fair Trade on first of all providing better prices to producers – preferably many and preferably immediately – to which more far-reaching objectives have been subordinated (ibid., 50). In his view, this development has been furthered by an increasing neo-Smithian theoretical orientation within the movement, which has opened the latter towards neoliberal policies of institutions like the WTO or the World Bank (ibid., 48-51). According to Fridell, the movement still encompasses both apologists of the vision that Fair Trade could be an alternative to neoliberal globalisation and those of envisioning it as an opportunity for producers from the global South to participate more successfully in neoliberal globalisation. However, with reference to Fair Trade's recent expansion and mainstreaming, he argues that the latter vision of it has obviously become the dominant one (ibid., 52-53).

Although for Reed, Fair Trade unquestionably belongs to SSE, he admits: "Not all actors involved in FT [Fair Trade] are SSE organisations, and many can be quite hostile to the SSE if it threatens their interests" (Reed 2015, 104). In that context, he particularly refers to corporate distributors and retailers with whom collaboration may be necessary in order to market Fair Trade products – especially when they are supposed to be marketed on a larger scale (ibid.). They are 'hostile' in the sense that requirements such as sharing knowledge with small-scale producers or encouraging the latter to move up the value chain are not in their interest (ibid., 110-111). On the contrary, those actors reintroduce the element of competition to Fair Trade. One of the incidents that made them access the Fair Trade network was the FLO's decision to allow estate production for the largest part of the certified products. This increased the attractiveness of Fair Trade for large processors, retailers, and distributors (ibid., 110). Paradoxically, small-scale producers have become disadvantaged within the Fair Trade network, which was supposed to be their refuge. They cannot compete with the cheaper products from large estates and plantations. The owners of the latter do not only profit from their lower costs of production and the 'fair' prices they receive, but also from the reputation of the Fair Trade label, which builds on advertisement for alternative trade with small-scale producers (ibid., 113). Peter Nickel presents another example of the dubious sides of Fair Trade. He deplores how, in Germany, the 'TransFair' certification mark was able to be granted to products that are sold by the supermarket chain 'Lidl', as the latter has a bad reputation in terms of social standards (Nickel 2008, 28-30). This could only happen either because sales figures count more for the organisation of certification than its own standards, or because of a double standard involving insisting on a set of standards for producers in the global South that do not apply to the sellers in the global North (ibid., 29-30). These problems show that Fair Trade is an approach that does not suspend the dependency of the global South on the benevolence of the global North. Cheryl McEwan points out how much the global North still fancies the idea that the global South depends on its benevolence and how this idea dominates Fair Trade discourse (McEwan 2009, 135). Utting likewise hints at the split in the Fair Trade movement that was caused by the turn of some of its representatives from its original focus on the empowerment of small-scale producers and rural communities towards big business with *Starbucks* and *Nestlé* (Utting 2015, 15). Reed concludes that the admission of corporations without serious restrictions led to "the degeneration of FT [Fair Trade] from an SSE movement to a corporate social responsibility practice", in which large corporations are the winners and small-scale producers are the losers (Reed 2015, 113-114).

Mirja Wuttke points to two other problems: One is also part of Fair Trade's tendency to widen its market. In the past, training producers on environmentally friendly production methods and on how to raise the quality of their produce was part and parcel of the 'alternative trade' approach. Meanwhile, those aspects have become *criteria* producers *must already fulfil* in order to become part of a Fair Trade network. This excludes the original target group of 'alternative trade', namely the smallest and most vulnerable producers in the global South (Wuttke 2006, 162-163). The second problem pointed out by Wuttke is a pre-existing one that neither 'alternative trade' nor Fair Trade have been able to tackle, namely tariffs on the import of processed products in the global North. The majority of agricultural produce being traded on 'fair' terms, such as coffee or cocoa, is being imported as raw material and processed in the global North, leaving the highest profit margins on the end product in the global North (ibid., 54). One of the core problems of unfair trade is thus not being tackled by the Fair Trade approach. Another aspect concerns the producer countries. Astrid Ohnmacht shows in her study of Mexican Fair Trade coffee producers that Fair Trade networks have tried to replace the services that had been successfully provided by the governmental Mexican Coffee Institute (INMECAFE) from the 1960s up to the late 1980s

(Ohnmacht 2007, 84-85). Although her study strongly supports Fair Trade endeavours, Ohnmacht admits that the latter are not capable of supporting small-scale farmers the way the governmental INMECAFE has done with regard to organising and financing the purchase and export of coffee on a large scale, technical assistance, and access to loans (ibid.). This suggests that governments of the global South are more effective in protecting their small-scale producers from exploitation than organisations from the global North – if neoliberal 'development' programmes do not prohibit them from doing so.

Despite all these shortcomings, alternative and Fair Trade do have positive effects. Producers profit to a certain extent from better prices for their products (Ohnmacht 2007, 59, 87; Wuttke 2006, 151-152), the reliability of long-term trade relations (Ohnmacht 2007, 64, 87; Wuttke 2006, 152), improved access to trainings (Ohnmacht 2007, 59, 64-65, 89, 92; Wuttke 2006, 153), and greater access to loans (Ohnmacht 2007, 64, 9; Wuttke 2006, 153-154). Positive psychological effects of Fair Trade, such as self-esteem or a feeling of economic and social security among small-scale producers exist, thought these are generally attributed to their membership in cooperatives rather than to membership in Fair Trade networks (Ohnmacht 2007, 63, 90-91). Nevertheless, such concepts are not able to overcome the problematic structures of the world economy. After having conquered a small 'fair' island for itself within the global capitalist world economy, Fair Trade has allowed the latter's exploitative structures to start re-colonising that island by softening the fair principles in return for wider market access. This does not absolve individual consumers or institutions in the global North from buying Fair Trade products rather than buying the same products from distributors and retailers that exploit producers in the global South even more. Neither does it make it a bad idea to bring Fair Trade products to the shelves of ordinary supermarkets. Carrying the topic out of its limited world-shop-sphere and, at the same time, providing more producers from the global South an opportunity to receive a better price for their produce are intentions that have merit. However, the sphere of agency lies in the global North, a finding that disqualifies Fair Trade as an alternative economic approach to be analysed in depth in the scope of my study.

4.3.3 SSE in relation to de-growth and Fair Trade

A major difference between SSE and de-growth is that the latter is a holistic, macroeconomic concept that needs many structural and political prevailing conditions in order to come into existence. Although the principles of de-growth are tested in small 'laboratories' like the so-called 'transition towns' (Muraca 2014, 83, see also 90), the concept has little applicable use on a small scale. This is different for SSE. Although SSE likewise has strong aspirations to change society as a whole, it is much easier to start implementing SSE activities on the smallest level with a tiny group of local people. It is a concept that is intended to move from micro- to macroeconomic dimensions. Implementing SSE is possible in the global South, as has been shown above, whereas applying de-growth to the global South is comparably difficult. When it comes to the global South, de-growth scholars and activists (e.g., Latouche 2015; see also chapter 4.3.1) tend simply to refer to the Post-Development approach (see chapter 2.2.3 for details). De-growth has so far developed *its own ideas* with regard to the *global North, in particular*. This makes perfect sense, for it is *the global North's* economic growth, excessive exploitation of natural and human resources, ever-increasing consumption, wastefulness, and pollution of the natural environment that has carried the global ecological and social crisis to extremes. The extension of the global middle class (Paech 2015; see also in chapter 2.2.3: Illich 1998; Sachs 1998) and progressive industrialisation start to aggravate such problems in the global South. Nevertheless, the global North is still responsible for the bigger share of consumption and production and, as a result, has more room for manoeuvre in terms of reducing both (Khor 2001, 125). However, SSE and de-growth have a lot in common and make up a good combination for drawing a utopia (or in Wallerstein's terms: 'utopistic', see chapter 3.4) of a global 'de-growth society based on solidarity'. For instance, Philip McMichael points out that de-growth's emphasis on "revaluing local resources" can lead to the promotion of activities "such as care work, barter, cooperatives, and resource-sharing" (McMichael 2012, 297). Barbara Muraca likewise presents cooperatives and social enterprises as natural elements of a de-growth economy (Muraca 2014, 88). Those are typical SSE activities. De-growth advocates call for "cooperation instead of competition" (ibid., 78, translation by E.K.). Among other things, they intend to replace the claim to 'intellectual property' within capitalist competition with creative commons (including scientific and technological knowledge) (ibid., 78-79). The de-growth model also emphasises solidarity and the common good instead of profit maximisation and capitalist expansion (ibid., 85). De-growth is certainly an ally that would harmonise well with SSE within a 'de-growth society based on solidarity'. While de-growth would first and foremost serve to transform the global North, SSE can be applied well to both the global North and the global South.

Fair Trade, even if we accept it as one of the approaches of SSE, as suggested by Reed, Singer, and Utting (Reed 2015; Singer 2008, 216; Utting 2015, 1), is obviously one of its weakest examples. While its vulnerability to be misappropriated by the capitalist world-system is being shared by the majority of alternative approaches to a certain extent, its biggest flaw in my view is that it does not touch upon the relations of power and dependency between the actors from the global South and the global North whom it connects. The actors from the global North decide on the rules, the criteria, and, in most cases, on the prices they are willing to pay. The actors from the global South receive more money, yet have little to no room for participation or emancipation. On the contrary, they must fulfil criteria that actors from the global North are not always required to fulfil in order to be labelled 'Fair Trade', e.g., fulfilling social standards (see chapter 4.3.2). Hence, Fair Trade is more akin to an act of philanthropy on the part of the global North than to a measure of emancipatory SSE implemented by actors from the global South.

SSE shares several aspects with de-growth and Fair Trade, first and foremost the critique of the exploitative practices of capitalism. As shown in chapter 4.2, there is no single and undisputed definition of SSE. The aspects of SSE that are emphasised depend very much on who is writing about it or which group is practising it. Some approaches, especially those of the Social Economy in the narrow sense, are capitalism-friendly or at least vulnerable to misappropriation by capitalism. Some are pro-growth and, as such, incompatible with the de-growth approach. Fair Trade can be counted among them. Others, especially those that are closer to the Solidarity Economy in the narrow sense, are more radically anti-capitalist. My study focusses on alternative economic practices in the global South. Among the three alternative concepts presented in this chapter, SSE seems to me the most promising in that regard, while others seem to have their primary sphere of agency in the global North. The role of actors from the global South within the scope of Fair Trade is rather passive, while in the de-growth approach, their role is a marginal one that is being 'outsourced' to the Post-Development school of thought.

4.4 Conclusion

Thinking about potential "alternatives to development", especially those that are based on "local culture and knowledge" and "localized, pluralistic grassroots movements", is one of the cornerstones[37] of the Post-Development approach (Escobar 2012, 215). From the world-systems perspective, Immanuel Wallerstein assigned the world population, and in particular Africans, the tasks of simultaneously implementing "short-run local meliorations" and "middle-run transformation of values and structures" (Wallerstein 2017, 65). This goes hand in hand with my conclusion on the '(post-)development'-chapter of this thesis: While reformist approaches are needed for the immediate 'melioration' of the suffering of the subaltern in the global South, *alternatives to* development, as suggested by the Post-Development school of thought, are desperately needed in the medium-to long term, as the current development model is neither socially, nor economically, nor ecologically sustainable (see chapter 2.2.4). In order to follow those recommendations, *decolonising* the epistemological basis of economic thinking in general, and development thinking in particular, is indispensable (see chapter 2.1.3). SSE is a concept that has the potential to fulfil all these criteria. As has been shown above, it can deliver short-term solutions for meliorations of the situation, e.g., by granting access to markets or loans to small-scale producers, or by providing mutual support in case of sickness or other casualties. At the same time, it promotes values that clearly oppose those of capitalism: cooperation instead of competition; making a living and distributing income justly among the members instead of profit maximisation for a few and exploitation for many; democratic control of means of production and decision making instead of accumulation and top-down management. In the medium to long term, this may contribute to a change in values that goes beyond the respective groups and eventually leads to structural change. Beyond that, SSE theorists also aspire to structural changes similar to those demanded by de-growth, such as the above-mentioned calls for monetary policies that reduce the power of money (Bender 2012, 97), a different understanding of property with respective legislation (Winkelmann 2012, 122-126), or the switch from the ideal of full-time employment to that of flexible part-time

37 In addition to that one, other cornerstones of the Post-Development approach encompass criticising the conventional concept of development and critically analysing specific areas of intervention within development policy (Kerner 2012, 112-113; see also chapter 2.2.3 of this thesis).

employment (Winkelmann 2012a, 158). The applicability of SSE to the micro- and macro-level in equal measure is one of the main reasons why I prefer it over other alternative approaches in this thesis. Although the focus of the study itself is clearly on the micro-level, a theoretical applicability of the concept to the macro-level increases its political relevance.

In chapter 4.3, de-growth and Fair Trade have been used as concrete examples to demonstrate major similarities and differences in comparison with SSE. De-growth has many parallels with SSE and can be combined with it very well. Yet, it is a radical and holistic concept for change that requires fulfilling many prerequisites for implementation. As such, it is a concept for long-term change rather than for short- to medium-term change. SSE can likewise evolve beyond the local level through international coordination between SSE initiatives (e.g., through umbrella associations or the *World Social Forum*), the creation of favourable legal and political frameworks for SSE on the national and the international level and, ultimately, the replacement of the capitalist world-system by diverse world-systems based on solidarity. For instance, in Brazil, a National Office for Solidarity Economy was created within the Ministry of Labour and Employment in 2003 as a result of a request from the *World Social Forum* – and of political will (Singer 2008, 215). However, though a favourable political framework at national and international levels is its objective and ideal, SSE does not need all those conditions in order to be practised. It is already being practised by innumerable initiatives, trying to make change from the bottom up. Fair Trade, in contrast, functions so well within the scope of the capitalist world-system that it does not show the way for serious change. Many of its positive effects can rather be traced back to its use of SSE organisations, namely cooperatives, than to its alternative approach to North-South trade. However, the greatest advantage of SSE in comparison with de-growth and Fair Trade is that it provides obvious and immediate options for agency that actors in the global South can and do implement. In contrast to that, actors from the global South play a passive role in Fair Trade and a marginal one in the de-growth approach.

Cooperatives are a form of activism that can be found in all three approaches and beyond them. As discussed in chapter 3.4, Immanuel Wallerstein calls upon social movements worldwide to implement decommodification as one of the steps to form more just and democratic principles for the world-system(s) to come after the upcoming demise of the current one. For him, this does not only encompass opposing the current tendency to commodify everything but also to reverse the commodification of industries, especially those that seem to be failing. Instead of nationalisation, he suggests the installation of "structures, operating in the market, whose objective is performance and survival rather than profit" (Wallerstein 2003, 271). Cooperatives (and other SSE activities like social enterprises or factories occupied by their workers) fulfil those criteria. The history of Ugandan cooperatives, from their inception until today, illustrates very well the ambiguity of the cooperative concept (see chapter 4.2.2). They were founded as an initiative of small- to medium-scale farmers who wanted to protect themselves from capitalist exploitation. At first sight, this makes them appear as the perfect SSE activity. However, their goal was first and foremost to provide direct access to the market to their members, which is in line with capitalism and the conventional approach to development. Cooperatives have been popular as an approach to 'rural development' under socialist, market-oriented, and neoliberal governments alike. Today, they are still promoted by development agencies, not because of their counterhegemonic potential, but due to the expectation that they can help marginalised people to 'develop' in the sense that has been criticised in chapter 2.2.3. Regardless, cooperatives are always among the examples provided for SSE and de-growth activities. Singer has hinted at their ability to 'oscillate' between capitalist and anti-capitalist behaviour (Singer 2007, 5-6; see also chapter 4.2.3). I follow Cooper (Cooper 2009, 47; see also chapter 4.1) as well as Santos and Rodríguez-Garavito (Santos/ Rodríguez-Garavito 2007, xxii-xxiii; see also chapter 4.2.1) in their assessments suggesting that the counterhegemonic potential of an activity is not necessarily visible at first sight. Apart from that, cooperatives are not the only form of SSE activities. They have been selected as an example to illustrate what such an activity can look like. Before starting my research, I expected to also encounter other activities in Busoga that fulfil the above-mentioned criteria for SSE activities. Indeed, they are there, and some of them are less ambiguous than typical cooperatives in one respect or another. I discuss this in detail in chapters 8.3, 8.4, and 9.2.

That the majority of SSE initiatives in Africa are results of people's day-to-day struggles for survival must not be taken as their liability but as one of their assets. Utting lauds that "much contemporary theorising on SSE is grounded in real-world practices" (Utting 2015, 33). This thesis is an attempt at such an examination of 'real-world practices'. I did not expect to find a fully developed Solidarity Economy in rural Uganda. Rather, my intention was to see what kind of structures that would fit into SSE definitions can be found at all – and what kind of experience people have had with them (e.g., success, disappointment, challenges, evolution over time). This research project is built on the assumption that "the rest of the world can learn a lot from Africa, meaning especially from the experience and principles of the 'People's Economy' " (Chipakupaku 2008, 138, translation by E.K.). Nevertheless, I am aware that this approach contains a certain danger of romanticising societies of the global South and creating dichotomies of their attitude of solidarity on the one hand, and concepts from the global North, like capitalism and the development paradigm, on the other (Ziai 2006, 200).

This research project traces solidarity structures in local economies in the Busoga region of Uganda. These economic activities should fulfil at least part of the criteria presented in chapter 4.2.1. I assume that the criteria suggested by Michelle Williams and Norman Chipakupaku capture the most essential characteristics of SSE without demanding too much and risking overlooking interesting approaches. Hence, in chapter 8.3, I apply those criteria to the groups encountered in Busoga in order to evaluate their alternative potential. According to Michelle Williams, the minimum criteria to be fulfilled by the Social Economy (Williams 2014, 46-47) *and* the Solidarity Economy alike are „cooperation, democratic decision making, collective ownership, bottom-up processes, caring and sharing" (ibid., 59). The principles of the People's Economy, which Chipakupaku defines as the African version of Social and Solidarity Economy (see chapter 4.2.1 or Chipakupaku 2008, 138-139), complement Williams' criteria. Those principles are: 1. joining economic efforts in order to earn a living; 2. being run by and for the sake of the local population; 3. creating local economic cycles that provide employment to locals, keeping money and facilities at their disposition; 4. preserving nature for future generations (Chipakupaku 2008, 138). Chipakupaku's criteria have been taken up in the interview framework in order to explain to the interviewees the kinds of groups and activities in which I was interested. Furthermore, respondents were asked whether those groups and their activities are autochthonous or modern; created by the people themselves, by the church or aid agencies; a counteraction to crisis or undisputed daily practices. Based on the information received, I analysed their relation to globalisation and economic liberalisation. In Brazil, Singer has observed a significant increase in SSE activities as a reaction to the crisis caused by neoliberal economic policies (Singer 2008, 215). In the course of this study, interviewees were requested to give their evaluation of evolutions over the past 30 years, which by that time referred to the period between 1987 (the advent of neoliberal policies in Uganda) and 2017. Apart from the change over time, the separation of autochthonous solidarity structures and modern SSE activities was particularly salient during the interviews.

As has been stated above, autochthonous solidarity structures should not be confused with SSE activities but they can have a strong influence on how people see and practise SSE (Develtere 2008, 2; Thomas 2015, 10-11).

5. Research design[38]

This chapter describes how the data for this study were collected and analysed, and why it was done in that particular way. The following paragraphs provide a very brief overview of the research design. Chapter 5.1 introduces postcolonial (or decolonial) research methodology. This is central to understand the way in which data collection and analysis were done and the choices made during that process. My application of postcolonial research methodology also demonstrates the influence of postcolonial theory on my study. Chapter 5.1 is sub-divided into five sub-headings meant to display the points of greatest concern for postcolonial research methodology. Chapter 5.2 and 5.3 describe the research activities in detail, namely the methods used and the steps taken in order to produce the research results presented in chapters 7 and 8. Chapter 5.4 comments on the extent to which the research project has managed to fulfil the demands of postcolonial research.

This is a qualitative research project. The primary method of data collection is a set of 30 problem-centred interviews with people in 21 communities in the Busoga region of Eastern Uganda ('main interviews', see chapter 5.2.1 for details). In line with the strategy of triangulation (Bowen 2009, 28; Denzin/ Lincoln 1994, 2-3), I have taken two additional steps to strengthen the quality of the research. One is the analysis of written material (see chapter 5.3). The other one is a set of ten so-called 'expert interviews' with representatives of the local administration and Ugandan academics (see chapter 5.2.2). Norman K. Denzin and Yvonna

---

38 Excerpts from this chapter have been presented in the scope of the talk "Postkoloniale Forschung in Uganda: Ein Werkstattbericht" ("Postcolonial research in Uganda: A report on work in progress") at the conference of the section "Development Theory and Policy" of the DVPW (Deutsche Vereinigung für Politikwissenschaft/ German Political Science Association), on 23 November 2017 in Kassel, Germany, and published in: Schöneberg, Julia/ Ziai, Aram (eds.) (2021): *Dekolonisierung der Entwicklungspolitik und Post-Development Alternativen.* Baden-Baden: Nomos, 81-101. Excerpts of this chapter have also been presented in the scope of the talk "Decolonising the Interview: Prospects and challenges" at the Conference "Rethinking Development" (22-23/08/18), within the panel "Rethinking Development Research – Objects and Subjects in Development Studies" on 23 August 2018 at the University of Gothenburg, Sweden.

S. Lincoln explain that "the use of multiple methods, or triangulation, reflects an attempt to secure an in-depth understanding of the phenomenon in question" and, as such, it "is not a tool or a strategy of validation, but an alternative to validation" (Denzin/ Lincoln 1994, 2). The aim of both additional activities is to gather background information about the economic situation – historically and contemporarily – of the concerned communities, and the effects of globalisation on Uganda in general.

I lived in Uganda from March 2016 up to December 2018, in Kamuli town, the capital of Kamuli District located in the heart of Busoga kingdom in the Eastern region of the country. My husband was working in a vocational training centre in Kamuli during that period and I stayed with him in a house on the compound of that training centre. Thus, I lived in the extended social environment of the interviewees (Kamuli/ Busoga) but not in their home communities.[39] During the first ten months I spent in Uganda, the primary research activities I undertook were learning the language of the region, Lusoga; preparing the instruments for data collection (interview guideline, informed consent form, short questionnaire; see chapters 5.2.1 and 5.2.2, and appendices); and applying for a research clearance from the *Uganda National Council for Science and Technology* (UNCST). In order to apply for the research clearance from the UNCST, I needed to first apply for a letter of approval from the *Research Ethics Committee at the School of Social Sciences of Makerere University* (MAKSS REC). For learning Lusoga, I took lessons every week, did exercises on my own, and tried to apply my language skills in everyday conversations. Apart from those research-related activities, I looked for a second academic supervisor (whom I found at *Makerere University*, Kampala) and conducted literature review. The first letter of approval from MAKSS REC was issued on 4 January 2017. It was valid for one year, such that, by the end of that year, I needed to apply for an extension of the approval in order to complete my research. The research clearance from UNCST was issued on 31 January 2017 and was valid for four years. However, I was obliged to deliver a progress report every 12 months as long as the research was ongoing, and a closure report. Together with it, I received a research clearance letter from the *Office of the President*, which I took to the *Resident*

---

39 Indeed, a few interviews were conducted in Kamuli town, with local residents and representatives of the local administration; however, Kamuli town is the district capital and as such rather anonymous and not comparable with a village, in which everyone knows everyone else. Other interviews were conducted in towns and villages in a considerable distance from Kamuli town.

District Commissioner of every district in which I was intending to conduct research. The same letter was needed in order to be granted access to any archive or to be supported by government institutions such as the *Office of the Prime Minister* or the library of the *Parliament of Uganda*, where I went in search of helpful documents on my research topic (see chapter 5.3). After having attained the research clearance, I started the data collection and analysis as described in chapter 5.2 and 5.3. Before going into detail about this, I present the methodological assumptions underlying these research activities.

5.1 Postcolonial research methodology

There is no uniform definition of postcolonial (or decolonial) research (Swadener/ Mutua 2008, 33-34). Some authors have nevertheless presented approaches widely accepted[40] among scholars, who want to give their research a postcolonial turn. As I show below, there are many parallels between postcolonial and feminist critique of research practice. This chapter is sub-divided into five sub-headings that display the greatest points of concern for postcolonial methodology. However, it is just an attempt to offer a clear overview, which is quite artificial because the issues overlap. For instance, *power* plays a significant role in all five sub-sections, not only in the one that bears the term in its title (chapter 5.1.3). *Self-reflexivity*, which includes acknowledging one's own *positionality* and *role* in the research process, is considered the most important prerequisite for being able to conduct postcolonial research. Those issues are introduced first, in chapter 5.1.1. Chapter 5.1.2 discusses a central question in qualitative research, namely whether or not the researcher is supposed to *'speak for'* (or 'give voice to') the researched – and what could be the alternative. After the above-mentioned sub-section on the central issue of *power constellations in qualitative research* (5.1.3), I address questions concerning *language and translation* (chapter 5.1.4). The sub-section closes with some remarks concerning the most difficult ethical issue in social science research, namely *reciprocity*, i.e., how to avoid exploitation of the researched by the researcher and make the research process rewarding for both parties (chapter 5.1.5). This may not be an exhaustive list of aspects to be considered in

40 I have verified this, on the one hand, through literature repeating the same or similar issues and, on the other hand, through talks and discussions within the scope of academic conferences and colloquia.

qualitative research from an ethical, and especially from a postcolonial, point of view. However, it encompasses the most frequently discussed issues.

5.1.1 Positionality and self-reflexivity

Many postcolonial approaches to research methodology emphasise self-reflexivity (e.g., Husseini de Araújo/ Kersting 2012, 139, 141-142; Kapoor 2004). Adhering closely to the work of Gayatri C. Spivak, Ilan Kapoor recommends the following steps for researching 'the subaltern': The researcher must accept that she is part of a cultural, geopolitical, and power constellation that always influences her view of the world. That does not absolve her from the responsibility of being critical but it keeps her from feeling morally superior about it. She needs to trace back the roots of the knowledge systems, prejudices, and representations with which she works and be honest with herself, the researched, and the reader regarding those influences. She must try to unlearn her privileges to the furthest extent possible, but openly reflect on the limits of that attempt (Kapoor 2004, 640-641). Finally, "learning from the subaltern requires an anterior step: learning to learn" (ibid., 641). That means being aware that the 'Western expert' is not coming up with universal solutions and that Western concepts are not universal (ibid., 642). Ramón Grosfoguel cautions that "we always speak from a particular location in the power structures" (Grosfoguel 2011, 5). He continues:

> "Nobody escapes the class, sexual, gender, spiritual, linguistic, geographical, and racial hierarchies of the 'modern/colonial capitalist/patriarchal world-system. [...] The main point here is the locus of enunciation, that is, the geo-political and body-political location of the subject that speaks. In Western philosophy and sciences the subject that speaks is always hidden, concealed, erased from the analysis. [...] By delinking ethnic/racial/gender/sexual epistemic location from the subject that speaks, Western philosophy and sciences are able to produce a myth about a Truthful universal knowledge [...]" (Grosfoguel 2011, 5, "Truthful" is capitalised in the original).

In her famous essay *Can the Subaltern Speak?*, Gayatri C. Spivak writes: "I am also far from averse to learning from the work of Western theorists, though I have learned to insist on marking their positionality as investigating subjects" (Spivak 1988, 296). Challenging the universality of theories from the global North and extending the influence of theorists from the global South is also among the measures Pavarti Raghuram and Clare Madge suggest for postcolonial research – as well as contextualising theories historically and geographically and interweaving them with practice (Raghuram/ Madge 2006, 277-281). Nikita Dhawan recommends historicising and contextualising concepts as well as theories from the global North in order to decolonise knowledge and enable its flow from South to North (Dhawan 2011, 20).

Kim England argues that feminism and other critical approaches in the social sciences have made a point of criticising the principles of neopositivist empiricism, among them the researcher's "carefully constructed public self as a mysterious, impartial outsider, an observer freed of personality and bias" (England 1994, 81). Drawing from a host of feminist literature, she calls the idea that any researcher could leave behind his or her biography and personal characteristics such as gender, lived experiences, or historical location while conducting research, "completely mythical" (ibid., 85). As one way of making the researcher – a subjective human being, not an 'objective' machine – visible again, she recommends using "the reflexive 'I'" when writing the research report (ibid., 82). She states: "A researcher is positioned by her/his *gender, age, 'race'/ethnicity, sexual identity*, and so on, as well as by her/his *biography*, all of which may inhabit or enable certain research method insights in the field [...]" (ibid., 85, emphases by E.K.). Denzin and Lincoln demand the researcher recognises that "research is an interactive process shaped by his or her *personal history, biography, gender, social class, race, and ethnicity*, and those of the people in the setting" (Denzin/ Lincoln 1994, 3, emphases by E.K.).

I came to Uganda as a privileged white woman from Germany. I had been able to travel there because I had been born in a country and a social class that allowed my sheltered upbringing, my possession of a passport that allows easy travelling, my earning of a widely acknowledged degree, and my access to the necessary financial means to conduct such a research project. It is a *sheer coincidence* that I was born among the small part of humanity that enjoys such privileges. As I have tried to depict above (chapters 2 and 3), I am of the view that it is *no coincidence* that the largest part of humanity, which includes the people I encountered during the research process, does not enjoy such privileges. I am aware that my complicity in the global power imbalances and exploitative relations (historical and current), which are responsible for that circumstance, is insurmountable. Nevertheless, I have chosen to adopt an active attitude and try to make a tiny change through my research, rather than to ignore my political responsibility (see chapter 5.1.2). After all, as Denzin et al. have put it: "Critical qualitative scholarship offers humble grounds and many unforeseen possibilities to seek and promote justice, critical global engagement, and diverse epistemologies" (Denzin et al. 2017, 482). However, I do not claim to be absolved from my complicity in global power imbalances as a result.

On the one hand, my origin in the global North, i.e., my privileged and historically-charged background (representing a people of colonisers), was visible to everyone at first sight. This circumstance threatened the basis of trust of the research encounter. I tried to reduce this potential distrust by several means, which I describe in the following chapters (e.g., learning the interviewees' language; sharing control over the research situation with them; obtaining approval from all concerned parties before getting in touch with interviewees). Beyond that, I did not bother the interviewees with the provocative dressing style or the brash, demanding behaviour that many Africans expect from white women (due to movies, TV shows, and in some cases, personal experience with tourists or young volunteers). This may have reduced potential reserve on their part, as well. When I conducted the interviews, I was in my mid-thirties. As Kim England points out, being a woman and being younger than the interviewees is not necessarily a disadvantage to the researcher, as it may lead to her appearing less 'intimidating' to them (England 1994, 85). I was younger than all interviewees, and significantly younger than the main interviewees, and we were from different sociocultural backgrounds. I had the impression that, due to these facts, many of them enjoyed teaching me about what I was obviously inexperienced about, namely their lifeworlds. In order to express that I was aware of that lack of experience on my side and had come to learn from them, the opening question of the interview guideline (see chapter 5.2.1 for explanations and appendices for the full text of the interview guideline) was supported by the sentence: "Please take your time and explain it in detail to me, as I am a foreigner". As has been mentioned in chapter 2.2.4, in the context of development practice, I belong to "a new generation of thinkers and 'doers' – particularly those whose personal field experience has led them to see things from the perspective of the peoples most concerned – [who] have now come to question many of their previous ideological certainties" (Rahnema 1998, 379). As a privileged white person, I do not claim to be able to look at things from the perspective of the alleged 'beneficiaries' of development projects; however, having seen their living conditions, heard their concerns, and witnessed the failure of the development apparatus to address the latter has significantly influenced the stance I have taken. In contrast to a theorist who undertakes a lengthy stay in the field for the first time, I had several years of experience working and living in Africa prior to conducting my research study. In contrast to a confident practitioner, I had turned towards critical reflection due to my disappointment with the development apparatus and its failure to address the actual causes of global inequality. I had decided to look for explanations for phenomena such as poverty and global power imbalances, as well as for potential solutions, at the scientific level. This attitude of mine was simultaneously a liability and an asset for my research. On the one hand, it was an asset because it had sensitised me to avoid a lot of pitfalls, as shown in this chapter 5. On the other hand, I needed to be constantly aware of the danger of allowing the bias resulting from my personal experience to influence the research process or results. However, as I explain in this chapter, *any researcher* needs to beware of that danger, no matter the details of his or her particular experiences. Previous life experience – be it academic, practical, or personal – cannot be erased before collecting or analysing data. On the contrary, as Ian Baptiste aptly points out, a researcher's "interests, ideological stance, and theoretical positions", regardless of whether they are conventional or critical, inevitably form his or her "systems of values and beliefs concerning research" (Baptiste 2001, [5]). What counts is to reflect on such influences thoroughly throughout the entire research process and to share a good part of those reflections with the reader instead of trying to give oneself an air of being "a mysterious, impartial outsider" (England 1994, 81), a "hidden, concealed" subject that produces "a Truthful universal knowledge" in an ivory tower in the global North (Grosfoguel 2011, 5). This is what I have been trying to do in these paragraphs. I also follow Kim England's recommendation to use "the reflexive 'I'" deliberately (England 1994, 82) – though in the course of my German academic training, I have been taught not to write in the first person.

5.1.2 Speaking for others?

Another frequent demand by postcolonial (e.g., Husseini de Araújo/ Kersting 2012, 140; Ziai 2006, 208) as well as feminist (e.g., Alcoff 1991, 6) critique of research methodology is that the researcher should not claim to speak for the researched or 'give voice' to them. Shadia Husseini de Araújo and Philippe Kersting complain that there is no clear guidance on how to do better. While some authors call for research projects to build on collaboration and for ensuring that research results are shared, others demand researchers from the global North to end their activities in the global South (Husseini de Araújo/ Kersting 2012, 140). Alcoff, in spite of her disapproval of any claim to be speaking for others, nonetheless does not want "the discursively privileged" to stop their research activities but encourages them to practice "a more receptive listening" (Alcoff 1991, 17). Otherwise, it would mean to ignore one's political responsibilities as a privileged person and to withdraw to a self-centred lifestyle (ibid.). Privileges would not be overcome but simply concealed (ibid., 17, 20, 24-25). Political responsibility is also an issue for Mario Rufer as well as Barbara Katz Rothman. Rufer urges scholars, instead of trying to 'speak for' the subaltern, to *listen* to them. He aptly points out that listening is an act of authority because it is a precondition for the act of speaking – if no one has listened, no act of speaking has taken place. Hence, whether to listen or not, or whom to listen to, are political decisions (Rufer 2012, 48, 62-63). He draws on Gayatri C. Spivak' argument that what the subaltern expect from her as researcher is to *speak about* them in a language they cannot speak themselves, namely the language of the powerful (ibid., 62). In an article on feminist research, Rothman defines her role towards the women she researches as "political representation" (Rothman 1996, 53). She states: "I am their representative to the world that reads my words, hears me speak" (ibid.). The world hears her because, unlike the researched, she speaks the language of the powerful. Even though she does not share the experience of the researched, she accepts that task of political representation for them (ibid., 52-53). The representatives of Enda Graf Sahel make a similar point:

> "To recognize the value of the know-how and the beliefs of the poor somehow ends up by becoming a political act: it amounts to attacking the bases of legitimacy of the dominant power. Working with the underprivileged means, first of all, rehabilitating the status of their beliefs and promoting them on the belief market." (N'Dione et al. 1998, 375)

Hence, listening to the subaltern and speaking about them in the language of the powerful in order to make the powerful listen as well, is a counter-hegemonic act. James Ferguson surmises that the anthropologist holds a special position as a mediator between two different spheres of life and two spheres of power, as he or she knows the researched "as real, flesh and blood human beings" (Ferguson 2014, 286). This entails his or her status as an 'expert' for their concerns, on the one hand, and the responsibility to use that status on their behalf, on the other hand (ibid.). Certainly, this can be applied to any scholar from the global North conducting research in the global South. Rufer's hypothesis is based not only on the above-mentioned assessment by Spivak but also on the argumentation in her famous essay *Can the subaltern speak?* A central part of her argument was that the subaltern cannot express themselves in a way that will make the powerful listen to them (Castro Varela/ Dhawan 2015, 197-199). Spivak presents the example of the controversial widow sacrifice, which was practiced by some groups in India. Spivak shows that those widows, as subaltern women, had no option to speak out, as anything they might have said would have been instrumentalised by either party in the quarrel: Either the British could have used it to prove that the widow sacrifice was barbaric or certain Indian traditionalists, claiming that the widows had the will to die with their husbands, could have used it to defend the ritual against its critics (Spivak 1988, 297-298). Any comment of those subaltern women, be it in favour of sacrificing themselves on their dead husband's pyre or in favour of wanting to live, would have been taken as the mere validation of the argument of one of those patriarchal parties, not as an autonomous opinion. As a result, they were not even asked. Spivak asserts that no account of their voices could be found at all (ibid., 297).

Rufer, however, warns the researcher "not to regard the 'voice' of the subaltern as a discursive unity" because that would be an act of romanticising it and adjusting it to the researcher's expectations (Rufer 2012, 48, translation by E.K.). He goes on to describe his struggle with incidents from his own research experience, which confronted him with statements from the researched that contradicted his expectations and contained inconsistencies (ibid., 45-48). Kapoor likewise demands sincere openness to unexpected statements uttered by the subaltern from a self-reflexive postcolonial researcher (Kapoor 2004, 642). Raghuram and Madge state:

> "But in advocating dialogue we certainly do not presume that all difference can be dissolved to attain a complete (rational) understanding of the other, for there will always be degrees of incomprehensibility and continuing spaces 'in between'. But working through these inbetween spaces can bring moments of enlightenment; glimpses of the world through someone else's reality [...]." (Raghuram/ Madge 2006, 276)

Thus, it is possible to catch a glimpse at subaltern lifeworlds if the researcher is genuinely interested in understanding and if, at the same time, she is ready to give up the illusion of herself being in the position of reaching a *full and objectively correct* understanding of 'the Other'. She must accept the insurmountable limits of her methods, her theoretical framework, her positionality and above all, the limits that the researched decide to set for her. It is their right to keep something for themselves and to set limits for the researcher. Husseini de Araújo and Kersting also employ the metaphor of "researching in between" in an article on postcolonial research (Husseini de Araújo/ Kersting 2012, 144, translation by E.K.). They borrow the image of *researching in between* from translation, which is subject to "inevitable shifts of meaning" when trying to transfer messages from one language to another, just like research that tries to transfer the voice of 'the Other' to the scientific community (ibid., 143, translation by E.K.). Their conclusion is that, what can be expected from both processes can only be a bridge built *in between* both sides, not a truthful representation of any of them (ibid., 144). The researcher must perform the balancing act of neither silencing the researched by completely ignoring them, nor doing so by pretending to be able to 'speak for them' authentically. In summary, postcolonial critique demands the researcher to abandon any belief of being able to understand the researched fully or represent them authentically. This means abandoning the belief in the omnipotent scholar, despite the centuries-old tradition this belief has in the global North. What the researcher can do instead, is to explore 'inbetween spaces' and build bridges in collaboration with the researched and publish the results in a 'language' that has a possibility of being listened to by decision-makers. However, this should be distinguished from 'speaking for the researched' or 'giving voice to them', as these ideas imply that the researcher is able to represent the researched authentically. What the researcher can do, is to speak *about her own experience she had in the interaction with* the researched.

5.1.3 Power constellations in qualitative research

Steinar Kvale and Svend Brinkmann state that "the research interview is not a conversation between equal partners", as the researcher is the one controlling the interview situation, defining the topic, and evaluating the answers (Kvale/ Brinkmann 2009, 3). Despite their generally positive attitude towards interviews, they raise concerns about the interview not being an ethically non-hazardous method, especially when it comes to power constellations (ibid., 18). These statements make believing in a decolonisation of the interview difficult. Nevertheless, persistent power constellations do not allow *any research method* to make researcher and researched fully equal. At the 2015 *International Congress of Qualitative Inquiry*, Yvonna Lincoln presented her argument that it is impossible for researchers to free themselves from power relations (Denzin et al. 2017, 483-484). She emphasised the importance of making those power relations a subject of discussion instead of labouring under the illusion that they might be eliminated (ibid.). Feminist scholar Kim England, despite providing much helpful advice for critical research, warns that following it should not make the researcher believe that she was absolved of responsibility, as "being sensitive to these power relations does not remove them" (England 1994, 85). What counts for her is to "*accept responsibility* for the research" instead of pretending to either be able to "'give voice' to the researched" (ibid., 86, emphasis by E.K.) or to be a neutral, objective analyst of social reality (ibid., 81-82). Husseini de Araújo and Kersting likewise state that, even in postcolonial research, to overcome power imbalances completely is desirable, but unattainable – hence, they should be named and not concealed (Husseini de Araújo/ Kersting 2012, 142). The extent to which power imbalances in the research process can be reduced depends, first of all, on the attitude with which the researcher prepares and undertakes the research. For the interview, this means that the researcher must let go of as much of the control over the interview situation as possible. Or, as Karen Ross explains, "to place me, the researcher, in vulnerable moments" in order to enable "*moments of empowerment* for research participants" (Ross 2017, [18], emphasis in the original). Drawing on several theorists of methodology as well as on his own research experience, Frederick Anyan demonstrates that this is possible because the interviewee is by no means powerless in the interview situation. Although the interviewer's position is the more powerful, interviewees have their own options to challenge it. They are the ones with the knowledge needed by the researcher, they control what they say and how they say it, or whether they simply refuse to begin or to continue the interview (Anyan 2013, 3-5).

In my research project, I tried to attain the goal of "*moments of empowerment* for research participants" (Ross 2017, [18], emphasis in the original) by first of all letting the interviewee decide when and where to meet. This corresponds with one of the strategies to empower research participants suggested by Ross (ibid., [33]). Most of my interviewees decided to meet me in their homes, a few met me in public places such as the office of a cooperative or an empty church. Not only that they had the power to take an important decision concerning our encounter, they also got the opportunity of choosing the place where they felt most comfortable. I, the researcher, complied with their wishes. Kim England suggests that fieldwork structured according to these principles is "a dialogical process in which the research situation is structured by both the researcher and the person being researched" (England 1994, 84). Secondly, I spent much time thinking about whether or not to offer a financial compensation for the interviewees' time. I ultimately decided not to do so, based on the rationale that this also strengthened the position of the interviewees. They were informed from the very beginning[41] that there would be no financial compensation for their time. This put me, the researcher, in the position of a supplicant. They knew that the success of my project depended on their good will and that they were free to decide whether or not to support me. Kim England recommends that a researcher should prefer supplication to other possible stances she could adopt in the research relationship, such as intimidation or self-promotion. This involves exposing her dependence on the researched. She states that "the appeal of supplication lies in its potential for dealing with asymmetrical and potentially exploitative power relations by shifting a lot of power over to the research*ed*" (England 1994, 82, emphasis in the original). In my case, to offer money to the interviewees would have changed that power constellation in favour of the researcher – an effect that I wanted to avoid. It is worth noting, however, that this approach might not have been appropriate in other cultural settings. For instance, in the Maori context, it is necessary as a form of request and a ritual of initiation to offer gifts of goods and money to the community that one wishes to research in (Gonzalez y Gonzalez/ Lincoln 2006, [17]). Accordingly, it is important to first become informed about the particular cultural context before taking such decisions. In the case of my field of research, the procedure that had to be respected in order to gain access to prospective interviewees, was a bureaucratic one. It started on the highest level, with the requirement of applying for research clearance from the *Uganda National Council for Science and Technology* (UNCST). From there, I descended the administrative ladder, from the district administration, down to the local council at the village level (LC 1). In order to gain permission to research in a certain village, as well as to win the trust and the consent of potential interviewees, I needed to prove that I had followed the entire procedure and I had the support of all concerned authorities.

41 Prospective interviewees were informed of the voluntary (i.e., unpaid) nature of their involvement in the study both during the first telephone call requesting their participation and in the interview context (as part of the content of the *informed consent form* that was read out, explained, and provided to them in written form before the actual interview started) (see chapter 5.1.5).

This process consumed much more time than I had anticipated, yet surrendering to it was a visible sign of respect for local hierarchies, which is an important virtue in the interviewees' culture.

Ross states that open-ended interviews "provide opportunities that empower participants by enabling them to focus on what is important to them, rather than to researchers" (Ross 2017, [23]). I suggest that we can attribute this quality to interview forms that are slightly structured, like the problem-centred interview, as well – if they are prepared and conducted appropriately. I tested this hypothesis in my research. For instance, in response to the same question about what material possessions were missing during an interviewee's childhood, one may produce a long list of things like salt, soap, clothes, or medicine, which people used to make from natural materials instead of buying them – while another one did her best to sensitise me to the current problem of modern seed varieties. The latter interviewee explained how she observed the so-called 'improved' seeds to produce crops much quicker but without the taste and the positive health effects that they previously had. This illustrates that even a problem-centred interview in which the overall topics are suggested by the researcher can still provide interviewees certain leeway to bring in those aspects of the topics they consider important. Another example is the issue of savings and credit groups, which I describe in the next paragraph.

In order to infuse research with a postcolonial turn, some authors suggest making research questions more flexible to the influence of the researched (Husseini de Araújo/ Kersting 2012, 144; Raghuram/ Madge 2006, 276). Olaf Kaltmeier assumes that, in the course of the research process, the topic naturally becomes redefined by the researched (Kaltmeier 2012, 28). In my case, the flexibility of the topic itself was limited, yet I was open to the influence of the researched on certain aspects. After the first phase of interviews, I took a break to revise what had been done so far and what should be considered in upcoming interviews (see chapters 5.2.1 and 5.2.4). The most significant change arising from that reflection was the opening of my research focus towards savings and credit groups. When it came to the keyword 'solidarity', I used to ask interviewees about groups carrying out economic activities in an alternative way, e.g., through cooperatives, associations, and the like. My original intention had been to focus on groups, which are active in production, and leave out savings and credit groups. Due to negative experiences I had with the latter in my professional life, I suspected that judging such groups fairly would pose a challenge to me. Still, when looking at the first set of interviews, I realised that savings and credit groups were the ones that interviewees talked about most frequently and which they cherished most. Consequently, in order to fulfil postcolonial research requirements, I had to overcome my own prejudice and yield to the priorities of the researched. In the remaining interviews, I took time to go into detail about those kinds of groups and the way they operate. This helped me to see the advantages they had for the interviewees and focus on *their* experience, rather than my own. Other examples of my attempts to reduce power imbalances in the research relationship can be found in the other sub-sections of this chapter 5.

5.1.4 Language and translation

Achille Mbembe deplores the lack of "patient, careful, in-depth research" on Africa as well as the general attitude among researchers that there is no need to learn African languages (Mbembe 2001, 7). In anthropology, learning the language of the researched is standard procedure (Fabian 2014, 105). Still, Johannes Fabian imputes to anthropological methodology that the aim of learning the language of the researched was either to use it as a tool for effective data collection or to facilitate grasping the 'essence' of the other culture through linguistics, both of which imply a rather "manipulative use of language" (ibid., 106). In order to achieve "a reversal of information and knowledge production so that they flow from South to North, and not always in the other direction", Kapoor borrows Spivak's idea of learning a language of the global South (Kapoor 2004, 642). Spivak compares it to the only other situation in which we manage to see the world through someone else's eyes: when reading a novel and surrendering ourselves to the actions and thoughts we are being told about. She recommends that researchers should try to approach the narratives of the researched in a similar way, preferably in the latter's own language, because that is when they can "name and define themselves" instead of being labelled from outside (ibid.). In my case, one of the main activities I undertook in my first year in Uganda was learning the local language of the region in which I was living and planning to research: Lusoga. My intention was to overcome the indifference deplored by Mbembe and the manipulative approach described by Fabian in order to get as close as possible to a "non-exploitative learning" from the self-description of the researched, as suggested by Kapoor (ibid.).

When I started the interview phase, my language skills were fair but not good enough to conduct the interviews without a translator. Edith Enzenhofer and Katharina Resch warn that over-estimating one's own language competence can lead to loss of valuable information in the interview situation (Enzenhofer/ Resch 2011, [35]). Moreover, I noticed that my Lusoga skills made some people feel insecure, both in everyday conversations and in the first research-related encounters. Gatekeepers who were to put me in touch with potential interviewees, often mentioned that it was a good idea to come in the company of a Musoga (person from Busoga), and that I should take her everywhere I go in order to create confidence on the part of the interviewees. Hence, the role of the translator during the data collection phase became a crucial one. As Enzenhofer and Resch point out, translation should not be regarded as an auxiliary service, but as a central step in the research process (ibid., [16], [86]). Among the measures they recommend to ensure this, one that I consider notably important is the acknowledgment of the complex task of translators (ibid., [87]). Another one is intensive communication between researcher(s) and translator(s) before as well as during the research process (ibid., [100], [102], [103]). As I further elucidate in chapters 5.2.1 and 5.2.3, I owe a lot of thanks to my Lusoga teacher (Nkonoka Victoria); to my co-researcher, who accompanied me from the beginning of the interview phase through the completion of the transcription of the interviews and the translation of the Lusoga transcripts (Nkonoka Hellen); and to the translator who joined us during the phase of transcription and translation of transcripts (Kaiso Moses).

5.1.5 Reciprocity

The most challenging question a researcher can be asked is that of reciprocity, especially when it comes to a case like mine, a doctoral research study. I am the main beneficiary of this research because, if all goes well, I will ultimately earn a doctorate. There is no equivalent I can give to the researched. Because of this imbalance, I must try even more fervently to reduce that element of exploitation in our relationship, as far as possible. First and foremost, the respondents should know in what kind of study they are participating and that they are free to withdraw at any time. The people I interviewed in the course of this study received a detailed *informed consent form* (see appendices) before engaging in the interview. The consent form was designed according to the standards of the *Research Ethics Committee at the School of Social Sciences of Makerere University* (MAKSS REC). Interviewees could choose whether they wanted it in Lusoga or English (both versions were approved by the MAKSS REC). It was read out to them and discussed with them in their preferred language. They signed two copies, one for me, one for themselves. Through this form, interviewees learned about the academic and personal intentions underpinning the study and issues concerning their rights to voluntariness, confidentiality, and potential risks and benefits. This is the absolute minimum of reciprocity that must be provided to research participants. I tried to do more than that.

For instance, I followed the demand for a "reverse flow of knowledge" (Husseini de Araújo/ Kersting 2012, 140, translation by E.K.), which can be found in the literature on postcolonial research methodology and was likewise uttered by my interviewees. By the end of my last year in Uganda (2018), I organised feedback workshops in order to share the preliminary research results with the interviewees and give them a chance to comment on them. This activity was not part of my original research design but came in during the research process as a result of my reflection on the above-mentioned influences from the literature as well as from the researched. The feedback workshops were held within the districts of residence of the interviewees, on 11 (Kamuli), 12 (Jinja), and 13 December 2018 (Buyende). This needed to be completed before the end of my stay in Uganda (15 December 2018) and therefore required that I present the results the way they were at that particular moment in time. I explained to the participants that the results I was presenting to them were provisional. The preparations included writing a report on the provisional results in a way that was understandable and interesting for the interviewees.[42] Every participant of one of the workshops could choose whether (s)he wanted a copy of this report in Lusoga or in English. Those who were not able to participate also received a copy in their language of choice. I also prepared a workshop concept and didactic materials (flipcharts) and organised a venue, breakfast, lunch, and transport for all participants. Many interviewees live far from main roads. Finding a central venue in their respective district, collecting all of them from home and transporting them there,

42 As I knew from the interviews, respondents were interested to know what other respondents said, e.g., in terms of their experiences with solidarity groups and how to make them work well. Some were interested in knowing what I would make of the things they told me, i.e., whether I understood well what they wanted to tell me and which aspects were important to them. The content of the workshops and the written reports was supposed to give them feedback on these points as well as the chance to correct me in case they would not agree with something I made of – or failed to make of – the things they had told me during the interviews.

and organising meals at the venue, turned out to be demanding but rewarding tasks. The feedback workshops were well-attended and highly appreciated by interviewees. We had invited 47 participants, including 33 main interviewees[43], ten expert interviewees, and four important gatekeepers. The workshops were attended by 32 people: 11 in Kamuli, ten in Jinja, and 11 in Buyende.[44] My co-researcher and I presented the provisional results in Lusoga and English. This input was supplemented with lively discussions with the participants. The workshops were only documented through notetaking as they were not part of the data collection instruments and transcribing and analysing the discussions again would have gone far beyond the scope of this research project.

According to Kvale and Brinkmann, the interview interaction can be rewarding for both parties (Kvale/ Brinkmann 2009, 15). This is a point of view that I also heard from several interviewees when asked how they liked the interview. Many said that they found it worthwhile reflecting on the topics we talked about. For instance, one interviewee said he was going to start teaching his grandchildren about the past and the traditions of Busoga. He had realised during the interview that this was an important task he had so far neglected. Another interviewee, who is a government worker, said that he was going to write a report on the problem of companies exploiting the region while bringing their own workers, such that the people of the region do not get jobs or any other benefit from them. He said that the interview conversation had made him aware of the urgency of this problem. There is no guarantee that they really did those things. Such comments from interviewees nevertheless showed me that the interview left them feeling they had invested their time well. Other efforts described under sections 5.1 and 5.2, like trying to reduce the power imbalance between the researcher and the researched (5.1.3), trying to fulfil my political responsibility towards them (5.1.2), learning their language (5.1.4), and doing my best to respect their cultural values and personal priorities, were also attempts to reduce the element of exploitation in the research relationship.

43 Including three tandem interviews (of which one was discarded from the analysis, still the interviewees were invited to the workshops), we had 34 main interviewees, but unfortunately, one was deceased in the meantime (for details on the main interviews and interviewees, see chapter 5.2.1).

44 The majority of expert interviewees were not available. In Buyende, the district administration sent other workers to represent them. A group of main interviewees from Buyende had been invited to a training by an NGO.

Nevertheless, *the researcher* decides whether and when to allow "potentially empowering moments" (Ross 2017, [31]) and what to do with the research results. Kim England and Karen Ross likewise emphasise this circumstance (England 1994, 86; Ross 2017, [31]-[32]). It is applicable to *any* research method, no matter how participative, collaborative, and horizontal it is. It is still the researcher, from a position of power, who decides to use that particular research method. In almost every case, the researched do not even have the knowledge to participate in that decision. Even if the researcher provides the researched with information on differing research methods and allows them to choose from those options, she was still the one deciding which information to present to them and how. In summary, the power imbalance in research as such cannot be overcome. Under these circumstances, eliminating exploitation and creating reciprocity in the research relation proves to be exceedingly difficult. Researchers must therefore try that much more fervently to get as close to the unattainable ideal as possible.

5.2 Qualitative interviews

As the aim of qualitative interviews is "to understand the world from the subject's point of view" (Kvale/ Brinkmann 2009, 1), they are centred on the interviewee, such that even slightly structured forms can be handled flexibly during the interview situation (Dannecker/ Vossemer 2014, 154; Hopf 2012, 350-351). Kvale and Brinkmann explain: "The knowledge is not merely found, mined, or given, but is actively created through questions and answers, and the product is co-authored by interviewer and interviewee" (Kvale/ Brinkmann 2009, 54). Against the background of postcolonial methodology, I consider as worthwhile entering in such a relationship, trying to explore "spaces 'in between'" (Raghuram/ Madge 2006, 276; see also: Husseini de Araújo/ Kersting 2012) with my interviewees. Nonetheless, interviews, most of all those with groups to which the researcher does not belong, contain the danger that interviewees do not trust or understand the researcher and, as a result, provide answers that are either not honest, candid, or helpful (Miller/ Glassner 2011, 134). Still, the same peril lies in many participative research methods. The researcher may hope to gain more trust from the researched because she is giving them more power over the research than an ordinary interviewer does. Yet, there is no guarantee for the fulfilment of that hope. My approach is that a general lack of trust or understanding can only be bridged by the attitude of the researcher, not by a method as such. If the researcher succeeds in convincing the researched of her genuine openness and trustworthiness, an interview can become a space for generating knowledge where both researcher and researched feel comfortable. If the researcher fails to convince the researched of her genuine openness and trustworthiness, even the use of collaborative methods may not bring out the desired results. Certainly, the most dangerous characteristic of the interview is that researchers can be tempted to conduct it without prior or concomitant reflexion (Kvale/ Brinkmann 2009, 1, 15). However, as I have shown in chapter 5.1, the obligatory preconditions for any kind of postcolonial research are intensive preliminary, concomitant, and subsequent (self-)reflexivity as well as a critical positioning in terms of power relations.

Two sets of interviews have been conducted in the scope of this study: 30 'main interviews' with people from a variety of communities in the Busoga region and ten 'expert interviews' with Ugandan academics, politicians, and representatives of the local administration. The growing criticism passed on the term 'expert interview' is acknowledged here, e.g., that it raises the expectation of the knowledge of those people being more valuable than the knowledge of others (Dannecker/ Vossemer 2014, 161-162). However, in my case, the term is used in order to distinguish one group of interviewees from another. The other group is called '*main* interviews', a designation that is supposed to demonstrate that the knowledge of *these people* is in the centre of attention of my study. Nevertheless, due to their powerful position, the so-called 'experts' have access to information that the main interviewees may not have. Hence, their knowledge is needed as a supplement in order to embed the main interviewees' observations in a broader context.

5.2.1 Main interviews

The primary data collection method for this research project are so-called problem-centred interviews, which work from an interview guideline that suggests certain questions that build on theoretical knowledge about the research topics (Kruse 2015, 153-155; Witzel 2000). Andreas Witzel developed the problem-centred interview (PCI) as an attempt to find a middle ground between the extremes of purely inductive ways of dealing with data (e.g., Grounded Theory) and purely deductive ways of working with data. While the former tends to downplay the role of theory in research, the latter reduces the data to mere 'evidence' for what has already been known thanks to theory. Both approaches tend to conceal the role of the researcher who actively designs and steers the processes of data collection and analysis, bringing in her own theoretical (and personal) socialisation (Witzel 2000, [3]). Witzel concludes: "In relation to a PCI, the insight gained through data collection and evaluation must much rather be organized as an inductive-deductive mutual relationship" (ibid.). I followed that recommendation during the data collection phase and during analysis (see chapter 5.2.4).

The data collection through PCI encompasses four instruments: "a short questionnaire, interviewing guidelines, tape recordings of the discussion and a postscript" (Witzel 2000, [5]). The short questionnaire (see appendices) serves to collect some background information about the interviewee prior to the actual interview, such that the latter is not disturbed by this process (ibid., [6]). In the case of my study, this procedure served to gather some personal information such as the criteria for interviewees, namely age and time of stay in Busoga. Concerning the next instrument, Witzel states: "*Guidelines* are a supportive device to reinforce the interviewer's memory on the topics of research and provide a framework of orientation to ensure comparability of interviews. In addition, some ideas for lead questions into individual topics and preformulated questions to start the discussion are included" (ibid., [7], emphasis in the original). I tried to realise this in my interview guideline (see appendices). The 'tape recording' was done with a digital audio-recorder and the recordings were fully transcribed, as recommended by Witzel (ibid., [8]). There was only one exception – an expert interview – when the interviewee refused to be recorded. In that case, I took detailed notes and wrote an extensive protocol of the interview, right after it had ended. This protocol was analysed together with the transcripts of the other interviews. In all cases, interviewees were asked in advance whether they were comfortable with recording. All but the above-mentioned expert interviewee agreed; some did after asking for some clarification on the purpose of recording. For recorded interviews, I did not write a detailed protocol. Instead, I took notes on observations before, during and after the interview that would save the most important information in case of a recording being damaged (which did not happen), and that would be helpful for the application of the fourth instrument. In the *postscripts*, all observations that accompanied the interview situation – before, during, and after – must be fixed, including the researcher's impressions and spontaneous ideas (ibid., [9]). I also used them to document how the interview had been arranged and how every interviewee was introduced to the study and to the informed consent form.

An *interview guideline* is supposed to be much more flexible than a *questionnaire*, with open questions and order and formulation that can be adjusted to each interview situation (Dannecker/ Vossemer 2014, 159-160). The *interview questions* are derived from *guiding questions*, which in turn are derived from the *research questions* of the study (ibid., 159). Petra Dannecker and Christiane Vossemer emphasise the requirement that *interview questions* must "be understandable and compatible with regard to the everyday language and the sociocultural context of the interviewee" (ibid., translation by E.K.). By 'compatible' they mean that scientific or technical terms as well as expressions from a sociocultural context other than that of the interviewee must be 'translated' into terms that are easily understandable to the respondent (ibid.). Apart from 'translation' in the sense of replacing one word by another, this can be done by giving examples and explanations. This is how I made 'globalisation' and 'Social and Solidarity Economy' understandable to the interviewees. Globalisation is a process that affects people all over the world (see chapter 3), even though many may notice its manifestations without tracing them back to the phenomenon itself or using the term 'globalisation' to describe it. Likewise, the 'Social and Solidarity Economy' is completely unknown to many people as a theoretical concept, though they may know and, in some cases, even *practise* its manifestations, such as cooperatives or other forms of solidarity structures. Preparatory work therefore required identifying potential manifestations of globalisation as well as solidarity structures in the everyday lives of the interviewees. Most helpful for doing this, and for creating questions for the interview guideline, were a study by Enda Graf Sahel with a similar research focus (N'Dione et al. 1995) as well as some informal conversations with people in Busoga. The latter were fixed in conversation records, which I have analysed together with the interviews (in total, there are three conversation records). Beyond that, the theoretical framework outlined in chapters 2, 3, and 4 of this thesis influenced the interview guideline. In the following paragraphs, I present some sample interview questions in order to illustrate their theoretical foundation as well as the contribution I expected them to make towards answering my research questions. The full text of the interview guideline is available in the appendices.

The interview guideline is divided into parts A to D, namely: A. opening question; B. exploration questions on 'the influence of globalisation on people's lives'; C. exploration questions on 'alternative economic activities based on solidarity'; D. balancing and closure questions. It was neither planned nor necessary to ask all questions in the interview guideline to every interviewee because many of them were answered automatically in the course of the narratives encouraged by preceding questions. Nevertheless, the interview guideline is very detailed for three reasons: 1. to enable the interviewer and the translator to observe easily that all important information has been provided; 2. in anticipation of the possibility that an interviewee may be very reserved and need a lot of encouragement to talk; 3. because the MAKSS REC and the UNCST wanted to know as precisely as possible the contents of the conversations I planned to have with respondents. The introductory question should be formulated openly and end on an explicit invitation to answer with a detailed explanation. This is supposed to animate the interviewee to delve into the research topic with a free narrative, instead of preparing for a yes-no investigation scheme (Witzel 2000, [13]). Though subsequent questions should still provide leeway to associate and formulate freely to the interviewee, they also serve to direct the conversation towards the aspects in which the researcher is most interested (ibid., [14]-[16]). My interview guideline starts as follows:

A. Opening question: How do people earn a living in this town/ village? Please take your time and explain it in detail to me, as I am a foreigner. The idea underlying this first question in my interview guideline is to encourage interviewees to talk about their everyday economic practices, which is the field in which I intended to examine both the influence of globalisation and solidarity structures. It was a deliberate decision to ask about 'the people' instead of addressing the interviewee directly by asking, 'How *do you* make a living?'. There are two reasons for this decision. First, this way of asking provided me with more information, as the interviewee would tell me all forms of making a living that he or she observed in his or her social environment, not only his or her own occupation. Second, I hoped this approach would make interviewees feel at ease because it was not a personal question. I observed in several interview situations that this expectation was fulfilled. Interviewees who had been excited up to that point, started to relax when they heard that question and started responding to it. Some said after the interview that they had been afraid of the questions being too difficult for them to answer (as a matter of courtesy, they were not asked whether they meant intellectually, politically, or personally 'difficult') and that they were glad to find out that this was not the case. This opening question was supposed to show them that, on the one hand, the questions that awaited them referred to *their* *sphere of experience* and, on the other hand, they were not going to be too personal.

Section "**B. Influence of *globalisation* on people's lives**" is sub-divided into five 'guiding questions' (see above; cf. Dannecker/ Vossemer 2014, 159) – or rather 'key aspects', as they are not formulated as questions and rather serve the researcher to structure the interview guideline. Each of them encompasses one to three sets of *interview questions*.

I. Development of the profitability of products (e.g., crops) produced in the region in the past 30 years. This 'key aspect' encompasses questions such as: "Which products are most commonly produced in this region? Are they produced for home consumption or for sale?" The underlying interest of those and related questions is to delve into the topic of production within the interviewee's home region. Many of the things reported by interviewees (see chapter 8.2) cannot be found in official statistics because this is not considered important for the macroeconomics of the (inter-)national economy. For the majority of the population, however, it is important, as they survive on it every day. Against that background, its political and economic significance cannot be denied. Further questions under this heading go into detail about cash crops and the mode of production. Martin Khor has pointed out the problem that many countries of the global South must still rely on primary commodities as their main exports. As a result, resources are invested in cash crops that may even turn out to be unprofitable (Khor 2001, 27-29; see also chapter 3.3). The questions under this key aspect can shed light on this issue in the context of Busoga. As Yash Tandon suggests, global warming, increasing fuel prices, land grabbing, the repurposing of land from food crop to cash crop production, financial speculation with food, and agricultural subsidies within the European Union and the USA directly threaten farmers in the global South (Tandon 2016, 37; see also chapter 3.3). Furthermore, the latter are dependent on market forces, intermediaries, and global fertiliser and seed producers, as a result of structural adjustment programmes reducing or abolishing governmental support for agriculture in countries of the global South (ibid.). The questions under this and the following key aspect can uncover whether the interviewees have experienced such phenomena.

II. Involvement of the town/ village in trade – locally, nationally, internationally. Under this heading are questions such as: "Do people in your town/ village sell crops in other villages/ towns, or to brokers, or traders? How is it organised? How was it organised in the past decades?" Those questions helped me to understand the local trade networks in the past and present alike. They were inspired by a study on peasant life in

Senegal by Enda Graf Sahel that took an approach similar to mine, namely interviewing elderly people in order to learn how they see changes in their social environment (in that case of farming practices, in particular) over the past decades (N'Dione et al. 1995, 18). Respondents of Enda Graf Sahel explained how they used to be exploited by traders until they managed to organise the transport of crops to the next market by themselves, and they praised the new means of transport that connected them to areas outside their village (ibid., 25-26). Another interesting point in that study was the account of how people used to produce clothes and other everyday commodities by themselves before it was possible – and necessary – to buy them in shops (ibid., 21-22). This inspired the interview questions: "Do you remember a time when there were no shops around? Where did people get the products from, which they buy in these shops nowadays?" Those questions provided insight into the involvement of the town or village in trade over time, as interviewees were animated to talk about evolutions such as barter trade and subsistence production turning into capitalist shop business. As discussed in chapter 3.2, a possible consequence of expanding capitalism is the effect that people let go of their biological, social, and cultural survival strategies in favour of the 'modern lifestyle' of a consumer-citizen (Hawley 2008, 26). This hypothesis relates to the above question as well as to the question that follows in the next paragraph and to the question about 'traditional' solidarity structures in section C of the interview guideline (question C.IV, see below).

III. Availability and origin of new products. Need for those products and ways to finance their purchase. The central interview question under this point is: "Which products can be found in most households nowadays that were not there during your childhood?" In the above-mentioned study by Enda Graf Sahel, respondents reported that people had developed needs that they did not previously have, such as the need for "curtains, sheets, radios" (N'Dione et al. 1995, 21). This goes hand in hand with Glenn's above-cited point that firms in a capitalist environment must innovate and expand permanently and, as a result, need to create "new social wants and needs" in customers, in their home markets or abroad (Glenn 2007, 10-11; see also chapter 3.1 of this thesis). As a result, it is safe to assume that one of the signs of the penetration of an area by global capitalism is the availability of new products that create those desires. As they are 'new' desires, the need for those products was either not there before, or it was satisfied in another manner, e.g., by people producing things themselves in order to satisfy those needs. This might be a sign of the neglect of former survival strategies in favour of the 'modern lifestyle' of a consumer-citizen, which Hawley describes (Hawley 2008, 26). And as they are 'social' desires, at least in some cases, the prestige of those new products may be more important than their practical usefulness. Hence, the availability of new products and an emerging 'need' for them – especially when there is no other explanation for that 'need' than the availability itself – can be taken as evidence for the penetration of the area of research by globalisation.

IV. Presence of companies/ individual business people from 'outside' (either Kampala or other big cities, or from abroad). This key aspect raised interview questions such as: "Did the population of business companies in this region increase in the past 30 years?" According to the promises of development institutions and international financial institutions, creating a favourable environment for investors should increase the number of business companies in a country. Uganda has undoubtedly tried to do this by implementing 'market-oriented' policies and adjustment programmes in the past 30 years (Reinikka/ Collier 2001). This question was supposed to test whether or not the success of policies and programmes for attracting foreign investment could be perceived by the interviewees. A growing number of business companies, no matter whether foreign or Ugandan, could be taken as an indicator of globalisation's increasing penetration into the region. Another question arising from this query is: "What are the effects those companies have on the welfare of the local population?"

V. Summary on globalisation. This concluding part of the interview guideline asks: "Nowadays, is it easier or harder to make a living than 30 years ago? From your point of view, what are the main reasons for that?" This offered the interviewees the chance to provide their personal evaluation of socio-economic developments in their region as they have experienced them over the past 30 years, the period of economic liberalisation in Uganda. Despite the critical attitude towards liberalisation I displayed in chapters 2 and 3 of this thesis, I formulated the questions in a neutral way so as to welcome positive and negative reactions even-handedly.

Section "**C. Alternative economic activities based on *solidarity***" is sub-divided into four 'key aspects' with one to four sets of interview questions each.

I. Existence of groups that fit into this category and their function(s). This section starts with a definition of solidarity structures as they have been defined in chapter 4.2: "With the headword 'solidarity', I mean that I would like to know whether there are any alternative ways of doing economy here, meaning groups that are run by and for the sake of the local population, keeping money and facilities at their disposal. Such groups could be cooperatives, associations, mutuals, or similar ones". In the following, interviewees were asked about the existence of such groups and, if they were knowledgeable about them, their function(s). Following the cooperative principles cited in chapter 4.2.2 (which can also be applied to other kinds of solidarity groups, to a certain extent), interviewees were asked about the ownership of the means of production in those groups, decision making, and redistribution among the members.

II. Motivation of people for founding/ joining such groups. This key aspect led to the interview question: "Why do you think people engage in such groups?"

III. Personal evaluation of such groups. Here, interviewees were asked: "How do you judge such groups/ activities?" Further enquiry referred to their *personal* motivation for belonging or not belonging to such groups. Interestingly, those seemingly similar questions led to notably different answers, in some cases. For instance, one interviewee could name many advantages of solidarity groups that motivate people to join them. She herself is not a member of such a group, however, as she is afraid of taking out a loan, being unable to pay it back, and ending up being pursued by the group.

IV. Other (traditional?) practices that can be mentioned here? The underlying idea of this key aspect was to find out about the autochthonous solidarity structures mentioned in chapters 4.1 and 4.2.2 that can serve as bases for modern SSE activities (cf. Develtere 2008, 2; Thomas 2015, 10-11). One of the questions asked in this section derived from a casual conversation I had with a woman in Busoga (which has been fixed in a conversation record). She had told me that, in the past, neighbours had been sharing many things, such as manure, whereas today, people made their neighbours and friends pay for everything. On the one hand, this sounded to me like evidence of progressing commodification, which is a typical sign of the expansion of capitalism into all spheres of life. On the other hand, asking interviewees about that practice of sharing could have revealed that it is still done. This could be interpreted as an autochthonous form of solidarity structures. In either case, the outcome was of interest to my research questions. In order to obtain more information on this point, I formed the following interview question: "Are there any things you used to get from your neighbours for free/ exchange with your neighbours, and now you have to buy them (e.g., manure)? If yes, how would you explain that change?" Another question under this point goes back to the above-cited Enda Graf study. Respondents talked about special rites with regard to the millet harvest, in which particular members of the community must help and have to receive their share of the harvest and a festive meal in return (N'Dione et al. 1995, 19). From this resulted the question in my interview guideline: "Are there any rites of giving/ redistribution (e.g., a certain group of people that has to get a share of each harvest, traditional support to widows, etc.)?" Those could be potential autochthonous solidarity structures. In general, these questions were also supposed to find out whether the following hypotheses in terms of globalisation apply to Busoga: Hawley's claim that people let go of their social and cultural survival strategies in favour of the 'modern lifestyle' of a consumer-citizen (Hawley 2008; see above and chapter 3.2); Escobar's contention that community ties in the global South were destroyed by these influences from outside (Escobar 2012; see chapter 2.2.3); and Ziai's assumption that the latter lead to "the increasing commodification of social relationships" (Ziai 2017, 106; see chapter 3.3).

The interview guideline ends with the short section "**D. Balancing questions/ Closure**". It has no 'guiding questions' or 'key aspects', but only two sets of interview questions. The first one goes as follows: "Is there any aspect that might be of interest for me, which we did not yet talk about? Or is there anything you would like to add to what was said?" Dannecker and Vossemer recommend asking the interviewee for such recommendations at the end of the interview (Dannecker/ Vossemer 2014, 160), a recommendation that makes perfect sense from a postcolonial point of view. After all, it helps to deconstruct the image of the 'omniscient researcher' and the 'passive research participant'. The second one, which is the conclusive set of questions for the whole interview, asks: "How did you like the interview? Is there any advice you would like to give me?" It has a similar function as the preceding question though this time focused on the interview itself, whereas the preceding question referred to the research topics.

There was no question in the interview guideline for main interviewees that directly asked them about the effects of liberalisation and privatisation. This was a deliberate choice I made in order not to influence their answers. There were, however, many chances for interviewees to mention such effects, and they frequently took those chances. For instance, during analysis, a code for the burden of school fees (a result of the privatisation of the education sector) was applied 28 times (in 19 distinct interview transcripts). Indeed, narratives concerning this problem came up as part of the answers to diverse questions, namely A. 1), B.I. 2) and 3), B.II. 1), B.III. 2), B.IV. 3), B.V. 1) and 2), C.I. 3), C.II. 1), C.IV. 1 and 3), and D. 1) (cf.

appendices). Although this information may not be very productive with regard to content here (for details, see chapter 8), I provide it in order to demonstrate the broad dispersion of that issue over very diverse interview questions, among which some may be predestined for it, while others are not. Hence, interviewees obviously felt a strong need to bring up that topic. The interview guideline was conceptualised in a way that *allowed* them to raise those issues yet did *not push* them to do so. The latter would have meant encouraging answers that would rather have been informed by the bias of my own theoretical stance mirrored in leading questions, which I sought to avoid.

Before starting the interview phase, I held a workshop with my co-researcher/ translator in order to provide an opportunity for her to gain a deeper understanding of the research topics, the research methodology and methods, as well as the objectives of the research project. As recommended by Dannecker and Vossemer, we conducted a pilot interview in order to see whether the questions were understandable and to determine the approximate duration of such an interview (Dannecker/ Vossemer 2014, 160). This pilot interview was not transcribed and analysed. The interviewee was informed beforehand that he was participating in a pilot interview. I held another workshop with my co-researcher after the first set of interviews (10 main and 4 expert interviews; see also chapter 5.2.4). Continuous discussions between her and me accompanied the research process.

For the main interviews, I chose participants from 21 communities in the Busoga region, out of which ten are rural, six are considered 'urban' according to local standards (trading centres in rural areas), and five are urban in the narrow sense (towns). The region has ten districts, from which I chose three: Buyende, Jinja, and Kamuli District. My plan was to conduct 30 main interviews. The Busoga region is wide and contains differing geographical and cultural influences as well as accents in the various sub-regions. Instead of conducting three interviews in each district and trying to compare what is incomparable, I decided instead to conduct ten interviews in three districts that are geographically close to each other and show similar cultural and linguistic patterns. Kamuli is the district in which I lived for 34 months and the others are neighbouring districts. I limited my research to the area that has the cultural background and speaks the accent that I know better than others. Furthermore, it made sense to choose the three districts on the Nile because, despite all they have in common, they can also show different facets of the Busoga region: Buyende is extremely rural and used to be sparsely populated. Nowadays, it receives a lot of migrants from Jinja and over-populated regions outside Busoga, who are looking for land there. Jinja is the most urbanised area in Busoga and its capital of the same name used to be Uganda's number one industrial city before Kampala took that over. Kamuli is located in between Buyende and Jinja – geographically, economically, and in terms of the extent of urbanisation.

In order to be able to ask interviewees about processes that span several decades, I decided to delineate inclusion criteria for interviewees, e.g., requiring they be above 40 years of age. I did not want to apply tribalist criteria, hence, it was not a requirement for them to be Basoga. They only had to speak either Lusoga or English and be residents of the respective area of study for at least 30 years. Indeed, the majority of interviewees were born in Busoga; however, some had moved to Busoga from other places, more than 30 years prior to the interview. I was obliged to reduce the original age limit from 'at least 50 years' to 'above 40 years' (the youngest interviewee was 43 years old at the time of the interview). In some cases, this was due to the fact that there was no group member above 50 (who was willing to be interviewed). In other cases, the prospective interviewee was warmly recommended to me, e.g., because (s)he is active in the community and, as result, an attentive observer of social life who can provide helpful information (and is ready to do so). In total, I interviewed 34 people in the course of the main interviews. Three interviews were "tandem interviews". On several occasions, my polite request to talk to the interviewee in private was not respected and other people (family members or other group members) stayed around during the interview. In those situations, I considered it more important that the interviewee felt at ease and had his or her will than to follow my own wishes. In most cases, those 'observers' were listening quietly or occasionally commenting. These comments were documented in the transcripts but not considered in the analysis of the interviews. In three cases, the observer talked as much as the actual interviewee. In those cases, I requested that person to sign an informed consent form (they had heard the content already, when it had been read out to the actual interviewees in their presence) and give me some information for the questionnaire as well, such that I could regard them as interviewees and consider their answers during the interview analysis. In one case, this was completely unproblematic because both the original interviewee and the 'observer' fit my criteria. In two of those 'tandem' cases, one of the interviewees suited my requirements regarding age and time of stay in the region, while the other did not. I deemed it acceptable to nevertheless include their comments in the analysis, as one of them was able to answer the questions concerning "the past 30 years". In one case, the tandem consisted of a member of a SACCO, who was by then 65 years old and had been living in the same place for his entire life. Hence, he fulfilled all my criteria perfectly. The 'observer' of the interview, who had put us in touch, and who became part of the interview, was an employee of that SACCO, who was 'only' 38 years old, yet had a lot of interesting information to contribute, especially when it came to the management of the SACCO. Due to that constellation, I decided to accept the interview the way it was because as an entity, it fulfils my criteria. In the third case, the interview turned out to be unfit for my research purposes. It did not bring out information that was promising to contribute to answering my research questions. The fact that one of the two interviewees did not match my criteria was one of the reasons for that, albeit not the only reason. I therefore decided to remove this interview from the data and did not transcribe or analyse it. In order to reach my target of 30 main interviews, I conducted an additional interview with an interviewee who suited my criteria. Out of the total number of 31 main interviews with 34 interviewees, transcription and analysis were thus done on 30 interviews (including two tandem interviews) with 32 interviewees. Out of those 32 respondents, 15 were female and 17 were male; 21 were aged between 50 and 70, while six were younger and five were older. Twenty had completed primary school, out of whom five had completed secondary school, and two were University graduates.

I reached the majority of interviewees using the gatekeeper approach. Prior to going to 'the field', I needed to respect the official hierarchy and approach the officers in charge of my field of study (*Community Development* and *Commerce*) on the district level. These officers always needed to first see my research clearance from the *Uganda National Council for Science and Technology* (UNCST). I presented my clearance letter and the content of my study to them and asked them for helpful contacts. As I was showing interest in solidarity groups, they gave me the contacts of some groups in their respective districts, plus the contacts of local officials that I should get in touch with before doing anything in their place (sometimes sub-county chiefs, sometimes village leaders). Referring to the district officers helped me gain the support of those local officials as well as the chairpersons of the groups, who, in turn, connected me to the majority of the interviewees. I always asked for an interview with one member of a group and one non-member from the same place. I also applied the criteria for which I had planned (see above). In each district, I contacted four groups in order to arrange eight interviews in this way. The last two,

I saved for spontaneous interests ('snowball method'), meaning that an interviewee told me about an interesting group or person and I asked him or her to put us in touch. This worked out very well and enabled me to obtain a balanced sample of solidarity group members and non-members.

As described further in chapter 5.2.4, I took a break from data collection and started first steps of analysis after completing the first set of interviews (10 main and 4 expert interviews). Meanwhile, my translator was working on the transcription of the main interviews, which had been conducted in Lusoga. When I had some preliminary results from first analytical steps, and my translator/ co-researcher had some revision of the interviews through transcription, we gathered our ideas on aspects to be considered in future interviews prior to continuing with the remaining interviews.

The findings of interview analysis are backed by the results of other methods used in triangulation. Certainly, the answers of the interviewees do not paint a picture of the 'real' situation. They gave me their *personal* view, the perception of the situation by the subaltern. In contrast, official statistics and other written sources, as well as economic literature, describe the situation the way it is presented by the powerful. As Linda Alcoff states, 'truth' is never objective, as it depends on the social position of the speaker, whether what (s)he says is taken as 'the truth' (Alcoff 1991, 12-14). I do not want to accept the common view that the 'official version' of government institutions and international organisations is 'true'. Apart from my support for the assumption that 'reality' is socially constructed, those institutions have good reasons to describe the situation in a way that casts a positive light on their policies – and their sources of information may be one-sided in many cases. Nor do I want to stylise the subaltern view as the (alternative) 'truth'. I take the view that both are partial views from a particular perspective, i.e., social constructions based on differing interests and resources. My interest in the subaltern view arises from the fact that it is seldomly taken into consideration seriously, such that the people, who are actually affected by certain developments (e.g., the effects of globalisation on their everyday lives), are silenced. Still, the subaltern view is not objective, and it needs to be contextualised with the help of specialist literature and the outcomes of expert interviews and document analysis.

5.2.2 Expert interviews

The term 'expert interviews' does not refer to a specific form of interviews, but to the target group of interviewees (Dannecker/ Vossemer 2014, 161). For expert interviews, I used problem-centred interviews built around an interview guideline rather than a questionnaire as I had done for the 'main interviews'. Due to their powerful position, namely as Ugandan academics, politicians, and representatives of the local administration, these individuals could access information that the main interviewees could not, e.g., academic knowledge or knowledge on government policies that concern my research topics. This kind of knowledge was needed in order to embed the main interviewees' observations into a broader context. Against this background, the approach used in this study can be considered a form of "systematizing expert interview" – in contrast to the explorative expert interview and the "[t]heory-generating expert interview" (Flick 2018, 237; see also: Dannecker/ Vossemer 2014, 162).

Under the rubric of 'experts', I interviewed the *Commercial Officer* and the *Community Development Officer* of all three districts I researched in (Buyende, Jinja, Kamuli), one economist in Kampala[45], the *Prime Minister* of *Busoga Kingdom*, and two politicians from Busoga region who had been active in the Ugandan cooperative movement and other developments that are of significance to my study. In total, I conducted ten expert interviews, which gave me very helpful information about my topic. It was unavoidable to have nine male and only one female expert interviewee as I had selected interviewees by their positions, which were mainly held by men. For the same reason, I could not consider age as a criterion for choosing them. Nevertheless, only one of them was below 43 years old by the time of conducting the interview.

The expert interview guideline is very similar to the main interview guideline. However, the 'experts' have a higher level of formal education (all are University graduates) than the majority of main interviewees and all are, or have been, active in politics, public administration, and/ or economic research. Consequently, I could ask the questions more directly, without eliminating technical terms (such as 'liberalisation') and linking

45 The economist was a research fellow at the *Economic Policy Research Centre* (EPRC) Kampala. Because I had conducted interviews exclusively with males, I had done some research in order to find a female academic who was knowledgeable about my research topic. This researcher had recently done some research on farmers' groups in Eastern Uganda.

the content of the questions to the interviewee's everyday life. For example, the opening question immediately addresses the issue of globalisation by asking: "How does globalisation influence people's lives in Uganda?" Another difference between the two interview types concerns the locality on which the interview guideline focused. Main interviewees were asked about their home region. For expert interviewees, the opening question was generally asked about Uganda. Subsequent questions were adjusted to the field of expertise of the interviewee, either asking about Busoga as a region or about a narrower region, e.g., a particular district or town about which the interviewee was particularly knowledgeable. Apart from these differences, sections B.I., B.IV., and C. are the same in the main and expert interviews. The interview questions in sections B.II and B.III are slightly different, though the overarching 'key aspects' are the same. Section B.II asks directly about the involvement of the region in trade and the effects of economic liberalisation, without taking the detour of the main interview guideline. The same applies to section B.III, in which experts are asked whether, in their view, new products are actually available to and affordable for people with low incomes. Section D. is the same across both interview types, with the exception of an additional closing question in the expert interviews, namely: "Is there any advice you would like to give me where to find further information?" Although all instruments of data collection were available in Lusoga and English, and the majority of expert interviews were conducted in the presence of the translator, all expert interviewees chose to be interviewed in English.

5.2.3 Transcription and translation of transcripts

There is no standard transcription system. Rather, it is up to the researcher to decide which information is necessary for conducting analysis. Uwe Flick cautions the over-enthusiastic transcriber that linguistically elaborated transcription systems should only be applied when the additional information is actually needed because the more detailed a transcript, the more time its production consumes and the more complicated becomes the extraction of contents from it (Flick 2018, 438-439). In my case, the transcription was done by two people, who were not very experienced in transcription, namely my co-researcher and me. It was very important to me not to 'outsource' this work but to have it done by the same people who had conducted the interviews and, to the greatest possible extent, by myself. I was planning to apply a method of analysis that focusses on what was said, not on how it was said (see chapter 5.2.4). For those reasons, I decided to work with a simple transcription system and with a simple transcription software. Following the recommendations from some methodology books, I chose *f4transcript* (Kruse 2015, 608; Kuckartz 2007, 38). Its basic functions like automatic rewind, setting of time stamps, or easy adjustment of play-back speed turned out to be helpful and easy to acquire.

I transcribed the expert interviews and two main interviews that were conducted in English. Other interviews were conducted partly or totally in Lusoga[46]. The translator, who had also been interpreting during the interviews, transcribed these interviews. This was very helpful because she had been communicating with the interviewees, knew their way of speaking and even remembered gestures interviewees had made during the conversation. For instance, when the audio record had only documented the interviewee saying "so many" and the translator had noted down or remembered how many fingers the person had been holding up to indicate the number, she would note in the transcript, in parentheses: "showing 2 fingers". When she had finished typing a transcript, we worked together to check back against the audio file and make any necessary corrections. We subsequently printed the transcript and translated it word-by-word into English. In order to save time, I engaged a second translator at that point in time, such that we could work in parallel: As the original translator was still transcribing, the new colleague and I could already do the checking and translation of the available transcripts. When all transcripts were ready, I worked with the two translators taking turns, six days a week, until we were through with all Lusoga transcripts. This very time-consuming but rewarding process enabled me to read the interview transcripts the way Kapoor recommends (Kapoor 2004, 642) and to get as close to what was actually said as a cultural, social, and linguistic outsider like me can expect to get. This was enabled by the language skills I had acquired but most of all by the permanent exchange with the translators as we translated and cross-checked together. That exchange provoked numerous discussions about latent, situational, or alternative meanings of a word or a statement. Moreover, a lot of cultural background information was given to me during that process.

46 Some interviewees spoke some Luganda as well, however, Lusoga and Luganda are so similar that my translators are fluent in both and I could cope with it, as well.

As it sufficed for the purposes of my analysis and facilitated the work with the Lusoga transcripts for me, I used a simple transcription system as described by Thorsten Dresing, Thorsten Pehl, and Christian Schmieder (Dresing et al. 2015, 27-33). A summary of the most important rules of this transcription system can be found in the appendices of this thesis. In the following sub-section, I elaborate on the steps of transcription, correction and (where necessary) translation of transcripts, all of which were part of my first step of analysis.

5.2.4 Interview analysis

Methods of data analysis should be reflected upon as critically as methods of data collection. Otherwise, a researcher's cooperative conduct towards the researched might be interpreted as a mere trick, aimed at effective data collection (Kaltmeier 2012, 35). While it is difficult to find literature on postcolonial methods of data collection, it is impossible to find literature on postcolonial data analysis. As a result, I took the criteria described in chapter 5.1, which either refer to data collection methods or to 'research' in general, and applied them to qualitative data analysis in particular. In qualitative research, it is common practice to start data analysis parallel to data collection (cf. e.g. Rapley 2011, 285-286). After the first set of interviews (10 main and 4 'expert' interviews), I paused data collection and started initial steps of analysis. After having produced some preliminary results that were helpful for the remaining process of data collection, I continued with both procedures. In qualitative research, the method of data analysis is chosen according to the properties of the data collected and the expectations of the researcher concerning the results (Dey 1993, 2; Schmidt 2012, 447). In my case, this meant first and foremost that the method of data analysis needed to match my postcolonial approach. As elucidated above, one of the central requirements of the latter is to occupy as little space within the research process as possible and provide leeway to the researched, as far as this is possible within the given power constellations. From this I drew the conclusion that a 'postcolonial' method of data analysis needs to comprise close examination of the original data rather than premature interpretation or adaptation of the data to precast theoretical frameworks. Hence, it must be a method that prioritises inductive analysis. Nevertheless, there is also the postulate to reflect on one's own background and refrain from pretending that the researcher was able to approach the data without any theoretical or personal prejudice. Hence, the method of choice needed to have inductive and deductive elements, with the clearest separation possible that makes the researcher's intervention visible. Certainly, another challenge is the fact that *any kind of analysis* inevitably makes something new out of the original data. Ian Dey uses an expressive image to illustrate this phenomenon: He compares the data to eggs and the analysis results to an omelette, the latter containing the essence of the former, though not being the same thing, anymore (Dey 1993, 30). This is another proof of what has been discussed in chapter 5.1.2, namely that a researcher is never able to 'speak for the researched' or to 'give voice to them'. Their *voices* (plural!) get more and more lost with every step of the way, beginning with the very first step. Nevertheless, a faint echo of those voices – blended with the researcher's voice and those of other people that have influenced the researcher, e.g., through literature, teaching, discussions, etc. – will come through in the research report. The task of the postcolonial researcher is to keep this echo as loud and authentic as possible *and* to be honest with herself, the researched, and the readers of the report concerning the unsurmountable limits to that endeavour.

For this difficult task, I had to choose the method that was most suitable for my data. Originally, I had planned to use Mayring's *Qualitative Content Analysis* (QCA). With regard to document analysis, I retained that approach. The material to be examined as well as my expectations of its analysis matched with QCA, as I explain further in chapter 5.3. The data set derived from *interviews* did not match well with QCA, however. The documents, in contrast, provide existing data and were chosen for analysis because of their known content. The interviews, conversely, had been a social process of shared knowledge production with a relatively open outcome. A social relationship was created between the actors through the process of knowledge production. The respondents as well as the researcher herself (through the theoretical framework and the considerations described in chapter 5.1) had developed certain expectations concerning the researcher's treatment of the collected data. As such, the interview data required a different approach. The more familiar I became with the interview data as well as postcolonial critique on research methods, the more I realised that QCA was not the right method for this part of the research project. I found QCA too exclusively descriptive and deductive. However, what disturbed me most about it was the notion of "consistency", saying that the quality of a coding frame had to be measured by proving that any other person – or, if that was impossible, the researcher, at a later point in time – would produce the same results using it (Schreier 2012,

6, 174-175; see also: Mayring 2008, 43). From a self-reflexive perspective, which postcolonial critique demands (Husseini de Araújo/ Kersting 2012, 139, 141-142; Kapoor 2004), this requirement appeared highly problematic to me. From this point of view, two people can never attain identical results in a qualitative study because they approach the data with their necessarily differing personal and theoretical backgrounds. Concerning the alternative of the same researcher doing the coding again after some time, the situation I am describing here is good evidence of how the theoretical background of a person can develop over the course of some months. Consequently, I needed a method through which those problems would be at least mitigated.

The method I ultimately chose is *Thematic Analysis*, as described by Virginia Braun and Victoria Clarke (2006). The term 'thematic analysis' has been accused of being "a somewhat 'diffuse approach' lacking sufficient agreed principles" (Mackieson et al. 2019, 969). Braun and Clarke call it "a poorly demarcated and rarely acknowledged, yet widely used qualitative analytic method" (Braun/ Clarke 2006, 77). While some authors consider it a *tool* that is used within the scope of other methods, Braun and Clarke claim that "thematic analysis should be considered a method in its own right" (ibid., 78). In order to make it *visible* and *usable* as such, they give a detailed step-by-step guide on their approach to thematic analysis. To a certain extent, their approach builds on Richard Boyatzis (1998), however, it has several unique features (Braun/ Clarke 2006). This step-by-step guide, on which I have built my own description of the process of analysis, serves the purpose of traceability. However, qualitative analysis is an iterative process, not a linear one. Without explicitly referring to it, Braun and Clarke share some important assumptions of postcolonial critique: They reject the suppositions – which can frequently be found in the literature on research methodology – of the researcher 'giving voice' to the researched, and that of codes or themes naturally "emerging" from the data (ibid., 80). Instead, they insist on the active role of the researcher, who purposively choses certain aspects from the data, bringing in his or her own, unique theoretical background (ibid.; see also 84). Thematic analysis can be described as "a search for themes that emerge as being important to the description of the phenomenon" under examination, an approach that first of all involves *careful and repetitive reading* of the original data (Fereday/ Muir-Cochrane 2006, 82). This approach matches the above-cited demands for "receptive listening" in critical research (Alcoff 1991, 17; see also: Rufer 2012, 48; see also chapter 5.1.2). The attempt to 'listen' to the researched actively can be sustained throughout analysis by reading their words carefully and repetitively – and by using an inductive approach to coding, deriving codes for analysis from their words[47]. The latter is not a requirement for thematic analysis. However, the method allows for it, as it is flexible to be used either in an inductive or deductive way, depending on the researcher's particular approach (Braun/ Clarke 2006, 83-85). Here, the above-cited suggestion to read the accounts of the researched like a novel, i.e., as open-mindedly as possible, in their own language, comes in (Kapoor 2004, 642; see also chapter 5.1.4). All interview transcripts have been analysed in the language, in which the interview was conducted. For the majority of main interviews, it was done in Lusoga. Only two main interviews and the expert interviews were conducted in English, at the request of the interviewees. Thematic analysis fulfils postcolonial requirements as well as Dey's clarion call for qualitative researchers to keep the balance "between an open mind and an empty head" when doing data analysis (Dey 1993, 63). Dey opines that it is neither possible nor desirable for a researcher to 'empty' her head of all knowledge – yet, she should not allow her own assumptions to overshadow the evidence in the data (ibid.). Meanwhile, "their [Braun's and Clarke's] approach to thematic analysis has become the most widely cited of the many different versions available" (Mackieson et al. 2019, 969). For instance, it has found its way into popular textbooks on qualitative research, such as Uwe Flick's *An introduction to Qualitative Research* (Flick 2018, 474-476).

Braun's and Clarke's thematic analysis consists of *six phases*, out of which some allow and others *require* working intensively on the original data (see below). Interpretation also plays an important role in it. However, its influence on the research results is made visible. The first phase, "***familiarizing yourself with your data***" (Braun/ Clarke 2006, 87, emphasis[48] in the original), starts with transcription or, if it is done by someone else, by "check[ing] the transcripts back against the original audio recordings for 'accuracy'" (ibid., 88). As described in the preceding sub-section, I used the phase of transcription and translation of transcripts for a very close examination of the original data. After this, the first phase of analysis was concluded by going through every single transcript anew, collecting ideas for coding and writing a list of them (see Braun/ Clarke 2006, 87-88). From this point onwards, the software MAXQDA was used for analysis.

47 However, it must be kept in mind that it is *the researcher* who derives the codes, not the researched nor any kind of 'natural' process.

48 Both italics and bold font. The same applies to the other headlines for subsequent steps of analysis by Braun and Clarke cited below.

The second phase is called ***"generating initial codes"*** (ibid., 88, emphasis in the original). Braun and Clarke borrow the definition of a unit of coding from Boyatzis, who calls it "the most basic segment, or element, of the raw data or information that can be assessed in a meaningful way regarding the phenomenon" (Boyatzis 1998, 63). I concluded from this definition that, for me, a unit of coding is *a group of words that contains information on a particular aspect* and that may vary in size, from three words up to several sentences. What is rather exceptional in the approach of Braun and Clarke, is their definition of a unit of analysis, which for them, refers to *a theme*. As such, it can only be defined after the themes have been established in the following phases of analysis (Braun/ Clarke 2006, 88; see below). Their key advice for this second phase is to code generously (in terms of number of codes), inclusively (in terms of context), and flexibly with regard to extracts of text being coded once, more than once, or not at all. Beyond that, the authors caution not to iron out contradictions within the data set, as they occur naturally (ibid., 89). This method of coding produces a lot of material. I went through the entire corpus of material for coding twice. After the first round of coding, I had 964 codes, which I reduced to 860 during the second round. Finally, I revised the coding frame. After that final revision, I remained with 658 codes. During coding, I kept in mind the following rules proposed by Boyatzis: In his view, a code needs a name or label, which should be formulated as closely to the data as possible because interpretation should be kept out of this early stage of analysis as far as possible. Furthermore, it needs a definition of its topic; a general description of when to apply it and possible criteria that lead to its application or non-application; and examples for clarification (Boyatzis 1998, 31-32).[49]

The third phase of Braun's and Clarke's thematic analysis is called ***"searching for themes"***, which means that codes are sorted into "overarching theme[s]" (Braun/ Clarke 2006, 89, emphasis in the original). During this phase, codes are sorted either into main themes, sub-themes, or they are discarded if they do not fit anywhere and if creating a new theme for them is futile (ibid., 90). Braun and Clarke provide the following definition of a theme: "A theme captures something important about the data in relation to the research question, and represents some level of *patterned* response or meaning within the data set" (ibid., 82, emphasis in the original). They explain that themes "are *where the interpretative analysis of the data occurs*, and in relation to which arguments about the phenomenon

49 The codebook is available upon request.

being examined are made" (ibid., 88, emphasis by E.K.). This change of strategy within the process of analysis is readily apparent in thematic analysis, especially when it is carried out in an inductive way, as I did in this study. During phases 1 and 2 of analysis, I had been completely focused on the original data. The coding frame was created with the intention to keep code names as close to the respondents' words and as free of interpretation as possible. This had resulted in a very long list of codes. Extracts were only subsumed under a certain code if the interviewee had really said what the code implied, not if the interviewee's statement required interpretation in order to be coded there. Subsuming these numerous, specific codes under overarching themes inevitably required generalisation and interpretation. Otherwise, 658 codes could have never been reduced to 60 themes.[50] However, the detailed knowledge of the original data I had gained during phases 1 and 2 enabled me to take this interpretative step with the priorities of the respondents in mind – though from this phase of the analysis onwards, they had to share my attention with theoretical considerations. Qualitative data analysis "is a process of resolving data into its constituent components, to reveal its characteristic elements and structure", followed by a "reconceptualization of the data" (Dey 1993, 30). Phases 1 and 2 consisted of 'resolving' the data. When entering phase 3, looking for themes, I began re-combining the data bits in order to make sense of them in relation to my research questions. As Braun and Clarke demonstrate in their step-by-step guide, in phase 3 the *list of codes* (or coding frame) is reduced to a comparably shorter list of overarching themes. In phases 4 and 5, it is further reduced to a progressively shorter and more distinct *list of themes* (Braun/ Clarke 2006, 89-92). I provide the final list of themes in chapter 8.1 of this thesis.

The fourth phase of thematic analysis sets the task of ***"reviewing themes"*** for the analyst (Braun/ Clarke 2006, 91, emphasis in the original). The "set of candidate themes" that has been produced in phase 3 is refined in this phase (ibid.). This means more than further reducing the number of themes in order to provide a clear and manageable structure for the analysis. Primarily, it means that the data extracts collected under one candidate theme are checked for coherence. This may lead to some themes being broken down into two, while others may need to be combined or discarded from the analysis (ibid.). I also encountered several cases in

50 Out of ten main themes, two had no sub-themes and the rest was composed of 58 sub-themes. This resulted in 60 themes having codes subsumed under them; see chapter 8.1 for the final list of themes.

which redundant themes needed to be *dissolved*, meaning that particular codes and sometimes even particular coded extracts were either transferred to other themes or codes, or they were discarded from the analysis. In some cases, even the codes themselves needed to be dissolved. This meant re-coding under other codes for some of the extracts subsumed under it, and deleting the coding for others that were not useful. In addition to that, the themes' validity must be checked against the entire data set (ibid.). The sensitive issue at this stage of analysis is to crosscheck against the data extracts and the whole data set that, in the attempt to introduce interpretation, the themes are not being *imposed on data* that they do not really match. On the contrary, at the end of this phase, the researcher must have assured herself of the themes telling a story about the data (ibid., 92). Themes should fulfil the criteria of "*internal homogeneity* and *external heterogeneity*", meaning that the data combined under each theme should form an entity, whereas the differences between themes should be obvious (ibid., 91, emphases in the original). As Braun and Clarke point out, although some re-coding can be necessary during this phase, the researcher should beware of getting lost in it. What counts is to get a coding frame that "fits the data well", neither more nor less (ibid., 92). They recommend thematic maps as a tool for visualisation of themes and their mutual relationships (ibid., 89-92). Following the recommendations outlined above, I concluded this phase with a thematic map of five main themes under which 21 sub-themes were subsumed. Those sub-themes contained the codes and data extracts that were going to tell the story about the data set in the final analysis.

The fifth phase of thematic analysis is called ***"defining and naming themes"*** (Braun/ Clarke 2006, 92, emphasis in the original). It began with a final revision of the thematic map, resulting in three main themes and 18 sub-themes with the data subsumed under them (see chapter 8.1). After having finalised the thematic map, I needed to "define and refine" the themes that were going to be presented in the final analysis and to analyse the data within them (ibid.). Braun and Clarke clarify: "By 'define and refine', we mean identifying the 'essence' of what each theme is about (as well as the themes overall), and determining what aspect of the data each theme captures" (ibid.). The groups of data extracts under each theme receive an "accompanying narrative" each (ibid.). Braun and Clarke emphasise that this does not mean to paraphrase the extracted data bits, but to describe "what is of interest about them and why" (ibid.). After all, this is a highly interpretative phase. This "detailed analysis" of each theme should not only tell the story of the theme itself but also define its role within the overall data set and with regard to the research questions (ibid.). Eventually, this is the point when all themes should get their final labels or names. This phase ends when the researcher has produced "a set of fully worked-out themes" (ibid., 93) with definite names, detailed analytic definitions, and a final thematic map (see chapter 8.1 for the final list of themes and the final thematic map). The sixth phase concludes the process of analysis by ***"producing the report"*** (ibid., emphasis in the original). This last step, also known as write-up, encompasses adducing analytical arguments as well as providing sufficient evidence from the original data to support those arguments (ibid.). Chapter 8 of this thesis is the outcome of phase 6 and bears the traces of all preceding phases. The complete definitions of the themes written in the course of phase 5 of the analysis are more extensive than the final analyses presented in chapter 8 and can be provided at any time upon request. The codebook for every step of analysis has been saved and can be provided at any time upon request.

The quality of a thematic analysis, according to Braun and Clarke, is determined according to a number of criteria. First, the researcher should "actually *analyse*" the data (Braun/ Clarke 2006, 94, emphasis in the original). This analysis should be grounded in the data but not reduced to mere paraphrasing or presenting a collection of data extracts. However, in order to make the theme convincing, examples should be numerous and conclusive. The researcher's analytic claims should be coherent with the theoretical framework *and* grounded in the data (ibid., 94-95). For instance, Braun and Clarke emphasise that contradictions and inconsistencies within the data set are normal. Attempts to iron them out would produce an "unfounded" analysis that is "open to suspicion" (ibid., 95). The authors caution the researcher to avoid "anecdotalism", i.e., interpreting as themes instances that occur only once or twice throughout the data (ibid.). Internal coherence and consistency of themes should be guaranteed, while overlap should be avoided wherever possible. The interview questions should not serve as categories or themes for analysis (ibid., 94). Just like all approaches of qualitative analysis, thematic analysis first and foremost requires transparency and rigor (ibid., 96). For this reason, I have described in detail all the activities I undertook within the scope of interview analysis (see chapters 5.2.3, 5.2.4, and chapter 8.1).

5.3 Document analysis

In order to provide contextual information for the results of the interview analysis, a document analysis has been undertaken in the scope of this study. Document analysis can be quite flexibly defined to refer to any item as 'document' that bears traces of human social activities (e.g., buildings, tools, works of art, etc.) (Mayring 2016, 27). In this study, however, I define document analysis more narrowly to include *textual* material, including paper as well as digital files. This approach complies with that of Glenn Bowen, in which document analysis is being defined as "a systematic procedure for reviewing and evaluating documents—both printed and electronic (computer-based and Internet-transmitted) material" (Bowen 2009, 27). As Bowen explains, document analysis is frequently used as part of a set of qualitative research methods in triangulation (Bowen 2009, 28; see also: Flick 2018, 376, 383). He states: "The analytic procedure entails finding, selecting, appraising (making sense of), and synthesising data contained in documents." (Bowen 2009, 28) In my study, document analysis fulfils the first of 5 possible purposes Bowen suggests for it, namely to "provide data on the context within which research participants operate—a case of text providing context" (ibid., 29). I decided to use documents for that very purpose because there is little literature on the Busoga region that can serve to contextualise the findings of the interview results and give the reader an impression of their setting. Apart from information about Busoga region in the narrow sense, I analysed documents that address the Ugandan cooperative movement or particular government policies. Those issues are not limited to Busoga, but they influence life in the region significantly, especially with regard to my research questions. Bowen states that, when document analysis serves the purpose of providing contextual information and is not the main source of data, "even a few [documents] can provide an effective means of completing the research" (ibid., 33). I have analysed 15 documents from very diverse sources.[51] I consider half of them (seven documents) 'historical' as they were written between the years 1965 and 1982, which precedes the period on which I focus in my study (yet they contain important historical background information about current phenomena). They have been accessed at *Jinja District Archives* and the Africana section of *Makerere University Library*. They encompass government reports and correspondence concerning topics of interest to me, e.g.,

51 I provide a list of those documents with some information about them in chapter 7.1.

activities of cooperatives or group farms in Busoga. I categorise the other half of the documents (8 documents) as 'current', as they were written between 2011 and 2018. These include reports on the Busoga region from various levels of Ugandan government institutions; government policy papers; newspaper articles; an annual report of the *Uganda Co-operative Alliance* (UCA); and an information sheet about the 'zero grazing' approach prepared by a UN agency. Those sources provided information about the Busoga region in general, about government policies and NGO activities that have a strong influence on (alternative) economic activities in the region, the Ugandan cooperative movement in general and its manifestations in Busoga in particular. Some of them were found during internet research, while the majority was provided by some of the institutions named below (for further details, see chapter 7.1).

Several Ugandan government institutions, namely the *Office of the Prime Minister* (Kampala); the library of the *Parliament of Uganda* (Kampala); the *Uganda Bureau of Statistics* (Kampala); *Makerere University Library* (Kampala); the *National Records Centre and Archives* (Kampala); *Jinja District Archives* (Jinja); and *Jinja Municipality* kindly opened their doors to me during my search for data on the current and historical economic background of Busoga. Apart from that, the *Prime Minister of Busoga Kingdom* (Bugembe) kindly shared with me some written and oral (expert interview) information on Busoga. The team of *Prime Solutions Ltd.* (Kampala), a provider of professional research services with whom the *Office of the Prime Minister* had kindly put me in touch also provided helpful information. Even though I did not find documents that I ultimately used in the analysis in all of them, it was important to gain an overview of the available holdings of documents. Indeed, I invested a lot of time in finding the few documents I ultimately chose. In the institutions in Kampala, it was difficult to find any documents that concerned Busoga. The place in which I had put the greatest hope, *Jinja District Archives*, has unfortunately been flooded several times in the past decades. I was lucky to reach there after a serious rearrangement of the archives had been done, such that the holdings were well-ordered and protected from further destruction. However, a very large part of the material had already been lost. This circumstance considerably reduced the expected outcome of my search for documents. I made inquiries on how to find some helpful documents at the local administrations of all three districts of Buyende, Kamuli, and Jinja, as well as at the municipalities of their capital cities. They all referred me to *Jinja District Archives*. Even the administration of *Busoga Kingdom* does not have its own archives but I nevertheless received one of the most helpful 'contemporary' documents from there.

Before visiting all these institutions, I had to decide what to do with the documents once I would find them. The 'contemporary' documents did not pose any challenge, as they were all provided to me as digital files. The 'historical' documents were a different case. At *Jinja District Archives*, making photocopies, photographs, or scans of any document was strictly prohibited. For that reason, I typed all interesting passages in a WORD-document, word-by-word, and noted all formal and material characteristics of the respective document as well as contextual information (where I found it, when I accessed it, my impressions of it). At the Africana section of *Makerere University Library*, I was given permission to photocopy *part* (but not all) of a report on *Busoga Growers Co-operative Union*. I proceeded with the first 15 pages the way I had done at *Jinja District Archives* and had the rest of the document (40 pages) photocopied. For analysing the other 'historical' documents, I uploaded the above-mentioned WORD-files with the extracted passages and additional information. As with the interviews, I analysed the documents using MAXQDA software. However, I established a separate 'project' for them in MAXQDA, as the coding frame and the method of analysis used for them are different from those used for interviews.

Document analysis consists of three comprehensive steps: "skimming (superficial examination), reading (thorough examination), and interpretation" (Bowen 2009, 32). As specific methods to carry out this endeavour, "all the methods of coding and categorizing [...] can be applied as well as conversation analytic approaches" (Flick 2018, 383). For this reason, I chose *Qualitative Content Analysis* (QCA) for this part of my study. Although I had found QCA unsuitable for the analysis of my interviews (see chapter 5.2.4), I used this approach for the documents, as they constitute a less complex kind of material than the interview transcripts and I approached their analysis with different expectations. While I view the interviews as my primary method of data collection, the document analysis should provide some contextual information from *another* (though not necessarily more objective) point of view. The interview analysis was expected to bring out the aspects of my research topic that the interviewees judged important – at the risk of producing large amounts of data. Conversely, the purpose of the document analysis was to *reduce* data and extract from the material what really adds value to my overall analysis as contextual information. As I explained in chapter 5.2.4, I consider the demand of "consistency" in QCA (Schreier 2012, 6, 174-175; see also: Mayring

2008, 43) highly problematic against the background of the positionality of researchers. However, when dealing with well-structured documents and theory-driven main categories (see below), that 'consistency' can be attained to a much larger extent than in the case of interview transcripts and an inductive approach. QCA can serve the purposes of this document analysis, if it is used the way Bowen suggests. He recommends using QCA in document analysis for separating information that is of interest for the research purpose from information in the texts that is not (Bowen 2009, 32). As it serves to "extract from the data and summarise material that concerns specific contents", Philipp Mayring's QCA technique of "content structuring" ("inhaltliche Strukturierung", Mayring 2008, 59, translation by E.K.)[52] has been applied in the scope of this document analysis. After selecting the material to be analysed, I analysed the respective documents with regard to their material, structural, and formal characteristics, including the context in which they were written (author(s), audience, purpose) (ibid., 54, see also: 29, 47; see also: Flick 2018, 378, 380, 382). Another aspect of interest is the accessibility of the documents under examination (Flick 2018, 377). Source criticism is an extremely important step in document analysis (Mayring 2016, 48). The researcher must "determine the authenticity, credibility, accuracy, and representativeness of the selected documents" (Bowen 2009, 33). The origin of the document should be unquestionable, the evidence contained in it unambiguous, correct, and characteristic of its kind (Flick 2018, 378). Apart from the two newspaper articles, the annual report of the UCA, and the information sheet on 'zero grazing', all documents analysed in the scope of this study have their origin in different institutions of the government of Uganda – and the UCA report is addressed, among others, to the government of Uganda. As a result, they are part of official communication processes between the government and the public. Additionally, most of them have been provided to me by government institutions, while the ones from the internet were found on the official websites of government institutions (for details, see chart 1 in chapter 7.1). Newspaper articles are a popular category of documents for such kinds of analyses (Bowen 2009). The ones I used in my study appear to be well-researched and have been found on the official website of the respective newspaper. The information sheet about 'zero

52 Mayring, the most renowned methodologist for QCA in German academia, defines seven forms of QCA: Summary, narrow context analysis, broad context analysis, formal structuring, content structuring, typifying structuring, and scaling structuring (Mayring 2008, 59).

grazing' has been produced by the *Food and Agriculture Organization of the United Nations* (FAO) and has been found on their official website. However, it is worth bearing in mind that all documents are not objective but are rather historically and socio-politically situated. Their emergence, their content, their wording, and the fact that they were kept (and possibly others were not) are influenced by this context (ibid., 32-33; see also: Flick 2018, 378). In this particular case, for instance, 'the government of Uganda' does not refer to the same entity with regard to all documents under examination. Depending on their date of origin, 'the government' was not only manned by other individuals but organised in a different way and geared towards different policies. However, this is part of what makes the examination of documents from distinct periods so interesting for my research project. Different governments had varying approaches to economic development. I will discuss this issue further in chapter 6.

I developed my research plan drawing on the work of Mayring, beginning with the "*definition of the units of analysis*" as step 1 (Mayring 2008, 84, translation and emphasis by E.K.; see also: 54). As *unit of analysis* (ibid., 53; Schreier 2012, 130-131), I chose each document. In case a unit of coding (see below) needs further explanation, *context units* must be taken into consideration (Mayring 2008, 53; Schreier 2012, 133-134). For that purpose, I chose the sub-section (in case of long, structured documents) or paragraph (in case of short and/ or unstructured documents), in which the unit of coding occurs. For selecting the unit of coding (Mayring 2008, 53; Schreier 2012, 131-133), I applied a "*thematic criterion*" (Schreier 2012, 136, emphasis in the original; see also 137-138). This was necessary because my material is not homogeneous in its structure, as it encompasses reports, letters, policy papers, an information sheet, and newspaper articles. A formal criterion for the selection of units of coding that requires a clear structure from the material (ibid., 134-136), was not the right choice in this particular case. As *unit of coding*, I chose the *unit between two changes of topic* (ibid., 136), the 'topic' of the selected extract "fit[ting] exactly one subcategory in [the] coding frame" (ibid., 138).

The following steps of QCA serve to conceptualise the coding frame. Mayring states: "Categories are developed in an interplay between theory (research question(s)) and the specific material, by means of rules of constitution and subsumption, and during analysis, they are revised and *crosschecked*" (Mayring 2008, 53, translation by E.K., emphasis in the original). Step 2 of the research plan encompasses the *theory-driven definition of main categories (or dimensions)*, which constitute the backbone of the coding frame (ibid., 84, 89; see also: Schreier 2012, 59). From the research questions of this study[53], I derived 4 main categories for the document analysis. This activity was followed by step 3, the *definition of sub-categories* (Mayring 2008, 84; see also: Schreier 2012, 60-61), which comprises step 4, the "formulation of definitions, examples, and coding rules for each category" (Mayring 2008, 84, translation by E.K.), and step 5, the process of *segmentation* of the material (ibid.; see also: Schreier 2012, 126-128, 139-141). My main categories are: 1. Socio-economic situation of Busoga (current); 2. Historical roots of the socio-economic situation of Busoga; 3. General information about Busoga; 4. The cooperative movement in Uganda, especially in Busoga. I provide a comprehensive list of all categories (i.e., these four main categories with their 30 sub-categories) in chapter 7.1. I used an inductive approach to the definition of sub-categories, which Margrit Schreier calls "subsumption" and which builds sub-categories on a combination of theory-driven main categories and extraction from the material (Schreier 2012, 115-116). I defined and revised sub-categories while working through the material, creating a new sub-category whenever an extract was of interest with regard to the research questions but could not be subsumed to any existing sub-category (ibid.; see also: Mayring 2008, 75-76). Step 6 consists of the actual process of coding (Mayring 2008, 84), which must include a pilot phase in order to prove the validity of the categories and their applicability to the particular material (ibid., 44; Schreier 2012, 146). My pilot phase encompassed one 'current' and one 'historical' document, each. As a result of the phase of reading and segmentation, I was aware that the 'current' *Busoga ten years strategic plan* was going to provide information with regard to all main categories, but primarily to main categories 1 and 3. The 'historical' annual report on the year 1975 by the *Department of Co-operative Development of Busoga Province* provides information for main categories 2 and 4. Both are among the medium to long documents within the corpus of material. These circumstances made them suitable for the pilot phase. As suggested by Mayring, step 7 was undertaken parallel to steps 3 to 6, namely *revising the coding frame, category definitions, and coding rules* (Mayring 2008, 84). Steps 8 to 10 are specific to *content structuring*: In the course of step 8, extracted material has

53 How have people in Busoga experienced changes in their socio-economic environment that can be traced back to globalisation, in the past 30 years? What kind of alternative economic activities based on solidarity do or did they practise? Did those activities persist in spite of, dissolve because of, or emerge as a reaction to globalisation? Do people consider such activities helpful in their situation, and why or why not?

been paraphrased, which was followed by summarising it per sub-category (step 9) and per main category (step 10) (cf. ibid., 89). The results can be found in chapter 7. As I had expected, QCA, with its rigorous structure and its tendencies to be theory-driven and descriptive, was the appropriate method for dealing with documents, whereas for the interview analysis, thematic analysis was the better choice.

5.4 Conclusion

Postcolonial methodology is an attitude, not a particular set of methods. Due to its above-mentioned principles (see chapter 5.1), it has a preference for qualitative rather than quantitative methods. The nature of qualitative methods allows the adjustment of instruments of data collection and analysis to the specific research project. Hence, it is up to the researcher to decolonise them in every particular case. For instance, qualitative interviews conducted by a researcher (or researchers) from the global North with interviewees from the global South resist their full decolonisation, especially when it comes to power relations. Yet, this resistance is shared with all other research methods. As shown under section 5.1, it is highly doubtful whether power asymmetries in research can ever be fully overcome. Certainly, in the constellation of a person from the global North – who is in the majority of cases privileged in comparison to the researched and even co-researchers – coming to the global South in order to conduct research, the power asymmetry is further fortified by global power constellations. As a result, researchers from the global North must make a difficult choice. If they refrain from conducting research in the global South, they make a good choice of avoiding entry into the unfair power relations that are immanent to this research situation. However, in doing so, researchers from the global North miss an opportunity to gain a better, though necessarily incomplete, understanding of 'the Other' and offer their own powerful position to the researched as an opportunity for political representation. Though the latter can never be an authentic representation (see chapter 5.1.2), the researched can make use of the research encounter to influence the researcher's point of view. If, on the other hand, researchers from the global North decide to conduct research in the global South, they may get the chance to enter "spaces 'in between'" (Ranghuram/ Madge 2006, 276) with the researched and start a process of creating knowledge with them. This process can be rewarding for both parties. However, global North researchers choosing this route have not chosen an easy task, but one that is subject to constant legitimate critique and requires permanent critical (self-)reflexion as well as sincere openness towards 'the Other'. As a member of this group of researchers, who has even decided to use an old-fashioned method like the interview, I am unable to discharge myself of some of this legitimate critique. Nonetheless, based on the arguments outlined above, I conclude that the qualitative interview can be decolonised to an extent that makes it suitable for postcolonial research. As a result of several years of professional experience in the sector of so-called 'development cooperation', I suggest that any kind of understanding of 'the Other' necessarily requires communication. For that reason, I consciously chose to conduct research in the global South. My approach matured thanks to the encounter with the researched and to the advancing study of literature on postcolonial methodology. I took the first steps, such as the conceptualisation of the research questions and the choice of methods of data collection, in a rather conventional way. The further the research process advanced, the more measures I undertook to decolonise it, from learning the language of the researched and trying to reduce the power imbalance between them and me, up to holding feedback workshops. In that regard, my research project is typical for the general situation of research that is currently being carried out in the global South. Participative and conventional approaches exist side by side, sometimes competing, sometimes blending into hybrid forms, as in my case.

As Husseini de Araújo and Kersting aptly point out, the demands of postcolonial critique towards research are perfectly legitimate but sometimes not fully attainable, be it due to global power constellations or to academic conventions (Husseini de Araújo/ Kersting 2012, 142, 144; see also Raghuram/ Madge 2006, 276). The circumstance that I lived in Uganda for 34 months gave me the great chance to conduct my research project following many recommendations on qualitative and postcolonial research methods, e.g.:

- being self-reflexive during the whole research process (cf. Husseini de Araújo/ Kersting 2012; Kapoor 2004); a stance that includes the personal attitude towards the researched as well as the methods of data collection and analysis;
- learning the language of the researched (Kapoor 2004);
- empowering the researched (Ross 2017) by respecting their social environment; in my case, this meant following all locally demanded procedures (e.g., acquiring a research clearance, respecting local hierarchies when getting in touch with interviewees), without using 'short-cuts';

- working very closely with linguistic and cultural translators (Enzenhofer/ Resch 2011);
- starting analysis parallel to data collection in order to improve on the quality of data collection methods and instruments (Rapley 2011);
- trying to create a "reverse flow of knowledge" (Husseini de Araújo/ Kersting 2012, 140, translation by E.K.) by providing feedback to interviewees by means of bilingual feedback workshops and written reports;
- choosing a method for interview analysis that harmonises with the tenets of postcolonial research and allows working intensively with the original data in order to sustain the approach of carefully 'listening to'/ reading the self-expression of the researched;
- making the whole research process as transparent as possible; an act that I owe to the researched as much as I owe it to all readers of the research report.

With regard to literature, I gave preference to authors from the global South wherever possible, throughout the whole thesis, and I took a critical stance towards the alleged universality of knowledge from the global North. In line with that, I constantly challenge the image of the all-encompassing competence and authority of 'the (Western) scientist', be it with regard to myself or to others. I value knowledge from the global South – an attitude that is reflected by my research methodology. Nevertheless, I do not hide behind the claim of 'giving voice' to the researched. Instead, I *take responsibility* for the research with all its shortcomings. The latter include the uncomfortable dominance of the word "I" in this paragraph. This is a result of the deliberate use of "the reflexive 'I'" (England 1994, 82), which serves the purposes explained in this chapter and summarised in these conclusive paragraphs. Chapters 7 and 8 present and discuss the results of the research process described above.

6. The setting: Uganda and the Busoga region

As stated in the introduction, this study is not principally intended as a work on Uganda or the Basoga people. It is rather supposed to be a work on traces of global capitalism and solidarity in a local economy – *in a particular setting*. Nevertheless, the *setting* has great influence on the particular shape the objects under examination (globalisation and solidarity) take in the hands of the people concerned. Consequently, I provide a brief introduction to the setting of this study in this chapter, drawing on literature review. The information provided here serve as contextual information for the study results presented in chapters 7 and 8. Chapter 6.1 provides an overview of Uganda's political history after independence and chapter 6.2 introduces the Busoga region, emphasising the aspects that are of special interest for this study.

6.1 Uganda

Uganda is a country with a very eventful history that could fill more than one book and with a multitude of groups that define themselves in terms of different categories (e.g., language, tribe, clan, social class). Many aspects would be worth further discussion or investigation, but do not concern the focus of my study. This small sub-section cannot do more than provide an overview of some basic data and some information that is important for understanding the research results presented in chapters 7 and 8.

Uganda is located in East Africa. It is landlocked, a circumstance that makes import and export activities costly (Mwase 2007, 63). The population is estimated at above 41 million people.[54] The country is home to more than 30 languages, with English as its lingua franca (Ofcanski 1996, 72). The earliest industrial towns of the country were Kampala (today the capital city), Jinja (in Busoga), and Mbale (close to the border with Kenya) (Mutibwa 2016, 204). Uganda has gone through ups and downs in

54 According to the "Population clock" on the website of the *Uganda Bureau of Statistics* (UBOS), the country had a population of 41,680,920 people on 26 August 2020, at 08:23 p.m. (https://www.ubos.org).

recent history. The British officially declared Uganda their protectorate in 1894 and, up to 1921, extended their actual sphere of influence gradually from Buganda[55] Kingdom to the rest of the territory covered by Uganda today (ibid., 66). They profited considerably from the land's production capacities by introducing cash crops, especially cotton and coffee, but also some others like tea and tobacco. In 1962, Uganda gained independence as one of the most promising economies in Africa and being self-sufficient in terms of food, thanks to its fertile soils and favourable climate (Ofcanski 1996, 93). As outlined briefly below, the euphoria of the 1960s was disappointed and the population went through a very difficult time in the 1970s and 1980s. Nevertheless, in the early twenty-first century, Uganda was again celebrated as a model for Africa. Its post-conflict recovery was praised as exemplary (e.g., Reinikka/ Collier 2001). Recently, the euphoria has again subsided.

After Uganda gained independence in 1962, the King of Buganda (Edward Mutesa II) became President of Uganda until 1966, when Prime Minister Milton Obote toppled him and abolished all kingdoms in Uganda with the constitution of 1967 that remained until 1995 (Mutibwa 2016, 204-211; see also Ofcanski 1996, 41). Nevertheless, as the office of the president was at the time merely "ceremonial" (Ofcanski 1996, 39), the government that ruled Uganda from 1962 up to 1971 is considered "Obote's government" and the policies of that period are associated with Obote, not with Mutesa (see for example Mutibwa 2016, 198-204). That period is also frequently referred to (in the literature as well as in everyday conversations) as 'Obote I', as he served a second term from 1980 to 1985. Up to the early 1970s, the business sector, including industries and trade, was in the hands of the community of Indian descent (Ofcanski 1996, 93). The British had brought from their colony, India, people to Uganda for constructing the railways and subsequently made them Uganda's commercial class[56] (Nayenga 1981, 187; see also: Larimore 1958, 24-25; McMichael 2012, 37). Obote made first attempts to "Africanize the economy" by forwarding legislations intended to grant Ugandans *of African descent* access to the business and trade sector (Ofcanski 1996, 93). Idi Amin, originally a comrade of Obote, toppled the latter on 25 January 1971 (ibid., 40-42). Although, at first, many people in Uganda praised the end of Obote's regime, the period of Idi Amin turned out to be much worse, as he became

55 The most powerful of the kingdoms on what was about to become Ugandan land.

56 This issue is discussed in detail in chapters 6.2.2 and 8.2.

a brutal, sadistic dictator (Mutibwa 2016, 272-276; Ofcanski 1996, 42-44, 47-48). In the 1970s, Idi Amin continued the policy of Africanisation in a more radical and violent way. In 1972, all people of Asian descent, whether Ugandan citizens or not, were expropriated and expelled from the country, followed by all foreigners (Mutibwa 2016, 260-261; Ofcanski 1996, 44, 94). This act was the beginning of Amin's economic policy, which was termed 'economic war' and officially aimed to reallocate Uganda's wealth into the hands of her citizens of African descent (Mutibwa 2016, 260-261). However, the fact that many expropriated properties were given out on the basis of favouritism suggests that Amin cared more about certain elites whose support he needed to remain in power, than about the population as a whole (ibid., 260-262; Ofcanski 1996, 94). The lack of business experience of the recipients of the expropriated assets led to the collapse of the majority of Uganda's supply chains, affecting consumption (Ofcanski 1996, 45, 94), agricultural and industrial production (Mutibwa 2016, 263-264; Ofcanski 1996, 45, 95). After having occupied the Kagera Salient (Tanzania) in October 1978, in April 1979 Amin was overthrown by Tanzanian forces in collaboration with Ugandan oppositional groups, headed by the *Uganda National Liberation Front (UNLF)* (Ofcanski 1996, 47; see also: Mutibwa 2016, 292-296).

In the 20 months that followed, Uganda went through several short-term governments that failed to establish themselves properly and, as a result, to bring peace or other significant changes to people's lives (Mutibwa 2016, 304). The first of those short-term governments was the one under President Yusuf Lule that lasted only 68 days (Ofcanski 1996, 47-49). The UNLF replaced him with Godfrey Binaisa on 19 June 1979 (ibid.). Binaisa never gained control over the situation, neither in terms of security (Mutibwa 2016, 312-314; Ofcanski 1996, 50) nor in terms of the devastated economy (Mutibwa 2016, 315-317). The UNLF split into various factions (Ofcanski 1996, 51). So did the security forces (Mutibwa 2016, 312-313). In May 1980, Binaisa was removed from office and replaced by a Military Commission, which prepared elections for December of the same year (ibid., 318-320). In December 1980, Milton Obote's UPC (*Uganda People's Congress*) won the elections under highly disputed circumstances and again made him President of Uganda (ibid., 328-330; Ofcanski 1996, 51). During this second presidency, he managed to somewhat stabilise the economy with the help of funds from the International Monetary Fund (IMF) and the World Bank, yet violence remained a daily occurrence (Mutibwa 2016, 349-350; Ofcanski 1996, 52). Various oppositional forces and rebel groups congregated and strove for Obote's fall (Mutibwa 2016, 335-341; Ofcanski

1996, 52-54). Apart from failure to restore public order, the government itself acted violently not only against the rebels but also against political opponents and civilians (Mutibwa 2016, 342-343; Ofcanski 1996, 52-55). The *National Resistance Army (NRA)/ National Resistance Movement (NRM)* under Yusuf Lule and Yoweri Museveni was most successful among the resistance movements in wearing down the government (Mutibwa 2016, 335-336, 363; Ofcanski 1996, 53-54). On 27 July 1985, Obote's second regime was ended by a coup headed by two of his army officers, Basilio Olara-Okello and Tito Lutwa Okello, who became the new head of state and ruled with the help of a Military Council (Mutibwa 2016, 362-368; Ofcanski 1996, 56-57). The six-months Okello government did not mitigate the situation, neither in terms of civil war, nor in terms of the economy (Ofcanski 1996, 95). The military junta of the Okellos did not come to terms with Museveni's NRM/ NRA (Mutibwa 2016, 369-372). On 26 January 1986, the NRA overthrew Okello and established a new government (ibid., 372-373; Ofcanski 1996, 58). Only three days later, Yoweri Museveni was sworn in as President of the Republic of Uganda (Mutibwa 2016, 388). Having been elected five times since then, he has remained in office until the time of writing.

Describing all the political complexities, the varying alliances, and the tactical measures the above-sketched events encompassed would exceed the scope of this study. Of note, however are three particularly intense impacts of the political events in Uganda on everyday life in Busoga.[57] First, especially from the 1970s through the mid-1980s, the permanent lack of public order and security considerably affected the everyday life of the population (Mutibwa 2016, 434; Whitworth/ Williamson 2010, 1). This was a humanitarian catastrophe and a serious obstacle for economic activities on all levels. As further discussed in chapter 8, it did not only affect industries in Jinja town but also agricultural cooperatives or small village shops. Brutal robberies made running any kind of business in the villages a dangerous endeavour. Second, this situation involved a severe scarcity of commodities, including consumer goods, spare parts for vehicles and machines as well as inputs for agricultural production and processing. People in Uganda in general and Busoga in particular were affected by this as producers (as individuals or cooperative members) and consumers. This experience has an impact on the way they perceive current developments in their socio-economic surroundings. Third, different governments had varying approaches to economic policies. The Obote I government followed a

57 All of them are discussed in detail in chapter 8.

course that oscillated between socialism and a mixed economy (Mutibwa 2016, 218-220), leading to policies like the promotion of import-substitution, marketing boards in control of export crops, and a general tendency towards state intervention into the economy (ibid., 199-201). Although Obote tried to reduce Uganda's dependency on cash crops by emphasising other business sectors like tourism, mining, and domestic industries (Ofcanski 1996, 93), cash crops remained the mainstay of Uganda's economy. Yet there were endeavours to supplement the typical cash crops like coffee, cotton, tea, and tobacco with other crops (Mutibwa 2016, 199-201). Idi Amin's 'economic war' mainly led to the breakdown of supply chains and export business. This was aggravated by the desperate situation in terms of security. Under Obote II and his IMF recovery programme were first attempts at economic liberalisation (Kiiza 2008, 190; Nabuguzi 1993, 55-56; Sørensen 2000, 21), yet political instability prevailed and made changes difficult. The other above-mentioned governments – apart from Museveni's NRM government – were too short-lived and too busy trying to establish their power to implement any significant economic policies. During their reigns, the general situation in the country was chaotic.

Under Museveni, a full structural adjustment programme was launched and economic liberalisation became fully evolved (Asowa-Okwe 1994, 173; Bonger 2004, 268; Kiiza 2008, 190). The *Economic Recovery Programme* for Uganda, which was sponsored and the rules of which were set by the International Monetary Fund (IMF) and the World Bank, was launched in May 1987 and it complied with the *Washington Consensus*[58] (Mutibwa 2016, 434-436). The programme began with a currency reform, i.e., a massive devaluation of the Ugandan Shilling (ibid., 435; Whitworth/ Williamson 2010, 4). There were adjustments on the exchange rate policy (from state-controlled to market-determined), tariffs, and taxes as well as a trade reform (Whitworth/ Williamson 2010, 32). The underlying objectives were economic liberalisation and growth as well as macroeconomic stability (ibid.). Governmental price controls were abolished (Kiiza 2008, 190; Mutibwa 2016, 436). Massive privatisation was undertaken (Collier/ Reinikka 2001a, 37-38; Kiiza 2008, 190-191) and complemented by other measures of promotion of the private sector, e.g., the creation of the *Ugan-*

58 For discussions of the IMF and the World Bank, see chapters 2.2 (from the perspective of development) and 3 (from the perspective of globalisation). For explanations on the *Washington Consensus* in particular, see chapter 3.3. For concrete impacts of those policies on the lives of people living in Busoga, see chapter 8.

da Investment Authority (UIA) and generous incentives for private investment like tax holidays and exemptions from import duties (Whitworth/ Williamson 2010, 13). In order to guarantee fiscal discipline, effective management of increasing foreign aid, and the successful implementation of the reforms, an institutional reform of the concerned ministries was undertaken (ibid., 32-33). On a *macroeconomic* level, these policies have reportedly had considerable success (see e.g., ibid., 27-30; Kuteesa et al. 2010; Reinikka/ Collier 2001). However, they cannot alone take credit for Uganda's good performance. In 1986, with a completely devastated economy, the country started anew from almost zero (Collier/ Reinikka 2001a, 15). The NRM government significantly improved the security situation (ibid., 17-23; Whitworth/ Williamson 2010, 27) and attracted large amounts of aid money to fill the state's empty purse (Collier/ Reinikka 2001a, 39-44; Whitworth/ Williamson 2010, 21-23). These were essential factors in Uganda's quick recovery (Collier/ Reinikka 2001a, 44-45). Apart from that, however, impressive macroeconomic indicators do not necessarily reflect improvements in the everyday lives of the majority of the population. More and more scholars have come to the conclusion that economic growth does not lead to a 'trickle-down' effect, i.e., benefit for all, but rather to constantly increasing social inequality (e.g., Paech 2015, 73-74; Shanin 1998, 70; Stiglitz 2002, 78-80). This issue is discussed in theory in chapters 2.2 and 4.3.1 – and in relation to the research results of this study in chapter 8.2. Two other important measures Museveni has undertaken during his period in office are the re-establishment of Uganda's kingdoms in 1995 (see chapter 6.2.1) and the invitation to expelled Ugandans of Indian descent and foreigners to settle in Uganda anew (see chapter 6.2.2). The latter had been attempted by Obote in 1982 but on unattractive terms, especially for Asians and Ugandans of Asian descent (Mutibwa 2016, 351). The NRM government was at first celebrated for Uganda's effective economic post-conflict recovery, which was attributed to the resolute implementation of the IMF programme (e.g., Kuteesa et al. 2010; Reinikka/ Collier 2001). In the meantime, euphoria has reduced. For instance, the UNDP (*United Nations Development Program*) deplores an "upsurge of poverty" in its 2017 report on Uganda (UNDP Uganda 2017, 3). As further discussed in chapters 7 and 8, there are signs that the Ugandan government is not satisfied with the outcomes of orthodox economic liberalisation and is tending to increase governmental regulation.

With "one of the most ambitious programs of economic liberalization on the African continent" (Collier/ Reinikka 2001, 1) and a cooperative movement with a history of about 100 years (for details, see chapters

4.2.2, 6.2.3, 7.5, and 8.3.2), Uganda is a good setting for this study. The country has 15 sub-regions[59], of which Busoga is one (UBOS 2018, 4). The following sub-section introduces the region, emphasising the aspects that are of special interest for this study.

6.2 Busoga

This section paints a rather fragmentary picture of Busoga, as the number of texts available and relevant to my research focus is limited. As a result, some aspects may appear to receive a lot of attention (e.g., the role of maize in Busoga's economy), while others are left out. This chapter is neither a complete bibliography on Busoga, nor a comprehensive description of the region. It is a general introduction to the region that amplifies aspects relevant to this study. In combination with this chapter and the document analysis (chapter 7), the interview results (see chapter 8) offer the fullest possible picture of the research topics.

Most of the detailed studies on Busoga draw on relatively old data, that is, data originating from the 1960s or earlier (Cohen 1972; Brandt et al. 1972; Fallers 1965; Hasselmann 1976; Larimore 1958; Nayenga 1981). This makes them helpful for understanding Busoga as it was during the childhood and youth of the study interviewees and to arrange in chronological order the things they talked about from that time, even though I had asked only for recollections from the previous 30 years (1987-2017). In some cases, interviewees expressed uncertainty about when exactly a certain occurrence had taken place, in others they expanded the scope of their narration in order to make recent developments understandable. As outlined in chapter 3.1, my approach to globalisation is "transformationalist", based on the assumption that globalisation is not new, but started with capitalist expansion – however, it has sped up and intensified in the last third of the twentieth and into the twenty-first century (Glenn 2007, 34, 66-67). In line with world-systems theory, I take colonialism as the first phase of capitalist expansion, as the colonialist countries integrated the colonised countries into the capitalist world-system (see chapter 2.3 and 3.4 of this thesis). From a postcolonial point of view, Sabelo Ndlovu-Gatsheni states that Africa was dragged forcefully into the Western-dominated capitalist world-system by means of "mercantilism, the slave trade, colonization, neo-colo-

59 Acholi, Ankole, Bukedi, Bunyoro, Busoga, Central I, Central II, Elgon, Kampala, Karamoja, Kigezi, Lango, Teso, Tooro, West-Nile.

nization, underdevelopment [in the sense of Walter Rodney, E.K.], structural adjustment programs, and neo-liberalism" (Ndlovu-Gatsheni 2018, 285). He draws a continuous line of Africa's integration into the capitalist world-system (ibid.). Consequently, even though my research focuses on the 30 year period beginning in 1987, a glance at earlier developments can inform my understanding of processes that span more than 30 years. Without this contextual information, I might have been tempted to regard phenomena, which have a long history in Busoga, as innovations. The following description of Lloyd A. Fallers' impressions is telling in that respect, as it shows how 'globalised' Busoga already was in the early 1950s:

> "The vast changes which the past century has brought to Busoga have rendered rather unreal to many a world in which there were no bicycles, no schools, no cash-crop cultivation of cotton and 'no religion' (*ddini*, by which is meant Christianity or Islam). [...] Recent change has been too exciting and too rewarding for many to look back with real nostalgia to a golden age." (Fallers 1965, 34, emphasis in the original)

A few recent academic works on Busoga can be found, indeed. Some of them deal with specific topics (e.g., in terms of health or marriage rituals), which do not concern my field of study. Others (e.g., Gonza et al. 2016; Nabuguzi 1993; Sørensen 2000) have been combined with the above-mentioned and other dated works in order to draw a picture of Busoga's economic structure over time in this sub-section. Political and cultural aspects have been taken into consideration where their direct influence on socio-economic transformations is evident.

6.2.1 Administrative and cultural setting

The Busoga sub-region of Uganda consists of several districts (UBOS 2018, 4). In the past, it has been ascribed differing kinds of federal status, e.g., as a territory or a district, while its inhabitants define Busoga first and foremost as a kingdom (see below). Importantly, *Busoga* refers to a place; the term *Basoga* refers to the people originating from there; *Musoga* an individual originating from there; and *Kisoga* a thing that has to do with the Basoga (e.g., Kisoga culture; Nayenga 2002, 42). *Lusoga* is the language spoken by the Basoga (ibid.). According to Richard Kayaga Gonza et al., the Basoga are "the descendants of the Bantu-speaking people in the interlacustrine group who started migrating into, and eventually settled in what is called '***Busoga***' today, from around the 15th century" (Gonza et al. 2016, 6, emphasis in the original). Among the ethnic groups residing in Uganda, they are the third largest (Nayenga 2002, 41). Though other ethnic groups are represented in Busoga as well (Ugandans of Indian and Arab descent as well as Ugandans of African descent, who migrated to the area from other regions of Uganda), the Basoga are by far the dominant group of residents (Sørensen 2000, 61-64). Busoga is referred to as *an island* because it is bordered by lakes in the North (Lake Kyoga) and the South (Lake Victoria) and by rivers in the West (River Nile) and in the East (River Mpologoma) (Gonza et al. 2016, 4; see also Nayenga 2002, 41). During the active research period of this study, Busoga consisted of ten districts, from North to South: Buyende, Kamuli, Kaliro, Luuka, Namutumba, Iganga, Jinja, Bugiri, Mayuge, and Namayingo (Gonza et al. 2016, xiii-xiv; 4). As the local government structure of Uganda is permanently subject to change, the number of districts into which the Busoga region was divided varied strongly over time, from one up to eleven[60]. However, this did not considerably affect the boundaries of the region as a whole, probably due to its natural boundaries (bodies of water) or its relative cultural homogeneity.

In my study, several interviewees spoke about Busoga's high population growth and the resulting shortage of land, which has serious implications for their economic situation (see chapter 8). After having "lost many people to severe famines, small-pox, plague, and sleeping sickness" at the turn of the century, Busoga's population had started to recover in the 1930s (Nanyenga 2002, 42) and has been on the rise since then. The census, which was carried out by the *Uganda Bureau of Statistics* in 2014, indicates a population of 3.6 million in Busoga.[61] In his 1993 article, Emmanuel Nabuguzi already diagnosed a rising shortage of land in Busoga (Nabuguzi 1993, 60-61). According to the *National Population and Housing Census 2014*, the districts in which interviews for this study took place had the following population sizes by then: 323,067 people in Buyende (UBOS

60 Iganga was divided into Iganga and Bugweri in July 2018 (Oguti 2019). This had no impact on my research, as it was already in the phase of analysis by then and as the concerned area was not part of the three districts in which I conducted interviews.

61 After having failed to find a current figure for the whole of Busoga, I added up the population figures for the ten districts of Busoga (in 2014, they were 10 and they encompassed 3,583,196 people, in total) that can be found on the interactive map on the home page of the *Uganda Bureau of Statistics* (UBOS): https://www.ubos.org, accessed on 29 June 2020, at 10:34 a.m..

2017a, 20); 471,242 people in Jinja (UBOS 2017b, 21); and 486,319 people in Kamuli (UBOS 2017c, 20). Of the three districts, Jinja is the most urbanised, a fact that is mirrored in the comparably low percentage of the population practicing either livestock farming or crop growing, namely 59.4% (UBOS 2017b, 28), compared to 95.2% in Buyende (UBOS 2017a, 27) and 92.5% in Kamuli (UBOS 2017c, 27). According to the 2014 census, the average nominal monthly household income in Busoga amounted to 222,000 UGX, whereas the national average was 416,000 UGX (UBOS 2018, 109). This shows that, apart from Jinja District, which encompasses the industrial town of Jinja, Busoga is a rural area, with comparatively low incomes primarily generated in the agricultural sector.

Before the arrival of the British, there was no political or administrative unit called 'Busoga'. The area consisted of "several small, more or less autonomous states" united by "enough cultural similarity to set them off from neighbouring social units, and a frequent interchange of persons" (Fallers 1965, 12). First and foremost, they shared a common legend of origin (Cohen 1972). Gonza et al. describe the process of their formation into a unit called 'Busoga' as follows: From 1894 on, the British *District Commissioner of Busoga* forced the major rulers of the 'district' of Busoga to collect taxes and assist in settling conflicts in the name of British rule. He established a council for the representatives of the eleven chiefdoms of Busoga, which, from 1906 on, met in Jinja, under the name "Lukiiko"[62] (Gonza et al. 2016, 173). The rulers in the council advocated for a *King of Busoga*. According to Gonza et al., they hoped to become a new political force that could stand the competition with neighbouring kingdoms like Buganda and demand privileges from the colonial administration (ibid., 178-180). However, in the first 20 years, the British allowed for only a *President of Busoga Lukiiko* (ibid., 180-186). Eventually, in 1938, a special kind of kingship was established: the *Kyabazinga*[63] would be *elected* by the Lukiiko and be their 'king', but *without personal or hereditary privileges* (ibid., 184). In the second *Lancaster House Constitutional Conference on Uganda* in London, in January 1962, a quasi-federal status was granted to Busoga, its name changed from "Busoga District" to "Busoga Territory", and its new constitutional powers were fixed in the 1962 *Uganda Constitution* (ibid., 201). As Gonza et al. point out, when in 1966 then Prime Minister of Uganda, Milton Obote, put himself into the position of the

62 Lusoga for "meeting".

63 Full title: "Isebantu Kyabazinga", meaning "father of all people" (Gonza et al. 2016, 179).

President and changed the constitution, the federal powers of Busoga Territory and of Uganda's officially recognised kingdoms were suspended. The Kyabazingaship was abolished in September 1967, together with the other kingdoms of Uganda (ibid., 208-209) and Busoga Territory returned to its former status as a "District" (ibid., 213). In 1973, under the regime of then President Idi Amin, Busoga was turned into a "Province" consisting of three districts – North Busoga, South Busoga, and West Busoga – and reaching up to the Kenyan border (ibid., 215). After the overthrow of Idi Amin in April 1979, the three districts of Busoga Province were re-named Kamuli (North), Jinja (South), and Iganga (East) (ibid., 215-216). The Busoga Lukiiko was re-installed on 15 May 1993 (ibid., 223). The 1995 Uganda constitution proclaimed "The institution of Traditional Cultural Leaders" in article 246 (ibid., 224). The new Kyabazinga was officially crowned on 11 February 1996, in the presence of President Yoweri Museveni and a huge audience (ibid.). However, the Kyabazingaship had been reduced from a political to a purely cultural institution, without any legislative, executive, or administrative powers, and without the right to engage in party politics (ibid., 225, 278-279). The institutions of the Lukiiko and the Kyabazinga helped to establish long-lasting economic structures in Busoga. The British colonial administration used them through its system of *indirect rule* to implement its policies (ibid., 180, 184-185). As Gonza et al. describe, the Lukiiko promoted the growing of coffee and cotton, which have become the most important cash crops in Busoga's economic history (see also chapter 6.2.2). It helped to introduce the commercial class of Indians and made the Basoga provide free labour for constructing railway lines and feeder roads in the area (ibid., 185). The *Busoga Ten Years Strategic Plan 2016-2025*, which has been examined in the course of document analysis (see chapter 7), suggests that these institutions continue to influence Busoga's socio-economic transformation.

An important social institution in Busoga are extended families or clans. These are both an important part of people's identity and function as their social safety net (Gonza et al. 2016, 9). The latter function makes clans particularly interesting for my research question concerning autochthonous solidarity structures and the influence of their transformation over time on modern phenomena of the Social and Solidarity Economy (see chapter 4, especially 4.1, and chapter 8.3.1). Gonza et al. state that "even highly trained technocrats or professionals in Busoga are often found participating in clan matters" because clans are still important in everyday life in Busoga (Gonza et al. 2016, 8). They borrow Cohen's definition of a Kisoga clan as "a patrilineal descent group, including all those who recognized a common ancestor through male lines" (Cohen 1972, 6; Gonza et al. 2016, 8; a very similar definition of Kisoga clans can be found in Nayenga 2002, 44). Peter Nayenga explains that, in the past, particular locations have been associated with particular clans and have been called "obutaka", which means "ancestral lands" (Nayenga 2002, 44). Cohen suggests that there used to be different categories of obutaka land, one of them being the land on which the members of a particular clan buried their ancestors (Cohen 1972, 16). Nayenga continues, explaining that, over time, "as a result of population growth, clashes within clans, catastrophes such as famines and sleeping sickness, and raids from neighboring states, many clans dispersed" (Nayenga 2002, 44). As will be shown in chapter 8 of this thesis, the research results of this study have not only confirmed the latter observation, but have made an additional one: The word "obutaka" has acquired an additional meaning, which bears traces of the old one, yet accommodates later events. It has become the synonym for burial support among village residents (see chapter 8.3.1 for details).

6.2.2 A short economic history of Busoga

Gonza et al. describe the first contacts of Busoga with the outside world as follows: Arab traders came to Buganda Kingdom and later to other parts of Uganda, from the 1850s onwards. The first Europeans whose visit to Busoga was documented were the famous British explorers John Hanning Speke and James August Grant, who came to Jinja in July 1862 in search of the source of the River Nile. They were followed by Christian missionaries and later by the *Imperial British East African Company (IBEACo)* (Gonza et al. 2016, 166-169). Busoga was among the regions that were integrated in the British 'Protectorate' very early, i.e., shortly after its establishment (Mutibwa 2016, 42). As Charles Asowa-Okwe points out, the majority of the Basoga were introduced to the cash economy through the imposition of taxes by the British colonial administration from 1900 onwards. The need to pay those taxes forced the people to either look for wage labour or odd jobs – both of which were hard to find – or to produce cash crops for export (Asowa-Okwe 1994, 149-150). This cycle of taxes and cash crop production was one of the typical approaches through which African countries were integrated into world trade during colonial times (Mbembe 2001, 40-41). It was a special feature of the Ugandan economy, from colonial times up to Idi Amin's coup, that its agricultural sector relied primarily on *smallholders*[64], who were in turn well-linked to the manufacturing sector (Bonger 2004, 254).

According to studies that were carried out in Busoga in the 1950s and 1960s, at that time, the staple food in the region, especially in the southern part of it, were plantains (Cohen 1972, 3; Fallers 1965, 46-49; Larimore 1958, 166-167). A well-kept plantain garden could be productive for several decades (Fallers 1965, 50-51), making it a sustainable source of food. As the natural conditions were less favourable for growing plantains in the northern part, the latter was dominated by cattle keeping and millet growing (Cohen 1972, 4-5; Fallers 1965, 46-47). Other food crops grown in Busoga were cassava and sweet potatoes (Cohen 1972, 4-5; Fallers 1965, 46-47). Cotton was the major cash crop by that time, supplemented by some maize (Fallers 1965, 46, 50). Groundnuts were grown for both personal consumption and sale (ibid., 50). Changes in terms of diet of the people living in Busoga as well as their cash crop portfolio are discussed in chapters 6.2.4 and 8.2. With regard to methods of farming, crop rotation and fallowing were encountered as local agricultural practices in Busoga in the 1950s and 1960s (for both see: Fallers 1965, 50; Larimore 1958, 167-168; for fallowing see also: Brandt 1972, 92).

In his micro-study of a village in Busoga (Buyodi village in Bulamogi) in the early 1950s, Fallers described "a number of village crafts carried on by part-time specialists who sell their products in the weekly village markets" (Fallers 1965, 54). He lists pottery; furniture made by local carpenters; bark cloth; weaved bags and baskets; and blacksmithing. He explains that bark cloth was "almost entirely superseded by cotton cloth for clothing purposes", yet it was still widely used as "traditional burial wrapping" and for household purposes (ibid.). Cohen still encountered those crafts in the 1960s (Cohen 1972, 6). Commenting on products from outside, which people used to buy in towns and trading centres, Fallers notes:

> "Although many of the fundamental needs of the Soga[65] homestead are met by the land itself and by local village craftsmen, three-quarters of a century of contact with the outside world have resulted in the *addition to the peasant's style of life of many items obtainable only from abroad in exchange for money. It is to the acquisition of such goods and services that cash crop cultivation is devoted.* [...] Since the staple foodstuffs

64 (in contrast to plantations)

65 "Soga" is an anglicised expression, which is used to avoid confusions of "Kisoga", "Musoga", "Basoga", "Busoga", and "Lusoga" (Nayenga 2002, 42).

> are produced by each homestead for its own use, this money income is very largely available for expenditure on such imported goods and services as bicycles, sugar, tea, clothing, utensils, tools, school fees and for the payment of taxes." (Fallers 1965, 55-56, emphasis by E.K.)

This importance of consumer goods in everyday life in Busoga is a central topic of the interview analysis. Before the arrival of the British, there was only little trade within Busoga. According to Nayenga, there was some exchange of bark cloth from the northern part or fish from the islands in Lake Victoria for pottery products or food from the southern part (Nayenga 2002, 43). Cohen states that: "A number of villages in South Busoga are remembered as pre-colonial markets, and trade extended from some of these across Lake Victoria to the islands and neighbouring lands" (Cohen 1972, 6). From 1895 onwards, the British introduced "[l]arge-scale commercial economic activities" to Busoga (Nayenga 2002, 43). They tried to introduce cotton, rubber, cocoa, and coffee growing, out of which cotton was most productive in Busoga "and by 1939 had become the chief source of cash earnings for the majority of the Basoga" (ibid.; see also: Nayenga 1981, 189). The Basoga "received from cotton sales earnings that enabled them to build modern houses, educate their children, purchase clothing, house utensils, bicycles, motorcars, or motorcycles" (Nayenga 1981, 185). After 1925, commercial coffee production on plantations was introduced to Busoga, but it turned out to be unprofitable due to the soil quality and a drop of coffee prices in the 1920s (Hasselmann 1976, 214). From the 1940s onwards, coffee production in Busoga was mainly practised by local farmers on a small- to medium-scale basis – a strategy that worked out much better and led to a significant extension of the sector (ibid., 222-226). According to Schubert, "the *coffee boom* in Busoga [...] began in 1957 and had fully set in by 1962" (Schubert 1972, 232, emphasis by E.K.). However, the colonial division of labour[66] kept the Basoga in their place as farmers

66 The colonial division of labour between the colonies as producers of cheap raw materials and the colonising countries as manufacturers and rich exporters (see e.g., McMichael 2012, 31-33) can be translated into a colonial division of labour *within the colony*, here Uganda: While the British had the hold on political and economic power, they had installed agents between themselves and the local population. As has been explained above, African local elites were used on the political level (Lukiiko). However, on the economic level, Indians were installed for that purpose. Quijano's concept of *coloniality of power* applies here in particular, as it focusses on the allocation of occupations and prospects within the economy by the category of race (Quijano 2000, 216-217; see chapter 2.1.2 of this thesis for details).

and labourers in crop processing but prevented them from building a commercial elite (Nayenga 1981, 189). The marketing was done by traders of Indian descent (ibid., 185). Over the course of time, Ugandan farmers of African descent started to form cooperatives in order to compete with the Indian and the few European traders in the cash crop market (Develtere 2008, 6; Kyazze 2010, 2; Nannyonjo 2015, 267, 271; see chapter 4.2.2 of this thesis for details). In Busoga, they started to gain influence when the first four cooperatives joined to form *Busoga Growers Co-operative Union* in 1951/52 (Hasselmann 1976, 228; see also chapter 6.2.3 of this thesis). Cotton marketing in the 1950s worked as follows:

> "Ginners buy cotton from the peasant growers *at government prices* recommended by the quasi-governmental Lint Marketing Board, and sell all cotton at a fixed price to the Lint Marketing Board which in turn sells the Uganda crop to exporters, by fixed price and by auction, in Kampala. […] The gins' function in this process is to buy seed cotton and process it into lint and cottonseed which are then sold to the Lint Marketing Board." (Larimore 1958, 142, emphasis by E.K.)

Cotton was processed by a variety of industries in Jinja (e.g., textile, oil, and soap factories) and could be grown parallel to food crops (Nayenga 2002, 43). Nabuguzi and Nayenga both trace the decline in cotton production in the 1970s and 1980s to the severe economic crisis caused by the policies of Idi Amin and the aftermath of his regime (see below). Nayenga mainly blames the breakdown of factories in Jinja town for the fact that cotton growing became unprofitable and was abandoned by the majority of farmers in Busoga (Nayenga 2002, 43). Nabuguzi identifies a similar situation at the national level, observing that, after having been Uganda's number one cash crop in the 1950s and 1960s, cotton ceased to be profitable in the 1970s because it became completely unmarketable. Processing became difficult because of insufficient quantities of baling materials and spare parts for ginneries, transport became a serious problem and – perhaps most devastatingly – there were no more buyers for cotton. While coffee farmers could at least sell their products to smugglers, unprocessed cotton was too bulky to allow for that solution (Nabuguzi 1993, 53). According to Paul Collier and Ritva Reinikka, most export crops of Uganda, including cotton, were made unprofitable by means of export taxation in the 1970s. They likewise attribute it to smuggling – in combination with its production being a long-term investment – that coffee survived that crisis best, with its export dropping by one third, while the export of other cash crops collapsed almost completely (Collier/ Reinikka 2001a, 31-32).

By that time, farmers in Busoga started to turn to "growing cash-generating foodstuffs such as corn, peanuts, and rice" (Nayenga 2002, 43). The crop that received most attention was maize, as will be further discussed in chapters 6.2.4 and 8.2. Although the above-cited authors accurately identify the significant contribution of political turmoil and economic collapse under Idi Amin to the breakdown of Busoga's traditional cash crops, coffee and cotton, the Ugandan government's request to Anne Martin for "a faculty study of the marketing of African-grown agricultural produce other than the major export crops" in 1961 (Martin 1963, v) suggests that the government must have had some inkling about the declining profitability of those crops long before. The rationale of the study commissioned was

> "the *unfavourable outlook for Uganda's major exports, coffee and cotton*, on the world market; and Government's desire both to reduce this dependence on only two export crops, and to make some change, if possible, out of their production into that of crops with a more hopeful future." (Martin 1963, 1, emphasis by E.K.)

Martin even mentioned World Bank endorsement for "diversifying Uganda's cash crop production" (ibid., 2). She stated that coffee prices had further dropped during the period in which she conducted her research and cautioned about the serious competition synthetic fibres posed to cotton. At the time of her study, Martin observed that all crops except coffee, cotton, and groundnuts were produced for sustaining only the farmers' families, not for sale (ibid., 1). Evidently, by then some political plans for diversification of the crops market had not yet reached the farmers' lifeworld.

Indians and Arabs introduced shops and thereby small trading centres to Busoga (Fallers 1965, 56; Larimore 1958, 26-27; Nayenga 2002, 43). According to Larimore, it was in the 1940s that "African peasants have begun to imitate the commercial practices of the Indian population and have established shops scattered through Busoga" (Larimore 1958, 129, see also 130-132). As trading centres and towns were the places where cash crops were exchanged for money and money for imported goods, Fallers comments on them in the 1950s: "In any case, their existence is a measure of the degree to which Busoga has passed from the isolation of subsistence cultivation *into the world-wide network of trade*" (Fallers 1965, 56, emphasis by E.K.). Brandt et al. suggest that the combination of farmers producing cash crops and crops for personal consumption, which was established during colonial times, left farmers with some cash money, after paying their expenses. Consumer goods were imported from Europe in order to meet the farmers' consumption desires (Brandt et al. 1972, 9). In other words, as they were not obliged to buy food, they could use their cash money to increase the profits of the colonial power by buying the consumer goods it imported for them. Thus, Busoga was 'globalised', i.e., integrated into the capitalist world-system, to a very large extent from the early twentieth century up to the early 1970s, when Idi Amin changed the situation for the whole country.

The Arabs had started their activities in Busoga by travelling "up and down the Lake Victoria region trading guns and cloth for slaves and ivory" (Fallers 1965, 59; see also: Larimore 1958, 26). Over time, some of them started to settle and – unlike Indian immigrants – to marry into the Kisoga population (Larimore 1958, 27). As immigrants of Arab descent were few in number, integrated into the local population to a considerable degree through intermarriage, and pushed out of many branches of trade by Indian immigrants, the Arab influence on the Ugandan and Kisoga society is not very obvious today – apart from the religious portfolio of Uganda, to which they have added Islam (Sørensen 2000, 69-70). The influence of Indians[67] and Ugandans of Indian descent on society and economy is much more prominent. There had been some little trading activities by Indians in Uganda in the nineteenth century, coming from Zanzibar, but the important role that Indians and Ugandans of Indian descent have been playing in the (economic) history of Uganda until today can only be explained by considering the intervention of the British colonial administration (Nayenga 1981, 186-187). The British brought to Uganda people from their colony, India, to construct the railways and afterwards made them Uganda's commercial class by refusing to give them land for cultivation and encouraging their trading activities (ibid., 187; see also: Larimore 1958, 24-25; McMichael 2012, 37). Only after European

67 Ugandans of African descent typically call everyone who appears to be of Indian descent an "Indian" (Luganda or Lusoga: "Muyindi"). I try to distinguish between "Indians" who are Indian citizens and have recently moved to Uganda and "Ugandans of Indian descent". Some families of Indian descent have been Ugandan residents for several generations. Though some of them decided to keep their British passports after independence (Mutibwa 2016, 201), they were still born and raised on Ugandan soil, and in many cases, their parents were also born there. Since 1982, both returnees (whose families had been expelled from Uganda in 1972) and new immigrants, who are Indian citizens and would define themselves as such, came to Uganda. I will make visible whether a comment refers to only one of these groups or to both. At times, I distinguish Ugandans with regard to their either African or Indian descent. The complicated wording is necessary to make clear to whom I am referring and to avoid discrimination.

planters had failed in Busoga did they start selling their land to Indians (Hasselmann 1976, 213). After 1900, immigrants from India started to come to Uganda to work in the colonial administration, as artisans, or in various business sectors (Fallers 1965, 44). Brandt et al. hypothesise that the immigrants were encouraged by the colonial administration to come and start their businesses because the latter feared that "traditional obligations of solidarity and loyalty towards family and tribal members" on the part of Ugandans of African descent would interfere with the "new behavioural norms" required by the market (Brandt et al. 1972, 10). In the 1950s, Larimore assigned the following business branches in Busoga to so-called "Indians": "import, export, and wholesaling of consumer goods" as well as the latter's supply to consumers through their shops, "the industrial supply and vehicle importing fields", "cotton buying", and "produce processing" (Larimore 1958, 24).

Jinja town has played an important part in Busoga's economic history since the early twentieth century. However, it was not a linear process of development. Nayenga explains:

> "Jinja's decline as Uganda's industrial town has exacerbated Busoga's economic difficulties. The opening of the Owen Fall Dam in 1954 catapulted Jinja to a position of potential economic leadership in Uganda. Jinja attracted several major industries, including textiles, blankets, spinning mills, copper smelters steel rolling mills, and breweries. Poor management during the 1970's resulted either in the underuse of these facilities or their closure." (Nayenga 2002, 43)

Jinja town originated as a trading post set up by the *Imperial British East Africa Company*, which emerged as the administrative capital of Uganda's Eastern Province in 1901 (Gerken 1972, 321). However, it was not until the 1940s that serious efforts began for a general industrialisation of Jinja town (ibid., 321-322; see also: Brandt et al. 1972, 10). However, many small business people of Indian descent did not limit themselves to Jinja town, but went to rural areas and called trading centres into being by opening shops and ginneries. Some moved to areas far away from any centre (Fallers 1965, 44; Larimore 1958, 25; Nayenga 1981, 188). In the 1920s, there were eleven cotton ginneries in Busoga, out of which nine were owned by Indians and two were owned by Europeans (Nayenga 1981, 188). Fallers diagnosed in the 1950s that the Ugandan population of Indian descent, by then consisting in part of third-generation born in Uganda members, was going to become a problem within Ugandan society. The main reason he gave was that Ugandans of African descent desiring social advancement were frustrated with Ugandans of Indian descent's occupation of the positions for which they strove (Fallers 1965, 44). He described the atmosphere between Basoga and so-called "Indians" he observed in the early 1950s as "an atmosphere of mutual hostility and rudeness" (ibid., 56). The British colonial administration had created a class struggle between the two groups by defining one as the commercial elite and the other as the peasantry. In 1972, under then President Idi Amin, all people of Asian descent, whether Ugandan citizens or not, were expropriated and expelled from the country, for Ugandans of African descent to get their chance in business (Mutibwa 2016, 260). According to Phares Mukasa Mutibwa, the expropriated properties were given out on the basis of favouritism, an approach that did not change the situation but rather replaced the old detested elite with a new one. In the following year, Britons were likewise told to leave the country and 500 foreign firms were appropriated by the Ugandan government (ibid., 260-262). As major reasons for the failure of Amin's strategy of "economic war", Mutibwa names the following: having expelled the commercial elite, bad economic approaches like the government's pricing policy for export crops, lack of business experience on the part of the recipients of the expropriated assets, lack of trust in the new Ugandan business people on the part of external trading partners, and difficulties financing business (ibid., 260-266). His observation that "the well-being of the average Ugandan declined considerably over that period", especially because of the high prices of consumer goods (ibid., 263), was confirmed by several respondents of my study, who also deplored the non-availability of commodities that led to smuggling (see chapter 8; see also: Mutibwa 2016, 263-264; Nabuguzi 1993, 55; Sørensen 2000, 48).

The second regime of Milton Obote had taken over a country and an economy devastated by Idi Amin and was forced to accept the conditionalities of the International Monetary Fund (IMF) in order to raise funds for rehabilitation (Sørensen 2000, 21; see also Nabuguzi 1993, 55-56). For that reason, Tenkir Bonger calls the year 1987 "the beginning of a full-fledged SAP" (structural adjustment programme), whereas "a limited one was undertaken during Obote II in 1981-85" (Bonger 2004, 268; see also: Asowa-Okwe 1994, 173). Julius Kiiza summarises the major elements of the first phase of structural adjustment as follows: "the replacement of state-managed foreign exchange rates with market-determined rates; the removal of state controls on product and factor prices; and the equalization of sales tax on imports and domestic products" (Kiiza 2008, 190). As the second term of Obote and the transition to the current government were not peaceful either, several authors regard the whole period as a continuous disaster (e.g., Mutibwa 2016, 434), as for instance the following statement by Alan Whitworth and Tim Williamson demonstrates: "Following Idi Amin's coup in 1971, Uganda suffered fifteen years of brutality, war, and civil war, which turned one of Africa's more prosperous economies into one of the poorest" (Whitworth/ Williamson 2010, 1). The oil crisis and falling world market prices for primary products (like Uganda's cash crops) made the situation even more disastrous for the Ugandan economy (Nabuguzi 1993, 54). Kiiza postulates that the second phase of structural adjustment, under President Museveni, went much further than the first one under Obote II. Trade and industry, capital and foreign exchange market were fully liberalised; jobs in the public service were more than halved between 1993 and 2000; many state-owned companies were subjected to privatisation (Kiiza 2008, 190).

Both the economic crisis and the adjustment policies had concrete implications for people's everyday life. For instance, Asowa-Okwe describes how the devaluation of the Ugandan Shilling in the course of the IMF programme accelerated social inequality and poverty among fisherpeople in Busoga as it made imported materials needed for fishing as well as consumer goods more expensive (Asowa-Okwe 1994, 173). In interviews, fisherpeople told Asowa-Okwe that "bribing of government officers is an old practice, but its tempo increased with the acceptance of the IMF conditionality", as decreasing salaries made government officials prone to corruption (ibid., 179). This goes hand in hand with Nabuguzi's assessment, as he suggests that "salary earners bore the brunt of structural adjustment policies" (Nabuguzi 1993, 57) yet he accuses national elites of having tried to secure their privileges in spite of those policies at the expense of the population (ibid., 56-57). Existing problems (corruption) and new problems introduced by structural adjustment programmes (wage cuts and increasing cost of living) appear to have exacerbated each other. Achille Mbembe emphasises the importance of government workers' salaries in Africa. As those salaries sustain not only the employee's nuclear family but a large group of poorer dependants in the wider sense (e.g., from the *extended* family or from the village of origin), Mbembe considers these an instrument of state power that can be used to create obedience among dependent groups (Mbembe 2001, 44-47). Every member of the community who has succeeded economically, must pay a "social tax" or "social debt" to his or her community of origin for the support received from there (ibid., 47). From the employee's point of view, this argumentation can elucidate how difficult the relationship of a government worker with his or her dependants becomes when his or her salary is cut. After all, in most

African countries, Uganda included, there is no governmental social safety net to which people can turn. Upon losing one's job, neither the poor dependants nor the government worker can rely on any social services provided by the state. As a result, many government workers will try to maintain their level of income and their support to their dependants, despite wage cuts. In case of unemployment or old age, they may need to return to their place of origin and rely on the support of their relatives and local community.

Upon coming into power in 1986, Museveni's NRM[68] government initially tried to resist the IMF conditionalities, yet from 1987 onwards, it accepted them (Sørensen 2000, 21-22). Initially, the NRM government's economic policy approach was "anti-market driven economy" (Mutibwa 2016, 433) or "dirigiste" (Whitworth/ Williamson 2010, 3). The state was supposed to "play a direct role in driving development through planning and through ownership of utilities, marketing, and industrial enterprises" (ibid.). However, because of "inheriting an empty Treasury" (Mutibwa 2016, 433) and because it needed to face the reality of global power constellations in which the Bretton Woods institutions decide who gets money, even from other donors, the NRM government had no choice but to accept the *Economic Recovery Programme* (1987), including all conditions of which many of its representatives did not approve (ibid., 435). This happened at the very time when the IMF's 'recommendations' had become binding 'conditionalities', in the 1980s (Teivainen 2009, 131). It can be taken as a case of "signing away control of their political economies to the international financial institutions to whom their nations are indebted" by governments of the global South, as it has been diagnosed, for example, by Rick Rowden (Rowden 1999, 170; see chapter 2.2.1 of this thesis for details).

As a result of the above-described reluctant acceptance, the first few years of operation of the NRM government displayed a contradictory mix of regulation and planning on the one hand and liberalisation on the other hand (Mutibwa 2016, 433-434; Nabuguzi 1993, 56-58; Whitworth/ Williamson 2010, 2-3). In one year, parastatals were given monopolies (*Produce Marketing Board*, *Uganda Hardwares Ltd.* in 1986); in the following year, other parastatals were abolished (*National Textiles Board*, *Uganda Advisory Board of Trade* in 1987) (Mutibwa 2016, 433-434). Some policies even cancelled each other, for instance, increased producer prices for export

68 NRM = National Resistance Movement, the ruling party of Uganda and President Museveni's party.

crops could not really become the incentive for production as intended because in combination with increased interest rates and a tendency to a decreasing exchange rate, they led to inflation (ibid., 434). The increased producer prices also did not have the desired effect due to high taxation and, at the same time, sharply increasing prices for consumer goods as well as the tendency of the parastatals to delay payment (Nabuguzi 1993, 58). As a result, people had little money at their disposition. Nabuguzi describes how the IMF's structural adjustment programme impacted on the marketing of cash crops and food crops as follows: Independent Uganda had inherited from colonial times state-run marketing boards, which strictly controlled the marketing of certain crops, like the *Produce Marketing Board* did for diverse food crops or the *Lint Marketing Board* for cotton (ibid., 56). In the disastrous political and economic situation of the 1970s, the boards lost the ability to pay acceptable prices to the farmers, such that the latter preferred to sell their products directly to the end consumer (if possible) or to private traders (ibid.). During the 1980s, the government started to liberalise its marketing system by gradually allowing private competition with marketing boards (ibid., 53). In the course of the liberalisation policies, the Obote II government invited the Ugandans of Indian descent to come back and reclaim their properties or receive compensation for their expropriation in 1982, yet on unattractive terms (Mutibwa 2016, 351). In the early 1990s, under Museveni, they were encouraged to come back and be compensated, once more (Collier/ Reinikka 2001a, 44; Sørensen 2000, 27). Pernille Sørensen postulates that the government did so because the World Bank had put pressure on it. Though the returnees are Ugandan citizens, she submits, "to the common mind, they are still Asians, i.e. non-Ugandans who are just out for Ugandan money" (Sørensen 2000, 27). This is the very attitude I encountered during my stay in Uganda in the years 2016-2018, both during interviews and informal conversations. The class struggle continues under a racist banner. This is a very short and selective presentation of Uganda's liberalisation measures. The focus of this study is not on macroeconomic policies but rather on the reactions of ordinary people to phenomena of globalisation in their everyday economic activities. Elaborate studies on those policies and their success in terms of a general recovery of Uganda's economy and its creditworthiness after the crisis include Kuteesa et al. (2010), Musisi/ Dodge (2002), and Reinikka/ Collier (2001). Those liberalisation and adjustment policies are included here because they are taken as a phenomenon of globalisation in my theoretical framework (see chapters 2 and 3 of this thesis) and traces of them can be found in everyday economy. Examples of their effects on everyday life have been found in the literature on Busoga and have been presented here. Others found during interviews are presented in chapter 8.

6.2.3 Cooperative societies in Busoga

In chapter 4.2.2., I provided a general overview of the history and current relevance of cooperatives in Uganda. Henceforth, cooperatives play an important role in the results of my document analysis and interview analysis. Here, I would like to consider only the information that the literature provides with regard to cooperatives *in Busoga* in particular. Most of this information refers to the renowned *Busoga Growers Co-Operative Union*. No study specifically addresses smaller cooperatives, so-called primary societies, in the past or present with special focus on Busoga. My study intends to contribute to closing that gap. Another approach of the 1960s that used to be combined with cooperatives for purposes of marketing, was *group farming* or *block farming*. This was mentioned by some interviewees and considered during document analysis. I address this approach in the last paragraph of this sub-section.

In his anthropo-geographical study of Busoga, for which he collected the data in the second half of the 1960s, Hasselmann provides the following summary on Busoga Growers Co-Operative Union: It started as an amalgamation of four cooperatives from Busoga in 1951/52. It had stores to which farmers could bring their products in exchange for money. From the stores, the products – namely coffee, cotton, and groundnuts – were taken to processing units, at the expense of the cooperative (Hasselmann 1976, 228). Hasselmann diagnoses a "tremendous development" ("stürmische Entwicklung") of Busoga Growers Co-Operative Union from 1951 to 1965 (ibid., 185, translation by E.K.). In 1964/65, *Busoga Growers* had 144 primary societies and marketed 55% of Busoga's cotton production as well as 40% of its coffee production, while almost every ninth Musoga was a member of that cooperative union (ibid.). During interviews, some respondents told me that they were members of such above-mentioned primary societies and one was even involved in the union itself (see chapter 8.3.2). Irrespective of membership or involvement, many respondents mentioned Busoga Growers. Even though most primary societies of that time have since collapsed and given way to a new kind of cooperatives, the idea many people in Busoga have about cooperatives has been strongly influenced by those forerunners (see chapter 8.3.2 and 8.3.6.). In 1966/67, Busoga Growers owned eight cotton ginneries – a quarter of all cotton ginneries in Busoga – one coffee processing unit, and one buying centre for groundnuts (Hasselmann 1976, 185). According to Bernd Schubert, the cooperative societies tried to take over the Ugandan maize market as well, but gave up because cotton marketing was already demanding for them and maize marketing was a "risky business" (Schubert 1972, 179). According to Hasselmann, the Ugandan government had contributed between 60 and 90% of the purchase price for the cotton ginneries and 50% of the purchase price for the coffee processing unit at Namulessa. He confirms the hypothesis forwarded by other authors (see chapter 4.2.2 as well as this chapter) and by the respondents of this study (see chapters 8.3.2) that this was done in order to expel cash crop buyers of Indian descent out of the market (Hasselmann 1976, 186). Signs for this "process of Africanisation" (ibid., 185) could also be found in other sectors of the Ugandan economy, e.g., the promotion of Africans' access to wholesale and retail trade through the *Uganda Development Corporation* (ibid., 189).

In the 1960s, Hasselmann described the failure of *block farming* or *group farming* that some respondents of this study talked about, from a contemporary perspective. Though he used a different term, namely "private agricultural cooperatives" (Hasselmann 1976, 208), it is clearly the same phenomenon. He reported that "[t]he land of these cooperatives is being divided into *10-acre-blocks*", which the members had to cultivate (ibid., translation and emphasis by E.K.). However, he identified severe problems in this approach: While the members' motivation to work in their own fields was higher than their motivation to work in the block farm, the marketing of the cooperatives' products did not work well, such that they had difficulties paying back their loans and acquiring money anew (ibid.). This corresponds with information on block farming gathered during document analysis and interviews (see chapters 7 and 8.3.2 of this thesis).

6.2.4 The rise of a new food and cash crop in Busoga: maize

Between 1962 and 1965, the area under cultivation in Busoga increased by 82% (Hasselmann 1976, 232). This can be traced back to both an extension of commercial agriculture and increased food production for the growing population (ibid., 233-235). For instance, Hasselmann observed a considerable increase in the cultivation of the staple food items, namely plantains, cassava, and millet, by that time. However, he found a much larger increase in terms of maize (more than 150%) and beans (125%) (ibid., 235). This appears to be an indicator of a development about which several respondents told me during the interviews: maize flour (posho) and beans replaced the staple food items plantains and millet and to a limited extent cassava and sweet potatoes (see chapter 8.2). This development is interesting because maize and beans have since become the staple food of the entire country and neighbouring countries, making them highly marketable. Based on her research undertaken in 1961 – not in Busoga in particular, but in Uganda – Anne Martin states that "maize flour (posho) now plays an important part in the diet in most parts of Uganda" and "significant quantities of flour (720 tons in 1961) are imported from Kenya" (Martin 1963, 3). This implies that already in the 1960s there was great potential for commercial maize production in Uganda. Martin claimed that, by then, maize had already become a cash crop in two regions of Uganda, including South Busoga (ibid., 4). In the meantime, maize has become a popular food crop and cash crop all over Busoga. According to the *National Population and Housing Census 2014*, in the three districts under examination, maize is currently the most popular crop. Of the three districts, Kamuli has the highest rate of maize growing: 86.0% of the households, which are involved in agriculture, grow maize, followed by beans (63.2%) and sweet potatoes (44.4%) (UBOS 2017c, 27). Coffee growing in Kamuli is low, yet at 6.7% slightly higher than the other two districts. Data on cotton growing were not even gathered (ibid.). In Buyende District, 85.1% of the households involved in agriculture grow maize, followed by sweet potatoes (54.0%) and beans (26.1%) (UBOS 2017a, 27). Only 1.5% grow coffee and data on cotton growing were not even gathered (ibid.). In Jinja District, 48.9% of the households involved in agriculture grow maize, followed by beans (42.1%) and sweet potatoes (25.5%) (UBOS 2017b, 28). Only 2.5% grow coffee and data on cotton growing were not even gathered (ibid.).

As a *food crop*, maize has long been disregarded by the population of Busoga (Sørensen 2000, 44). According to Schubert, maize found its way onto the Kisoga menu as follows: The first consumer of maize flour in Uganda was the army, followed by other government institutions like schools and prisons but also commercial enterprises like plantations, ginneries, or sugar factories that started to feed their workers on maize flour (Schubert 1972, 186-187). Schubert states that before World War II, the production of maize was of no economic significance in Uganda. Only when the stationing of increasing military units in Kenya and Tanganyika led to shortages of maize supply, did the colonial government show interest in maize production and set up a respective *Department of Supplies*, which held the monopoly in maize marketing up to 1954 (ibid., 172-173). During the war, maize prices rose and cotton prices fell (due to limited export possibilities), such that maize production increased and cotton production decreased accordingly. After the war, the colonial government was interested in reversing this development again, in order to improve Uganda's export performance (ibid., 173). However, meanwhile, "a certain home demand had developed": maize had become popular as cheap food being supplied to workers of processing plants and plantations (ibid.), town dwellers, and people in regions affected by sporadic famines (ibid., 175). Correspondingly, between 1954 and 1968 the retail prices for plantains, the original staple food of Busoga, especially southern Busoga, increased by 75% in Jinja Central Market (ibid., 230). A cheaper alternative was clearly needed. The solution to this dilemma was a very strong regulation of the Ugandan maize market, such that neither more nor less maize than required would be produced (ibid.). Maize mills, a prerequisite for producing mush, had started to spread across Uganda after World War II (Sørensen 2000, 31-32). At first, they had to be authorised by the department and their number was strictly controlled (Schubert 1972, 175). As of 1954, the Ugandan maize market was liberalised, such that everyone was allowed to trade in maize domestically, even without a license (ibid., 177). In Jinja town, a business sector of professional maize mills developed in the course of the 1950s (ibid., 178). During the second wave of industrialisation in Jinja town, from 1964 onwards, "a new type of enterprise, the small mill, first developed" and "their share in the market grew rapidly" (ibid., 179). In the 1960s, Busoga had become one of the major maize-producing regions in Uganda (ibid.). Nowadays, small maize mills play a significant role in Busoga's economy, far beyond Jinja town, as will be shown in chapter 8.2.3 of this thesis.

Drawing on information generated in the 1990s, Sørensen claims that, in Uganda, maize has never become a major staple crop as in Kenya, where maize "united the country" by being eaten as mush everywhere and by everyone (Sørensen 2000, 44). As I observed in Uganda in 2016-2018 and as I was told in the interviews conducted for this thesis, this situation has changed profoundly. Posho (mush made from maize flour) with bean sauce is the uncontested everyday standard food in Uganda, including Busoga. It 'unites' the country, as it has done in Kenya before. Several interviewees deplored this development and longed for the times when their staple food was still plantains. However, they also told me that plantains and all kinds of banana plants have been almost totally wiped out by diseases (see chapter 8.2.2). A report of the *International Food Policy Research Institute (IFPRI)* dated 2008 stated (yet without providing any specification of the respective period): "Banana yields in Uganda are severely reduced by several pests and diseases" (Kikulwe et al. 2008, 3). As clarified in the text, this statement refers to all kinds of banana plants grown in Uganda, including those used for cooking, making beer, or the sweet varieties that are eaten raw or used for making juice (ibid.). Over the years, they have been severely attacked by weevils, nematodes, the Panama disease and black leaf spot disease (both fungal), and bacterial wilts (ibid.). The scarcity created through this severe decimation has led to a steep increase in price and a wide-spread loss of subsistence plantain gardens.

The commercialisation of food crops is a major topic in the interviews I conducted in the scope of this study (see chapter 8.2.1). Sørensen suggests that the commercialisation of food crops followed the political and economic crisis of Uganda under the regime of Idi Amin, the dropping world market prices for cash crops, market liberalisation, and the inability of cooperative societies and the Ugandan government to absorb those shocks and offer attractive prices to farmers. She has observed a significant increase in maize production between the late 1980s and 1995. She traces it to the *export diversification policies* following the 1989 coffee price drop, the arising interest of the *World Food Programme* in Ugandan maize from 1990 onwards, and the opening of the Kenyan border for the import of maize from Uganda in 1993 (Sørensen 2000, 34-35). Sørensen emphasises that, during the first wave of liberalising food crop prices (1986), five of the most important food crops of Uganda were excluded, namely: maize, beans, groundnuts, sesame seeds, and soya beans. They were still marketed by the *Produce Marketing Board (PMB)*[69] until 1988, when the government put an end to the control of producer prices and to the PMB's monopoly in export marketing as well as domestic marketing, e.g., as sole supplier to government institutions (ibid., 24-25). While the PMB has been in fierce competition with other parastatals and private companies in the liberalised Ugandan market for maize exports since the late 1980s, it has found new customers in the World Food Programme and other relief agencies (ibid., 25-26). Another factor that has been promoting maize production in Uganda is the increase of meat production, in connection with the promotion of maize as animal feed (ibid., 32, 52). Sørensen conducted her research in Iganga town, which is not part of the three districts examined in this thesis, yet it is part of Busoga, not far from Kamuli, and there is no reason why it should be profoundly different from my geographical

69 The Produce Marketing Board had been established in 1968 (Schubert 1972, 172).

area of research. Consequently, it does not come as a surprise that the two studies complement each other to some extent, especially with regard to the commercialisation of food crops and the increasing relevance of maize as a cash crop (see chapter 8.2.1). The findings in terms of maize *as a food crop* differ, yet within 20 years, such things may change. In contrast to Sørensen's study, my research project has been started without any particular interest in maize production and marketing, but it developed by itself, as numerous respondents spoke about maize during discussions of major products of their area.

6.3 Conclusion

Busoga has gone through many transformations. From a group of small states united by a common cultural background and framed by bodies of water, it has been transformed into a part of the British Protectorate and, later, of the independent Republic of Uganda. It went through being a district, a territory, a province, a kingdom, and a sub-region. Since the eradication of killer diseases like sleeping sickness in the first half of the twentieth century, its population has been increasing steadily and quickly. It is a predominantly agricultural region, with comparably low incomes and industrialisation traditionally limited to Jinja town (the current situation is not yet well-documented but information about it can be found in chapter 8.2 of this thesis). The majority of Busoga's inhabitants have been living on a combination of cash crop farming and subsistence farming since colonial times. Both the staple food (plantains and millet) and the major cash crops (cotton and coffee) have changed over time. They have been replaced to a great extent by maize, which is being eaten as mush all over Busoga and sold as a cash crop on the local market, the national market, the regional relief market, and to neighbouring countries. However, there are also other food crops like rice, which have recently pushed into the market. From 1900 onwards, the British colonial administration introduced the cash economy to Busoga by creating a need for cash through the imposition of taxes, offering cash for certain crops (cotton and later coffee), and providing consumer goods on which the balance could be spent. Busoga was 'globalised', i.e., integrated into the capitalist world-system, to a very large extent from the early twentieth century up to the early 1970s, when then President Idi Amin provoked the breakdown of the Ugandan economy. It was mostly cut off from international trade, the local economy was almost brought to a standstill, and a great deal of the remaining economic activities were pushed into the illegal sector (smuggling). After Amin, Busoga's recovery took quite a long time in comparison to the recovery of the country as a whole. Due to neoliberal economic recovery programmes of the 1980s and 1990s, today's Busoga has a liberalised, diversified economy, which builds primarily on the production of food crops, both for personal use and for sale. It is a sub-region with eleven districts and a cultural kingdom with a strong cultural identity.

7. Method and results of document analysis

This chapter complements the fragmentary picture of Busoga that has been painted in chapter 6.2 with some further fragments from historical and contemporary documents. I selected and analysed the documents presented in this chapter with the intention of collecting contextual information on issues mentioned by study interviewees. In combination with this chapter 7 and the literature analysis (chapter 6), the interview results (see chapter 8) provide a thorough understanding of the research topics. This chapter starts with a list of the documents I analysed, followed by a list of the main and sub-categories applied to the texts during *content structuring Qualitative Content Analysis* (chapter 7.1). The sub-sections are divided according to the main categories, as the last step in content structuring Qualitative Content Analysis involves summarising by main category the content extracted from the data set. These summaries are presented in sub-sections 7.2 to 7.5, together with their interpretation in the respective concluding paragraphs. The chapter closes with a short conclusion (chapter 7.6).

7.1 Method

I have used a combination of 'historical' and contemporary sources in the scope of document analysis (see chapter 5.3 for detailed explanations). Many of the analysed documents, e.g., government reports and correspondence (accessible at *Jinja District Archives* and the Africana section of *Makerere University Library*), were written between 1965 and 1982. The 'contemporary' documents written between 2011 and 2018 encompass reports on Busoga region from different levels of Ugandan government institutions; government policy papers; newspaper articles; a paper prepared by an UN agency; and an annual report of the *Cooperative Alliance of Uganda*. I present the results of the analysis of these documents in chapters 7.2, 7.3, 7.4, and 7.5, with a conclusion in chapter 7.6. I outlined the methodological approach of Content Structuring Qualitative Content Analysis in detail in chapter 5.3. In the following, the list of documents (chart 1) and list of categories applied in the analysis (chart 2) can be consulted.

Chart 1: Documents used in the analysis

Title	Short	Information	Significance for this research project	Source
280,000 coffee farmers in Busoga decry lack of market	Daily Monitor 2018	Newspaper article by Philip Wafula, published in the established Ugandan newspaper "Daily Monitor" on 9 Jan. 2018.	Information on what has happened to the famous Busoga Growers Co-operative Union; information on coffee marketing in Busoga.	Online, last access 22 March 2018, on: http://www.monitor.co.ug/News/National/280000-coffee-farmers-Busoga-decry-lack-market/688334-4256034-aet9siz/index.html
BUSOGA DEVELOPMENT PLAN. Baseline Survey Report. Status of Socio-economic and demographic development indicators in Busoga	Dev. Plan 2017	Report dated March 2017, submitted to the *Permanent Secretary of the Office of the Prime Minister (OPM)*, Kampala, Uganda, by *Prime Solutions Limited*, Workers House, Plot 1 Pilkington Road ,P. O. Box 72397, Kampala, Uganda. *Prime Solutions* is a provider of professional research services.	General statistical information about Busoga and its development challenges.	The report was provided to me as a soft copy by the team of *Prime Solutions Ltd*. In response to my official request for helpful information, a representative of the OPM had introduced me to the team of *Prime Solutions.*
How to reap big from zero grazing in cattle	Daily Monitor 2017	Newspaper article by Denis Bbosa, published in the established Ugandan newspaper "Daily Monitor" on 6 Aug. 2017.	Information about the "zero grazing" strategy.	Online, last access 30 April 2020, on: https://www.monitor.co.ug/Magazines/Farming/How-to-reap-big-from-zero-grazing-in-cattle/689860-4045362-quwq4vz/index.html
UGANDA COOPERATIVE ALLIANCE LTD. ANNUAL REPORT For the year 2016/2017	UCA 2017	The UCA is the official umbrella organisation of the Ugandan cooperative movement, according to the cooperative societies act. It is obliged by its statutes to provide an annual report to the public. The report is dated Sept. 2017 and was published on the official website of the UCA.	Information about the cooperative movement in Uganda.	Online, last access 21 March 2020, on: https://uca.co.ug/wp-content/uploads/2018/ 06/AGM-FINAL-REPORT-2016-17.pdf

Zero-grazing of improved cattle breeds using drought-tolerant fodder in Uganda	FAO 2017	Information Sheet prepared by the *Food and Agriculture Organization of the United Nations (FAO)* in 2017, under the ID 8926, and published on the official FAO website.	Information about the "zero grazing" strategy.	Online, last access 30 April 2020, on: http://www.fao.org/3/CA2565EN/ca2565en.pdf
BUSOGA TEN YEAR STRATEGIC PLAN FOR THE PERIOD 2016 -2025	OBB 2016	Strategic Plan, dated June 2016, prepared by the administration of *the Kingdom of Busoga (Obwa Kyabazinga Bwa Busoga, OBB)*.	General statistical information about Busoga; information about the OBB and its development priorities for Busoga.	Provided to me as a soft copy by the Prime Minister of the OBB, in response to my request.
NATIONAL AGRICULTURAL EXTENSION POLICY	NAEP 2016	Policy paper by the *Ministry of Agriculture, Animal Industry and Fisheries* of the Republic of Uganda, dated Oct. 2016.	Information about extension services, which were mentioned by many interviewees and are important for Busoga as agricultural region.	Provided to me as a soft copy by *Prime Solutions Ltd*. (see above).
NATIONAL CO-OPERATIVE POLICY	NCP 2011	Policy paper by the *Ministry of Trade, Industry and Cooperatives*, dated 10 January 2011 and published on the ministry's website.	Information about the current approach to cooperatives of the government of Uganda; information about the Ugandan cooperative movement.	Online, last access 2 April 2020, on: http://www.mtic.go.ug/wp-content/uploads/2019/09/Final-Copy-of-Cooperative-Policy.pdf
YOUR AGR. 163/1 OF 18th FEBRUARY, 1982 – STATUS OF FORMER GROUP FARMS.	Group Farms 1982	Letter addressed to *The Commissioner for Agriculture, P. O. Box 2, Entebbe*. From the *Department of Agriculture, Kamuli District, P.O. Box 149, Kamuli*, 31 March 1982, with the memo requesting for that information.	Information about the approach of "group farms", about which some interviewees spoke and which used to be combined with cooperatives for marketing.	Jinja District Archives
DEPARTED ASIANS' PROPERTIES	Busoga Province 1976	Letter addressed to *All District Commissioners, Busoga Province.*, by the *Provincial Governor's Office, Busoga Province, P.O. Box 1551, Jinja, Uganda.*, 5 July 1976.	Information about the situation in Busoga during Idi Amin's regime and the impacts of his "economic war" on everyday economy and on cooperatives in the region.	Jinja District Archives

DEPARTMENT OF CO_OPERATIVE DEVELOPMENT _ ANNUAL REPORT 1975: BUSOGA PROVINCE	Busoga Coop. Dept. 1976	Report addressed to *The Commissioner for Co-operative Development, P.O.Box 3585*, Kampala, from the *Dept. of Co-operative Development* of *Busoga Province*, Jinja, 1 April 1976.	Information about the impacts of Idi Amin's "economic war" on everyday economy and on cooperatives in the region; historical information about the cooperative movement in Busoga.	Jinja District Archives
GOVERNMENT WHITE PAPER on the Report of the Committee of Inquiry into the Affairs of the Busoga Growers Co-operative Union	BG Inquiry 1966	Government White Paper printed by the Government Printer*, Entebbe, in 1966.	Information about the government's reaction to the report on Busoga Growers Co-operative Union (see below) and the consequences for the Ugandan co-operative movement.	Makerere University Main Library (Africana Collection)
The report of the Committee of inquiry into the affairs of the Busoga growers co-operative Union Limited	BG Inquiry 1965	Report dated on 27 April 1965, addressed to *The Commissioner for Co-operative Development, P.O. Box 3585, Kampala*, by the *Committee of inquiry into the affairs of the Busoga growers co-operative Union Ltd.* The Commissioner gave the order for the inquiry by his letter of 23 Nov. 1963, as described in the letter that commences the document.	Information about Busoga Growers Co-operative Union (BG) at the peak of its activities; historical information about the Ugandan cooperative movement.	Makerere University Main Library (Africana Collection)
NAIRIKA PROPOSED GROUP FARM	Nairika 1965	Letter addressed to *The District Agricultural Officer, Busoga Territory, P.O.Box 67, Jinja*, by the *Asst. Agric. Officer i/c Luuka County (S.J. Ibanda)* from the *Department of Agriculture, Kiyunga Luuka, P.O.Bulongo/Jinja*, 11 Aug. 1965.	Information about the approach of "group farms", about which some interviewees spoke and which used to be combined with cooperatives for marketing.	Jinja District Archives

Ref. Your C/330/65/1299 of 10/6/65. Group Farms.	Group Farms 1965	Letter addressed to *M/S. Smith McKenzie & Co. Ltd., P.O. Box 657, Kampala* from the *Department of Agriculture, Special Development Section, Busoga Territory, P.O. Box 67, Jinja, Uganda.*, 16 June 1965, with the letter requesting for that information.	Information about the approach of "group farms", about which some interviewees spoke and which used to be combined with cooperatives for marketing.	Jinja District Archives

* Established in 1902, today called Uganda Printing and Publishing Corporation (UPPC; see: https://www.uppc.co.ug).

I present the categories I applied to the above-listed documents in the course of Content Structuring Qualitative Content Analysis (see chapter 5.3 for details) in chart 2. In the subsequent sub-sections, I present the results of the document analysis according to each main category.

Chart 2: Categories of document analysis

Categories of document analysis		
Main categories (4)	**Sub-categories (30)**	**Coded extracts**
1. Socio-economic situation of Busoga (current)	high production/ marketing capacities	130
	low production/ marketing capacities	
	limited access to agricultural inputs and training	
	limited value addition	
	poor quality of outputs	
	low-level techniques of production	
	cash crops	
	destruction of the environment	
	socio-economic infrastructure (positive)	
	socio-economic infrastructure (deficits)	
	population growth/density	
	poverty	
	shortage of land	
	zero grazing	
	liberalisation/ privatisation	
	gender inequality	
	agricultural policies influencing Busoga's economy (current)	
2. Historical roots of the socio-economic situation of Busoga	past economic strength of Busoga	24
	economic decay of Busoga	
	indigenous knowledge ignored	
	agricultural policies influencing Busoga's economy (past)	
3. General information about Busoga	geographic and administrative structure	50
	social organisation (e.g. clans)	
	occupation(s) of population	
	regional dispersion across Busoga	
4. The cooperative movement in Uganda, especially in Busoga	information about cooperatives in Uganda	155
	historical information about cooperatives in Busoga	
	information on Busoga Growers Cooperative Union	
	information about cooperatives in Busoga today	
Total number of coded extracts		359

7.2 Socio-economic situation of Busoga (current)

In this section, I present the main category "socio-economic situation of Busoga (current)". This *main category* (of *document* analysis) provides background information for the *main theme* (of *interview* analysis) "Busoga's economy under globalisation" (chapter 8.2), a theme that, in turn offers answers to the research question: *How have people in Busoga experienced changes in their socio-economic environment, which can be traced back to globalisation, in the past 30 years?* This document analysis provides important context for a number of topics about which study respondents spoke, e.g., the conditions of agricultural production, the impacts of liberalisation, the socio-economic infrastructure of the region, development strategies like "zero grazing" and the *National Agricultural Extension Policy*. For this main category, the following documents have been used: Daily Monitor 2018, Dev. Plan 2017, Daily Monitor 2017, UCA 2017, FAO 2017, OBB 2016, NAEP 2016, NCP 2011.

Busoga is an agricultural region. The 2008 agricultural census found out that Busoga region delivered 24.6% of the maize and 24.4% of the rice produced throughout Uganda (Dev. Plan 2017). Both are locally consumed products that are simultaneously being exported to neighbouring countries (ibid.). Beyond that, Busoga accounts for 31.2% of Uganda's sweet potato production, 15.5% of Uganda's cassava, 10.4% of the country's soya beans, and 7.4% of its groundnuts (ibid.). However, the agricultural production of Busoga has been reducing due to climate change, reduced soil fertility, weeds, and pests (ibid.). Another challenge is the limited access to certain inputs. For instance, only 1.41% of Busoga households own a tractor and 44.5% have an option to hire or borrow a tractor (ibid.). Of course, hiring a tractor requires more than its availability, the main challenge is to raise the money. Anyway, 54% of the population have no access at all to mechanisation of agriculture (ibid.). As a result of such constraints, farmers in Busoga must resort to simple methods of agriculture (OBB 2016). The hand hoe is the dominant agricultural tool (Dev. Plan 2017). There is also limited value addition to agricultural products in Busoga (ibid.). Income from agriculture is little due to the low quality of many agricultural products (ibid.).

Rural population growth in Busoga is very high (OBB 2016) and according to the population census of 2014, at 2.9%, comparable to the national average of 3% (Dev. Plan 2017). However, compared to the national population density, Busoga's population density is almost twice as high, with 397 people per square kilometre (ibid.). As a result, land is scarce (ibid.).

The average household size of 5.1 (OBB 2016) is above the national average of 4.7 people (Dev. Plan 2017). This results in a high dependence ratio and limitations on the households' abilities to save or invest, as cost of living is high for large households (Dev. Plan 2017). Land fragmentation, i.e., the division of land into small parcels, is a problem (OBB 2016). Numerous study respondents spoke about it posing a major challenge to their economic development and sometimes even subsistence (see chapter 8.2.2). As most families in Busoga have many children, land has been fragmented, such that individuals or families have small portions of land at their disposition for growing food (Dev. Plan 2017). Shortage of land results in food insecurity, land conflicts among the population, and pressure on the natural environment. Deforestation and the loss of wetlands are rampant (OBB 2016) and cause drought (Dev. Plan 2017). Trees are cut in large numbers for the purposes of clearing land for agriculture, construction, charcoal production, or getting firewood for cooking (Dev. Plan 2017).

The so-called *zero grazing* strategy is being regarded as the future for farmers in Uganda in view of the increasing shortage of land (Daily Monitor 2017). Some respondents of this study discussed the advantages and disadvantages of zero grazing during the interviews (see chapter 8.2.2 and 8.3.1). According to the *Food and Agriculture Organization of the United Nations* (FAO), one of the promoters of this strategy in Uganda, zero grazing is a system that serves to effectively keep high-performance cattle breeds (FAO 2017). In the zero grazing system, the cattle stays in the farm instead of wandering around and is provided with food and water by the farmer (Daily Monitor 2017; FAO 2017). The main objective of zero grazing is to enhance animal productivity (ibid.). Yet, it works with a relatively small piece of land (Daily Monitor 2017; FAO 2017). Dung can be collected and used as manure in the farm easily (FAO 2017). Zero grazing reduces conflicts that otherwise arise when a farmer's cattle eats the neighbours' crops (ibid.). However, to build an enclosure for four cows costs between 700,000 and 800,000 UGX (ibid.), which is barely affordable for most people in Busoga. The so-called improved breeds, which are supposed to be kept in this way, are costly and delicate (ibid.). Nevertheless, zero grazing has many advantages, namely the provision of manure, effective use of land, milk for personal consumption and income realisation, and the production of biogas by means of cow urine and dung (Daily Monitor 2017). The NGO *Heifer International* has been promoting zero grazing since its beginnings in Uganda, in 1982 (ibid.). According to some respondents of this study, the greatest challenge for farmers is the provision of water and food to the cattle. Nevertheless, they consider zero grazing an option to deal with the increasing shortage of land that impedes allowing the cattle to graze as it was done in the past (see chapter 8.2.2 of this thesis). In chapter 8.3.1, I examine the implications of zero grazing for the social practice of sharing and giving.

Busoga suffers from a lack of food security, particularly in the areas with plenty of sugar cane (Dev. Plan 2017). In March 2017, seven sugar cane factories were found in Busoga, which together account for 54% of Uganda's sugar production, among them *Kakira Sugar Ltd.* (Jinja District, owned by *Madhvani group of companies*), which alone produces 42% of Uganda's sugar (ibid.). In addition to 180,000 tonnes of sugar, the company's 9,366 employees annually produce 20 million litres of ethanol and 50MW of 'green' electricity (ibid.). Kakira Sugar Ltd. grows 35% of its sugar cane on its own fields that cover approximately 10,000 ha (ibid.). The remaining 1,200,000 tons of sugar cane are produced by more than 7,000 outgrowers on 19,000 ha (ibid.). Kakira paid about 100,000 UGX per ton to its outgrowers in 2015/16 (ibid.). Although, on average, this implies an annual payment of 17 million UGX per outgrower, in practice distribution is unequal and sugar cane growing causes a lot of poverty and food insecurity (ibid.). It is common for a (male) head of household to rent out a piece of the family's land to sugar cane growers for four seasons, which means about eight years, as sugar cane needs 18 months to mature (ibid.). At the going rate of about 600,000 UGX per acre for three harvests (i.e., six years), a landowner receives 8,333[70] UGX per month, an amount that cannot sustain a family (ibid.). As a result, some families borrow money from the very person who rented their land, such that the renting period is being prolonged to account for the loan (ibid.). Food security is permanently endangered by this situation (ibid.).

The socio-economic infrastructure in Busoga tends to be weak. As of March 2017, 7,933 people are served by one health facility in Busoga (Dev. Plan 2017), compared with the national average of 6,664 (ibid.). Though the guidelines of the Ministry of Health demand every district of Uganda to have a district hospital, only four of Busoga's ten districts have one, namely Jinja, Kamuli, Iganga, and Bugiri (ibid.). While each county is supposed to have a health centre IV and each sub county a health centre III, there are six counties and 28 sub counties that do not have them (ibid.). Medical equipment and drugs are lacking in many health facilities in Busoga (ibid.). The infrastructure of schools in the region is deficient (ibid.). There are not enough housing facilities for teachers, furniture for

70 As of October 2020, that would be less than 2 Euro.

classrooms, latrines, and even classrooms (ibid.). The latter are often in bad conditions (ibid.). Roads in Busoga are very vulnerable to rain that destroys their weak sub-base and makes them impassable (ibid.). Several urban centres in Busoga have no electricity (ibid.). As power lines serve only main roads, many communities have no access to them (ibid.). Some social indicators in Busoga are also worrying. Busoga is weaker than all other regions of Uganda in terms of poverty reduction (Dev. Plan 2017). In the 2017 baseline survey report, 24.3% of Busoga's population are defined as poor (without further definition of poverty), 50.5% as non-poor, but insecure (i.e., prone to returning to poverty as soon as a shock occurs), and only 25.2% as middle class (ibid.). There are social problems within many families due to the conditions in which they have to live (OBB 2016). Many dwelling units are of poor substance and not well-equipped with household items (ibid.).

Another social challenge is gender inequality. Though there has been considerable progress in terms of gender equality in Busoga recently, the prevailing gender norms still disadvantage women and girls heavily (OBB 2016). As a result, many of them are affected by financial and social insecurity (ibid.). For instance, women and girls are widely excluded from access to land (Dev. Plan 2017). Their standing is particularly difficult when it comes to contracts for selling or renting out land, e.g., to sugar cane companies (ibid.). Land inheritance in Busoga is practised to the disadvantage of women and youth (ibid.). The majority of women in Busoga (4 in 5) have no say in major decisions in their households (OBB 2016), e.g., the use of land (Dev. Plan 2017). The high level of gender inequality shows also in he prevalence of child marriages, polygamy, and domestic violence (ibid.). The transition rate from secondary school form 4 to form 5 is 27.4% for boys in Busoga and only 18.7% for girls and indicates that girls tend to leave school earlier than boys (Dev. Plan 2017).

Economic liberalisation has considerably impacted Busoga's everyday economy. Though the following information about it (from the documents) refers mostly to Uganda as a whole, chapter 8 of this thesis shows how they also apply to Busoga, in particular. Due to globalisation, market liberalisation, and privatisation, global agriculture is rapidly transforming (NAEP 2016). Since economic liberalisation, commercial enterprises, especially multinational ones, have taken over the medium to upper level of the business sector in Uganda (NCP 2011). As a result, cooperatives, which in the past played a major role in Uganda's economy, have been pushed to the lower ranks through competition (ibid.). This circumstance poses a threat for the development of cooperatives (ibid.). Another competitor to cooperatives is the so-called "middleman"[71], individuals or firms that purchase agricultural products from farmers (ibid.). As middlemen pay immediately, or even in advance, cooperatives have a hard time competing with them (ibid.). However, middlemen exploit farmers with their unfair practices and often do not care much about quality standards (ibid.). In addition to that, cooperatives are affected by counterfeit and low-quality goods, e.g., industrial or agricultural inputs that can enter the Ugandan market easily because of liberalisation (ibid.).

According to the *National Agricultural Extension Policy (NAEP)*, the neoliberal reforms of the 1990s have exacerbated the uncoordinated and fragmented structures of extension services in Uganda by allowing more players in the field and impeding their regulation (NAEP 2016). For that reason, the field has become non-transparent and the information spread in it has grown inconsistent (ibid.). The policy defines agricultural extension services as services provided by public or private organisations with the objective to allocate knowledge and technologies to farmers' organisations, facilitate their interaction with other relevant actors, and assist them in capacity building (ibid.). There are diverse methods in extension services, e.g., group training sessions; demonstrations in the field; agricultural shows and fairs; communication through mass media or publications like booklets and posters, etc. (ibid.). The main objective of the *NAEP* is to lead farmers from subsistence farming to commercial farming (ibid.). Another challenge posed by liberalisation policies to the achievement of that goal is the reduction in staff budget caused by these policies (ibid.). In 2014, the ratio of extension worker to farmers, which is supposed to be at 1:500, was at 1:5,000 (ibid.). As a result, according to the writers of the policy paper, farmers' associations have become weak and the application of new technologies is minimal (ibid.). The first lesson learnt from the confusion created by liberalisation, i.e., the new strategy for extension services in Uganda, is to establish a hybrid approach that allows many actors in the field, but subjects them to governmental coordination and regulation (ibid.). The second lesson learnt from previous experience is a widening of the focus beyond production, emphasising value addition and marketing (ibid.). Various agricultural policy approaches on the national level may influence life in Busoga in the long run. Apart from NAEP, the Ugandan government has launched programmes for the commercialization of agriculture, rural finance provision, enabling

71 "Middlemen" or intermediaries are usually Ugandans, sometimes people from neighbouring countries. For details, see chapter 8.2.

market access, creating employment, and supporting industrialisation, in order to fight poverty, e.g., the *Rural Development Strategy* (NCP 2011). The *Uganda Co-operative Alliance* (UCA) has a partnership with CAIIP (*Community Agriculture Infrastructure Improvement Program*) (UCA 2017). CAIIP provides infrastructure like roads, electricity, and equipment for the processing of agricultural products (ibid.). An expert interviewee informed me that CAIIP is implementing activities in Busoga (Expert 2, 2017). The UCA has influenced legislation on the level of local government on behalf of farmers, e.g., with regard to post-harvest handling of crops, counterfeit agricultural inputs, etc. (UCA 2017).

The information collected under this main category shows that Busoga is an agricultural region that contributes significantly to Uganda's supply of food crops. Hence, beyond contributing to subsistence, food crop production is of high significance to farmers in Busoga. Yet farmers face many challenges related to land shortages, loss of soil fertility, climate change, pests, poverty, and low capacities of the socio-economic infrastructure of the region. The quality of agricultural products from Busoga is often low, in part due to production challenges, i.e., limited access to improved farming methods (especially post-harvest handling), tools, and inputs. This is exacerbated by marketing circumstances, i.e., the involvement of middlemen who prefer buying cheaply regardless of quality. Low returns on the crops hinder future investments in better techniques or inputs. Land shortages are caused both by high population growth and density as well as the increasing occupation of land by sugar cane. Sugar cane growing has turned out to be a lucrative business for few and a poverty trap for many (see above: Dev. Plan 2017, in this chapter; this topic is also discussed in chapters 8.2.1 and 8.2.2). As such, it increases income disparity and food insecurity in the region. Various agricultural policy approaches at the national level (some, such as agricultural extension services, mentioned by study respondents) have already influenced life in Busoga or may influence it on the long run. Extension services are an attempt by the Ugandan government to bridge the gaps between the free-market economy, governmental regulation, and the social economy. While those services are intended to promote commercial agriculture and value addition (free-market), the government intends to increase their regulation in order to improve service provision efficiency. The services are provided to farmers' groups, not to individuals. They thus actively promote the social economy by encouraging farmers to form groups. This could also contribute to the mitigation of some of the above-mentioned problems, e.g., the low quality of agricultural products, as groups could help their members to access better inputs and technologies. Furthermore, they could increase their bargaining power for better prices. After a period of massive liberalisation, the government of Uganda is taking some steps towards regulation and promoting the social economy in response to lessons learnt from the inefficiency of extension services under liberalisation and the decline of cooperatives (on the last point, see also chapter 7.5).

7.3 Historical roots of the socio-economic situation of Busoga

This main category provides background information for the main theme "Busoga's economy under globalisation" (chapter 8.2), which in turn delivers answers to the research question: *How have people in Busoga experienced changes in their socio-economic environment, which can be traced back to globalisation, in the past 30 years?* This section contextualises a number of topics about which study respondents spoke, e.g., the comparison of Busoga's past and present economic status and former agricultural policies that permanently influenced the region's economy. Unfortunately, the historical information found at *Jinja District Archives* is fragmented because the archives have lost many documents due to flooding over the past years. For this main category, the following documents have been used: Dev. Plan 2017, OBB 2016, NAEP 2016, Group Farms 1982, Busoga Province 1976, Busoga Coop. Dept. 1976, Nairika 1965, Group Farms 1965.

In the past, Busoga was known for its agricultural products, mainly cotton, coffee, groundnuts, and sugar cane (Dev. Plan 2017). Jinja town played a central role as an industrial town of East Africa (ibid.). As a result of political and economic upheaval throughout the country following independence, Busoga lost its strong status (ibid.). The documents under examination correspond with the literature (chapter 6) and the interview results (chapter 8), as they report on serious supply shortages of virtually everything during Idi Amin's regime in the 1970s. For instance, in the mid-1970s, transport was very problematic in Busoga (Busoga Coop. Dept. 1976). Cars and bicycles lacked spare parts and tyres and thus did not move (ibid.). If spare parts could be found, the prices for them were extremely high (ibid.). Bus service reduced and ceased to reach certain areas completely (ibid.). Any public transport that existed was very expensive (ibid.). A 1976 document reports that expropriated Asian businesses were not being used well by individuals or groups who received them (Busoga Province 1976). Some had not yet been allocated to anyone and were beginning to decay (ibid.). Machines of expropriated Asian businesses were dismantled and sold or taken to other places (ibid.). Hence, the expropriation and expulsion of the community of Asian descent in 1972 had not benefitted Ugandans of African descent to the extent expected. The businesses were not only affected by ineffective allocation, but also by severe supply bottlenecks. In contrast to Uganda as a whole, Busoga region has not recovered well from that breakdown (Dev. Plan 2017). In its *Ten Years Strategic Plan*, the *Obwa Kyabazinga Bwa Busoga* (OBB or *Kingdom of Busoga*) offers the following explanation: The autochthonous socio-political setup of Busoga has been disregarded and subjected to diverse impacts over time (OBB 2016). As a result, it has been devitalised and confused (ibid.). Cultural issues and indigenous knowledge have been condoned and degraded (ibid.). For those reasons, the socio-cultural fabric of the Basoga has lost its vitality, including its potential to renew itself and the living conditions of the Basoga (ibid.). Several attempts to work with the people have failed due to those problems (ibid.). Nevertheless, the Basoga are proud of their culture and try to ensure its continuous existence and practice (ibid.).

As Busoga is an agricultural region, government's attempts to build up its economy have in most cases been implemented through agricultural policies (apart from the industrialisation of Jinja town in particular). Over time, several agricultural policies have left their mark on Busoga. Apart from the cooperative movement (see main category number 4), these policies included: group farms (or block farms), tractor hire services, and extension services, all of which study respondents mentioned (see chapters 8.2.1 and 8.3.2). The *Food Production Campaign* was not mentioned by respondents yet is of interest because of its contribution to the turn from so-called traditional cash crops, namely cotton and coffee, to food crops for sale in Busoga. In 1975, two programmes were implemented in Busoga: the *Cotton Double Production Campaign* and the *Food Production Campaign* (Busoga Coop. Dept. 1976). The result was a trend towards food crop production and a reduction in cotton output (ibid.). In 1965, Busoga had four *group farms*, with 150 to 472 acres of land each (Group Farms 1965). A group of farmers from Nairika village requested another group farm that same year (Nairika 1965). The land for group farms was provided by private land owners. In case of Nairika proposed group farm, 27 people offered to make their land available for it (ibid.). By 1975, there were no longer any registered group farms in Busoga (Busoga Coop. Dept. 1976). The report on the *tractor hiring service* in that year contained mainly complaints about the number of tractors being too low and the availability of spare parts posing a serious challenge (ibid.). A 1982 document mentions *one group farm* in Kamuli District, Nabirumba, about seven miles North of Kamuli Town, consisting of 230 acres that had been re-occupied by the local people who had previously owned the land (Group Farms 1982). At the time, the *tractor hiring service* was still operational in Busoga (ibid.). This was all the information I could find on the two programmes in Busoga at *Jinja District Archives*. Though it is not much, it can serve as context for the mentions of those programmes in the interviews. In chapter 6.2.3, I introduced Hasselmann's conceptualisation of *group farming* as "private agricultural cooperatives" (Hasselmann 1976, 208). Indeed, it was a cooperative that wanted to start a *group farm* in Nairika in 1965 (Nairika 1965).

According to the 2016 National Agricultural Extension Policy, the Ugandan government had previously undertaken numerous approaches to extension services, yet with varying and sometimes disappointing results (NAEP 2016). The first activity in terms of agricultural extension in Uganda was the so-called 'kiboko' of 1898, which is called "a regulatory system" in the policy paper (ibid.). It was followed by "the supply-led progressive farmers approach of the 1950s" and the "educational approach" in the 1960s (ibid.). The 1970s are sometimes called the "non-directional period" because there were no activities going on (ibid.). In the 1980s and 1990s, the "Training and Visit agricultural extension model" was implemented (ibid.). Preceding extension programmes have reached only 22% of the target group (ibid.).

The information collected under this main category has provided some evidence to support study respondents' claims that the supply of goods in Busoga had collapsed during the 1970s. This is an important point with regard to the respondents' evaluation of today's opportunities for consumption (see chapter 8.2.4). Beyond that, this finding differentiates the picture of Busoga's economy, which has neither undergone linear development nor stagnation in the past 100 years. After having been in good condition up to the early 1970s, it was completely destroyed by Idi Amin's economic war and by actual civil war. In comparison to some other regions of the country, Busoga has not recovered well from that shock. The administration of the *Kingdom of Busoga* offers a cultural explanation for this phenomenon. It might be one of several reasons. A differentiated analysis exceeds the parameters of this study but would be of interest for further research. As Busoga was an agricultural region throughout the twentieth century, the national policies with the strongest impact on its economy (apart from Amin's economic war) have always been *agricultural* policies. Some were mentioned by study respondents. Background information that could be found on them in documents has been provided above. One of them, namely the provision and governmental regulation of extension services, is still significant today (see also chapters 7.2 and 8.2.1). Others have been mentioned as more or less successful approaches of the past.

7.4 General information about Busoga

This main category provides background information for the main theme "Busoga's economy under globalisation" (chapter 8.2), which in turn delivers answers to the research question: *How have people in Busoga experienced changes in their socio-economic environment, which can be traced back to globalisation, in the past 30 years?* Some general statistics on the region from the analysed documents complement the information drawn from the literature in chapter 6.2. Special attention is paid to the comparison of the three districts under examination in this study – Buyende, Jinja, and Kamuli – with regard to important indicators like population, urbanisation, and socio-economic infrastructure. Beyond that, there is also some background information for the main theme "SSE – Social and Solidarity Economy" (chapter 8.3), which in turn delivers answers to the research questions: *What kind of alternative economic activities based on solidarity do or did people in Busoga practise? Did those activities persist in spite of, dissolve because of, or emerge as a reaction to globalisation? Do people consider such activities helpful in their situation, and why or why not?* This main category of the document analysis provides some background information about clans and cultural institutions that can enhance the understanding of autochthonous forms of solidarity, which are examined in chapter 8.3.1. For this main category, the following documents have been used: Dev. Plan 2017, OBB 2016, Busoga Coop. Dept. 1976, BG Inquiry 1965.

Ten per cent of Uganda's population and 40% of the population of the Eastern Region live in Busoga (OBB 2016). Only 14% of Busoga's population live in urban centres (Dev. Plan 2017). Jinja District has the highest urbanisation rate (36.6%), followed by Iganga and Bugiri (ibid.). The remaining districts have an urbanisation rate below the national average of 21.3% (ibid.). The level of urbanisation of Kamuli District is 12.3%, equalling to rank four among the ten districts of Busoga (ibid.). The level of urbanisation of Buyende District is 7.2%, equalling to rank seven within Busoga (ibid.). The mainstay of Busoga's economy is agriculture (OBB 2016). The main occupation in Busoga is subsistence farming, which is based on family labour and does not engage in value addition (Dev. Plan 2017). However, it is often accompanied by some cash crop farming and /or livestock keeping (ibid.).

The official major concern of the *Obwa Kyabazinga Bwa Busoga* (OBB or *Kingdom of Busoga*) is to unify the four million people of Busoga, who as of June 2016 belong to 11 chiefdoms, 350 clans, and 750,000 households (OBB 2016). The current *Kyabazinga* is William Wilberforce Gabula Nadiope IV (ibid.). The allocation of tasks among the OBB and the local government looks as follows: The Kingdom is in charge of cultural norms, values, and aspiration of the Basoga (ibid.). The local government of the Republic of Uganda is in charge of the legal framework, national policies, strategic investments, infrastructure, and social services (ibid.). Article 246 of the 1995 *Constitution of Uganda* grants the institution of traditional and cultural leaders (ibid.). Uganda's heritage is supposed to be promoted, as long as human rights and dignity, democracy, and the Constitution of Uganda are not compromised (ibid.). According to the *Ten Years Strategic Plan* of the Kingdom of Busoga, clans are the most important social institution in Busoga that has an influence on every person living there (ibid.). So-called *traditional leaders* fulfil various tasks in Busoga, especially in terms of local customs, values, cultural laws, and the provision of cultural and social direction to the people (ibid.). The administration of the Kingdom plans to institutionalise and facilitate their work (ibid.).

The regional dispersion of all development indicators within Busoga varies strongly. In all cases, Jinja is the district of Busoga that performs best. Buyende is usually the last or second-last. Kamuli ranges somewhere in the middle, depending on the indicator, slightly below or above the average. In some few cases, it performs quite well. For instance, the dispersion of health facilities across Busoga varies, with Jinja at the top (53) and Buyende at the bottom (ten) (Dev. Plan 2017). Jinja and Buyende Districts mark at the two ends of the spectrum with regard to the average number of people attended to by one health facility: 4,144 people per health facility in Jinja and 13,933 people per health facility in Buyende (ibid.). Among the counties that lack health centre IV facilities are Budiope East in Buyende District and Bugabula North in Kamuli District, yet no county in Jinja District (ibid.). The highest number of government schools can be found in Kamuli (180) and the second-lowest in Buyende (91) (ibid.).

The comparison of these three districts shows that they represent different stages in terms of urbanisation and the provision of various kinds of infrastructure within Busoga. As a result, they provide a good overview of

Busoga as a region with different facets. A certain rural bias is unavoidable, as even in Jinja, the most urbanised district of the region, a large part of the population lives in rural areas and is involved in agricultural activities. At the interface of local administration and social organisation, there is the *Obwa Kyabazinga Bwa Busoga* (OBB or *Kingdom of Busoga*). While local government authorities control administration in the narrow sense, legislative activities, and the implementation of national policies, the OBB is in charge of the cultural concerns of the population. However, as its *Ten Year Strategic Plan* (OBB 2016), which has been analysed in the scope of this study, shows, the OBB is also concerned with the improvement of the living conditions of people in Busoga and produces strategies for socio-economic transformation. Clans and traditional leaders play an important part in people's everyday life. Those findings are of interest with respect to chapter 8.3. Clans and other cultural systems of mutual support are considered in relation to autochthonous solidarity structures (chapter 8.3.1). Beyond that, as further elaborated in the next main category, the OBB is committed to promoting farmers' groups.

7.5 Cooperatives in Uganda, especially Busoga

This main category provides background information for the main theme "SSE – Social and Solidarity Economy" (chapter 8.3), which in turn delivers answers to the research questions: *What kind of alternative economic activities based on solidarity do or did people in Busoga practise? Did those activities persist in spite of, dissolve because of, or emerge as a reaction to globalisation? Do people consider such activities helpful in their situation, and why or why not?* Drawing from the documents I analysed, I provide context for a number of topics about which study respondents spoke, e.g., the comparison of cooperative societies of the past with their contemporary counterparts, the history of the Ugandan cooperative movement in general and of the renowned *Busoga Growers Co-operative Union* in particular. These topics are vividly remembered by the people in Busoga and have formed their image of cooperatives and other kinds of solidarity groups. Unfortunately, the historical information found at Jinja District Archives is fragmented because the archives have lost many documents due to flooding over the past years. Information from the *National Cooperatives Policy* of the Ugandan government and from the *Strategic Plan* of the Kingdom of Busoga reveal the approaches to cooperatives of these institutions. Both are likely to influence the future of cooperatives in Busoga. For this main category, the following documents have been used: Daily Monitor 2018, Dev. Plan 2017, UCA 2017, OBB 2016, NAEP 2016, NCP 2011, Busoga Coop. Dept. 1976, BG Inquiry 1966, BG Inquiry 1965, Nairika 1965.

Since 1996, there has been a permanent increase in the number of cooperative members in Uganda (NCP 2011). In 2010, there were over 10,746 cooperatives in the country, with approximately four million members (ibid.). In September 2017, approximately 18,000 cooperatives were registered countrywide (UCA 2017). Their main fields of intervention are agriculture (production and marketing, 55%) as well as savings and credit (25%) (NCP 2011). The current government of Uganda has high expectations of cooperatives. According to the 2011 National Cooperative Policy, cooperatives can provide for basic human needs, reduce poverty, and provide employment (ibid.). They involve the poor in the development process and produce economic growth (ibid.). As cooperatives are spread all over Uganda, they are a good medium for delivering services to the population (ibid.). The *National Cooperative Policy* is an attempt to improve the conditions for cooperatives in terms of leadership, capitalisation, information and knowledge, as well as the legal framework (ibid.). The government is to regulate cooperatives in an effective way and provide them with resources, e.g., technical support (ibid.).

Today, there is a four-tier vertical structure: A primary society must have at least 30 members and can form a secondary society, together with at least one other primary society (NCP 2011). Tertiary societies can be formed by at least two secondary societies and they can be specialised service providers, e.g., for finance, insurance, transport, or housing (ibid.). The apex is formed by secondary and tertiary societies (ibid.). Out of Uganda's 10,746 cooperatives, as of 2010, 10,621 were primary societies, 121 were secondary societies (including 80 area cooperatives), four were tertiary societies (transport, creameries, insurance, finance), and one was an apex, namely the *Uganda Co-operative Alliance Ltd. (UCA)* (ibid.). The UCA was established in 1961 (UCA 2017). It is the umbrella organisation for the Ugandan cooperative movement and represents it on the national as well as international level (ibid.). An important task of the UCA is political lobbying for the cooperative movement (ibid.). For instance, it has been involved in consultations concerning amendments of the cooperative law and has influenced decision making on behalf of cooperatives from the local level up to the international level (ibid.). It connects cooperatives with decision makers on various levels (ibid.). Through advocacy, the UCA has accomplished a tax exemption for SACCOs for the period of 2017 to 2027 (ibid.). The Ministry of Agriculture, Animal Industry and Fisheries provides support to farmers through the member organisations of the UCA, e.g., under programmes like NAADS (*National Agricultural Advisory Services*) and *Operation Wealth Creation* (OWC) (ibid.), both of which were mentioned by several study respondents. The UCA collaborates with the Ministry of Finance in terms of promoting savings and credit cooperatives (ibid.). There are plans for a cooperative bank that is to grant access to finance to cooperatives on favourable terms (ibid.). Another core task of the UCA, according to the cooperative societies act, is the conciliation of conflicts within the cooperative movement (ibid.). The UCA provides tractor hire services to farmers' cooperatives at subsidised prices (ibid.).

The first 'cooperative' of Uganda – yet a very small one comprised of only four people – was founded in Mubende District in 1913 (UCA 2017). It was an attempt of farmers to escape exploitation by business people of Asian descent (ibid.). The first larger cooperative was formed through the amalgamation of four small farmers' groups in the central region, in 1920 (ibid.). The National Cooperative Policy postulates that the year 1946 can be taken as the birth date of the Ugandan cooperative movement and the *Co-operative Department* (NCP 2011) as 1946 is the year of the legalisation of cooperatives through the first governmental *Cooperative Societies Ordinance* (Nannyonjo 2015, 267). By then, there were 75 organisations in Uganda that could be considered cooperatives, 50 dealing in marketing of agricultural products, eight in shopkeeping, six in consumer stores, and 11 in other businesses like fishing or dairy (NCP 2011). Cooperation in Busoga began with small cooperatives (BG Inquiry 1965). It was the *Department* that encouraged them to increase the size of the groups (ibid.). Between 1946 and 1970, the number of cooperatives in Uganda grew, especially in the sectors of coffee and cotton marketing (NCP 2011). Between 1952 and 1970, the Ugandan cooperative movement flourished (UCA 2017). Plenty of coffee, tea, tobacco, and cotton was marketed by cooperatives (ibid.). In 1963, a cooperative college was initiated and, in 1964, a cooperative bank was established as a service provider to cooperatives (ibid.). According to the UCA, by 1965, the Ugandan economy was dominated by the cooperative movement (ibid.). In that year, cooperatives handled 61% of Ugandan cotton, 40% of Robusta coffee, and 90% of Arabica coffee (NCP 2011). This gave the farmers a considerable amount of power (UCA 2017). By that time, a cooperative union had to invest only 10% to open a new cotton ginnery and the government would provide the balance of 90% for the project (BG Inquiry 1965). The savings and credit movement initially took root only in Jinja District as it targeted industrial workers (Busoga Coop. Dept. 1976). Thanks to the registration of 1,991 members of *Nytil*[72] *Employees Savings and Credit Co-operative Society Limited*, the membership increased from 320 to 2,311 people in the year 1975, while the number of registered societies increased from four to five (ibid.). The Nytil employees' savings and credit society was a joint production of the *Uganda Co-operative Savings and Credit Union* (which provided trainings and technical advice), trade unionists, the Nytil management, and the group's committee (ibid.).

Several study respondents mentioned Busoga Growers Co-operative Union, which used to be a regional umbrella organisation for the agricultural cooperatives of Busoga, particularly those dealing in coffee and cotton. Busoga Growers Co-operative Union is among the oldest Ugandan cooperative unions and, in 1964, it was the largest (BG Inquiry 1965). In the first ten years of its existence, it was very successful and one of the most creditworthy unions in Uganda (ibid.). Its management committee asked for advice from the Cooperative Department on a regular basis and implemented it well (ibid.). Government officers carried out accounting and supervision in it permanently (ibid.). However, the close supervision of Busoga Growers Co-operative Union by government officers stopped in 1963 due to shortage of staff at the Cooperative Department (ibid.). Up to 1965, no new officer had been sent to Busoga, but the whole Ugandan cooperative movement was supervised from Kampala (ibid.). *Busoga Growers'* financial capacities collapsed between 1960 and 1964 (ibid.). This happened in spite of the union's assets increasing, from three ginneries in 1960/61 to seven ginneries and one coffee factory in 1963/64 (ibid.). The committee members spread ginneries all over Busoga, beyond the production capacities of the members, trying to push the government to fulfil its announcement to grant a monopoly for coffee and cotton marketing to the cooperative movement (ibid.). At that time, Busoga Growers dealt mainly with cotton, and, less so, with coffee and groundnuts (ibid.). Some primary societies no longer wanted to sell their products to Busoga Growers but were forced to do so by the Ministry of Agriculture and Co-operatives (ibid.). The cotton season begins towards the end of the year, when farmers need money for the festive season, for paying school fees and taxes (ibid.). Yet, at that time, Busoga Growers was not prepared to gin cotton and to pay out money to the members (ibid.). As a result, they preferred to sell their cotton to commercial ginneries at that time of the year (ibid.).

72 Nytil is a prominent textile factory in Jinja town.

In 1965, a committee of inquiry was sent to Jinja in order to report on the situation of the union and provide recommendations for improvements. One of the main purposes of the various amendments to the cooperative law since 1946 was to make cooperatives more democratic (BG Inquiry 1965). However, as the committee of inquiry found out, government left a power vacuum that was filled by the committee, not by the members (ibid.).[73] Several informants of the 1965 inquiry into the problems of Busoga Growers Co-operative Union complained that the government had left them hastily (ibid.). According to the report of the committee of inquiry, there was no control of finance in Busoga Growers, as the union was being regarded as an endless supply of money by its own management committee and the member societies alike (ibid.). The committee of inquiry blamed the low level of education of Busoga Growers' management committee for the poor financial management and deplored the neglect of the professional accountant they had employed (ibid.). Fraud was also a problem among Busoga Growers. Committee members, staff, and representatives of member societies were found to be involved in the following activities: falsifying weight notes, raw cotton being stolen from and resold to Busoga Growers, theft of lint and cotton seed (ibid.). The committee consisted of nine members (ibid.). They held monthly meetings, which were supposed to take maximum two days (ibid.). However, they met much more often and for longer periods in order to receive higher allowances (ibid.). There were several other ways in which they abused their position (ibid.). In 1966, building on the report of the committee of inquiry on the situation of Busoga Growers Co-operative Union, the government planned to enhance its power over and guidance of the cooperative movement (BG Inquiry 1966). After all, the Ugandan government was planning to put the processing of cotton exclusively in the hands of the cooperative movement (BG Inquiry 1965). Problems like those that were diagnosed in Busoga Growers were typical of cooperative unions of that time (BG Inquiry 1966). As a result, the government decided to apply the lessons learnt from the inquiry to the movement countrywide (ibid.). In the 1960s, relevant training programmes were provided by the Ministry of Agriculture and Co-operatives, by the Department of Co-operatives, and by the Ministry of Education, yet the report of the committee of inquiry diagnosed a need for expansion of training programmes for cooperative staff and committees (BG Inquiry 1965). In case a cooperative was in

73 The same insight was gained by Herment Mrema in his study of the Ugandan cooperative movement (Mrema 2008, 155-156; see chapter 4.2.2. of this thesis).

financial trouble, the Co-operative Societies Act allowed the registrar and the ministry in charge to intervene in its management (ibid.). In 1966, the government planned to send more staff to Busoga Territory to supervise the cooperative movement and it got involved in the election of the chairman of Busoga Growers (BG Inquiry 1966). That same year, the central government raised the requirements for the qualification of committee members of cooperative societies and unions (ibid.).

The decline of cooperatives started with the civil wars of the 1970s and 1980s in which the groups lost members and assets (UCA 2017). Apart from that, the economic policies of the regime of Idi Amin (1971-1979), especially the expulsion of people of non-African descent from the country, led to extreme scarcity of goods and funds and to a wide-ranging economic isolation of Uganda (see chapter 6). This situation, which was described by several study respondents (see chapter 8.2, especially 8.2.4), affected not only individuals and companies but also cooperatives. Some cooperative societies in Busoga had received the assets of expropriated and expelled people of Asian descent, like jaggery mills, shops, etc. (Busoga Coop. Dept. 1976). In 1975, they operated them, yet without much success (ibid.). For instance, three of Busoga's six sugar cane cooperatives were assigned jaggery mills that had belonged to people of Asian descent before (ibid.). While the groups without jaggery mills suffered from lack of transport and marketing facilities for their members' sugar cane, the groups with mills also encountered challenges as those mills needed constant repair (ibid.). The activities and numbers of cooperative societies in Busoga in 1975 were as follows: five thrift and loan societies (2,311 members); one consumer society (27 members); no traders societies; 175 producer societies (including hides and skins, poultry, transport, carpenters, and dairy; 101,249 members); one producer union (153 member societies) (ibid.). Though the prices were higher than in the previous year, the turnover of cotton and coffee in cooperatives declined in 1975 (ibid.). The reason for this was a trend in favour of planting food crops (instead of cotton and coffee), not marketed through cooperatives (ibid.). In previous years, *Busoga Growers Cooperative Union* had given loans to member societies for buying so-called controlled produce (ibid.). These food crops were marketed through the Produce Marketing Board (PMB). In 1975, due to lack of material that even impaired the core business of the union, cotton and coffee, this practice was stopped (ibid.). A few member societies managed to buy their members' food crops with their own money (ibid.). They sold it directly to the PMB, not through Busoga Growers (ibid.).

In the 1970s, Busoga Growers was considerably affected by the general shortage of materials (Busoga Coop. Dept. 1976). As the only union in Busoga, it was in charge of all cotton and coffee processing of the region (ibid.). However, it lacked means of transport, e.g., from primary societies to the union's processing units or from there to the Lint and Coffee Marketing Board (ibid.). If it was at all possible, it was costly (ibid.). Busoga Growers also lacked materials for cotton processing and packaging like hessian squares, baling materials, gunny bags, and machinery spare parts (ibid.). In 1975, the seasons for cotton and coffee processing were prolonged due to those shortages of materials (ibid.). Worldwide inflation and the prolonged cotton season led to a widespread failure of primary societies to return cotton crop finance (ibid.). In 1972, Busoga Growers had added five tractors to the fleet provided by the tractor hire service programme (ibid.). However, by 1975, only two of them were operational (ibid.). There were a lot of problems with Namulesa Coffee Factory in 1975 (ibid.). It remained unused almost permanently due to various reasons, e.g., transport difficulties or lack of materials (ibid.). Inflation led to the union's payment of coffee commission to the societies being too low to cover their operational expenses (ibid.). Another problem was fraud. The Department's 1975 report deplores six major cases of embezzlement within primary societies (ibid.).

During the 1970s, cooperatives were greatly mismanaged (NCP 2011). As described above, they were also affected by destructive political and economic developments around them. However, they could not recover from the shock, as the structural adjustment programmes of the 1990s, especially economic liberalisation, forced upon them competition with multinational corporations (UCA 2017). According to the UCA, the downfall of the cooperatives was advanced by these economic policies (ibid.). Hence, there were two waves of cooperative demise, one in the 1970s and one that began in the 1990s. The NCP locates the second wave of cooperative demise between 1992 and 2006 (NCP 2011). For instance, cooperative handling of coffee marketing dropped from 22% in 1992/93 to 2% in 2001/02 and again to 1% in 2006/07 (ibid.). The breakdown of cooperatives has led to a decline in value addition, storage facilities, and marketing opportunities for farmers in Busoga (Dev. Plan 2017). While the cooperatives demised, multinational companies pushed into the Ugandan coffee market, increasing their share from 14% to 83% between 1992 and 2006 (NCP 2011). While cooperative *marketing* declined, other cooperative activities increased, especially SACCOs, i.e., savings and credit cooperatives (ibid.). Between 2004 and 2008, the registration of 2,351 SACCOs took place (ibid.). In the 1990s, the UCA had established so-called *village banks*, which later became SACCOs (UCA 2017).

In 1982, Busoga Growers Cooperative Union owned one cotton ginnery and one coffee processing plant each, plus several commercial and residential houses in Jinja town (Daily Monitor 2018). Meanwhile, all its assets were sold off (ibid.). In 2015, the organisation itself was purchased by *Agroways Limited* (ibid.). Since then, Busoga's coffee farmers complain that their products are no longer properly marketed for them (ibid.). Since its inception in the 1950s, Busoga Growers had been promoting coffee farmers' capacities for production and marketing (ibid.). In 2015, it ceased to exist due to mismanagement (ibid.). Agroways Limited, a private company, is specialised in cereals, not in coffee (ibid.). As a result, it concentrates on large-scale coffee farmers, who do not need much assistance and deliver large quantities (ibid.). The small- to medium-scale farmers, who used to rely on Busoga Growers Cooperative Union to assist them in post-harvest handling of their crops, feel neglected by Agroways and long for the times when Busoga Growers was still there (ibid.). With the loss of their cooperative union, farmers lost bargaining power (ibid.).

In some respects, the cooperative movement of today has similar problems like the historical one, e.g., dominant elites and inactive members. In practice, members are widely failing to implement the democratic principles of cooperatives (NCP 2011). They do not necessarily elect the most able leaders and employ the most qualified staff (ibid.). This hinders the success of many cooperatives in Uganda (ibid.). The groups are poorly managed and members are exploited due to lack of knowledge about cooperative business (ibid.). The government institutions concerned with cooperatives lack staff and other resources for being able to serve the movement sufficiently (NCP 2011). Cooperatives themselves do not have the resources to employ qualified personnel, either (ibid.). Members must pay entry fees, share capital, and annual subscription fees (ibid.). They find it difficult to raise the money for those purposes (ibid.). As a result, the organisation remains poor and must take out loans at high interest rates, e.g., 29% per annum (ibid.). Because of liberalisation, cooperatives have lost the specific banking system on which they used to rely (Daily Monitor 2018). Commercial banks are not willing to support them (ibid.), especially with regard to agricultural activities (NCP 2011).

Due to Uganda's historical experience with cooperatives, many people in the country view them negatively (NCP 2011). The current approach of the Ugandan government is to keep the cooperative movement autonomous while government provides support on all levels: regulation, technical support, and infrastructure (ibid.). The 2011 National Cooperative Policy sets the following tasks for the government: find out what the cooperative movement needs to be re-vitalised and provide for these needs; encourage the creation of new cooperatives; foster tertiary cooperatives, such that the provision of certain services to cooperatives can be improved; improve the public image of cooperatives; strengthen cooperatives; encourage the Ugandan cooperative movement to collaborate with regional and international movements (ibid.). The UCA has replaced the old model of the cooperative unions – which were not close to the farmers and dealt only in traditional cash crops – with the new Area Cooperative Enterprise (ACE) model, which is supposed to be closer to the farmers and more diverse in terms of products marketed (UCA 2017). It initiated the tripartite linkage model, i.e., a link between a SACCO (finance), cooperatives (production), and an ACE (processing and marketing) (ibid.). The Obwa Kyabazinga Bwa Busoga (OBB or Kingdom of Busoga) has a policy of promoting agricultural cooperatives and their forerunners like farmers' associations, with the intention to market products from Busoga, locally and globally (OBB 2016). Through those organised groups, agriculture in Busoga is supposed to be transformed from subsistence and small-scale farming to competitive business, at least on the regional level (ibid.). The Kingdom's *Financial Sector Development Strategy 2015-2020* focusses particularly on the *Busoga SACCO*, which is supposed to revolutionise rural credit and micro-finance and develop the local capital market (ibid.).

The information collected under this main category complements the general impression received from the literature (see chapter 4.2.2): The Ugandan cooperative movement has been steered by the government since the latter got involved in 1946 by providing a legal framework and establishing the first government authority in charge of such groups, the Co-operative Department. Since then, there has always been a ministry that had cooperatives in its name, though over time it changed from the ministry in charge of agriculture to the ministry in charge of trade and industry. After having neglected cooperatives for about 15-20 years, beginning in the 1990s, the Ugandan government has returned to an approach of heavy intervention with its National Cooperative Policy of 2010/11. It expects co-operatives to solve the socio-economic problems of large parts of the population and thus has a strong interest in making them succeed. However, today's government control over cooperatives is not as intensive as it was in the 1950s and 1960s. At the time, the government could force primary societies to sell their products to the local cooperative union and could send staff to cooperatives of all levels to audit them and intervene in their management. Today, in Uganda there is a relationship of mutual influence between the cooperative movement and the government. Through the Uganda Co-operative Alliance, the movement advocates for its concerns and influences policy making, taxation, and political decision making. The reasons for the breakdown of the original cooperative movement of Uganda are manifold. One was their strong dependence on guidance by the government. As soon as the government withdrew a little from them, they were overtaken and mismanaged by elites. This inability of the members to take the management of their cooperative societies and unions into their owns hands likely reflects the dominant role played by the government in the movement from the very beginning. Members have been relying on it instead of taking democratic cooperative structures seriously. However, the civil wars of the 1970s and early 1980s as well as the economic policies of the 1970s were exogeneous factors that ruined many cooperatives because they left them bereft of funds, assets, materials, and members. In the 1980s and 1990s, economic liberalisation policies further weakened cooperatives by exposing them to competition with domestic and international business enterprises. It has turned out that cooperatives need a specific banking system for the financing of their activities. There are efforts to re-build such a system in Uganda through a combination of SACCOs on the local and regional level and a revival of the cooperative bank on the national level. All in all, the relationship between cooperatives and the government has proven to be complicated and at the same time essential. If a cooperative movement on a large scale is supposed to succeed, it needs governmental support, e.g., in terms of a legal framework, finance, and other resources. Yet, too much government intervention violates cooperative principles by impeding ownership and commitment on the part of the members. In Busoga, the cooperative movement has been very strong at its heyday, in the 1950s and 1960s. From the 1970s onwards, it was affected by the above-mentioned processes. More information about its current status can be found in chapter 8.3, especially 8.3.2.

7.6 Conclusion

This document analysis has complemented the fragmentary information from the literature about Busoga as a region, the evolution of its socio-economic situation over time, and the manifestation of the Ugandan co-operative movement in Busoga. It has been identified as an agricultural region in which food crop production beyond subsistence is becoming increasingly important. The comparison of the three districts under examination in this study has shown that they provide a good overview of the different facets of the region, e.g., in terms of varying levels of urbanisation. However, Busoga is also a low-income region with many challenges in agricultural production as well as socio-economic infrastructure. Sugar cane, once the region's hope as its new major cash crop, has been found to exacerbate income disparity and food insecurity.

This retrospective supports the information from the literature concerning Busoga's economy neither having undergone linear development nor stagnation over the past century. After having been in good condition up to the early 1970s, it was devastated by Idi Amin's economic war as well as by actual civil war. The impacts were felt by private businesses and individuals, agricultural production and marketing, and cooperatives alike. In comparison with some other regions of the country, Busoga has not recovered well from that shock. The latter was followed by economic liberalisation, which has left its mark on the region, as could be learnt from documents on different topics. In crop trade, the free-market middlemen system has been found promoting low quality standards and low prices for the farmers, in comparison to the period when cooperatives were still the major buyers of some crops. The competition with those middlemen and (multinational) business enterprises, as well as the loss of its specific banking system, were negative impacts of economic liberalisation on the Ugandan cooperative movement. These impacts on the Ugandan cooperative movement occurred after it had already been weakened by the turmoil of the 1970s and by elite capture and inappropriate dependency on the government in the 1960s. These tendencies of the national movement could be observed well in Busoga, as it had a dynamic cooperative landscape and one of the oldest and largest cooperative unions in the country.

I have examined some past and present government policies because study respondents mentioned them during the interviews. A prominent example, as it has existed in varying forms from 1898 up to the present, is the approach of agricultural extension services. The latest extension policy of the Ugandan government is an attempt to bridge the gaps between the free-market economy, governmental regulation, and the social economy. The case of the latest cooperative policy, which has been examined in order to evaluate its potential influence on the cooperative movement in Busoga, looks similar: Cooperatives are supposed to be promoted and supported, yet not as an alternative to capitalist production, but as a tool for disadvantaged groups to benefit from capitalist development. They are supposed to be integrated into capitalist marketing chains, yet the government's approach to making them succeed is regulation. It appears that the Ugandan government is trying to combine the different approaches of a market-economy, governmental regulation, and elements of a social economy. In order to allow their combination, the doctrines of all three approaches are being watered down. Otherwise, a social economy would conflict with a neoliberal market economy (the way the latter is prescribed by structural adjustment programmes) – and both would disapprove of governmental regulation. None of the approaches that have been tried out in Uganda after independence – neither socialism with a strong state under Obote I, nor economic war under Idi Amin, nor economic liberalism under Obote II and Museveni – seem to have served cooperatives well. They had their best time under Obote I, yet the foundations for their decline were also laid there (dependency on the government). Nonetheless, they continued to exist and the government felt obliged to deal with them in one way or another. Cooperatives have been an integral part of Uganda's history and economy from the beginning of the twentieth century up to the present. Today's relationship between the cooperative movement and the government is one of mutual influence. Through the Uganda Co-operative Alliance, the movement advocates for its concerns on all levels of decision making. There are efforts to re-build a cooperative-friendly banking system, with SACCOs on the local and regional level and a cooperative bank at the national level. In addition to national policies and local government authorities, the Kingdom of Busoga, cultural leaders, and clans play a significant role in Kisoga society (see chapter 7.4). They form autochthonous systems of mutual support and have an impact on socio-economic transformation. As the Kingdom of Busoga and the National Cooperative Policy both have announced the massive promotion of cooperatives and similar groups, an increase in such activities in Busoga can be expected.

8. Method and results of interview analysis

Qualitative interviews have been the major data collection tool in this study. I explained the methods of data collection and analysis in detail in chapter 5.2. In this chapter, I present the results of the thematic analysis of the 30 main interviews and ten expert interviews. These findings are embedded in the context outlined in chapters 6 and 7. The latter is clearly distinguished from the information derived from the interview analysis. Chapter 8.1 presents the list of themes and the thematic map I created during the interpretative phases of the analytic process. Towards the end of the analytic process, I remained with two main themes, of which one has seven sub-themes and the other one has six sub-themes. The rest of this chapter is divided accordingly. Chapter 8.2 bears the title of the first main theme: "Busoga's economy under globalisation". Its sub-sections are named after the respective sub-themes and present the results of the analyses of those sub-themes. I apply the theoretical framework of chapters 2 and 3 of this thesis to the results of the interview analysis that concern globalisation. The last sub-section (8.2.8) presents the key findings of the first main theme. Chapter 8.3 bears the title of the second main theme: "SSE – Social and Solidarity Economy". Its sub-sections are named after the respective sub-themes, plus chapter 8.3.7 with the key findings of the main theme as a whole. I apply the theoretical framework of chapters 2, 3, and 4 to the results of this main theme. Finally, chapter 8.4 provides a summary of the key findings of both main themes, i.e., of the interview analysis as a whole and conclusions on their theoretical implications. This involves elements of the theoretical framework of chapters 2, 3, and 4.

8.1 Method: the themes

"A theme captures something important about the data in relation to the research question, and represents some level of *patterned* response or meaning within the data set" (Braun/ Clarke 2006, 82, emphasis in the original). Looking for themes and developing them is "where the interpretative analysis of the data occurs, and in relation to which arguments about the phenomenon being examined are made" (ibid., 88). In my case, I generated the codes inductively, operating as closely to the original data as possible. At the stage of creating themes, I began to *actively* involve my theoretical framework (though it certainly had an implicit influence on all the research work I did before). In chapter 5, I explained in detail the methodological reflections (5.1) and practical steps (5.2) on which this interview analysis is based. Below, I present the final list of themes and the final thematic map.

Chart 3: Final list of themes

Final List of Themes		
Main themes (2)	**Sub-themes (13)**	**Number of coded extracts**
Busoga's economy under globalisation	Business enterprises in Busoga	326
	Access to consumer goods	538
	Cost of living	158
	Obstacles to benefitting from the market economy	72
	Trade in food crops and animal products new mainstay of Busoga's economy	889
	New challenges in farming	160
	Other effects of globalisation on life in Busoga	197
SSE	Autochthonous solidarity structures survive partly	146
	Cooperatives	414
	Savings and credit groups (S&C)	183
	Mukenkede/ Gema Kumwino groups	20
	Muno Mukabi groups	38
	Respondents' experience with SSE groups	378
Total number of coded extracts		3,519

Chart 4: Final thematic map

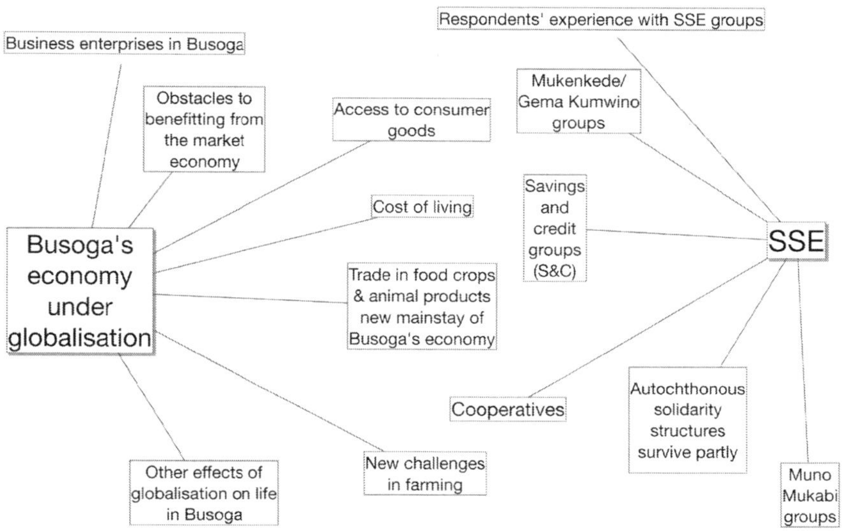

The thematic map shows relationships between themes by their proximity to each other on the map. For instance, "Cooperatives" mainly correlate with "Trade in food crops & animal products [being the] new mainstay of Busoga's economy", i.e., the major products of agricultural cooperatives have changed over time from the so-called traditional cash crops, coffee and cotton, to food crops and animal products. Beyond that, cooperative members are confronted with "New challenges in farming", just like individual farmers in Busoga. "Savings and credit groups (S&C)" provide finance for agriculture, "Cost of living", and "Access to consumer goods" alike. However, as is usual with graphic visualisations, especially those containing a considerable amount of data, the representation is necessarily imprecise. It can help to gain a first impression but is insufficient for undertaking a detailed analysis. The final list of themes is mirrored in the structure of the remainder of this chapter, which presents my interview analysis.

8.2 Busoga's economy under globalisation

This main theme provides answers to the research question: *How have people in Busoga experienced changes in their socio-economic environment, which can be traced back to globalisation, in the past 30 years?* The theme paints a picture of the way respondents have perceived the transformation of their everyday economy over time. According to James Ferguson, what can be found in Africa nowadays is "not a lamentably immature form of globalization, but a unique 'advanced' and sophisticated mutation of it" (Ferguson 2006, 41). My study was informed by an interest in getting to know more about the features of this 'mutation', especially with regard to its impacts on the lives of the general public. The results must look different in particular countries and regions of Africa, depending on the respective local circumstances. This study provides a glimpse into the specific experiences of people in Uganda's Busoga region with globalisation's effects on their everyday lives.

Postcolonial analysis of globalisation sees globalisation's historical roots in colonialism (e.g., Castro Varela/ Dhawan 2015, 78; Dhawan/ Randeria 2016, 562; Gandhi 2019, 125; Ndlovu-Gatsheni 2013 and 2018; see chapter 3.2 of my thesis). I take a position that John Glenn would call 'transformationalist' (see chapter 3.1 of my thesis and Glenn 2007, 34, 66-67). As my approach is partly based on world-systems analysis, I do not see the beginnings of globalisation in the twentieth century but rather in the sixteenth century, when the formation of the capitalist world-system began (see chapters 2.3.2 and 3.4 of this thesis). The 'globalisation' we experience today (see chapter 3 of this thesis) is a phenomenon of the last 30 to 40 years with roots in the sixteenth century onwards. Colonial expansion initiated this process in the global South and the liberalisation policies that have been promoted by the IMF and the World Bank since the Reagan-/ Thatcher-era have fuelled it. Hence, in my analysis, I considered both the way liberalisation policies paved the way for globalisation in the narrow sense and the historical structures on which this process was built.

The following seven sub-sections present the sub-themes of this main theme (chapter 8.2.1 to 8.2.7). Each of them concludes with a short summary of the respective sub-theme. They are followed by a presentation of the key findings of this *main theme* as a whole (chapter 8.2.8). In all these sub-sections, I use some information from chapters 6 and 7 to supplement information that was fragmentary in the interviews. Beyond that, I apply elements from the theoretical framework of this study (chapters 2 and 3) to the results of this main theme.

8.2.1 Trade in food crops and animal products is the new mainstay of Busoga's economy

The majority of respondents identified agriculture – practised on one's own land or as a worker for someone else – and livestock breeding as the most important survival strategies in Busoga. Urbanised areas offer more diverse occupational options than rural areas. Yet study respondents described those job opportunities as scarce and as primarily low-profile jobs. These findings justify taking a closer look at the agricultural sector. A central finding of this sub-theme is that the system originating from colonial times, which combined subsistence farming of food crops with the production of inedible cash crops for sale (see chapter 6.2.2), has changed. It is being replaced by commercial production of food crops and animal products (live animals for meat production, eggs, milk) for sale. An expert interviewee told me about the government policy that encouraged this development: "In general, since economic liberalisation, the idea was diversion in production. People diverted from the traditional crops where government had market. And they changed to products where their market starts with their neighbour" (Expert 5, 2017). By "the traditional crops where government had market", he referred to the export crops coffee and cotton. As elaborated in chapter 6.2.2, the Ugandan government exercised stringent control on the marketing and pricing of agricultural export products through marketing boards through to the 1980s, when liberalisation policies partly abolished those institutions and partly exposed them to competition with other buyers. In this thesis, I view Uganda's liberalisation policies as a product of globalisation because they have been prescribed by the IMF through economic recovery programmes (see chapter 6.2.2) with their usual conditionalities (see chapter 3.3). As outlined in the theoretical framework, in this thesis the neoliberal[74] orientation of the IMF's economic programmes as well as its powerful position[75] in the world economy are taken as phenomena of globalisation[76]. For instance, Joseph Stiglitz calls the IMF, the World Bank, and the WTO "the three

---

74 See chapters 2.2.1 (especially Teivainen 2009) and 2.2.2 (especially Rowden 1999) for details.

75 See chapter 2.2.1 (especially Mbembe 2001, McMichael 2012, Teivainen 2009) for details.

76 See chapter 3.2 (especially Eckert/ Randeria 2009) for that argumentation from a postcolonial point of view and chapter 3.3 (especially Khor 2001, Stiglitz 2002) for the corresponding argumentation from the point of view of development studies.

main institutions that govern globalisation" (Stiglitz 2002, 10) and postulates that through conditionalities, "the IMF became a permanent part of life in most of the developing world" (ibid., 14). Uganda is no exception to this process.

The respondents of this study predominantly reported that, in their area, commercial crop production has been extended to food crops over the past decades. The following comment by a main interviewee from Buyende District, who used to live on cotton production for sale and food crop production for subsistence in the past and meanwhile has become a successful local food crop trader and ceased to grow cotton[77], is typical:

> "So, these days, there is what? Market. Even people have increased doing what? Cultivating. Because what you cultivate, you sell, but there [in the past], although you cultivate, you cannot do what? Sell. It is just there for eating, just eating. So, these days, people have even increased as, uh (considering), now, in cultivating, there is what? Income." (Main 4, 2017, translation by E.K. and N.H.[78])

As outlined in chapter 6.2, the commercial production of food crops in Busoga started slowly in the 1960s, with the gradual introduction of maize (see chapter 6.2.4). In the following decades, food crops and cash crops shared the fate of not being properly marketable during the turmoil of 1971 to 1986 and being subject to market liberalisation from the late 1980s onwards (see chapter 6.2.2). Export diversification policies had come up due to the 1989 price collapse in terms of coffee, yet the Produce Marketing Board had already in 1988 lost its monopoly on the marketing

77 As will be further analysed in chapter 8.3, this interviewee has been doing both activities in cooperatives. He has been one of the co-founders of the crop trading cooperative he has succeeded with.

78 As explained in chapter 5.2.3, the transcripts of interviews, which were conducted in Lusoga, have been translated through intensive collaboration between me and the two translators with whom I worked in the course of this study, my co-researcher Nkonoka Hellen, and our colleague Kaiso Moses. Our intention was to leave the original statement as authentic as possible, even if that meant to have imperfect English texts. Wherever the extract that is being presented was originally in Lusoga, I indicate this by adding "translation by E.K." and either "N.H." or "K.M.", depending on who worked with me on that particular transcript. All expert interviews and two main interviews (7 and 20) were conducted exclusively in English. Some other interviews contained a few passages in English while the majority was in Lusoga (and sometimes Luganda, though the difference between the two is not very big). Wherever the passage was in English in the original, there is no comment about translation.

of major food crops in terms of export and domestic marketing alike (see chapter 6.2.4).

Among the locally produced items in Busoga that respondents listed, agricultural products considerably outrank all the others. There are very few non-agricultural products and most of them are only relevant to the local market, e.g., tables or doors being produced in wood or metal workshops. Only very few industrial products, produced exclusively in Jinja town, have economic relevance beyond Busoga's borders (e.g., iron sheets, hoes, brewery products across the country; processed fish beyond Uganda's borders). The commercial production of food crops is being promoted by export orientation as well as by domestic factors. Export orientation primarily refers to export to neighbouring countries. Apart from sugar and coffee, maize was mentioned as export crop frequently. A main interviewee from Jinja town talked about *processed* maize (flour) being exported: "Because they can grind the flour, mill from here, they export them, some to Sudan. Mm (affirmative). Flour, cassava also, they export it outside" (Main 20a[79], 2017). However, some minimal export beyond those boundaries was also mentioned by the above-cited expert:

> "Uhm (considering), let's take the marketing, any of, uh (considering), FARM PRODUCE[80]. You have crops, which are consumed far beyond Uganda, like coffee and cocoa, uh (considering), in the past, cotton, but these days, there isn't much cotton grown, uh (considering), a FEW horticultural products find their way into Europe." (Expert 6, 2017)

Since cotton and coffee had become unprofitable as export goods, there was a need for alternatives. Primarily maize (and some fish and sugar) is being exported to the neighbouring countries, while fish and fruit have started to move to international markets. Some factors that made this development possible are: improvements with regard to transport facilities for products; new export opportunities, e.g., thanks to the East African

---

79 As explained in chapter 5.2.1 of this thesis, two interviews conducted in the scope of this study were tandem interviews. In both cases, there was an original interviewee and an observer who turned out to talk as much as the actual interviewee. As a result, that person was included as an additional interviewee, with his or her own informed consent form and questionnaire. When those two cases are quoted here, an "a" behind the number of the interview indicates the "original" interviewee and a "b" indicates the additional respondent.

80 Capitalisation indicates a special emphasis set by the respondent (see transcription rules, Appendix 1).

Community (EAC); and people having "learnt to sell" things that they did not sell before. The latter is not further explained in the extracts. However, it is an effect of economic liberalisation and urbanisation, supported by population growth and improvements with regard to security. "Learning to sell" something can only mean to discover that there is a market for it. Economic liberalisation has indeed created markets. Respondents told me that when everybody had the same food in their home and even a filled granary, there was no need to buy or sell such things. Domestic factors that enhance production encompass a change of diet in Busoga and possibly other regions, which has made maize flour the staple food of the whole of Uganda (see below for more information). It is complemented by high population growth, which increases the demand for food. Urbanisation is another typical effect of globalisation about which interviewees spoke and which creates markets for foodstuff, as the following statement by an interviewee from a village in Kamuli District close to an urban centre shows:

> "A-ha (affirmative), what caused the market to come in, that one, I know it very well. Education was little, when the majority, in every home, on every ten people, three go to town. Today, of ten children born, eight go to town, and then, that causes high demand for food. [...] People have increased, but cultivating, they/ the people have increased, they refuse to engage in cultivating. Eh (affirmative), those who are just eating are many, the farmers are few, the crop increased because in town, they are longing for it. Longing for it, have you understood it?" (Main 21, 2017, translation by E.K. and N.H.)

Several respondents made similar comments about town dwellers, especially young people, being major customers for food crops, as they do not grow food themselves. All these factors have created markets for food crops and animal products – local, national, regional, and, to a very limited extent, international – and contributed to a significant increase in their production in Busoga. While in 25 interviews, the motivation for cultivating food crops was depicted as more or less balanced between personal consumption and sale, in nine interviews, sale was named as the major motivation, and only in four interviews, subsistence farming was described. Hence, the dominant type of farmer in Busoga is the small-scale farmer who wants to sell some of the harvest yet depends on producing food for the family as well. While the majority depends on family labour, those who have a little more land can afford to employ some workers.

According to study respondents, livestock is reserved for selling. Cows, goats, chicken, and pigs are kept for the sole purpose of making money. Keeping and trading cattle has long been a prestigious business in Busoga. As meat consumption increases in the big cities of East Africa, it gains in economic relevance as well, though it is in fierce competition for land with sugar cane and food crop production. Expert interviewees were more likely to make a direct reference to globalisation, taking it as a factor that provides markets for farmers' products, as exemplified by the following comment from a representative of Buyende District:

> "Mm (considering), globalisation has significant influence on the people of Uganda, positively and negatively. On the positive note, globalisation has widened the market for our people. For instance, in Buyende, here, we have the biggest livestock market in the sub-region. So, we get people from Juba, Southern Sudan, they come and buy cattle, goats, and chicken, at a reasonably higher price. And that is GOOD." (Expert 1, 2017)

Many comments of this nature came from Buyende, part of the original area dominated by cattle keeping, Northern Busoga. However, such comments were not limited to Buyende. For instance, the following statement came from a main interviewee from Kamuli District:

> "And rearing is a very important thing, there is a lot of money in it, to the one who knows (laughs), eh (affirmative), there is money in it. [...] Nawantale[81]. They bring cows, like 200, 180, every Tuesday. But they get finished. Every cow a million, eight hundred thousand, seven hundred thousand. Again, at Buyende like that (inc.)[82]. So, there are a lot of riches in rearing. [...] My small cow, I will take the evening milk myself, and that of the morning, I will take it there and get some money for school fees or what [...]." (Main 22, 2017, translation by E.K. and K.M.)

Another central finding of this sub-theme is that maize has profoundly changed Busoga. It has done so not only by becoming its most popular crop and export article (though for export to neighbouring countries, on-

81 A major marketplace.

82 The expression "(inc.)" refers to "incomprehensible", i.e., a word or (partial) sentence that was not identifiable during the process of transcription due to low quality of audio recording, noise in the background, or mumbling on the part of the speaker (see transcription rules, Appendix 1).

ly). At the same time, the relatively new[83] habit of eating mush has created a field of activity for many people who have some little capital or can get a loan for buying a maize mill and running a small-scale enterprise with it (see chapter 8.2.3). A main interviewee from Buyende District reported in detail that maize used to be there exclusively for roasting single cobs. As a result, it was just planted in mixed gardens, not on its own fields, until "in nineties, maize started as a business" (Main 6, 2017). Several other respondents mentioned those aspects (maize being eaten per cob, not very popular, intercropping) separately. Together, all these respondents created the impression that eating mush has become popular in Busoga during their lifetime. Furthermore, out of three popular occupations for average people in today's Busoga (agriculture, small-scale businesses like maize mills, shopkeeping), the most prevalent are based on maize (*running maize mills* depends on maize completely, *agriculture* to a large extent). While there have been attempts to introduce other crops like rice, quantitatively and qualitatively the strong emphasis respondent placed on maize is not comparable to any other crop.

Economic liberalisation has turned Uganda's highly regulated agriculture-based economy into a free market economy. Cooperative societies, marketing boards, and the combination of subsistence farming and cash crop production have been replaced by commercial food crop production, which relies on a middlemen-system for marketing. Several respondents explained the system as follows: Middlemen[84], who are often, though not always, from the very area, move around and buy agricultural products from the farmers. They get the order and the money for buying those products from traders, who bulk the products and take them to the next central market. In some cases, there are two or three levels of traders, who take the products to local markets, regional markets (e.g., in big towns or on the borders to neighbouring countries, especially Kenya), or directly to neighbouring countries. On the one hand, the advantages of the middlemen system are the low effort of marketing for farmers (as their

83 It has been traced in the literature that the introduction of maize as a food crop in Uganda started after World War II and proceeded gradually, with commercial maize production starting in two regions, among them some areas of Southern Busoga in the 1960s and expanding from there (see chapter 6.2.4).

84 The term is used for intermediaries of any gender. It is the term used by my translators and by all interviewees who talked about that issue in English. That is why I decided to use it here. Though roaming around in order to buy things from people is rather a male-dominated occupation (which may explain the usage of the term), it is not impossible to find female "middlemen".

products are collected from them) and the creation of job opportunities (for those who act as middlemen and traders). On the other hand, the combination of high cost of living and lack of alternative markets for farmers provides middlemen with such a high bargaining power that farmers do not have a chance to escape exploitation. They must accept the prices that middlemen, who try to keep as much of the money from the trader as possible for themselves, are ready to give them. A respondent in a rural area of Buyende District described the situation as follows:

> "Uh (considering), there are middle people[85] who come with their fake weighing scales, they come and try to buy from them at any price they see. Also, our local farmer, here in Bubugudo, Bugaya, all together in Buyende, they don't have a permanent market. So, that buyer, the middleman[86], comes with his/her price and our local person, here, asks the rich, (s)he[87] says to him/her: 'For how much do you buy beans? For how much do you buy coffee?' So, (s)he is like, (s)he doesn't have a permanent market or the true market that can sell the produce and (s)he is able to look like (s)he gets money that can help him/her. They cheat them a lot in the situation of selling the crops [...]" (Main 8, 2017, translation by E.K. and N.H.)

Another respondent noted that some farmers, who have very good bargaining skills, may profit from the system. Nevertheless, the majority makes a loss in it, as several respondents pointed out. Ugandan scholar and politician Yash Tandon describes this dependency of farmers of the global South on "the vagaries" of middlemen as a consequence of their involvement in the free market economy (Tandon 2016, 35-37; see chapter 3.3 of this thesis). The only chance for farmers to escape this situation would be taking care of the transport and marketing of their crops by themselves. However, the majority of small-scale farmers have neither the volume of production nor the means of transport that would allow them to do this individually (more on alternatives under the main theme "SSE",

85 In the original, he used a mix of Lusoga and English: "bamido person", "ba" signalling that he was talking about people in plural and "mido" being onomatopoeia for "middle".

86 Here, he used the English term "middleman" in the original, though the rest was in Lusoga.

87 In Lusoga, there are no personal pronouns. A prefix of the verb shows that, in this case, it is third person singular. Whenever there is no hint in the context whether the respondent talked about a male or a female person, "(s)he", "him/her", or "his/hers" has been used in the English translation.

especially chapters 8.3.2 and 8.3.6). Some private-based trading activities in food crops in Busoga existed prior to liberalisation, though they seem to have been moderate, compared to today. In general, farming is considered profitable by respondents, though this depends on the portion of land a person has at his or her disposition and external factors like drought, pests, (in)fertility of the soil, and prices paid by middlemen for the products. Respondents regard Busoga as an important producer of agricultural products, especially food crops, for other parts of the country and the neighbouring countries but not as a significant player in global trade. They observe that products of the region are frequently taken to towns in different parts of Uganda, to regional markets on the borders[88], and to neighbouring countries. Only a few reported on products, namely small quantities of coffee, fish, or fruit, being taken to other continents.

The above-described promotion of commercial food crop production – as well as the advancing cash crop sugar cane – have replaced Busoga's so-called 'traditional cash crops' cotton and coffee. Cotton (mentioned in 37 extracts) dominates the extracts that deal with Busoga's 'traditional' cash crops, while coffee ranks second (mentioned in 18 extracts). As long as coffee and especially cotton were still profitable, they occupied the fields that were not needed for the provision of food for the family. Hence, there was no need for selling other crops – even if there had been any demand for them. There were two ways to sell cotton in Busoga by then: cooperative societies and so-called 'Indians' (i.e., Indians and Ugandans of Indian descent). The latter were private business people. Respondents told me that cooperative societies had started up their own ginneries in order to acquire better prices for their members' cotton than they received from the owners of private ginneries. However, the accounts on cotton are predominantly historical, as cotton has become a marginal crop in Busoga after it had "lost market", as several respondents called it. Nevertheless, cotton has left a mark on Busoga that respondents have not yet forgotten. Coffee had been a popular crop in the past but then "got lost" for a while. Some people[89] believe it was due to "lack of market" (which may refer to declining world prices as well as the loss of cooperative societies that used to do the marketing for the farmers), but most of them blame it on

88 Theoretically, products can be exported beyond the region from there. Yet the nature of the products that are taken there, namely primarily maize and fresh foodstuff, suggests that their final destination is a neighbouring country, not another continent. Some respondents even said that explicitly.

89 Study respondents as well as people I had informal conversations with.

a pest, which exterminated almost all the coffee plants in Busoga (and possibly other regions). Some respondents lauded coffee for having been very profitable for them in the past. Government programmes like NAADS (National Agricultural Advisory Services) or Operation Wealth Creation (OWC) have been trying to bring coffee back to Busoga as a cash crop. However, it is far from attaining anew its former importance. Under the given circumstances, it is very unlikely that coffee and/ or cotton will ever again gain their former importance. The resources for their production, especially land, have been allocated to other purposes. Land is needed for the construction of homesteads for the rapidly increasing population. Furthermore, land is needed to plant food crops, and to keep farm animals – businesses that have become profitable and will not readily give way to something else.

Beyond that, a lot of land has been allocated to sugar cane production, which occupies it for several years. Sugar factories have started to spread over urban and rural Busoga alike. The companies establish their own plantations for which they buy and rent a lot of land from the local population. They also encourage farmers who have a considerable portion of land to become their 'outgrowers' and plant sugar cane for them. Some factories provide seeds and chemicals to those outgrowers and oblige them to pay back with a part of the harvest and sell the rest of the harvest to the same company. The interviews suggest that sugar cane production divides the local population socially. Those, who are relatively well-off because they have much land or the capital to buy or rent land from others, can earn good money from it. Other segments of the population, especially those depending on purchasing food, are disadvantaged by sugar cane production. As the latter reduces the land available for food production, the food prices increase. I provide more information on this in chapter 7.2. A respondent who lives nearby *Kakira Sugar* factory run by the *Madhvani Group of Companies* said that

> "those who are a bit okay, those who are able to cultivate, they planted sugar cane. Because they take it to Madhvani and they sell it. Don't you see? So, the food, still, you find that, again, itself, it has reduced because of people planting sugar cane. [...] So, as we, the people of down, as we don't have, still we don't have. [...] While the food has reduced." (Main 26, 2017, translation by E.K. and K.M.)

Several scholars have diagnosed such processes of increasing social inequality, i.e., small groups accumulating more and more capital, whereas the majority of the population is worse off than before, as side-effects of neoliberalism (e.g., Ostry et al. 2016; Schmidt/ Schröder 2016; see chapter 2.2.1 of this thesis; see also: Santos 2014, 36) and globalisation (e.g., Hall et al. 2015a; Stiglitz 2002; see chapter 3.1 of this thesis). The development of Busoga's social inequality is typical for a globalised economy, i.e., the income gap grows (see also chapter 8.2.7) and access to resources is polarised (see above for land; see chapter 8.2.5 in terms of access to education and health services as well as food prices).

Currently, the general trends in farming in Busoga are commercialisation, diversification, and 'modernisation' (in terms of trainings and application of inputs such as chemical fertilisers, herbicides, and pesticides, ox-ploughs, tractors, etc.). A very interesting trend is that the Ugandan government uses tools in order to achieve the above-mentioned goals, which seem at first sight to contrast with liberalisation (promotion of cooperatives, provision of free farming inputs). As farming is done at the level of the family and without a serious tendency to form large-scale farms, cooperatives are supposed to serve as a basis for large-scale agribusiness. The promotion of trade in food crops and animal products as the new mainstay of Busoga's economy is supported by those measures in favour of commercialisation, diversification, and 'modernisation'. The change from pre-liberalisation policies to liberalisation policies from the 1980s onwards was of high significance for this development. The old policies were aimed at promoting coffee and cotton on the one hand and food security on the other. The agricultural sector was highly regulated. As several interviewees could still recall, "in the past, the crops had fixed prices", which were announced on the radio (Main 23, 2017, translation by E.K. and N.H.). This contrast between the ancient agricultural policies and those after liberalisation makes them interesting for this study. For the promotion of agriculture, there were various programmes like the *tractor provision scheme*, which made available tractors to farmers and groups, and so-called *camp* or *group* or *block farming*. Several respondents reported that those programmes were there, but they failed. For instance, a main interviewee in Buyende District summarised it thus:

> "'cause, formally, there used to be what we used to call camp farming, whereby could get a block and a farmer grow their harvest, then sell under this group chairman according to the number they have (inc.), mm (affirmative), but that one collapsed. Ya. (...) And that power, it collapsed cause they used to be given a tractor from the agriculture sector, which, today, is not there. [...] the management section of the group used to swindle money from their fellow group members. So, they gave up." (Main 7, 2017)

Other respondents likewise assumed that the breakdown of the tractor provision service contributed to the collapse of group farms and agricultural cooperatives. Without tractors, it was not possible to cultivate the large portions of land of those groups.[90] This led to their disorganisation. Apart from those group approaches to commercial agriculture, there were programmes for food security.[91] Some respondents mentioned that, in the past, they used to have granaries where they kept the surplus of the food crop harvest. According to the following comment by a respondent from Kamuli District and to my translator, who explained that comment to me, there were times when the government even obliged people to store food in order to ensure food security:

> "Selling food, we have started in [19]80- what? But that food used not to be sold. When they say that, 'that this food is for something compulsory'. So, when all of you, you have to cultivate/ […] You cultivate, but when/ which means, you eat your food yourself." (Main 13, 2017, translation by E.K. and K.M.)

It was "compulsory" to grow food and to store it instead of selling it. The new policies, in contrast, focus on diversification and on commercialisation of all kinds of farm products. Those policies, in combination with other factors like increasing *cost of living* and *new challenges in farming* (see corresponding sub-themes, chapters 8.2.5 and 8.2.2), threaten food security. For instance, one respondent explained that "the government encourages people, everything you do, to sell a part of it and leave a part for consumption" but that the problem has become that people sell two thirds and keep only one third – a behaviour that can cause famine (Main 23, 2017, translation by E.K. and N.H.). However, the commercialisation of food crops and animal products is being successfully promoted through trainings by both government actors (like NAADS or OWC) and NGOs as well as through the promotion of modern farm inputs. The volume of production, though it is still relatively low, has already been increased considerably in that way. The most appreciated agricultural policy, past and present, is the government service of extension workers. While in the past, those agronomists used to train groups and individuals alike, they have meanwhile become limited to training only groups. This limitation may

90 At the time, land was still available in Busoga, as the population was much lower.

91 Some background information about the *tractor hire service*, *group farms*, and a programme for the promotion of food security can be found in chapter 7.3 of this thesis.

contribute to the formation of more farmers' associations and agricultural cooperatives in the future, as many respondents rated extension services very positively.

In summary, a fierce commercialisation of edible farm products of all kinds, yet with special focus on maize and animal products, has been underway in Busoga in the past decades. The government has liberalised the market and continues to encourage the commercial production of those products, e.g., through trainings and provision of seeds, especially through NAADS and OWC. People in Busoga react to the changes in the crop market by increasing the production and sale of foodstuff, to the extent that food security is threatened by their desire to sell (almost) the whole harvest. In the liberalised market system, small-scale farmers depend on middlemen to buy their products and they are in a weak position in terms of price negotiations. The so-called 'traditional cash crops' of Busoga, coffee and cotton, have become unprofitable. Sugar cane, which once was expected to become the 'new' major cash crop of the area, is only an option for those with much land. Others depend on food crops and animal products. A main interviewee from Jinja District nicely summarised the commercialisation of food crop production. In the context of food crop production, she said that, in the past, "we didn't know that cultivating was a job, but cultivating is a job" (Main 28, 2017, translation by E.K. and N.H.).

8.2.2 New challenges in farming

The greatest recent challenges in terms of farming are shortage of land, the loss of soil fertility, pests and livestock diseases, and the shifting of rainy seasons. Technical innovations intended to enhance productivity, such as fertilisers, pesticides, and modified seeds, have advantages as well as disadvantages (details below). In the interviewees' youth, shortage of land in Busoga was unthinkable and migrants from other regions came to the region because it was known for offering a lot of unused land. During that time, nobody bothered farm animals wandering around and grazing. Every field could rest after the harvest because the owner had enough land left to cultivate in the following season. Enda Graf in Senegal has observed a change from regular fallowing to permanent exhaustion of land as a result of increasing cost of living and desire for consumption among the population (N'Dione et al. 1995, 21-22). I asked study respondents about fallowing in order to ascertain whether comparable tendencies exist in Busoga. Indeed, the permanent exhaustion of land is partly caused by those factors. Yet a strongly aggravating factor is shortage of land. If people had much land at their disposition, most likely their limited means would not even allow them to pay for inputs and labour to cultivate all of it every season. The reason study respondents most frequently provided for the emergence of shortage of land is that "the population increased and the rate of birth a year is at a terrific speed, so, the land has become actually SCARCE" (Main 7, 2017). As fathers must give a portion of land to each son and as men in Busoga have many children, often from several wives, the portions of land per person have shrunk significantly over the past generations. Several interviewees from both groups explained this issue to me. In the following example, a representative of Buyende District expressed this particularly clearly:

> "Land is being divided and this has been worsened by our land tenure system. Our land tenure system is that, when I have land, and I have three sons/ here, land is mostly given to MEN because women marry off and they belong to their/ to the families where they marry. So, it is mostly given to men. So, the man will divide his piece of land into the five sons. So, the land that was originally twenty acres, will reduce to each one having three-three or four-four acres. And the process will continue when the grandfather gives his son, the sons gives the other, so, that is the challenge. And it is affecting production." (Expert 1, 2017)

Another reason for shortage of land is that "because of eating[92], others sold some of it [...] selling to people who came to settle", while others "sold to those people of sugar cane, the majority rent out, just rent out" (Main 18, 2017, translation by E.K. and K.M.). The rent or purchase price does not compensate them properly for the loss in agriculture that they make over time, as was deplored by some interviewees (see also chapter 7.2 on that issue). Nevertheless, immediate need for money makes them sell the land in spite of that problem. A main interviewee from Kamuli District put it as follows: "You, who had land, they come and rent and they give you money and you eat it,[93] but when the other one, the rich, is the one who has cultivated there and he has gained from there a lot" (Main 21, 2017, translation by E.K. and N.H.). As a result of those occurrences, people have started to cultivate the same portion of land repeatedly, ex-

92 Meaning "because of the need to eat/ the need for money to buy food".
93 Meaning "you spend the money on food and it is finished rapidly".

hausting the soil and creating dependency on fertilisers. Shortage of land significantly limits the agricultural production capacities of people living in Busoga. This applies to cash crops, food crops, and animal products alike. As a region that has always been a hub for cattle trade, Busoga has been changed profoundly by the 'zero grazing' strategy. The latter had originally been introduced by NGOs for the promotion of exotic cattle breeds and enhancement of animal productivity (see chapter 7.2) but is now being pushed by shortage of land. For instance, a main interviewee from Kamuli District, who is a member of a dairy cooperative, said that "the land is small for people to rear animals. So, mostly, here we are trying to organise our people so that we rear the animals on zero grazing" (Main 14, 2017). In order to prevent farm animals, especially cattle, from wandering around and causing conflicts by eating other people's crops in the fields, farmers have started to keep their animals in paddocks or cowsheds. This reduces the number of animals a household can manage to keep. Apart from building the cowshed, the biggest problem is to provide the animals with fodder and water – a procedure that was not necessary when they were still allowed to graze. The above-cited respondent added the following information: "Today, we buy the feeds, hm (seeking confirmation)? For animals. But, formerly, that was not there" (Main 14, 2017). Another main interviewee, from Buyende District, likewise said that "now that zero grazing came in, we even started buying plantain stems, grass, that elephant grass" for feeding cows (Main 1, 2017, translation by E.K. and N.H.). This issue is taken up under the sub-theme "Autochthonous solidarity structures survive party" (chapter 8.3.1), as the newly created market for formerly unmarketable items has changed practices of sharing and giving for free among neighbours in Busoga. A form of "increasing commodification of social relationships and nature" that Aram Ziai counts among the central concepts of neoliberalism (Ziai 2017, 106; see chapter 3.3 of this thesis) has been introduced to the region by the NGO-concept 'zero grazing'.

Several interviewees expressed the feeling that, in spite of technical innovations, farming becomes more and more laborious while the yield decreases. For instance, they have the impression that due to shortage of land, fertilisers *can at best keep up* the quantities of crops harvested but they *cannot raise* them. Fertilisers are needed to balance the loss in production, which arises from smaller fields and decreasing soil fertility due to overuse. Old methods like fallowing can no longer be practised. One of the respondents who mentioned this issue explained that "because the population increased and the land is small, it [production] reduced, but every season, you have to plant in the same area, there is no chance of resting for the land" (Main 9, 2017, translation by E.K. and N.H.). Another problem is the prevalence of counterfeit fertilisers on the market. Pesticides are hardly perceived as an improvement because they came at the same time as the pests. According to several interviewees, prior to the availability of pesticides, they were also fewer pests, so pesticides were not needed. One of them put it as follows: "And that virus, so to say, now, in the past, we used to cultivate, but when we don't spray [pesticides], hm (seeking confirmation)? But now, if you cultivate and you don't spray, you don't eat" (Main 17, 2017, translation by E.K. and K.M.). Furthermore, both pesticides and fertiliser can have negative impacts on the natural environment. Nevertheless, according to several respondents, pesticides are urgently needed these days. Pests and livestock diseases attack all kinds of crops and farm animals and have already driven some plant species (plantains and coffee plants) to the verge of extinction within Busoga. The above-cited respondent continued describing that process: "Because they [pests] started in coffee. They ate the coffee. Time reached and they turned even on plantains. The plantains, now, we no longer get plantains" (Main 17, 2017, translation by E.K. and K.M.). This has led to a change in staple food for many people living in Busoga (from plantains to other crops, especially maize). Study respondents typically explained something along the lines of the following statement: "because today plantains somehow got spoilt, the main food that we eat now are posho[94] and sweet potatoes" (Main 11, 2017, translation by E.K. and K.M.). People in Busoga perceived the loss of their former staple food as a drastic change in their lives. Another technical innovation in agriculture are modified seeds. Study respondents felt that they are expensive and produce crops and fruit that may grow fast but do not taste as good as the old varieties. Furthermore, some of them yield for only one season, whereas the older varieties used to last longer. Nevertheless, they are provided by agricultural programmes like NAADS and sold in shops, whereas old varieties are difficult to find. A respondent from Jinja town who emphasised this topic, summarised some of those issues:

> "The g-nuts of those days would yield and they are good. But, now, another problem also we have in the production of/ in producing in the garden, the NAADS issue. More so, the seeds are not natural. They

94 posho = mush made from maize flour, most popular food in Uganda, incl. Busoga

> are now in NAADS and then you find some people don't like it. It yields very fast, like matooke[95] for NAADS, the mixed one, it grows very fast, you cut, the moment you chop one, the/ the whole thing dies. Yet, we used to have matooke where we plant, it grows, it takes some time longer than the NAADS things, and we get the matooke. When you chop this one, another one is growing, the suckers are growing. But these days, for the NAADS, it is only one and that is that. And then, the beans are very big, they get ready very fast, or they die very fast. [...] When the weather is bad, they go. And many people, when you cook the beans for the NAADS, they find that the taste is not good. [...] So, they take shorter period and they are not very tasty, like the time I was born." (Main 20b, 2017)

Another phenomenon I was told about in several interviews and informal conversations and which I observed myself during the 34 months I spent in Busoga, is that the rhythm of the rainy and dry seasons is no longer reliable. As the above-cited main interviewee summarised: "At times, you plant your things in the garden, they all dry because there's no rain, yet the rain had started, then it stopped all of a sudden. And then you find a period where there should be no rain, there is a lot of rain" (Main 20b, 2017). This development threatens food security and (petty) commercial agriculture alike.

In summary, farmers in Busoga are challenged by shortage of land, pests and livestock diseases, the shifting of rainy seasons, and the loss of soil fertility. Technical innovations such as fertilisers, pesticides, and modified seeds, have so far alleviated the effects of those problems to some extent yet they have not managed to significantly increase productivity due to land shortage and because they are too expensive for many farmers. Moreover, such innovative inputs are at times counterfeit, produce poor quality crops, or impact negatively on the natural environment. Many of those aspects have been listed by Yash Tandon as reasons for food insecurity in the global South, caused by its involvement in the global trade regime (see chapter 3.3). Among them are: high prices for fertiliser and dependence on "global seed and fertiliser corporations"; land grabbing by large-scale farmers and commercial enterprises; re-allocation of land from food production to the production of commercial commodities[96] (Tandon 2016, 37). In

95 matooke = plantains

96 Tandon refers to biofuels in particular; however, I extend the idea to food crops that are being produced for sale and to sugar cane (which is partly produced as raw material for biofuel).

the context of increasing food insecurity in the global South, Tandon also mentions unusual weather patterns resulting from climate change (ibid.). Hence, the agricultural production challenges Busoga is currently facing are typical for an agriculture-based region in a globalised economy in the global South. A representative of Jinja District summarised the situation as follows: "These days, you cannot longer throw there a cassava stem and it gets the yields you want. [...] A farmer of tw/ 30 years ago cannot survive as of now" (Expert 8, 2017).

8.2.3 Business enterprises in Busoga

In addition to the production of and trade in agricultural products, three kinds of businesses are relevant in Busoga: shops, small-scale enterprises, and factories[97]. For the local population, shops and small-scale enterprises are of higher importance than factories.

In the past 30 years, shopkeeping has become a very popular business activity among the people living in Busoga. Up to the expulsion of the commercial class (foreigners and especially Ugandans of Indian descent) by then President Idi Amin, the colonial division of labour had survived (see chapter 6.2.2). The latter had been preventing Ugandans of African descent from engaging in business activities other than cattle trade and production of and, to a limited extent, trade in crops. Aníbal Quijano described as the *coloniality of power* the phenomenon of colonisers inventing racial categories and applying them to the division of labour they established in the colonies. Occupations and prospects within the colonial economy were allocated to differing classes defined by the category of race (Quijano 2000; see chapter 2.1.2 of this thesis for details). In Uganda, that *coloniality of power* has left a permanent mark on society, creating conflicts between the commercial class of so-called 'Indians' (i.e., Indian immigrants and Ugandans of Indian descent) and the peasant class of Ugandans of African descent. The latter were deprived of access to many branches of business in colonial times and, to a lesser extent though, in

97 Note on terminology: The Lusoga word „eikolero" (plural: „amakolero") does not distinguish between business companies, firms, corporations, factories, industries, or small-scale enterprises. In order to understand what a respondent talked about, the context had to be taken into consideration. Maize mills are sometimes called "ebyuma" (machines) but even here, the context is needed to be sure as there were cases in which interviewees referred to sugar factories using that word. Usually, the context is unequivocal.

the 1960s. As further explained below, the 1970s and early 1980s were not much better, though for different reasons. Several respondents enthusiastically told me that these days, Ugandans of African descent (often people from the very village) open their own shops. In the following example, the interviewee even spoke about shopkeepers as "children themselves", not referring to minors but rather to people who have their parents, i.e., their home in the village in which they open a shop:

> "We, this side, children themselves come up/ people of the village themselves, (s)he starts a small business, (s)he opens up a shop, we, people of the village, they don't come from outside like in the past, it was a generation for Indians, who could come up with shops, but now, it is us, the Blacks." (Main 9, 2017, translation by E.K. and N.H.)

Apart from the emancipatory aspect, the fact that more and more shops are run by local people has economic advantages as well. The shops provide employment and income – and the shopkeepers spend at least a part of that income locally. Nevertheless, there are still some shops run by people the respondents referred to as "outsiders" (Indian immigrants, Ugandans of Indian descent, Ugandans from other regions, other Africans). During Idi Amin's regime and its aftermath, extreme scarcity of commodities due to the breakdown of supply chains led to a standstill of shop business (see chapter 8.2.4 for details). Since the 1980s, it has become easy for locals to open a shop, buy commodities in bulk (to a great extent from foreigners or Ugandans of Indian descent, who have either returned or were born in Uganda after 1982) and sell them in their shops. In towns and larger trading centres, they usually share a shop because the rent is expensive, whereas in villages shops can be operated by individuals.

The second business category respondents spoke about are small-scale enterprises. In this study, small-scale enterprises are defined as businesses that can be initiated with low capital investment, such that a large number of people can afford to found them, e.g., financed through microcredit or personal savings. Usually, they are operated by a small number of people and allow for only modest profit expectations. Interviewees from both groups mentioned various kinds of small-scale enterprises, e.g., mobile popcorn machines, carpentry or metal workshops (with basic tools), tailor's shops, and video halls. However, the majority of comments referred to maize mills in particular. Respondents observed that the number of maize mills and other small-scale enterprises has increased recently. A main interviewee from Namwendwa, a trading centre in Kamuli District that has grown into a small town over the years, said about small-scale businesses that

> "they increased a bit because, in the past, there, we had one maize mill. But now, we have many, about six. [...] we have here even carpentries that were not there, we have even a video hall, so, those used not to be there." (Main 11, 2017, translation by E.K. and K.M.)

While it is difficult for some small-scale entrepreneurs to find customers, maize mills are very popular. The popularity of maize mills seems to correlate with the rise of food crops in general and maize in particular, from unmarketable products to the major economic factors in Busoga. However, a lot of maize that these mills grind is intended for personal consumption. Changes in people's diet have thus made possible the triumph of maize mills, as maize flour has only recently gained its status as staple food in Busoga. Maize mills are also associated with the extension of livestock breeding by providing maize bran as animal feed. The usefulness of maize mills is rated so high that, for the interviewees, they outweigh their discontents (noise, dust, metal residues from the mills in the maize flour). Hence, maize mills are a relatively new form of small-scale enterprises in Busoga and, at the same time, the most important. A typical example of respondents' appreciation for the service provided by maize mills is the following extract:

> "The good aspects that are there, they have brought services nearer to the people. [...] we used to take maize from here to Kamuli, to Buwenge. But now, distance, they reduced it. [...] Secondly, when we grind, we are able to get form there some maize bran, which we give to our chicken, when the services are near for us, which we give to pigs, which we give the cows." (Main 15, 2017, translation by E.K. and K.M.)

Small-scale enterprises, and in particular maize mills, are dominated by Ugandans of African descent. In a similar way as the respondent of interview Main 9 stated above with respect to shops, a main interviewee from Buyende District commented that "these small millers, ourselves, some of them are our sons, some are our fathers, on the side of maize mills" (Main 6, 2017).

The third category of business enterprises in Busoga are large-scale companies mainly found in the form of factories. Globalisation is often associated with the expansion of international corporations that exploit natural resources and labour in the global South (e.g., Glenn 2007; Greig et al. 2007; Stiglitz 2002; see chapter 3.1 of this thesis). Accordingly, study respondents were asked about the existence and origin of business companies in their region as well as about their impacts on the life of the local population. In this context, the history of Jinja town must be taken into account as it was outlined in broad terms to me by respondents (for more information, see also chapter 6.2.2). Up until Idi Amin expelled foreigners and the Ugandan population of Asian (especially Indian) descent in 1972, Jinja had been an industrial hub of Uganda. Factories were numerous and not yet highly automated, while the population of Busoga was still much lower than today. As a result, those factories provided a relatively (i.e., in comparison with today) high proportion of the population with jobs. When the factories were closed or their activities reduced because their owners and managers were expelled from the country, it was a shock for the employees and their extended families who lost an important source of income. This historical experience explains the local population's positive attitude towards factories and the longing for them to return to the region. Only those living nearby Jinja or Kamuli towns could tell me about their actual observations regarding big business companies or factories, while others had to speculate because there are no companies or factories in rural areas of Busoga. Study respondents believe that the Ugandan government has a strong will to (re-)industrialise Busoga, especially Jinja town. As a result of government promotion, business people (especially Indians and Ugandans of Indian descent, but also investors from diverse countries and a few Ugandans of African descent) begin to start large-scale enterprises in the region. Respondents observed that industrialisation depends on the level of urbanisation. It is perceived to be strongest in Jinja town and its area of influence, minimal in Kamuli and some other towns of Kamuli District and absent in the whole of Buyende and rural areas of Kamuli and Jinja Districts. Improved transport facilities (roads, availability of trucks and spare parts for the latter) have made transporting raw materials from various production sites in Uganda to central processing plants in or nearby the capital city more attractive than having many small production plants all over the country. This has considerably reduced Busoga's relevance as a site for the processing of agricultural products and industrial production. A representative of Kamuli District explained:

> "'Cause formally, they used to say that companies have to follow where the raw materials are and what. But these days, most companies are located in Kampala. Because of the market, that big market. So, you find, if something get a bit produced here, it goes to Kampala. From Kampala, then, it is brought back here." (Expert 4, 2017)

However, as the desired industrial locations in and nearby Kampala have become crowded and expensive, investors have once again developed an interest in Jinja. At the same time, the increasing interest in sugar cane and the fact that it is a challenging transport good have started to make sugar cane processing factories advance into semi-rural areas of Busoga. They are the only factories that can be found beyond Jinja town, as the following statement by a main interviewee from Buyende District illustrates:

> "Also, we shall say, I will say that they increased because in the past, there, the companies were far from us, we cannot know unless they are near, for example in Jinja, it's where they were found but now, you find when there are companies for sugar, if you move even here in Kamuli, which is next door to us, they are found there, if you go to Kaliro, you find it there, I have given an example of sugar. That means, I see that those companies are increasing." (Main 5, 2017, translation by E.K. and N.H.)

The two respondents of the tandem interview Main 20 who live in Jinja town agreed that industries have started to come back. One of them stated that "people has just come back, mostly the Indians. Some came back, the former people, but most of them are new. So, they are constructing theirs. Mm (affirmative), they are still constructing" (Main 20a, 2017). To my question whether those industries were only opened by so-called "Indians", she answered "Indians and the Bazungus" (=whites), while her fellow respondent added: "The Ugandans themselves are also building" factories (Main 20b, 2017). It is safe to assume that the latter referred to Ugandans of African descent, in contrast to the Ugandans of Indian descent, who had been mentioned earlier. The two also provided the example of a British-American company. Of the other main interviewees who talked about the ownership of companies and factories, some likewise named "the whites and the Blacks" (Main 23, 2017, translation by E.K. and N.H.) or people from both "outside" and "inside here, Uganda" (Main 13, 2017, translation by E.K. and K.M.). It appears that Jinja's evolving industrial sector is going to encompass some companies owned by Ugandans of African descent, though they may still not be the main group among the factory owners and they must not necessarily be Basoga. None of the respondents of this study named a single company owned by a Musoga (beyond the level of a small-scale enterprise). Those who are constructing factories in Jinja town currently can be assumed to be business people from Kampala, as they are the ones who have the capital for such endeavours.

Respondents expressed mixed feelings about factories. On a positive note, there is a very high level of agreement among the respondents that factories are supposed to provide jobs and some interviewees reported that there are actually jobs in factories in their region. For instance, a respondent from Kakira (Jinja) said that "Kakira sugar/ Madhvani group of companies is in our area. [...] The population of our area, most people are labourers" (Main 29, 2017). Others spoke about job opportunities hypothetically, expressing the conviction that one day, if factories come to the area, they are going to provide job opportunities. The above-cited extract praising Kakira sugar factory for employing many locals referred to *Madhvani group of companies*, which was started in Busoga and still has one of its core businesses there (see chapter 7.2). However, the situation is different with respect to other industries, especially if their owners come from Kampala or from abroad. A representative of Jinja District complained about them as follows:

> "Most of the companies in Lusoga regions, to me, they have not benefitted the Basoga. Basoga to mean every person, who is in the Busoga. (...) First of all, most of them come with their employees. 'We go to Busoga to work', but they come with the people, who are going to do the work. They don't employ. The/ they RARELY do/ They do it, but not a scale that would easily/ that would equally affect the lives of people." (Expert 8, 2017)

Apart from this complaint about companies bringing their own staff, respondents deplored that they automate their production processes instead of employing people; that the few locals they employ are assigned only to low-skilled, poorly paid jobs; and that the working conditions are bad. Apart from employment, respondents stated that factories can be a source of income for the local population in different ways, e.g., by buying agricultural products from them (especially sugar cane), supplying local shopkeepers, or paying salaries to their workers who in turn buy things from local farmers and shopkeepers. Nevertheless, some respondents complained that farmers do not get fair prices for their crops from the companies. Numerous interviewees also praised companies for making commodities available and affordable to the local population, as in the following statement:

> "Mm (considering), those companies, they make soap. Eh (considering), food, they sell to the people food of every kind. The traders from here buy from the others and they bring the things to the village, and

people buy, even the poor buy." (Main 22, 2017, translation by E.K. and K.M.)

Nonetheless, some interviewees deplored that people could not even afford to buy the products they had produced with their own hands, either by working in the factory or by providing the agricultural inputs for production (e.g., sugar cane). Another positive effect of the presence of factories in the region is the improvement on infrastructure, e.g., the road network (constructed by the companies themselves or by the Ugandan government in order to attract or facilitate companies). On a negative note, study respondents demonstrated a keen awareness concerning the destructive effects of factories on people's health and the natural environment, especially through air pollution. They perceive decision makers to prioritise industrialisation rather than environmental or health protection, as the following example illustrates:

> "Pollution is a serious problem in Jinja. Often, you come to Jinja, you see there are those times when the smell/ Jinja town/ [...] While it was smelling all over, the blame was put on the Mayor. But the Mayor cannot refuse the industries." (Main 24b, 2017, translation by E.K. and K.M.)

Other well-known effects of industrialisation mentioned by interviewees include migration to the cities and the displacement of people living in the cities in favour of companies. In this context, a main interviewee from Jinja town said:

> "And then, also, about what we have been talking, a conclusion: IF at all, the government would HELP in those industries, which are coming up, they should try to think of the local people, also. So that the local people also can be happy and the industry also grow up. And then, also, let them try to compensate the people whom they are taking their plot. Even if it is small, let them compensate them, so that they can also go and get somewhere to settle." (Main 20b, 2017)

Though the interviewee showed her understanding of the 'necessity' of industrialisation and even displacement, she appealed to decision makers and industrialists to pay more attention to the needs of the local population. The last two comments are clear illustrations of the "massive shift of power and resources from public to private, from state to market" (Hall et al. 2015a, 10) and the resulting prioritisation of the concerns of business companies over those of the local population (Castro Varela/ Dhawan 2015, 80, 204) postcolonial scholars have analysed (see chapter

3.2). It is worth noting, however, that although respondents were asked about the origin of those companies or factories and indicated that some are domestic and others are run by foreigners, the main interviewees did not distinguish between the two categories in their further description and evaluation of companies. In their view, there is no difference between national and international business enterprises with regard to their conduct, their advantages, and their disadvantages. Only expert interviewees made a few comments specifically regarding companies from abroad. They deplored that such companies could leave at any time, taking away not only the jobs they had been providing (regardless of their number and quality) but also their knowledge, technology, and innovation – things that have not yet developed properly in Uganda because of the dominance of companies from abroad.

In summary, there are two kinds of business enterprises in Busoga. On the one hand, there are shops and small-scale enterprises like maize mills. Both can be found in villages, trading centres, and towns alike. They can be started with little capital, enabling a relatively high (though still limited, as few people have access to any capital at all) number of people to make a living off them. At the same time, they benefit their customers by making available goods and services at affordable prices – even in the villages. On the other hand, there are factories and large companies. Respondents mainly appreciate them from the point of view of customers. Though factories are expected to provide many jobs, most of them do not fulfil that expectation, some due to automation, others because they bring their own workers from elsewhere. The number of factories and business companies in Busoga, especially in Jinja town, is increasing slowly, yet they are not owned by Basoga. On the side of making a living, all three options serve only limited groups of people. In comparison, shops and small-scale enterprises provide employment to more local people than large business companies and factories. With respect to all three, respondents observed the greatest advantages from the perspective of consumers. One main interviewee's comment (from Kamuli District) about small-scale enterprises can be applied to the other two types as well, as other respondents made very similar comments about them: "the service is nearer, so people are benefiting" (Main 14, 2017).

8.2.4 Access to consumer goods

One of the main findings of this sub-theme is that, with respect to the limited purchasing power of the majority of people in the region, consumption patterns in Busoga have adapted to globalisation to the greatest possible extent. However, this turned out to be a non-linear process that started much earlier than 30 years ago. An undisputed characteristic of globalisation is that it makes new commodities available to prospective customers either through stimulation of local production and technology transfer or through trade (see chapter 3.1 of this thesis, e.g., Glenn 2007; Stiglitz 2002). I found evidence of this phenomenon in the data set. Respondents frequently discovered many items in their surroundings that were not yet available during their childhood. These items concern diverse spheres of everyday life: Among them, there are manifold household items, textiles, plastic products, electrical appliances, electricity for running them, means of transport, machines for food processing, food items, and construction materials. Some of those items were indeed there during their childhood albeit only in small quantities and at a high price, reserved for the relatively 'rich'. Today, they are affordable either for the majority of people (e.g., imported clothes, mosquito nets, radios, mattresses, blankets) or at least a larger part of the population than in the past (e.g., bicycles, iron sheets for roofing and other construction materials). A representative of Buyende District commented on the issue of affordability: "Ya, I think they can afford them. […] Like, for example, products from CHINA, they are very cheap, really. And, you know, cheap things also go with poor quality" (Expert 2, 2017). Another expert interviewee likewise mentioned consumer goods being imported from China, while a third one added that "junk goods, sub-standard goods have flooded these markets of ours" and he named India and America as examples for their origins (Expert 4, 2017). There are also commodities that were not known at all in the past, e.g., solar panels, mobile phones, plastic basins. Many of those commodities have become available and in some cases cheaper through import. When asked from where consumer goods come, several interviewees had no idea about the respective countries but noted that the commodities are being imported. Others listed countries of origin that came to mind, including (from the highest to the lowest frequency): China (5), Japan (3), Britain (3), India (2), Germany (2), America (2, in both cases without further specification), Korea (1), and Pakistan (1). This list does not necessarily reflect reality but rather mirrors the respondents' impressions of which countries interfere most in their daily life by providing consumer goods to them.

While experts tended to complain about low quality, main interviewees rather lauded the availability and affordability of commodities. However, some respondents also mentioned that some items are nowadays being produced in factories in Jinja or Kampala (though those factories are not necessarily owned by Ugandans).

In the past, as many items were not available or affordable, people made them by hand. Respondents listed many items made by most people in the villages, in some cases by local craftspeople. Among them are manifold household items, bark cloth as a precursor to textiles, pottery and smithery products, tools for food processing (mortars, grinding stones), food items (salt, sweetener), and natural fertiliser (though the latter was not used much as the soil was still quite fertile). Almost all of these things have since been replaced by industrially produced and commercially distributed commodities (see above). One of the few exceptions to this is natural fertiliser. Though there is a chemical replacement, manure has become even more popular nowadays due to its promotion by NGOs and government programmes. However, care must be taken with respect to the timeline. Busoga is not a place where people made their own salt, moulded their clay dishes, wore bark cloths, etc., until the liberalisation policies of the 1980s brought them industrial products and taught them how to behave as consumers. Indeed, none of the respondents of this study could remember a time when Busoga was self-sufficient. The role of coffee and cotton production in Busoga must therefore be taken into consideration, as these cash crops were the reason for the introduction of the first commercial structures in Busoga in the early twentieth century (see chapter 6.2.2).

Study respondents generally agreed that the so-called "Indians" (i.e., Indians and Ugandans of Indian descent) introduced consumer goods into Busoga even before the interviewees were born. From their introduction by the British colonial administration through to their expulsion by then President Idi Amin in 1972, they dominated the shop business in Busoga. This corresponds to a large extent with the information collected from the literature in chapter 6.2.2 of this thesis: Though the very first traders in Busoga were Arabs, serious trade and immobile shop business were promoted by people who immigrated from India from the beginning of the twentieth century onwards as well as their descendants who were born in Uganda. A typical comment on that point by study respondents was: "The first shops were for the Indians" (Main 2, 2017, translation by E.K. and N.H.). As a result, the latter were the ones who introduced the local population to consumer goods, whether they were produced in Ugandan factories (e.g., sugar) or imported (e.g., porcelain plates and cups, etc.).

A typical example is the claim of a main interviewee from Jinja District that "the Indians brought us those cups of this time" (Main 24, 2017, translation by E.K. and K.M.). A main interviewee from Kamuli described how, when she was young, she became accustomed to sugar as a giveaway (sprinkled on her hand) in an "Indian" shop: "if you go to buy something there, from the Indian, maybe that sugar: *'come get, get'*, (s)he scoops for you, you go while licking. *'It's sweet'*, then you go as you lick" (Main 13, 2017, translation by E.K. and K.M.). Before their expulsion, the shops of so-called "Indians" were located exclusively in urbanised areas and local traders carried their products to rural areas to sell them on weekly market days or as hawkers. A main interviewee from Buyende District explained:

> "Eh (affirmative), these ones, other people, they used to carry things on their heads. [...] they were Ugandans from here [...] Also, we had a man, I think he was hardworking, he was on that side, down there. He could get those things from Kamuli, when he sets off here at 7 a.m., he goes, then comes back by 11 a.m. He went to Kamuli and he could carry things up to here and help his colleagues by selling things to them." (Main 3, 2017, translation by E.K. and N.H.)

Respondents spoke about a time when commodities were not available and people had to make their things themselves or line up in order to get at least some industrially produced commodities. However, this was not a distant past followed by a linear 'development' but rather a serious cut during their lifetime, namely the regime of then President Idi Amin. Prior to Amin's rule, people had become accustomed to certain consumer goods and had ceased making home-made equivalents themselves. With the expulsion of all foreigners as well as Ugandans of Indian descent, Idi Amin robbed the country of all its importers, traders, factory owners and managers as well as shopkeepers – without creating feasible alternatives. The businesses were allocated to Ugandans of African descent, of whom many had neither received the required training nor did they have any capital to invest or the personal networks required to keep up the supply chains. Until then, the colonial division of labour, in which the majority of Ugandans of African descent, especially those from rural areas, were not promoted beyond the level of basic education and the production of – and sometimes trade in – agricultural products, had still persisted. As a result, supply chains broke down, factories and shops were closed and commodities became extremely scarce. Up to this point, the information provided by the interviewees, the documents (chapters 7.3 and 7.5), and the literature (chapter 6.2.2) were in congruence with one another. The following additional information was provided by the interviewees: Representatives of the army or other government bodies sold commodities to people in their purview. As those commodities were extremely scarce, people had to fill out lists and wait in line. A main interviewee from Jinja District summarised that situation as follows:

> "The one with the shop, maybe an individual person, when (s)he works for government, when (s)he goes and brings those things, puts in his/her shop, for us, we go and take the names and we line up, (s)he reads the names. 'So, where are you?' For you and they give you what/ what you're going to take, maybe sugar, eh (affirmative), like that we used to buy in the past, in that era, that of Amin." (Main 17, 2017, translation by E.K. and M.K.)

Study respondents reported that, sometimes, despite waiting in line, people did not receive anything. As a result, another respondent from Jinja stated, "other people used to do '*magendo*'/ they smuggle things from Kenya, from our neighbouring countries" (Main 30, 2017, translation by E.K. and K.M.). The following testimony by a main interviewee from Buyende District explains the ambiguous role played by the army – as looters taking away the shops of private people and as peacekeepers accompanying the official distribution of commodities to the population by government authorities:

> "Now, you see, during that time, first of all, the Asians had been sent out of the country. So, the Asian shops were located to Ugandans, who knew nothing about business. At the same time, when someone located those shops, AGAIN, army men came and took over by force. Let me say, almost more or less looting. So, the whole issue became a problem, and there, that's when the government started bringing in items like salt, some soap, and some clothes at the same time. It was again government also involved in bringing clothes for the community. […] They used to send the so-called, by then, county chiefs plus army commanders to attend to sell those things. In a LINE, you queue, we used to queue." (Main 7, 2017)

This experience made a strong impression on people in Busoga (and most likely Uganda as a whole but such information cannot be derived from my research results). After having been used to modest but frequent access to consumer goods from the beginning of the twentieth century up to the early 1970s, that time of scarcity was a shock to the population. This experience has led to a high level of appreciation for today's availability of consumer goods. Study respondents generally agreed that the new consumer goods are better than their old equivalents that people had to make themselves. They prefer to sleep on a mattress instead of mats or grass; to cook with saucepans instead of clay pots; or to wear 'modern' fabrics instead of bark cloth. Hence, though the disadvantages of some commodities – e.g., negative health effects of cooking oil, the dangers of counterfeit products, poor quality as a result of low prices – are known, the overall rating of the increasing availability and affordability of consumer goods is positive. In terms of affordability, a representative of Jinja District explained to me that

> "the providers of these products in Uganda are reading the market so well in terms of who is able to buy WHAT. [...] Like for example, we may have about ten phone sets here, which are similar. But one may be costing 20,000 [shillings] and the last one may be costing two millions. So, the people, the global market is conscious of that. Uhm (considering), to the extent that they are trying as much as possible to provide items in relation to ability of particular people to pay for them." (Expert 8, 2017)

While some of those commodities actually make the lives of people much easier, others are status symbols. Yet to the majority of commodities both applies, e.g., to mobile phones. In either case, availability creates desires. As John Glenn points out, firms in a capitalist environment must create "new social wants and needs" in their (potential) customers permanently, either back home or in new markets, in order to remain competitive (Glenn 2007, 11; see chapter 3.1 of this thesis). The long-term practice of this strategy trains consumers to long for more consumption. Néstor García Canclini suggests that, under globalisation, people in the global South have started to define themselves through "commodity consumption and the mass media" rather than through their citizenship (García Canclini 2008, 15; see chapter 3.2 of this thesis). I am not certain whether that process is already underway in Busoga, as I did not discuss interviewees' citizenship. Based on the research results, I can nevertheless assume that the strong desire for consumer goods described by García Canclini exists in Busoga. In either case, the firms and the consumers need intermediaries. While weekly market days and hawkers were the only supply channels for rural areas in the past (see above), nowadays they are still existent but complemented by a dense network of shops. Those shops can be found in both urban and rural areas, run by Basoga, other Ugandans of African descent, in few cases other Africans, Indians, and Ugandans of

Indian descent. What is special for many respondents is that shops and trading centres have come closer to them. For instance, a main interviewee from Kamuli District explained that "today, even at night, you can go and buy paraffin, soap, sugar, everything. But, at my ten years, we used to buy sugar or soap at a distance of eight kilometres" (Main 14, 2017). In addition to liberalisation, improved security has contributed significantly to the spread of shops to rural areas. Hence, all that hinders excessive consumption of new and well-known consumer goods is the challenge of low incomes. Even though many items have become cheaper, increasing *cost of living* (see corresponding sub-theme: chapter 8.2.5) and low incomes make it difficult for people to raise the money to buy consumer goods. By far the most popular way of raising it is through agricultural practices, followed by related activities such as livestock breeding or trade in agricultural products. Respondents noted some other options but agriculture and related fields were clearly predominant. This confirms the finding that farming is the most important survival strategy in Busoga. A main interviewee from Buyende District said:

> "Buying them [consumer goods], we sell this food, it is where we get the money, we begin buying things like those ones that are used in homes, like plates, flasks, these chairs – we buy from people, who make them from our trees – mattresses, bed sheets, blankets, we get from what we cultivate. [...] And from what we rear, when you sell a cow like that one, you can buy those things." (Main 9, 2017, translation by E.K. and N.H.)

Some study respondents reported purchasing consumer goods through their private savings. However, joining groups is more popular than saving individually. Respondents explained that, in order to get access to certain consumer products, they join either savings and credit groups (especially ROSCAs and SACCOs; see chapter 8.3.3) or Mukenkede/ Gema Kumwino groups (small consumer associations; see chapter 8.3.4). In the past, borrowing and sharing items like tools, clothes, salt, etc. among households was another common way of gaining access to them. Today, it is no longer common. Study respondents generally agreed that nowadays, everybody has to try his or her best to get his or her own things (see also chapter 8.3.1).

Although barter trade is also no longer an option, it has outlasted the introduction of commercial structures in Busoga much longer than self-sufficiency. Several respondents reported that barter trade was still common throughout the 1970s. This seems logical in view of the general situation during that time. A representative of Buyende District explained to me that, in Uganda, "before liberalisation, we had barter trade. [...] But the cash economy, which came as a result of liberalisation and globalisation, has completely killed that one. Everything is now for what? For money [...]" (Expert 1, 2017). Prior to their expulsion, even some of the so-called 'Indians' had accepted an exchange of cotton for products from their shops. Today, shopkeepers accept only cash, explained a main interviewee from Jinja town:

> "Nobody in the shop can go with your kawunga[98] that, 'Give me soap, I go and use it, you take the maize.' No, they don't. They use money now. That's why people are selling their things, so that they get money to buy what they cannot grow from their garden." (Main 20b, 2017)

Liberalisation introduced institutions that cannot accept payment in kind, e.g., an education system that costs the parents a lot of money, as it is based on austerity and privatisation (see chapter 8.2.5). As a result, everybody (including shopkeepers) needs cash money, such that they can no longer accept payment in kind.

In summary, consumption patterns in Busoga have adapted to globalisation to the greatest possible extent, with respect to the limited purchasing power of the majority of people in the region. A process of commercialisation can be observed here. During their lifetimes, study respondents have gone through a number of phases of availability of consumer goods: limited availability (which was nevertheless availability, before Idi Amin); extreme scarcity (during Idi Amin's reign); increasing availability; abundance (in the sense of more goods being available than people can afford to buy, not in the sense of extreme abundance that can be observed in the global North). As a result, consumer goods – both new consumer goods and those that were previously available and got lost for a while – are appreciated and desired. People work hard to mobilise the funds to buy these goods, especially as sharing, borrowing, and barter trade are considered outdated. They appreciate the new dense network of shops and trading centres that nowadays make such goods available to them, even in rural areas. To conclude on this sub-theme, I would like to use the words of an expert interviewee, who has travelled the world and likewise played a significant role in Ugandan politics and in Busoga. He said about the region: "Wherever you go, you'll meet a plastic chair. And deep in the village. That's globalisation" (Expert 5, 2017).

98 kawunga = Luganda for maize flour

8.2.5 Cost of living

The main finding of this sub-theme is that the cost of living in Busoga is increasing permanently and more rapidly than the incomes. Health care and educational expenditures pose enormous challenges to respondents and the people in their social environments. One of the numerically strongest codes in the whole study is the one capturing respondents' massive complaints about the burden of educational expenditures[99]. A comprehensive description of this dilemma is the following statement by a main interviewee from Buyende District:

> "You want to educate a child now, you are over-working, but you get little money, yet at school, they tell us that children, it's for free, and you find yourself when it's for money. […] You go and find yourself, a child of Primary 7 there, they are telling him/her 120,000 [shilling] per term. […] Now, where are the free things? That one of Primary (...) 1, they want from him/her money, maybe 6,000, don't you see? And it is not easy to get it. It is going to be got in the season, but they are sending the child home today.[100] Today, you find that children are not in UPE schools." (Main 1, 2017, translation by E.K. and N.H.)

Parents are aware that education is necessary for their children, so they work hard and some take out loans in order to pay for it. They may even take out loans in order to pay back other loans, which they had taken out for paying school fees. A main interviewee from Jinja District described how the members of her savings and credit group use the loans from the group for such purposes:

> "For us to form our group, as I have told you that we used to help each other in good times and bad times. If we contribute that small

99 In Uganda, educational expenditures encompass official school fees in private schools as well as expenditures that can incur in both private and state-run schools: 'requirements' (materials that are needed in order to attend school like a uniform; exercise books; pens; in case of boarding a mattress etc.; often, this comprises money for photocopies, printing of reports, school meals, etc.) and 'teachers' motivation' (a half-official extra 'fee' that is raised because of low teachers' salaries). As a result, in spite of the 'Universal Primary Education' (UPE) and 'Universal Secondary Education' (USE) programmes (which are not universally available anyway), education is expensive for many families.

100 He referred to his own child that had been expelled from school on the day of the interview because some fees had not yet been paid to the school. This is common practice in private and state-run schools alike.

> money and we give you, or you have a problem at home that you have come with, we help you and you solve it. When you have not gone to the place of so-and-so to tell him/her that, 'my friend, lend me', you will reach there when (s)he has money in the house and (s)he will tell you that, 'I don't have.' […] But when you come knowing that on Sunday, we are going to sit, even if the other one is bad to you, you say that, 'my friend, help me, on Sunday, we are going to do what?' […] 'We are going to sit, I will tell the members to give me money, I will give you, and I finish this problem, maybe, I take my child to school.'" (Main 28, 2017, translation by E.K. and N.H.)

Hence, the loan from the group is used as a security for a private loan from another individual, and all this is made necessary by the high level and urgency of educational expenditures. Many respondents observed a significant increase in the level of education and the number of children attending school. They appreciated those improvements yet hoped that the affordability of education would further improve in the near future.

In terms of health services, I was told repeatedly and empathetically by respondents that they pose a big challenge to the people in Busoga. Health services are not available at all in some places and are not helpful or very expensive in others. People have to buy medicine from private dealers – at high costs and without proper guidance on their application. Although respondents reported that, compared to 30 years ago, the number of health facilities has increased significantly, their accessibility and the services provided remain limited. For instance, a respondent from Kamuli District stated that "in the past, when a person/ the drugs in the health facilities were for free, but now, if you don't have money, you die" (Main 11, 2017, translation by E.K. and K.M.). Respondents reported that crops are stored at home until 'a problem' occurs, e.g., the children's school demands money or a medical bill. Then, the crops are being sold in order to solve that problem. In contrast to the past, when food crops were stored in granaries to feed the family up to the next harvest, nowadays crops are stored for short periods of time and with the objective to sell them at short notice when money is needed. For most people in rural Busoga, this is the only form of capital or security they have. However, the high cost of living – especially educational and health expenditures – prevents them from keeping some of it or at least selling it at a high price in times of scarcity. Instead, they are pressured to sell it at whatever price they can get when there is an urgent need for money. A main interviewee from Jinja District reported that

> "we have those small, small health facilities, those Health Centre II, Health Centre III, and so on. Except that the drugs are not there, but the nurses are there, when you go, (s)he examines you, gives you advice, and when you return this way, when you have your beans, you sell, you go and you get drugs, and you treat yourself, when at least you got some advice from there." (Main 16, 2017, translation by E.K. and K.M.)

Though people are trying to raise their agricultural activities to a higher level, there are many challenges that prevent them from doing so (see chapter 8.2.2). Apart from educational and health expenses, high prices for food and consumer goods pose serious challenges to the majority of Busoga's population. The perceived inflation is high. A main interviewee from an urbanised area in Jinja District compared the situation of today with that of the past[101], when she was a young adult, as follows:

> "Now, me, I remember, I was working at Kakira[102], when I used to get a salary of 300 shillings. But while I eat from it, I also buy a dress for my mother, a whole month on those shillings. Yet, when it was me who studied a bit. The porters used to get 54 shillings. But now, this era, a person gets one million, (s)he finds him-/herself to pay house rent, when (s)he has a family, (s)he can't sustain him-/herself. Because a bunch of plantains, only, is at 40,000, 35,000, hm (seeking confirmation)? Still, (s)he can't even buy it for him-/herself. Others, we are on posho and beans. We can no longer eat well. We eat badly. Still, the people now, the majority in Uganda here are eating food, a meal this?[103] [...] Only. If (s)he eats lunch, does not eat supper, if (s)he eats supper, does not eat lunch, (s)he uses tea, and (s)he just survives. So, this era now, it has become very difficult, more than the other time." (Main 30, 2017, translation by E.K. and K.M.)

Certainly, the amounts she mentioned cannot be compared with today. Yet, importantly, when she was young, her salary allowed her a standard of living with which she was satisfied, whereas today she says about herself and others with a relatively high income that they cannot even afford to buy the food they like. Economic liberalisation has created more expenses for all (education; health; increasing food prices; desires for and availability

101 She could not specify the year but was most likely talking about the late 1960s or early 1970s.

102 She referred to Kakira Sugar factory in Jinja.

103 She showed one finger.

of consumer goods) but very limited opportunities of earning money for people who do not have capital (e.g., for investing in a small-scale enterprise). Respondents feel frustrated by a permanent pursuit of money that is never sufficient to cover even the most urgent needs. With regard to the biggest stress factor, education expenditures, a main interviewee from Kamuli District explained that even increasing production of crops for sale cannot cover them:

> "Especially education for the children. Children are overstraining us. Because now, much money must be paid, yet things that are cultivated are there, produce has increased a bit, but again, there are very many necessities." (Main 11, 2017, translation by E.K. and K.M.)

In summary, the cost of living in Busoga is increasing permanently and more rapidly than the incomes, such that frustration, poverty, and indebtedness pose a threat to a large portion of the population. Health care and educational expenditures as well as high prices for food and consumer goods pose enormous challenges to respondents and the people in their social environment. The respondent's suggestion above that a patient without money has to die resembles James Ferguson's report from 1989 Zambia, where structural adjustment programmes (SAPs) had led to the abolition of free health care and deprived many people of access to treatment (Ferguson 2006; see chapter 3.3 of this thesis). As described in my theoretical framework, privatisation[104] and fiscal austerity are typical measures of the Washington Consensus and have been frequently applied to the sectors of education and health care (see Stiglitz 2002 in chapter 3.3 of this thesis and Schmidt/ Schröder 2016, 27, in 2.2.1). However, Uganda's health care system, "considered to be one of the best in Africa" until the 1970s, was ruined by the political turmoil under Idi Amin and its aftermath, not by SAPs (Hutchinson 2001, 407). Nevertheless, in the late 1990s, after more than ten years of IMF recovery programmes, Hutchinson encountered the same problems in the health sector that I was told about by interviewees another 20 years later: Medical personnel was rare[105], gov-

---

104 The website of the Ugandan Ministry of Education indicates: „Since the government of Uganda decision in 1993 to liberalize the education sector, thousands of schools and institutions have been set up by private investors. In the secondary sub-sector, the number of private schools, at about 4000, is more than double the number of government-funded schools." (http://www.education.go.ug/private-schools-institutions/ accessed on 25 April 2020, 08:47a.m.)

105 According to Hutchinson, medical personnel was rare because they went to neighbouring countries after training due to poor payment in Uganda

ernment-run health facilities had no materials and charged their patients fees, just like NGO-run health facilities (ibid., 411-413, 431). Within those 30 years, there has been neither great improvement in services, nor in affordability of those services. Though a thorough analysis of the reasons would exceed the scope of this study, it is likely a combination of austerity, privatisation, and corruption (the latter is further discussed in chapter 8.2.7). Unofficial fees (e.g., 'teachers' motivation'; 'nurses' motivation' for delivery, which should be for free) and the lack of materials in schools and hospitals could be a result of austerity (low salaries, low budgets for purchase of materials) and corruption. Privatisation aggravates the situation by answering the demand for more schools and health facilities with the provision of expensive private institutions to which few people have access. In terms of food prices, besides food subsidies being cut under IMF-programmes (McMichael 2012, 118; Stiglitz 2002, 20; Tandon 2016, 37), financial speculation influences them in countries that have been integrated in the global trade regime (Tandon 2016, 37), like Uganda (see chapter 3.3 of this thesis). As Daniel Bendix and Aram Ziai aptly point out, "[i]ncreased income can nevertheless mean growing impoverishment, if formerly free resources (water, education, health) are provided against payment" (Bendix/ Ziai 2015, 163, translation by E.K.; see also chapter 2.2.1). In a nutshell, as a main interviewee from Kamuli District put it, "cost of living, these days, is very high" (Main 11, 2017).

8.2.6 Obstacles to benefitting from the market economy

As has been shown thus far, Busoga has become a free market economy with liberalised trade in crops and animal products of all kinds, consumer goods, and services; with very little state intervention; and without barter trade. However, several interviewees deplored the absence of significant improvement in their life situation. Various reasons for that circumstance could be revealed from their descriptions of the general situation. One is that the infrastructure of the area is weak in terms of different aspects, such as roads, health facilities, etc. Among the three districts under examination, Buyende is the weakest in that respect (confirmed by the statistics in chapter 7.4). As a representative of Buyende District explained: "Now, for example, Buyende, it's/ we are really a hard-to-reach-area. It's a remote

(Hutchinson 2001, 411). Fiscal austerity usually leads to low salaries in all kinds of government institutions, including health facilities.

area. And you find that also those companies, we don't have them here" (Expert 2, 2017). A main interviewee living in Buyende District likewise stated that the road network "does not allow these big vehicles travelling to come and buy crops or bring in items so easily" (Main 7, 2017). However, rural areas in the other two districts are likewise affected by that problem. Furthermore, there are almost no jobs available in Busoga that suit the skills and the salary expectations of young, educated people and their families, who have struggled to invest money in their education (see chapter 8.2.5). A main interviewee from Jinja District expressed her disappointment about this as follows:

> "[...] we have gone through hardships and educated the children, but the children we have educated don't have jobs. Me, I have four of them. [...] They have degrees. [...] I have educated them, but they don't have jobs. They are not working. This time, they are still depending on me, but when I even sold land to enable a child to study and do what? (S)he finishes and gets a degree. Now, me, how have I benefited from it, hm (seeking confirmation)?" (Main 17, 2017, translation by E.K. and K.M.)

As families invest large parts of their income in a training that does not result in paid employment, families do not have at their disposition the money they would need in order to participate in the market economy by investing, saving, or consuming. Instead, they have an increasing number of members who depend on them permanently in spite of the high investment in their training.

Another problem is that the financial demands are so overwhelming for many that they lose sight of their families' other needs. Since food crops, fruit, and animal products such as eggs or meat have become highly marketable, people try to solve their financial problems by selling the biggest part of their production of such commodities. In the following example, a main interviewee from Kamuli District described how this situation leads to malnutrition, which in turn causes expenses for the family, as the treatment in the health facility is expensive:

> "Eh (affirmative), because there is rearing chicken, a person says that, 'My chicken at home is not for eating, or the egg', but when even a child, you are taking it to the health centre and it takes from you all that you got through selling all of them. Because this egg, you have not given it to the child." (Main 19, 2017, translation by E.K. and K.M.)

In the past, the harvest was kept in granaries and animals were mainly kept in order to provide meat, eggs, and milk *for the family*. Today, they are sold in order to pay for educational and health expenditures as well as consumer goods. Eventually, the producers who have sold all their products must again buy food and suffer from high food prices. In the following statement, a main interviewee from Jinja District explained about the open market having replaced granaries and endangered food security:

> "In the last 30 years, people had not known about export. Growing and sending out food. They were using it WITHIN the peop/ the family. So that famine doesn't enter in the home, they have ginne/ the granary where they keep the foodstuff from the garden. So, they don't go bad, and they continue eating, so that there's no famine. But now, as time is going, people are learning more things. They have learnt how to SELL food in the market, in the open market. They sell it outside, so that they remain without food at home, and they are crying because of famine. There is no food at times. Like now, the weather when food doesn't come out well. The little they get, they sell it away. They are now more interested in money than keeping the foodstuff in the family." (Main 20b, 2017)

Due to lack of education and the overwhelming daily struggle for survival, many people cannot properly calculate household expenses, much less investments in small-scale enterprises and agricultural activities. People often sell their products or provide their services at prices that do not allow them to make any profits, either due to lack of education (as they do not calculate a minimum price they must demand in order to make a profit) or due to lack of bargaining power in the liberalised market. The latter is being explained in the following expert's comment:

> "Today, everybody sells maize. To the extent that, because you have opened up, you've globalised the market, hm (seeking confirmation)? Uh (considering), some people sell BELOW a threshold they shouldn't. So, soon, they find themselves without food in the homes." (Expert 6, 2017)

While liberalisation has created markets, it has led to a high cost of living (see chapter 8.2.5) and small profit margins for the economic activities of the majority of the population (see chapters 8.2.1, 8.2.3, and 8.2.7). As a result, it has created a socio-economic environment favourable only to elites. This is a typical effect of liberalisation policies (see e.g., Rowden 1999, 157). Those with capital to invest in factories, large-scale agriculture or trade, high-quality education for their children, and high-level health care can indeed profit from Busoga's liberalised market economy. The vast majority of the population however does not have any capital, such that they do not have a realistic chance of succeeding within this system. Instead, they grow food and sell it for the price offered by the first interested middleman and then spend the earnings on educational expenditures, paying the outstanding hospital bill or buying medicine, and, should any money remain, indulging in consumption. In other words, they do what they are expected to do in an economically liberalised system. However, due to their lack of capital (and increasing lack of land), they end up having spent their money long before any further income (e.g., from the next harvest) can be expected. This study provides evidence for the division of the world population into a global middle-class and a global lower class, a finding by Ivan Illich as well as by Wolfgang Sachs. Both of them postulated that small numbers of people from the global South are joining the former, enjoying the comfort of capitalist development, especially in terms of consumption, while the majority joins the latter and is worse off than before (see chapter 2.2.3 of this thesis).

With regard to another problem, comments from several interviewees confirmed my observations in Uganda as well as Uganda's reputation in that respect: corruption is rampant and disables economic and social development on all levels. As pointed out in chapters 6.2.2 (Asowa-Okwe 1994) and 8.2.5 (Hutchinson 2001) of this thesis, the history of corruption in Uganda began prior to economic liberalisation. An analysis of its exact starting time and all its causes and effects would require a separate study. I do not assert that globalisation, or any other single issue, can be held responsible as 'the cause' of corruption in Uganda. However, globalisation has the potential to *aggravate* existing corruption and *promote* new corruption, e.g., through lowering salaries in all kinds of government jobs, as discussed in chapters 3.3 (Ferguson 2006) and 6.2.2 of this thesis. Several scholars have postulated that problems like corruption must be regarded in relation to colonial experience (Amin 2004; see chapter 3.3 of this thesis) as well as in relation to the role of national elites in the neo-imperialist system that has been established by the global North (Cooper 2009; Gruffydd Jones 2018; Ngũgĩ wa Thiong'o 1988; see chapter 2.2.1 of this thesis). Nevertheless, as corruption is an obstacle to social and economic transformation of any kind, it must also be included in the factors that prevent Ugandans from benefitting from the market economy.

In summary, large parts of Busoga's population do not benefit from the liberalised market economy. Rather obvious reasons are corruption and deficits in infrastructure as well as in the provision of qualified jobs. However, subtler reasons are also responsible for this inequality in the effects of the liberalised market economy, such as its insistence on selling foodstuff small-scale farmers produce rather than storing it and using it for subsistence. Due to the high cost of living, many sell unreasonably high portions of their products for unreasonably low prices, further entrenching poverty and sometimes even malnutrition. Liberalisation has created a socio-economic environment favourable for elites with capital to invest but unfavourable for the largest part of the population. This appears to me to be the principal problem as it has been created by globalisation itself. As a problem integral to the system, it is much more difficult to find solutions to it than to others, such as lack of infrastructure. For that reason, and because there is no extract in the data set that enumerates all above-mentioned problems at once, I would like to close the analysis of this sub-theme on a comment from a representative of Jinja District that refers to this principal problem:

> "VOLUMES which are going out have become much, which is also causing another problem at local level. The desired sale is creating food insecurity. Somebody would rather sell/ NOT even is CONDITIONED to sell to get the money without thinking so much about tomorrow." (Expert 8, 2017)

8.2.7 Other effects of globalisation on life in Busoga

All the sub-themes of the main theme "Busoga's economy under globalisation" encompass to some extent *effects of globalisation on life in Busoga*. However, some effects are so important for the analysis – due to a combination of their role in the theoretical framework and their prevalence in the data set – that it was worthwhile and even necessary to create separate sub-themes for them. Others are not sufficiently important – or numerically strong – to warrant their own sub-theme, yet are too important to be altogether discarded from the analysis. Codes containing information of that latter kind have been subsumed under this sub-theme. Apart from the phenomena captured in the other sub-themes of the main theme "Busoga's economy under globalisation", this sub-theme captures *the remaining* effects of globalisation on the lives of people in Busoga, as found in the data set. As a result, this sub-theme is very diverse.

Technical innovations – most of all the telephone, which enables easy communication and circulation of information – are highly appreciated by respondents. The same applies to improvements in transport. When describing the situation of the past, some respondents spoke about people having been obliged to walk everywhere they wanted to go, even if that meant getting up in the middle of the night or spending several nights away from home, on journeys taking several days. In the following statement, a main interviewee from Buyende District rejoiced in the possibilities that open up when combining innovations in transport and communication, for example by calling a motorcycle-taxi with the mobile phone:

> "I can just make a call, and I say that I want this, then it comes, hm (seeking confirmation)? I just call a motorcyclist that I'm here, and then he picks me, hm (seeking confirmation)? I can access what I want, I can travel in a bus, and they are there." (Main 9, 2017, translation by E.K. and N.H.)

Thanks to liberalisation, there are countless taxis in the shapes of busses, motorcycles, and bicycles, whose owners have easy access to spare parts and are in fierce competition with each other. As a result, transport is cheap and always available, all over Busoga (though in Buyende, it is still more difficult than in Kamuli and Jinja Districts). Conversely, that means that transport providers have low profit margins, except if they have a large armada of taxis.

On a cultural – yet, at the same time material – level, the generational conflict in Busoga is strongly influenced by the media and their Euro-American contents that make young people desire to consume the way people do in the global North. Many examples given by interviewees for that phenomenon, as well as for Western behaviour threatening local culture in general (e.g., indecent dressing styles that are spread via the media) are typical and could likewise be noted by conservative Europeans. In such cases, what makes those comments interesting, is that they show the strong influence of globalised phenomena, like the media, in Busoga. A main interviewee from Kamuli District echoes the sentiment of several respondents in noting that

> "the only problem that has come about is that the children have got spoilt, going to the disco, film, in of now. They watch things that are not good on TV. The children grow up when they are not easy to handle, they are not easy to handle, those of this time." (Main 15, 2017, translation by E.K. and K.M.)

The new ('Westernised', 'modernised', or 'globalised') lifestyle for which young people are longing is to a large extent defined by their participation in a particular *material* culture. They must *consume* in a particular way in order to be part of it. They must purchase certain status symbols like commercial music, films, clothes, and technical assets that allow them to participate in social media. All these things cost money, which is difficult to earn in Uganda, where jobs are rare. Respondents attested that new wants and needs are created within the young generation in Busoga, without realistic chances of satisfying them. The dissatisfaction caused by the impossibility of fulfilling those wishes (due to low purchasing power) leads to ill-mannered, sometimes even delinquent behaviour among youth. Some respondents complained about theft, prostitution, and drug abuse among youth (using the word "abaana", which literally means "children" but can refer to any young, unmarried person). One respondent from an urbanised area in Jinja District lamented:

> "Our children don't want to work, that is why these other ones are selling themselves. […] They are stealing. (S)he sees that that one will make him/her get the money quickly, not being patient, and wanting to get money quickly, it is what is causing hardships." (Main 28, 2017, translation by E.K. and N.H.)

In addition to the challenges faced by and with youth, respondents named several new phenomena that, in their view, have led to a sharp increase in theft, namely: rapid climate change (which makes survival difficult), the need for hard work to survive, selling food crops instead of storing them as well as availability of and desire for numerous new commodities. For instance, a main interviewee from Kamuli District claimed that, in the past, in terms of food crops, "there never used to be selling […] and there was no theft like this today, which is there of these days […] that they are going for stealing and selling" (Main 13, 2017, translation by E.K. and K.M.). According to the respondents, adults likewise have desires for participation in new material cultures, for instance having lavish wedding parties like the ones they see on TV. This is what Arjun Appadurai calls global "mediascapes": people all over the world developing their own image of the lifeworlds and consumption patterns of others, based on what they see on the omnipresent media, and desiring to position themselves in relation to what they see (Appadurai 1990, 298-299). This also corresponds with García Canclini's finding that, due to globalisation, the combination of "commodity consumption and the mass media" gains more and more in importance in the lives of people in the global South (García Canclini

2001, 15). In that regard, Busoga shows typical signs of penetration by globalisation. Commodities like technical assets have become important status symbols (e.g., mobile phones, radios, TVs). As an expert interviewee noted, it "is a lifestyle now, you must BE SEEN carrying, uh (considering), a cell phone in your hand, hm (seeking confirmation)? Then, they think you're okay" (Expert 6, 2017). Low incomes make it hard for the majority of people to make a living at all (see chapter 8.2.5), let alone fulfilling their wishes for participation in the global consumer class. Two examples of descriptions of income disparity are cited below, the first from a charcoal seller from an urbanised area in Jinja District, the second from a farmer and cattle keeper from a rural area in Kamuli District:

> "Oh dear, you see that maybe the development has still failed, it's little, it's little. So, there are those who developed, but that is not for those who are down. Like for us, the people of down, we are still being oppressed because we don't have a way in which we can help ourselves [...]." (Main 26, 2017, translation by E.K. and K.M.)

The farmer and cattle keeper compared himself to government workers as follows:

> "Because those workers are well. [...] For us, what we say that 'they are well' because we are not able to reach it ourselves. You go and hear that a worker gets a million [shilling], every month. Every month, (s)he gets 800,000. But for you, a man, you go and work a full season. Eight hundred thousand, you might not even get it a year of a season[106]. So, you see that the number of farmers is very low. So, if they would add some money in crops business, it would make a person cultivate, who wouldn't have cultivated before. Because (s)he is seeing that if (s)he sells a bag of coffee or maize, what is coming out is maybe 400,000 or 300,000. But from a bag, you get 100,000, 150,000, yet when the needs at home are many." (Main 12, 2017, translation by E.K. and K.M.)

These descriptions of income inequality evoke of the social disparities described by interviewees with respect to landowners profiting from sugar

---

106 It is not clear what he meant by "a year of a season". In this context, it does not make a big difference. Depending on the weather, the agricultural year has two to three seasons in Busoga. His point remains the same: What government employees earn *per month* is more than he earns either once or maximum thrice per year, i.e., in any case, they are much better off than he is.

cane cultivation, whereas small-scale farmers and the landless suffer from food insecurity (see chapter 8.2.1; see also chapter 7.2 on that point). Essentially, Busoga's inequitable development is typical for an economy that is penetrated by globalisation. The latter connects it to the capitalist world economy and adjusts its national economy to capitalist principles (see chapter 3). Busoga's situation represents precisely what Immanuel Wallerstein noted with regard to the capitalist world-economy, namely that its "guiding principle of the ceaseless accumulation of capital *requires* and *generates* ever-greater polarization of real income" (Wallerstein 2017, 59, emphases by E.K.; see chapter 2.3.2 of this thesis).

Just like the above-cited main interviewee, several respondents from both groups made requests during the interview for the government to re-introduce agricultural subsidies, guaranteed markets, and fixed prices. For instance, a farmer and stockbreeder from Buyende District disdained the middlemen-system of liberalised crop trade and wanted back the times of governmental price regulations:

> "Uh (considering), the markets, there is need, if it is possible, the government to put there, uh (considering), fixed amounts rather than saying that, 'Let the other person come and buy maize at 300 shillings, the other one at 500, the other one at 200, the other one buys at what/' [...] As it was in the generations of our grandfathers and our fathers, those generations were doing very well." (Main 8, 2017, translation by E.K. and N.H.)

Nevertheless, numerous interviewees reported that, if someone is ready to work hard, there are more opportunities to gain today, e.g., from small businesses (like selling charcoal) or trade in food crops, than in the past. There was general appreciation for the circumstance that these days, hard work pays off, whereas in the past, this was not the case. For instance, a main interviewee, who succeeded as a rural crop trader in Buyende District, gave me the following testimony:

> "Because I am going to give an example of myself. There, in the past, we used to cultivate when we don't gain, but this time, I cultivated, I resorted to trading, and I started getting money, then, I constructed a house. Also, that is my development. Also, my friends in the region have gone on doing what? They cultivate and get money, then, they make a living." (Main 4, 2017, translation by E.K. and N.H.)

However, several respondents referred to the downsides of the promotion of commercial (food crop) farming, especially the destruction of natural resources (e.g., deforestation) and the endangering of human health and long-term livelihood (e.g., climate change, pollution). For instance, a main interviewee from Kamuli District complaining about his harvest having halved, gave the reason that "what made production reduce is cutting down forests, rain has become little" (Main 15, 2017, translation by E.K. and K.M.). Several other respondents also mentioned deforestation in favour of the expansion of agricultural production and used this to explain why the attempt to produce larger quantities of crops for the domestic and export markets ends in a disaster for small- to medium-scale farmers who have no financial cushion. Some of them blame poor harvests on climate change and climate change, especially drought, on deforestation. As a result, some respondents called for their government to provide guidance on how to deal with climate change, especially in farming.

Business relations with foreigners were rated as helpful or desirable for their region by some respondents. For instance, one respondent who runs a garage and a spare parts shop in Jinja town was not at all afraid of competition from abroad. On the contrary, he longed for spare part suppliers from abroad to open shops in Jinja, such that the local businesses could be supplied by them directly:

> "Now, that is why, you see, I like a lot people who bring development in the area. Hm (seeking confirmation)? If, let's say, in case there was/ there comes a person, who comes from outside, when (s)he says that, 'Me, I have gone to bring here spare parts for vehicles, all of you, you are going to be coming to buy here.' We would not/ may we go/ to look for them in Kampala, again? Or even others going to Dubai. But now, if we get shops like those, which are strong, those of the investors, and they come here and they begin to bring their things in here, we are going to be well." (Main 25, 2017, translation by E.K. and K.M.)

On a negative note, seven of the ten expert interviewees complained that Ugandan producers cannot compete with their international counterparts. According to them, Ugandans feel overwhelmed by international competition and they speculated that the chances of Ugandan producers (both industrial and agricultural producers) to succeed within the current neoliberal structures is very low. For instance, one expert interviewee raised the issue of the lower price of imported agricultural products at the local market compared with local goods, using the example of rice produced in the Eastern region of Uganda, including the swampy areas of Busoga:

> "I would say, despite this, uhm (considering), globalisation overall has been good for Uganda. But also, it has opened us up for competition. And, uh (considering), sometimes, we are not/ we don't have a comparative advantage, we cannot compete with other people. And (...) that has worked against us. It has, uh (considering), I'll give an example like, in Uganda, we ca/ Eastern region can grow rice and they, indeed, it's one of the/ it might even be their major crops. They are growing rice, but you find Kenya is growing rice even more cheaply. Or even imported rice from Pakistan, from elsewhere, is more cheap than our own. So, I mean, it disadvantaged the common, the poor man, majority who are farmers. They are left disadvantaged. Cause households in urban areas will buy the imported rice and not the one that is locally grown, so." (Expert 9, 2018)

Another expert interviewee postulated that, in his view, a local company would never get a chance to win the contract for constructing a road in Uganda because there are many more competitive international companies in the Ugandan market. The following extract from his explanation serves to illustrate his argument:

> "Look at the construction industry. If there is a road to be dug, or to be constructed because you are getting moneys from international banks, you must go for competitive bidding. [...] So, the Germans will come, the Italians will come, the French don't get involved in this business very much. But the British will come, and, of late, the Chinese will come. [...] So, the local ones, whom I'm calling the weaker ones, will never succeed. So, then, you say, 'Uh (generous), let the big company get the contract, then, they can sub-contract you.' So, you get the peanuts. So, globalisation (...) promotes the bigger fellows to grow bigger and suffocates the smaller ones. [...] Liberalisation is the big ones eat the weak ones, kill them off. [...] Look at Uganda today. And show me any of these roads they are constructing with a local company." (Expert 6, 2017)

As Ha-Joon Chang (2002; see chapter 2.2.2 of this thesis) and Joseph Stiglitz (2002; see chapter 3.3 of this thesis) have pointed out in general, and Julius Kiiza (2008; see chapter 2.2.2 of this thesis) with regard to Uganda in particular, premature liberalisation leads to a situation in which local producers have no chance to succeed. If they are not allowed to grow strong by means of protective policies prior to the opening of the national economy, they are overrun by international competition. Certainly, the usefulness of neoliberal globalisation and capitalist development can be questioned in general (see chapters 2.2, 2.3, 3, and 4 of this thesis). However, even the three above-cited authors, who follow rather developmentalist (though to differing extents reformist) approaches, postulate that premature liberalisation is disastrous for local producers.

Irrespective of companies' origins, several respondents called upon their government to regulate them. For instance, a main interviewee from Jinja town was worried about their effects on peoples' health: "Now, things like those, the factories are good. But again, we don't have an arrangement, which is good, which goes and helps people not to get diseases from them" (Main 25, 2017, translation by E.K. and K.M.). Others deplored low workers' salaries, low prices in case the companies buy products from local farmers, and the practice of bringing their own workers instead of employing locals at all. In all these points, respondents did not distinguish between Ugandan companies and international ones. In their view, they all behave in the same way and there is a need to regulate them. Some expert interviewees however complained about counterfeit, second-hand, and low-quality *imported* goods flooding the Ugandan market. One of them even called Uganda "a dumping society" because other countries just send their scrap (e.g., second-hand fridges/ cars) to Uganda instead of disposing of it properly (Expert 10, 2018).

According to some expert interviewees, the Ugandan government also has some concerns about the impact of liberalisation policies. One of the expert interviewees who is active in national and regional politics alike explained to me that the Ugandan government was disappointed with the outcomes of orthodox liberalisation:

> "There are things that the market cannot produce for the society, which need to be produced publicly. And this happens all over the world. But when we did our liberalisation in this country, we liberalised everything. Now, we are going back to government participating and regulating. Yes. So, our strategy in this country is now what we call a quasi-market economy. […] Quasi-market economy. What that means is that, eh (considering), there is private/ the economy is private-led, government-regulated, okay? Government-regulated, and there's government provision where there are market failures. […] We closed cooperatives, cooperative banks, and whatever, and we are starting another. We sold all our banks, and we are seeing that we have a problem with interest rates." (Expert 10, 2018)

A representative of Buyende District spoke about a return to the provision of free farming inputs by the government because the farmers have been found to be in dire need:

> "Mhm (considering), really, the government is trying to make sure that maybe it REVIVES what it used to do because, right now, we have Operation Wealth Creation. Operation Wealth Creation, they're providing the inputs for these peasants. But, however, we realized that, ONE, the inputs are just VERY FEW because a person like having three acres, and you are given only two kilogrammes of maize, really, it cannot do MUCH. So, we hope that, with TIME, when they realize that they can add them more, it will do better. OR, if they reduce the taxes on these inputs, such that they can be affordable, then, that one can yield more? Success. In the production." (Expert 2, 2017)

It appears that the Ugandan government has been observing the course of liberalisation and globalisation, realising that some measures did not bring out the desired effect but rather negative ones. My analysis of the current National Agricultural Extension Policy (NAEP 2016) and the National Cooperative Policy (NCP 2011) in chapter 7 confirmed that assumption. They provide for more governmental intervention in spheres that had previously been fully liberalised, aiming to correct the "shortcomings" that have been encountered in the de-regulated environment (NAEP 2016). It remains to be seen which long-term developments these and other new policies will bring and whether the complete opening of the economy for three decades can be reversed at all.

In summary, it is clear that globalisation has left its mark on Busoga, as has been shown in this sub-theme and in the overarching main theme as a whole. This particular sub-theme mirrors the diversity of perspectives on globalisation. It contains positive and negative accounts as well as assessments that cannot readily be sorted into one of those categories. Technical innovations and improvements in the sectors of transport and communication were absolutely lauded by respondents. On the other hand, technical innovations raise desires and grant access to information that study respondents perceive as "spoiling the youth". The current generational conflict in Busoga is strongly influenced by the media and its globalised contents. Basoga of all age groups seek to participate in the global consumer culture they see on TV and on the internet. Low incomes that do not suffice to pay for the desired lifestyle and income disparity lead to dissatisfaction. While making money has become easier than in the past, the high cost of living cancels this effect for many people. This applies especially to farmers, who are the disadvantaged party in liberalised crop trade, from which middlemen and traders profit much more than the mass of producers. Another serious challenge to agricultural production is climate change. The position of Ugandan (industrial and agricultural) producers in competition with international rivals is perceived as unpromising, even in the home market. The sub-theme contains requests to the government to re-introduce regulations and subsidies. According to some expert interviewees, the government itself has realised some of these problems and decided to correct some market failures in the future. From the point of view of a politician and government worker, an expert interviewee described the situation as follows:

> "Yes, it [globalisation] is a double sword, which is affecting our people, but either way, the positives and the negatives. So, the most important thing for us, now, is how do we deal with mitigating the negatives that come with globalisation? Cause we can't stop it." (Expert 10, 2018)

8.2.8 Key findings of the main theme "Busoga's economy under globalisation"

This main theme addresses the first part of my research hypothesis, namely that *everyday economy in Uganda shows signs of penetration by globalisation*. It also provides answers to the research question: *How have people in Busoga experienced changes in their socio-economic environment, which can be traced back to globalisation, in the past 30 years?* The key findings of this main theme are the following:

1. Everyday economy in Busoga shows signs of penetration by globalisation.

Over the past 30 years, Busoga has become a free market economy with liberalised trade in crops and animal products of all kinds, consumer goods, and services; with little state intervention; and without barter trade. This process was initiated and guided by policies of economic liberalisation. Other typical processes of globalisation that can be observed in the region are: the dispersion of technical innovations that facilitate communication and transport; increasing availability and affordability of consumer goods thanks to cheap imports; urbanisation; and climate change. Cost of living and income inequality are increasing (for details, see findings 3 and 4). Beyond that, this study found evidence of the *process of commodification* in Busoga in the shape of former subsistence crops having become cash crops and formerly unmarketable items having become commodities in high demand, e.g., as cattle feed or manure (due to 'zero grazing'). Apart from the spheres of modernisation and commercialisation of agriculture and livestock breeding, this process of commodification also takes place in the sectors of education and health care. Gaining access to those services has become a serious financial challenge to the majority of households in Busoga.

2. The involvement of the residents of Busoga in the global market *as producers* has *reduced*, while their involvement in the global market *as consumers* has *increased.*

Farmers in Busoga have adjusted their production portfolio to the demands of the global market. In fact, the global market demand for products from Busoga has reduced significantly. At the moment, only small quantities of coffee, fish, and fruit can be marketed beyond the neighbouring countries. As a result, the production of unprofitable export products for the global market (cotton and coffee) has been widely replaced by the production of crops for the local, national, and regional markets (the latter referring to trade with neighbouring countries). Those are products like food crops (especially maize), animal products, sugar, and small quantities of industrial goods produced in Jinja town, e.g., brewery products and iron sheets.

The consumption patterns of people in Busoga have likewise been adapted to globalisation to the greatest possible extent, as far as the limited purchasing power of the majority of people in the region allows. However, this was a process that started much earlier than 30 years ago and that was not linear. The respondents of this study have gone through different phases of availability of consumer goods during their lifetime: limited availability (which was after all availability; up to Idi Amin's regime); extreme scarcity (during the times of Idi Amin and their aftermath, i.e., the 1970s and early 1980s); increasing availability; abundance (in the sense of more goods being available than people can afford to buy, not in the sense of extreme abundance that can be observed in the global North). As a result, they appreciate today's high availability of consumer goods and the dense network of shops that reaches even the smallest village. They struggle to participate in the global consumer culture as far as their limited means allow, even if that means taking out loans. It is of particular importance to them to get *their own* things. Practices of sharing and borrowing of the past are being regarded as out-dated (see also chapter 8.3.1). An achievement of globalisation from which even low-income households in Busoga benefit is the import of cheap vehicles[107] and spare parts, mobile phones, and other items for daily use. Yet, the consequences of this consumer behaviour for the lives of the people who produce those cheap items (mainly in Asia) and for the natural environment cannot be examined in the limited scope of this study.

3. Cost of living in Busoga has been increasing sharply.

The cost of living is increasing permanently and more rapidly than the incomes. Due to privatisation, austerity, and corruption in the sectors of education and health care, the greatest challenges households face are educational expenditures followed by health expenditures. Other important matters of expense are high food prices and the desire to purchase consumer goods. The combination of high demand for money to meet those requirements and ready market for farming products makes people who would otherwise be able to survive on their own agricultural production, sell a high portion of their yields and, as a result, suffer from food insecurity. Others sell or rent out their land to sugar cane growers in order to quickly obtain money, yet they end up with the same result, as they spend the money quickly and the loss of land reduces the agricultural production capacity of the household.

4. Social inequality is prevalent and increasing in Busoga.

Incomes of the majority of Busoga's population are low and not likely to increase soon because the profit margins of the popular commercial activities of people in Busoga are low. The majority lives on the production of food crops, which have a very low profit margin, especially given the weak position of farmers in price negotiations with intermediaries in the free market economy. Other income-generating activities in which at least some people can afford to engage include shopkeeping and running small-scale enterprises like maize mills. However, their profit margin is not high, either. Profitable jobs are extremely rare in the region. People with capital they can invest in factories, large-scale agriculture or trade, high-quality education for their children, and high-level health care, can indeed profit from Busoga's liberalised, globalised market economy. The vast majority of the population does not have any capital, so that they do not have a realistic chance of succeeding within this system. In terms of social inequality, Busoga develops typically for a globalised economy, i.e., the income gap grows and access to resources (e.g., land, education and

107 The majority cannot afford them, but uses them in the shape of taxi-busses, -motorcycles, and -bicycles.

health care services) is polarised. As a result, liberalisation has created a socio-economic environment favourable only to elites.

The majority of these findings are congruent with the theoretical framework of this study and can serve as evidence for the penetration of Busoga's economy by globalisation. The findings combined under number 2 are exceptional. At first sight, they appear contradictory to each other and, at the same time, to some elements of the theoretical framework. The finding that the involvement of the residents of Busoga in the global market *as producers* has *reduced*, conflicts with assumptions that globalisation promotes the expansion of the exploitation of natural resources and labour in the global South by the global North (e.g., Glenn 2007; Greig et al. 2007; Stiglitz 2002; in chapter 3.1 of this thesis). It rather seems to confirm the assumption that globalisation produces a steadily increasing global mass of people that is "marginalized" because it has nothing to contribute to global capitalism (Dirlik 2004, 519; see chapter 3.2 of this thesis). With regard to Africa, Samir Amin emphasises how the continent has been integrated in the system since colonial times, rather than 'marginalised' (Amin 2004; see chapter 3.4 of this thesis). As James Ferguson has pointed out, Africa has since colonial times been divided into two categories, while capital concentrates on "[u]sable Africa" and ignores "unusable Africa", based on its own logic regarding which parts are easily and effectively exploitable, e.g., because they are rich in valuable resources and politically unstable (Ferguson 2006, 39-41; see chapter 3.3 of this thesis). Frederick Cooper has laid forth a similar hypothesis, adding to it that the categorisation has changed over time, with capital concentrating on a decreasing number of places in Africa that turned out to be most profitable (Cooper 1993; see chapter 3.3 of this thesis). It appears that, from the perspective of the global North, Busoga has been downgraded from the status of 'usable Africa' (when there was still much demand for Ugandan coffee and cotton) to that of 'unusable Africa'. However, this does not really match with the finding that the involvement of the residents of Busoga in the global market *as consumers* has *increased*. Consumers are not marginal but rather essential to capitalism. Yet, though a few products from Europe or America can be found in shops in Busoga today[108], the majority of products come from Asian countries, especially from China, as several interviewees told me and as I could observe myself. Hence, even the hypothesis that the global North creates markets for its products in the global South (e.g., Stiglitz 2002; see chapter 3.1 of this thesis) applies to Busoga to only a

108 Those are mainly tools, not many household items or consumer goods.

limited extent. Asian suppliers have started to overtake the market, making many products cheaper, i.e., available for people who had not previously been able to afford them.

World-systems analysis can help to understand the situation. Once integrated in the capitalist world-system, a peripheral area fulfils its role in it (see chapters 2.3.2 and 3.4 of this thesis). In this case, the semiperiphery has taken the core's place in relation to the periphery. As explained in chapter 3.1, firms in a capitalist environment must continuously expand in order to remain competitive and to accumulate capital. They need to constantly create "new social wants and needs" in potential customers either in their home markets or in new markets (Glenn 2007, 10-11). This is not limited to firms in core countries of the capitalist world-system. It applies to *all firms in a capitalist environment*. Semiperipheries receive "pressure from core states and [put] pressure on peripheral states", pouring their products on the latter's markets (Wallerstein 2007, 29-30). The semiperipheries must do this in order to at least keep their status – or advance to become a core country (see chapter 2.3.2 of this thesis). After colonialism had accustomed the population of Busoga to cash crop production, the cash economy, and consumer goods, the liberalisation policies of the 1980s and 1990s have opened it up to the market economy. When the Bretton Woods institutions (representing the interests of the global North; see chapter 3) introduced these liberalisation policies, they did not do it with the intention of exploitation, as by that time, Uganda, and especially Busoga, did not have resources in which the global North was interested any longer. However, economic liberalisation was part of the universal project of neoliberal globalisation that was applied to all countries of the global South by its three managers, the IMF, the World Bank, and the WTO (see chapter 3.3). A possible explanation why this was done is Joseph Stiglitz's argument that it was well-intended but "bad economics" (Stiglitz 2002, 17; see chapter 3.3 of this thesis). This may be the case for some individuals within those institutions, yet given the high political influence and the number of highly educated staff of the three above-mentioned institutions, I rather suspect an intention behind their policies than a simple error. I support the view presented in chapter 2.2.2 of this thesis that the imposition of neoliberal economic policies on the global South was an act of "kicking away the ladder" (Chang 2002) under the unofficial policy that Rick Rowden calls: "No More NICs!"[109] (Rowden 1999, 156), i.e., making sure that no more peripheral countries advance too far within

109 NICs = newly industrialised countries

the economic world order and become serious competitors to the global North, as some NICs (or semiperipheries) have previously done (see also Cooper 1993; Kiiza 2008; Teivainen 2009; in the same chapter of this thesis).

Despite the global North's lack of interest in Busoga, neoliberal globalisation still had many effects on the region. One effect is that the role of exploiters of local resources and of the local consumer market has been filled again – by actors satisfied with lower profit margins. Exploitation of local resources, especially land and labour for the production of food crops, animal products, and sugar cane, is being done by local forces, i.e., Ugandan players and some from neighbouring countries. The local consumer market is mainly supplied by the semiperiphery, i.e., producers from Asian countries. Some products sold in local shops are also produced in factories within Uganda, whose ownership is diverse: Ugandan, Asian, and various nationalities from the global North. However, this is no longer the main field of intervention of the global North in Uganda. It can rather be found in the sector of big infrastructure projects in which firms from the global North are still involved, though competition from China is also arising in this field. For Busoga, this means that the players have changed and the emphasis has changed – from production to consumption – yet the game has remained the same: globalisation.

This is Busoga's specific form (or, as Ferguson put it, 'mutation') of globalisation. As other key findings are showing, more typical features of globalisation can also be found in the region. Busoga's role as a peripheral region in the capitalist world-system explains why, though the population is doing better in comparison with the catastrophic period of 1971-1986, it is not doing better in comparison with the time prior to that period. Neoliberal developmentalists and globalists may have expected economic liberalisation to improve the situation. Based on the argumentation of critics of the global North's domination over the global South, an amelioration of the situation because of the withdrawal of the global North may have been expected. Yet, the firm position of Uganda and Busoga as peripheral areas of the capitalist world-system has even been consolidated through the IMF-led economic recovery programmes, which aligned Uganda's economy to neoliberal orthodoxy. As a result, the opportunities for exploitation of the residents of Busoga as producers and consumers for purposes of capital accumulation have been consolidated as well. The role of the exploiters has just been passed from one player in the system to another, who is working on his own advancement within the system. This ostensibly contradictory key finding corresponds with James Ferguson's argument that globalisation theorists from neither political camp write a lot about Africa because the latter fails to fulfil their expectations. While neoliberals wonder about the complete failure of structural adjustment programmes to make Africa join the winners of globalisation, some supporters of the 'anti-globalisation' movement equally miss a basis for their usual argumentation, e.g., problems arising from "being overrun with Western factories and consumer goods" (Ferguson 2006, 26, see also 21). On the one hand, Ferguson paints a rather simplified picture of the alter-globalisation movement. On the other hand, I share his experience that Africa does not fit in the usual theoretical frameworks very well, especially when the researcher is limited to a single framework. Hence, he may have a point in assuming that this phenomenon discourages research on Africa while this research is desperately needed if globalisation ought to be understood. According to Ferguson, research on the specific forms of globalisation that are evolving in Africa "may in fact reveal key features of how the 'global' works today, and how it might work in the future" (ibid., 48).

In summary, the key findings of this main theme suggest that the living conditions of people in Busoga have changed in the past 30 years due to a variety of factors, of which not all, yet quite a number could be traced to globalisation. The global North has lost interest in Busoga's export products, such that production is mainly for the local, national, and regional market (i.e., for neighbouring countries). As a result, the production portfolio has been adapted to the demand of those markets, from cotton and coffee to food crops (especially maize) and animal products. Though the involvement of the region's residents in the global market as producers has reduced, their involvement as consumers is constantly increasing. Yet, their suppliers have changed, from the global North to primarily Asian countries. Though the buyers of its raw materials and the suppliers of its shops are new, Busoga's role remains the same: a peripheral area within the capitalist world-system. On the one hand, in comparison with the disastrous times of civil war, economic war, and short-term governments from the early 1970s up to the mid-1980s, there have been significant improvements in many sectors, e.g., availability of commodities, potential sources of livelihood (selling food crops, running shops or small-scale enterprises) and general security. However, several negative impacts of globalisation on the livelihood of people have been found. Those are climate change, aggravating income inequality, sharply increasing cost of living, processes of commodification (which increase cost of living and investments required for farming), and a weak position of farmers within the free market economy, while farming is the major source of income in Busoga. Chapter 8.3 will examine activities of the Social and Solidarity Economy (SSE) as possible solutions for some of the above-described challenges in everyday life posed by globalisation. For instance, it has been shown above that some people in Busoga react to the conflict arising from sharply increasing cost of living and desires for consumption on the one hand and low incomes on the other hand by turning to groups, especially savings and credit groups and small consumer associations (see chapters 8.3.3 and 8.3.4 for details).

8.3 SSE – Social and Solidarity Economy

This main theme provides answers to the research questions: *What kind of alternative economic activities based on solidarity do or did people in Busoga practise? Did those activities persist in spite of, dissolve because of, or emerge as a reaction to globalisation? Do people consider such activities helpful in their situation, and why or why not?* The following six sub-sections present the sub-themes of this main theme. Each of them concludes on a short summary of the respective sub-theme. They are followed by a presentation of the key findings of this main theme as a whole (chapter 8.3.7). In all these sub-sections, I use some information from chapters 6 and 7 to supplement information that was fragmentary in the interviews. Beyond that, I apply elements from the theoretical framework of this study (chapters 2, 3, and 4) to the results of this main theme. In the first sub-section (8.3.1), autochthonous solidarity structures in Busoga are being examined. In the following four sub-sections (chapters 8.3.2 to 8.3.5), I portray 'modern' solidarity groups. The latter are not specific to Busoga. The term 'modern' is used here in the absence of a better word that encompasses the meanings of being both *relatively* new and influenced by transformations that affect local culture from outside. Some of those groups have their origins somewhere else than in local culture (e.g., having been introduced by NGOs from the global North). Others have their origin in local culture, but they are a new version of the 'traditional' variant that evolved because capitalist development changed the social structures in a way that hinders the implementation of the older variants (for details see below, especially chapter 8.3.7, key finding 2). However, this should not create the impression that 'modern' solidarity structures are either more or less valuable than autochthonous ones. The distinction between them is just a matter of fact, without judgement. These four sub-themes encompass an evaluation of the respective kinds of groups in terms of some of the criteria for SSE-activities presented in chapter 4.2.1 of this thesis. In my view, the criteria proposed by Michelle Williams and Norman Chipakupaku capture the most essential characteristics of SSE without demanding too much and risking missing interesting approaches. The minimum criteria to be fulfilled are the common characteristics shared by the *Social Economy* (Williams 2014, 46-47) *and* the *Solidarity Economy* according to Michelle Williams, namely „cooperation, democratic decision making, collective ownership, bottom-up processes, caring and sharing" (ibid., 59). The principles of the *People's Economy*, which Chipakupaku defines as the African version of *Social and Solidarity Economy* (see chapter 4.2.1 of this thesis; or see: Chipakupaku 2008, 138-139), complement Williams' criteria. Those principles are: 1. joining economic efforts in order to earn a living, not to make profits; 2. being run by and for the sake of the local population; 3. creating local economic cycles that provide employment to locals, keeping money and facilities at their disposition; 4. preserving nature for future generations (Chipakupaku 2008, 138). Beyond that, I evaluate the alternative potential of the groups. In chapter 8.3.6, I present the general experience with solidarity groups about which respondents spoke. This section on the main theme "SSE" concludes with the key findings of this main theme (chapter 8.3.7).

8.3.1 Autochthonous[110] solidarity structures survive partly

As elaborated in chapter 4, SSE is a modern phenomenon and I want to avoid using clichés of an allegedly 'traditional African society' that is

110 I used the word 'traditional' – or in Lusoga the word for 'traditional' and 'cultural' alike, 'kya bughangwa' (or 'kya buwangwa') – during the interviews to create a common understanding with the interviewees. The word 'autochthonous', which I prefer to use (see chapter 2.4, headword "Traditional"), could have been incomprehensible to them, as it is to the majority of people who have not yet dealt with the related discussion. It is a technical term. What is more, while 'traditional' can have a negative connotation when used by people from the global North ('backward'), for the people in Busoga, it has a positive meaning. Something 'traditional' is created by the Basoga themselves and belongs to their identity, whereas the counterpart, 'modern' describes things that may be desirable but that come from outside and are not their own creations. Their lifeworlds do not only contain both of those aspects but also current ones, which have been developed by themselves. However, as this is not a cultural but an economic analysis, I cannot take the discussion beyond this

still based on reciprocity or a kind of cultural solidarity. I rather want to present a differentiated picture of today's Busoga, with autochthonous as well as endogenous aspects, new and old ones. Nevertheless, autochthonous solidarity structures are important for this study. On the one hand, they can be an indicator for testing the hypotheses that globalisation "broke down community ties" (Escobar 2012, 22; see chapter 2.2.3 of this thesis) and leads to "the increasing commodification of social relationships" (Ziai 2017, 106; see chapter 3.3. of this thesis). On the other hand, the existence of autochthonous solidarity structures in a community favour the acceptance of modern forms of SSE (Develtere 2008; Thomas 2015; see chapters 4.1 and 4.2.2 of this thesis). Consequently, I did not take for granted that solidarity structures or groups about which respondents spoke were 'traditional' or autochthonous structures. Instead, I asked respondents explicitly about such kinds of solidarity structures in contrast to 'modern groups', i.e., SSE activities.

To date, autochthonous solidarity structures have been reacting to globalisation in a variety of ways. While some such structures have been almost eradicated by globalisation, others have transformed in order to adjust to it and a few even flourish under globalisation. By far the most important solidarity structure for the respondents of this study is burial support. Death is omnipresent and dealing with the loss of a relative is emotionally and also financially and practically demanding. Burial support exists in three forms: two autochthonous forms (clan support and village support) and a modern form (Muno Mukabi). While I address the first two within this sub-theme, the latter of these is described in a section of its own (chapter 8.3.5). Almost every person in Busoga is served by one of them, some even by more than one. This is not unusual. Burial support is a burning issue in many African countries and takes various shapes. For instance, Patrick Develtere, though essentially sceptical about the autochthonous roots of solidarity groups in Africa, counts "burial societies" among the activities that "in most countries have always involved large parts of the population" (Develtere 2008, 2; see chapter 4.1 of this thesis). While this seems to refer to rather small-scale, autochthonous activities, Ngewnya Barbara Ntombi describes burial societies in Botswana, of which some operate on a high professional and financial level and are officially registered (Ntombi 2004).

---

clarification of terms. Hence, when I quote interviewees directly or indirectly or when I use the word in a context where this distinction between 'ours' and 'theirs' is important, I use the word 'traditional'. In my interpretation, I use 'autochthonous'.

She explains that having to bury a related person is a socially and financially sensitive issue to people of all income brackets (ibid., 16-17). The latter applies to Uganda as well, as will be further explained below. The social institution of the *clan* [111], which used to be the most important social institution in Busoga and used to have many functions beyond burial support, has lost a good part of its influence. Another autochthonous form of solidarity is the culture of *sharing and giving for free*. It has been terminated to a great extent, though not yet completely, by the changes in everyday life brought about by globalisation. Other collective activities discussed with the respondents are *rotating farming support* and a phenomenon that I have termed *'Christmas groups'*: A group of people pools money in order to buy an animal that will be slaughtered on a special holiday. Neither the respondents, nor my translators, nor other people I asked about it in Busoga could think of a name for that practice. As I needed a handy name for it for coding and as it occurs most frequently (though not exclusively) around Christmas, I called it 'Christmas groups'. It is the only form of autochthonous solidarity structures that flourishes under globalisation. In the following, I present in detail the above-mentioned forms of autochthonous solidarity structures.

Sharing and giving

In the past, people in Busoga used to share farming inputs and foodstuff among themselves. A person could go to a neighbour to ask for seeds or cow dung that could serve as manure. It would be given to him or her without further obligations. Seven respondents said that it is still done that way. According to two of them, the giver expects a favour in return at some point in the future. This is the common principle of reciprocity. In contrast to that, ten respondents said that this is a system of the past and that today, nobody would give anything for free, as it was said in the following example from Buyende District:

> "There, previously, at times, like seeds, you could go to your neighbours' and you request that, 'eh (affirmative), help me with your seeds and I plant something', mm (affirmative). But, nowadays, things

111 While this term has negative connotations in some settings and is often replaced by other terms like 'extended family' or 'kinship network', I use it because the Basoga themselves use it, with positive connotations (identity, belonging, social protection; see below and chapter 6.2.1).

turned into money, (s)he can't just give you anything." (Main 10, 2017, translation by E.K. and N.H.)

The sentiment expressed in this last sentence was typical among respondents. Several other respondents made statements like "now, everybody knows that everything is for money" (Main 19, 2017, translation by E.K. and K.M.). Food crop production has changed from a subsistence activity to a business (see chapters 6.2.4, 7.2, and 8.2.1); hence, farming inputs have become merchandise. When asked why people no longer give such things to their neighbours for free, respondents explained that on the one hand, farmers prefer selling their products that can be re-used as inputs (especially cow dung, sometimes seeds or seedlings) to giving them away for free and seeing somebody else make money from them after harvesting his or her crops. On the other hand, the marketability of foodstuff made people insist on property rights about which they had previously not cared much. Three ways in which new markets for certain items have been created in Busoga in the last 30 years could be traced in the data: a) turning commons into private property; b) formerly useless items becoming marketable thanks to new functions; c) commercialisation of food crops and animal products. I address these, next.

a) Turning commons into private property has created scarcity and, consequently, demand. Respondents gave the concrete examples of fruit and vegetables. While fruit used to be commons in the past, nowadays, every fruit tree is the private property of a person, who, according to respondents, does not hesitate to call the police in case someone takes fruit from his or her tree. A representative of Jinja District traced this change to the circumstance that "everything, as of now, there's a value attached. Yes. Thirty years ago, people just pass by and somebody picks a passion fruit from your tree. But these days, you'll be arrested" (Expert 8, 2017). His formulation "your tree" suggests that, even if in theory the tree has always been the property of a person because it grows on his or her land, that person has only recently begun caring about those property rights. Private property rights are among the "key institutions" being promoted in the scope of capitalist development (see e.g., Chang 2002, 1; Wolf 2018, 25-26, 46-47) and neoliberal globalisation (Altvater/ Mahnkopf 2002, 263). Only if the fruit tree owner has exclusive rights to her tree can she profit from it. Otherwise, there would be no commodity to sell (as fruit had been eaten) and no demand, that is, no market for the commodity (as everybody could eat fruit for free). Only when private property has created scarcity and, consequently, demand, is there a market. However, in a place where purchasing power is extremely low, profits remain minimal, whereas (potential) customers are endangered by malnutrition because they cannot afford to buy appropriate quantities of healthy food. With regard to land, it is first and foremost the high population growth that has made people insist on property rights. In the past, nobody cared about other people grazing their animals on his land, as there was more than enough and it was fertile. As described in detail in chapter 8.2.2, shortage of land is increasingly becoming a problem in Busoga due to population growth, migration, and sugar cane production. Land has been turned from private property that has been used as commons (with the owners not caring about it) into private property that is being protected. Shortage of land has contributed significantly to the commodification of certain items. The following paragraph examines the latter in detail.

b) New functions attach value to formerly useless items. This aspect correlates with the preceding one. Shortage of land forces the owners of farm animals to keep the latter in paddocks or cowsheds. The 'zero grazing' strategy has been introduced by NGOs in order to teach Ugandan farmers how to keep exotic cattle breeds efficiently and how to use their excrement as manure (see chapter 7.2 for details) – the latter being known and done prior to the introduction of this strategy but often not necessary because the land was still fertile. However, respondents reported that shortage of land was the factor that led this strategy to success in Busoga (see chapter 8.2.2). As a result, people must provide their farm animals with food and water, whereas in the past they simply needed to accompany them as they wandered around, grazing and drinking from rivers, lakes, and swamps. This has introduced the new concept of fodder, attaching economic value to (guinea) grass and the left-overs of plantain plants after harvest. A main interviewee who had moved from Jinja to Buyende, compared the two locations in that respect. He reported from both of them that cattle keepers had started to buy cattle feed because of *zero grazing*, as this extract demonstrates:

> "Now, in Jinja, mm (considering), I have been rearing cattle, but now, 'zero grazing' came in, we even started buying banana stems, grass, that elephant grass, we started buying them in Jinja also, even the banana stem, they buy it for money. […] The banana stem/ Eh (affirmative), when you have cut from it the bunch of bananas, it fell there, you buy it and cut it into pieces, for the cow to eat. Mm (affirmative), and the elephant grass." (Main 1, 2017, translation by E.K. and N.H.)

At the same time, three factors came together to make manure another marketable product: One is the very development described above, as it facilitates – and even makes necessary – the collecting of dung that accumulates in paddocks and cowsheds. Parallel to this, soils became exhausted by overuse, due to shortage of land. At the same time, extension workers and NGOs encouraged farmers to use manure to increase their yield. Those three factors complemented each other perfectly. Dung, which used to be a waste product given free of charge to the few people who used it as manure, has become a commodity in high demand. A farmer and animal keeper from Jinja District explained her business with cow dung as follows:

> "[...] now, these cows are on 'zero grazing'. You may find yourself when, within six months, you have like two tonnes of cow dung. You have not been able to use all of it, neighbours take it and they do what? They use it. [...] Okay, they buy it. [...] Eh (affirmative), it is also there as one of the business items." (Main 29, 2017, translation by E.K. and K.M.)

Cow urine has likewise become a commodity, since it has been discovered to be a good ingredient for an organic insecticide (e.g., against the 'army worm' that represents a serious challenge to maize farmers). A landscaper from Jinja District who does some additional farming at home described the way he deals with that product as follows:

> "In the past, they were not there. But this time, it is there, so/ to go to the neighbour, you buy there cow urine/ [...] Now, like us, we have cows here, when even the urine collection pit is there. So, while that urine (inc.) your friends, you bring. [...] You go and put in ash, you put in red pepper, you put in tobacco, you pour it on what? On your fruit. And it survives." (Main 24a, 2017, translation by E.K. and K.M.)

c) The liberalisation of the crop market has adjusted it to the trends of the international crop market. Busoga's so-called 'traditional cash crops', coffee and cotton, are no longer profitable. They have given way to the new dominant cash crop, sugar cane, and especially to trade in food crops and animal products (see chapter 8.2.1). For instance, a farmer and stockbreeder from Buyende District explained that:

> "Uh (considering), what caused that, it is like someone is looking for development of his/her living conditions because (s)he has his/her seeds of groundnuts, but if (s)he just gives you, (s)he will not afford to buy a dress, or just giving you for free, (s)he can't go and buy a plate

> in the market. If (s)he just gives freely, (s)he can't buy a bicycle, if (s)he just gives it to you, (s)he cannot afford to access what (s)he wants. So, it changed in terms of money that, 'my colleague, I have my seed of groundnuts, maize, soya bean, and other things, so, give me money for those things, and I also buy what I want'. Eh (considering), terms like that, devel/ they are after developing, development. That is why they have changed purely." (Main 8, 2017, translation by E.K. and N.H.)

After all, in the past, food crops were planted for subsistence, only. Any extra produce was of no use, which made it easier to share. Today, there is no 'surplus' or 'leftovers'. Every little bit that would be given to other people for free would reduce the profit margin, which is already low for small- to medium-scale farmers. The above-described developments, in combination with a high population growth and other factors (see chapters 8.2.2 and 8.2.5) led to commodities being hard-fought and living conditions being demanding for a large part of the population. As there are many people in most families, with many needs, sharing with others and giving out things for free has become difficult if not impossible for many people living in Busoga. When respondents spoke about their fellows being into money, they were not necessarily speaking about greed but rather about the new structures of everyday life in which money has come to play a central role, while attaining that money is not easy (see chapter 8.2.5). What is more, problems like shortage of land, loss of soil fertility, climate change, and pests limit the production capacities of farmers (see chapter 8.2.2). A main interviewee from Jinja District compared the situation of past and present times as follows:

> "In the past, they used to be there: While you go at your friend's, even if they would be beans, there, they were in plenty, when (s)he says/ when (s)he says that, 'you go and get'/ [...] Iih (affirmative), while (s)he says, 'Uh (consenting), plantain, you go there and you cut the plantain you want and you carry.' But now, it is not there. [...] If you go to get it, (s)he is burdened, (s)he has got little, and yet even him/her, it does not/ sometimes, at home (s)he is seeing that, also, it is not enough. So, (s)he decides, (s)he refuses to give you. Because him-/ herself, also, his/her family, is likewise using it sparingly, for him/her to see that (s)he does what? It sustains them. And yet, again, if (s)he will share it, again, (s)he also, the other day, how will (s)he do?" (Main 26, 2017, translation by E.K. and K.M.)

As a result, everybody tries to get his or her own things in order to be independent of the decreasing generosity of others. Some respondents, including this teacher from Kamuli District, stated that borrowing or sharing has become embarrassing:

> "Mm (considering), again now, there in the past, we use things like those, you can go to your friend's, and you get fire. Now, these days, a person seeing you going at your friend's' with a shard to get fire, now, it is very embarrassing. There, in the past, when a person goes and requests for salt. But these days, mh-mh (negative), this modernisation[112] here, everyone, you have to work for yourself. And there, in the past, we used to borrow even clothes. But now, a-ah (negative), no, a person has to work, to have your own at home. Because of this modernisation that came about." (Main 11, 2017, translation by E.K. and K.M.)

Other respondents claimed that, thanks to new developments, borrowing has become unnecessary. One main interviewee, a farmer, talked about new technologies making borrowing obsolete, e.g., artificial insemination in animal breeding replaced 'borrowing' a bull or a cock from the neighbour. Some others referred to increasing incomes, which allow people to buy their own things instead of borrowing, as in the following example:

> "Mm (affirmative), the other times, while a person goes and requests for salt, (s)he requests for a knife, (s)he requests for fire. This time, it's very difficult for a person to go do what? [...] Request. The majority of the people can get things themselves. [...] The income increased. Mm (affirmative), every person can reach for him-/herself a small thing to be used in the home." (Main 29, 2017, translation by E.K. and K.M.)

This quote can serve as an explanation for the previous one. Borrowing has become embarrassing because people are expected to have their own things. Those who do not have their own things are considered poor. An earlier[113] quote from an expert interviewee bears repeating here: "you must BE SEEN carrying, uh (considering), a cell phone in your hand, hm (seeking confirmation)? Then, they think you're okay" (Expert 6, 2017). In other words, then, they assume that you are not poor. Globalisation has increased the incomes of some people and has simultaneously brought a new preoccupation with one's prestige that does not allow people to admit lack of certain items.

In summary, sharing, giving things to friends or neighbours for free, and borrowing used to be common practices in Busoga until recently.

112 The word "modernisation" was said in English, both times.

113 See sub-theme "Other effects of globalisation on life in Busoga", chapter 8.2.7.

Most of these practices are phasing out, for a variety of reasons. One of those reasons is the commercialisation of food crop farming, which turned foodstuff and certain farming inputs, e.g., manure, into commodities. Commercialisation also led to the implementation of property rights (e.g., on fruit trees) on what used to be commons that have recently been discovered as assets in commodity production. Shortage of land and the 'zero grazing' strategy have not only fuelled the above-described developments, they have also attached value to formally useless items such as plants that are given as fodder to animals that used to graze freely. Though incomes are rising, respondents have the impression that the fight for survival becomes harder as the need for money increases constantly. Though sharing, borrowing, and giving for free would be helpful under these circumstances, they are actually phasing out – apart from a few exceptions. People struggle to acquire their own things, such that they do not have to depend on others who might reject their requests or consider them poor.

Clan support

One important aspect of which I was unaware prior to starting the research and that was emphasised strongly by some respondents and other people with whom I conversed in Busoga, is the role of clans in the lives of the Basoga (see also chapter 6.2.1). A Kisoga clan is "a patrilineal descent group, including all those who recognized a common ancestor through male lines" (Cohen 1972, 6). In the course of the interviews it turned out that, depending on the respective clan, these structures may still be very strong and even the most important form of solidarity and cooperation that people know. Modern forms of solidarity and cooperation might even be unnecessary, or merely be weak supplementations. An expert interviewee who is very engaged in cultural issues of Busoga explained:

> "Actually, our culture stands on the principle of solidarity. People coming together, clans. [...] There is a clan structure, which brings people together, who work common, who have to behave in a certain way, hm (seeking confirmation)? And who have to live in a certain way. And those clans are the basis." (Expert 10, 2018)

Clan affiliation leads to certain obligations but also to the right by birth to enjoy the clan's protection (to differing extents, depending on the rules in the respective clan and the individual's position within it). In case a man dies, the clan is supposed to take care of his wife, or wives, and children. In that context, the above-cited respondent added:

> "But otherwise, every child produced in a family remains a family child and a family responsibility. And that's the basis of marriage. When you come to introduce[114], you introduce to the family, to the entire/ actually, the entire clan. [...] It's a major, major, major thing in Busoga." (Expert 10, 2018)

However, in many cases, especially in places with a lot of migration, the clan structures have been destroyed to varying extents. People who migrate do *not necessarily* lose touch with their clan, though it happens. The most important support people receive from their clan is assistance for burying a deceased relative. Several respondents spoke about this point. For instance, a main interviewee from Buyende commented about the clan: "In terms of losing someone, they help you. They bury you" (Main 2, 2017, translation by E.K. and N.H.). As this extract shows and others in the data set confirm, the clan is supposed to help both when a member dies and when a member is bereaved of a relative (who must not necessarily be from the same clan, e.g., as is the case with a spouse, who is never from the same clan). However, when asked about any other support from the clan, she noted that, in her area, "it is not there" (ibid.). In the past, the whole clan used to take care of every member in case (s)he was facing a problem, for instance becoming a widow or an orphan. However, several interviewees deplored that today, nobody takes care of orphans and widows any longer. Another main interviewee from Buyende echoed this observation: "It's not there, they just talk, it's not there, no one fulfils the promises" (Main 9, 2017, translation by E.K. and N.H.). A main interviewee from Kamuli District elaborated: "They, orphans and widows, are so badly off. They are deserted, were left there, and badly off, the majority are not well, and there is a lot of poverty" (Main 22, 2017, translation by E.K. and K.M.). In those cases, modern forms of solidarity and cooperation can be particularly important because the old forms have been lost. For example, in such areas, I often observed that autochthonous burial support has been replaced by Muno Mukabi groups, which copy the old system while they are a modern phenomenon with its own rules (see corresponding sub-theme: chapter 8.3.5).

In summary, clan structures were the original solidarity structures in Busoga. Over time, their importance started to pale in comparison to the

114 "Introduce" meaning to present your future spouse to the family.

past. This process appears to be moving at varying speed in different clans, depending on many factors, e.g., migration and a changing social environment with new values and priorities. There are also internal reasons like conflicts within clans, as explained in chapter 6.2.1. The most important support a clan can give to its members – and at the same time the kind of support that is still most frequently given by clans – is burial support. I discuss burial support further in the following paragraphs. Other forms of clan support still exist in some places but have decreased significantly over the past decades.

Burial support

When asked about "traditional" forms of solidarity or mutual support, the majority of main interviewees immediately began talking about burial support with the name *obutaka*[115] or *abataka.*[116] *Obutaka* works as follows: A person who lost a relative receives support from all residents of the village. The village residents' obligation respondents most frequently mentioned – and which is always fulfilled by women – is to bring food, water, and firewood for the funeral service. The original practice, which is still implemented in many places, involves all members of the extended family and of the village community ceasing work and attending the funeral service. An expert interviewee described it thus:

115 As noted based on the literature review in chapter 6.2.1, the word *obutaka* has an older meaning: It refers to 'ancestral lands', which were associated with particular clans (Nayenga 2002, 44) and could even refer to the very land on which the members of a particular clan *buried their ancestors* (Cohen 1972, 16). The latter appears to create the connection between the old and the new meaning. Both my translators told me that 'abataka' means 'village residents'. This translation is confirmed by Fountain's *Lusoga-English Dictionary*, which defines the singular form "mutaka" as "resident of a village" but also as "citizen" (Gulere 2009, 172). MK's *Lusoga-English Dictionary and English-Lusoga Dictionary* defines "mutaka" as "citizen", "landholder", or "peasant" (Gonza 2007, 152). This word is closely related to the word "eitaka", which means "land" (Gulere 2009, 355; Gonza 2007, 35) or "soil" (Gonza 2007, 35). The MK dictionary confirms the meaning of "obutaka" as "the basic source of support as of a village community", among other, related ones like "community membership" or "society" (Gonza 2007, 190). The Fountain dictionary rather sticks to the original meanings like "family estate" or "ancestral place" and adds "citizenship" as the only abstract interpretation (Gulere 2009, 22).

116 The support itself is called obutaka and the group of people practicing it is called abataka.

> "We even have what we call butaka, where people come together to solve misfortune, like death. Is a communal thing here. [...] Because if somebody passes, we don't expect anybody to be digging[117] that day. They bring food, they bring [...]." (Expert 10, 2018)

In the past, the mourning period could take several days or weeks but today, it has been shortened significantly due to the need to go back to work. Nevertheless, even if the mourners stay for only one day, hosting them is expensive. In addition to that, the bereaved has other expenses like the coffin and the priest. Men from the village used to dig the grave and build a shade where the visitors could sit. Today, they do this occasionally but more often they contribute money and someone gets paid for rendering those services. As a respondent from Jinja District explained: "the woman brings the food, the man brings money" (Main 17, 2017, translation by E.K. and K.M.). The following example is the abridged version of a typical description of *obutaka* as it was given to me various times, here by a main interviewee from Buyende District:

> "Mm (affirmative), it is there, the residents cultivate, if you get a problem, they bring for you food, they fetch for you water to add on the food, they also put vegetables and firewood, mm (affirmative), when you have got a problem.[118] [...] We, women, we cook food and fetch water. [...] Money is for men. [...] it is also mandatory [...] In the past, they took like those/ they just take firewood, food, water, and also the shade, when they make tarpaulins, men used to cut grass, they reach there and mount tarpaulins, mm (affirmative)." (Main 10, 2017, translation by E.K. and N.H.)

The above-mentioned clan support in case of death is the oldest form of burial support in Busoga. *Obutaka* has copied its activities from this kind of support. Nevertheless, all respondents who spoke about *obutaka* consider it 'traditional'. When asked since when she knew the *obutaka* system, a respondent from Buyende answered: "By the time I was born,

---

117 'To dig' is a typical description in Lusoga for working in the field or cultivating the land, such that many Basoga even express it that way when they speak English, as is the case here.

118 'To get a problem' (okufuna ekizibu) is a typical expression used by Basoga to paraphrase the case of death of a person, especially a person for whose burial one is responsible (a relative or a spouse). A more direct way of saying it, which was also used by the respondents frequently, is 'okufirwa', meaning 'losing (someone)'.

it was there" (Main 2, 2017, translation by E.K. and N.H.). Obutaka also shares many characteristics with clan support, e.g., being obligatory for the target group and encompassing a taboo on working on the day of the burial. The modern *Muno Mukabi* groups do not have any of those characteristics. In the following extract, a main interviewee from Buyende explained that the difference between the local Muno Mukabi group and the local obutaka is voluntariness:

> "Eh (affirmative), agreement, coming together for providing help of such kind. But again, the residents [abataka], we have a difference/ [...] That it is a must that this area [...] every resident of it is responsible for being a resident, if (s)he does not work hand in hand with us, we blame him/her for staying with us and (s)he doesn't do what? That is there as a law because of his/her being a resident in this area. But the other group we are in, it was formed by agreement [...]" (Main 5, 2017, translation by E.K. and N.H.)

While membership in a Muno Mukabi group is voluntary, not participating in obutaka would result in conflicts with the community. The main difference between obutaka and clan support is the condition for membership. Nowadays, obutaka still exists in some places, while in others it has taken a new shape as a Muno Mukabi group (see chapter 8.3.5) or again given way to the more flexible clan system. This has a lot to do with migration, as in obutaka, membership depends on residency. In the past, everyone died in the place where (s)he was born. As a result, it was easy for the village community to cater for the burial. Now that people are constantly moving and often live far from their ancestral home for decades, this has become difficult. Nevertheless, taking care of a dead person is a big challenge because there are very few funeral services, they are way too expensive for most of the population, and there is no insurance or governmental assistance on which to rely in case of a relative's death. One possible solution is the clan system. In former times, the clan system coincided with obutaka because the clan was living in one place, though at times, a village was a smaller unit than the area of residence of the whole clan. Today, practically all clans have their members more or less scattered across Busoga or even across the country. It varies between just a few young people living in towns (because they are looking for work there) and the majority of clan members having left the ancestral place. As a result of the dispersal of its members, the clan tries to reach out beyond the boundaries of the village, obliging each member of the clan to pay a contribution to the so-called 'bank' (a treasurer who keeps the money) for burial support, regardless of where the member lives. In the following extract, an expert interviewee from Kamuli District explained the system in detail:

> "For example, if this is your ancestral home and this is where you're likely to be buried, when a death occurs within that community, even if you are in Kampala, uh (considering), you send a contribution. How is that contribution done? There is a leadership. You have a chairperson, a secretary, and a treasurer. So, what we do, those who don't live within the village, you come and deposit, they call it banking, by the way. You put money, you deposit your money with the treasurer. And they have a rate, uh (considering), which they decide and it varies from community to community. So, when somebody dies, they look at your account, they deduct what is due and they pay. So, you are okay. So, even IF/ EVEN/ even when we bring, we've started bringing funeral services and so on, still, this thing must work. For that's where everybody gets assured." (Expert 6, 2017)

The latest approach to burial support is 'Muno Mukabi', which has nothing to do with the affected person's origin but borrows the focus on residency from obutaka. The membership is voluntary (distinguishing it from the other two systems). As I have classified it as an SSE activity, 'Muno Mukabi' has its own sub-theme under which more information about it can be found.

Against that background, burial support in Busoga is a typical example of a phenomenon described by Bruno Baeriswyl: In many African countries, "various forms of *collaboration within the socio-economic system of the extended family* played an important role" until the "*dissolution of traditional social structures* brought about further development of these collaborations into new organisational forms with a co-operative nature" ("… mit genossenschaftlichem Charakter"; Baeriswyl 1988, 17-18; translation and emphases by E.K.). Baeriswyl uses "autochthonous savings and credit associations" as an example for such groups, which evolved out of the need to "face the requirements of a changing social and economic order" (ibid., 18; translation by E.K.). Burial support in Busoga has gone through this very process. It started out as an unquestioned responsibility of the clan towards its members. Migration and other social changes caused the first transformation into burial support at the village level (obutaka). As the interviewees called that village support 'traditional' and noted that it was there before they were born, it can be assumed that the changes in the first half of the twentieth century led to the transformation. These included epidemics that forced people to leave certain areas for a period of time and the establishment of Jinja town with its employment opportunities in numerous factories (see chapter 6.2). As a result, there was a lot of migration within the region during that time. Presumably, this caused the dissociation between clan support and village support, whereas in the far past, the two coincided, as most people were born and died in the same place. Eventually, the continuous "dissolution of traditional social structures" (Baeriswyl 1988, 17-18; translation by E.K.) caused by globalisation in the subsequent decades led to further transformation into the so-called Muno Mukabi groups. They have been identified as a new form of burial support, as they are based on voluntary membership rather than cultural obligation.

Chart 5: Comparison of membership criteria for different kinds of burial support in Busoga

Comparison of membership criteria for different kinds of burial support in Busoga			
Membership criterion	**clan support**	**obutaka**	**Muno Mukabi**
compulsory	yes	yes	no
residency	no	yes	yes
by birth	yes	no	no

In summary, burial support is one of the most important manifestations of solidarity and mutual support for the respondents of this study. Consequently, it exists in many variations: 1. an autochthonous form, which is losing ground due to changing living conditions (clan support); 2. a newer but still autochthonous form that arose as an attempt to adjust to the new living conditions, especially migration (obutaka); 3. a yet newer form, which fulfils the criteria for an SSE activity (Muno Mukabi groups). The differences can mainly be found in the membership criteria, plus one criterion that distinguishes the two autochthonous forms from Muno Mukabi groups: a taboo on working the day of burial. It is difficult to distinguish the different forms from each other based on activities undertaken, as the newer forms build on the older ones and even the older forms have started to transform over time and integrate money in the support given to the bereaved. As the death of a relative or spouse is part of daily reality in Busoga and as there is no help in sight for dealing with this difficult situation – neither from the government, nor from any players in the market economy – people keep up their mutual support in any form that suits their current life situation.

Other collective activities (rotating farming support, 'Christmas groups')

Rotating farming support refers to a group of people (e.g., the residents of a village or a neighbourhood) agreeing to work in one member's field on one day, in another member's field on the other and so on, until all members have harvested successfully. It used to be an autochthonous practice that was formalised by agricultural government programmes in the 1960s. Some interviewees call it "kampu" (camp) because they refer to that formalised version. For instance, a main interviewee from Kamuli District said that "they were many: camp. […] when ten people work in the field, then/ they work in the field of the other one, and they work in the field of the other one. […] But they faded away" (Main 22, 2017, translation by E.K. and K.M.). It makes sense that a practice that was carried out without reflection until then remained with the name of its formalised version. Moreover, the majority of interviewees was still young in the 1960s and does not remember very well the time prior to that. Consequently, it is quite possible that they actually saw only the formalised groups, not the original ones. Many remember those 'camps' but few can name a place where it is still practiced. Where it is practiced, it is usually a marginal activity of a formally organised group (e.g., a savings and credit group), not as a cultural practice. The latter was already destroyed by the (unsuccessful) attempts to formalise it in the 1960s, according to an expert interviewee. One of his colleagues blamed it on the harder living conditions in the free market economy where everything has become expensive, such that people prefer to concentrate on their own business:

> "Cause even formally, when it came farming, people can/ could come and say even: 'We have got for/ Today, we are going to cultivate for this one, the other day, it is for that.' Those things have stopped. They are no longer there. […] These days, people have become individualistic, almost. So, some people, they laugh. Those days, as maybe this thing of like education, urbanisation has a lot of, a LOT of necessities. Formally, things almost were free, eh (seeking confirmation)? They will come (inc.), it will be free. But, now, with education, with WHAT, moderniSATION, a LOT of NECESSITIES and WHAT, (chuckles), when resources are not even enough." (Expert 4, 2017)

Hence, farming has mainly become an activity for individuals who depend on family labour or hired workers. People are no longer willing to sacrifice their time for cultivating in a neighbour's field without pay. What was not said by respondents but can be assumed, is that this attitude also has to do with shortage of land. When farmers had larger fields, they benefitted from the group working on their own field, such that they were willing to help the others for free, in return. Today, the fields of many people are small, such that they can manage to cultivate them using only family labour, which is naturally without cost. Hence, rotating farming support in a group becomes unappealing for them. Even in agricultural cooperatives, as is discussed further in the subsequent sub-theme, the main activity is *marketing* crops that the members have grown in their own fields. Common work in the field is still practiced by some organised groups in Busoga (see chapter 8.3.6), yet, according to my research results, by very few.

The term *'Christmas groups'* is my own invention that was never used by any respondent. The kind of associations I labelled 'Christmas groups' has no official name. It refers to groups that come together in order to prepare for Christmas or other big days of the year. The members contribute money, such that the group can buy an animal for slaughtering on the celebrated day. Due to increasing cost of living, being able to afford to buy meat or to slaughter one's own farm animal, which is supposed to be sold, becomes more and more difficult. As a result, those groups flourish. In some cases, every family receives its share and eats alone; in other cases, the members share their feast jointly. A main interviewee from Kamuli District provided the following account:

> "[...] like nowadays, the big days, like Easter, or (if it is?) any day/ [...] Eh (affirmative), Christmas. People, they come together. Every person contributes small money and buys maybe a cow or a goat that they will eat on that big day. Uh (considering), and also women were/ of that area, they join together, the women and men, to see what is done by women, they get involved, they join together because they are the ones who bring firewood, they bring water and they are the ones who cook. Eh (affirmative), that is there up to now, it is still there." (Main 23, 2017, translation by E.K. and N.H.)

Only two respondents could name any *other informal solidarity structures* in their social environment than those that have been described thus far. The ones they listed are emergency measures: residents of an area coming together and contributing when one of their fellows is sick or 'has a patient', i.e., a seriously sick dependant in the hospital. The above-cited respondent postulated that "in our culture as Basoga, if someone gets a problem, (s)he is rescued and helped. Mm (affirmative), maybe losing someone, falling sick, or having a patient" (ibid.). A main interviewee from Buyende District put it as follows:

> "[...] like the old method as it was, when a person hears that maybe who has got a problem, you have to gather and go to rescue your friend or help your friend. [...] Losing someone/ [...] Falling sick/ [...] Mm (affirmative), let me get the motorcycle, we join hands and make sure that our friend is taken for medical treatment." (Main 3, 2017, translation by E.K. and N.H.)

In summary, autochthonous solidarity structures have not been reacting uniformly to globalisation. While burial support is constantly transforming in order to withstand it, others like rotating farming support or the culture of sharing and giving, have been almost eradicated by it. The hypothesis that globalisation leads to "the increasing commodification of social relationships" (Ziai 2017, 106; see chapter 3.3. of this thesis) has been confirmed by the information gathered from the data. The only form of mutual support that flourishes under globalisation is the one I named 'Christmas groups', which refers to a kind of temporary consumer associations. They form for buying and consuming something conjointly (meat for a feast) and dissolve afterwards. The situation described under the main theme "Busoga's economy under globalisation" (see chapter 8.2, particularly 8.2.8), especially increasing cost of living and income inequality, increases the need for such arrangements. So far, social relationships still work, as people come together to help each other achieve what they could not achieve on their own. In contrast to that, the culture of sharing and giving for free has been terminated to a great extent by the effects of globalisation. The commercialisation of food crops, formerly useless items (e.g., plants that have become fodder), and things that have been treated as commons in the past (land, fruit) has led to the commodification of social relationships. Neighbours and friends who used to share things for free, have been turned into buyers and sellers. Money has replaced the long-term reciprocal relationship that used to be established between them by exchanging favours, e.g., one giving seeds for free, knowing that one day, the neighbour will return the favour by sharing the harvest. Nevertheless, there is still a relationship among the people, though it is being commodified.

The hypothesis that globalisation "broke down community ties" (Escobar 2012, 22; see chapter 2.2.3 of this thesis) may be applied to a certain extent to kinship networks. The clan, which used to be the most important social institution in Busoga, has lost a good part of its influence. The extent to which the clan still has an important function in people's lives varies strongly, from large in some cases to non-existent in others. In many cases, the last important function it still fulfils is burial support. In general, its function as social safety net has been seriously damaged by internal factors on the one hand and work-related migration as well as the new priority of earning money rather than fostering social relations, on the other hand. Here, the argumentation that people let go of their biological, social, and cultural survival strategies in favour of the 'modern lifestyle' of consumers comes in (Hawley 2008; see chapter 3.2 of this thesis). Kinship networks as well as the above-mentioned culture of sharing and giving used to be important social and cultural survival strategies in Busoga. Though their living conditions imply that they still need them, people let go of them because they do not fit in the new lifestyle. As has been demonstrated with several quotes from the interviews above (in this sub-theme and in chapter 8.2.4), globalisation has introduced a new preoccupation with one's material prestige. Having to borrow things from the neighbours or to ask them for free gifts used to be normal but now, it has become embarrassing. People want to be seen with their own household items, their own mobile phones, etc., such that the others do not consider them poor.

Any other solidarity structures about which interviewees spoke are relatively new, formalised group activities and could be classified as SSE groups (see subsequent sub-themes). Some respondents claimed that certain modern self-help groups (like Muno Mukabi or Mukenkede, see corresponding sub-themes) build on autochthonous models. When speaking about SSE groups in general, a main interviewee from Buyende District speculated that they have been modelled on autochthonous social structures:

> "Mm (considering), I think that it originated from our grandparents because those ones, by that time, they were/ when, mm (considering), they were few, they could come together, for example on Christmas days, they could just take their local beer as a group, uh (considering), Christmas, they work together, they play drums, so, we are following our culture." (Main 8, 2017, translation by E.K. and N.H.)

8.3.2 Cooperatives

In the theoretical part of this study, I define cooperatives based on the definition of the International Co-operative Alliance (ICA) as follows (see chapter 4.2.2): "Cooperatives are based on the values of **self-help**,

self-responsibility, **democracy**, **equality**, **equity**, and **solidarity**. In the tradition of their founders, cooperative members believe in the ethical values of honesty, openness, social responsibility and caring for others" (ICA 2020, emphasis in the original). The internationally acknowledged "seven cooperative principles" of the ICA are: "1. Voluntary and Open Membership", "2. Democratic Member Control", "3. Member Economic Participation", "4. Autonomy and Independence", "5. Education, Training, and Information", "6. Cooperation among Cooperatives", "7. Concern for Community" (ICA 2020; see also: Santos/ Rodríguez-Garavito 2007, xxvii). Hence, members are supposed to join cooperatives without any pressure to do so or not to do so; they should be part of rule-setting and decision-making; with their financial contribution, they become owners of and decision-makers in the cooperative; they can decide for their cooperative to enter into collaboration with governments or other organisations, yet this has to be implemented without damaging the cooperative's autonomy; they have a right to be trained by the cooperative and an obligation to be disseminators of cooperation in their social environment; they should strive for "local, national, regional and international" collaboration with other cooperatives; and they should show concern for their home community (ICA 2020; see also: Santos/ Rodríguez-Garavito 2007, xxvii). The daily administrative business is done by an executive committee that is elected by all members (ICA 2020a; Singer 2007, 3). Whenever authors or activists list examples for alternative economic activities or SSE activities (regardless of their respective definition of those terms), the *cooperative* is among the examples they cite. Singer even states that "[t]he production cooperative is the basic unit of the solidary economy", followed by other forms of cooperatives, such as commercial, consumer, and credit cooperatives (Singer 2007, 4). Hence, it was not really a question whether cooperatives are or are not SSE activities. However, existing cooperatives needed to be distinguished from the cooperative societies of the past, with which Uganda has a significant tradition (see chapters 4.2.2; 6.2.3; and 7.5). That tradition is very important for understanding the history of solidarity and cooperation in Busoga. However, the cooperatives that exist today are different from the historical ones. One type of cooperatives existed from 1913 up to the 1980s. Their history is well-researched and has been presented in chapter 4.2.2 of this thesis, with additional information in terms of Busoga in chapters 6.2.3 and 7.5. After the breakdown of the Ugandan economy in the 1970s and the new start under the liberalisation policies of the 1980s and 1990s, a new kind of cooperatives arose. In the following, I distinguish the two by calling them 'cooperative societies of the past' (as they were commonly called 'cooperative societies' by then) and 'current cooperatives' or 'cooperatives of the present'. Towards the end of the analysis of this sub-theme, I compare cooperative societies of the past and currently existing cooperatives in relation to the ICA-criteria. This sub-theme deals only with non-financial cooperatives. I examine cooperatives that render financial services (SACCOs) under the sub-theme "Savings and credit groups (S&C)". Furthermore, cooperatives must be distinguished from other kinds of SSE groups, e.g., associations or community-based groups. In Uganda, as in many other countries of Africa and of the world, cooperatives are required to officially register and to follow legislation, including paying taxes. This requires a certain scope of the group's activity and, as a result, a certain number of members. In contrast to that, associations or community-based groups are smaller, have less capital, and are not necessarily registered.

Cooperative societies of the past

Respondents had a lot to say about the cooperative societies that existed prior to economic liberalisation. However, these cooperatives are not central to the research questions of this study because they have ceased to exist decades ago and have been replaced by new cooperatives that are different in several regards. Nevertheless, the importance of those historical cooperative societies lies in the way they have shaped the respondents' perception of cooperatives and of SSE activities in general. What I refer to as 'cooperative societies' are, in technical terms *primary societies* headed by overarching regional *cooperative unions*. According to a main interviewee from Kamuli District who is involved in the current cooperative movement, cooperative societies used to handle farmers' products as follows: "The society is the one that used to pick it from here and take it to the union. The union processes and they sell, they come, and they give them, such that they pay the people" (Main 15, 2017, translation by E.K. and K.M.). The primary societies were the link between the union – which had the processing plants and the access to export markets – and the farmers. The union in charge of Busoga was *Busoga Growers Co-operative Union* (often referred to simply as *Busoga Growers*). It was in charge of Busoga's export goods, i.e., mainly coffee and cotton, and to a limited extent, groundnuts. Several respondents said that Busoga's former economic success had been built on cooperative societies and the products they marketed. Some even referred to cooperative societies as organisations and to Busoga as a region as "rich". This is different from the current situation. An expert interviewee expressed it this way:

> "Busoga was one of the richest regions in this country. […] But this was based on a cash crop, which was cotton and coffee/ […] And the existence of co-operators. That together, you can sell, together, you can market, you can, you can fix the highest price, and that you can share the profits." (Expert 10, 2018)

Another expert interviewee claimed that, in the past, "cooperatives drove the economy of this country" and he added: "There was Busoga Growers Co-operative Union. It had even industries, it had coffee, a processing industry in Namulessa […]" (Expert 5, 2017). Four respondents were involved in the cooperative movement of that time, including one woman, who was involved in Busoga Growers Co-operative Union. Being asked about its advantages or disadvantages, she responded:

> "In terms of advantages, the people educated from there their children. Like me, I used to work in Busoga Growers, I educated from there my children. I managed to buy from there pieces of land because even this land, I bought it when I was working in Busoga Growers/ […] The time reached and I/ and I was loading coffee/ […] and I go to Kampala. While it was me on the lorry." (Main 17, 2017, translation by E.K. and K.M.)

The products marketed by cooperative societies of the past in Busoga were mainly cotton and coffee. To a limited extent, they also marketed groundnuts and dairy (yet, groundnuts were marketed 'on the side', not as the main activity of any cooperative, and for dairy, there was no umbrella organisation like the Coffee Marketing Board or the Lint Marketing Board that regulated the market, as it was not meant for export). When it comes to the advent of cooperative societies in Uganda, the relationship of cooperative societies and so-called 'Indians' (i.e., Indian immigrants and Ugandans of Indian descent) must be taken into consideration. Busoga's first cash crop, cotton, was initially bought by traders who belonged to that group. They were the owners of the ginneries in Busoga. As cotton farmers believed the ginnery owners cheated them, they founded cooperatives and opened their own ginneries. A main interviewee from Kamuli District describes a common sentiment among respondents:

> "That they [farmers] were taking [cotton] to the society. The other times, there were even the Indians, but they were again before that. That even they were coming to the store, but the Indians also, they

> were thieves. They were also on a price like these ones [middlemen] of these days. When every day, (s)he comes up with another price. But now, societies were the ones that were true. [...] Because they were the ones with a permanent price." (Main 12, 2017, translation by E.K. and K.M.)

This is a common narrative among many people (in the scope of the interviews and beyond) and in the literature (see chapter 4.2.2). Respondents agreed that farmers received more money for their cotton and later also their coffee from the cooperative societies than they could acquire from private buyers (i.e., so-called 'Indians'). Moreover, the cooperative societies' prices were fixed throughout the whole season and did not vary as the middlemen's prices do today. Respondents' views on *the reliability* of payment differed. The cooperative societies were commissioned to sell their members' crops – a system that worked well in many cases and caused problems in others, as members waited in vain for their money. There was a special kind of agricultural cooperatives respondents referred to as 'block farms' or 'group farms'. As has been discussed in chapter 6.2.3, Hasselmann, who encountered them in the scope of his research in Busoga in the 1960s and found them already in crisis, termed them "private agricultural cooperatives" (Hasselmann 1976, 208). One of the main interviewees of my study who has participated in that activity reported:

> "Usually, they used to share equally because they used to, as I told you, they used to make their block garden or farm, maintain, cause the money was coming in for the group as a society, and after harvesting, they SELL. The distributors, they leave some money for their, uh (considering), management, and the rest, distribute out to the members. [...] Nowadays, those groups have collapsed. [...] I've been one of the members in those groups." (Main 7, 2017)

Group farms or block farms were another attempt to formalise mutual farming support, akin to the so-called 'camps' (see chapter 8.3.1). Those approaches did not succeed well in Busoga, neither in the past nor today, as the low support for small farmers' associations shows (see chapter 8.3.6).

As the respondents who were involved in the cooperative movement of that time told me, farmers were *members of cooperatives*, not mere suppliers. They also claimed that the members took decisions together. Yet, there was a lot of government intervention and a tendency towards domination by elites, such that the democratic structure of those cooperative societies is questionable. Several respondents reported believing that the historical cooperative societies were government institutions. A typical comment by a respondent not herself involved in the movement noted: "Those cooperatives were for the government" (Main 9, 2017, translation by E.K. and N.H.). Respondents who *were involved* in such groups explained to me that they were farmers' initiatives, yet government intervention was intensive and government actively promoted them. For instance, a main interviewee who was the co-founder of a dairy cooperative in the 1960s, when asked who initiated such groups, answered: "People. It [the cooperative] was an organisation" (Main 22, 2017, translation by E.K. and K.M.). When asked more explicitly whether the government was involved in the management of cooperatives, he replied: "But when government was the one that was giving them the advice that, 'you put there'[119]" (ibid.). He described how a Cooperative Officer from a government agency came to audit their books and told them exactly how to use their profits:

> "The Cooperative Officer used to come and audit, he audits us. He used to come and audit us, eh (affirmative). He counts the total, 'Now you are doing well. Now, this month, you are going to get like this.' And for us, 'Yes'. 'Profit that you eat from a bit will be like this', for us, 'Yes'. 'You will leave some for the group', for us, 'Yes'. […] He used to come from Kamuli, he comes and audits the books." (Main 22, 2017, translation by E.K. and K.M.)

This interviewee viewed these audits in a positive light because they helped the group to succeed. Such intensive government intervention, however, contradicts the idea of a cooperative being member-owned and self-organised. The way the executive committee simply replied "yes" to all the officer's demands shows that the members were not in control of their cooperative. Another respondent reported that government intervention had introduced corruption into his cooperative society for cotton, such that he stopped cultivating cotton and became suspicious of government and elite intervention in groups. In his current cooperative, they do not trust educated people in the executive committee and they remove a committee member from his or her post as soon as they suspect that the person might abuse his or her power. This is a telling example of a lesson learnt from historical cooperative societies. The respondent expressed it thus: "If we see that you have extreme knowledge, you remind us of previous tears […] we take away your responsibilities, we give them to someone else who can do what? Whom we can trust" (Main 4, 2017, translation by E.K. and N.H.). After selling the products, cooperative societies used to share

119 Meaning: 'Go ahead and set up a cooperative!'

the profits among the ordinary members, the members of the executive committee who received an extra payment for their commitment, and some re-investment in the group's activities.

Respondents frequently spoke about the circumstance that cooperative societies "died", "collapsed", or were even "killed". They provided multiple reasons for this, foremost among them fraud among the members (especially on the part of the committee members). Others blamed robbers, the termination of the *tractor provision scheme*, and mismanagement within the groups. Certainly, all of those factors contributed to the decline of cooperative societies in Uganda in the 1970s and 1980s. As analysed in chapters 4.2.2 and 7.5, the tight government control in the 1960s and the power vacuum it left behind favoured abuse of power and embezzlement on the part of the committee members. This was followed by a period in which the processing and official marketing of the cooperatives' products became almost impossible due to political turmoil and economic breakdown (1970s to mid-1980s). Eventually, the liberalisation policies of the 1980s and 1990s sounded the death knell for cooperative societies (Mrema 2008; Nannyonjo 2015; see chapter 4.2.2 of this thesis). Some respondents of this study mentioned rumours about cooperative societies having become too powerful and, as a result, having been destroyed for political reasons. In either case, the liberalisation policies of Uganda's recovery phase were destructive to cooperatives, as they exposed them to competition and deprived them of essential government support at a point in time when the cooperatives were already weakened by previous occurrences. Hence, liberalisation may have created a false impression of intentional sabotage or it may have served as a pretext for it. To investigate whether there was such a motivation behind it would go beyond the scope of this study and may not even be traceable. In either case, the Ugandan cooperative societies of the past had no chance to survive after decades of events that had impacted them negatively. Nevertheless, numerous interviewees felt that farmers benefitted from those historical cooperative societies. Not only did cooperative societies buy farmers' products for a good and stable price, respondents noted, they also provided inputs (e.g., seeds) to their members. However, it is safe to assume that the fixed prices did not come from the cooperative societies but rather from the marketing boards. Nevertheless, the population associates those fixed prices with cooperative societies. As a result, currently existing cooperatives must appear disappointing to some, as they depend on the liberalised market and cannot grant fixed prices to their members.

Cooperatives of the present

Out of 32 main interviewees, 12 are currently members of cooperatives. This is not representative of Busoga, as I had told the gatekeepers that I was interested in interviewing people who are members of such groups. Consequently, the ratio of people involved in cooperatives (and other kinds of groups) in my sample is likely to be higher than the ratio within Busoga as a whole. Out of those ten[120] cooperatives, four deal in dairy, two[121] deal in food crops, one deals in mushrooms, one in coffee, one in eco-friendly briquettes made from pressed rubbish, and one in handicrafts. The most important advantage of these cooperatives, according to the respondents of this study, is their ability to grant access to markets to their members. Individual small-scale farmers are neither able to produce the quantities required for wholesale activities, nor do they have the bargaining power needed in such a setting. Many cooperatives – of course depending on their size and management – are able to sell their members' products at national and regional markets (i.e., markets from where many things are taken to neighbouring countries). A representative of Jinja District explained to me the following about coffee marketing:

> "Ya, it is produced at household level. But what happened, when it comes to marketing, those household, uh (considering), come up with groups, or sometimes cooperative organisations to attain the level of collective bargaining. Okay? Uh (considering), collective bargaining, and when they collect their produce together, they ca/ and achieve ONE, uh (considering), improved quality, two, better prices for? Their? Market items, out of collective bargaining and bulking. […] The major ones, actually, when it comes to marketing, they are mostly cooperatives that bring different stakeholders, different households together to ensure that they market their produce." (Expert 7, 2017)

Irrespective of coffee, one of his colleagues from Buyende District mentioned how different kinds of cooperatives collaborate these days:

---

120 The respondents of two interviews were members of the same cooperative. I interviewed the second person because he had participated in the original cooperative movement and could compare the two very well. In another case, the two respondents of a tandem interview were members of the same cooperative.

121 One of them is an *area cooperative*, i.e., an overarching marketing arm for several smaller cooperatives, comparable to the cooperative unions of the past; see chapter 7.5 for details.

> "UNDER the cooperatives, at least we have one of our marketing arms, called Bugaya Area Cooperative Enterprise. Is associated to one of the SACCOs, which are financial institutions, so, the SACCOs, they provide finances, then that Area Cooperative gives them the marketing arm." (Expert 2, 2017)

A respondent who is involved in an area cooperative explained its marketing channels as follows:

> "[...] the farmers carry from the other small stores there, so, the truck comes at once and collects what has been covered, what has been collected by the farmers. [...] Mm (considering), sometimes, we sell to the schools, sometimes we have Agroways[122], sometimes we have our buyers, sometimes we do value addition, we sell to the/ these Serena hotels, they come for posho[123]." (Main 6, 2017)

He added that the area cooperative even provides on credit materials such as seeds, fertiliser, and pesticides to the members (ibid.). These illustrative examples, drawn from a multitude of data extracts, suggest that cooperatives open up for farmers marketing opportunities they would not have without cooperatives. As elaborated in the main theme "Busoga's economy under globalisation" (chapter 8.2), the only marketing alternative for small- to medium-scale farmers is selling their products to middlemen. As such farmers depend heavily on middlemen, the former have a weak negotiation position vis-à-vis the latter and gain little from selling their products through this marketing channel. Farmers also lack means of transport to take their products to a supra-regional market or a major customer such as a hotel. A cooperative can achieve all this, as the products of all members make up the required quantities and money for transport can be collected from its members. The members can pool their resources, not only for organising transport, but also for other purposes, e.g., buying or renting materials like tractors or milk coolers. Beyond that, the group can grant farmers access to resources that only a group can acquire. For instance, it can buy materials in bulk and provide them to the members

---

122 See chapter 6.2.4: Agroways is a private enterprise that bought Busoga Growers Co-operative Union in 2015. In contrast to Busoga Growers, Agroways specialises in food crops, first of all maize and rice. The area cooperative the respondent mentions likewise specialises in maize and rice.

123 posho = maize flour (posho can also refer to mush made from maize flour, but here, he means that the hotels buy the flour from the area cooperative in order to prepare mush for their customers)

at a cheaper price or get them for free from an NGO or government programme that supports groups but no individuals. Some cooperatives take up loans from SACCOs (see chapter 8.3.3) that would be too expensive for many of their individual members. In general, an additional savings and/or credit component is common in the new cooperatives. With regard to their non-financial main activities, members do the work at home (e.g., rearing and milking cattle; growing mushrooms, maize, or coffee) or in the group's premises (e.g., producing briquettes or grinding maize). Some cooperatives engage in value addition, e.g., by grinding and packaging maize and rice (like the above-mentioned area cooperative), drying and packaging mushrooms, or processing milk. A member of a dairy cooperative in Kamuli District explained the process as follows:

> "The milk that comes from it, as we are in this group of ours, we collect it here and we make yoghurt, eh (considering), that milk, we give to where it came from, to the members, and they get paid. The profit that comes with it is kept in the group." (Main 12, 2017, translation by E.K. and K.M.)

His observation that the money "is kept in the group" refers to the group's expenses (e.g., running the milk cooler, packaging materials, marketing) as well as to future investments and possibly an annual share for the members, in addition to the money they receive immediately for their delivered milk. Another advantage for cooperative members is the ability to access advice on their economic activities from the group. For instance, a main interviewee from Kamuli District said that his cooperative books agricultural experts from time to time:

> "Now, let me talk of the groups, farming group. When one wants, let's say, to plant maize, we can go and help because, eh (considering), we have the (...) technical people, who go and demo/ teach how we should plant the maize. Planting banana, we go and dig the ditches, where we/ and we have the technical people to do that. Eh (affirmative), that's how we go and assist one another." (Main 14, 2017)

Apart from those advantages, which benefit only their members, some cooperatives also support non-members from their community. For instance, they buy their crops or let other people use their facilities at a moderate price. A respondent from Jinja District who has founded with some other women a cooperative for the production of eco-friendly briquettes said that any woman, even a non-member, can come and use their press if she leaves some briquettes behind for the group:

> "When you come, if you make three basins [of briquettes], the machine, you leave for it 20 briquettes, when it's not for the group, when you, you have come to make when you are not in the group. You come and you make yours because it is for women." (Main 27, 2017, translation by E.K. and K.M.)

After having been offered a training and a machine for the production of such briquettes by a government agency, that respondent had animated other women to form a group with her or to form groups in their places. According to her, the other groups received the same support as hers.

In my study, I did not encounter any signs of elites dominating the cooperatives. Though some of them had received some support from the government (e.g., seeds, a press for making briquettes) or from NGOs (e.g., a milk cooler), the interviewees insisted that the groups had been founded on the initiative of some of the members. This insistence was supported by the relatively long operational period of the groups. This would not have been the case had the groups been formed without the members' commitment, e.g., because they were formed by government agencies or NGOs, or with the sole purpose of earning support from such institutions, sharing it, and dissolving the group (see chapter 8.3.6 for details on this point). It is safe to assume, instead, that these groups were formed through bottom-up processes by people looking for a source of livelihood together. Local people run the cooperatives themselves in order to profit from them themselves. In terms of membership, I encountered two variants. Apart from a one-time membership fee at the time of joining, members must either buy shares in the cooperative or pay a regular contribution. The system with shares is more common and the original variant, as the underlying idea of cooperatives includes collective ownership. It is also the variant that works better. The representatives of the groups that tried out the alternative with regular contributions reported more problems in their group than the representatives of cooperatives in which members are shareholders. The means of production are partly provided by government programmes[124] or NGOs and partly rented or bought by the cooperative (e.g., land). In either case, the group usually owns them as a whole. For instance, when asked about the ownership of the assets of his dairy cooperative, a main interviewee from Kamuli stated: "Cooperative,

124 As Justine Nannyonjo (Nannyonjo 2015, 275-281; see chapter 4.2.2 of this thesis) has pointed out and as could be seen from the 2011 National Cooperative Policy (see chapter 7.5), the Ugandan government has again started to promote cooperatives intensively.

they just elect us, it has no owner, even if (s)he is the chairperson, they elect him/her and (s)he leaves, they belong to the society[125]" (Main 21, 2017, translation by E.K. and N.H.). Hence, neither individuals nor the executive committee own the assets. Rather, the group as a whole owns them. Only in few cases are the assets given to the members and become their property (e.g., two dairy cooperatives give cows to their members and they become the members' properties). The profits of cooperatives are shared according to the members' input. If the members deliver products like crops, milk, or handicrafts, they get paid the purchase price for them either at the moment of delivery or when the products have been sold. A member of a crop marketing cooperative explained to me why his group had so far failed to make the outcome equal for all members:

> "In that group, we sit and discuss when we have collected that food, we take it to the market, we come back and we show to our friends how we did what? How we sold. We give out some money for helping themselves, we leave the other money in what? [...] In the group. [...] We wanted also to make it equal, now, we told people, we said that, 'Our colleagues, every person should make how many bags? Two.' [...] but the situation of other people/ one can manage, but the other cannot manage. So, we are like we are moving at that pace." (Main 4, 2017, translation by E.K. and N.H.)

Hence, the profit a member makes depends on his or her production capacities. Additionally, in the annual or biannual general meeting, the executive committee must communicate to all members the profits made and pay them their dividends according to the share capital they have invested (see above). For instance, in a dairy cooperative in Kamuli District, it is done as follows: "You sit, the interest you made in a year, (s)he gets some small money on that money you contributed for share capital, the 10,000 [shilling] (s)he put" (Main 21, 2017, translation by E.K. and N.H.). Usually, there is a minimum but not a maximum number of shares a member must buy. Another part of the profits is usually re-invested in the groups' activities, e.g., for purchasing or maintaining machines. While many continue to regard the cooperative societies of the past as government institutions (see above), currently existing cooperatives are instead

125 The interviewee was asked whether he referred to *cooperatives* here and he answered in the affirmative. He used the terms "cooperative", "chairperson", and "society" (which was inspired by the old expression 'cooperative society') in English.

founded and operated by the people themselves. Government regulates them to a certain extent and may provide some material support, but it is not involved in their daily business. For instance, a main interviewee from Jinja District told me how she convinced some friends and neighbours to start a cooperative for mushroom production. Though she organised some support from the government programme NAADS and the local town council, the initiative was hers and her fellow members joined in, as this extract from her detailed narration shows:

> "I just read in a newspaper, I saw someone, who was growing mushroom. […] I came up with the mind, I took/ I got some members. […] They said, 'Now, for us, we are interested in growing mushroom, but you first do it alone. If you will come up well'/ […] After beginning, we made a group with this one, NAADS. Now, I shared it with those people at the town council. They supported us that, 'We are going to give you what? The mushroom seeds.' So, they bought us mushroom seeds and we began/" (Main 29, 2017)

Nevertheless, the Ugandan government has a keen eye on cooperatives, as the following comment by a representative of Buyende District shows:

> "Only that government comes in to regulate. For instance, when you want to form a cooperative, there are procedures you have to follow. There are by-laws you have to agree with. And there are offices you MUST WORK WITH. So, PRODUCTION is controlled in such a way that it is managed by members. It is ONLY in AREAS of arbitration conflicts that these officers now come in to intervene and put back the what? The organisation on track. And there are QUITE often those conflicts arising out of sharing of dividends, profits. Mm (affirmative). So, those groups are there, they are engaged in production, they sell their produce, they get profits, and their production is governed by the members themselves. As government, we come in to control or to intervene in areas of conflicts that tend to tear the organisation apart. Mm (affirmative), that's when we come in. But we don't go ahead to tell them that: 'This is how you should manage your thing, this is how you should share your profit.' Ah-ah (negative), don't do that." (Expert 1, 2017)

Though I demonstrated in the analysis of the 2011 National Cooperative Policy (see chapter 7.5) that cooperatives are still an important policy instrument (NCP 2011), nevertheless, the government has left behind the previous approach of intensive intervention into the groups' daily business. In an above-cited extract from a main interview, the respondent spoke about the audits of his dairy cooperative by a Cooperative Officer in the 1960s in which the members and the committee had nothing to say but "yes". In the new cooperatives, the members are the decision-makers. Apart from certain legislations[126] with regard to cooperatives, they are free to conduct their organisation the way they want. They elect an executive committee, which sometimes has sub-committees and, in some cases, even a supervising committee. Those committees are in charge of the everyday business but must report to the members. Major decisions are taken conjointly during the general assemblies. When asked who takes decisions in her briquette-producing cooperative, the above-cited respondent answered: "All of us, with the members" (Main 27, 2017, translation by E.K. and K.M.). The respondent, whose cooperative markets crops and learnt its lessons from elite domination in the cooperatives of the past, replied to the same question: "Ourselves. [...] We come together, we discuss, and we decide" (Main 4, 2017, translation by E.K. and N.H.). Comparing cooperatives of the past and of the present, as someone who has been involved in both, this respondent came to the conclusion that today's cooperatives are much better. The reason he gave is the following: "Because we, ourselves, we organise ourselves and we elect within ourselves, who heads us, the treasurer, everything, we are like, we have done what? We are working on it ourselves" (ibid.). No respondents said that the decisions in currently existing cooperatives are taken by elites, by the executive committee, or by any government representatives. However, some complained about some members not being committed to the group's activities because either some members are more successful than others in that activity or the cooperative has disappointed their price expectations. The first case has been reported by the founder of a mushroom-growing cooperative in which the members have to pay a regular contribution instead of buying a share:

> "So, now, as you know, in groups, groups grow, others collapse, hm (seeking confirmation)? There are some members/ there are some members, who say, 'Uh (with disgust), after all', like when a season has not come up well, he can go and influence other members/ [...] That, 'Why are we doing this? Hm (seeking confirmation)? Anyway, as

126 The Ugandan Ministry of Trade, Industry and Cooperatives website indicates that registering a cooperative involves considerable effort (http://www.mtic.go.ug/cooperatives-registration/). Cooperatives are also required to pay taxes. However, none of the respondents of this study mentioned either of those issues.

> if we are just giving the bank, as if we are just giving those, who are/ who are successful in every season.' Things like that." (Main 29, 2017)

The other case has been reported with regard to a dairy cooperative in the following extract:

> "[...] milk has no money in it, so, it has given us that even that thing disorganises even people to leave, they say that, 'Uh (negative), me, in the village, I sell at 500 [shillings] per cup, now when I take to the dairy, where do I benefit?' It's like it has given us an image that people have broken off from us because we don't have market." (Main 3, 2017, translation by E.K. and N.H.)

Indeed, the complaint about prices came up only with regard to milk. Cooperative members were generally satisfied with the money they received for all other products, compared to other marketing options (middlemen, organising the marketing by themselves individually). Members of cooperatives characteristically expect a certain financial profit. If they do not achieve it, or if the extent to which members achieve it varies too much, the harmony of the group is endangered. As noted above, these expectations have their historical roots in the Ugandan cooperatives of the past and their close relationship with the government. Thanks to market monopolies and marketing boards, the cooperatives of the past had been able to guarantee stable and relatively high prices to their members. In a free market economy like the economy of today's Uganda, such guarantees are inexistent, likely leading to disappointment and, as a result, difficulties in terms of commitment on the part of the members. Hereinafter, I compare cooperatives of the past and of the present in terms of the seven cooperative principles of the International Cooperative Alliance (ICA). After that, I examine the potential of currently existing cooperatives as SSE groups.

Chart 6: Comparison of contemporary cooperatives and cooperative societies of the past with regard to the 7 Cooperative Principles (ICA)

Comparison of contemporary cooperatives and cooperative societies of the past with regard to the 7 Cooperative Principles (ICA)			
7 Principles	**Cooperatives (present)**	**Cooperative societies (past)**	**Comparison**
1. Voluntary and Open Membership	It depends on the group. Many cooperatives are founded and joined by people at their own initiative. However, there are also cases in which government pushes people to found or join them (see chapter 8.3.6). I have not found out about any restrictions that prevent people from joining cooperatives.	It depended on the group. Some cooperatives were founded and joined by people at their own initiative. However, there were also cases in which government pushed people to found or join them (one expert said that the government wanted *everybody* to be a member). I have not found out about any restrictions that prevented people from joining cooperatives.	Basically, membership has always been and still is voluntary and open. However, the higher the motivation of the respective government to promote cooperatives as a means of economic development, the higher the pressure on people to found or join them. This pressure was high during the peak period of cooperative societies (1950s-1970s), dropped considerably in the 1980s, and is currently rising again.
2. Democratic Member Control	In the cooperatives about which I learnt during the interviews, the members take decisions conjointly, without domination by elites, government or other parties.	In theory, members were supposed to take decisions together. In practice, government used to intervene (e.g., through audits, which included telling the committee how to use the profits made by the group). The executive committees were rather dominant in relation to the 'ordinary' members.	As one respondent said explicitly, and as can be concluded from the reports of other respondents, democratic member control is much more serious in the cooperatives that exist today than it was in the cooperative societies of the past.
3. Member Economic Participation	In most cases, members are shareholders of the group. In two cases, the group tried to replace that system with regular contributions but it did not work well. However, there is no maximum number of shares a member can buy. As a result, the ownership of the group is not necessarily equal. Apart from that, members certainly participate economically by giving their products to the cooperative and receiving money in return – though	In terms of member economic participation, I have not been given any specific information by the respondents. Drawing on the information that members received an annual bonus from the cooperatives' profits and that the membership could be passed on to a relative, I assume that, most likely, members bought shares. Apart from that, members reportedly participated economically by giving	In the currently existing cooperatives, member economic participation is granted. Members buy shares in order to become a member and market their products through the group. However, their participation is not equal, as some members may buy more shares or deliver higher quantities of products than others. I received only scare information on that point with regard to cooperative societies of the past and can therefore

	this is also not equal and depends on the respective member's capacities.	their products to the cooperative and receiving money in return.	not make definitive declarations. At best, it is reasonable to cautiously assume that the system worked in the same way in the past.
4. Autonomy and Independence	The cooperatives about which I was told during the interviews appeared to be autonomous and independent.	The autonomy and independence of the cooperative societies of the past were limited by intensive government intervention.	While cooperatives that exist today are autonomous and independent, study respondents remember cooperative societies of the past as strongly regulated or even *operated* by the government.
5. Education, Training, and Information	Several interviewees reported that education and training is very important in their cooperative.	None of the respondents of this study spoke about education, training, or information in the cooperative societies of the past.	Education and training used to be of little importance in the historic cooperatives but are of high importance in the ones of today.
6. Cooperation among Cooperatives	Cooperatives and SACCOs cooperate on loans; cooperatives and area cooperatives cooperate on processing and marketing. Apart from that, I did not encounter any collaboration between cooperatives.	Cooperatives and cooperative banks cooperated on loans; cooperatives and cooperative unions cooperated on processing and marketing. Apart from that, I was not told about any collaboration between cooperative societies.	There is no difference between Ugandan cooperatives of the past and of the present. They collaborate with cooperatives that provide them with services such as granting loans or assisting them in processing and marketing on a higher level. Yet I have found neither evidence for their collaboration with other Ugandan cooperatives that operate on the same level nor with cooperatives from other countries.
7. Concern for Community	This point is difficult to grasp. In three cases, respondents reported that a cooperative does not exclude non-members from their activities. They support them by buying their products or letting them use their materials for a fair price. Women cooperatives tend to be sensitive to issues concerning women beyond their group. Apart from that, I was not told about any activities in the communities. Several groups have additional components such as loans or burial support but they are reserved for members.	None of the respondents of this study spoke about concern for community in the cooperative societies of the past.	Concern for community beyond the groups' members seems to be weak in today's cooperatives in Uganda and even weaker in those of the past.

In summary, there are significant differences between cooperative societies of the past and currently existing cooperatives. The only point in which they are the same pertains to *cooperation among cooperatives*. Both contemporary and former cooperatives show evidence of vertical collaboration with cooperative service providers, but neither of horizontal nor of international collaboration. The cooperatives of today are much stronger than their forerunners in terms of *voluntary and open membership*; *democratic member control*; *autonomy and independence*; and *education, training, and information*. A few of these show some *concern for community* beyond their members but this is barely more than in the past. The data did not allow me to draw a conclusion concerning *member economic participation* with respect to the past. At present, it is strong, though not equal. Overall, the cooperative societies of the past were weak in relation to the definition of the ICA and are not likely to fulfil the criteria for SSE groups. I examine their successors in this regard below. A representative of Kamuli District nicely summarised the characteristics of cooperatives of the past and of present days in Busoga:

> "They look not like the other old/ they were/ cause there used to be other old cooperatives, where government used to come in to do EVERYTHING. They used to come in to give them money, what they call CROP FINANCE. Eh (affirmative), they used to look for MARKETS for these people, INPUTS for them, they used to put even STAFF in these cooperatives, eh (affirmative), to monitor. But rather that's no cooperative. A cooperative is MEMBER-OWNED. [...] the whole group is supposed to own this thing. They are supposed to control it, they are supposed to elect their leaders, they also put in their money, we would call share capital [...]." (Expert 4, 2017)

To examine the SSE-potential of the various kinds of groups I encountered in Busoga I use the criteria suggested by Michelle Williams and Norman Chipakupaku (see chapters 4.2.1 or 4.4 of this thesis, or the introductory paragraph to this chapter 8.3). They capture the most essential characteristics of SSE and, in the chart below, will be applied to cooperatives as they currently exist in Busoga.

Chart 7: Criteria for SSE groups: Cooperatives (as currently existing in Busoga)

Criteria for SSE groups: Cooperatives (as currently existing in Busoga)	
Michelle Williams' criteria for the Social Economy and the Solidarity Economy (2014, 59):	
cooperation	Cooperatives build on the principle of cooperation, i.e., people coming together, joining efforts, and pooling resources in order to overcome a common problem.
democratic decision making	They are founded and operated by the members. The government is no longer involved in cooperatives' daily business. The members are the decision-makers. They elect an executive committee that must report to the members. Major decisions are taken conjointly during the general assemblies.
collective ownership	Members must either buy shares in the cooperative or pay a regular contribution. The system with shares is more common and more successful. The means of production are partly provided by government programmes or NGOs, partly rented or bought by the cooperative. In either case, the group usually owns them as a whole. Only in few cases, the assets are given to the members and become their individual property.
bottom-up processes	In this study, I did not encounter any signs of elites dominating the cooperatives. Neither did I encounter signs of government pressure or NGO projects leading to the formation of the groups (which does not mean that they do not exist). The groups I encountered were formed through bottom-up processes, by people looking for an income-generating activity together.
caring and sharing	Several cooperatives have additional components like loans or burial support for their members. Women cooperatives tend to be sensitive to the issues of women both within and beyond the group.
Norman Chipakupaku's principles of the People's Economy (2008, 138):	
joining economic efforts in order to earn a living	Though in practice, the income that the members earn seldomly allows for more than the satisfaction of basic needs, in theory the goal is to become a prospering enterprise and succeed in the market. Though profits are meant to be distributed among the members (more or less) equally, members receive their money according to the input they bring (e.g., crops or milk) and the number of shares they buy. Hence, the idea of the People's Economy of equal distribution of modest income to many participants is only partially fulfilled.
being run by and for the sake of the local population	This criterion is being fulfilled, see "Bottom-up processes".
creating *local economic cycles* that provide employment to locals, keeping money and facilities at their disposition	Local people run the cooperatives themselves, employing themselves. Their products are often taken to supra-regional, sometimes even to international markets. Hence, the economic cycles created are seldom local. This is no surprise, as cooperatives have been introduced to Uganda as marketing instruments for export crops. However, the people making a living on those activities are locals and their incomes are primarily spent locally.

Generally speaking, the cooperatives that exist in Busoga today can be categorised as SSE groups according to Michelle Williams' definition. They fulfil all her criteria as a forum for *cooperation*, with *democratic decision making*, *collective ownership* of the means of production and the group itself via buying shares, *bottom-up processes*, and *caring and sharing* among the group members. The only shortcoming of cooperatives in relation to this definition is in the area of *collective ownership*, as it is not equal and, sometimes, some assets are the individual property of members. With respect to Norman Chipakupaku's definition of the People's Economy, cooperatives fulfil only one criterion perfectly, *being run by and for the sake of the local population*, and the others only partly. Though their primary purpose is to *earn a living for ordinary local people*, cooperatives cannot escape their history. They have originally been initiated in Uganda for the purpose of export marketing. Hence, very few of them create *local economic cycles*. Their purpose is to provide to local people access to profitable markets, which usually means markets outside of Busoga. However, the incomes earned are primarily spent locally. The slight lack of accord with the criteria of the People's Economy may be explained by Chipakupaku's perception of a *specifically African version* of SSE, while the concept of co-operatives originates from Europe (see chapter 4.2.2). In summary, though cooperatives do not fit Chipakupaku's definition perfectly, they are also not antithetical to them. In combination with their good compatibility with Williams' SSE-criteria, cooperatives as they exist in Busoga today are manifestations of the Social and Solidarity Economy. Though their principles are not always oppositional to capitalist principles (e.g., market access, profit-orientation, economies of scale), cooperatives are the only option for small- to medium-scale farmers in regions like Busoga to escape exploitation by the free market system through middlemen (see chapter 8.2.1).[127] After all, Ugandan farmers founded the cooperative movement in the first half of the twentieth century "to help each other survive the market forces" (Nannyonjo 2015, 271; see chapter 4.2.2 of this thesis). The only exception is made by those (such as dairy farmers) who have a good local market. They do not depend on middlemen and sometimes not even on cooperatives for selling their products. They rather like cooperatives because they provide them with trainings, materials, and sometimes cows. This shows that the concept of cooperatives, the way it is implemented in Busoga, is not a model for a localised economy but for the participation of small- to medium-scale producers in markets outside the region. As such,

---

127 As described in chapter 8.2.1 of this thesis, intermediaries tend to bargain farmers down or to cheat them by manipulating their weighing scales or lying in terms of the prices for commodities in the regional markets, in order to keep their own profit as high as possible.

it is closer to the *Social* Economy in the narrow sense[128] and to approaches of poverty eradication[129] and development than to the *Solidarity* Economy and to *Post*-Development approaches, which rather look for *alternatives to* capitalist development (for the latter, see chapter 2.2.3). In view of Immanuel Wallerstein's call for alternatives to the current capitalist world-system, cooperatives can serve the need for "interim, middle-range goals" by mitigating the negative effects of the old system as long as it still exists (Wallerstein 2003, 271; see chapter 3.4 of this thesis). They can also contribute to the process of "experiment[ing] with alternatives" in order to find long-term solutions for "the better (not the perfect) society" (ibid., 271-272).

8.3.3 Savings and credit groups (S&C)

Savings and credit (S&C) groups are among the most popular community-based groups in Busoga. A main interviewee from Buyende District explained the popularity of these groups by noting: "They help them to be able to save a little money. Because, if you have it [the money] at hand, at any time, it gets finished. A problem comes and you use it – but when you have not saved" (Main 2, 2017, translation by E.K. and N.H.). In Jinja District, a respondent said about an S&C group that "when you have got

128 Some authors distinguish the *Social Economy* from the *Solidarity Economy* by defining the former as an attempt to mitigate the negative effects of capitalism on the lives of some social groups without questioning the system as such and the latter as a forum for *alternatives to* capitalism (see chapter 4.2.1 for details). As elaborated in chapter 4.2.1, I argue that the two cannot be clearly distinguished in practice and that it makes sense to work with the combined term *Social and Solidarity Economy*. In order to be of interest for this study, it is sufficient that a group complies with the principles of the Social *and* Solidarity Economy (SSE). Nevertheless, in the analysis, I examine the question whether they end at the attempt to make capitalism more bearable for disadvantaged social groups (i.e., the *Social* Economy *in the narrow sense*) or whether they have alternative potential (i.e., the *Solidarity* Economy *in the narrow sense*).

129 Poverty eradication is an objective shared by all approaches in this list. However, some of them, namely *Post*-Development approaches, Wallerstein's approach to *long-term* transformations in world-systems analysis, and the *Solidarity* Economy, agree on the point that fighting poverty means changing the system that causes it. In contrast, conventional approaches to development and poverty eradication regard poverty as a technical problem. They are based on the belief that the poor can 'catch up' with the global middle-class when they are provided with some capital and/ or advice.

some money and, yet you are finding it difficult to keep it in the house, then you can take it there" (Main 16, 2017, translation by E.K. and K.M.). A main interviewee from Kamuli District explained her positive attitude towards S&C groups as follows:

> "Yet, if you were alone, you wouldn't be keeping those two thousands[130] every month. But here, you are forced to/ to at least, to save, to save that twenty thousand every month, so that you can be able to, at least, to work upon something that you want." (Main 11, 2017, translation by E.K. and K.M.)

Another interesting point was mentioned by a respondent from Jinja District, namely that groups replace social obligations to help friends and relatives in financial distress – or to ask friends and relatives for help when being in financial distress:

> "For us, to form our group, as I have told you, we used to help each other in good times and bad times. If we contribute that small money and we give you, or you have a problem at home that you have come with, we help you and you solve it. You don't have to go to so-and-so to tell him/her that, 'My friend, lend me', you will reach there when (s)he has money in the house and (s)he will tell you that, 'I don't have.'" (Main 28, 2017, translation by E.K. and N.H.)

All these extracts illustrate, as the respondent of interview Main 16 expressed it, the difficulty of keeping money in the house. Whenever people acquire of some money, they either spend it quickly because there are many necessities – or someone comes to ask for it. As elaborated under the main theme "Busoga's economy under globalisation", high costs of living (e.g., educational and health expenditures, or basic material needs like food, clothes, household utensils) and an increasing desire to participate in material consumer cultures collide with low incomes in Busoga (see chapter 8.2). As a result, saving is extremely difficult. And, as the last quote shows, to say "no" to someone, who asks for financial assistance when one has money in the house, is considered unfriendly. S&C groups provide the only solution to that problem. They replace the obligation to help friends and family members in need with an obligation to comply with the rules of the group. The responsibility towards friends and family is replaced with the responsibility towards the fellow group members. This

130 She spoke about "ten two thousands", i.e., twenty thousand shillings, the typical Lusoga way of counting.

is socially acceptable, whereas saying "no, I am saving the money for my own purposes" is not. It would lead to the social isolation of the person who refused to help, such that he or she could not expect any help from the community in case of emergency. As a result of this, such groups could be accused of even *destroying solidarity* in favour of selfishness, capital accumulation, and personal consumption. To a certain extent and depending on one's definition of 'solidarity', this is the case. If solidarity is being defined as the social cohesion between family and community members not organised in a group, S&C groups are destructive. However, it depends on the perspective one takes. As an alternative to commercial loan providers[131], those groups have the merit of introducing elements of solidarity and mutual support to the credit business. Another factor that requires consideration is the key finding of the sub-theme "Autochthonous solidarity structures survive partly" (chapter 8.3.1): in many places within Busoga, social safety nets like the extended family (clan) or neighbourhood have started to deteriorate or become commercialised due to the impact of globalisation. As a result, many people may not even have any other solidarity structures beyond their groups on which they can rely. Consequently, S&C groups take a position between the local community, the autochthonous solidarity structures of which (if existent) they disturb, and commercial loan providers. In comparison to commercial loan providers, the level of solidarity within S&C groups is high. For instance, Milford Bateman, a prominent critic of formal microfinance who calls the latter a "poverty trap" (Bateman 2010, 166), lauds "forms of community-based credit, such as credit unions" as a much safer option for low-income earners to gain access to loans (ibid., 168). As will be further discussed in subsequent parts of this section, there are various kinds of S&C groups

131 Apart from banks, commercial loan providers encompass formal microfinance institutions (MFIs). They are organisations that give out small loans to people without collateral (Wichterich 2015, 471). It is an approach to poverty reduction, yet the interest rates and other fees can culminate in up to 40% (ibid.; Rahaman 2014, 54-58) and MFIs are known for putting high pressure on their debtors when they fail to pay back on time (Rahaman 2014, 56). Uganda has a broad microfinance sector with formal and informal as well as local and international organisations, including the American organisation FINCA (Bibangambah 2001, 174-177). BRAC, one of the "big players in microcredit business in Bangladesh", "the cradle of microcredit" (Rahaman 2014, 53, translation by E.K.), can also be found in Uganda. In Busoga, BRAC and FINCA are the dominant formal microcredit providers.

that show differing degrees of solidarity among their members. In terms of formal credit providers, an expert explained that

> "very few, uh (considering), households are able to afford credit from, uh (considering), formal financial institutions. Majority cannot afford because their interest rates are high. So, the other objective is, they are coming together to just be able to fund their own activities, using their personal savings. The other is also to be able to gain access to formal credit. Because some financial institutions feel safer to lend to a group. If one member fails to pay, the bank might lose. Most of these people don't even have the collateral. But when we attain chances that, uh (considering), at least eight of us will organise ourselves and be able to pay, are higher than when you deal with an individual. So, they are coming together to also be able to access credit from financial institutions. Which is one of the constrains that they are normally facing. They lack access to credit and because of that, they are unable to invest in certain things they would wish to invest in." (Expert 9, 2018)

A main interviewee from Jinja District likewise deplored that for "those banks, you must have a big security that they have to get before you get money" (Main 30, 2017, translation by E.K. and K.M.). Furthermore, she added that banks[132] do not finance small income-generating projects but only businesses that are already running. She compared this practice to the S&C group to which she belongs, coming to the conclusion that

> "the banks, while they don't give [money] to a person, who has not yet started to do something, hm (seeking confirmation)? […] But for us, when we look at a person, like now, we did among ourselves that we are residents. You'll not run. We can even give a person, even though

132 On terminology: Ugandans tend to call savings and credit groups or clan cashboxes for burials "banks". I had to examine from the context whether respondents were speaking about a bank in the international sense of the term. Another confusion is that, in some cases, the comments on "banks" may also refer to formal microfinance institutions (MFIs). This is difficult to distinguish in some cases. However, this is not problematic, as I simply want to contrast *commercial* financial service providers with those that operate within the scope of SSE. In that categorisation, commercial banks and MFIs anyway belong in the same non-SSE category. In the case of Main 30, I assume that she meant banks in the narrow sense, as she said that they do not finance start-ups, whereas this is the very purpose of MFIs and a common practice in S&C groups that belong to the SSE-category.

> (s)he is starting, just starting business, when (s)he has explained to us well what (s)he is going to do. Which may not be possible in what? In the bank. Because, in the bank, they have to inspect what you do, and then, they give you money. But for us, one can say that, 'Friends, I don't have what to do, still, I don't have what I'm feeding the children. But I want to begin with charcoal, hm (seeking confirmation)?' We say that, 'Oh-ho (affirmative), you want to begin with charcoal. You want to begin with how many bags, that maybe five?' We/ (s)he calculates a bit, (s)he/ we give him/her the money for the five bags, and (s)he begins from there, selling as (s)he brings back [money]." (Main 30, 2017, translation by E.K. and K.M.)

Members benefit from their social capital, that is, from their fellow members knowing and trusting them. In that case, it does not matter whether it is 'old' social capital (e.g., related to kinship relations or other 'traditional' obligations to support certain people) or 'new' social capital (stemming from association with a group of people that has recently decided to collaborate, e.g., because they have moved to the same neighbourhood or because they have realised that they are having a common problem). In S&C groups, any kind of "capital of relationships", which the representatives of Enda Graf Sahel from Senegal call "the main wealth of the poor" (N'Dione et al. 1998, 370; see chapter 2.2.3 of this thesis), can replace the collateral demanded by banks. However, in many cases, the loan is not used as productively as presented in the above-cited extract from Main 30. More commonly, loans – irrespective of their source – are used to cover daily expenses, a phenomenon that is well-known from borrowers with low incomes in other countries (see e.g., Bateman 2010, 29-30 (Bangladesh, India, Tanzania, Uganda); Rahaman 2014, 56 (Bangladesh); Wichterich 2015, 479 (India)). A main interviewee from Jinja District stated that "another thing we have that sustains us, we go to banks and we borrow" (Main 27, 2017, translation by E.K. and K.M.). She later added: "We take from there a loan, we educate the children" (ibid.). Paying school fees and other cost of living does not help the debtors to pay back the loan. Apart from that problem, there are other obstacles, like being bereaved of someone, falling sick, or having a sick relative in the hospital. The latter means bringing that person food (though the hospital might be far away) because this is not part of the services provided by hospitals in Uganda. As a result, there is no time left for working to earn the money for debt repayment. The above-cited respondent compared being in such a situation when having a loan from the bank and from her S&C group as follows:

> "And also, there, the people of the group, the way they demand is not how a bank demands. [...] For us, you can be considerate with your friend. So to say, (s)he has a patient in the hospital and (s)he has not been able to bring back the money, but has a patient in the hospital, (s)he has not been working, and you say that, 'Okay, (s)he'll bring it back next month', and you leave him/her to go to attend to his/her patient, and (s)he brings the money later. But the bank, for it, it doesn't know that you are sick, it doesn't know maybe you have lost someone, it doesn't know challenges." (Main 30, 2017, translation by E.K. and K.M.)

Another respondent from Jinja District reported that people in his area had bad experiences with formal microfinance institutions. He complained about their high interest rates and claimed that even the government had realised how much they had "harmed" the local population. In his view, this finding made the government promote S&C groups at the village level:

> "Okay, mainly like these groups, which are here these days that maybe microfinance, finances those, these maybe FINCAs those, I don't know BRAC, BRAC [...] okay, they have helped. But, at the end of the day, again, they end up harming us. [...] So, now, when we saw that those so-and-so, they are harming us, now, even this government also saw that/ when/ Okay, in fact even government also saw that the groups are harming us a lot. Then, government is to come in with the groups and told us to form those groups. In case we have formed a group, then government also will come to see what the group is doing, then, the group/ eh (considering), government will have its ways to help us. So, that's why you see we started there/ we put there small groups, those groups, in the villages." (Main 16, 2017, translation by E.K. and K.M.; "microfinance", "finances", "okay", and in some cases "group" were English in the original)

A similar account was given by another main interviewee from Jinja District who was the co-founder of an S&C group. She told me how women in her area suffered from the tough measures taken by "banks" in order to make their debtors pay (in that case, it is not clear whether she meant banks in the narrow sense or MFIs, but for this analysis, it makes no difference, as both are formal loan providers in contrast to SSE groups). Consequently, they founded their own S&C group to escape formal loan providers, as she narrated:

> "For that group of ours, we started it in 2010. […] When the objective/ when women used to run away because of the bank, if they have not paid, they take away their things, if they have found you with your TV, they take it, they sell it/ […] But we, here, we look after each other […]." (Main 28, 2017, translation by E.K. and N.H.)

Other respondents likewise said things like "those of the bank, they come with the police officers" (Main 27, 2017, translation by E.K. and K.M.). All things considered, S&C groups are an option for people to: 1. save money, an activity that they can hardly undertake individually; 2. deal with the problem that they are not eligible to formal loans, either by giving loans to each other, or by accessing formal loans as a group; and 3. secure more favourable conditions for paying back their loan (lower interest rates, softer conditions for paying back) than they could acquire from banks or formal MFIs. Furthermore, those groups provide a forum in which solidarity among the members can develop. Apart from the above-mentioned understanding of challenges in everyday life that people can expect from fellow members but not from formal financial institutions, other levels of cooperation exist. For instance, a main interviewee from Kamuli District, who was a member of a SACCO and a VSLA (for details on types of S&C groups, see below), said about the latter, i.e., the smaller group: "Mm (affirmative), and that is where you see that, now, the groups come to be good, now, if you get sick, your friends can help you" (Main 13, 2017, translation by E.K. and K.M.). Many main interviewees judged S&C groups positively. Concluding remarks on them like the following one by a respondent from Buyende District are typical: "They are helpful because, in case you have gone as an individual and they give you a big amount of money, you have to find what to do that can help you in your life or in your household" (Main 10, 2017, translation by E.K. and N.H.).

However, S&C groups also have potential downsides. For instance, all kinds of credit providers, regardless of their size or level of professionalism, find themselves in trouble when their members delay or even refuse to pay back their loans. For instance, the above-cited respondent and co-founder of a S&C group (a VSLA) in Jinja District told me:

> "So to say, when they come together, the money, they come together, they lend it to people. Other people don't pay back. They run away with it. So, their friends have made a loss. But still, there are some groups, which are doing well. Me, like mine, the one that I'm in. We removed from it those people, who run away with the money, and we

> remained with few people, there." (Main 30, 2017, translation by E.K. and K.M.)

Later, she continued explaining that: "Now, we remained 25 people. […] At the very beginning, we were 60 people/ […] We used to give people and they fail to pay back to us/ […] Others, we used to confiscate the TV from them“ (Main 30, 2017, translation by E.K. and K.M.). Hence, the members of her group have been reduced to the house owners who reside permanently in the place. The members who had only rented a house or a room have been excluded from the group because, for them, it was easy to disappear overnight before paying back their loan. From the point of view of the group, this measure makes perfect sense, as the group may collapse if too many members do not pay back (on time). However, the neediest group, those who cannot afford to buy a plot and build a house in the area, has been excluded from the group activity. This respondent also mentioned that the group used to take away the properties of members who had not paid back. This is evidence of the tough methods of smaller groups such as this VSLA copying the ways of formal microcredit institutions. It also illustrates the ambivalence between solidarity on the one hand (understanding each other's challenges) and social control on the other hand (taking away each other's properties to enforce repayment) in such groups. Another main interviewee from Jinja District described the situation from another point of view:

> "We have groups, but for me, I don't enter groups for a reason. Why I don't enter a group, you will go and borrow money, or they give money, you will fail to do what? […] To pay it, and they bring the police here, they come and they take all the things, they take them out, so to say, sometimes, you get ashamed in front of the people." (Main 17, 2017, translation by E.K. and K.M.)

These examples illustrate a general impression I gathered from the data: Savings and credit groups are highly ambivalent. On the one hand, they can be a means of emancipation from financial restraints and the power of formal financial institutions as well as a space in which people understand each other's challenges. On the other hand, they are prone to develop into the very thing from which they were supposed to protect their members, namely oppressive institutions that try to realise payment by all means. There are different forms of S&C groups that are based on solidarity to differing extents. A representative of Jinja District explained their hierarchy by stating that "when they promote themselves from a ROSCA, they can become a ViSiLA[133], or they can become a SACCO" (Expert 7, 2017).

In the following, I present the three kinds of savings and credit groups that have been encountered in Busoga in the scope of this study. At the end of each presentation, I apply to the various kinds of S&C groups the characteristics shared by the Social Economy (Williams 2014, 46-47) *and* the Solidarity Economy according to Michelle Williams as well as the principles of the People's Economy, which Norman Chipakupaku defines as the African version of Social and Solidarity Economy (Chipakupaku 2008, 138-139; see chapter 4.2.1 of this thesis). This has been done with cooperatives above and will be done with the remaining kinds of SSE groups in subsequent sub-themes. I compare the results at the end of this sub-theme in order to see which kind of savings and credit groups has the highest potential in terms of SSE.

ROSCAs – Rotating Savings and Credit Associations

Rotating Savings and Credit Associations (ROSCAs) are pure *saving* groups (despite the word *credit* in their name) that are small and easily manageable. In a ROSCA, people contribute a fixed amount at every meeting, e.g., every week. Every time, the total amount of contributions is given to one member. This process continues until every member has been a recipient, upon which most ROSCAs immediately start a new cycle. The defining elements of a ROSCA that distinguish it from a VSLA (see below) are the *element of rotation* together with the *absence of loans* and, as a result, *of interest*.[134] The way ROSCAs function has been explained to me as follows:

> "A ROSCA, a ROSCA is a small group of people. It involves a small group of people, who come together and they normally stay in a particular area. […] at end of a certain period of time, they contribute a certain amount of money, and give it to one individual. […] It

133 The correct abbreviation is VSLA, i.e., Village Savings and Loan Association (see below). However, Ugandans turn the abbreviation into a word, as it is done more easily with the abbreviations SACCO and ROSCA. In case of VSLA, it becomes "ViSiLA" in speaking. This is how it was spelled in the transcripts.

134 This description is based on the findings drawn from this study's data. It corresponds with Shirley Ardener's description of ROSCAs (Ardener 1995, 1), which helped me to categorise the described groups.

continues rotating from one person to another, until the last person is what? Is also served." (Expert 7, 2017)

Main interviewees did not use the term ROSCA. Instead, they often spoke about "saving groups" or simply "small groups" but the activities and rules they described categorised them unambiguously as ROSCA. A main interviewee from Buyende District explained her ROSCA in a simple and clear way by saying that

> "every member has to contribute 10,000 [shillings], we choose a member we are going to give money, every month [...] Every month, we give to how many people? [...] Two. [...] Mm (affirmative), on 15th/ [...] Even on 30th." (Main 10, 2017, translation by E.K. and N.H.)

Given that, even in the remaining interview she never spoke about interest or about having to pay back that money, she was clearly referring to a ROSCA, not a VSLA or a SACCO (see below). The members pool money twice per month and give the whole amount to one person, each time. There is no need to pay back the money or to pay interest because there is no loan. As a result, those groups are not attractive for people with money to invest. Instead, they are ideal for people with low incomes because they are easy to handle, there is no need to find a storage place for the money and the amount to be saved every time is the same, i.e., it is predictable. ROSCAs are the safest variant of savings and credit groups. I have not been told about any ROSCA that failed. Two main interviewees from Buyende District and one from Kamuli District told me that they are members in such groups.

Chart 8: Criteria for SSE groups: ROSCAs

Criteria for SSE groups: ROSCAs	
Michelle Williams' criteria for the Social Economy and the Solidarity Economy (2014, 59):	
cooperation	Members cooperate. Their activity (contributing money and giving it to one or two members) takes place during their meetings, which all members are required to attend (otherwise, the system does not work). Thus, a member cannot miss any important information, decision, etc.
democratic decision making	Members must agree among themselves how to operate. Elites do not tend to dominate because groups of this nature are not attractive to well-off people. There is no interest and the amounts saved are small.
collective ownership	Until the cycle has been completed, all the money circulating in the group remains common property. Every member is responsible for ensuring that all other members get their savings accordingly. They collectively own the group activity.

bottom-up processes	Such groups are initiated by the members themselves. There may have been NGOs or other institutions that brought the idea but the latter has grown independent of them. Such groups multiply by themselves, without government promotion or any other incentive.
caring and sharing	People like such small groups because the members know each other well. If a member is genuinely unable to pay back on time, e.g., because of sickness or being bereaved of someone, the fellow members can check it, understand it, and allow the member to delay the payment. This would be impossible in a SACCO (see below), a formal MFI, or a commercial bank.
Norman Chipakupaku's principles of the People's Economy (2008, 138):	
joining economic efforts in order to earn a living	Members regard ROSCAs as an option to pay for daily expenses and to make small investments like materials for house construction, small income-generating activities, etc. The amounts they get do not exceed the amount that the individual member has actually saved by the end of the cycle, and there is no interest on the savings. Everybody gets the same amount, nobody profits more than the other members.
being run by and for the sake of the local population	This criterion is fulfilled, see "cooperation" and "bottom-up processes".
creating local economic cycles that provide employment to locals, keeping money and facilities at their disposition	The money remains among the members until one member takes it out to buy things or pay bills with it. However, this is likely to happen within the surroundings of the members, in most cases.

In summary, ROSCAs are SSE groups. They fulfil all of Williams' criteria as a forum for *cooperation* with *democratic decision making*, *bottom-up processes*, and *caring and sharing* among the group members. With regard to the criterion of *collective ownership*, it is debatable whether it is fulfilled or not. After all, the money belongs to the individual members. However, in comparison to other S&C groups, ROSCAs provide more space for collective ownership, as the financial contributions and the responsibility for the group activity are shared equally among the members. ROSCAs fulfil the criteria of Chipakupaku's definition of the People's Economy. They help their members to save money, which is very difficult for them in everyday life. Nevertheless, they serve to make survival in the globalised economy easier, rather than to question it. In that sense, they are closer to the Social Economy in the narrow sense and to approaches of poverty eradication and development than to the Solidarity Economy and Post-Development approaches, which rather look for *alternatives to* capitalist development. Nevertheless, ROSCAs also have features that qualify them for the Solidarity Economy and for Post-Development approaches. As the members receive only their own savings without interest and without the obligation to invest the money into a business, ROSCAs lack capitalistic elements such as growth or profit-orientation. Their activity illustrates mutual assistance in planning of household expenses rather than raising capital. There is almost no room for exploitation, apart from a member running away with the money at the beginning of the cycle. Yet, this is unlikely to happen (though not impossible) because ROSCAs are small and the members know each other well, such that the inhibition threshold to betray the fellow members is high. The lack of interest makes ROSCAs unattractive for well-off people and protects them from elite capture (see SACCOs on that point). Considering these characteristics, ROSCAs – though they are concerned with the cash economy and consumption – offer the most radical alternative approach within the scope of savings and credit groups. Beyond that, they are the most accessible option for support in saving, as even the poorest can start them, as long as they find some fellow members among their friends, relatives, or neighbours. In view of Wallerstein's call for alternatives to the current capitalist world-system, such groups can serve both medium-term and long-term goals (Wallerstein 2003, 271; see chapter 3.4 of this thesis). In the medium term, they can contribute to the mitigation of the situation of households that suffer from low incomes, high cost of living, and lack of possibilities for saving. In the long term, they can offer *an alternative to* commercial savings and credit business, while other kinds of S&C groups just try to copy them, on a lower scale (see below). ROSCAs are closely related to *Mukenkede* and *Gema Kumwino*-groups (see chapter 8.3.4), which operate in the same way, but instead of cash, the recipient is given 'gifts' by the comrades.

VSLAs – Village Savings and Loan Associations

Though ROSCAs are the safest variant of S&C groups, *the most attractive variant*, according to respondents, are *Village Savings and Loan Associations* (VSLAs). This is mirrored in the high number of VSLA members among the study respondents. While only three were members of a ROSCA, 12 were members of a VSLA (5 in Buyende, 4 in Jinja, and 3 in Kamuli District). Though the term VSLA (spoken: "ViSiLA") is more commonly used in Busoga than the term ROSCA, not all main interviewees used it. However, with the help of their descriptions of activities and rules of the respective groups, they could be unambiguously identified as VSLAs. According to Anyango et al., the model of VSLAs was introduced to several African countries, including Uganda, by the organisation CARE and has ever since been promoted by numerous NGOs all over Africa (Anyango et al. 2007, 11-12). Hence, it is very likely that one of these NGOs has brought the idea to Busoga, though it is no longer traceable, which NGO was responsible for this. The idea has spread and become independent, as all the respondents involved in them claimed that the group was formed on their own initiative. Anyango et al. postulate that "[a] VSLA is a time-bound accumulating savings and credit association (ASCA)" (ibid., 12). It makes sense to distinguish it from a ROSCA in that way because the ROSCA *rotates* permanently, while the VSLA *accumulates* over a certain period of time that has been agreed upon by the members in advance. The respondents of this study described the system as follows: VSLAs collect savings for a fixed period of time (in most cases one year) and lend them out throughout this period, such that the borrowers provide interest for the savers. However, the borrowers and the savers are the same people: the members of the group. A main interviewee from Jinja District described the activities of her VSLA as follows:

> "We sit every week. When we sit, every week, we decide and say that it depends on someone's earning, in a week, you put 10,000 [shilling]. Are you getting me? In a week, put 10,000, now, there, for these other emergencies, you put 1,000. Now, these emergencies, if we lend that money to someone, because that money is for problems, we don't put interest. […] A child has fallen sick, so to say, that problem that comes when you are not prepared for it, you get a loan, then you take two weeks and bring back the money. There is no interest. This saving that we save, we say that, 'you end on 10,000 depending on your earning, whether you can manage 10 or, ah-ah (negative), we want to be what? Equal.' […] We start from 2,000 up to 10,000. […] we do it for a full year […]." (Main 28, 2017, translation by E.K. and N.H.)

Two aspects in this description are of particular interest. One is typical, though not obligatory, for VSLAs in Busoga: It has two cash boxes, one for the regular savings and credit activities and one for emergency loans in case a member is in trouble. I discuss this practice further in chapter 8.3.5. The second aspect is special and was encountered only twice in the scope of this study: There is not only a minimum amount for the regular savings but also a *maximum* amount for the regular savings. The respondent explained that circumstance by saying that the members want to be "equal". This may be a hint to elite capture, which is a serious problem in many SACCOs (see below). Obviously, this VSLA wants to be unattractive to people with a higher income, who may put much money in the group's cash box and refrain from taking out loans, waiting for their fellow members to increase their profits by taking out loans and paying them back with interest. In the above-cited case, the members want to remain in control of their group. At a later point, the respondent particularised the group's mode of operation as follows:

> "We lend out the savings, but when there is interest on them. [...] We give depending on the month, depending on what you are going to do, the reason for taking that money: one month, two months, three months, and we end there at four." (ibid.)

Though details vary, the above describes the basic functioning of a VSLA in Busoga. Variations can be found in the time intervals between the regular meetings (e.g., once per week or every two weeks), in the amount to be saved in every meeting (sometimes, there is a fixed amount or a limit, sometimes not), in the time limit for payment (usually between two weeks and four months) and in the regulations concerning emergencies. What respondents liked most about VSLAs is the regular payout[135] – or as the established term in Lusoga translates: "breaking the box". After having paid their contributions for six to twelve months (depending on the regulations of the respective group), the money has accumulated and, if all went well, the borrowers have not only brought it back, but added interest on it. A main interviewee from Buyende District described it as follows:

> "We have a group, we collect money, we save, we take ten months, then we break the box. Now, by the time of breaking the box, the amount of money, you don't expect that you can have it, you benefit from it immensely." (Main 2, 2017, translation by E.K. and N.H.)

With one exception in which the chairperson behaved rather dominantly, in most cases those groups are managed conjointly by the members and decisions are made together by the members. For instance, a respondent from Kamuli District said about VSLAs in general that "they are managed by the people themselves" (Main 12, 2017, translation by E.K. and K.M.). VSLAs are governed through by-laws the members themselves design. The co-founder of a VSLA in Jinja District, who was cited at the beginning of this chapter, described that process as follows:

135 Anyango et al. made the same observation in the course of their study of VSLAs in Zanzibar (Anyango et al. 2007, 19, 21).

> "For us, we start to meet and we get our friends. Those friends of ours, when we get them and we reach the number that we want, we elect the chairperson, secretary, treasurer, and the members. […] we make a constitution and put up even laws. […] We agreed on every law by law. […] Like: 'My friends should this one work?' In case there is where they are changing, they say like: 'Ah-ah (negative), here, it is too hard, let us lessen a bit.'" (Main 30, 2017, translation by E.K. and K.M.)

VSLAs are frequently combined with other group activities. The combination with burial support is most popular. Some have more far-reaching social support components, like the group described by one of its members, a respondent from Jinja District, in the following:

> "Our friend, a member, in case (s)he has fallen sick, we come in to help him/her out, in case (s)he has lost someone, we come in to help those widows, the disabled/ Because, eh (considering), all those categories, in our group, we welcomed them, we are with them. […] Mm (considering), now, we send assistance in this way: For you, if you are maybe a widow, or you have a kind of disability on your body, but when you have something that you are doing, maybe a small thing, you can come in the group and we have a way, in which we support you a bit. Eh (considering), when we have not said that maybe, again, bring back interest or do like this. Our friend, if (s)he is a member in the group and has fallen sick, but when (s)he does not have a way/ […] So, for that one, we also have a purse, from which we can manage to help him/her. That one, I'm speaking on behalf of our group/" (Main 16, 2017, translation by E.K. and K.M.)

Here, burial support is extended by support in case a member falls sick. There are interest-free loans for widows and members with disabilities. The same group provides an additional service of buying seeds in bulk and providing them to the members on credit. In order to fill its cash box, it has an income-generating activity of renting out party equipment:

> "Because it is so easy, today, we have a tent, we have chairs, plastic chairs/ […] those ones, we hire them out. You, in case you want, as long as you know that, 'Uh (considering), I have my party, but I need some chairs, I need this and that, uh (considering), here, the one who has things/' 'Uh (considering), you go in the group called Tukoome, they have chairs, they have those tents.' And for you, you come and you give us this-and-that and we hire them out to you." (ibid.)

This group is special because it has exceptionally many and diverse activities. It has acquired some of its materials, for instance the tents and chairs, by applying to the local administration for funds, and it occasionally borrows money from a SACCO. The last two are important activities that motivate people to join groups. Many resources provided by the government, NGOs, or financial service providers are reserved only for groups. Members appreciate when their group grants them access to those resources. In the worst case, they form or join the group only for that purpose, which can lead to the group's disbandment as soon as the resource is finished. In the best case, it is one of many advantages enjoyed by the members of a functioning group. Though I did not encounter a second group with such diverse activities as the above-mentioned Tukoome group, many have some kind of combination of two or three activities (e.g., savings and credit, plus burial support, plus agriculture). If savings and credit is the most important activity for them, they present their group as a VSLA. This is more often the case than the opposite, e.g., presenting the group as a farmers' association with a credit component. This illustrates the popularity of S&C groups in Busoga. A few VSLAs are also involved exclusively in savings and credit. Like ROSCAs, VSLAs are small groups of people with low incomes. As a result, the savings and credit business is manageable and, in case a member fails to pay back the loan on time, the comrades examine the situation and often decide to prolong the grace period when they see that there are good reasons, like sickness or being bereaved of someone. This is the reason why VSLAs work well and are very popular, though the social peace and financial success within them are fragile. If failure to pay back loans occurs too often and maybe even members disappear with the money, those groups can either collapse or take tough measures on their default borrowers, as SACCOs and commercial microfinance institutions (MFIs) do.

Chart 9: Criteria for SSE groups: VSLAs

Criteria for SSE groups: VSLAs	
Michelle Williams' criteria for the Social Economy and the Solidarity Economy (2014, 59):	
cooperation	Most of the VSLAs about which I was told cooperate well. Some have the usual problem of S&C groups that members fail to pay back their loans, which endangers the whole system, financially and socially. In S&C groups, cooperation is always prone to turn into social control and serious sanctions. It is a fragile kind of cooperation, yet very much appreciated by many interviewees. As long as the system works, VSLAs are among the most popular SSE groups and the spirit within them seems to be positive.

democratic decision making	Apart from a single case, in which the chairperson seemed to be very dominant, most respondents described VSLAs managed conjointly by their members. Members reportedly decide together on their by-laws and the conditions, under which their group operates.
collective ownership	Throughout the year, the money belongs to the whole group, as it can be borrowed to any member at any time and the borrower is supposed to pay it back *to the group*, not to an individual member. The group bears the risk as a whole. When the annual payout comes, the savings and interest become the individual property of each member.
bottom-up processes	The concept of VSLAs was most likely brought to Busoga by NGOs, yet it has since grown independent of them. VSLAs multiply by themselves, without government promotion or any other incentive. One group reported having been supported by an NGO but only after they had been operational for a while.
caring and sharing	People like such small groups because the members know each other well. If a member is really unable to pay back on time, e.g. because of sickness or being bereaved of someone, the fellow members can check it, understand it, and allow the member to delay the payment. This would be impossible in a SACCO (see below), a formal MFI, or a commercial bank. However, cooperation in S&C groups is fragile and always prone to turn into pressure and fear. In either case, many VSLAs have additional components of mutual care, like burial support or other forms of social protection (e.g., emergency fund in case of sickness, interest-free loans for widows).
Norman Chipakupaku's principles of the People's Economy (2008, 138):	
joining economic efforts in order to earn a living	One objective of the members of a VSLA is to make profits through the interest on their savings. However, those interests are very low. The more interesting aspects for the members are the possibility of receiving a loan easily when they need it and to receive their accumulated savings at the end of the cycle (as explained above, to save individually is impossible for most people). VSLAs operate on a financial level that does not allow high profits. It is rather a possibility for people with low incomes and no capacity to save on an individual basis to get hold of a *relatively* high amount of money once or twice per year, e.g., for paying school fees, buying some construction materials, or investing in a small business. Hence, in a VSLA, members join economic efforts in order to make a living.
being run by and for the sake of the local population	This criterion is fulfilled, see "bottom-up processes". Members implement their activities together, in their regular meetings.
creating local economic cycles that provide employment to locals, keeping money and facilities at their disposition	VSLAs do not really provide employment and their assets are purely financial. However, they are a means of keeping the members' money at their disposition, without giving it to a bank, which keeps some of it as account fees and speculates with it. The money circulates only among the members. Certainly, in most cases, the group has no control over the way members spend their loans and savings. However, they are likely to spend them within the area.

In summary, VSLAs do not perfectly fulfil all criteria for an SSE group but they have many elements of SSE and are greatly appreciated by respondents. They fulfil most of Williams' criteria, apart from collective ownership, to a certain extent, though the cooperation within them is fragile and depends on the members' discipline with regard to paying back the loans. VSLAs fulfil the criteria of Chipakupaku's definition of the People's Economy. They help their members to save money, which is very difficult for them in everyday life, and to receive an accumulated amount with added interest once or twice per year. The most important traits of a VSLA are the very ones that distinguish it from a ROSCA: the elements of credit, interest, and the annual payout (i.e., accumulation instead of rotation). The interest paid on the loans is what makes VSLAs more attractive than ROSCAs, but it also makes them more prone to failure. To pay the same amount on a regular basis is easier for most people than to pay back a loan within a short period of time - especially when the money was not invested productively (e.g., for paying school fees or for consumption), or when the investment, e.g., a small business, has failed. Even more than ROSCAs, VSLAs don't question the globalised economy but rather facilitate survival within it. They are closer to the Social Economy in the narrow sense and to approaches of poverty eradication and development than to the Solidarity Economy and to Post-Development approaches. In contrast to ROSCAs, they encompass the capitalistic elements of growth and profit-orientation. Their goal is to raise capital, though on a very low level. There is room for exploitation, as well-off members can invest comparably high amounts of money and wait for the borrowers to bring them profits. In practice, the activities of VSLAs are on such a low level that this is not as frequent a problem in them as in SACCOs (see below). In addition to that, VSLAs are small and the members know each other well, such that the inhibition threshold to betray the fellow members is relatively high. Nonetheless, they often have trouble with members who do not pay back their loans. VSLAs are the most accessible option for taking out loans for people with low incomes. Due to their emphasis on accumulation of capital and profit-orientation, VSLAs can rather serve "interim, middle-range goals" while they fall short of contributing ideas to the search for *long-term* future alternatives to the current capitalist world-system (as demanded by Wallerstein, see: Wallerstein 2003, 271; see chapter 3.4 of this thesis). As they likewise have the elements of *cooperation, caring and sharing, bottom-up processes, democratic decision making, collective ownership*, local orientation, and especially as they are often named first as SSE activities by respondents, VSLAs must be understood as SSE groups – though with certain reservations.

SACCOs – Savings and Credit Cooperatives

Savings and Credit Cooperatives (SACCOs) are the latest descendants of the cooperative movement in Uganda. As the research at *Jinja District Archives* revealed, at least up to the 1970s, SACCOs were run only by the employees of large industries (see chapter 7.5). Today, their target group has been extended to every person who lives in Uganda. They are the only type of cooperative that has not suffered but rather flourished under the policies of economic liberalisation (Kyazze 2010; see chapter 4.2.2). SACCOs essentially work like VSLAs but on a larger scale: Apart from size, the major difference is that members must buy shares, as they do in other kinds of cooperatives (see chapter 8.3.2). They buy shares and save money on their account like VSLA members. They can request a loan at any time and must pay it back with interest within a predetermined period of time. In SACCOS, their yield on capital depends on the number of shares they have bought, as explained in the following statement by an employee of a SACCO:

> "That money that we got, they call it dividends, at the end of the year. And these dividends come from their shares, share capital. [...] And the person who qualifies to get the dividends, is the one who has the shares. If you don't have a share, then you don't own dividends. [...] The more shares you have, the more dividends. That's how we give out. [...] And we use the shares now, to borrow as loans to different people. [...] The interest from the borrowed money, it's what we use to give them, to give back to the members." (Main 24b, 2017, first sentence translated by E.K. and K.M.; the rest was in English in the original)

As a result, there is a risk of well-off people buying a high number of shares in order to receive dividends from the interest paid on loans by their less well-off fellow members (elite capture, see below). The comments of diverse members of SACCOs among the respondents of this study implied that they feel like account holders, not comrades or decision makers. The initiative to form a SACCO usually comes from the government. Evidence of this circumstance are comments like the following by a main interviewee from Kamuli District: "SACCOs are there, government put them there" (Main 22, 2017, translation by E.K. and K.M.). A representative of Jinja District explained that many groups, among them numerous SACCOs, which had been formed hastily in order to profit from government funding, collapsed quickly:

> "And, eh (considering), government has done a very big job in encouraging people to come together in order to address their concerns. And government has even gone ahead to put in place an enabling environment in terms of people accessing resources they may desire from those institutions created by government. And when government did that, people responded. People hurried. People formed community-based organisations, people formed associations, people FORMED cooperative societies. SACCOs mushroomed everywhere. [...] People thought government was just going to dump money there, without restrictions [...] For SOME reasons, some associations, which were formed without expecting much from government, have survived." (Expert 8, 2017)

Massive government promotion, i.e., the persuasion of people to found SACCOs in combination with the provision of funds to SACCOs, has led to the reputation of those groups as a chance to pocket government funds easily without having to pay back. This does not apply only to SACCOs. However, their structure makes them particularly prone to that phenomenon. They are large, anonymous, in many cases artificially compound groups. As a result, the repayment morale in many SACCOs is poor. The groups either collapse as soon as the start-up funds from government are finished or the committee takes tough measures on the members, who have not paid back. In general, SACCOs tend to suffer from elite capture, as the above-cited expert explained:

> "Most of these groups are suffering from elite capture/ [...] I call it elite capture because, wherever there's a need to form a group, there are always people at the forefront. [...] They control everything and their intention is to get what they want to get and GET OUT." (ibid.)

Like his earlier comment, this did not refer only to SACCOs. However, SACCOs were included in the groups he referred to and his comment corresponds with what an employee of a SACCO in Busoga (not the one cited above) told me in a spontaneous conversation: If those elites see their dividends in danger because the less well-off members fail to pay back their loans (on time), they put much pressure on them to pay, e.g., through seizing their possessions or imprisoning them (Conversation Record, May 2018). Hence, they act just like formal MFIs. In terms of decision-making processes, a main interviewee from Jinja District said about his SACCO that "the leaders, four people, they teach the people what to do, then, they decide" (Main 24a, 2017, translation by E.K. and K.M.). At best, this can be the result of well-meant paternalism on the part of educated 'leaders' while, at worst, it is a form of exploitation of the weaker members. For instance, a main interviewee from Jinja town reported that he had left the SACCO, in which he had once been a member, because the committee had abused its power and embezzled the members' money. When asked about decision making processes in the respective SACCO, he answered:

> "Now, there used to be a small committee, that small one, it was the one that decides. Now, it decides that, 'We are going to take out money like this.' And the people were taking out money while they have not informed the other people, and they just go there. [...] So, now, me, I left them." (Main 25, 2017, translation by E.K. and K.M.)

In that case, the committee did not even wait for the dividends but just embezzled the group's money. This was facilitated by the fact that the other members were neither involved in decision making, nor in the daily business of the SACCO. In most cases, the daily work is done either by the executive committee or by employees but not by the members. All the members meet only seldomly, for instance once per year, at their annual general meeting. This leads to a serious lack of control of the majority of members over their group. Apart from the above-described problems with dishonest committee members, many SACCOs are challenged by the fact that members do not know each other well. The groups are too big for the people in charge to control properly, whom they can give how much money, according to the person's ability to pay back. For the same reason, they often refuse to accept the challenges in the lives of their members that lead to delayed payments. In cases like sickness or being bereaved of a relative, in most small groups like ROSCAs or VSLAs, the other members would understand the problem and allow the borrower to delay the payment a bit. Most SACCOs, as they don't know their members well, would react by taking away all of that member's properties or by putting the person in prison.

Nevertheless, SACCOs perform some important functions. As explained above, under the sub-theme "Cooperatives", SACCOs can be financial service providers for other cooperatives. Furthermore, SACCOs can be useful as a link between individuals or institutions that have some money to invest (local elites, NGOs, MFIs, government agencies) and small groups like farmers' associations or VSLAs that sometimes need loans for their activities. For individuals with low incomes or no permanent income at all, taking out a loan from a SACCO is very risky (comparable to a formal MFI). These conclusions can be drawn from elements of the data like the following comment by the above-cited member of the multi-purpose VSLA *Tukoome*:

> "Then, we, as small groups, in case when we've entered a SACCO, then we can also go to borrow that money from the SACCO, we bring it in our group and we manage to distribute it to the people. So, you find that those SACCOs, again, their interest is very high [...]." (Main 16, 2017, translation by E.K. and K.M.)

Hence, SACCOs can make resources available to smaller groups. Furthermore, they can grant their members access to certain resources that are reserved for groups. Two respondents reported having received support through their SACCO, which in one case was provided by a government programme and in another case by an NGO. While four respondents reported currently being a member of a SACCO, three said that they had been members of SACCOs that have collapsed. Though these figures are not representative due to the small size of the sample, they still suggest a relatively high rate of failure.

Chart 10: Criteria for SSE groups: SACCOs

Criteria for SSE groups: SACCOs	
Michelle Williams' criteria for the Social Economy and the Solidarity Economy (2014, 59):	
cooperation	Though, by definition, SACCOs are cooperatives, in practice they are more like financial service providers. In most cases, elites that occupy the executive committee and paid workers operate the daily business. When members fail to pay back their loans (on time), they are taken to prison or their properties are taken away. Members do not feel like comrades but rather like customers.
democratic decision making	Many SACCOs are affected by elite capture. Though their by-laws are supposed to secure democratic structures (after the model of cooperatives), in practice, most members are excluded from decision making. The members meet seldomly and decisions are usually taken by the executive committee.
collective ownership	The money circulating in the group belongs to the group. However, the level of participation of a member depends on the amount of money (s)he has saved and the number of shares (s)he has bought. In many cases, members are *forced* to pay back their loan, or they fail to pay back. Hence, there is no collective ownership.
bottom-up processes	Many SACCOs are formed because government promotes them aggressively. Some of them collapse as soon as there is no (more) government funding for them.
caring and sharing	In the SACCOs about which I was told, members either felt like customers of a bank, or they were afraid of the measures the SACCO can take when they do not pay back. In large SACCOs, the members do not know each other. They consider the committee to be the SACCO, not the community of members. Though some SACCOs grant access to additional benefits like support from NGOs to their members, this can rather be regarded as another 'service provision' than caring and sharing among the members.

Norman Chipakupaku's principles of the People's Economy (2008, 138):	
joining economic efforts in order to earn a living	By definition, SACCOs are cooperatives. Indeed, cooperatives have the goal of making profits to a certain extent – and those profits are not equally distributed among the members, as their payout depends on their input. On the one hand, members with low incomes are prone to exploitation. In some SACCOs, there is an elite that buys many shares in order to make profits from the interest paid by less solvent members, who depend on taking out loans. On the other hand, some members with low incomes may succeed in starting an income-generating activity or another project that improves their livelihood with a loan that either the individual or a smaller group to which (s)he belongs has received from a SACCO. Hence, the idea of the People's Economy of equal distribution of modest income to many participants is fulfilled to a *very limited* extent.
being run by and for the sake of the local population	This criterion is fulfilled to a limited extent, as the members of the executive committees and the paid workers in the SACCOs are also local people. However, most members do not really 'run' the SACCO, i.e., have little to no control over the daily business and decision-making. Whether the group is run for their sake or for the sake of local elites that want to exploit them or just because a government institution has encouraged people to form a SACCO, differs from case to case.
creating local economic cycles that provide employment to locals, keeping money and facilities at their disposition	SACCOs do not provide employment to their members, only to a few workers. Though the latter are also local people, the idea of the People's Economy is rather to provide employment to as many people as possible, preferably the members of the group. The assets of SACCOs are purely financial. However, they are a means of keeping the members' money at their disposition, without giving it to a bank, which keeps some of it as account fees and speculates with it. The money circulates only among the members. However, as elaborated above, there are different 'classes' of members. Certainly, in most cases, the group has no control over the way members spend their loans, savings, and dividends. Yet, they are likely to spend them within the area.

Of Williams' five SSE-criteria, SACCOs fulfil none. In terms of Chipakupaku's People's Economy, the groups' performance looks better, though not satisfactory. Each of the criteria is being fulfilled only to a limited extent. While the weak point of other kinds of cooperatives in relation to SEE was the fact that their focus is not on the local economy, this is the only strength of SACCOs through an SSE perspective. Though the loans may technically be used for projects that go beyond the local scale, this is not very likely, given the relatively small amounts (apart from the purchase of commodities, which have been produced elsewhere). All things considered, the SSE-potential of SACCOs must be judged on two levels: as a group composed of individual members and as a provider of essential services to other SSE groups. When SACCOs are judged as member-based organisations, especially for individual members with low incomes, the judgement is devastating. Even in terms of the Social Economy in the narrow sense and approaches of poverty eradication and development, SACCOs do not deliver good results. They can even aggravate poverty and harm their members' dignity when the latter are unable to pay back – or when elites abuse SACCOs to drain surplus value from low-income earners. In terms of the Solidarity Economy or Post-Development approaches, SACCOs lack any alternative potential, as they work like formal MFIs, only on a smaller scale. However, the role of SACCOs does not end there. In an alternative economy, funding and even loans may still be needed. For instance, as long as there is a cash economy, agricultural production will require some kind of crop finance, as farmers incur expenses prior to harvesting and selling their yield. As has been elaborated under the respective sub-theme (chapter 8.3.2) and in chapters 4.2.2 and 7.5, production cooperatives face a serious challenge when trying to get a loan from formal financial service providers. For smaller groups like farmers' associations, it is not even worth a try to go to a bank and ask for a loan. In that context, a modified kind of SACCOs that does not involve individual low-income earners but rather connects SSE groups to sources of finance, would be needed. What qualifies SACCOs for that task is that they are cooperatives. As such, they can appreciate the potential of other SEE groups and grant loans to them while other financial institutions would not. Beyond that, they could make sure that the transaction between the lender and the borrower complies with SSE-principles and they would not indulge in financial speculation. For low-income earners, the involvement in S&C groups beyond the scope of ROSCAs and VSLAs makes no sense. The risks are higher than the potentials, regardless of some exemplary cases in which the borrower succeeded well. In view of Wallerstein's call for alternatives to the current, capitalist world-system (Wallerstein 2003, 271; see chapter 3.4 of this thesis), SACCOs can serve both medium-term and long-term goals, yet only as financial service providers for other SSE groups, not as SSE groups that serve individual members.

Summary on savings and credit groups (S&C)

In summary, Savings and Credit groups (S&C) are highly ambivalent and have a difficult standing within the Social and Solidarity Economy. Few SSE activities have the potential of S&C groups to be simultaneously helpful and destructive. They are supposed to be associations in which people who have a problem but not the means to solve it on their own come together and support each other in solving their problem. By that definition, savings and credit groups are SSE activities like cooperatives and many others. As the analysis has shown, in practice, they oscillate between the ideal of solidarity among the members on the one hand and rough methods of recovering money, which are not different from formal microfinance institutions, on the other hand. The safest variant of S&C groups encountered in Busoga in the scope of this study are ROSCAs, rotating saving associations without loans and without interest. Riskier, yet more attractive in the view of the respondents are VSLAs, village savings and loan associations. They save for a fixed period of time during which they give out loans to the members. When the period is over, the members receive their savings, together with the interest delivered by the borrowers. In both ROSCAs and VSLAs, a member who has a good reason to delay paying back has a good chance of encountering understanding among the fellow members. After all, they usually know each other, live close to each other, and have a similar life situation. In a SACCO (Savings and Credit Cooperative), which works like a VSLA yet on a larger scale and with an obligation for the members to buy shares, understanding is replaced by means of coercion, as there is no personal relationship and no trust among the members. However, I have also observed such conduct in some VSLAs. Anyway, I have seen good and bad examples of different kinds of groups in Busoga. My conclusions regarding ROSCAs, VSLAs, and SACCOs represent the average judgement that I have come to after analysing and comparing them.

Savings and credit groups support capital accumulation, profit-orientation (profits for the members though), and personal consumption (depending on what the group members do with their savings/ loans). Consequently, they cannot promote values that are in opposition to capitalism. Their major goal is to make survival in the globalised economy easier for the members, not to question it. This locates them closer to the Social Economy in the narrow sense and to approaches of poverty eradication and development than to the Solidarity Economy and to Post-Development approaches, which rather look for *alternatives to* capitalist development. In view of Wallerstein's call for alternatives to the current, capitalist world-system, they appear to rather serve as "interim, middle-range goals" of mitigation of the current situation than alternatives for the future (Wallerstein 2003, 271). However, as an alternative to commercial loan providers, those groups introduce elements of solidarity and mutual support to the credit business. Moreover, each type of group must be judged separately. ROSCAs offer the most radically alternative approach imaginable within the scope of S&C groups. VSLAs are more profit-oriented and risky, yet they fulfil many SSE-criteria and are very popular with respondents. SACCOs, when judged as member-based organisations, especially for individual members with low incomes, do not pass the SSE-test. However, SACCOs in a modified shape are needed in order to facilitate the activities of other SSE groups, which may need funding for their activities from time to time. They can connect those groups to sources of funding like NGOs, government programmes, or local 'investors' and supervise the SSE-compatibility of the transactions.

Originally, I had not planned to include savings and credit groups in this study, as explained in chapter 5.1.3. The interviewees were the ones who wanted to speak about them. They are the kind of group that was most frequently mentioned and many mentions were positive, especially with regard to VSLAs and ROSCAs. As my postcolonial research approach required me to respect the priorities of the researched, I was obliged to include S&C groups in the interviews and the analysis. Many respondents reported liking these kinds of groups because saving as an individual is almost impossible. As soon as money enters the house, it is immediately used up in one way or another. The obligation to take it to the next group meeting helps. Though a few interviewees preferred commercial banks to groups, the majority felt the opposite. Many would not even be eligible for a loan from a bank and should they get a bank loan or a loan from a formal microfinance institution (MFI), they fear the measures those institutions take in case a borrower fails to pay back on time (seizing their properties, imprisonment). In contrast to (small) groups, those institutions show no understanding for the living conditions of their customers, e.g., having to delay the payment because sickness or the death of a relative has destabilised the financial situation of the household for a while.

The kind of government promotion currently done on behalf of SACCOs in particular is not helpful. A slow but sure development of well-organised VSLAs, in which members know and trust each other, would be more helpful than the current promotion of the formation of SACCOs from scratch. However, this development of VSLAs into SACCOs should not be enforced. Member trainings on dealing with money properly would be much better than providing money to the groups. They should build their activities on their own money. This may not allow for big projects, yet the prospects of success are much better and the risk of exploitation is lower. In this way, the members can be in control of their groups and protect themselves from pseudo-members who either want to grab government funds and leave – or buy a lot of shares in order to profit from the interest paid on their loans by less well-off members. In general, this study has led to the finding that what S&C groups need most in order to be supportive to the totality of their members is trust, reliability, and understanding among the members (though with regard to SACCOs, it is questionable whether they can serve individual members beyond a small elite, at all). In order to be able to build such a relationship between the members (especially in VSLAs and ROSCAs), the group must be formed from the bottom up by people who know each other and who have comparable financial capacities. They must live close enough to each other to be able to visit a default borrower and evaluate his or her personal situation. As concluding quote on S&C groups, I have chosen a positive one because, in spite of some critical voices and of the problems I have seen and interpreted myself, the majority of respondents who talked about those groups, were in favour of them. A main interviewee from Kamuli District noted:

> "Mm (considering), now, as we are now trying to form groups, we are trying to simplify everyone's mind. Because when we/ you are more than one, you can at least be saved and get something that can help." (Main 14, 2017, translation by E.K. and K.M.)

8.3.4 Mukenkede/ Gema Kumwino groups

Mukenkede (Lusoga for: "my beloved one") – also called Gema Kumwino (Lusoga for: "hold on to your friend" or "support your friend") – groups are based on a revolving scheme that works exactly like a ROSCA, only that the recipient of the regular collection of funds does not receive the money in cash but rather in gifts. They meet regularly (usually every two to four weeks) and contribute goods for one member who then receives gifts from his/ her fellows, usually household utensils, e.g., cookware, plates, plastic chairs, sometimes also building materials, depending on what the group has decided upon. Either every member buys one item for the recipient or the group pools the money in order to buy one big item. They rotate until every member has been served and then start a new round with other items. A main interviewee from Kamuli District, who is a member of a group of that kind, explained:

> "That group, we sat and we saw that in terms of household items, we are badly off. So now, we were how many people? Twenty. While after every weeks like this [gesture: 3], we give to a person a bar of soap, one kilogramme of sugar, we give to him/her 30,000 [shillings]. That 30,000, when 20,000 from it are used to buy an asset. That thing is collective. This other 10,000 does what? It helps to host the visitors on that day. Now you, yourself, the person, you know, a gift that you buy

> for me, hm (seeking confirmation)? You may buy for me to say/ you ask me, you say that, 'My friend, in terms of what are you badly off, what is it?' And I say that, 'Maybe a blanket, or a mattress, or a bed, or what?' So, a person buys for you those, eh (considering), (s)he has bought for you a blanket, has bought for you a bed, (s)he who buys for you saucepans, (s)he who buys for you plates, (s)he who buys for you/ So to say, all those things, they bring them for one person. In those three weeks. Now, when we go at 'so-and-so's', I know that 'so-and-so', (s)he bought for me a mattress, that is what (s)he wants from me, too. Even me, in those three weeks, it's for him/her that I do what? I buy it for him/her." (Main 19, 2017, translation by E.K. and K.M.)

Mukenkede/ Gema Kumwino groups are new. It is quite possible that an organisation has come up with the idea, yet I have not found any evidence of that. The majority of respondents who talked about those groups were uncertain about the origins of that idea. Only one main interviewee proposed a hypothesis: She is a member of such a group and assumed that it is a new version of an old system of solidarity, as she explained in the following statement:

> "Mukenkede, it is like / let me tell you, like you, those people of the past, hm (seeking confirmation)? They used to cut/ they used to carry out blood pact, whereby the other person becomes your brother or sister, but when they cut themselves [...] that is the past blood pact, which is now in place, but now, we don't cut ourselves, but we use trust, (s)he is a real person, every problem, (s)he is so close, (s)he is your relative." (Main 9, 2017, translation by E.K. and N.H.)

In her view, building trust through the exchange of blood in the blood pact has been replaced by exchanging gifts. However, I have heard about the existence of such kinds of groups in Rwanda, where they are considered a special form of savings and credit groups. Both NGOs or local initiatives could be the origin of such groups. In either case, the above-cited explanation of the respondent suggests that the concept suits Kisoga culture very well, as the respondent takes very seriously the responsibility of the group members for one another. She likewise emphasised that it is important to give the fellow members exactly what they have given to oneself: "But these other groups of contributing for each other things like, uh (considering), maybe we have given my colleague this, you also buy the same" (Main 9, 2017, translation by E.K. and N.H.). This creates reciprocity and peace within the group. At the end of the cycle, every member has received the exact equivalent to the amount of money he or she has spent. At the same time, he or she has received more than he or she would have ever acquired alone due to the challenges of saving money on an individual basis, as explained above (see chapter 8.3.3). For respondents, it is better to have an obligation to give the money to a group. The social obligation towards fellow members outweighs other obligations. Consequently, many interviewees regard those groups as a great chance to improve their household situations, as daily necessities make it impossible to save enough money to buy all the things, which one receives on the big day. When asked how people manage to afford household utensils and other consumer goods, a main interviewee from Kamuli District answered: "Now, the people, presently, to buy those things, the majority, especially the ladies, these days have developed themselves much in groups" (Main 13, 2017, translation by E. K. and K.M.). She spoke about the above-described system and regretted that she could not herself afford to join such a group. After all, a member cannot refuse to return all the gifts to his or her fellow members, one by one, after having received them on his or her big day. That means, he or she must be sure in advance that he or she can afford the regular purchases. Otherwise, as the group members know each other well – after all, they meet very regularly – members who do not fulfil their responsibilities may get in trouble. However, I have not been told about any conflicts in such groups. People seem to take them more seriously than, for instance, savings and credit groups or cooperatives in which conflicts with members who are not really committed are normal. This finding suggests that Mukenkede/ Gema Kumwino groups are based on autochthonous solidarity structures, as people feel much commitment and ownership for them. Three main interviewees reported that they are members of such groups and many other respondents also spoke about them. Those groups seem to have additional activities quite often. Out of the three I encountered, two had additional savings and credit activities as well as burial support. This circumstance suggests a high level of harmony in those groups. If this was not the case, the groups would not tend to start more and more activities.

Chart 11: Criteria for SSE groups: Mukenkede/ Gema Kumwino groups

Criteria for SSE groups: Mukenkede/ Gema Kumwino groups	
Michelle Williams' criteria for the Social Economy and the Solidarity Economy (2014, 59):	
cooperation	Members cooperate by pooling their money and completing the cycle in order to serve every single member. With their joint efforts, they manage to purchase more items than each of them would have bought alone.

democratic decision making	Decisions are taken at the beginning of a cycle, e.g., regarding the time interval in which the group is going to meet, what amount of money the members have to contribute in each meeting, the order of members in the cycle, and the way the gifts will be distributed (collectively, individually, with a wish list, randomly, etc.). For each new cycle, those questions may be discussed again, based on the experience of the previous cycle. Yet, when a cycle is running, no decisions are to be taken until it is over. As the groups are based on voluntary membership and serious commitment on the part of the members (conflicts would arise quickly as soon as a member would fail to fulfil his/ her obligations), decisions can only be taken if agreed upon by all members.
collective ownership	The gifts are handed over to individual members and some get theirs earlier than others, who come later within the cycle. Nevertheless, the money and the commodities that circulate in the group cannot become the full property of the recipient before the cycle is completed. (S)he must first fulfil his/ her obligation to contribute to the gifts for all other members. When the cycle is completed, the group's activity is over and the assets become the individual members' property. However, in most cases, the group starts a new cycle right away. However, this criterion is not fulfilled.
bottom-up processes	These initiatives are started by people by themselves. There is no government intervention, no elite capture. It is quite possible that the original idea was introduced by NGOs. If that is the case, it has become independent of them.
caring and sharing	The alternatives to joining such a group would be either individual saving or taking out a loan for buying the desired items. As both is very difficult for most people in Busoga and the latter is even expensive and dangerous (see chapter 8.3.3), people have come together to take care of their problems conjointly. They put their resources together. In one case, solidarity among the members that goes far beyond the group activities has been described (see quoted extract): the members become "relatives" to each other and help each other in all spheres of life. Yet, this is not necessarily the case in all of these groups.
Norman Chipakupaku's principles of the People's Economy (2008, 138):	
joining economic efforts in order to earn a living	In this economic activity, nobody makes any profit. At the end of the cycle, every member has spent the amount of money that (s)he would have spent on the items (s)he has received if (s)he would have bought them. The balance is zero. However, what is helpful about those groups is that they are an alternative to individual saving (which is impossible for most people, see above) and taking out loans. Another side effect is that they help to plan well the expenses for buying commodities. All of this can help people to make a living and plan well for other expenses.
being run by and for the sake of the local population	This criterion is fulfilled, see "bottom-up processes". Though the producers of the respective commodities also profit from the system, the main objective is to make life easier for the local population.
creating local economic cycles that provide employment to locals, keeping money and facilities at their disposition	The economic cycles created are not purely local, as many of the commodities bought in the scope of those groups are not being produced in Busoga. Hence, the money may often leave the region when the purchase is done and employment opportunities being supported (in production and trade) may be somewhere else. However, the local people can decide on what they want to spend their money. This situation is similar to S&C groups. However, the money from S&C groups is frequently used for local activities like paying school fees (i.a., financing the teachers' salaries), financing agri-

	culture, starting small businesses, or buying food. It may also be used for buying consumer goods (which are usually produced elsewhere) sometimes. However, in Mukenkede/ Gema Kumwino groups, the latter is the only objective.

Mukenkede/ Gema Kumwino groups are SSE activities. They completely fulfil Williams' criteria of being a forum for *cooperation* with *democratic decision making*, *bottom-up processes*, and *caring and sharing* among the group members. The only shortcoming of Mukenkede/ Gema Kumwino groups in relation to this definition can be found in the area of *collective ownership*, as the assets become the property of the individual members. With respect to Norman Chipakupaku's definition of the People's Economy, Mukenkede/ Gema Kumwino groups fulfil two criteria but fail to *create local economic cycles*, as many consumer goods are either imported or produced in Kampala. Those groups may look materialist at first sight because their aim is to purchase goods. This circumstance makes their potential to promote values that oppose capitalism – which would be the prerequisite for them to be recognised as a phenomenon of the Solidarity Economy and many Post-Development approaches – highly questionable. They appear to be closer to the Social Economy in the narrow sense and to approaches of poverty eradication and development than to approaches, which rather look for *alternatives to* development and capitalism. However, a closer look at those groups reveals that there is more to them than materialism. First, the gifts being exchanged are not luxury goods. Rather, the groups serve to grant their members access to materials needed to fulfil basic needs (household necessities, construction materials, clothes). These groups also have a striking social dimension. Members meet once or twice a month and have an enjoyable time together while giving the gift shower to one of them. For them to meet so regularly, the groups must be small and made up of people who live close to one another. This potentially strengthens collaboration among neighbours beyond the group meetings (which has been described for one case, see above). In times of deteriorating social networks (see chapter 8.3.1), those groups can help to re-build those networks or establish new ones (e.g., in places with a lot of migration where the neighbours do not know each other well). All things considered, those groups have potential in terms of the Social *and* the Solidarity Economy as well as Post-Development approaches. In terms of Wallerstein's call for alternatives to the current, capitalist world-system, they first of all can serve the medium-term mitigation of the problem that many people do not have access to basic necessities. In the long term, political solutions for this problem would be more desirable than such self-help approaches. Though the number of Mukenkede/ Gema Kumwino groups encountered was not high – maybe because the approach is still new – the attitude towards them was very positive. The only negative thing I was told about them is that one interviewee deplored that she did not have enough money to join one. There were no reports about members not being committed, as in some cooperatives or savings and credit groups. The above-cited main interviewee from Kamuli District, who is a member of such a group, concluded as follows:

> "Anyway, now, what makes us be involved in, you may work alone where you fail to advance. So, in case your friend has given you that thing, (s)he also has given you a task to be done seriously for you to pay back that one that (s)he gave you. Finally, you find yourself when still, even you, you have accumulated those ones that your friends have given you. […] Because you may work sincerely when you are alone and you fail to advance." (Main 19, 2017, translation by E.K. and M.K.)

8.3.5 Muno Mukabi groups

"Muno Mukabi" can be loosely translated as "Your friend in bad times". Muno Mukabi groups are a modern version – sometimes a replacement, sometimes a supplement – of autochthonous forms of burial support, i.e., clan support or support at the village level (*obutaka*; for both see chapter 8.3.1). A main interviewee from Buyende District who is a member in both a Muno Mukabi group and the obutaka activity in his place, distinguished them as follows:

> "There is another group that I am in, let me say that of burying each other, helping in times of problems, when the other one has got a problem. […] It had its initiators, they explained it, it was like it changed/ not for saying that it gets residents (abataka), it gets/ it is a law that every resident in this region or person on that land that is taken by the resident council is meant to be. But this one where I am, it builds on agreement. […] Eh (affirmative), agreement, coming together for providing help of such kind. But again, the residents (abataka), we have a difference/" (Main 5, 2017, translation by E.K. and N.H.)

The obutaka activity is obligatory for everybody who lives in the village and is perceived as having always been there. In contrast, the Muno Mukabi group has been founded by some people ("initiators") and membership in it is based on voluntariness ("agreement"). Burial support is a very important issue in Busoga, as discussed above (see chapter 8.3.1). The activities of Muno Mukabi groups can include the following, depending on the specific arrangements of the group in question: Their most common activity is collecting what they call 'condolence fees', money that each member contributes in case one of them dies or loses a dependant (some define what kind of dependants they cover – e.g., only parents, spouse, and children – others cover any person for whom the member feels responsible). The money can be used to organise the burial ceremony and host the visitors who may stay near the burial location up to several days. If the dead body needs to be taken to an ancestral home that is far away, the money is used for the transport, including one or more people who accompany it. This collection of activities is common to all Muno Mukabi groups that I encountered. For some groups, they constitute the entirety of their activities. In other groups, members provide more assistance to their comrade, e.g., bringing food, water, and firewood to the burial ceremony like it is done by obutaka. In that case, the money can be used for other purposes, e.g., as balance for the loss the bereaved makes during the mourning ceremony by not being able to work. Some Muno Mukabi groups have even more activities, like attending the burial ceremony, bringing the required materials for serving the visitors (saucepans, plates, etc.), or providing support to members in other situations that come with unexpected expenses like sickness or major events in the lives of their children like graduations, weddings, or introductions (to the future family-in-law). In many cases, Muno Mukabi is integrated into other forms of SSE activities, namely cooperatives or savings and credit groups (see chapters 8.3.2 and 8.3.3). I encountered nine cases in which it was integrated into a savings and credit group and five cases in which it was integrated into a currently existing non-financial cooperative. A typical example is the following by a respondent from Buyende District: "Eh (affirmative), we made our small SACCO, then, those for burial, where there is collecting condolences in case of problems, and even lending, we, ourselves. But, again, government has not come to assist us" (Main 1, 2017, translation by E.K. and N.H.). In two cases, the burial support was even integrated in a group with savings and credit activities *and* Mukenkede activities (for details on the latter, see chapter 8.3.4). The two members of a cooperative in Jinja town with whom I spoke in a tandem interview told me about their group also having a burial component. One of them explained:

> "And also, when you lost someone in the group, we use to bury five people/ […] You, the member, the husband of the member, the chil/

> the son or the daughter of the member, the father of the member, the mother of the member. Mhm (affirmative). That whoever lost someone, we go let/ or/ we collect some little, little funds." (Main 20a, 2017)

Herment Mrema states with regard to Ugandan cooperatives: "Typically for African organizations, *social protection mechanisms are built in* by the members" (Mrema 2008, 169, emphasis by E.K.). Burial support is among the examples he gives for such kinds of built-in social protection mechanisms (ibid.). Muno Mukabi activities fulfil this function quite often, yet there are also many independent Muno Mukabi groups. Irrespective of whether the burial support is an independent group activity or integrated in another kind of group, there are different ways in which the collection of 'condolence fees' is organised. In some cases, the members contribute spontaneously for a comrade in trouble, as described above. In others, there is a permanent cash box for the contributions, which is re-filled by the members whenever needed. In case the Muno Mukabi activity is embedded in a savings and credit group, there are usually two separate cash boxes. For instance, a main interviewee from Kamuli town said that her VSLA (see chapter 8.3.3) collects an extra-contribution of 10,000 UGX from the members for burial support. Being asked whether that money is being lent out as loans (like the savings), she responded:

> "Ah-ah (negative), I've told you that we keep those 10,000 [shilling], we put them in what? In the group, here, the treasurer keeps it and we don't give it, we don't lend it. [...] Mm (affirmative), that one, we don't lend it. Because we may have lent it to you, and there could be a person who dies." (Main 19, 2017, translation by E.K. and K.M.)

Muno Mukabi groups have been included in the analysis as a form of SSE, though they may not look like an economic activity at first glance. They do not serve the purpose of making money. However, as a form of insurance, they do serve an 'economic' purpose in a wider sense. Having to bury a person is a serious economic challenge in Uganda. Nobody has a commercial burial insurance, and there is no support from the government. When a person dies, the family and the rest of the village are not supposed to work but rather to mourn together with the next of kin or the spouse. All these people must be served, sometimes for several days. Even the priest needs to be paid for the burial service. Handling all these expenses would be impossible for the majority of people, if there was no support from burial groups of any kind (obutaka, clan bank, Muno Mukabi). As a result, those groups can indeed be considered economic groups, as their function is primarily an economic one and their equivalent in the market economy are commercial insurance companies, which must certainly be considered economic organisations. Muno Mukabi groups are also very interesting because they emerged from autochthonous social structures of mutual support (obutaka, clan support) and because they often occur as part of a larger SSE activity, namely a cooperative or a savings and credit group. Numerically, Muno Mukabi are the strongest SSE activities in the data set, as 19 main interviewees reported being involved in them. The attitude towards them was generally positive. The only negative statement about them was similar to the only negative one regarding Mukenkede groups, yet this time it was voiced by a main interviewee from Jinja District. She deplored that: "Okay, there are those, who have them, I think. But they just want money, you enter with money, now/ where do you get 200,000 [shilling] from, for entering? So, other people have them, we don't have, those who are not able" (Main 26, 2017, translation by E.K. and K.M.). This was the only time I was told about such a high financial requirement to enter a Muno Mukabi group. Usually, the contributions to the cash box ranged between 1,000 UGX and 30,000 UGX and there was no entry fee or need to buy shares.

Chart 12: Criteria for SSE groups: Muno Mukabi groups

Criteria for SSE groups: Muno Mukabi groups	
Michelle Williams' criteria for the Social Economy and the Solidarity Economy (2014, 59):	
cooperation	The members of Muno Mukabi groups cooperate by coming together to solve a common economic problem: How to deal with the expenses caused by the death of a relative (or one's own death). Members cooperate by providing the money when it is needed. In some cases, they add other forms of assistance copied from autochthonous forms of burial support, i.e., bringing food, water, and firewood for the funeral service.
democratic decision making	There are not many decisions to be taken. When the groups is founded, members decide on the amount they are going to contribute and on whether they intend to support each other in case of death of any relative, or just in case of death of the closest relatives (e.g., parents, children, and spouse, only). After that, the groups work automatically and there are no more decisions to be taken. However, those decisions at the beginning are discussed and taken by the members conjointly.
collective ownership	The funds of the group are owned collectively and granted at short notice to whoever is in need. All members have the same right to the money.
bottom-up processes	Such groups are founded voluntarily by people who decide to do so by themselves. There is not even promotion of those groups by the government or by NGOs.
caring and sharing	Caring and sharing is the most important principle for supporting a person in case of death (of a relative).

Norman Chipakupaku's principles of the People's Economy (2008, 138):	
joining economic efforts in order to earn a living	Members join their efforts to establish and keep up an emergency fund that can serve any member at any time. There is no profit for anybody. Whoever gets money from the fund has become eligible to it by being bereaved of a person who was close to him or her. Yet, though there is no profit, there is protection from an economic loss following the social and emotional one. This is supposed to help the member to make a living, even after the burial.
being run by and for the sake of the local population	This criterion is fulfilled, see "bottom-up processes".
creating local economic cycles that provide employment to locals, keeping money and facilities at their disposition	Money is kept at the dispositions of the locals. An alternative would be burial insurances from commercial insurance companies, as they are common in Germany, for instance. This would mean that the people invest their money in such a company, which is likely to be at least located in the capital city, if not even abroad. In Muno Mukabi groups, the money does not leave the region and, most likely, less money is invested here than would be invested in a commercial insurance. While the latter requires a monthly contribution, Muno Mukabi only requires a contribution from time to time, when a case of death occurs. As a result, the money that is not needed for contributions in other months can be invested in other things likely to be located in the region, as well.

The special feature of Muno Mukabi groups that distinguishes them from other forms of burial support and makes them a SSE activity by definition is *voluntariness*. All other forms of burial support are not only autochthonous but also compulsory (obutaka is compulsory for all residents of a village or neighbourhood in a town; clan affiliation is compulsory by birth, but independent of residency; see also chart 5 in chapter 8.3.1). In contrast to that, Muno Mukabi are like all other SSE groups: Members form or join the group because they have decided to join efforts in order to address a common problem. Just like most of the other groups, membership also makes sense only for people from the same place, as the group must work together (this is different in case of clan affiliation, where strong family ties can overcome distances). In the following typical example, a main interviewee from Buyende District described the very basic function of every Muno Mukabi group, keeping in mind that "to get a problem" (okufuna ekizibu) in this context means being bereaved of someone: "We are in the groups of burying, Muno Mukabi, even if you get a problem, your colleagues contribute for you money" (Main 9, 2017, translation by E.K. and N.H.).

8.3.6 Respondents' experience with SSE groups

This sub-theme deals with positive and negative accounts of groups, conditions under which they work well, government promotion of groups and its effects and the internal organisation of groups. Beyond that, I examine at the outset of this sub-theme some forms of small groups that have not yet been dealt with as they occurred only once or twice in the whole data. In many cases, interviewees spoke simply about "ebibiina", i.e., "groups", without further specification, especially when it came to general comments or concluding remarks on them. Other comments subsumed herein were made with regard to different kinds of groups[136]. Groups mentioned included VSLAs, ROSCAs, SACCOs, women groups, agricultural groups for certain age groups (youth or the elderly), contemporary cooperatives, Muno Mukabi, Mukenkede/ Gema Kumwino groups, and multi-purpose groups. Some SSE groups are exclusively for women or men, for the young or the elderly. Most groups however have a mixed membership in terms of gender and age. The groups with specific criteria in those regards have the same activities as the others. Groups for certain age groups encountered in the scope of this study were exclusively agricultural, whereas women groups can be found predominantly in the sphere of savings and credit. For instance, a main interviewee from Kamuli District explained:

> "Uh (considering), (...) for example, like/ (...) we, the elderly, we don't work together with the youths because our energy is lower than that of the youth. So, uh (considering), if those groups for old people are there, eh (considering), we join them, at our place there, there is a group, but I have forgotten its name, for the elderly. [...] Government, also, it is where it lends a hand to us, maybe for rearing hens, or rearing goats, eh (affirmative), we are together." (Main 23, 2017, translation by E.K. and N.H.)

There are few agricultural groups like this one. Agricultural activities are limited almost exclusively to cooperatives. Though nine respondents spoke about the existence of smaller agricultural associations, only three main interviewees claimed to be a member of one of them. Another trait of those groups is that they do not rely exclusively on agriculture. They have additional activities, usually savings and credit activities. The group of one

136 Theoretical example: only one respondent said that his savings and credit group has by-laws but another said that about her SACCO, and another one about her agricultural cooperative.

main interviewee from Buyende District is involved in agriculture, animal breeding, crop trading as well as savings and credit:

> "We cultivate as a group, we rear as a group and we save money as a group. [...] Cultivating and rearing as a group, after harvesting those crops, we put them in the store, we get a day scheduled for market and we sell them and share the money according to how someone has stocked." (Main 8, 2017, translation by E.K. and N.H.)

This corresponds with the results of other sub-themes suggesting that agriculture is not really profitable except if a large quantity can be produced, such that the products can be sold on supra-regional markets or to major customers. Nevertheless, there is no widespread culture of farmers' associations in Busoga. When asked about farmers' associations, most respondents said that they do not exist within the region or that they are very few. There are some agricultural cooperatives, yet most of them deal only in crop marketing, while the production itself is done by each member individually. Cooperatives are more popular than smaller farmers' groups perhaps because of their higher bargaining power (due to larger numbers of members, who consequently deliver a higher total quantity of crops) or because they are well-known from the times of historical cooperative societies, whereas small farmers' groups do not seem to have any tradition in Busoga.

A cumulative assessment of respondents' judgements of the various types of groups in general shows that positive accounts (131 codings) are numerically stronger than negative accounts (32 codings). On a positive note, agricultural groups in particular (including cooperatives) are appreciated for granting to their members access to markets beyond middlemen. According to the respondents, escaping exploitation by middlemen is the main motivation for forming or joining agricultural groups. Respondents also expect from such groups the opportunity to earn a slightly higher income, compared to working as an individual. An expert interviewee commented on farmers: "When they are together, their bargaining power is higher. They've always been cheated by middlemen, especially in the East, even including Busoga region" (Expert 9, 2018). A main interviewee who is a member of a dairy cooperative in Kamuli District summarised some advantages, saying that "in a cooperative, you may take milk there, and you borrow medicine from there, you may take milk there and you all have a joint voice [...]" (Main 21, 2017, translation by E.K. and N.K.). People hope to improve their financial situation more quickly than they could without the support of groups. A main interviewee from Buyende

District noted that "what I think, those groups, when they are together, you can work together, even development becomes quick" (Main 1, 2017, translation by E.K. and N.H.). Another element of such groups that several respondents appreciated is that they make people work. As a higher outcome can be expected when people join their efforts (in terms of labour or in terms of finance), groups push the motivation of their members to work. Respondents appreciate savings and credit groups in particular for teaching their members how to save money. Groups in general have taken over many functions that were originally fulfilled by the (extended) family and neighbourhood. In the social surrounding of several interviewees, there are no more solidarity structures or social safety nets that could assist people in case they experience a challenging situation (e.g., sickness or death of a relative). They must rely on their group(s). For instance, a main interviewee from Buyende District described the situation as follows:

> "Those groups have raised us to another level, us, the people of this generation. How have they raised us? Those groups, if you have a problem, like these groups for money, someone cannot go to someone and you tell him/her that, 'Give me or lend me money now'. But in the other group/ if you have been saving money, it is very easy to say that, 'My colleagues, give such amount' and they give you. But as an individual, now, to say that, 'Lend this amount', (s)he can ask you when you are paying it back, you are going to use/ (s)he asks anything and everything. But here, you just go and say that, 'My colleagues, I need this amount', there is no problem. So, the situation has changed due to the formation of groups. Those groups have helped us/" (Main 9, 2017, translation by E.K. and N.H.)

A member of a dairy cooperative in Kamuli District gave another example:

> "[…] your child has fallen sick, you are in Jinja and you make a call, then the other one gets to know that you are a member. It is easy to give you some small money and you move out of the problem. Sometimes, you don't borrow from your sister or brother; you just call your chairperson, like me, that chairperson, you have got such and such a problem, 'get me some money', me, I just run to the treasurer, then we send you money, immediately." (Main 21, 2017, translation by E.K. and N.H.)

This means that social structures on the levels of family, neighbourhood, and community are falling apart and groups are the only source of support many people have in their social environment. Post-Development scholar

Arturo Escobar deplores that "the spread of the market economy broke down community ties" in the global South and thus deprived many people of an important resource for survival (Escobar 2012, 22; see chapter 2.2.3 of this thesis). As has been discussed above (especially in chapter 8.3.1), this is the case in Busoga to a certain extent. For some respondents, their modern SSE groups seem to be good substitutes. They find there trust, comfort, advice, and spontaneous help in case of a problem. A main interviewee from Kamuli District who is a member of another dairy cooperative said about groups:

> "Also, you have many ideas. Every person has to give ideas. You, what you wouldn't have done when you don't know, when you are together, there will be your colleague who helps, and you understand what you are doing, such that the result is beneficial." (Main 12, 2017, translation by E.K. and K.M.)

Hence, members share their knowledge and experience with comrades. A main interviewee from Jinja District who has been involved in Busoga Growers Cooperative Union in the past and who is a member of a Muno Mukabi group today, said about groups in general:

> "But when for them, they are good, mm (affirmative), groups are good. […] Because you go and you are together, you, so to say, you solve problems, eh (considering), you converse, hm (seeking confirmation)? So to speak, if you are annoyed and you are there, you laugh, you are happy because you are together." (Main 17, 2017, translation by E.K. and K.M.)

At least in some groups, though certainly not in all of them, there is some social interaction and warmth. Some respondents mentioned feeling relieved from their daily worries when they are in the group, as in the above-cited example. Others spoke about members supporting each other beyond the group activities (see above). Apart from that, groups have introduced opportunities to gain access to new resources. Many people join them in order to profit from the trainings they provide. The main interviewee from Jinja District who is a member of the above-mentioned multi-purpose group Tukoome with its diverse activities as a VSLA, an agricultural association, a renting agency for party equipment, etc., said:

> "Because we come, we are in groups, and we learn, we study. Because even those government, in case when they are bringing their things in something, still, they want the people who are together. So, we got a lot of trainings." (Main 16, 2017, translation by E.K. and K.M.)

Most likely, he referred to extension services. As discussed above, they have been reduced to a demand-driven service that is provided only to groups. In view of two female respondents, women also appreciate having an opportunity to make a living with the help of groups, without being dependent on a husband. In summary, the majority of the main interviewees of this study who commented on the usefulness of groups, said that they are helpful for their members.

Nevertheless, there were also negative accounts of groups. Numerically weakest among the negative accounts of groups, nevertheless important to consider, is the assertion that groups lack market. Selling agricultural products as a group works better than individually, yet it remains difficult to find a good market with fair prices. In terms of milk in particular, the wholesale price per litre may even be lower than the prices paid by individual customers in the village – a phenomenon that seriously challenges dairy cooperatives. In contrast to the picture painted above of groups full of trust and mutual support, there were also other more negative accounts. Several respondents reported of fraud within groups, among the ordinary members as well as on the part of the executive committee. The following observation by a main interviewee from Buyende District combines the two problems, with emphasis on fraud by the committee:

> "Groups here have been there but maybe later they get tired, I don't know. It is there, it finishes one year, those who want to eat a lot come in and especially the heads of the group […] they are the ones who destroy them." (Main 1, 2017, translation by E.K. and N.H.)

The following statement by a main interviewee from Kamuli who is a member of an agricultural group likewise contains that aspect but also an additional one, namely the problem that some groups are founded without any intention to run them permanently:

> "Sometimes, uh (considering), people are (...) they are stupid, if they give them the things, they share them there and then. […] That is what makes those groups collapse. Uh (considering), the third[137] point: even leadership, lacking trust, corruption." (Main 23, 2017, translation by E.K. and N.H.)

Many groups are formed in order to gain access to financial or material support from NGOs or from the Ugandan government. In some cases, the

137 The first point he had mentioned was that human beings are naturally prone to failure.

motivation to start the activity was there before, yet the financial means to start the activities were lacking. In other cases, as has been deplored above, the only motivation for the members (or the committee) is to pocket the money or materials for themselves, not to start any group activities. As elaborated earlier, under the corresponding sub-theme (chapter 8.3.3), VSLAs and SACCOs in particular have problems with members who frequently run away with the money they have borrowed. Cooperatives[138] – those providing financial services as well as those engaging in production and marketing – are prone to elite capture. This does not come as a surprise, as cooperatives are the largest SSE groups in Busoga and, as result, offer the highest profit margins. This makes them more attractive to elites than smaller formats like VSLAs or farmers' associations. Burial societies and groups based on revolving schemes like ROSCAs or Mukenkede/ Gema Kumwino groups do not offer any incentive to elites, as there is no profit in those groups.

Beyond the dichotomy of positive and negative accounts of groups, I extracted the conditions under which, according to the interviewees, groups can work well, as many respondents and gatekeepers had requested me to do so. They wanted to know how other groups are doing and what makes groups work. Several (main) interviewees had very concrete ideas regarding what groups need in order to be as successful as they could be. Many groups are small and their members have little to no capital. As a result, regardless of their activity and their motivation, they are unable to make big profits. Several respondents wished for material support, e.g., from the government, such that they could increase their outcome more quickly. However, as discussed above, financial or material support for groups is a double-edged sword. Government promotion of groups, especially cooperatives of all kinds, has recently been fairly intense. In many cases, this has been destructive. If it is pushed too aggressively, it leads to the phenomenon described in the two above-cited extracts and mentioned by some district officers during expert interviews: Some district officers estimated that maximum ten per cent of the SSE groups officially registered are actually operational.[139] They suggested that the other groups have been created only on paper in order to acquire government or NGO funds for the alleged members. Nevertheless, government support for groups

138 For SACCOs, see chapter 8.3.3; for other cooperatives, see chapter 8.3.2.

139 This is even worse than the estimate presented by Mrema that, in the year 2000, more than half of the cooperatives registered in Uganda were 'dormant' (Mrema 2008, 158; see chapter 4.2.2 of this thesis).

is desired and needed. On the one hand, more attention should be paid to the kind of groups that are being supported. Small groups that have been formed bottom-up by committed members should be prioritised. Currently, according to several respondents, this is not the case. A main interviewee from Jinja District noted the following:

> "Instead of helping the people who are what? Hm (seeking confirmation)? […] Who are badly off. Still again they help those who are what? Those who are somehow. […] you may see when there is a group, someone has put there a group, that 'this is a group,' but is a group, but shadow group, hm (seeking confirmation)? […] A-haa (affirmative), because there is something to get from, or up there, that group will be active that time. But you can find that these groups which are/ […] creative, they are not supported well." (Main 29, 2017, translation by E.K. and K.M.)

This respondent and others demanded that the focus of group promotion should shift from big groups with influential members to small groups with committed members. The results of my analysis support this demand. Furthermore, my analysis led to the conclusion that the focus should shift from financial inputs to trainings and, in the agricultural sector, material inputs. A respondent from Jinja town who quit his SACCO because of mismanagement on the part of the committee, complained about the current focus on financial support rather than trainings:

> "Uh (considering), that the groups need to be taught, government comes out and they teach the people. […] They teach the people how the groups must be. But government goes and says that, 'You people, make a SACCO, and we give you money'." (Main 25, 2017, translation by E.K. and K.M.)

A main interviewee from Kamuli District who is involved in a coffee cooperative, said about other smaller groups that are still evolving:

> "That, now, we talked about these groups/ which are there. But the people are lacking professionals, who are needed to continue to come to teach those groups, to take them from the level they are on to another level." (Main 15, 2017, translation by E.K. and K.M.)

Another main interviewee, from Buyende District, had another suggestion in that context:

> "Mm (affirmative), I could think, on the side of development, exchange visits, it could be done for our people because someone, if you

> visit somewhere, you can say, 'Ooh (challenged), I'm so big behind', you can pull up your socks and then you determine to do that thing." (Main 6, 2017)

Trainings in all respects (e.g., agriculture, saving culture, management, etc.) could certainly be a helpful form of support for groups. Another important issue concerning groups in Busoga (and presumably elsewhere) is trust. To a certain extent, this may be a natural human condition and not at all surprising. However, in Busoga, people have had some experiences in the past decades that make trusting their comrades even harder for them. On the one hand, there is their experience with the cooperative societies of the past, which were good for a while and then collapsed – many people say because of fraud (see chapter 8.3.2). It has continued in recent times in the shape of SACCOs (see chapter 8.3.3) and some other forms of groups that are aggressively promoted by government, such that they earned the reputation of giving out government money without conditions (see above). Such groups – as well as savings and credit groups in general – have attracted people who are not looking for cooperation but for easy money. In savings and credit groups, trust is most important, yet most fragile. A main interviewee from Buyende District commented:

> "Ya, and THEN, in these saving groups, if people keep TRUST, they could develop very fast. But what makes them to collapse, is untrustworthy. Yeah. Not keeping their promise [...] Otherwise, they are very good, if the motto put for it followed." (Main 7, 2017)

In order to build trust and stability, it is helpful when groups include as criteria for membership both social homogeneity and permanent residency in the location of the group activity. In some VSLAs, there is a maximum amount that can be saved per week, such that the group cannot be taken over by members who save a lot, expecting high dividends from the interest that their comrades pay on their loans – as it happens in some SACCOs (elite capture, see chapter 8.3.3 for details). When members live close to one another and know each other, trust is easily built. In areas with a lot of newcomers and tenants who can move away anytime, conflicts arise more easily. Though this finding provides a helpful solution for the permanent residents to stabilise their groups, it raises a problem for the newcomers and tenants. Usually, they are the ones most in need of support, as they have left behind the social safety nets of their native region. Hence, leaving aside permanent residency, social homogeneity, i.e., a comparable level of financial capacities of the members, remains an important criterion to protect groups from domination and even exploitation by elites. Furthermore, groups should be formed from the bottom up and based on a common vision. Being pushed by short timelines of NGOs or government programmes is not helpful to them, as the following comment by an expert interviewee illustrates:

> "We have tried, at a government level, to organise people, but MOST groups that have been organised, they tend to die. Of a perio/ of/ in a short while. MAINLY because, not mainly, but partly because much of the government intervention and NGOs, uh (considering), they work in a method of (...) periods. For example, if an NGO came here today to promote, uh (considering), a certain activity like how to (...) how to make clean water, they'll come, it is a project, it is two years, after two years, they disappear, go to another one. They are not permanent. Government programmes also have got these timelines. And, then, government programmes suffer from impatience." (Expert 6, 2017)

Groups, like any social institution, need time to evolve. Savings and credit groups in particular could stabilise themselves significantly by giving their members trainings and follow-up on how to deal with money, e.g., making a business plan or planning household expenses. Lack of permanent income, in combination with high cost of living, additional desires created by the availability of more and more consumer goods, and in many cases a low level of education, leads to a high risk of borrowed money being spent quickly, without a realistic chance of paying it back on time. As respondents have aptly pointed out here, the most helpful means of changing that situation for the better would be to help borrowers with their financial calculations, such that they can learn to plan sustainably. Two groups have had good experience with that strategy: the VSLA of the respondent of interview Main 30 (see chapter 8.3.3) and the cooperative of the respondents of the tandem interview Main 20, all of them living in the suburbs of Jinja town. The cooperative primarily markets handicrafts for the members but also has a savings and credit component. One of the members explained that, in case a member is in need of an additional income-generating activity, other members

> "will come and tell you: 'You see, you have to do this, in order to do this, borrow a loan from the group, you get that revolving loan, it will help you buy what you want, and you SELL. When you sell, you get the profit. The profit will help you. Because when you sit like this, it will not help you. Maybe, you are growing worse, down. So, please, do this and that.' And we FOLLOW you with the loan we have given you, we follow and see how you're using it. Are you using it correctly?

> Or you just want to eat it? Because there are some people, when they get the loan, they get excited. They go and buy with it/ [...] They buy MEAT. [...] They buy things in the house, and it gets finished, there is no way they can pay back. But this one, we always try to be with you. So that you can KNOW that, 'Let me do this, and I PAY. And then'/ [...] The interest I have, I use." (Main 20b, 2017)

In general, the revolving scheme on which ROSCAs as well as Mukenkede and Gema Kumwino groups are based, is a low-risk model for SSE groups. It has been adopted from the provision of agricultural inputs and is used in some multi-purpose groups and cooperatives in that form. An expert explained its origin as follows:

> "Like I said, government doesn't work with individuals. You have to be organised in a group. Uh (considering), especially that was the case under NAADS. If you were going to receive, for example, inputs, you had to belong to a group. And it's because NAADS was using the model of, uh (considering), revolving scheme. Like, if we are a group of five, I might be the first beneficiary of say, uhm (considering), uh (considering), say, an improved variety of maize. When I plant my maize and I've harvested, I'm supposed to pass on to the next person in the group." (Expert 9, 2018)

Several SSE groups have adopted that principle, e.g., when they distribute agricultural inputs to their members. There is no paying-back to an anonymous group but rather passing-on to a concrete person, a fellow member. In ROSCAs and Mukenkede groups, every member makes the same contributions and receives the same outcome. The contribution does not disappear on a mysterious bank account or in a cash box. Rather, it is passed on to a concrete fellow member (either in cash or in form of a gift). In a revolving scheme, everybody gets the same, yet only if all members deliver their contribution as promised. That principle works better than others in Busoga.

In terms of the internal organisation of groups, most of them appear to have democratic structures in which decisions are taken together. As a main interviewee from Buyende District who is a member of a Muno Mukabi group explained, "when we have gathered as a group, which wants to work, its decision, it depends on the explanation, if there's no consensus, we make an election for that reason" (Main 5, 2017, translation by E.K. and N.H.). Even down to the lowest level, SSE groups in Busoga are structured and organised with an executive committee of at least three people and with by-laws. The power of the executive committee varies. In the majority of low-level groups, it is very limited. The means of production are usually controlled by the group as a whole. The member of the multi-purpose group Tukoome from Jinja District claimed that "in case they [government] have given us something, they have given it to us as a group, we call the members, they come and they sit, they are there and they decide" (Main 16, 2017, translation by E.K. and K.M.). Most groups are formed by the members themselves, just a few have been initiated by organisations. A main interviewee said about her VSLA that it has received some support from an organisation but only after the group had already started its activities: "Now, we started, there was an organisation that bought for us a small cash box, after us sensitising that, 'My friend, let us save money for ourselves', but it found us when we are already there [...]" (Main 28, 2017, translation by E.K. and N.H.). However, in many cases, it is impossible to tell whether the initiative really came from the members or rather from government representatives promoting material or financial support that is reserved for groups, not for individuals. After all, this does not make a difference as long as the group is serious about its activities and does not dissolve as soon as the members have received their money or assets.

In summary, positive accounts of groups have been more numerous than negative accounts. On a positive note, agricultural groups in particular (including cooperatives) are appreciated for granting access to markets beyond middlemen to their members. People hope to improve their economic situation more quickly than they could without the support of groups. They appreciate groups for providing trainings and motivating people to work. Groups in general have taken over many functions that were originally fulfilled by the (extended) family and neighbourhood. Some people find trust, comfort, advice, spontaneous help in case of a problem, and sometimes even friendship in their groups (only). However, many respondents spoke about the opposite situation: fraud and lack of trust among the members of small groups, elite capture in the bigger ones. Some groups also have difficulties finding a market with fair prices for their products. Many groups have been created only on paper in order to acquire government or NGO funds for the alleged members. Several (main) interviewees had very concrete ideas about what groups need in order to be as successful as they could be, noting in particular financial and material inputs, as their members have no capital. However, financial and material support can also be destructive. Trainings would be the better choice if government agencies or NGOs want to support groups. In that regard, my findings correspond with those of Justine Nannyonjo who has analysed that Ugandan SACCOs do not profit from external funding as long as it is not accompanied by trainings and sensitisation for the members (Nannyonjo 2015, 277). Most of all, groups need trust among the members in order to be stable. Social homogeneity, i.e., a comparable level of financial capacities of the members, is an important criterion to protect groups from elite capture. Furthermore, groups should be formed bottom-up, based on a common vision, and with sufficient time to evolve. In general, the revolving scheme on which ROSCAs as well as Mukenkede and Gema Kumwino groups are based is a low-risk model for SSE groups. In a revolving scheme, everybody gets the same, yet only if all members deliver their contribution as promised. That principle works better than others in Busoga. In terms of the internal organisation of groups, most of them appear to have democratic structures. Even down to the lowest level, SSE groups in Busoga are structured and organised with an executive committee of at least three people and with by-laws. This may be part of the extensive experience with cooperative societies in the region. New groups, even the smallest, are modelled on their example. The means of production are usually controlled by the group as a whole. The majority of groups are formed by the members themselves. A main interviewee from Kamuli town who is a member of a SACCO and a Mukenkede group with a Muno Mukabi component concluded on groups as follows:

> "For me, I think that they are very good because, if you form them, you have where to start from. Mm (affirmative), you know where to start from. Because now, your friends would be building you up, and you, too, you are building them up and, for me, I encourage that, my friend, when we would be helping each other in what? In those groups. [...] we continue to lift each other or to carry the luggage for each other." (Main 19, 2017, translation by E.K. and K.M.)

Another main interviewee who has had bad experiences with a SACCO that failed, stated more critically, yet hopefully:

> "Now, not/ groups, I still like them, but trust/ [...] In my colleagues. Eh (affirmative), because you can be together with them, there, you think that you are thinking what? The same. But when the other one has a different motive." (Main 1, 2017, translation by E.K. and N.H.)

8.3.7 Key findings of the main theme "SSE"

This main theme addresses the second part of my research hypothesis, namely that *everyday economy in Uganda shows signs of alternative economic approaches, out of which some can be counted among the Social and Solidarity Economy (SSE)*. In addition to that, it provides answers to the research questions: *What kind of alternative economic activities based on solidarity do or did people in Busoga practise? Did those activities persist in spite of, dissolve because of, or emerge as a reaction to globalisation? Do people consider such activities helpful in their situation, and why or why not?* The key findings of this main theme are the following:

1. In Busoga, some autochthonous solidarity structures have been reacting to globalisation by starting to dissolve, while others transform and very few flourish.

The culture of sharing and giving as well as mutual farming support have been almost eradicated by the effects of globalisation, namely by the commercialisation of agriculture and the commodification of social relationships (see finding number 3). In contrast to that, groups that form temporarily for buying meat for a feast conjointly are the only flourishing autochthonous solidarity structure respondents could name. The clan, which used to be the most important social institution and safety net in Busoga, has lost much of its influence. In many cases, the last important function it still fulfils is burial support. The latter is the solidarity structure that went through the most interesting transition over the past decades. It is one of the most important manifestations of solidarity and mutual support for the respondents of this study and exists in three variations simultaneously: 1. an autochthonous form, which is losing ground due to migration and a shift of priorities from social relations to earning money (clan support); 2. a newer, but still autochthonous form, which came up as an attempt to adjust to the new living conditions, especially migration (obutaka/ village support); 3. a yet newer form, which fulfils the criteria for an SSE activity (Muno Mukabi groups). The differences can mainly be found in the membership criteria (clan: compulsory by birth; obutaka: compulsory by residency; Muno Mukabi: voluntary).

2. Several kinds of modern SSE groups have been encountered in Busoga, namely: cooperatives, savings and credit groups (SACCOs, VSLAs, and ROSCAs), small consumer associations (Mukenkede/ Gema Kumwino groups), burial groups (Muno Mukabi), and multi-purpose groups.

The term 'modern' is used here in the absence of a better word that encompasses the meanings of being both *relatively* new and influenced by transformations that affect local culture from outside. Some of those groups, especially cooperatives of the present and some kinds of S&C groups, have their origins somewhere else than in local culture (e.g., having been introduced by NGOs from the global North, government programmes that have been informed by international development programmes, or missionaries). Others, like Muno Mukabi groups, have their origin in local culture (clan support, obutaka), but they are a new version of the 'traditional' variant. They evolved because capitalist development has changed the social structures in a way that hinders the implementation of the older variants. In terms of Mukenkede/ Gema Kumwino groups, the question whether they were introduced from outside (e.g., by NGOs) could not be answered in a satisfactory manner. In either case, they are based on autochthonous solidarity structures to a certain extent. However, they are a reaction to new requirements, which came up as a result of capitalist development and the lifestyle associated with it. All these kinds of groups are not specific to Busoga (even modern burial groups and small consumer associations can be found elsewhere). Nevertheless, the way people perceive them and implement their group activities is specific to Busoga. Though the basic models for some 'modern' kinds of groups may come from elsewhere, the local culture and historical experience of the people living in Busoga are decisive for the attitude with which they judge and practice them in everyday life. The Ugandan cooperative movement has a special history, which I briefly summarise in chapter 8.4.3 (for details, see also chapters 4.2.2, 7.5, and 8.3.2). It was an indigenous initiative moulded by the colonial administration into an organisational form originating in Europe. Today's cooperatives are different from the original ones that existed up to the 1980s. The contemporary ones comply with international cooperative standards and SSE criteria much better than did their forerunners. Savings and credit groups are the SSE activities that respondents like best, especially Village Savings and Loan Associations (VSLAs). Apart from the latter, there is the safer yet less attractive variant of the Rotating Savings and Credit Association (ROSCA) and the largest groups of that kind, Savings and Credit Cooperatives (SACCOs). Another kind of SSE groups encountered in Busoga are small consumer associations (Mukenkede/ Gema Kumwino groups) that buy household necessities for their members on a rotating basis. All these kinds of groups are also known in other countries and are promoted by NGOs. As a result, I assume that most of them have also been introduced to Busoga by NGOs. Busoga does not have a tradition of small farmer's associations and has resisted all political efforts to introduce them. Farmers in Busoga prefer to cultivate their field on their own (or, if possible, with the help of paid workers) and unite only for the purposes of processing and marketing (the latter being a job for cooperatives). I encountered only very few small farmers' associations in the course of this study and none of them relied exclusively on agriculture. They all had additional activities, mostly savings and credit. Some presented themselves as VSLAs with a little agriculture, not the other way around. Others were veritable multi-purpose groups, with three or more activities. Eventually, there are modern burial groups (Muno Mukabi), the genesis of which has been explained in brief under finding number 1 (and in detail in chapters 8.3.1 and 8.3.5).

3. Globalisation has led to a commodification of social relationships and destruction of community ties, processes with which solidarity structures correlate in a complex way.

The major social institution of the clan as well as neighbourly help have been declining due to the effects of globalisation on everyday life in Busoga. The commercialisation of food crops, formerly useless items (e.g., plants that have become fodder), and things that have been treated as commons in the past (land, fruit) has led to the commodification of social relationships. Neighbours and friends who used to share things for free have been turned into buyers and sellers. Money has replaced the long-term reciprocal relationship that used to be established between them by exchanging favours. In general, modern SSE groups can replace the mutual support that used to be a matter of course in the past but has got lost in many places (though not yet everywhere). Those groups can be forums for cooperation, trust building, the exchange of advice and mutual help, even beyond the group's activities. However, this is the ideal case that reflects reality in many cases and not in others. With respect to social relationships, the position of savings and credit groups is most complicated. On the one hand, they contribute to the destruction of community ties. The obligation to take money to the next group meeting can serve as an excuse for disregarding social obligations like helping a relative or neighbour in need of money. On the other hand, where community ties are already weak or destroyed, such groups are an option to rebuild social safety nets. As the people living in Busoga cannot prevent their involvement in the liberalised Ugandan economy and in the global economy with their respective effects, they have found a constructive way to cope with this circumstance through building new social cohesion in SSE groups.

4. The potential of solidarity groups to be both helpful for their members' livelihood and to offer an alternative to capitalist development is highest

when the members are few and know each other well, such that every member has trust in the others and a good overview of the activities.

If they start like that and allow their activities to grow slowly and naturally, those groups have great potential to diversify and expand their activities and admit more members. These processes take time, as members must go through learning processes. Their capital is very low, such that the groups' activities grow very slowly. However, as soon as these processes are pushed, either by inserting external capital (e.g., from NGOs or elites) or by persuading the group to admit more members or 'professionalise' its activities when it is not ready (e.g., by government or NGO agents), the group runs the risk of being disorganised. The only kind of support that all groups need regardless of their size, experience, or the nature of their activities, is training. The low level of education of many members bears the risks of exploitation by elites and of failure to successfully plan group activities, to support individual members accordingly, and to keep the group alive through transparent accounting. The latter is essential not only for protecting the group from bankruptcy but likewise for keeping up the trust among the members. For these reasons, small groups perform better than large ones. On this low level, values like cooperation and reciprocity that oppose the capitalist logic of permanent growth, endless accumulation of capital, and competition among individuals can much more readily be put into practice. As soon as the groups and their activities grow too big, members lose track of them and become demotivated. The executive committee of such a group usually reacts with sanctions and means of coercion.

5. Members are most committed in groups that are based on revolving schemes.

Another factor that I have identified as helpful for the success of SSE groups are revolving schemes. Groups that are based on this principle (ROSCAs, Mukenkede/ Gema Kumwino groups) or use it to distribute materials to their members (agricultural groups) have fewer problems than do other groups (VSLAs, SACCOs, other cooperatives) with members who are not committed. In ROSCAs or Mukenkede/ Gema Kumwino groups, one member receives something (e.g., the savings of the week, gifts) in every meeting, until the cycle is over and every member has received something. Usually, the group starts a new cycle right away. In some groups, seeds or farm animals are distributed among the members by giving them to some individuals who pass them on after their reproduction (e.g., seeds passed on to another member after the harvest or a young goat passed on after the one initially received has given birth). From my individualistic

Western point of view, I would have expected a high temptation for the first people in the cycle to run away with the support received – and a high level of frustration on the part of those whose turn comes last. The research results proved my expectations wrong. Respondents regard revolving schemes as particularly fair because every member receives the same. As a result, the commitment to ensuring that this really happens is very high and these groups have a higher level of trust than others. There are certainly exceptions but the interview results suggest that this is the rule. It is quite possible that the following hypothesis of N'Dione et al. shows through in this finding:

> "Many African societies still live according to the model of reciprocity. 'I receive, therefore I exist. I give, therefore I am respected.' According to this logic, the gift is the main point of reference […] it is never an isolated act: the gift creates or reinforces the social ties; it calls for a counter-gift […]" (N'Dione et al. 1998, 371).

Though I want to avoid romanticising alleged 'African reciprocity', in this particular case, the explanation fits well. Nevertheless, as N'Dione et al. state in their article (ibid., 372) and as my research results suggest, the logic of capitalist exchange has spread widely in Africa and has started to destroy social relationships (see key finding 3). Yet, some social relationships and autochthonous solidarity structures have survived until today (see key finding 1). The preference for revolving schemes indicates the survival of another element of reciprocity in Kisoga society. In groups with revolving schemes, the relationship between the members is comparable to that between people exchanging gifts. The giver is assured of his or her right to a counter-gift, so he or she can wait patiently for it, even if he or she is the last in the cycle. As it is a 'modern' form of reciprocity, and as the social structure is already weakened, an additional element is needed for building trust: every member contributes and receives *exactly the same* amount of money or material gifts. This element supports the sense of fairness, as several respondents emphasised. In contrast to that, the obligation to pay back a loan to a VSLA or to engage in the activities of a cooperative has no such reference in everyday life that creates trust in the other members to deliver also their contributions. As long as there is no assurance of the other members bringing their contribution, it is hard for an individual to trust them and to be committed to the group.

6. The SSE groups encountered in Busoga are only partly alternatives to capitalist development and partly rather a strategy of survival within capitalist structures without any element of challenging those structures.

As suggested in chapter 4.2.1, activities in the scope of the Social and Solidarity Economy (SSE) can serve as both *slightly* alternative *strategies of* capitalist development (see e.g., Utting 2015, 5, 9-10) or *alternatives to* capitalist development (e.g., Santos/ Rodríguez-Garavito 2007, xx-xxiii). Abdou Salam Fall's image of "social and solidarity economy as a laboratory to question the dominant paradigm in development processes" (Fall 2013, 96) is very apposite. In a laboratory, ingredients of different origins are mixed and new substances are tried out – a process that does not bring out the ideal result at the first attempt but requires trial and error. In the 'laboratory' of SSE, capitalistic and non-capitalistic ideas are mixed, Western and non-Western approaches, autochthonous forms of solidarity and those initiated by influences from outside, old and new forms of mutual support. These mixtures bring about different results that can serve as valuable experience whether or not their outcome can be rated as successful. Village Savings and Loan Associations (though with reservations), Rotating Savings and Credit Associations, Mukenkede/ Gema Kumwino Groups, Muno Mukabi groups, and cooperatives that deal in production and marketing have been found to serve the local population (including disadvantaged groups) very well in terms of coping with the negative effects of globalisation on their everyday life. In terms of the potential of the above-mentioned groups to promote alternatives to capitalist development, it can be said that all of them promote values of solidarity, cooperation, and distributive justice that challenge the capitalist principle of the exploitation of many in favour of endless accumulation of capital by few. However, as they all currently exist within the capitalist world-system and the liberalised local economy, they are also tolerant to some capitalistic principles, e.g., profit-orientation (though the profit is meant to be distributed justly among all members of the groups) or, in case of cooperatives, market access. If SSE is supposed to exist within the scope of the capitalist world-system, it *must mitigate* capitalism's negative effects to a certain extent. Not doing so would mean that it would bring no improvement to people's lives. If that was the case, SSE would neither convince people of practising it today, nor to include it in their visions for the future. Only ROSCAs and Muno Mukabi groups can be taken for *radical alternatives* to capitalist development. In ROSCAs, members support each other in planning their household expenses, without interest or profit orientation, based on a revolving scheme, which people in Busoga rate as the fairest system. In Muno Mukabi groups, there is also no profit orientation. Instead, there is mutual support in case of economically and emotionally demanding life situations. Cooperatives are a special case, as they are at the same time the only chance for small-scale farmers to mitigate their exploitation by the capitalist structures of the liberalised economy, whereas cooperatives themselves are based on capitalist principles (profit-orientation, economies of scale). The popular reproach of SSE being 'capitalism's repair workshop' can be directed to them with more justification than to any other SSE activities. Moreover, the way the concept of cooperatives is implemented in Busoga is not a model for a localised economy but for the participation of small- to medium-scale producers in markets outside the region. Nevertheless, cooperatives fulfil many SSE criteria and are the type of groups most frequently named as an example for SSE groups. Savings and Credit Cooperatives (SACCOs) have been found to be a complete failure, even in terms of mitigation of capitalism's negative effects on people's lives, as long as they are regarded as associations of individual members. Nevertheless, cooperative financing is needed in an alternative economy model. Hence, as a link between other SSE groups, especially small ones like VSLA or farmers' associations, and sources of finance, SACCOs can play an important role.

In summary, the key findings of this main theme suggest that the everyday economy of the Busoga region displays various elements of the Social and Solidarity Economy. These elements – the autochthonous as well as the 'modern' ones – correlate in complex ways with the effects of globalisation on people's lives. While some of these SSE activities are called into being by the effects of globalisation, others are attacked by them. In either case, they are both part of the same complex and hybrid everyday life of the local population, not of separate spheres. Solidarity groups work best when they are composed of few members who know each other well or have enough time and geographical proximity to get to know each other through the group activity. The critical factors constituting solidarity groups are *trust* among the members and *time* to build that trust and to develop the group activities. If one of those factors is lacking, the group – regardless of its activity or capital – is unlikely to succeed. Trainings, either in terms of group management, accountancy, or the groups' specific activities, can be very helpful for groups. In contrast, external capital can be destructive. It may raise the group activity to a level at which the members can no longer keep an overview of it. It is also an incentive for embezzlement, as it makes the financial situation of the group less transparent for the majority of members. All things considered, SSE activities as they can be found in Busoga are neither the perfect solution for challenges like poverty or social inequality, nor a countermodel to capitalism. Nevertheless, they are a means of survival within the liberalised market-economy, for people as well as for values that emphasise cooperation and reciprocity rather than competition, exploitation, and accumulation of capital.

8.4 General theoretical implications of research results and conclusion

The research hypothesis of this study has been verified: Everyday economy in Busoga shows signs of penetration by globalisation as well as alternative economic approaches, out of which some can be counted among the Social and Solidarity Economy (SSE). The research questions have been answered. The *way in which people living in Busoga have experienced changes in their socio-economic environment that can be traced back to globalisation* has been described in detail and condensed in four key findings in chapter 8.2. The remaining research questions have been answered in detail in chapter 8.3, leading to six key findings. Chapter 8.3 has provided a comprehensive *presentation of all forms of solidarity structures that have been encountered* in the course of this study. Their *relationship with globalisation* has been analysed. It has been elaborated, *whether – or rather under which circumstances – they are helpful in the life situation of the researched*. This chapter provides some reflections on the general theoretical implications of the research findings (8.4.1). Furthermore, it provides conclusions on both aspects of Busoga's everyday economy that have been under examination in this study, the impacts of globalisation (chapter 8.4.2) and the Social and Solidarity Economy (8.4.3). These conclusions are *based on the information provided in chapters 6, 7, and 8*. This chapter closes with some reflections on the situation of women and girls in Busoga – and the implications of globalisation and SSE for them (8.4.4.).

8.4.1 General theoretical implications of research results

Various elements of the theoretical framework of this study that correlate with concrete research findings have already been applied to them in the preceding chapters. However, the research results also lead to some general theoretical implications. I discuss the latter in this sub-section.

In the interview study, I found evidence of Sally Matthews' hypothesis that "the poor and the oppressed [...] are indeed actively and effectively responding to their situation" (Matthews 2007, 135; see chapter 4.1 of this thesis). People in Busoga react in manifold ways to globalisation's impacts with regard to high cost of living and increasing desires for consumption without opportunities for sufficient income to cover any of them. Some try to cope with this on their own by working very hard – especially in agriculture but also as shopkeepers or by running small businesses such as maize mills – and taking out loans from any source available to them (e.g., private loans, formal microfinance institutions). Others join efforts in groups. They pool their resources in order to market their products more profitably, to save money together, lend each other money, buy household necessities together, or insure themselves against strokes of fate. They live in a 'modern', globalised lifeworld, not in a 'traditional', idyllic community. As a result of external influences that started to impact on the region at the very beginning of the twentieth century, social structures in Busoga have changed profoundly. Autochthonous solidarity structures like the culture of sharing and giving or the social safety net of the extended family have declined to a great extent (though not yet completely) due to these transformations. In some cases, the destruction made any kind of solidarity among the people impossible, as various cases of groups in which members cheated each other, have demonstrated. The pressure to pay for daily expenses, especially educational expenses, is too high for some people to wait for the outcome of group activities, such that they steal from their fellow group members. Nevertheless, in many cases, groups have succeeded and helped members to more sustainably cope with their difficult life situation.

The findings of this study contribute, at least in terms of Busoga region, to the confirmation of James Ferguson's hypothesis that Africa is "a place of bricolage and creative intervention, where bits and pieces of what used to be called Western modernity are picked up, combined with local (and not-so-local) resources, and put back together" (Ferguson 2005, 172). Elements of 'Western modernity' have been picked from the fields of globalisation and development, the latter including SSE activities that have been transformed (cooperatives) or introduced (savings and credit groups) by government programmes or other organisations. They have been combined with local resources, namely local culture; historical experience; the labour, ideas, and social capital of the local people. Furthermore, non-local resources have been added in some cases, namely further material or non-material support from NGOs or government programmes. In some cases, the groups came up with very creative models, like the above-described VSLA *Tukoome* that has over time developed into a multi-purpose group (see chapter 8.3.3). Its members have used diverse government programmes to apply for support and have managed to successfully integrate all those aspects into the portfolio of their activities (e.g., renting out party equipment, cultivating a demonstration garden conjointly, savings and credit, etc.).

Though they are indeed active, effective, and creative in their adaptation to their changing socio-economic environment, the people living in Busoga still live in the periphery of the capitalist world-system. Immanuel Wallerstein postulated that the expectations of disadvantaged people all over the world, and particularly in Africa, for "equality, living as well as, as comfortably as, people do in the North" will neither be fulfilled by the state nor by the market, due to the structure of the capitalist world-system (Wallerstein 2017, 59). However, though "ordinary people" all over the world may increasingly find that their governments do not fulfil their expectations and that they do not have the power to influence political decision making individually, they still have agency (Wallerstein 1998, 50). They establish "collective extrastate self-defence structures" (ibid.). Such structures are also of interest to representatives of the Post-Development approach (see chapter 2.2.3). In search of alternatives to the hegemonic discourse of Western development, Arturo Escobar sees high potential in existing local practices (Escobar 2012, 222-223). He emphasises their hybridity on the one hand and their rooting in "concrete local settings" on the other hand, as they can show how "modernity and development" have been taken up and transformed in a particular way by people with a particular cultural background (ibid., 223). He deplores that, in many studies, their focus on political economy tends to neglect that aspect of cultural peculiarity, whereas in others, the focus on (hybrid) culture obstructs their view for "the capitalist dynamics that circumscribe the local cultural constructions" (ibid., 98). Majid Rahnema makes a similar point when stating that "a deeper and unbiased knowledge of how different cultures have solved their problems and of what they learned to cherish or dislike through the ages would be instructive for all those in search of alternatives to our own dilemmas" (Rahnema 1998, 381). This study has been an attempt to overcome the shortcomings deplored by Escobar. Modern approaches of the Social and Solidarity Economy (SSE), which do not have their origin in Busoga yet are practiced in a particular way there, have been analysed as well as autochthonous solidarity structures. The former are hybrid practices, formed by modernity and discourses of capitalist development on the one hand and by local circumstances, including Kisoga culture and the historical experience of the people living in Busoga, on the other. Global capitalist structures, local circumstances (historical and current), and the attitude of the researched have been taken into account during the research.

Alternative economic practices in the globalised economy of the Busoga region first and foremost are means of survival for the local population. This means that they are expected to make life *within* the capitalist world-economy easier, especially for social groups that are usually disadvantaged by it. This corresponds with Norman Chipakupaku's description of the People's Economy, his 'African version' of Social and Solidarity Economy (SSE), as a necessity for survival in Africa (Chipakupaku 2008, 138-139). Elisabeth Voß points out that, even in Germany, it is hard to survive on SSE activities. Either those activities must be successful in the conventional market economy or, especially when they are truly alternative in nature, the members need additional sources of income in order to make a living (Voß 2008, 64). As survival in Africa in general, and particularly in Busoga, is even more difficult than in Germany, it is clear that SSE activities need to be viable within the existing liberalised capitalist market-economy. Otherwise, people have no resources to spend on such activities. From a Post-Development point of view, Sally Matthews' caution that the development discourse is still too powerful to allow for the existence of any alternative that is completely antithetical to it, is relevant (Matthews 2018, 174-179). Matthews notes that "opposition is possible even where is escape is not" (ibid., 179). As a result, alternatives to development that already exist cannot be perfectly antithetical to it, yet they are important for evolving more radical alternatives over time. The same applies to alternatives to capitalism. Boaventura de Sousa Santos and César A. Rodríguez-Garavito have identified "emancipatory potential" in the forms of economic and social organisation and in the values of cooperation and solidarity SSE activities encompass. They emphasise that this applies even to the ones that can also function within the scope of capitalism (Santos/ Rodríguez-Garavito 2007, xxiii). In their view, the "ability to survive in a capitalist context" is even an important characteristic of alternative economic practices because it ensures their feasibility (ibid., xxi). And, as I would like to add, it ensures their *attractivity*. Only if people have good experiences with them, they will consider them as a model for the future. People who struggle for survival every day do not invest time and effort into seemingly unrealistic or unpractical approaches.

The alternative economic practices discussed in this study have a limited yet significant potential to provide alternatives to capitalist development. In the ideal case, they can rebuild social safety nets and relationships that have been damaged or destroyed over time. They can replace capitalist competition with cooperation and reciprocity. However, one of the most important lessons learnt from SSE groups in Busoga in this context is their opposition to the capitalist values of permanent growth and endless accumulation of capital at any price. Their practical experience goes hand in hand with the following statement by Post-Development scholar Majid Rahnema:

> "On another level, a shift of focus from bigness and quantity to the right size and quality could help us to understand that a *small, human-sized and familiar group* of friends, who *know and trust* one other, is often the ideal place for them to learn from each other, to act in truth and eventually to change the only worlds they can truly love and care for. In such concrete and recognizable worlds, people are no longer abstractions to each other." (Rahnema 1998, 394, emphases by E.K.)

Indeed, the alternative practices examined in the scope of this study worked best when the groups were small, members knew each other well, lived close to each other, and implemented activities of which every single member could keep track. As soon as groups were too large, there were problems with members who were not committed, with elite capture, and with cheating. Government programmes and NGOs tend to push solidarity groups to admit many members, accumulate much capital, and rapidly implement large activities, thinking that rapid and successful development is enforceable. This study has provided evidence for the stance of many Post-Development scholars (e.g., Escobar, Rahnema) that this approach should be thoroughly reviewed in terms of its goals, methods, and underlying assumptions (see chapter 2.2.3 for details). This finding poses a challenge to conventional development models based on capitalist principles like rapid growth and endless accumulation.

I did not get the impression from the interviews that SSE activities de-politicise and pacify people, as they are sometimes accused of doing (see chapter 4.2.3). For instance, Frédéric Thomas described how several governments of global South countries 'outsourced' social services to SSE actors because structural adjustment programmes forced them to reduce their expenses for social services (Thomas 2015, 11). In such cases, there is a risk of people getting used to solving their problems on their own and stopping to demand what they have a right to, i.e., social service provision by their government. However, this is not the case in Busoga. In spite of the manifold self-help initiatives in which many of them were involved, several respondents of this study used the interviews as a forum to utter concrete requests for the amelioration of their situation to their government. As Matthews, Ferguson, Wallerstein, Escobar, and Chipakupaku suggest, they are committed and creative to solve their everyday challenges together. Nevertheless, they emphasise their government's responsibility towards them.

8.4.2 Conclusion on globalisation in Busoga's everyday economy

The key findings of the interview study on the effects of globalisation on Busoga's everyday economy are the following (see chapter 8.2.8 for details): 1. Everyday economy in Busoga shows signs of penetration by globalisation. 2. The involvement of the residents of Busoga in the global market *as producers* has *reduced*, while their involvement in the global market *as consumers* has *increased*. 3. Cost of living in Busoga has been increasing sharply. 4. Social inequality is prevalent and increasing in Busoga.

Busoga is a sub-region of Uganda (consisting of 11 districts) and a cultural kingdom. Its population of about four million people is increasing quickly. Busoga's integration into the capitalist world-system started in the early twentieth century. The cash economy was introduced to the region from 1900 onwards by creating a need for money through the imposition of taxes, offering cash for certain crops (cotton and coffee), and providing consumer goods, on which the balance could be spent. Furthermore, the colonial administration introduced a commercial class made up of immigrants from India and their descendants to Uganda in general and Busoga in particular. The colonial division of labour allocated the role of a peasant class to Ugandans of African descent. As a result, it initiated a class conflict between Ugandans of African and of Indian descent that persists until today. Since colonial times, the population of Busoga has mainly been surviving on a combination of cash crop production for income realisation and food crop production for subsistence. However, the region's cash crops became unprofitable in the 1970s and 1980s. Since then, food crops and animal products have replaced them. This was due to lack of export markets for coffee and cotton on the one hand, and to a new domestic and regional market for food crops, especially maize, on the other hand. The commercialisation of food crops has led to confusions. It threatens food security as the prices for those products are low and small-scale farmers sell large portions of their harvest without keeping enough food to sustain the family. Sugar cane, once the region's hope as its new major cash crop, was found to exacerbate income disparity and food insecurity. The combination of the commercialisation of agriculture and shortage of land has led to the commodification of many items that have not previously been marketable. This process of commodification has even extended to social relationships to a great extent. The regime of Idi Amin (1971-1979) marked a watershed in the socio-economic history of Busoga and in the everyday lives of its residents. Violence was the order of the day that affected all spheres of life. The expulsion of people of non-African descent in 1972 led to a general breakdown of supply chains. This affected the population of Busoga as individual producers (no more processing and marketing of their cash crops, lack of inputs and transport facilities), co-operators, and consumers (scarcity of consumer goods). This experience has deeply impressed the population. In comparison to some other regions of the country, Busoga has not yet recovered well from that shock. The latter was followed by economic liberalisation. In crop trade, the free-market middlemen system led to poor quality of crops (as intermediaries prefer paying little to insisting on quality standards) and exploitation of small- to medium-scale farmers, as the latter have a very low bargaining power. Other negative effects of economic liberalisation on the region are the above-mentioned process of commodification, increasing income inequality, and rising cost of living. The latter include exploding educational and health expenses, which arise from austerity and privatisation in those sectors as well as from omnipresent corruption. All those aspects are at least partially caused by policies of economic liberalisation. Climate change, a phenomenon that is aggravated by capitalist development and globalisation, endangers food security in Busoga. Positive effects of globalisation on the region encompass technical innovations, especially in the field of communication, the facilitation of the transport sector, increasing availability and affordability of consumer goods. Urbanisation and industrialisation start slowly in Jinja town and some other small but growing towns of Busoga. While agriculture is the major occupation of people living in Busoga, those who manage to raise some capital open shops or start small-scale enterprises like maize mills or workshops. However, the profit margins of those businesses are low. The most profitable businesses, namely factories, large-scale trade, and sugar cane production on large fields, are reserved for people with much capital, i.e., investors from Kampala or abroad, or people of Indian descent (returnees, immigrants, or those born in Uganda after 1982). The combination of low incomes and high cost of living poses a great challenge to the majority of people living in Busoga.

8.4.3 Conclusion on the Social and Solidarity Economy in Busoga

The key findings of the interview study on the Social and Solidarity Economy (SSE) in Busoga's everyday economy are the following (see chapter 8.3.7 for details): 1. In Busoga, some autochthonous solidarity structures have been reacting to globalisation by starting to dissolve, while others transform and very few flourish. 2. Several kinds of modern SSE groups have been encountered in Busoga, namely: cooperatives, savings and credit groups (SACCOs, VSLAs, and ROSCAs), small consumer associations (Mukenkede/ Gema Kumwino groups), burial groups (Muno Mukabi), and multi-purpose groups. 3. Globalisation has led to a commodification of social relationships and destruction of community ties, processes with which solidarity structures correlate in a complex way. 4. The potential of solidarity groups to be both helpful for their members' livelihood and to offer an alternative to capitalist development is highest when the members are few and know each other well, such that every member has trust in the others and a good overview of the activities. 5. Members are most committed in groups that are based on revolving schemes. 6. The SSE groups encountered in Busoga are only partly alternatives to capitalist development and partly rather a strategy of survival within capitalist structures without any element of challenging those structures.

In the scope of this study, some autochthonous solidarity structures were encountered in Busoga. The culture of sharing and giving has declined significantly due to the effects of globalisation on everyday life. Clan structures have been the original social safety net in Busoga but have also started to decline. Another autochthonous solidarity activity profits from globalisation: people come together to buy an animal for slaughtering on an important holiday. Increasing cost of living and commercialisation of agriculture lead to the situation that they either do not have their own farm animals, or they prefer selling them in order to earn some money. As a result, they rather pool a little money with other families and receive a small quantity of meat than rearing and slaughtering their own farm animal for the feast. Beyond that, four categories of SSE groups were identified: cooperatives, savings and credit groups (SACCOs, VSLAs, and ROSCAs), small consumer associations (Mukenkede/ Gema Kumwino groups), and modern burial groups (Muno Mukabi). Some of them, such as burial support, have a long history in Busoga. Burial support is the most important and most survivable autochthonous form of mutual support. Without any intervention from the government or NGOs, the local population has repeatedly over time transformed it to suit the current circumstances. Due to the regional differences of the impacts of globalisation on the social fabric and everyday life, two autochthonous forms and one modern form (see below) of burial support currently exist side by side. Almost every person living in Busoga is served by at least one of them, many by more than one. While the autochthonous clan support is reserved for Basoga, the autochthonous village support (obutaka) and the modern Muno Mukabi groups with their focus on residency are also open to other Ugandans of African origin living in the region. Many SSE groups with other main activities (e.g., cooperatives, savings and credit groups) additionally have burial support integrated in them.

An example of a completely different kind is that of cooperatives. The Ugandan cooperative movement started in 1913 as a reaction to exploitation by the colonial division of labour. However, the colonial administration appropriated it and turned it into a national instrument of export marketing. This was continued in the scope of national development by post-independence governments. By introducing the respective legislation, the colonial administration turned farmers' initiatives into organisations after the model of European cooperatives, yet with the difference that the Ugandan cooperatives were subject to stringent government control. After independence, the Ugandan governments kept a firm hand on the cooperative movement. It was, however, also granted monopolies and other support, e.g., financing of processing plants. Inappropriately high dependency on the government in the 1960s and economic as well as political turmoil in the 1970s significantly weakened the cooperative movement. Under these circumstances, it was particularly affected by the policies of economic liberalisation of the 1980s and 1990s. It could neither cope with the competition with middlemen and (multinational) business enterprises, nor with the loss of the cooperative banking system. These tendencies of the national movement could be observed well in Busoga, as it had a dynamic cooperative landscape and one of the oldest and largest cooperative unions in the country. The current government had first let go of the cooperative movement in the course of liberalisation but has recently re-discovered it as a development strategy. It expects from cooperatives to solve the socio-economic problems of large parts of the population and thus has a strong interest in making them succeed. After having neglected cooperatives for about 15-20 years, starting with the 1990s, the Ugandan government has returned to an approach of heavy intervention with its National Cooperative Policy of 2010/11. The analysis of the latter (see chapter 7.5) suggests that the Ugandan government is trying to combine the different approaches of a market-economy, governmental regulation, and elements of a social economy. In order to allow their combination, the doctrines of all three approaches are being watered down. Otherwise, a social economy would conflict with a neoliberal market-economy – and both would disapprove of governmental regulation. None of the approaches that have been tried out in Uganda after independence – neither socialism with a strong state under Obote I, nor economic war under Idi Amin, nor economic liberalism under Obote II and Museveni – seem to have served cooperatives well. They had their best time under Obote I, yet the foundations for their decline were also laid there (dependency on the government). Nonetheless, they have existed over time and every government felt obliged to deal with them in one way or another. Cooperatives have been an integral part of Uganda's history and economy from the beginning of the twentieth century up to present days. Today's relationship between the cooperative movement and the government is one of mutual influence. Through the Uganda Co-operative Alliance, the movement advocates for its concerns on all levels of decision making. There are efforts to re-build a cooperative-friendly banking system, with SACCOs on the local and regional level and a cooperative bank at the national level.

Cooperatives are by far the largest, best organised, politically most influential SSE groups that exist in Uganda. Nevertheless, they are not the most popular groups in Busoga. This may have to do with their bad reputation originating from mismanagement, embezzlement, and excessive government control in the 1960s and 1970s. The current massive government promotion of cooperatives (including SACCOs) raises people's suspicion, as it seems to announce revived government control and to attract alleged members who want to grab government funds and leave. These factors, in combination with cooperatives' general tendency to be at least partly based on capitalist principles (access to markets, economies of scale) and to reach beyond the local economy (export markets), make cooperatives a difficult kind of SSE groups. This applies to cooperatives in general and with regard to the specific history of the cooperative movement of Uganda in particular. Nevertheless, the history of Uganda's cooperatives with all its pitfalls is very instructive. Some lessons have already been learnt from it, as the comparison of the cooperative societies of the past (existing up the 1980s) and contemporary cooperatives has shown (see chapter 8.3.2). The cooperatives of today comply much more with international cooperative standards than their forerunners. The government intervention announced in the National Cooperative Policy is not as intensive as it was in the 1960s. It will be interesting to observe how the new Ugandan cooperative movement develops under these circumstances.

Other kinds of SSE groups encountered in the course of this study are savings and credit groups and small consumer associations (Mukenkede/ Gema Kumwino groups). In both cases, the idea was probably introduced to Busoga by NGOs or government programmes. Apart from that, the Uganda Co-operative Alliance reports having introduced "village banks" (possibly referring to VSLAs) to rural areas in the 1990s, which later became SACCOs (UCA 2017; see chapter 7.5). On the one hand, this is an SSE-internal source, as it is the national cooperative alliance. On the other hand, the initiative came from 'outside', from the point of view of the people living in Busoga. For instance, a respondent of this study believed that the government had introduced small savings and credit groups because it had realised that formal microfinance institutions had become a burden to the local population (Main 16, 2017; see chapter 8.3.3). Irrespective of their origin, those groups have been embraced enthusiastically by the local population. They are highly ambivalent. If the members deliver their contributions and repayments reliably, those groups make a great contribution to the members' livelihood and create strong solidarity among them, even beyond the group activity. In many cases, especially in small groups of people who know each other well, even failure to pay back on time is treated with understanding and support. However, in other cases, the members put considerable pressure on one another. Trust and solidarity in those groups can easily turn into conflict and fear. Size and trust are the critical factors: As soon as a group is too big and anonymous, trust and social capital are replaced by intimidation and means of coercion. Other critical factors are social homogeneity and geographical proximity. Groups in which the members have comparable financial capacities and live close to each other have better chances to succeed than others. However, according to study respondents, savings and credit groups, especially VSLAs (Village Savings and Loan Associations), are the most popular SSE groups in Busoga. This shows how much the population is affected by the exploding cost of living. They use every opportunity to gain access to money, even if it is risky. They are not able to save individually because any money they receive must be spent at once. Hence, though they are ambivalent, savings and credit groups are needed.

Solidarity groups correlate with globalisation in complex ways. On the one hand, it is globalisation that makes them necessary in many cases. As a result, they must be compatible with the capitalist, liberalised market-economy because they are intended to help their members survive within it. Cooperatives should help small- to medium-scale farmers to participate in profitable markets from which they are excluded, instead of being exploited by intermediaries. The aim of savings and credit groups is to help their members cope with increasing cost of living. Consumer associations are meant to grant access to consumer goods to their members. Burial groups serve to insure their members against one of the greatest financial risks in everyday life, namely having to arrange the burial of a relative. Sometimes, those groups can even be harmful for community ties, e.g., when modern burial groups replace autochthonous forms of support or when having to take one's money to a savings and credit group becomes an excuse for refusing to assist relatives or neighbours. On the other hand, solidarity and mutual support can be (re-)built through these groups. They can promote values oppositional to capitalist logic, like distributive justice and reciprocity (see key finding number 5). All things considered, the everyday economy of the Busoga region of Uganda is being formed by the complex interaction of two opposing forces: globalisation and solidarity.

8.4.4 Implications for the situation of women and girls in Busoga

The power constellations in Ugandan society tend to privilege men in relation to women in terms of "the distribution of resources, rights and decision making" (Kasente 2002, 186). Access to essential resources such as education and land has been limited for Ugandan women and girls for long time (Lucas 2007a, 102). The findings of this study indicate that Busoga region is a case in point. According to the results of the document analysis, though there have been certain ameliorations in terms of gender equality in Busoga recently, the prevailing gender norms still disadvantage women and girls (see chapter 7.2: Dev. Plan 2017; OBB 2016). Many of them are affected by financial and social insecurity due to their disadvantaged position as women and girls (OBB 2016). Polygamy and domestic violence are prevalent in the region (Dev. Plan 2017). Girls tend to leave school earlier than boys (Dev. Plan 2017). Deborah Kasente aptly points out that high absentee and dropout rates among girls in Uganda are caused by the increasing workload of their mothers, who demand the girls' assistance at home (Kasente 2002, 189). Sylvia Tamale likewise states that women's workload has increased as, due to globalisation in general and the consequences of structural adjustment programmes in particular, they have to attend to the families' increasing need for cash money, "[i]n addition to their traditional reproduction and production roles in the domestic arena" (Tamale 2002, 174). In my study, male and female respondents[140] equally deplored the pressure of a sharply increasing need for money (see chapter 8.2.5). In general, the effects of globalisation on people's everyday lives described in chapter 8.2 affect women and men. However, against the background of the above-described predicament of women and girls in Busoga, there can be little doubt that they bear the brunt of the negative effects. Support for this interpretation comes from several studies on globalisation's effects on women's lives, especially in the global South, coming to the conclusion that those effects are ambivalent, yet with a clear tendency to the disadvantage of women (cf. e.g. Lucas 2007, 4-5; Wichterich 2009; with a focus on Uganda: Tamale 2002, 165-166). Furthermore, the land tenure system as well as the decision-making structure in the majority of households in Busoga hinder women's control over land (see chapter 7.2 of this thesis: Dev. Plan 2017; concerning the land tenure system, see also chapter 8.2.2: comment by Expert 1, 2017). In view of the increasing financial responsibilities on the one hand and agriculture being the main source of income on the other hand (cf. chapters 7.2, 7.4, and 8.2.1 of this thesis), this circumstance makes the situation of women even more difficult. Frequently, it is the male head of the Ugandan household deciding over the use of the proceeds from women's work (Lucas 2007a, 105-106).

Activities of the Social and Solidarity Economy can provide women with opportunities for empowerment. According to two female respondents, women appreciate having an opportunity to make a living with the help of SSE groups, without being dependent on a husband (see chapter 8.3.6 of this thesis). The story of another respondent, who had lost her husband early and financed the education of her children through her engagement with Busoga Growers Co-operative Union, seems to support this appraisal (see chapter 8.3.2: comment by Main 17, 2017). In general, women groups have been found implementing the same activities as groups with a mixed membership: especially savings and credit, but also others like production or Mukenkede/ Gema Kumwino activities (see chapter 8.3.6 of this thesis). However, there is a tendency of wom-

140 As has been pointed out in chapter 5.2.1, out of the 32 respondents of the main interviews, 15 were female and 17 were male. Although gatekeepers tended to recommend men as potential interviewees to me, I emphasised that I would also like to speak to women, in order to keep the gender ratio balanced. The fact that it was difficult to find at least one respondent for an expert interview, as the relevant positions were almost exclusively held by men, speaks volumes.

en groups emphasising the aspect of caring and sharing, while in other groups, that aspect is implemented to varying extents. As has been stated in chart 7 (chapter 8.3.2), women cooperatives tend to be sensitive to the issues of women both within and beyond the group. In one case, the members of a women cooperative emphasised the mutual support among the members, especially in case one of them is very vulnerable. In her comment quoted in chapter 8.3.6, one of the respondents of the tandem interview Main 20 described how experienced members of their women cooperative encourage vulnerable ones to start income-generating activities and how they support them during the implementation (see chapter 8.3.2: comment by Main 20b, 2017). When speaking about her cooperative and women groups in general, she remarked that groups can ease women's lives significantly. Her colleague spoke about the cooperative members supporting each other in case of death of a relative (see chapter 8.5.8: comment by Main 20a, 2017). In two other cases, a female respondent used support from a government agency as an opportunity to encourage other women to join the activity, partly with her, partly within their own groups (see chapter 8.3.2: comments by Main 27, 2017 (briquette production); Main 29, 2017 (mushroom production)). This shows, on the one hand, that women can benefit from government (or NGO) support for groups in particular. On the other hand, it shows cases of women supporting each other and SSE groups being a useful tool for that mutual support. A similar case of mutual support was introduced in chapter 8.3.3: Women founded a savings and credit group in order to escape the rigorous practices of commercial loan providers trying to recover their money from female borrowers. The respondent emphasised that "women used to run away because of the bank" whereas, within the group, they "look after each other" (Main 28, 2017, translation by E.K. and N.H.).

In summary, the situation of women and girls in Busoga is difficult. In many cases, they are excluded from decision-making in the household and from access to essential resources. The Social and Solidarity Economy provides them with opportunities to gain access to resources (through income-generating activities, savings and credit, mutual support on various levels). This may either strengthen their position within the family or enable them to survive with their children, without being dependant on a male head of the household. Beyond that, women encountered in the scope of this study tend to show a high level of solidarity. Some of them have discovered SSE groups as means of supporting each other in their daily struggle for survival. This finding is consistent with the general impression from the literature (see chapter 4 of this thesis) and the results of this study (see chapters 8.3; 8.4; 9): SSE activities serve the most disadvantaged groups in a society to survive and even empower themselves within the scope of the system that puts them at a disadvantage. The cases of women gaining independence and self-esteem through their SSE activities show how this process can (slowly) lead to social change.

9. Conclusion

In this study, I have examined the impacts of globalisation on the everyday economy of the Busoga region of Uganda, with special emphasis on alternative economic practices. The term 'everyday economy' emphasises that the focus of this study is on the economic activities on which the majority of people in Busoga survive. This includes subsistence activities, alternative economic activities, the informal economy, 'official' microeconomic activities, and the grey areas between those spheres. In chapters 6.2, 7, 8.2, and 8.3, I traced the formation of this everyday economy in the Busoga region over time, its current structure, and the impacts of globalisation on it. In chapters 4.2.2, 6.2.3, 7.5, and 8.3, I examined the alternative practices within that economy. I devised the theoretical framework for this examination in chapters 2, 3, and 4. However, theory needs to be applied to practice and practice needs to be reflected theoretically. Postcolonial theory, which I discussed in detail in chapter 2.1, has been the foundation of my research methodology and my general attitude towards the research topics. I interpreted the research results from the standpoint of critical development studies, including the Post-Development approach (see chapter 2.2), and world-systems analysis (see chapter 2.3) and embedded these into the reflections on globalisation and the Social Solidarity Economy (SSE) in chapters 3 and 4. In this final chapter, I provide conclusions on my empirical findings about globalisation and solidarity in Busoga (9.1), on my findings concerning radical and feasible alternatives (9.2), and on my methodology, methods, their limitations, and recommendations for future research (9.3).

9.1 On empirical findings about globalisation and solidarity in Busoga

As James Ferguson aptly points out, Africa's potential for enriching the understanding of "how the 'global' works today, and how it might work in the future" is widely underestimated (Ferguson 2006, 48). The results of this study support his observation. The Busoga region has gone through a very specific process of globalisation. In the early twentieth century, it was integrated into the capitalist world-system in the typical manner, i.e., by the colonial administration extracting raw materials from it and introducing the need for cash money (by means of introducing taxes and consumer goods). Meanwhile, the region has developed in a way that, at first glance, seems to prove wrong the complaints of many representatives of postcolonial studies and the Post-Development approach, namely that the global South is being exploited by Western[141] countries. Local forces exploit the people living in Busoga as producers, while predominantly actors from semiperipheral countries in Asia profit from them as consumers. World-systems analysis has been helpful in shedding light on this constellation. The roles of Uganda and Busoga as peripheries of the capitalist world-system dominated by the global North, have not changed. A natural process within this world-system has taken place in the Busoga region: The centre (Western countries) has given up a field of intervention that is no longer sufficiently profitable for it and actors of the system, who are satisfied with smaller profit margins, have replaced it. Aspiring semiperipheries[142] have taken the lead in the provision of consumer goods. Agricultural production has been localised and intermediaries from Uganda, often even from the same village as the local farmers, wield their bargaining power over those farmers. As obviously even the semiperiphery has no interest in Busoga's agricultural products (at the moment), the next lower level in the system has to stand in for it. Without the income from agricultural production, the farmers would not be able to buy consumer goods in the shops. Hence, the system works and Busoga serves in it as a typical periphery, enriching higher levels of the system more than itself. The people living in the region are increasingly affected by exploding cost of living, whereas the chances for the majority of them to earn higher incomes are nowhere near the level that would be needed to cope with this situation. Income inequality is rampant and worsening, with very few people profiting from the situation (e.g., through large-scale trade or sugar cane production) and the majority living under worsening conditions. On the one hand, the local population appreciates some achievements of globalisation in their environment like technical innovations, easier com-

141 See chapter 2.4, keyword "The West".

142 Especially (though not exclusively) Asian countries and among them particularly China. It is disputable whether China is on the verge of becoming a new part of the centre of the capitalist world-system. However, China is not in the focus of this study, such that this question cannot be discussed in detail. In my view, it is safe to assume that, at the moment, it is still a semiperiphery, as the latter is defined by a combination of core-like and peripheral production processes (see chapter 2.3.2) and China continues to have a lot of peripheral production processes.

munication, transport, and availability of consumer goods. On the other hand, their daily struggle for improvement of their financial situation seems to be like tilting at windmills, as the surplus value of their work is drawn from them by actors of the liberalised market-economy in manifold ways. For instance, intermediaries pay the lowest prices possible for local farmers' products; the educational system that has been formed by austerity and privatisation forces families to spend much money on children's education; firms advertise their consumer goods and make families spend their money on them. Upon closer examination, the full integration of the population into the capitalist world-system becomes visible.

Some people in Busoga have discovered cooperation as a means of opposing their above-described exploitation. They are involved in various kinds of solidarity activities. Autochthonous forms of mutual support have declined to a large extent (though not completely) due to the effects of globalisation on life in Busoga, especially the commodification of many items and of social relationships as well as the destruction of community ties (see chapter 8.3.1 for details). Modern forms of the Social and Solidarity Economy (SSE), i.e., structures like cooperatives, savings and credit groups, etc., have taken their place. The way in which they are implemented suggests that they are informed by the principles of autochthonous solidarity structures rather than capitalist principles. First, those activities do not thrive on permanent expansion of membership and capital, but rather on small groups of people, who know one another, trust each other, and together implement activities of which every member can easily keep track. Second, trust is built most effectively when the groups are based on a revolving scheme (for details on both findings, see chapter 8.3.7). In theory, this system may be tempting for the first recipient in the cycle to run away with the money or assets received and frustrating for the last person in the cycle. In practice, however, my study findings suggest that people in Busoga regard it as the fairest system. It suits their sense of reciprocity and can serve best to build trust among them. While, in sum, there were in my study more positive than negative accounts of SSE groups, some groups are affected by lack of commitment or even by fraud because the above-described conditions for their functioning are not fulfilled. All SSE-activities encountered in Busoga in the course of this study are compatible with capitalism – and many of them are part of the portfolio of agents of conventional development (NGOs, government programmes). As a result, it is worth considering whether they are alternative practices or whether they are another symptom of capitalist development in Busoga.

9.2 On radical and feasible alternatives

Through this study, I hope to make a contribution to critical development studies. One question has been repeatedly discussed throughout this thesis: How radical must an alternative be in order to be an alternative? With the distinction in the heading, I do not want to suggest that radical alternatives are generally not feasible and feasible alternatives cannot be radical. I want, instead, to indicate which of those two elements is dominant within them. While a 'feasible' alternative may be tolerant to some principles of the conventional system in favour of easier implementation, a 'radical' alternative opposes the conventional system more resolutely. The latter may be more difficult to implement, however, or people may even refrain from implementing it because they consider it unfeasible (though it might not be). In chapter 2.2, I compared reformist developmentalist approaches with Post-Development approaches. The former follow the conventional development approach and try to make communities and nations catch up with the global North. The latter question the idea of Western development itself and call for alternatives. While reformist developmentalists challenge *the measures* of the development project, representatives of the Post-Development school of thought challenge *both the measures and the objectives*. In spite of this fundamental difference, they have in common two important aspects. First, they both deplore the disadvantaged position of the global South in the international economic and political order. Hence, they reject the basic assumption of the conventional development approach that poverty and development are technical, not structural problems. Second, they both look for paths that disadvantaged people, communities, and nations can choose for a better future. Reformist developmentalists stop at that point, whereas the Post-Development approach goes beyond it and also questions the socially and ecologically unsustainable way of life in the global North. Representatives of the Post-Development approach demand *alternatives to* capitalist development for both the global South and the global North – and reject the global North's claim to its conventional capitalist development paradigm being without alternative. My conclusion on that controversy is that both are desperately needed. *Alternatives to* conventional capitalist development are essential, as the latter is neither socially nor ecologically sustainable. Social inequality, the destruction of the natural environment, and the exploitation of both nature and people are immanent features of capitalism (see chapters 2 and 3). Consequently, capitalist development cannot be expected to eliminate them. Yet, radical alternatives need time to evolve and to win recognition.

The structure of the capitalist world-system and the strong hegemony of the conventional development paradigm make this process a demanding task. In the interim, people in the global South need solutions that work for them right now, as many of them struggle for survival every day. Hence, the two approaches should not engage in rivalry but rather combine their efforts and enrich each other's positions.

I have discussed the radicality and feasibility of alternatives in a similar way in chapters 4.2 and 8.3. The question whether activities of the Social and Solidarity Economy (SSE) must be oppositional to capitalism (and capitalist development) or whether they make sense as a means of survival *within* the capitalist world-system has been discussed in theory (4.2) and with regard to the research results of this study (8.3). My contention is again that both feasible short- to medium-term alternatives and radical medium- to long-term alternatives are indispensable. Whether we analyse the capitalist world-system as a whole (Wallerstein) or one of its branches, the conventional development apparatus (e.g., Ferguson, McMichael, Ziai), we find that they are still hegemonic – despite their gradual weakening by the world population's disappointment about their failure to provide wealth to all. As a result, radical alternatives are still scarce and have a long way to go before they can seriously challenge the hegemonic system on a larger scale. In that situation, less radical but feasible alternatives are needed for two tasks: First, they can help disadvantaged people to survive (better) within a system that cannot be expected to change profoundly from one day to another. Second, those feasible alternatives can pave the way for more radical ones – in the global South as well as in the global North. The circumstance that radical change cannot be realised from one day to another must not discourage the search for alternatives. As Wallerstein has put it, the negotiations about long-term alternatives need time and, in the interim, short- and medium-term alternatives can mitigate the most urgent problems (Wallerstein 2003, 270-272). On the one hand, they can promote values like solidarity, cooperation, and reciprocity. The hegemony of capitalist values like endless growth and capital accumulation, exploitation, and competition can be challenged. On the other hand, people in the global South have long been told by colonialists and 'development experts' that their way of life is 'backward' and capitalist development is without alternative. Feasible alternatives can help them to re-discover their creativity and self-esteem in evolving their own ideas. Some of the modern SSE groups encountered in the scope of this study are telling examples of such processes. On the one hand, they are meant to help members survive within the current system, such that they could be taken for capitalism-friendly development approaches. On the other hand, they rebuild social structures and values that have been destroyed to a large extent by the tough living conditions and individualistic, competitive values that have spread under globalisation and conventional approaches to development for decades. For instance, Muno Mukabi groups are replacing autochthonous forms of burial support where they no longer exist. Members support each other financially – and sometimes organisationally and emotionally – in one of the most demanding situations that can occur to them: being bereaved of a relative. There is not a single capitalist principle in those groups, neither profit-orientation nor growth, competition, or exploitation. The latter applies to ROSCAs (Rotating Savings and Credit Associations) as well, as their members do neither more nor less than assist each other in putting aside some money every week and planning their household expenses. Members receive only their own savings, without interest. Other groups, like cooperatives or VSLAs (Village Savings and Loan Associations), have some capitalist features like access to external markets, economies of scale, interest, and general profit-orientation – or in case of Mukenkede/ Gema Kumwino groups, purchase of consumer goods. However, those groups serve as alternatives to exploitation of their members through the free-market system (intermediaries, commercial loans) and, in the ideal case, they can be forums for cooperation, solidarity, and the (re-)building of networks of mutual support. My contention, based on the theoretical discussions in chapters 2 to 4 as well as on my research results, is that these groups, these feasible alternatives, are a necessary step on the way to more radical alternatives. The latter can emerge from them or can be built upon them. As I have shown in chapter 8.4.4, with regard to women groups, 'feasible' SSE activities can also provide disadvantaged groups with an opportunity for empowerment. In that way, they can contribute to social change in favour of such disadvantaged social groups.

So far, radical alternatives are few in Busoga (burial support, ROSCAs), yet there is potential for them (e.g., preference of revolving schemes, remnants of autochthonous solidarity structures). Feasible alternatives are many (cooperatives, VSLAs, small consumer associations, multi-purpose groups). As elaborated in chapter 8.3.6, all kinds of solidarity groups are anyway in need of education and trainings. Hence, if those trainings would be provided, it could be decisive by whom and with what intention. Though the groups certainly have their own orientation, trainings could support their development into one direction or another. Such trainings could be important instruments in the SSE landscape of the Busoga region and possibly beyond its boundaries.

9.3 On methodology, methods, limitations, and recommendations for future research

As has been described in detail in chapter 5, I based the research activities for this study on a postcolonial approach. The major rules of conduct this approach made me keep in mind during the entire research process were a high degree of transparency and a strong emphasis on the point of view of the researched. During the preparation phase, I studied the language of the researched region and followed all bureaucratic requirements, from the application for a research clearance up to the need to inform the people in charge on *every* administrative level about my research activities. During the entire research process, I endeavoured to be self-reflexive and mind my positionality (see chapter 5.1.1), including my complicity with the global power imbalances and exploitative relations (historical and current) that put me in a privileged position. Although those power imbalances are unsurmountable, I have chosen to rather adopt an active attitude and try to make a *tiny* change through my research, than to ignore my political responsibility as a privileged person (see chapter 5.1.2). However, I do not claim to be absolved from my complicity with global power imbalances or to be able to 'give voice to' the researched because of that. Persistent power constellations – on a global scale as well as in the nature of the research situation – do not allow any research method to make researcher and researched fully equal (see chapter 5.1.3). Nevertheless, I tried to make the best of the situation by *listening* carefully and consciously to the researched and by researching *'in between'* us (see chapter 5.1.2).

During the data collection phase, I tried to reduce power imbalances by sharing with the respondents the control over the research situation. They decided where to meet and whether they wanted somebody to sit with us (e.g., a family member or the gatekeeper, who had put us in touch). My major method of data collection were problem-centred interviews, which are a semi-structured form of qualitative interviews. They do not belong to the set of participative research methods because the role of the researched is relatively passive. Nevertheless, as postcolonial research is not a set of particular methods but rather a stance, I was confident that interviews could be undertaken in a decolonised way (see chapter 5.2 for details of that discussion). I experienced the interviews as great interpersonal interactions. The diversity of responses mirrored in the multitude of codes[143] and themes[144] in the analysis (see chapters 5.2.4 and 8.1) provides evidence of the freedom respondents had to introduce the aspects *they considered important* with regard to the suggested topics. In accordance with this, I expanded the research topic with respect to the priorities of the researched. Originally, I had planned to exclude savings and credit groups from this study because I had previously had bad experience with them during my professional practice. Yet, the respondents wanted to speak about them. Their general evaluation of those groups was very positive. As a result, I changed my approach and started to enquire about those groups in detail, such that I learnt about their special features and the reasons why respondents liked them. This has yielded very interesting results (see chapters 8.3.3, 8.3.6, and 8.3.7). For instance, one type of savings and credit group, the ROSCA, has turned out to be among the most radically alternative types of SSE groups (see chapters 9.2 and 8.3.3). Another attempt to respect the priorities of the researched involved asking them at the end of the interview whether they had anything to add to the conversation and to integrate those comments into the analysis (see chapter 5.1). The most challenging question a researcher can be asked is the one about reciprocity, especially when it comes to a case like mine, a doctoral research study. I am not able to offer any equivalent to the benefit I hope to earn through the study to the respondents. All I could do to thank respondents for supporting me through their participation was to treat them respectfully and to share information with them. They were informed in detail about the contents and the purpose of the study prior to the interview. Beyond that, towards the end of my stay in Uganda I organised feedback workshops[145] for them. During those workshops, respondents could hear what I had made out of their answers up to that point, to discuss it with me and with each other. Those who had told me during the interviews that they wanted to know how other groups work and under which circumstances groups are most successful, were able to get some answers and reflect on

143 After I had concluded the phase of coding, there were 658 codes with 4,183 coded extracts. After the following phases of analysis, which were focused on themes, yet included some re-coding and discarding of codes and coded extracts from the analysis (see chapter 5.2.4), I remained with 500 codes and 3,519 coded extracts.

144 The initial list of themes contained 68 themes, which I reduced to 15 themes in further phases of analysis (see chapter 5.2.4).

145 Those workshops took place on 11 (Kamuli), 12 (Jinja), and 13 December 2018 (Buyende). For details, see chapter 5.1.5 of this thesis.

them with other respondents and with me. Many of them appreciated that opportunity for feedback and exchange.

My analysis process began with transcription and translation. I transcribed the interviews that were conducted in English and I proofread and translated the Lusoga-transcripts together with the translators (see chapter 5.2.3 for details). This procedure enabled me to gain a deeper understanding of the data. As my postcolonial approach demanded a strong focus on the researched, I worked very closely to the original data in the first steps of analysis. I diverted from my original plan to use *Qualitative Content Analysis* (QCA) for the interview analysis because it appeared too deductive. Having said that, other 'purely inductive' methods of analysis likewise turned out to be unfit for my approach. It was important for me to emphasise that the researcher is not a mysterious, objective medium for 'true knowledge' but rather plays an active role, bringing in her theoretical and personal background. The research results can neither be true to the original concerns of the researched, nor do they 'naturally' emerge from the data. They are produced by the researcher, who can indeed prioritise either theory or original data, yet in either case, produces *her version* of the analysis. What I needed was a method that encompasses both high commitment to the original data (i.e., the contribution of the researched) and an honest reflection of the researcher's contribution to the outcome. For these reasons, I chose *Thematic Analysis* as described by Braun and Clarke (see chapter 5.2.4 for details). It encompasses six phases of which the first two can be conducted inductively (which I did) and the subsequent phases involve increasing levels of interpretation. This method turned out to suit my approach very well. For the document analysis, as it dealt with less complex material and was intended merely to deliver contextual information for the interviews, I retained my plan to use QCA. While the thematic analysis of the interviews produced a lot of data and turned out to be very work-intensive and time-consuming, the QCA enabled comparably quick and effective *reduction* of the information contained in the documents. Hence, each method suited the data to which it was applied and the expectations I had towards the results. Thematic analysis allowed intensive reflection on and relatively detailed presentation of the contents of the interviews, yet with a clear focus on the research topics. QCA helped to condense the information contained in the documents with less effort.

All in all, my approach has turned out to be very laborious and time-consuming, especially in the phases of preparation and data analysis. I was in a luxurious position, having the time and the financial means to conduct all the above-described activities thoroughly and to spend 34 months in Busoga. In a study with a more limited timeframe, this might not have been possible. However, as elaborated above, my contention is that being privileged obliges me to use my privilege on behalf of others, in that case the researched. Though I am not in the position to judge whether the result does them justice, I did my best to conduct the kind of "patient, careful, in-depth research" for which Achille Mbembe calls in the context of Africa (Mbembe 2001, 7). However, every method has its limitations. If I was to conceptualise the study once again, I would think of a more participatory approach to the conceptualisation of the research questions and to data collection. However, I had to go through the theoretical reflections and practical experience of this research project in order to come to that conclusion.

One of the objectives of this research project was to challenge the epistemological monopoly of the global North (see chapter 2.1.3). I am aware that, no matter what I do, I remain a privileged white person. Regardless of the level of respect I pay to the researched, regardless of the number of scholars from the global South I quote, the standpoint I present in this and any other study I conduct remains a standpoint from the global North. My complicity with global power imbalances and social inequalities, from which I have been profiting immensely all my life, does not disappear because I name it. Yet, by retreating, I cannot make it disappear either. In my view, facing the people on the other side of the line, listening to them, learning from them, and passing on that knowledge (i.e., my version of what I have learnt) is better than simply retreating. At least, the contributions I am making to the above-mentioned discussions have been informed by my encounter with people in Busoga, with a glimpse of their everyday life and their reflections about it.

For further research about Busoga, the question why the region did not recover well from the shock of the 1970s, like other regions of Uganda did, would be of interest. Furthermore, it would be interesting to observe how the socio-economic situation of people in Busoga transforms on the long run, in relation to other regions of the country in which capitalist development has led to more impressive development indicators – yet, possibly also to more side-effects (see chapter 2.2). In terms of the Ugandan cooperative movement, a worthwhile approach for future research could be to observe how the latest occurrences, namely the increasing impacts of globalisation like competition with commercial enterprises on the one hand and the new approach of the Ugandan government with more emphasis on regulation on the other hand, influence cooperatives over time. In general, the latest attempts of the Ugandan government to combine the approaches of a market-economy, governmental regulation, and elements of a social economy (see chapter 7.6) is an interesting aspect for future research. It could be observed, in which of the three directions future policies move and what effects they have on the life of the population. In case the policy makers keep on combining them, it would be interesting what kind of outcomes this approach produces.

This study has delivered information about the *specific* forms of globalisation and solidarity structures *in the Busoga region of Uganda*. This narrow regional focus was necessary in order to provide a detailed analysis of the phenomena under examination. Furthermore, what can be said about Busoga is not necessarily true for other regions of Uganda, for Uganda as a whole, or for Africa as a whole. The results can hopefully enrich the understanding of "how the 'global' works today, and how it might work in the future" (Ferguson 2006, 48). Nevertheless, more studies on the various "'advanced' and sophisticated mutation[s] of" globalisation in the diverse countries and regions of Africa are needed (ibid., 41). Moreover, studies from global South countries beyond Africa need to be combined with them. While some may bring out similar results as this study, others may provide completely different ones, due to differing circumstances. In order to create a picture of 'the global', a mosaic of countless tesserae is needed, of which this study is one. The same applies to the search for alternatives. Economic activities with potential to be alternatives to Western 'development' and to capitalism may look different and teach distinct lessons in various research locations.

List of References

Alcalde, Javier Gonzalo (1987): *The Idea of Third World Development. Emerging Perspectives in the United States and Britain, 1900-1950*. Lanham: University Press of America.

Alcoff, Linda (1991): *The problem of speaking for others*, in: *Cultural Critique, 20*, 5-32.

Altvater, Elmar (2015): *Genossenschaft und gutes Leben: Der Sozialismus des 21. Jahrhunderts*, in: Blätter für deutsche internationale Politik (ed.) (2015): *Mehr geht nicht! Der Postwachstums-Reader*. Berlin: Blätter Verlagsgesellschaft mbH, 275-284.

Altvater, Elmar (2006): *Solidarisches Wirtschaften: prekär oder emanzipativ?*, in: Altvater, Elmar/ Sekler, Nicola (eds.) (2006): *Solidarische Ökonomie*. Hamburg: VSA-Verlag, 9-21.

Altvater, Elmar/ Mahnkopf, Birgit (2002): *Globalisierung der Unsicherheit. Arbeit im Schatten, schmutziges Geld und informelle Politik*. Münster: Westfälisches Dampfboot.

Amin, Samir (1990): *Delinking: Towards a Polycentric World*. London: Zed Books.

Amin, Samir (1998): *Capitalism in the Age of Globalization: The Management of Contemporary Society*. London: Zed Books.

Amin, Samir (2004): *Globalism or Apartheid on a Global Scale?*, in: Wallerstein, Immanuel (ed.) (2004): *The Modern World-System in the Longue Durée*. Colorado: Paradigm Publishers, 5-30.

Anyan, Frederick (2013): *The influence of power shifts in data collection and analysis stages: A focus on qualitative research interview*, in: *The Qualitative Report, 18(18), 1-9*, accessed on 5 August 2018, on: http://nsuworks.nova.edu/tqr/vol18/iss18/2/.

Anyango, Ezra/ Esipisu, Ezekiel/ Opoku, Lydia/ Johnson, Susan/ Malkamaki, Markku/ Musoke, Chris (2007): *Village Savings and Loan Associations – experience from Zanzibar*, in: *Small Enterprise Development*, Vol. 18, No. 1, 03.2007, 11-24.

Appadurai, Arjun (1990): *Disjuncture and Difference in the Global Cultural Economy*, in: Featherstone, Mike (ed.) (1990): *Global Culture: Nationalism, globalization and modernity*. London: SAGE, 295-310.

Ardener, Shirley (1995): *Women Making Money Go Round: ROSCAs Revisited*, in: Ardener, Shirley/ Burman, Sandra (eds.) (1995): *Money-Go-Rounds. The Importance of Rotating Savings and Credit Associations for Women*. Oxford: Berg, 1-19.

Arrighi, Giovanni (2002): *The rise of East Asia and the withering away of the interstate system*, in: Bartolovich, Crystal/ Lazarus, Neil (eds.) (2002): *Marxism, Modernity, and Postcolonial Studies*. Cambridge: Cambridge University Press, 21-42.

Asowa-Okwe, Charles (1994): *Capital and Conditions of Fisher Labourers on Lakes Kyoga and Victoria Canoe Fisheries,* in: Mamdani, Mahmood/ Oloka-Onyango, Joe (eds.) (1994): *Uganda. Studies in Living Conditions, Popular Movements, and Constitutionalism.* Wien: JEP Book, 143-182.

Bartolovich, Crystal (2002): *Introduction: Marxism, modernity, and postcolonial studies,* in: Bartolovich, Crystal/ Lazarus, Neil (eds.) (2002): *Marxism, Modernity, and Postcolonial Studies.* Cambridge: Cambridge University Press, 1-17.

Baeriswyl, Bruno (1988): *Die transkulturelle Übertragbarkeit der Genossenschaftsbank.* Zürich: Schulthess Ploygraphischer Verlag AG.

Baptiste, Ian (2001): *Qualitative Data Analysis: Common Phases, Strategic Differences* [42 paragraphs], in: *Forum: Qualitative Sozialforschung/ Forum: Qualitative Social Research, Vol. 2, No. 3, Art. 22,* accessed on 19 December 2016, on: http://nbn-resolving.de/urn:nbn:de:0114-fqs0103226.

Bateman, Milford (2010): *Why doesn't microfinance work? The destructive rise of local neoliberalism.* London: Zed Books.

Bender, Harald (2012): *Schuldgeld oder öffentliches Kapital – Grundzüge solidarwirtschaftlicher Finanzverfassung,* in: Bender, Harald/ Bernholt, Norbert/ Winkelmann, Bernd/ Akademie Solidarische Ökonomie (eds.) (2012): *Kapitalismus und dann? Systemwandel und Perspektiven gesellschaftlicher Transformation.* München: oekom, 79-112.

Bender, Harald/ Bernholt, Norbert/ Winkelmann, Bernd/ Akademie Solidarische Ökonomie (eds.) (2012): *Kapitalismus und dann? Systemwandel und Perspektiven gesellschaftlicher Transformation.* München: oekom.

Bendix, Daniel/ Ziai, Aram (2015): *Emanzipation durch Entwicklungspolitik? Einige Überlegungen zu Fragen globaler Ungleichheit,* in: Momentum quarterly: Zeitschrift für Sozialen Fortschritt, Vol. 4(3), 161-173.

Bhabha, Homi K. (2004): *The location of culture. With a new preface by the author.* London/ New York: Routledge (Classics).

Bibangambah, Jossy R. (2001): *Africa's Quest for Economic Development. Uganda's Experience.* Kampala: Fountain Publishers.

Birkhölzer, Karl (2006): *Soziale Unternehmen: Ausweg aus Arbeitslosigkeit, Armut und Ausgrenzung?,* in: Altvater, Elmar/ Sekler, Nicola (eds.) (2006): *Solidarische Ökonomie.* Hamburg: VSA-Verlag, 62-72.

Bonger, Tenkir (2004): *Uganda: Strategic Trade and Industry Policy-Making in Africa,* in: Soludo, Charles Chukwuma/ Ogbu, Michael Osita/ Chang, Ha-Joon (2004): *The Politics of Trade and Industrial Policy in Africa: Forced Consensus?* Trenton, NJ: Africa World Press, 253-270.

Bowen, Glenn A. (2009): *Document Analysis as a Qualitative Research Method,* in: Qualitative Research Journal, Vol. 9 (2), 27-40, accessed on 15 March 2020, on: DOI 10.3316/QRJ0902027.

Boyatzis, Richard E. (1998): *Transforming Qualitative Information: Thematic Analysis and Code Development.* Thousand Oaks: Sage.

Brand, Ulrich (2005): *Gegen-Hegemonie. Perspektiven globalisierungskritischer Strategien.* Hamburg: VSA-Verlag.

Brandt, Hartmut (1972): *Part 1: The Organization of Peasant Farms under the Influence of Industrial Towns: The Case of Jinja/ Uganda*, in: Brandt, Hartmut/ Schubert, Bernd/ Gerken, Egbert (eds.) (1972): *The Industrial Town as Factor of Economic and Social Development: The Example of Jinja/Uganda*. München: Weltforum Verlag, 25-136.

Brandt, Hartmut/ Schubert, Bernd/ Gerken, Egbert (1972): *Introduction: Approach and Results of the Case Study Jinja/ Uganda*, in: Brandt, Hartmut/ Schubert, Bernd/ Gerken, Egbert (eds.) (1972): *The Industrial Town as Factor of Economic and Social Development: The Example of Jinja/Uganda*. München: Weltforum Verlag, 7-23.

Braun, Virginia/ Clarke, Victoria (2006): *Using thematic analysis in psychology*, in: Qualitative Research in Psychology 3, 77-101.

Burchardt, Hans J. (2004): *Zeitenwende. Politik nach dem Neoliberalismus*. Stuttgart: Schmetterling.

Burgmann, Verity (2008): *Striking Back against Empire: Working-Class Responses to Globalization*, in: Krishnaswamy, Revathi/ Hawley, John C. (eds.) (2008): *The Postcolonial and the Global*. Minneapolis: University of Minnesota Press, 238-251.

Castro Varela, María do Mar/ Dhawan, Nikita (2015): *Postkoloniale Theorie. Eine kritische Einführung*. Bielefeld: transcript.

Césaire, Aimé (2000): *Discourse on Colonialism*. New York: Monthly Review Press.

Chang, Ha-Joon (2002): *Kicking Away the Ladder: Development Strategy in Historical Perspective*. London: Anthem Press.

Chakrabarty, Dipesh (2000): *Provincializing Europe. Postcolonial Thought and historical difference*. Princeton: Princeton University Press.

Chipakupaku, Norman (2008): *People's Economy in Afrika*, in: Giegold, Sven/ Embshoff, Dagmar (eds.) (2008): *Solidarische Ökonomie im globalisierten Kapitalismus*. Hamburg: VSA Verlag, 136-139.

Chossudovsky, Michel (2003): *The Globalization of Poverty and the New World Order*. Montréal: Global Research.

Cichon, Peter/ Hosch, Reinhart/ Kirsch, Fritz Peter (eds.) (2010): *Der undankbare Kontinent? Afrikanische Antworten auf europäische Bevormundung*. Hamburg: Argument.

Cohen, David William (1972): *The Historical Tradition of Busoga: Mukama and Kintu*. London: Oxford University Press.

Collier, Paul/ Reinikka, Ritva (2001): *Introduction*, in: Reinikka, Ritva/ Collier, Paul (eds.) (2001): *Uganda's Recovery: The Role of Farms, Firms, and Government*. Kampala: Fountain Publishers (published with the permission of the World Bank), 1-11.

Collier, Paul/ Reinikka, Ritva (2001a): *Reconstruction and Liberalization: An Overview*, in: Reinikka, Ritva/ Collier, Paul (eds.) (2001): *Uganda's Recovery: The Role of Farms, Firms, and Government*. Kampala: Fountain Publishers (published with the permission of the World Bank), 15-47.

Conrad, Sebastian/ Randeria, Shalini (2002): *Geteilte Geschichten – Europa in einer postkolonialen Welt,* in: Conrad, Sebastian/ Randeria, Shalini (eds.) (2002): *Jenseits des Eurozentrismus. Postkoloniale Perspektiven in den Geschichts- und Kulturwissenschaften*. Frankfurt am Main: Campus, 9-49.

Cooper, Frederick (1993): *Africa and the World Economy,* in: Cooper, Frederick/ Isaacman, Allen F./ Mallon, Florencia E./ Roseberry, William/ Stern, Steve J. (eds.) (1993): *Confronting Historical Paradigms: Peasants, Labor, and the Capitalist World System in Africa and Latin America*. Madison: University of Wisconsin Press, 84-201.

Cooper, Frederick (2009): *Afrika in der kapitalistischen Welt,* in: Randeria, Shalini/ Eckert, Andreas (eds.) (2009): *Vom Imperialismus zum Empire: Nicht-westliche Perspektiven auf Globalisierung*. Frankfurt am Main: Suhrkamp, 37-73.

Dannecker, Petra/ Vossemer, Christiane (2014): *Qualitative Interviews in der Entwicklungsforschung. Typen und Herausforderungen,* in: Dannecker, Petra/ Englert, Birgit (eds.) (2014): *Qualitative Methoden in der Entwicklungsforschung*. Wien: mandelbaum verlag, 153-175.

Delheim, Judith/ Schlosser, Irmtraud (2008): *Solidarische Ökonomie als Türöffner des Neoliberalismus?,* in: Giegold, Sven/ Embshoff, Dagmar (eds.) (2008): *Solidarische Ökonomie im globalisierten Kapitalismus*. Hamburg: VSA Verlag, 89-91.

Denzin, Norman K./ Lincoln, Yvonna S. (1994): *Introduction: Entering the Field of Qualitative Research,* in: Denzin, Norman K./ Lincoln, Yvonna S. (eds.) (1994): *Handbook of Qualitative Research*. Thousand Oaks: Sage, 1-17.

Denzin, Norman K./ Lincoln, Yvonna S./ MacLure, Maggie/ Otterstad, Ann Merete/ Torrance, Harry/ Cannella, Gaile S./ Koro-Ljungberg, Mirka/ McTier, Terrence (2017): *Critical Qualitative Methodologies. Reconceptualizations and Emergent Construction,* in: *International Review of Qualitative Research, Vol. 10, No. 4,* 482-498. DOI: 10.1525/irqr.2017.10.4.482, accessed on 6 August 2018, on: http://irqr.ucpress.edu/content/10/4/482.full.pdf+html.

Develtere, Patrick (2008): *Cooperative Development in Africa up to the 1990s,* in: Develtere, Patrick/ Pollet, Ignace/ Wanyama, Frederick (eds.) (2008): *Cooperating out of poverty: The renaissance of the African cooperative movement*. Geneva: International Labour Organization, 1-37.

Dey, Ian (1993): *Qualitative Data Analysis: A user-friendly guide for social scientists*. London: Routledge.

Dhawan, Nikita/ Randeria, Shalini (2016): *Perspectives on Globalization and Subalternity,* in: Huggan, Graham (ed.) (2016): *The Oxford Handbook of Postcolonial Studies*. Oxford: Oxford University Press, 559-586.

Dhawan, Nikita (2011): *Transnationale Gerechtigkeit in einer postkolonialen Welt,* in: Castro Varela, María do Mar/ Dhawan, Nikita (eds.) (2011): *Soziale (Un)Gerechtigkeit. Kritische Perspektiven auf Diversity, Intersektionalität und Antidiskriminierung*. Berlin: LIT Verlag, 12-35.

Dirlik, Arif (2004): *The Postcolonial Aura: Third World Criticism in the Age of Global Capitalism,* in: McClintock, Anne/ Mufti, Aamir/ Shohat, Ella (eds.) (2004): *Dangerous Liaisons: Gender, Nation and Postcolonial Perspectives*. Minneapolis: University of Minnesota Press, 501-528.

Dresing, Thorsten/ Pehl, Thorsten/ Schmieder, Christian (eds.) (2015): *Manual (on) Transcription. Transcription Conventions, Software Guides and Practical Hints for Qualitative Researchers.3rd English Edition*. Marburg, accessed and downloaded on 3 March 2017, on: http://www.audiotranskription.de/english/transcription-practicalguide.htm (available only online).

Eckert, Andreas/ Randeria, Shalini (2009): *Geteilte Globalisierung*, in: Randeria, Shalini/ Eckert, Andreas (eds.) (2009): *Vom Imperialismus zum Empire: Nicht-westliche Perspektiven auf Globalisierung*. Frankfurt am Main: Suhrkamp, 9-33.

Engels, Bettina/ Dietz, Christina (2011): *Land grabbing analysieren: Ansatzpunkte für eine politisch-ökonomische Analyse am Beispiel Äthiopiens*, in: *PERIPHERIE* 2011, 31 (124), 395-416.

England, Kim V.L. (1994): *Getting Personal: Reflexivity, Positionality, and Feminist Research*, in: The Professional Geographer, 46 (1), 80-89.

Enzenhofer, Edith/ Resch, Katharina (2011): *Übersetzungsprozesse und deren Qualitätssicherung in der qualitativen Sozialforschung* [111 paragraphs], in: *Forum: Qualitative Sozialforschung/ Forum: Qualitative Social Research, Vol. 12, No. 2, Art. 10*, accessed on 9 August 2018, on: http://nbnresolving.de/urn:nbn:de:0114-fqs1102106.

Escobar, Arturo (2007): *'Post-development' as concept and social practice*, in: Ziai, Aram (ed.) (2007): *Exploring Post-development: Theory and practice, problems and perspectives*. London: Routledge, 18-31.

Escobar, Arturo (2012): *Encountering Development. The Making and Unmaking of the Third World*. Princeton: University Press.

Esteva, Gustavo (2019): *Development*, in: Sachs, Wolfgang (ed.) (2019): *The Development Dictionary: A Guide to Knowledge as Power. Third Edition*. London. Zed Books, 1-23.

Fabian, Johannes (2014): *Time and the other: how anthropology makes its object*. New York: Columbia University Press.

Fall, Abdou Salam (2008): *The Senegalese cooperative movement: embedded in the social Economy*, in: Develtere, Patrick/ Pollet, Ignace/ Wanyama, Frederick (eds.) (2008): *Cooperating out of poverty: The renaissance of the African cooperative movement*. Geneva: International Labour Organization, 330-365.

Fall, Abdou Salam (2013): *The social and solidarity economy response to global social needs*, in: Jeantet, Thierry (ed.) (2013): *Social and Solidarity Economy: A response to international challenges*. Paris: Éditions Le Manuscrit, 87-101.

Fallers, Lloyd A. (1965): *Bantu Bureaucracy: A Century of Political Evolution among the Basoga of Uganda*. Chicago: The University of Chicago Press.

Fanon, Frantz (1967): *Racism and Culture*, in: Fanon, Frantz (1967): *Toward the African Revolution. Political Essays*. New York: Grove Press, 29-44.

Fanon, Frantz (2004): *The Wretched of the Earth*. New York: Grove Press.

Fanon, Frantz (2008): *Black Skin, White Masks*. New York: Grove Press.

Feierman, Steven (2002): *Afrika in der Geschichte. Das Ende der universalen Erzählungen,* in: Conrad, Sebastian/ Randeria, Shalini (eds.) (2002): *Jenseits des Eurozentrismus. Postkoloniale Perspektiven in den Geschichts- und Kulturwissenschaften.* Frankfurt am Main: Campus, 50-83.

Fereday, Jennifer/ Muir-Cochrane, Eimear (2006): *Demonstrating Rigor Using Thematic Analysis: A Hybrid Approach of Inductive and Deductive Coding and Theme Development,* in: International Journal of Qualitative Methods 5 (1), accessed on 25 October 2017, on: https://journals.sagepub.com/doi/pdf/10.1177/160940690600500107.

Ferguson, James (2005): *Decomposing Modernity: History and Hierarchy after Development,* in: Loomba, Ania/ Kaul, Suvir/ Bunzl, Matti/ Burton, Antoinette/ Esty, Jed (eds.) (2005): *Postcolonial Studies and Beyond.* Durham: Duke University Press, 166-181.

Ferguson, James (2006): *Global Shadows. Africa in the Neoliberal World Order.* Durham: Duke University Press.

Ferguson, James (2014): *The Anti-Politics Machine. "Development," depoliticization, and bureaucratic power in Lesotho.* Minneapolis: University of Minnesota Press.

Flick, Uwe (2018): *An introduction to qualitative research: 6th edition.* London: Sage.

Foucault, Michel (2010): *The Archaeology of Knowledge And The Discourse on Language.* New York: Vintage Books.

Frank, André Gunder (1966): *Die Entwicklung der Unterentwicklung,* in: Schmidt, Lukas/ Schröder, Sabine (eds.) (2016): *Entwicklungstheorien: Klassiker, Kritik und Alternativen.* Wien: mandelbaum, 170-185.

Fridell, Gavin (2015): *Fair Trade Coffee: The Prospects and Pitfalls of Market-Driven Social Justice.* Toronto: University of Toronto Press.

Friedman, Thomas L. (2005): *The world is flat: a brief history of the twenty-first century.* New York: Farrar, Straus and Giroux.

Gandhi, Leela (2019): *Postcolonial Theory: A critical introduction.* New York: Columbia University Press.

García Canclini, Néstor (2001): *Consumers and Citizens: Globalization and Multicultural Conflicts.* Minneapolis: University of Minnesota Press.

George, Susan (2004): *Another world is possible if….* London: Verso.

Gerken, Egbert (1972): *Social Structure and the Industrial Town. The Case of Social Change in Jinja and Busoga/Uganda,* in: Brandt, Hartmut/ Schubert, Bernd/ Gerken, Egbert (eds.) (1972): *The Industrial Town as Factor of Economic and Social Development: The Example of Jinja/Uganda.* München: Weltforum Verlag, 291-441.

Giegold, Sven/ Embshoff, Dagmar (eds.) (2008): *Solidarische Ökonomie im globalisierten Kapitalismus.* Hamburg: VSA-Verlag.

Glenn, John (2007): *Globalization: North-South perspectives.* London: Routledge.

Gonza, Richard Kayaga (2007): *Lusoga-English Dictionary and English-Lusoga Dictionary.* Kampala: MK Publishers Ltd.

Gonza, Richard Kayaga/ Nabwiso, Frank/ Muzaale, Dias/ Oloka, Fred (eds.) (2016): *Evolution of Busoga's Eleven Hereditary Chiefdoms and Kyabazingaship in Uganda 1600-2016*. Jinja: Cultural Research Centre.

Gonzalez y Gonzalez, Elsa M./ Lincoln, Yvonna S. (2006): *Decolonizing Qualitative Research: Non-traditional Reporting Forms in the Academy*, in: *Forum: Qualitative Social Research, Vol. 7, No. 4, Art. 1*, accessed on 4 August 2018, on: http://www.qualitative-research.net/index.php/fqs/article/view/162/360.

Greig, Alastair/ Hulme, David/ Turner, Mark (2007): *Challenging Global Inequality. Development Theory and Practice in the 21st Century*. Houndmills: Palgrave Macmillan.

Grosfoguel, Ramón (2008): *World-System Analysis and Postcolonial Studies: A Call for a Dialogue from the "Coloniality of Power" Approach*, in: Krishnaswamy, Revathi/ Hawley, John C. (eds.) (2008): *The Postcolonial and the Global*. Minneapolis: University of Minnesota Press, 94-104.

Grosfoguel, Ramón (2011): *Decolonizing Post-Colonial Studies and Paradigms of Political-Economy: Transmodernity, Decolonial Thinking, and Global Coloniality*, in: TRANSMODERNITY: Journal of Peripheral Cultural Production of the Luso-Hispanic World, 1(1), 2-38, California Digital Library, University of California: https://escholarship.org/uc/item/21k6t3fq, publication date: 13 May 2011, accessed 11 December 2019.

Gruffydd Jones, Branwen (2018): *African Anti-colonialism in International Relations: Against the Time of Forgetting*, in: Iñiguez de Heredia, Marta/ Wai, Zubairu (eds.) (2018): *Recentering Africa in International Relations. Beyond Lack, Peripherality, and Failure*. Cham, Switzerland: Palgrave Macmillan, 187-223.

Gulere, Cornelius W. (2009): *Lusoga-English Dictionary: Eibwanio*. Kampala: Fountain Publishers.

Hall, Stuart (2002): *Wann gab es "das Postkoloniale"? Denken an der Grenze*, in: Conrad, Sebastian/ Randeria, Shalini (eds.) (2002): *Jenseits des Eurozentrismus. Postkoloniale Perspektiven in den Geschichts- und Kulturwissenschaften*. Frankfurt am Main: Campus, 219-246.

Hall, Stuart/ Massey, Doreen/ Rustin, Michael (eds.) (2015): *After Neoliberalism: The Kilburn Manifesto*. London: Lawrence & Wishart.

Hall, Stuart/ Massey, Doreen/ Rustin, Michael (2015a) *Framing Statement: After neoliberalism: analysing the present*, in: Hall, Stuart/ Massey, Doreen/ Rustin, Michael (eds.) (2015): *After Neoliberalism: The Kilburn Manifesto*. London: Lawrence & Wishart, 9-23.

Hasselmann, Karl-Heinz (1976): *Untersuchungen zur Struktur der Kulturlandschaft von Busoga/Uganda*. Berlin: Selbstverlag des Geographischen Instituts der Freien Universität Berlin.

Hawley, John C. (2008): *Agencies for Resistance, Prospects for Evolution*, in: Krishnaswamy, Revathi/ Hawley, John C. (eds.) (2008): *The Postcolonial and the Global*. Minneapolis: University of Minnesota Press, 22-32.

Hindess, Barry (2016): *'Slippery, like a fish' The Discourse of the Social Sciences*, in: Huggan, Graham (ed.) (2016): *The Oxford Handbook of Postcolonial Studies*. Oxford: Oxford University Press, 489-505.

Hirsch, Joachim (2001): *Die Internationalisierung des Staates: Anmerkungen zu einigen aktuellen Fragen der Staatstheorie*, in: Hirsch, Joachim/ Jessop, Bob/ Poulantzas, Nicos (eds.) (2001): *Die Zukunft des Staates: Denationalisierung, Internationalisierung, Renationalisierung*. Hamburg: VSA-Verlag, 101-138.

Hopf, Christel (2012): *Qualitative Interviews – ein Überblick*, in: Flick, Uwe/ von Kardorff, Ernst/ Steinke, Ines (eds.) (2012): *Qualitative Forschung. Ein Handbuch*. Reinbeck bei Hamburg: Rowohlt-Taschenbuch-Verlag, 349-359.

Husseini de Araújo, Shadia/ Kersting, Philippe (2012): *Welche Praxis nach der postkolonialen Kritik? Human- und physisch-geographische Feldforschung aus übersetzungstheoretischer Perspektive*, in: *Geographica Helvetica*, 67, 139–145.

Hutchinson, Paul (2001): *Combating Illness*, in: Reinikka, Ritva/ Collier, Paul (eds.) (2001): *Uganda's Recovery: The Role of Farms, Firms, and Government*. Kampala: Fountain Publishers (published with the permission of the World Bank), 407-449.

Illich, Ivan (1998): *Development as Planned Poverty*, in: Rahnema, Majid/ Bawtree, Victoria (eds.) (1998): *The Post-Development Reader*. London: Zed Books, 94-101.

International Co-operative Alliance (ICA 2020) *Cooperative identity, values and principles*: https://www.ica.coop/en/cooperatives/cooperative-identity, accessed on 6 March 2020.

International Co-operative Alliance (ICA 2020a): *History of the cooperative movement:* https://www.ica.coop/en/cooperatives/history-cooperative-movement, accessed on 6 March 2020.

Jeantet, Thierry (ed.) (2013): *Social and Solidarity Economy: A response to international challenges*. Paris: Éditions Le Manuscri.

Jones, Andrew (2010): *Globalization: Key Thinkers*. Cambridge: Polity Press.

Kaltmeier, Olaf (2012): *Methoden dekolonisieren. Reziprozität und Dialog in der herrschenden Geopolitik des Wissens*, in: Kaltmeier, Olaf/ Corona Berkin, Sarah (eds.) (2012): *Methoden dekolonisieren. Eine Werkzeugkiste zur Demokratisierung der Sozial- und Kulturwissenschaften*. Münster: Westfälisches Dampfboot, 18-44.

Kapoor, Ilan (2004): *Hyper-Self-Reflexive Development? Spivak on Representing the Third World 'Other'*, in: *Third World Quarterly*, 25/4, 627-647.

Kasente, Deborah (2002): *Assessing Social Development in Uganda: Taking Gender Relations Seriously*, in: Musisi, Nakanyike B./ Dodge, Cole P. (eds.) (2002): *Transformations in Uganda*. Kampala, Uganda: Makerere Institute of Social Research, 183-193.

Kerner, Ina (2012): *Postkoloniale Theorien zur Einführung*. Hamburg: Junius.

Khor, Martin (2001): *Rethinking Globalization: Critical issues and policy choices*. London: Zed Books.

Kikulwe, Enoch/ Wesseler, Justus/ Falck-Zepeda, José (2008): *Introducing a Genetically Modified Banana in Uganda: Social Benefits, Costs, and Consumer Perceptions.* IFPRI Discussion Paper 00767, May 2008, International Food Policy Research Institute, Washington D.C.: https://www.ifpri.org/publication/introducing-gene tically-modified-banana-uganda, accessed on 25 June, 2020.

Kiiza, Julius (2008): *Mercantilism and the Struggle for Late Industrialization in an Age of Globalization*, in: Mensah, Joseph (ed.) (2008): *Neoliberalism and Globalization in Africa: Contestations from an Embattled Continent*. New York: Palgrave MacMillan, 177-202.

Kruse, Jan (2015): *Qualitative Interviewforschung. Ein integrativer Ansatz. 2., überarbeitete und ergänzte Auflage*. Weinheim/ Basel: Beltz Juventa.

Kuckartz, Udo (2007): *Einführung in die computergestützte Analyse qualitativer Daten. 2., aktualisierte und erweiterte Auflage*. Wiesbaden : VS Verlag für Sozialwissenschaften.

Kuckartz, Udo/ Dresing, Thorsten/ Rädiker, Stefan/ Stefer, Claus (2008): *Qualitative Evaluation – Der Einstieg in die Praxis*. 2., aktualisierte Auflage. Wiesbaden: VS Verlag.

Kuteesa, Florence/ Tumusiime-Mutebile, Emmanuel/ Whitworth, Alan/ Williamson, Tim (eds.) (2010): *Uganda's Economic Reforms*. Oxford: Oxford University Press.

Kvale, Steinar/ Brinkmann, Svend (2009): *InterViews : learning the craft of qualitative research interviewing*. 2nd edition. Los Angeles: Sage.

Kyazze, Lawrence M. (2010): *Cooperatives: The sleeping economic and social giants in Uganda*. CoopAFRICA working paper No. 15. Dar es Salaam: International Labour Office, accessed on 28 August 2018, on: http://www.ilo.int/public/english/employment/ent/coop/africa/download/wpno15cooperativesinuganda.pdf.

Larimore, Ann Evans (1958): *The Alien Town: Patterns of Settlement in Busoga, Uganda. An Essay in Cultural Geography*. Chicago: The University of Chicago Press.

Latouche, Serge (2015): *Farewell to Growth*. Cambridge: Polity Press.

Latouche, Serge (2019): *Standard of Living*, in: Sachs, Wolfgang (ed.) (2019) *The Development Dictionary: A Guide to Knowledge as Power. Third Edition*. London. Zed Books, 279-294.

Logan, Ikubolajeh B. (1995): *Can Sub-Saharan Africa Successfully Privatize Its Health Care Sector?*, in: Mengisteab, Kidane/ Logan, Ikubolajeh B. (eds.) (1995): *Beyond Economic Liberalization in Africa: Structural Adjustment and the Alternatives*. London: Zed Books, 56-74.

Lucas, Linda E. (2007): *Unpacking Globalization: Markets, Gender and Work*, in: Lucas, Linda E. (ed.) (2007): *Unpacking Globalization: Markets, Gender, and Work*. Lanham: Lexington Books, 3-10.

Lucas, Linda E. (2007a): *Locating Women: Structure and Work in the Ugandan Macroeconomy*, in: Lucas, Linda E. (ed.) (2007): *Unpacking Globalization: Markets, Gender, and Work*. Lanham: Lexington Books, 101-115.

Mackieson, Penny/ Shlonsky, Aron/ Connolly, Marie (2019): *Increasing rigor and reducing bias in qualitative research: A document analysis of parliamentary debates using applied thematic analysis*, in: Qualitative Social Work, Vol. 18(6), 965-980. DOI: 10.1177/1473325018786996, accessed on 4 March 2020.

Martin, Anne (1963): *The Marketing of Minor Crops in Uganda: A Factual Study. Overseas Research Publications No.1*. London: Her Majesty's Stationary Office.

Matthews, Sally (2007): *What, then, should we do? Insights and experiences of a Senegalese NGO,* in: Ziai, Aram (ed.) (2007): *Exploring Post-development: Theory and practice, problems and perspectives.* London: Routledge, 131-144.

Matthews, Sally (2018): *Alternatives to Development in Africa,* in: Iñiguez de Heredia, Marta/ Wai, Zubairu (eds.) (2018): *Recentering Africa in International Relations. Beyond Lack, Peripherality, and Failure.* Cham, Switzerland: Palgrave Macmillan, 167-186.

Mayring, Philipp (2008): *Qulitative Inhaltsanalyse: Grundlagen und Techniken. 10. Auflage.* Weinheim: Beltz.

Mayring, Philipp (2016): *Einführung in die qualitative Sozialforschung. 6. Auflage.* Weinheim: Beltz.

Mbembe, Achille (2001): *On the Postcolony.* Berkeley: University of California Press.

McEwan, Cheryl (2009): *Postcolonialism and Development.* London: Routledge.

McMichael, Philip (2012): *Development and Social Change: A Global Perspective. Fifth Edition.* Los Angeles: SAGE Publications.

Mensah, Joseph (2008): *Introduction: Neoliberalism and Globalization in Africa,* in: Mensah, Joseph (ed.) (2008): *Neoliberalism and Globalization in Africa.* New York: Palgrave Macmillan, 1-14.

Mignolo, Walter (2012): *Local Histories/ Global Designs. Coloniality, subaltern knowledges, and border thinking.* Princeton: Princeton University Press.

Miller, Jody/ Glassner, Barry (2011): *The „Inside" and the „Outside": Finding Realities in Interviews,* in: Silverman, David (ed.) (2011): *Qualitative Research. Issues of Theory, Method and Practice.* Los Angeles: Sage, 131-148.

Mohanty, Chandra Talpade (2004): *Under Western Eyes: Feminist Scholarship and Colonial Discourses,* in: McClintock, Anne/ Mufti, Aamir/ Shohat, Ella (eds.) (2004): *Dangerous Liaisons: Gender, Nation and Postcolonial Perspectives.* Minneapolis: University of Minnesota Press, 255-277.

Morris, Rosalind C. (2010): *Introduction,* in: Morris, Rosalind C. (ed.) (2010): *Can the Subaltern speak? Reflections on the history of an idea.* New York: Columbia University Press, 1-18.

Morton, Adam David (2007): *Unravelling Gramsci: Hegemony and Passive Revolution in the Global Political Economy.* London: Pluto Press.

Mrema, Herment A. (2008): *Uganda: Starting All Over Again,* in: Develtere, Patrick/ Pollet, Ignace/ Wanyama, Frederick (eds.) (2008): *Cooperating out of poverty: The renaissance of the African cooperative movement.* Genf: International Labour Office, 153-174.

Mudimbe, Valentin Y. (1988): *The invention of Africa: Gnosis, Philosophy, and the Order of Knowledge.* London: James Currey.

Muraca, Barbara (2014): *Gut leben: Eine Gesellschaft jenseits des Wachstums.* Berlin: Wagenbach.

Musisi, Nakanyike B./ Dodge, Cole P. (eds.) (2002): *Transformations in Uganda.* Kampala, Uganda: Makerere Institute of Social Research.

Mutibwa, Phares Mukasa (2016): *A History of Uganda. The first 100 years 1894-1995*. Kampala: Fountain Publishers.

Mwase, Ngila (2007): *Sub-Saharan Africa: Globalization, Trade Liberalization and Impact on the Lives of the Poor*, in: Lucas, Linda E. (ed.) (2007): *Unpacking Globalization: Markets, Gender, and Work*. Lanham: Lexington Books, 59-70.

Nabuguzi, Emmanuel (1993): *Peasant Response to Economic Crisis in Uganda: Rice Farmers in Busoga*, in: *Review of African Political Economy*, No. 56, Challenging Gender Inequalities in Africa (March 1993), 53-67.

Nannyonjo, Justine (2015): *Enabling agricultural cooperatives in Uganda: The role of public policy and the state*, in: Utting, Peter (ed.) (2015): *Social and Solidarity Economy: Beyond the Fringe*. London: Zed Books, 266-283.

Nayenga, Peter F.B. (1981): *Commercial Cotton Growing in Busoga District, Uganda, 1905-1923*, in: *African Economic History* No. 19 (1981), 175-195.

Nayenga, Peter F. B. (2002): *Basoga*, in: Ember, Melvin/ Ember, Carol R./ Skoggard, Ian A. (eds.) (2002): *Encyclopedia of World Cultures: Supplement*. New York : Gale Group/ Thomson Learning (Macmillan Reference), 41-46.

N'Dione, Emmanuel/ De Leener, Philippe/ Ndiaye, Mamadou/ Jacolin, Pierre/ Perier, Jean-Pierre (eds.) (1995): *The Future of Community Lands. Human resources*. London: Intermediate Technology Publications.

N'Dione, Emmanuel Seni/ de Leener, Philippe/ Perier, Jean-Pierre/ Ndiaye, Mamadou/ Jacolin, Pierre (1998): *Reinventing the Present : The Chodak Experience in Senegal*, in: Rahnema, Majid/ Bawtree, Victoria (eds.) (1998): *The Post-Development Reader*. London: Zed Books, 364-376.

Ndlovu-Gatsheni, Sabelo J. (2013): *Coloniality of Power in Postcolonial Africa: Myths of Decolonization*. Dakar: CODESRIA.

Ndlovu-Gatsheni, Sabelo J. (2018): *Against Bringing Africa "Back-In"*, in: Iñiguez de Heredia, Marta/ Wai, Zubairu (eds.) (2018): *Recentering Africa in International Relations. Beyond Lack, Peripherality, and Failure*. Cham, Switzerland: Palgrave Macmillan, 283-305.

Ngũgĩ wa Thiong'o (1988): *Decolonizing the Mind: The Politics of Language in African Literature*. London: James Currey.

Ngũgĩ wa Thiong'o (2014): *Globalectics. Theory and the politics of knowing*. New York: Columbia University Press.

Niane, Djibril Tamsir (2010): *Der Afrikaner soll sich schuldig fühlen*, in: Cichon, Peter/ Hosch, Reinhart/ Kirsch, Fritz Peter (eds.) (2010): *Der undankbare Kontinent? Afrikanische Antworten auf europäische Bevormundung*. Hamburg: Argument, 251-273.

Nickel, Peter (2008): *Fairraten und verkauft? "Fairer" Kaffeehandel*, in: Giegold, Sven/ Embshoff, Dagmar (eds.) (2008): *Solidarische Ökonomie im globalisierten Kapitalismus*. Hamburg: VSA Verlag, 28-30.

Nkrumah, Kwame (1965): *Neo-Colonialism. The Last Stage of Imperialism*. London: Thomas Nelson.

Norberg, Johan (2005): *The Wealth of Generations. Capitalism and the Belief in the Future, 22nd John Bonython Lecture, Sydney*, accessed 26 September 2020, on: http://www.cis.org.au/app/uploads/2015/07/op98.pdf.

Ntombi, Ngwenya Barbara (2004): *Evading household indebtedness through participation in group solidarity coping strategies in contemporary Botswana,* in: Eastern Africa Social Science Research Review (EASSRR), Volume 20, Number 2, June 2004, 1-30 (Article), accessed on 22 Jan. 2016, on: DOI: 10.1353/eas.2004.0009.

Ofcanski, Thomas P. (1996): *Uganda: Tarnished Pearl of Africa*. Boulder: Westview Press.

Oguti, Bernard (2019): *LC5 elections in newly created districts set for tomorrow,* in: New Vision, 24 July 2019, accessed online, 28 June 2020, on: https://www.newvision.co.ug/news/1504160/lc5-elections-newly-created-districts-set-tomorrow.

Ohnmacht, Astrid (2007): *Fair trade and poverty alleviation: A critical analysis on the impact of fair trade network*, Aachener Schriften zur Betriebswirtschaft, Bd. 1. Aachen: Shaker Verlag.

Opratko, Benjamin (2014): *Hegemonie. Politische Theorie nach Antonio Gramsci*. Münster: Westfälisches Dampfboot.

Ostry, Jonathan D./ Loungani, Prakash/ Furceri, Davide (2016): *Neoliberalism: Oversold?,* in: *Finance and Development* 53 (2), 38-41.

Otto-Walter, Renate (1979): *Unterentwicklung und Subsistenzreproduktion: Forschungsansatz der Arbeitsgruppe Bielefelder Entwicklungssoziologen*, in: Arbeitsgruppe Bielefelder Entwicklungssoziologen (eds.) (1979): *Subsistenzproduktion und Akkumulation*. Band 5 Bielefelder Studien zur Entwicklungssoziologie. Saarbrücken: breitenbach, 7-12.

Paech, Niko (2015): *Das Elend der Konsumwirtschaft: Von Rio+20 zur Postwachstumsgesellschaft,* in: Blätter für deutsche internationale Politik (ed.) (2015): *Mehr geht nicht! Der Postwachstums-Reader*. Berlin: Blätter Verlagsgesellschaft mbH, 71-78.

Pfeifer-Schaupp, Ulrich (2005): *Die Schatten der Globalisierung und die Soziale Arbeit,* in: Pfeifer-Schaupp, Ulrich (ed.) (2005): *Globalisierung und Soziale Arbeit. Grundbegriffe, Problemfelder, Perspektiven*. Hamburg: VSA-Verlag, 11-51.

Prempeh, Edward Osei Kwadwo (2008): *The Anticapitalism Movement and African resistance to neoliberal globalization,* in: Mensah, Joseph (ed.) (2008): *Neoliberalism and Globalization in Africa*. New York: Palgrave Macmillan, 55-69.

Quijano, Aníbal (2000): *Coloniality of Power and Eurocentrism in Latin America,* in: *International Sociology* Vol 15(2): 215-232.

Raghuram, Pavarti/ Madge, Clare (2006): *Towards a method for postcolonial development geography? Possibilities and challenges,* in: *Singapore Journal of Tropical Geography*, 27, 270-288.

Rahaman, Andrea (2014): *Mikrokredite gegen Armut: Dichtung und Wahrheit in Bangladesch,* in: Klas, Gerhard/ Mader, Philip (eds.) (2014): *Rendite machen und Gutes tun? Mikrokredite und die Folgen neoliberaler Entwicklungspolitik*. Frankfurt: Campus Verlag, 53-60.

Rahnema, Majid (1998): *Towards Post-Development: Searching for signposts, a new language and new paradigms,* in: Rahnema, Majid/ Bawtree, Victoria (eds.) (1998): *The Post-Development Reader*. London: Zed Books, 377-403.

Randeria, Shalini (2007): *The State of Globalization: Legal Plurality, Overlapping Sovereignties and Ambiguous Alliances between Civil Society and the Cunning State in India,* in: Theory, Culture & Society, Vol. 24(1): 1-33.

Ranger, Terence (1984): *The Invention of Tradition in Colonial Africa,* in: Hobsbawm, Eric/ Ranger, Terence (eds.) (1992): *The Invention of Tradition*. Cambridge: University Press, 211-262.

Rapley, Tim (2011): *Some Pragmatics of Qualitative Data Analysis,* in: Silverman, David (ed.) (2011): *Qualitative Research: Issues of Theory, Method and Practice*. London: SAGE, 273-290.

Reed, Darryl (2015): *Scaling the social and solidarity economy: opportunities and limitations of Fairtrade practice,* in: Utting, Peter (ed.) (2015): *Social and Solidarity Economy. Beyond the fringe*. London: Zed Books, 100-115.

Reinikka, Ritva/ Collier, Paul (eds.) (2001): *Uganda's Recovery: The Role of Farms, Firms, and Government*. Kampala: Fountain Publishers (published with the permission of the World Bank).

Roberts, J. Timmons/ Hite, Amy (eds.) (2000): *From Modernization to Globalization. Perspectives on Development and Social Change*. Oxford: Blackwell Publishers.

Ross, Karen (2017*): Making Empowering Choices: How Methodology Matters for Empowering Research Participants,* in *Forum: Qualitative Social Research, Vol. 18, No. 3, Art. 12,* accessed on 4 August 2018, on: http://www.qualitative-research.net/index.php/fqs/article/view/2791/4134.

Rothman, Barbara Katz (1996): *Bearing Witness: Representing Women's Experiences of Prenatal Diagnosis,* in: *Feminism and Psychology, Vol. 6(1)*, 52-55.

Rowden, Rick (1999): *Developing Savages, Spreading Democracy: Popular Conceptions of North-South Relations,* in: Berkeley Journal of Sociology: A Critical Review, Volume XXXXIII, 1998-1999, University of California, 149-187.

Rufer, Mario (2012): *Sprechen, zuhören, schreiben. Postkoloniale Perspektiven auf Subalternität und Horizontalität,* in: Kaltmeier, Olaf/ Corona Berkin, Sarah (eds.) (2012): *Methoden dekolonisieren. Eine Werkzeugkiste zur Demokratisierung der Sozial- und Kulturwissenschaften*. Münster: Westfälisches Dampfboot, 18-44.

Sachs, Wolfgang (1998): *The need for the home perspective,* in: Rahnema, Majid/ Bawtree, Victoria (eds.) (1998): *The Post-Development Reader*. London: Zed Books, 290-300.

Said, Edward (1994): *Orientalism*. New York: Vintage Books.

San Juan, Jr. Epifanio (2002): *Postcolonialism and the problematic of uneven development,* in: Bartolovich, Crystal/ Lazarus, Neil (eds.) (2002): *Marxism, Modernity, and Postcolonial Studies*. Cambridge: Cambridge University Press, 221-239.

Santos, Boaventura de Sousa (2007): *Preface,* in: Santos, Boaventura de Sousa (ed.) (2007): *Another Production is Possible: Beyond the Capitalist Canon*. London: Verso, vii-xvi.

Santos, Boaventura de Sousa (2014): *Epistemologies of the South. Justice against Epistemicide*. London: Routledge.

Santos, Boaventura de Sousa (2017): *The end of the cognitive empire: The coming of age of epistemologies of the south*. Durham: Duke University Press.

Santos, Boaventura de Sousa/ Rodríguez-Garavito, César A. (2007): *Introduction: Expanding the Economic Canon and Searching for Alternatives to Neoliberal Globalization*, in: Santos, Boaventura de Sousa (ed.) (2007): *Another Production is Possible: Beyond the Capitalist Canon*. London: Verso, xvii-lxii.

Satgar, Vishwas (2014): *The crisis of global capitalism and the solidarity economy alternative*, in: Satgar, Vishwas (ed.) (2014): *The Solidarity Economy Alternative. Emerging Theory and Practice*. Scottsville: University of Kwazulu Natal Press, 1-34.

Schmidt, Christiane (2012): *Analyse von Leitfadeninterviews*, in: Flick, Uwe/ von Kardorff, Ernst/ Steinke, Ines (eds.) (2012): *Qualitative Forschung: Ein Handbuch*. Reinbeck bei Hamburg: Rowohlt-Taschenbuch-Verlag, 447-455.

Schmidt, Lukas/ Schröder, Sabine (2016): *Einleitung: Liberalismen*, in: Schmidt, Lukas/ Schröder, Sabine (eds.) (2016): *Entwicklungstheorien: Klassiker, Kritik und Alternativen*. Wien: mandelbaum, 20-37.

Schreier, Margrit (2012): *Qualitative Content Analysis in Practice*. London: SAGE.

Schubert, Bernd (1972): *Food-Marketing under the Impact of Urbanization and Industrialization: The Case of Jinja/Uganda*, in: Brandt, Hartmut/ Schubert, Bernd/ Gerken, Egbert (1972): *The Industrial Town as Factor of Economic and Social Development: The Example of Jinja/Uganda*. München: Weltforum Verlag, 137-289.

Seibel, Hans Dieter (1987): *Ländliche Entwicklung als Austauschprozeß*. Saarbrücken: breitenbach.

Shanin, Teodor (1998): *The idea of progress*, in: Rahnema, Majid/ Bawtree, Victoria (eds.) (2018): *The Post-Development Reader*. London: Zed Books, 65-71.

Singer, Paul (2007): *The Recent Rebirth of the Solidarity Economy in Brazil*, in: Santos, Boaventura de Sousa (ed.) (2007): *Another Production is Possible: Beyond the Capitalist Canon*. London: Verso, 3-42.

Singer, Paul (2008): *SENAES – Eine brasilianische Erfahrung der Politik Solidarischer Ökonomie*, in: Giegold, Sven/ Embshoff, Dagmar (eds.) (2008): *Solidarische Ökonomie im globalisierten Kapitalismus*. Hamburg: VSA Verlag, 215-223.

Spivak, Gayatri Chakravorty (1988): *Can the Subaltern Speak?*, in: Nelson, Cary/ Grossberg, Lawrence (eds.) (1988): *Marxism and the Interpretation of Culture*. Chicago: University of Illinois Press, 271-313.

Sørensen, Pernille (2000): *"Money is the True Friend": Economic Practice, Morality and Trust among the Iganga Maize Traders in Uganda*. Hamburg: LIT.

Steyerl, Hito (2008): *Die Gegenwart der Subalternen*, in: Spivak, Gayatri Chakravorty (2008): *Can the Subaltern Speak? Postkolonialität und subalterne Artikulation*. Wien: Verlag Turia + Kant, 7-16.

Stiglitz, Joseph (2002): *Globalization and its discontents*. New York: Norton.

Swadener, Beth Blue/ Mutua, Kagendo (2008): *Decolonizing Performances. Deconstructing the Global Postcolonial*, in: Denzin, Norman K./ Lincoln, Yvonna S./ Smith, Linda Tuhiwai (eds.) (2008): *Handbook of Critical and Indigenous Methodologies*. Los Angeles: Sage, 31-44.

Tamale, Sylvia (2002): *The Gender and Globalization in Contemporary Uganda*, in: Musisi, Nakanyike B./ Dodge, Cole P. (eds.) (2002): *Transformations in Uganda*. Kampala, Uganda: Makerere Institute of Social Research, 159-182.

Tandon, Yash (2016): *Trade is War*. Dar es salaam: Mkuki na Nyota Publishers.

Teivainen, Teivo (2009): *Globalisierung der ökonomischen Überwachung: Der Internationale Währungsfonds als moderner Priester*, in: Randeria, Shalini/ Eckert, Andreas (eds.) (2009): *Vom Imperialismus zum Empire: Nicht-westliche Perspektiven auf Globalisierung*. Frankfurt am Main: Suhrkamp,105-136.

Thomas, Frédéric (2015): *L'économie sociale et solidaire: enjeux, défis et perspectives*, in: Alternatives Sud, Vol. XXII (2015) 2: *L'économie sociale et solidaire, levier de changement?*, 7-23.

UBOS - Uganda Bureau of Statistics (2017a) *The National Population and Housing Census 2014 – Area Specific Profile Series: Buyende District*. Uganda Bureau of Statistics: Kampala, Uganda.

UBOS - Uganda Bureau of Statistics (2017b) *The National Population and Housing Census 2014 – Area Specific Profile Series: Jinja District*. Uganda Bureau of Statistics: Kampala, Uganda.

UBOS - Uganda Bureau of Statistics (2017c) *The National Population and Housing Census 2014 – Area Specific Profile Series: Kamuli District*. Uganda Bureau of Statistics: Kampala, Uganda.

UBOS - Uganda Bureau of Statistics (2018) *Uganda National Household Survey 2016/2017*. Uganda Bureau of Statistics: Kampala, Uganda.

UNDP Uganda (2017): Uganda Annual Report 2017, accessed on 26 August 2020, on: https://www.ug.undp.org/content/uganda/en/home/library/undp-in-uganda-/UNDP_Uganda_Annual_Report_2017.html.

Utting, Peter (2015): *Introduction: The challenge of scaling up social and solidarity economy*, in: Utting, Peter (ed.) (2015): *Social and Solidarity Economy. Beyond the fringe*. London: Zed Books, 1-37.

Voß, Elisabeth (2008): *Solidarische Ökonomien als Alternativen zum Neoliberalismus*, in: Giegold, Sven/ Embshoff, Dagmar (eds.) (2008): *Solidarische Ökonomie im globalisierten Kapitalismus*. Hamburg: VSA Verlag, 62-64.

Wade, Robert Hunter (2009): *Welche Strategien bleiben den Entwicklungsländern heute? Die Welthandelsorganisation und der schrumpfende "Entwicklungsraum"*, in: Randeria, Shalini/ Eckert, Andreas (eds.) (2009): *Vom Imperialismus zum Empire: Nicht-westliche Perspektiven auf Globalisierung*. Frankfurt am Main: Suhrkamp, 237-269.

Wai, Zubairu (2018): *Africa in/ and International Relations: An Introduction*, in: Iñiguez de Heredia, Marta/ Wai, Zubairu (eds.) (2018): *Recentering Africa in International Relations. Beyond Lack, Peripherality, and Failure*. Cham, Switzerland: Palgrave Macmillan, 1-29.

Wallerstein, Immanuel Maurice (1998): *Utopistics, or, Historical choices of the twenty-first century*. New York: The New Press.

Wallerstein, Immanuel Maurice (2002): *Social Conflict in Post-Independence Black Africa: The Concepts of Race and Status-Group Reconsidered*, in: Balibar, Etienne/ Wallerstein, Immanuel Maurice (2002): *Race, Nation, Class. Ambiguous Identities*. London: Verso, 187-203.

Wallerstein, Immanuel Maurice (2003): *The Decline of American Power: The U.S. in a Chaotic World*. New York: The New Press.

Wallerstein, Immanuel Maurice (2007): *World-Systems Analysis: An Introduction*. Durham: Duke University Press.

Wallerstein, Immanuel Maurice (2011): *The Modern World-System I: Capitalist Agriculture and the Origins of the European World-Economy in the Sixteenth Century*. Berkeley: University of California Press.

Wallerstein, Immanuel Maurice (2011a): *The Modern World-System II: Mercantilism and the Consolidation of the European World-Economy, 1600-1750*. Berkeley: University of California Press.

Wallerstein, Immanuel Maurice (2011b): *The Modern World-System III: The Second Era of Great Expansion of the Capitalist World-Economy, 1730s-1840s*. Berkeley: University of California Press.

Wallerstein, Immanuel Maurice (2011c): *The Modern World-System IV: Centrist Liberalism Triumphant, 1789-1914*. Berkeley: University of California Press.

Wallerstein, Immanuel Maurice (2017): *The World-System and Africa*. New York: Diasporic Africa Press.

Whitworth, Alan/ Williamson, Tim (2010): *Overview of Ugandan Economic Reform since 1986*, in: Kuteesa, Florence/ Tumusiime-Mutebile, Emmanuel/ Whitworth, Alan/ Williamson, Tim (eds.) (2010): *Uganda's Economic Reforms*. Oxford: Oxford University Press, 1-34.

Wichterich, Christa (2009): Gleich, gleicher, ungleich: Paradoxien und Perspektiven von Frauenrechten in der Globalisierung. Frankfurt: Ulrike Helmer Verlag.

Wichterich, Christa (2014): *Kleine Kredite, große Geschäfte und die andere Finanzkrise: Finanzialisierung des Alltags durch Mikrokredite für Frauen in Indien*, in: Klas, Gerhard/ Mader, Philip (eds.) (2014): *Rendite machen und Gutes tun? Mikrokredite und die Folgen neoliberaler Entwicklungspolitik*. Frankfurt: Campus Verlag, 45-52.

Wichterich, Christa (2015): *Mikrokredite, Rendite und Geschlecht: Von zuverlässigen armen Frauen und finanzieller Inklusion*, in: *PERIPHERIE* 2015, 35 (140), 469-490.

Williams, Michelle (2014): *The solidarity economy and social transformation*, in: Satgar, Vishwas (ed.) (2014): *The Solidarity Economy Alternative. Emerging Theory and Practice*. Scottsville: University of Kwazulu Natal Press, 37-63.

Williams, Raymond (1988): *Keywords. A vocabulary of culture and society*. London: Fontana.

Winkelmann, Bernd (2012): *Eigentum in einer Solidarischen Ökonomie*, in: Bender, Harald/ Bernholt, Norbert/ Winkelmann, Bernd/ Akademie Solidarische Ökonomie (eds.) (2012): *Kapitalismus und dann? Systemwandel und Perspektiven gesellschaftlicher Transformation*. München: oekom, 112-126.

Winkelmann, Bernd (2012a): *Neue Arbeits- und Sozialkultur*, in: Bender, Harald/ Bernholt, Norbert/ Winkelmann, Bernd/ Akademie Solidarische Ökonomie (eds.) (2012): *Kapitalismus und dann? Systemwandel und Perspektiven gesellschaftlicher Transformation*. München: oekom, 154-170.

Witzel, Andreas (2000): *The Problem-Centered Interview* [26 paragraphs], in: *Forum: Qualitative Sozialforschung/ Forum: Qualitative Social Research, Vol. 1, No. 1, Art. 22*, accessed on 19 December 2016, on: http://nbnresolving.de/urn:nbn:de:0114-fqs0001228.

Wolf, Martin (2018): *Why globalization works*. New Haven: Yale University Press.

World Bank (World Bank 2020) *Organization:* https://www.worldbank.org/en/about/leadership, accessed on 16 September 2020.

World Bank (World Bank 2020a) *Voting Powers: Allocation of Votes by Organization:* https://www.worldbank.org/en/about/leadership/votingpowers, accessed on 16 September 2020.

Wuttke, Mirja (2006): *Fairer Handel: Chancen und Schwierigkeiten eines alternativen Marktkonzepts*. Oldenburg: Paulo Freire Verlag.

Young, Robert J.C. (2001): *Postcolonialism: an historical introduction*. Oxford: Blackwell Publishers.

Zaoual, Hassan (1998): *The Economy and Symbolic Sites of Africa*, in: Rahnema, Majid/ Bawtree, Victoria (eds.) (1998): *The Post-Development Reader*. London: Zed Books, 30-39.

Ziai, Aram (2000): *Globalisierung als Chance für Entwicklungsländer? Ein Einstieg in die Problematik der Entwicklung in der Weltgesellschaft*. Hamburg: LIT Verlag.

Ziai, Aram (2006): *Post-Development: Ideologiekritik in der Entwicklungstheorie*, in: Politische Vierteljahresschrift, 47/2, 2006, 193–218.

Ziai, Aram (2007): *Development discourse and its critics: an introduction to post-development*, in: Ziai, Aram (ed.) (2007): *Exploring Post-development: Theory and practice, problems and perspectives*. London: Routledge, 3-17.

Ziai, Aram (2016): *Postkoloniale Studien und Politikwissenschaft. Komplementäre Defizite und ein Forschungsprogramm*, in: Ziai, Aram (ed.) (2016): *Postkoloniale Politikwissenschaft. Theoretische und empirische Zugänge*. Bielefeld: transcript, 25-45.

Ziai, Aram (2017): *Development Discourse and Global History: From colonialism to the sustainable development goals*. London: Routledge.

Appendices

Appendix 1: Transcription rules

For transcription of the interviews in this study, the transcription system described by Thorsten Dresing, Thorsten Pehl, and Christian Schmieder was used (Dresing et al. 2015, 27-33). In the following, I summarise the most important rules of this transcription system:

1. Literal transcription;
2. informal contractions like 'gonna' are transcribed in standard language, i.e. 'going to' (this was particularly helpful for me when working with the Lusoga transcripts during analysis);
3. word doublings are only transcribed if they indicate an emphasis on something; half sentences end on a slash;
4. punctuation is adapted to legibility;
5. pauses are marked with '(…)';
6. monosyllabic sounds like 'mhm' produced by the interviewer are only transcribed when they are meant as an answer, and in that case an interpretation is added in brackets, like '(affirmative)' or '(negative)';
7. capitalisation marks words with special emphasis;
8. every speech act has its own paragraph with a time stamp;
9. sighs, laughter, or similar utterances have to be transcribed in brackets;
10. for incomprehensible words, '(inc.)' is used; incomprehensible passages receive an explanation in addition, e.g., '(inc., wind)', and assumed but unclear words are written in brackets and marked with a question mark, like '(globalisation?)';
11. the interviewer is called 'I', the interviewee 'P' for participant (I added 'T' for translator and 'E' for expert);
12. transcripts are saved as rtf-files. (Dresing et al. 2015, 28-30)[146]

---

146 This transcription system suggested by Dresing et al. is an improved version of the transcription rules suggested by Udo Kuckartz, Thorsten Dresing, Stefan Rädiker, and Claus Stefer in Kuckartz et al. 2008, p. 27-28, which are based on experience made through extensive application of those rules in several qualitative research projects (Dresing et al. 2015, 27).

Appendix 2: Interview Guideline (Main Interviews)

A. Opening question:
   1) How do people earn a living in this town/ village? Please, take your time and explain it in detail to me as a foreigner.
B. Influence of *globalisation* on people's lives:
   I. Development of the profitability of products (e.g., crops) produced in the region in the past 30 years.
      1) Which products (e.g., certain crops) are most commonly produced in this region? Are they produced for home consumption or for sale? Are they produced by individual families or in groups (what kind of groups)/ companies?
      2) For those who are meant for sale: Since when have they been produced here on a large scale? How did the volume of production develop in the past 30 years? (If it decreased: Is it because producing this product does not generate enough income, anymore?)
      3) Did the mode of production change (common/individually; crop rotation/fallow fields/permanent exhaustion) in the past 30 years? If yes, how do you explain this?
   II. Involvement of the town/ village in trade – locally, nationally, internationally.
      1) Do people in your town/ village sell crops in other villages/towns or to brokers or traders? How is it organised (individuals, cooperative, informal union of farmers/traders, government...)? How was it organised in the past decades?
      2) Do you remember a time when there were no shops around? Where did people get the products, which they buy in these shops nowadays? (Did they make them themselves? Did they have them at all?)
   III. Availability and origin of new products. Need for those products and ways to finance their purchase.
      1) Which products can be found in most households nowadays that were not there during your childhood? Do you know where they come from?
      2) How do people afford to buy them? How do you judge this development?
   IV. Presence of companies/ individual business people from "outside" (either Kampala or other big cities, or from abroad).

1) Who runs the shops in this town (individuals from here or elsewhere, cooperatives, church)? How was it organised in the past decades?
2) Did the population of business companies in this region increase in the past 30 years? If there are any nowadays, do you think the percentage that comes from outside the region has changed?
3) What are the effects those companies have on the welfare of the local population?

V. Summary on globalisation.
1) So far, we have been talking about many aspects of your region's relationship with the world economy. Would you give me a short summary of how you see that relationship, please?
2) Nowadays, is it easier or harder to make a living than 30 years ago? From your point of view, what are the main reasons for that?

C. Alternative economic activities based on *solidarity*:

I. Existence of groups that fit in this category and their functioning.
1) With the headword "solidarity", I mean that I would like to know whether there are any alternative ways of doing economy here, meaning groups that are run by and for the sake of the local population, keeping money and facilities at their disposition. Such groups could be cooperatives, associations, mutuals, or similar ones.
2) Who owns the means of production in those groups (according to each case, I am going to replace the term "means of production" by the concrete things that the respective group may need for production, like fishing boats and nets or tools needed for agriculture/ crafts or bicycles/ other vehicles needed for transport etc.)?
3) How are decisions made in those groups?
4) How is the outcome of the activities redistributed to the members?

II. Motivation of people for founding/ joining such groups.
1) Why do you think people engage in such groups? [After the interviewee has given his/her own answer, I may ask whether these might also be some of the reasons, if they have not been mentioned: Is it due to lack of alternatives? Is it because people like engaging in a job where they have a say instead of being an employee who receives orders? Is it because people expect a bet-

ter income than they could achieve individually? Is it because economic activities of that kind have a tradition here? If yes, which one? Is it because the groups were created by NGOs or the church?]

III. Personal evaluation of such groups.
   1) Are you a member of such a group?
   2) How do you judge such groups/ activities?

IV. Other (traditional?) practices that can be mentioned here?
   1) Are there any things you used to get from your neighbours for free/ exchange with your neighbours, and now you have to buy them (e.g., manure)? If yes, how would you explain that change?
   2) Are there any rites of giving/ redistribution (e.g., a certain group of people that has to get a share of each harvest, traditional support to widows, etc.)?
   3) Can you name any other practices of that kind in your region? If they are no longer practised: Can you estimate since when? In your opinion, why do or did people stop to practise them?

D. Balancing questions/ Closure:
   1) Is there any aspect that might be of interest for me that we did not yet talk about? Or is there anything you would like to add to what was said?
   2) How did you like the interview? Is there any advice you would like to give me?

Appendix 3: Interview Guideline (Expert Interviews)

Note: Most interviewees will have special knowledge in a certain field (e.g., economics; NGO-work with rural population in Busoga; expertise on the respective region). Accordingly, one or more sections can be left out in case they concern a field of knowledge that the interviewee is not comfortable with.

A. Opening question:
   1) How does globalisation influence people's lives in Uganda?
B. Influence of *globalisation* on people's lives in Uganda, especially in the Busoga region [the following aspects can be asked about if they were not yet mentioned (in depth) above]:
   I. Development of the profitability of products, especially crops, produced in Uganda/ the Busoga region/ the town/village of _____ in the past decades.
      1) Which products, especially crops, are most commonly produced in Uganda/ the Busoga region/ the town/village of _____? Are they produced for home consumption or for sale? Are they produced by individual families or in groups (what kind of groups)/ companies?
      2) For those meant for sale: How did the volume of production develop since the economic liberalisation in 1987? (If there was any change: Why do you think people changed their attitude towards those products?)
      3) Did the mode of production change (common/individually; crop rotation/fallow fields/permanent exhaustion)? If yes, how do you explain this?
   II. Involvement of the Busoga region/ the town/village of ______ in trade – locally, nationally, internationally.
      1) How is the Busoga region/ the town/village of _____ involved in trade – locally, nationally, internationally?
      2) Is there any difference compared to the times before economic liberalisation (1987)? If yes: Why did those changes occur? What are the effects those changes have on the welfare of the local population?
   III. Availability and origin of new products.
      1) Globalisation opens the Ugandan market to many products from abroad. Other products, which are relatively new to the Ugandan market, are produced by companies of foreign origin inside Uganda. In your opinion, which ones are available even

to poor people, or to people who are living in villages, upcountry?

IV. Presence of business companies from "outside" (either Kampala or other big cities, or from abroad) in Busoga/ the town/village of _____.

1) Did the population of business companies in Busoga/ the town/ village of ________ change in the past 30 years? If there are any nowadays, do you think the percentage that comes from outside the region has changed?
2) What are the effects those companies have on the welfare of the local population?

C. Alternative economic activities based on *solidarity*:

I. Existence of groups that fit in this category and their functioning.

1) With the headword "solidarity", I mean that I would like to know whether there are any alternative ways of doing economy here, meaning groups that are run by and for the sake of the local population, keeping money and facilities at their disposition. Such groups could be cooperatives, associations, mutuals, or similar ones.
2) Who controls the means of production in those groups?
3) How are decisions made in those groups?
4) How is the outcome of the activities redistributed to the members?

II. Motivation of people for founding/ joining such groups.

1) Why do you think people engage in such groups? [After the interviewee has given his/her own answer, I may ask whether these might also be some of the reasons, if they have not been mentioned: Is it due to lack of alternatives? Is it because people like engaging in a job where they have a say instead of being an employee who receives orders? Is it because people expect a better income than they could achieve individually? Is it because economic activities of that kind have a tradition here? If yes, which one? Is it because the groups were created by actors like NGOs, the church, etc.?]

III. Other (traditional?) practices in the Busoga region that can be mentioned here?

1) Are there any things people in the Busoga region used to get from their neighbours for free/ exchange with their neighbours, and now they have to buy them (e.g., manure)? If yes, how would you explain that change?

2) Are there any rites of giving/ redistribution (e.g., a certain group of people that has to get a share of each harvest, traditional support for widows, etc.)?
3) Can you name any other practices of that kind in the Busoga region? If they are no longer practised, can you estimate since when? In your opinion, why do or did they cease to exist?

D. Balancing questions/ Closure:

1) Is there any aspect that might be of interest for me that we did not yet talk about? Or is there anything you would like to add to what was said?
2) How did you like the interview? Is there any advice you would like to give me?
3) Is there any advice you would like to give me where to find further information?

Appendix 4: Questionnaire (Personal Information, Main Interviews)

Date and place of interview: ______________________________

After introduction of my person and my request – orally and by handover and signature of the *Informed Consent Form* – I would like to request you to give me the following information about you. After that, we are going to start the interview itself. It will be like a conversation between you and me, but first of all I request you to take your time and give me your views on the questions I ask or the topics I suggest. Thank you.

As stated in the *Informed Consent Form*, this information will be used for my research, only. If you want your statements to be made anonymous in case I quote them in my thesis, please, tick the box. Of course, you can also decline to give me this information without any negative effect for yourself. Anyhow, it would help me a lot in analysing my research if you would give me the following information:

What is your name? ______________________________
How old are you? ______________________________
Gender: ____________________
Living in which District ________________ since when __________?
Living in which town/village ____________ since when __________?
What is your occupation? ______________________________
What is your level of education? __________________________
Do you have any special function in the town/village?

____

Are you running your own business? If yes, which one?

____

Other information? ______________________________
Do you agree if I mention your name in my thesis? □ YES □ NO

Thank you very much.

Appendix 5: Questionnaire (Personal Information, Expert Interviews)

Date and place of interview: ________________________________

After introduction of my person and my request – orally and by handover and signature of the *Informed Consent Form* – I would like to request you to give me the following information about you. After that, we are going to start the interview itself. It will be like a conversation between you and me, but first of all I request you to take your time and give me your views on the questions I ask or the topics I suggest. Thank you.

As stated in the *Informed Consent Form*, this information will be used for my research, only. If you want your statements to be made anonymous in case I quote them in my thesis, please, tick the box. Of course, you can also decline to give me this information without any negative effect for yourself. Anyhow, it would help me a lot in analysing my research if you would give me the following information:

What is your name? ________________________________

How old are you? ________________________________

Gender: ____________________

Living in which District ________________ since when ___________?

Living in which town/village ____________ since when ___________?

What is your occupation? ________________________________

What is your level of education? ____________________________

Do you have any special function in the town/village?

____

Other information? ________________________________

Do you agree if I mention your name in my thesis? □ YES □ NO

Thank you very much.

Appendix 6: Informed Consent Form (Main Interviews)

Introduction

Good morning/ afternoon. My name is Esther Kronsbein. I am a PhD student from Germany, but currently living in Kamuli, Eastern Uganda. This is a study for my PhD in Political Science at the University of Kassel, Germany. My affiliated organisation in Uganda is Makerere University. I am requesting you to participate in my study. If you agree, I will continue. Thank you.

Explanation about the research project

This study is focused on "political economy", so on a topic that is first of all focused on economic issues. I will not ask for your opinion on politics, but on your observations of economic developments in your region in the past 30 years. You can answer my questions as detailed as you like. There are no correct or incorrect answers. I am interested in your personal view on the respective developments.

The title of my thesis is "Globalisation and Solidarity. Lessons to be learnt from Ugandan everyday economy". In fact, I would like to learn from you and from your region. I would like to learn about the impacts of globalisation on people here. With the headword "solidarity", I mean that I would like to know whether there are any alternative ways of doing economy here, especially those that are based on: 1. mutual support; 2. being run by and for the sake of the local population; 3. creating local economic cycles that provide employment to locals, keeping money and facilities at their disposition; 4. having democratic structures instead of a boss-employees-relationship; 5. preserving nature for future generations.

You have been chosen as a research participant because you have been living in this area for long time, so that you could observe developments taking place over the years. I am eager to know how you saw them.

Expected outcome of the research project

After doing a certain number of interviews, I hope to be able to draw some conclusions from them and present them in my PhD thesis. About globalisation, I hope to find out how people in Uganda are affected by it, and whether they judge it good or bad. About economic alternatives, I want to see what kind of practices exist in Uganda, why people practice them and whether they feel that they help them or not. In my conclusions, I want to offer "Lessons to be learnt" from Ugandans for people all over the world, which may question or compliment the current understanding of economic and social development.

Risks/ Benefits

This study has no risks because one of the reasons it is asking about developments you have observed within your area. Therefore, you will not be affected in any way. You will not benefit directly from this study, but we shall share the findings with you and other stakeholders in different media to enable you to benefit from the recommendations.

Voluntariness/ Confidentiality/ Recording

Your participation is voluntary. You can stop this interview at any time – without suffering any negative consequences. This interview will take 1 hour. If you agree, I will record this interview. I will inform you when I turn the record on/off. If you change your mind during the interview, we can still turn the record off at any time you wish. Your statements will only be used anonymously and only for research purposes. They will be kept under key and lock and will only be accessed by the research team.

Do you agree to be recorded? □ Yes □ No

Contact

A short summary of my research results can be provided to you on request. In case of any question after the interview, please, do not hesitate to contact me: Esther Kronsbein, 0778328311, or Prof. Dr. Julius Kiiza, Makerere University, Department of Political Science and Public Administration, P.O.-Box 7062, Kampala, Uganda.

In addition, for your human rights, you may contact: Dr. Stella Neema, the Chairperson Makerere University School of Social Sciences Research Ethics Committee (MAKSS REC), Seminar Room 7, P.O.-Box 762, Kampala, Uganda, or Dr. Ndemere Peter, Executive Secretary, Uganda National Council of Science and Technology, Kimera Road 6, Ntinda, P.O.-Box 6884, Kampala, Uganda.

Place ____________________ Date _____________________________

Name of Interviewee ____

Signature or Fingerprint of Interviewee___________________________

Witness (for interviewees, who are illiterate):

Place ____________________ Date _____________________________

Name of Witness ____

Signature or Fingerprint of Witness______________________________

Place ____________________ Date ______________________________
Name of Researcher ____
Signature of Researcher____

Appendix 7: Informed Consent Form (Expert Interviews)

Introduction

Good morning/ afternoon. My name is Esther Kronsbein. I am a PhD student from Germany, but currently living in Kamuli, Eastern Uganda. This is a study for my PhD in Political Science at the University of Kassel, Germany. My affiliated organisation in Uganda is Makerere University. I am requesting you to participate in my study. If you agree, I will continue. Thank you.

Explanation about the research project

This study is focused on "political economy", so on a topic that is first of all focused on economic issues. I will not ask for your opinion on politics, but on your observations of economic developments in Uganda. You can answer my questions as detailed as you like.

The title of my thesis is "Globalization and Solidarity. Lessons to be learnt from Ugandan everyday economy". In fact, I would like to learn about the impacts of globalization on people in Uganda. With the headword "solidarity", I mean that I would like to know whether there are any alternative ways of doing economy here, especially those that are based on solidarity, fulfilling some of the following requirements: 1. mutual support; 2. being run by and for the sake of the local population; 3. creating local economic cycles that provide employment to locals, keeping money and facilities at their disposition; 4. having democratic structures instead of a boss-employees-relationship; 5. preserving nature for future generations.

This is an *expert interview*, so you have been chosen as a research participant because of your expertise concerning certain aspects of the study. The main research activity of my study are interviews with people in communities of the Busoga region. The *expert interviews* are supposed to provide me with background information that will help to prepare and analyse the main interviews.

Expected outcome of the research project

After doing a certain number of interviews, I hope to be able to draw some conclusions from them and present them in my PhD thesis. About globalisation, I hope to find out how people in Uganda are affected by it, and whether they judge it good or bad. About economic alternatives, I want to see what kind of practices exist in Uganda, why people practice them and whether they feel that they help them or not. In my conclusions, I want to offer "Lessons to be learnt" from Ugandans for people all over the world, which may question or compliment the current understanding of economic and social development.

Risks/ Benefits

This study has no risks because one of the reasons it is asking about developments you have observed within your area. Therefore, you will not be affected in any way. You will not benefit directly from this study, but we shall share the findings with you and other stakeholders in different media to enable you to benefit from the recommendations.

Voluntariness/ Confidentiality/ Recording

Your participation is voluntary. You can stop this interview at any time – without suffering any negative consequences. This interview will take 30 to 45 minutes. If you agree, I will record this interview. I will inform you when I turn the record on/off. If you change your mind during the interview, we can still turn the record off at any time you wish. Your statements will only be used anonymously and only for research purposes. They will be kept under key and lock and will only be accessed by the research team.

Do you agree to be recorded? □ Yes □ No

Contact

A short summary of my research results can be provided to you on request. In case of any question after the interview, please, do not hesitate to contact me: Esther Kronsbein, 0778328311, or Prof. Dr. Julius Kiiza, Makerere University, Department of Political Science and Public Administration, P.O.-Box 7062, Kampala, Uganda.

In addition, for your human rights, you may contact: Dr. Stella Neema, the Chairperson Makerere University School of Social Sciences Research Ethics Committee (MAKSS REC), Seminar Room 7, P.O.-Box 762, Kampala, Uganda, or Dr. Ndemere Peter, Executive Secretary, Uganda National Council of Science and Technology, Kimera Road 6, Ntinda, P.O.-Box 6884, Kampala, Uganda.

Place ____________________ Date ____________________________

Name of Interviewee ____

Signature or Fingerprint of Interviewee___________________________

Witness (for interviewees, who are illiterate):

Place ____________________ Date ____________________________

Name of Witness ____

Signature or Fingerprint of Witness______________________________

Place ______________________ Date ________________________________

Name of Researcher ____

Signature of Researcher____